"Because so much of Bavinck's corpus has only recently been translated, we in the English-speaking world have not yet had the full benefit of Bavinck's rich thought, which seems unique in how it stays fully biblical while taking into account the history of the church, of philosophy, and of social currents. But no one can grasp the theology of an Augustine or Aquinas, a Calvin or Luther, without knowing their life and context. Eglinton has provided this in his new critical biography of the greatest Reformed theologian of the twentieth century. It is a very important yet highly readable volume."

—**Timothy Keller**, pastor emeritus, Redeemer Presbyterian Church of New York City

"Of obvious interest to those concerned with Reformed and neo-Calvinist traditions, this probing biography also speaks to the enduring questions of 'Christ and culture' as it explores how one Christian inhabited his orthodox faith in a complex and changing world. Indeed, the range of timeless topics that Bavinck explored with wisdom and prescience is staggering. As Eglinton invites us into Bavinck's faithful and creative engagement with pluralism, psychology, Nietzsche, education for women, evangelism, missions, racism in America, and politics, we see that we still have much to learn from this member of the great cloud of witnesses."

—**Kristen Deede Johnson**, Western Theological Seminary

"In 1910, a Scottish theologian who had recently visited the Netherlands referred in a lecture to Herman Bavinck as 'Dr. Kuyper's loyal and learned henchman.' Now, a hundred and ten years later, another Scottish scholar sets the record straight. James Eglinton demonstrates that Bavinck was no one's 'henchman,' but a brilliant, creative theologian in his own right. This important book confirms what many of us have been convinced of for some time now: Bavinck's time has come as a world-class theologian for our own day."

—**Richard Mouw**, president emeritus, Fuller Theological Seminary

"Scholarly but accessible, this biography offers an account of Bavinck's life and work in its historical context, resisting the temptation to co-opt him to, or interpret him via, the concerns of later theological parties and conflicts. A wonderful companion volume to the *Dogmatics*."

—**Carl R. Trueman**, Grove City College

"In James Eglinton, Herman Bavinck has the biographer he so richly deserves, his own Scottish James Boswell. Especially illuminating is the additional material on Herman's father, Jan Bavinck; the young Herman; Herman's wife,

Johanna Schippers-Bavinck; and the legacy of their daughter and grandsons, all noteworthy on their own. This will be the definitive Bavinck biography for generations."

—**John Bolt**, Calvin Theological Seminary (emeritus)

"For too long, Bavinck studies has operated on the assumption that he was often at odds with his confessionally orthodox self in his alleged adulteration of Christianity with modern thought and culture. Eglinton's narrative critically debunks assumptions of this sort and convincingly portrays Bavinck's multifaceted life as a testimony to his eclectic theology, which concertedly endeavored to remain committed to Christ at every single point of creaturely existence."

—**Shao Kai Tseng**, Institute of Religious Studies, Zhejiang University, China

BAVINCK

BAVINCK

A Critical Biography

JAMES EGLINTON

ℬ Baker Academic

a division of Baker Publishing Group
Grand Rapids, Michigan

Published by Baker Academic
a division of Baker Publishing Group
PO Box 6287, Grand Rapids, MI 49516-6287
www.bakeracademic.com

Printed in the United States of America

Library of Congress Cataloging-in-Publication Data
Names: Eglinton, James Perman, author.
Title: Bavinck : a critical biography / James Eglinton.
Description: Grand Rapids, Michigan : Baker Academic, a division of Baker Publishing Group,
    2020. | Includes bibliographical references and index.
Identifiers: LCCN 2020007054 | ISBN 9781540961358 (cloth)
Subjects: LCSH: Bavinck, Herman, 1854–1921.
Classification: LCC BX9479.B35 E45 2020 | DDC 230/.42092 [B]—dc23
LC record available at https://lccn.loc.gov/2020007054

20   21   22   23   24   25   26   7   6   5   4   3   2

In keeping with biblical principles of creation stewardship, Baker Publishing Group advocates the responsible use of our natural resources. As a member of the Green Press Initiative, our company uses recycled paper when possible. The text paper of this book is composed in part of post-consumer waste.

So in practice man is the greatest puzzle that man has. He needs to know himself, in order to live and to make himself recognizable to other people. But at the same time he must remain concealed from himself in order to be able to remain alive and free. For if he ever finally got "behind himself," and could establish what was the matter with him, nothing would any longer be the matter with him, but everything would be fixed and tied down, and he would be finished. The solution of the puzzle what man is would then at the same time be the final release from being human. As we experience being human, we experience it as a question, as freedom and as openness.

—Jürgen Moltmann, *Man*

Contents

A Note on Sources

By chronicling many of his own experiences in journals (*dagboeken*) and letters, Herman Bavinck left his future biographers with a richly textured window into a significant portion of his life. These particular primary sources provide this biography with much of its rhythm and substance, and they will be referred to throughout. To aid readers in distinguishing between them, I have italicized quotations from the dagboeken and have left excerpts from his letters unitalicized. To date, one or both sides of three particularly important sets of correspondence—with his friends Christiaan Snouck Hurgronje, Henry Elias Dosker, and Geerhardus Vos—have been transcribed and published, respectively, under the titles *Een Leidse vriendschap*,[1] *"Men wil toch niet gaarne een masker dragen": Brieven van Henry Dosker aan Herman Bavinck, 1873–1921*,[2] and *The Letters of Geerhardus Vos*.[3] Unless otherwise indicated, all other letters cited in this biography, alongside Bavinck's dagboeken and unpublished manuscripts, have been accessed in the archives of the Historisch Documentatiecentrum voor het Nederlands Protestantisme (1800–heden) at the Vrije Universiteit Amsterdam, the Stadsarchief in Kampen, and the Archief- en Documentatiecentrum van de Gereformeerde kerken in Nederland, also in Kampen.

A great deal of information on Bavinck's life is found in the Dutch-language newspapers of the nineteenth and twentieth centuries. These were published in his native Netherlands, in the Dutch East Indies, and in conservative Dutch diasporic communities in North America. His lifetime was one in which the recent democratization and liberalization of society had an obvious consequence for the press. In his youth, the abolition of stamp duty on Dutch newspapers made daily newspapers affordable and numerous.[4] In that context, Bavinck's newly empowered social group made abundant use of their new media. As the course of Bavinck's life can also be traced across the pages of these newspapers, I will make regular recourse to them. Unlike some, I have chosen not to translate the names of Dutch newspapers into English. When they travel internationally, *The Guardian*, *Le Monde*, and *Die Zeit* retain their names—and so should *De Bazuin*, *De Heraut*, and *De Standaard*.

Unless an English source is cited, the translations of foreign-language material in the book are my own. The original text is usually included in an endnote.

Acknowledgments

While this book is the story of someone else's life, writing it has changed my own in many ways. The first five chapters were written in 2017, while I was on sabbatical as a visiting researcher at the Theologische Universiteit Kampen. It was a great pleasure to interact with many friends and colleagues there over a number of months, and to write in the beautiful city so central to the book itself. To Roel Kuiper, Dolf te Velde, Erik de Boer, Hans Burger, Janneke Burger-Niemeijer, Jos Colijn, Jolanda van Gelder-Bastiaan, Jolanda Zweers, Geert Harmanny, Marjolijn Palma, Koert van Bekkum, Ad de Bruijne, Wolter Rose, Wolter Huttinga, and above all George Harinck and Dirk van Keulen—who receive their own honorable mention a few paragraphs down—*zeer bedankt voor jullie gastvrijheid*. During those months, I spent many days working in the Stadsarchief Kampen, the Archief- en Documentatiecentrum Kampen, and the Historisch Documentatiecentrum voor het Nederlands Protestantisme (1800–heden) at the Vrije Universiteit Amsterdam: my sincere thanks to all at these institutions, in particular, Wim Koole, Ab van Langevelde, Merijn Wijma-van der Veen, and Hans Seijlhouwer. In those months, I was also invited to present my research at both the Vrije Universiteit's Amsterdam Centre for Religious History and, thanks to the hospitality of the John Owen Society, at the University of Oxford. To both, I extend my gratitude.

While preparing this book, it was my privilege to meet and interview a number of people descended from figures who played prominent roles in its narrative. Wim Bavinck, a great-nephew of Herman, and Emilie Bavinck-van Halsema welcomed me to their home, and gave me boxes of material—published and unpublished—that have proved invaluable to this project. It was an honor to meet the Minister of State Piet Hein Donner, a great-great-great grandson of Rev. J. H. Donner, who graciously welcomed me to his office in the Raad van State to discuss the history of his illustrious family. Another of Rev. J. H. Donner's descendents, Jerphaas Donner, kindly shared his own research into his family history. To each of you, *hartelijk bedankt.*

The remainder of the book came together at New College, where I am blessed to work with a group of outstanding PhD students. To my doctoral students past and present—Cory Brock, Nathaniel Gray Sutanto, Bruce Pass, Gustavo Monteiro, Cameron Clausing, Greg Parker, Ximian Xu, Richard Brash, and Israel Guerrero Leiva—I wish simply to say, *Thank you.* Working with each of you has been a joy and privilege. I do not take it for granted. Many of our interactions have influenced this book. I hope you enjoy it just as I have delighted in learning from your own research.

I remain grateful for many conversations with colleagues in the New College staff room, each of which pushed the book—sometimes in subtle but important ways—a bit further along. In some cases, colleagues have helped my work by sharing from their own areas of expertise. In all cases, my colleagues have offered valued words of encouragement, and shown remarkable patience in indulging my obsession: David Fergusson, Joshua Ralston, Zachary Purvis, Susan Hardman-Moore, Simon Burton, Naomi Appleton, Matthew Novenson, Sara Parvis, Paul Parvis, Ulrich Schmiedel, Emma Wild-Wood, Brian Stanley, Jolyon Mitchell, Paul Foster, Helen Bond, Hannah Holtschneider, Mona Siddiqui, Stewart J. Brown, and Alexander Chow (who receives his own special mention below). May our college's culture of intellectual hospitality never fade. The Edinburgh-based part of this project also owes a great deal to the efforts of Dmytro Bintsarovskyi, whose digitization work on behalf of the Theologische Universiteit Kampen's Neo-Calvinism Research Institute is exceptional.

Particular notes of gratitude are due to the following colleagues and friends. To Alexander Chow, who read the early chapters and provided helpful feedback, 谢谢. To Richard Oosterhoff, my sincere thanks for your critique and encouragement as the project drew to a close. To Dirk van Keulen and George Harinck, both of whom read the manuscript in detail and provided rich and stimulating interaction throughout, and to the ever-patient Marinus de Jong, who answered so many queries about archaic Dutch vocabulary and grammar: I am deeply indebted to each of you and hope you are pleased with the end result. *Bedankt, allemaal.* To Oliver Crisp, who provided the artwork for the book's cover: thank you for being both a Bezalel and a Barnabas to many, myself included, in the realm of academic theology.

For this book, I could not imagine a better publisher than Baker Academic: like Bavinck himself, Baker has deep roots in Dutch Calvinism and a keen eye to the wider world of Christian theology. Thank you Dave Nelson, Brandy Scritchfield, and James Korsmo, for your professionalism and enthusiasm.

To my parents, Jim and Ishbel, and my parents-in-law, Alasdair and Peigi-Mairi: thank you for your kindness and support in these busy years of research and writing.

Beyond all of these individuals, this book—written as it was in a demanding, wonderful, and hard season of life—has depended on the love and encouragement of my children, Seumas, Anna, Eachainn, and Mìcheal, and my wife, Eilidh. This book is for you.

Mìle beannachd oirbh uile. A thousand blessings upon you all.

Introduction

Prolegomena

Why does Herman Bavinck (1854–1921), a prolific theologian who worked within the Dutch neo-Calvinist movement, deserve a biography? In his own era, the answer to that question would have been fairly obvious: in the early twentieth-century Netherlands, Herman Bavinck was a household name. To his contemporaries, he was known not only as a brilliant theologian. To them, he was also—among other things—a pioneer in psychology, a pedagogical reformer, a champion for girls' education and advocate of women's voting rights, a parliamentarian, and a journalist. He was, and in some circles today *remains*, a person of international significance. In 1908, for example, Bavinck gave the prestigious Stone Lectures in Princeton, before which President Theodore Roosevelt received him and his wife at the White House. Bavinck was the kind of Dutchman whose foreign travels were chronicled in the national press and who would then return to give sold-out lectures across the country on his impressions and experiences overseas. A century later, a growing international audience reads his works in a host of languages.

His rise to national and international prominence was all the more striking given his family background: the Bavincks belonged to a formerly clandestine denomination that had left the Dutch Reformed Church earlier in the nineteenth century and, until shortly before Herman's birth, had faced state-led persecution on account of its religious dissent—with all the crippling social prospects that accompanied their pariah status. Viewed in that light, the significance of Bavinck's remarkable life was all too clear: born shortly after the Netherlands had committed itself to liberal democratic social ideals, he was something of a poster boy for that new age of opportunity, equality, and freedom.

Given this background, it might be more natural to ask why someone would *not* write a biography of Herman Bavinck. That question, however, has already occurred to a number of people in the century since his death. After all, to prospective biographers, the fascinating lives of polymaths are like honey to the bees. Indeed, prior to this book, six previous writers have set out accounts of Bavinck's life. Taking their works into consideration, one faces the pressing question of why another Bavinck biography should appear now. Why does Herman Bavinck deserve a *new* biography?

In short, this biography's new reading of Bavinck's life is part of a movement that has challenged a number of long-standing assumptions on how his works ought to be read. In the second half of the twentieth century, much secondary literature on Bavinck relied on a puzzling set of terms to describe him as something of a "Jekyll and Hyde" figure in the Reformed tradition. In reading works that noted his unusual combination of conservative Calvinist orthodoxy and apparent modernism, I encountered the regular description of two separate Herman Bavincks: one orthodox and the other modern. In these sources, the presence of these orthodox and modern elements of his life and thought was consistently attributed to two irreconcilable impulses. Bavinck was (or rather, as I had often read, the two conflicted Herman Bavincks were) pushed and pulled by opposing and contradictory forces and never able to settle on one direction. As for its impact on the growing field of Bavinck studies, this portrayal was seen, for example, in Jan Veenhof's classic description of the "two Bavincks" and "two poles" in Bavinck's thought[1] and eventually led to Malcolm Yarnell's unfortunate use of the language of "schizophrenia" as a descriptor for Bavinck's theological efforts.[2]

The direct result of this was the creation of a widely accepted hermeneutical lens through which Bavinck was read. When the reader noticed a section in Bavinck's work that appeared to reflect his confessionally Reformed roots, it became standard to identify that as the work of the "orthodox Bavinck." Conversely, it became normal to label sections that showed Bavinck's engagement with modernity as the writings of the "modern Bavinck." Brian Mattson's *Restored to Our Destiny* insightfully observed the application of this hermeneutic in Eugene Heideman's *Relation of Revelation and Reason in E. Brunner and H. Bavinck*, a book that tries to discern "which Bavinck," the "biblical" or the "idealist, scholastic" Bavinck, wrote particular sections of the *Reformed Dogmatics*.[3]

In that light, I began to wonder whether the future of Bavinck studies was simply one of Balkanization, as his "orthodox" and "modern" admirers carved up and claimed portions of his oeuvre for themselves. My first book, *Trinity and Organism*, grew out of my curiosity in that regard.[4] I began to ask questions about the scope of Bavinck's own theological vision. A former teacher's quip (originally from Cicero)—that consistency is a virtue of small minds—made me wonder whether Bavinck's mind might have deemed it possible to hold orthodoxy and modernity in some kind of critical equipoise. My first book, then, was an extended argument that specific nuances in Bavinck's doctrine of God (which stress divine unity-in-diversity in a number of ways) created the scope for him to develop a particular view of the world within which diverse parts are somehow organically connected. That work's central axiom is that "a theology of Trinity *ad intra* leads to a cosmology of organism *ad extra*": Bavinck's understanding of God had considerable consequences for his view of the world, which entailed consequences for his self-understanding as a human agent within it.

In rejecting the dominant set of tools used by most Bavinck interpreters for the last few decades, *Trinity and Organism* advanced a new reading of Bavinck. He was no longer the "Jekyll and Hyde" of Reformed theology. Without denying the hard challenge he set for himself or the difficult lived reality emanating from the tensions in his thought, it argued for Bavinck as a creative thinker whose theological imagination allowed him to envision a distinctive articulation of the historic Christian faith within his own modern milieu.

In making this argument, *Trinity and Organism* attempted to avoid a rapidly impending (and fruitless) impasse in Bavinck studies. And it ended on a bold note: "The breakdown of the 'two Bavincks' model calls for nothing less than a paradigm shift in Bavinck studies."[5] Its conclusion was that the rejection of the "two Bavincks" hermeneutic has consequences for all future readings of Bavinck. In view of this, it is no longer acceptable for his readers simply to annex portions of his thought or writings for their own "camp." Rather, they must wrestle with both sides of this tension in exploring Bavinck's example of modernity not denying orthodoxy and orthodoxy not precluding participation in modernity.

In the conclusion to *Trinity and Organism*, I noted that it was primarily concerned with Bavinck's *theology* rather than with Bavinck the *theologian*.[6] My goal was to explore the workings of a theological system that might allow him to maintain difficult tensions (and even to find this desirable). However, my conclusion left open a conversation that I am now picking up again: that of how this particular theologian came into, and developed within, the struggle to be an orthodox Calvinist participant in a rapidly modernizing culture. *Trinity and Organism* could be followed up by a number of theologically focused sequels probing different areas of his thought in its newly reunited form.

However, my current book plots a different kind of sequel in an altogether different literary genre: biography. If we are no longer justified in speaking of *two* Bavincks, what bearing might that have on how we tell the story of his life? What distinctive shape might his biography take in view of the collapse of the "two Bavincks" hermeneutic?

Bavinck, as I noted above, has already been the subject of a number of biographies. Within a year of his death, one (particularly hagiographical) English and two Dutch accounts of his life had been published: of these Dutch accounts, Valentijn Hepp's was the only extensive retelling of Bavinck's story.[7] A. B. W. M. Kok's Dutch biography, *Dr Herman Bavinck*,[8] followed by J. Geelhoed's *Dr. Herman Bavinck*, kept this interest alive into the mid-twentieth century,[9] although these works were all surpassed by R. H. Bremmer's 1966 publication, the excellent *Herman Bavinck en zijn tijdgenoten* (Herman Bavinck and his contemporaries).[10] More recently, however, the English translation of Bavinck's magnum opus, the *Reformed Dogmatics*,[11] has prompted several writers of English-language publications to introduce their works with short biographical sketches.[12]

In 2010, a longer English biography appeared: Ron Gleason's *Herman Bavinck: Pastor, Churchman, Statesman, and Theologian*.[13] My biography, however, is quite different from Gleason's, which was written as a largely derivative—and not always accurate—amalgam of Hepp's and Bremmer's contents. While my biography engages with Hepp and Bremmer throughout, it does so critically and prioritizes an *ad fontes* approach over reliance on the works of earlier biographers. Beyond this, Gleason's forays away from Bavinck's story into contemporary applications of "orthodox versus liberal" debates perhaps support locating his work somewhere in the Balkanization that my own *Trinity and Organism* politely declines.[14]

My biography has a particular aim: to tell the story of a man whose theologically laced personal narrative explored the possibility of an orthodox life in a changing world. Its foundations in *Trinity and Organism* lend no motivation to ignore or downplay either crises of faith or resolute Reformed convictions on Bavinck's part. It does not intend to draw contemporary applications of Bavinck for either self-professedly "orthodox" or "modern" readers. To the contrary, its disavowal of the "two Bavincks" model means it is set free from those obligations. As a consequence, this freedom entails the opportunity to consider his life anew. In that light, this biography is an attempt to retrace the narrative of his life and, in so doing, to chart the development of his (single, rather than divided) theological vision.

At this point, a few final prolegomenous comments are necessary. In setting out the life and times of Herman Bavinck, this biography makes abundant reference to three key terms: *modern*, *orthodox*, and *science*. By way of historical chronology, our story treats the events of 1848—the Spring of Nations so central to the eventual trajectory of Bavinck's life—as the point at which the last stage of the *early modern* period in the Netherlands gave way to its *late modern* successor. It marks the transition from one distinct phase of what can broadly be termed "modern European culture" into another and informs this account of Bavinck's life profoundly. Alongside that, this book's handling of the *modern* also leans heavily on Shmuel Noah Eisenstadt's notion of "multiple modernities." This is the view that modern people continually reconstructed the cultures they inhabited, negotiating which parts of modernization they would embrace and which they would reject. There was no single "modernity" or "modern culture"—just as there is no single "modern theology." Rather, "modernisation" was a process realized in a myriad of ways.[15] Bavinck, a theologically conservative Calvinist, was one such modern European. (It will probably be helpful for the reader to note that this book deals with *both* generic *modern theology*—a widely used umbrella term for a complex web of post-Enlightenment Protestant theologies—*and* a homonymous but quite particular branch of Dutch theology, "*de moderne theologie*," which defined the University of Leiden's theological faculty during the second half of the nineteenth century. When referring to the Leiden school of thought and its exponents, I have capitalized *Modern*. References to the catch-all *modern theology* and its practitioners remain in lowercase.)

This biography also frequently refers to *orthodoxy*. This term is used to denote a set of intellectual, theological, and ecclesiastical commitments maintained by Bavinck throughout his lifetime—albeit sometimes in moments of doubt and struggle. In that regard, this book handles *orthodox* as a synonym for Bavinck's unwillingness to follow the Enlightenment tendency to devalue and disregard the contribution of pre-Enlightenment (and specifically Christian) intellectual tradition. Positively, it points to his allegiance and willingness to submit to the texts, creeds, confessions, and an institution (the church) brought forward across two millennia by previous generations of Christians, and in his own particular context by the historic Dutch Reformed tradition.

The term *science* also plays a key role in this account of Bavinck's life. Although this book has been written in English, it primarily describes and interacts with sources written in Dutch. Like its German cognate *Wissenschaft*, the Dutch term *wetenschap* is appropriately rendered in English as *science*. Unlike its English equivalent, however, *wetenschap* has a purview not limited strictly to the hard (or soft) sciences. Rather, it deals broadly with higher forms of reflective knowledge and is used to describe humanities disciplines like theology just as much as physics, chemistry, and biology. Bavinck himself was aware of this linguistic difference and was publicly critical of the anglophone tendency to privilege the natural sciences over other avenues of inquiry by denying them their right to use that one mighty word.[16] Accordingly, this book translates *wetenschap* as *science*. A failure to do so would project today's anglocentric assumptions about higher forms of knowledge onto Bavinck quite inappropriately.

It is with these definitions that I present my subject as a modern European, an orthodox Calvinist, and a man of science.

This is the story of Herman Bavinck.

Chronology

1854, Dec. 13   Herman Bavinck born to Rev. Jan and Geziena Bavinck, in Hoogeveen, the Netherlands.

1857   Bavinck family moves to Bunschoten.

1862   Bavinck family moves to Almkerk.

1871   Herman becomes a student at the Zwolle Gymnasium.

1873   Enrolls as a student at the Theological School in Kampen.

1874   Enrolls as a theological student at the University of Leiden.

1880   Declines post at the Free University of Amsterdam, awarded doctoral degree at Leiden, and passes theological exams in Kampen.

1881   Accepts call to pastor Christian Reformed congregation in Franeker.

1882   Declines position at the Free University of Amsterdam; appointed at the Theological School in Kampen.

1889   Declines position at the Free University of Amsterdam; overlooked for professorship at the University of Leiden.

1891   Marries Johanna Adriana Schippers.

1893   Declines position at the Free University of Amsterdam.

1894   Birth of daughter Johanna Geziena Bavinck.

1895–1901   Publishes four-volume *Reformed Dogmatics*.

1902   Accepts position at the Free University of Amsterdam.

1911   Elected as parliamentarian in the First Chamber.

1921, July 29   Dies in Amsterdam at age sixty-six; buried in Vlaardingen.

Map of the Netherlands

PART 1

Roots

1

The Old Reformed Church in Bentheim

"From the farmhouse to the town"

The Modern European Experience of Upheaval

Insofar as it is seen as a story of upheaval, the history of nineteenth- and twentieth-century Europe forms a striking backdrop to Herman Bavinck's own life story. Tim Blanning portrays the experience of modern Europeans—including, by implication, our subject—as characterized by the conviction that "the ground [was] moving beneath their feet."[1] Theirs was an epoch of staggering, broad, and often dramatic social, political, intellectual, and religious shifts. As the nineteenth century dawned, the French Revolution had finished and was followed by the Napoleonic Wars. The First Industrial Revolution, which had begun in the eighteenth century, was in full swung. Europeans of that era saw the rise of nationalisms and the peak of the age of Eurocentric world empires. Europe at the time was the birthplace of new liberal democratic political ideals. In the twentieth century, its inhabitants knew the Great Depression and World Wars and watched as their world reoriented itself from modernization to globalization. Modern Europe was the garden in which diverse species of secularism bloomed.

In the Netherlands, more specifically, Bavinck was born into a tumultuous period of political, industrial, and religious change. In the decade before his birth, King William I, the authoritarian ruler of the nondemocratic Dutch state, abdicated. In 1848, his successor, King William II, consented to a new liberal constitution. Overnight, the Netherlands became a constitutional monarchy, the king's powers were constrained, and a new set of modern democratic civil liberties became the framework that guided Dutch social interaction. With the advent of parliamentary democracy and enlarged suffrage came a basic set of rights—the freedoms of assembly, religion, and education. The immediate social context into which Bavinck was born, as the son of a preacher in a movement of ecclesiastical secession from the established Dutch Reformed Church, was also one of flux: it was a cultural moment in which religious affiliations were regularly realigned, often with drastic consequences.

Bavinck entered the world in the midst of a period busy with its own reinvention—a constant setting of change that spanned the entirety of his lifetime. Indeed, the worlds into which he was born (in 1854) and died (in 1921) were dramatically different places. The backdrop to our story is thus anything but static. Had Bavinck been disengaged from this relentless process of social change, his biography would likely take a distinct shape. It would be the story of a theologically orthodox monolith, unyielding and immutable, weathering decades of storm, grounded in bygone and seemingly better days. That, however, is not the story to be told in this book. Our subject was profoundly aware of his social and historical context. To borrow Blanning's phrase again, Bavinck had no difficulty in recognizing that the ground was moving beneath his feet. The fact of this movement, however, was not inherently problematic to him—and often enough, he would be the one willing that ground to move in particular ways. The bare fact of change was not Bavinck's enemy. As he would articulate later, the only thing in this world that grace opposes is sin itself. In his eyes, this process of constant *becoming*, including perpetual change in human culture, was a basic feature of the created order. The great challenge of Bavinck's life was, rather, where he—as an orthodox Calvinist—should place his feet in this ever-shifting terrain.

If not read carefully, the basic details of Bavinck's early life could tempt the reader to caricature his life in a certain fashion. Following his upbringing in a pious Reformed family in small towns, he chose to study under the leaders of the unorthodox "Modern theology" movement at a secular university in a large city.[2] If not read carefully, that move to Leiden might be seen as a rejection of the conservative subculture that nurtured him. And his decision to study under that university's heterodox theologians might then be read as his first intellectual foray into the modern world. Our story will present Herman Bavinck quite differently, showing that the direction of his life was not to break with his tradition, as though he was simply a force of nature who moved forward into modern European culture while his fellow orthodox Calvinists were retreating from it. Rather, he emerged at the forefront of an already established social movement in the Dutch Reformed world that developed as early modern Europe was consumed by revolution and as a newly ordered form of late modern culture arose from its ashes.

As will be explained, in the mid-nineteenth century—the end phase of early modern culture—a movement of spiritually reawakened Dutch Reformed Christians seceded from the Dutch Reformed Church and were pushed to the periphery of their society as a result. As that century reached its midpoint, their society underwent seismic change. The early modern period came to a close and was superseded by a considerably different expression of late modern culture—one in which power shifted from the monarch to the people.

This new age's social conditions presented these marginalized Protestants with a set of possibilities, one of which was the chance to reenter a newly liberalized democratic society as equal participants. Herman Bavinck emerged as one of the most noteworthy and outstanding figures in that period, speaking in a recognizably orthodox voice as his movement negotiated its place in the late modern Netherlands. Bavinck's story might be remarkable, and is certainly unique, in that he stood at the forefront of a much larger movement and played a distinctive role within it. However, it remains the story of one person whose outstanding contribution was enabled and compelled by the lives of others. When approached through their stories, Bavinck's own life begins to take a particular, fascinating shape.

Saint Bavo's Wandering Children

To trace Bavinck's roots, we must begin in the early nineteenth century, in Bentheim, on the eastern side of the then-porous Dutch-German border. Bentheim, the capital of Lower Saxony, was his father's birthplace and had been home to generations of Bavincks.

Although Herman's life was spent in the Netherlands, he was well aware of his Lower Saxon heritage. In 1909, shortly before his own father died, Herman supplied the editor of *De Zondagsbode*—a Dutch Mennonite newspaper—with an account of their family's history in Bentheim, which was Mennonite on one side and a mix of Lutheran and Reformed on the other.[3] In the distant past, if the family folklore is to be believed, the Bavincks were Bauingas, Bavingas, Bauinks, and Bavinks—the offspring of a sixteenth-century Roman Catholic from Bauingastede (now Bangstede, a hamlet in northern Germany) who became a Lutheran and moved south to Bentheim. Bauingastede was named in honor of Saint Bavo, a seventh-century Catholic hermit, as were the subsequent generations of Bauingas, Bauinks, Bavinks, and Bavincks who all bore Bavo's name in Bentheim through the centuries that followed.[4]

Some of those descendants left the Lutheran church, becoming Mennonites who moved to the Netherlands in search of greater religious tolerance. (One of Herman's own contemporaries, the Dutch Mennonite preacher Lodewijk Gerhard Bavink [1812–90], descended from this branch of the family.)[5] Of those who remained in Bentheim, more still left the Lutheran church to become Reformed. While that ecclesiastical realignment did not push the first Reformed Bavincks to leave their hometown, subsequent developments in the mid-nineteenth century would eventually lead one of their clan—Herman's father, Jan—to look across the border, as his Mennonite cousins had done, in search of freedom to follow his religious conscience. Across its history, even into the nineteenth century, the Bavinck line was well acquainted with enforced religious sojourn. In that regard, they remained the sons and daughters of Saint Bavo—a man whose own conversion experience led him to abandon the comforts of home and hearth in favor of a long missionary journey through France and Flanders.

Lower Saxony and the Netherlands in Modern Europe

The capital of Lower Saxony, Bentheim had a long-standing, diffuse cultural identity, with its historically bilingual population reflecting its frontier location. However, and perhaps typical of its location as a border town, its history was marked by annexations and conquests. Swenna Harger has described this as producing a local population of resilient and independent spirit: "They became Hanoverians; they were invaded by Napoleon. Prussia took them over in 1866. They lived under the Kaiser and under Hitler. Through all this they came with good courage. If you ask them today about their identity, they just might tell you, 'Wy bin't Groofschappers' (We are from the County)."[6] Bentheim's nineteenth-century history was also one of emigration—in the case of different branches of the Bavinck family, from Germany to the Netherlands, but in many instances from Bentheim to North America.[7]

Although Bentheim's cultural identity straddled the Dutch-German border, it was nonetheless a German town, and the ecclesiastical ties of Herman's branch of the Bavinck family were to German denominations. At some earlier point, these particular Bavincks had left the Lutheran church and joined the (German) Reformed church (Reformirte Kirche),[8] although Herman's father would leave the church of his birth to join the Evangelical Old Reformed Church in Lower Saxony (Evangelisch-altreformierte Kirche in Niedersachsen).

In order to understand their family history, however, we must look beyond their context in Lower Saxony, beginning instead with earlier historical developments across Europe, and then, more specifically, in the Netherlands.

Nineteenth-Century Secessions and Revivals

Across Protestant northern Europe, much early nineteenth-century theology had been profoundly affected by the values and beliefs of the Enlightenment, which, in turn, had produced (and given dominance to) a liberal, antisupernatural, rationalistic form of Christianity. Alongside this, by the mid-nineteenth century, the reordering of society along liberal democratic lines raised new questions on the church's relationship to other centers of social power. In response to this combination of factors, a range of movements arose that tried to recover (to differing degrees) personal piety, a higher view of the authority of Scripture, a greater emphasis on personal Christian experience, and a reassertion of the contrast between sin and grace. The eighteenth and early nineteenth centuries thus saw the rise of pietism in Germany, evangelical awakenings in the English-speaking world, and the Réveil emanating from Switzerland across a range of European settings. A concurrent movement of devotionalization among nineteenth-century Dutch Catholics also mirrored this series of Protestant revivals.

How did this play out in the Netherlands, and how did that come to affect the Bavinck family in Bentheim, and then as they moved into Dutch society?

The Netherlands was also subject to the conditions of upheaval described at the outset of this chapter. In 1815, the Batavian Republic came to an end as William I became ruler of a new Kingdom of the Netherlands (Koninkrijk der Nederlanden). In this role, he set out to provide political unity between the Netherlands and Belgium, a task complicated by the religious division between Catholics and Protestants in his new kingdom. William I's ideal was to join them in a single, enlightened denomination that would then exist to a particular end: to serve the state by educating the people in civic virtues.[9] Ultimately, this unification proved impossible, leaving William I to work with the preexisting Christian division. In general, early nineteenth-century Dutch Catholics rejected the king's ideal of a single church redefined in line with the values of the Enlightenment and proved less than willing to be co-opted into his plan. The king's attention thus came to focus on the Dutch Reformed Church, which proved more receptive to his own Enlightenment-inspired influence,[10] and through which he believed he could promote a practically oriented, enlightened "Christianity above doctrinal division."[11]

William I had inherited governmental Departments for Religious Affairs established in 1808[12] and a state that, in 1814, had taken upon itself the task of providing stipends for Reformed ministers. The state attempted to exert considerable influence on Protestant worship, especially through its promotion of the (often moralistic) hymnbook *Evangelische Gezangen* (1807). This growing influence created a context in which the evangelical Réveil movement spreading through France and Switzerland would also see growth among Dutch Protestants. Conventicles were formed, increasing numbers of Reformed preachers began to emphasize the Réveil's "sin and grace" religion, and the works of the theologians of the older Dutch Further Reformation (Nadere Reformatie) experienced renewed popularity.

A further reaction to the state's appropriation of the Dutch Reformed Church for its own goals was seen in the Secession of 1834 (Afscheiding). Hendrik de Cock (1801–42), a Reformed minister who had experienced a pietistic conversion, began to protest and preach openly against the dominant liberal spirit within the Dutch Reformed Church. In 1834, he and his congregation formally seceded from the church. In the same year, he authored the foreword to a book opposing the aforementioned hymnbook, *"The Evangelical Hymns" Tested and Weighed and Found to Be Too Light*,[13] by Jacobus Klok, a businessman from Delfzijl.[14] This particular religious insurrection drew clergy and laity alike.

Klok's criticism of the substance and purpose of these hymns is instructive in demonstrating the atmosphere in the emerging secessionist circles. Attacking its supporters as "so-called Reformed teachers and their followers" who he claimed were, in reality, "Arminian, Pelagian, and Socinian," Klok wrote in damning terms. "Viewed as a whole, these 192 hymns are, in summary, in my opinion, the love songs of sirens, sung to rid the Reformed—already singing—of their sanctifying doctrine and to replace it with a false and deceptive doctrine and to coax all the parties outside of the church in order to unite them."[15]

This feeling began to spread more widely.[16] Within two years, approximately 2 to 3 percent of the Dutch Reformed Church's membership had joined the newly formed Seceder Church (which, from 1869, would be styled as the Christelijke Gereformeerde Kerk [Christian Reformed Church]), which had gathered some 130 congregations.

Their church came into existence before full freedom of religion was allowed in the 1848 constitutional revision. Prior to this, from 1815 onward, a limited degree of religious freedom had been established, whereby Dutch Roman Catholics, Lutherans, Remonstrants, and Mennonites were granted toleration. However, the freedom to be Reformed did not entail the right to leave the established Reformed Church in order to start another denomination. Therefore, the first Seceders (Afgescheidenen) faced considerable state persecution on account of their departure from the mother church. Indeed, they were among the last Europeans to experience the state-sanctioned billeting of troops in their homes (and be charged for the cost of the billeting).[17] As a result, many immigrated to North America, founding Dutch Reformed colonies in the United States and Canada. As will be seen, those who remained eventually came to occupy a more settled place in modern Dutch society and saw their denomination grow rapidly in that context.

At the time of the Dutch Secession, Herman's branch of the Bavinck family was in Bentheim, where the Afscheiding's impact resonated in a parallel movement in the local German Reformirte Kirche. There, in 1838, four years after the secession in the Netherlands, another secession took place as a small Reformed church was birthed: the Evangelisch-altreformierte Kirche (Old Reformed Church) in Niedersachsen, the denomination in which Herman Bavinck's father, Jan, would come to play an important role.[18]

Central to this movement were the Bentheimers Harm Hindrik Schoemaker (1800–1881) and Jan Barend Sundag (1810–93). As a young man, Sundag, the son of pietistic German Reformed parents, came to believe that the ministers in the local Reformirte Kirche had abandoned the true Reformed faith. He formally broke with the church in 1837 and quickly gathered and led a small group of like-minded believers who met for Sunday worship in a conventicle. Schoemaker underwent a conversion experience at the age of twenty-three and (in 1837, the same year that Sundag left the Reformed Church) formally aligned himself with the Dutch Seceders.[19]

Together, Sundag and Schoemaker became the focal point of a local movement to recover living piety and orthodox doctrine—a movement that looked toward the Dutch Secession and its theological leaders. As was the case for the early Seceders in the Netherlands, the first Reformed Christians to leave the Reformirte Kirche in Bentheim were subject to state persecution. Ordinary members of the Old Reformed Church received fines, while their ministers were regularly imprisoned.[20] These fines increased each time a person was caught attending illegal church services, which were often broken up by armed police.[21] When the Dutch Seceder minister Albertus van Raalte led a movement of persecuted Seceders to pursue a better life in North America, he was joined by many Old Reformed Christians from Bentheim.[22]

The Spring of Nations

The Old Reformed Church's lot changed considerably in the midst of the revolutions of 1848. During these revolutions—the Spring of Nations—political upheavals led to the implementation of new, modern, liberal social ideals across much of Europe. As has already been mentioned, in the Netherlands this meant the adoption of a new constitution under King William II, which turned the country into a modern liberal democracy (and included the freedom to form new Reformed denominations).

In Bentheim, the Old Reformed Christians felt the impact of the revolutions in that they were also granted freedom of religion, albeit in stages. Until 1847, it was illegal for citizens of Bentheim to leave the Reformirte Kirche in order to start another denomination. A qualified degree of religious freedom was first introduced in 1848, ending the persecution of Old Reformed believers and granting them tolerance, but not making them equal subjects under the law. Until the Kingdom of Hanover (to which Bentheim belonged) joined Prussia in 1866, the local Reformirte Kirche minister could demand forced declarations from Old Reformed members, stating that they had never intended to leave the Reformirte Kirche. Until 1873, all Reformed births had to be registered in the Reformirte Kirche, and every Reformed couple wishing to marry first needed the permission of the local Reformirte Kirche minister: no exemption was granted to the Old Reformed. The practice of taxing Old Reformed believers in order to fund the Reformirte Kirche only stopped universally in 1900.[23]

Religious freedom entered into the Old Reformed experience gradually. In comparison to the Netherlands, Lower Saxon society (and the place occupied by the Old Reformed within it) liberalized slowly. And therefore, the pace at which they had to process their newfound relationship to a pluralistic religious context was different from the pace at which the Dutch Seceders had moved. However, the Spring of Nations did change the Old Reformed Church's lot definitively, if not immediately. Their place in society, as a religious group that styled itself as *Old* insofar as it sought to revive pre-Enlightenment Christian tradition, was forever changed by the implementation of a distinctly *new* modern, liberal social ideal championed by the likes of Immanuel Kant and Gotthold Lessing—namely, the belief that people should not be persecuted for their lack of adherence to the beliefs of the state church.

Although some previous Bavinck biographers have tended to view Bentheim romantically, as though its relative obscurity and communal Reformed identity made it an "almost ideal place for Christians to live,"[24] a retelling of its history should also make plain that early nineteenth-century Bentheim was a part of this broader context of Europe-wide upheaval. It was profoundly affected by the onset of modernity.[25] While it was a place of great natural beauty, mid-nineteenth-century Bentheim was also a challenging locale for Reformed Christians who did not align themselves with the established Reformed

Church. By the time Jan Bavinck was born, Bentheim was a typical northern European town at the end of the early modern period. Its favored religion was established, moralistic, and antisupernatural, and its social structure (with rapidly modernizing judicial and medical systems) was characteristic of its era.

Orthodox Participation in Modern Society

Herman Bavinck's Lower Saxon roots contribute in no small way to the eventual course of his life. They also provide a corrective to the assumption that prior to his move to Leiden, or his own emergence as a prominent theologian who self-consciously tried to combine orthodoxy and modernity, he and his family had inhabited a premodern bubble and were in no sense children of their times.

It would be wrong to homogenize the various modernities developing in diverse nineteenth-century Europe[26] and, in so doing, for example, to ignore the piety and strongly Reformed identity that marked many people in nineteenth-century Bentheim. However, it remains to be said that Herman Bavinck's father was born into a modernizing world and that this cultural legacy was bequeathed to Herman. The question of how to inhabit the modern world while maintaining a vital connection to pre-Enlightenment orthodox Christianity was not Herman Bavinck's own creation. Rather, it was inherited from his father and was *already* central to the story of the secessions in the Netherlands and Lower Saxony in the 1830s and the revolutions of 1848.

An intriguing picture thus begins to emerge. The church Jan Bavinck would join styled itself "Old" rather than "New," and in so doing, it rejected one of the key tenets of the Enlightenment's modern program—namely, the claim that that tradition was laden with irrationality and superstition and should be shunned in favor of the new, the modern, and the rational.[27] In the face of this, the Old Reformed Church reasserted an older identity and orthodoxy. However, by accident more than design, its existence post-1848 was as a curiously modern social institution in a society reimagined by the implementation of modern liberal values. In short, the relationship that will be seen between Jan Bavinck's tradition and the modern world is already a complex one, where the rejection of one modern tenet was enabled by the application of another. Evidently, for the orthodox and the modern alike, finding one's feet in this new, late modern world was a game of give-and-take.

This is not to imply, of course, that either the Dutch Seceders or the Old Reformed in Bentheim were universally glad to join in this game. In the Dutch case, the Seceder movement was marked by a strong divergence between those who wanted to be recognized as the true Dutch Reformed church (and thus to replace the current established church in an otherwise untouched early modern social order) and those who wanted to exist as a minority group, alongside the established church, free to practice their beliefs (in a new social order). The latter group, led by the likes of Albertus van Raalte (1811–76) and Hendrik Pieter Scholte (1805–68), called enthusiastically for the liberalization of Dutch social space. The former group, however, was not quick to celebrate and affirm a liberal notion like religious pluralism, however much this newfound freedom transformed their existence.

Neither secession, then, should be seen as homogenous in its impulses or intentions. Believing that the existing Reformed churches had departed from the true Reformed tradition, the Afgescheidenen certainly saw themselves as reasserting the identity of *the* true Reformed church. However, the manner in which this reassertion was envisioned was complex and diverse. To recall Pieter Stokvis's memorable description, the majority impulse in the Dutch Secession was to restore "a mythical Calvinist church state."[28] De Cock's concerted efforts to have William I convene a synod to recognize the Seceders as the true Reformed church perhaps typify this desire. Alongside this, though, was a significant minority that called instead for an end to their persecution through the separation of church and state.

But for the majority of Seceders, their new post-1848 status—as a minority group tolerated in a pluralistic liberal social setting—was not one of their own design or choosing. Nonetheless, it was the new situation thrust upon them, benefiting them in unexpected ways and challenging them in others.

While the modern Dutch constitution reflected William II's willingness to establish more distance between church and state,[29] it did not establish a new, rigidly defined religious landscape. Its effect, rather, was to create a modern environment within which multiple religious forces could assert their own identities and existences. As James Kennedy and Jan Zwemer have argued, "A return to the situation before the Constitution was no longer conceivable,"[30] insofar as the social structure introduced in 1848 made it impossible for any one religious group to carry on its pre-1848 existence. And with that, the realization of the quest to be the only true Reformed church and be treated accordingly by society became very difficult indeed. From now on, no religious group would be persecuted or privileged by the state.[31] Seceders were, however, free to gather for worship and create their own space in this new society—but only insofar as they were prepared to accept their government's basic conditions (in this case, the separation of church and state and the religious pluriformity necessitated by the freedom of religion).

As was also true of the mainline Reformed (Hervormd) and the political Liberals (Liberalen), not all Seceders and Old Reformed were willing to engage in this new mode of inhabiting their societies, which would have meant accepting that they had become "new religious forces [who had] to contend for their own place in [a pluralistic] society."[32] Those who were unwilling to strike a deal with this new society could, of course, exercise their religious freedom by resuming a peripheral place in society. The right of religious freedom did not oblige religious groups to involve themselves in any other part of society, and therefore it became perfectly possible to use religious freedom to continue calling for a pre-1848 goal—however much more difficult the attainment of that goal had now become. And of course, in immigration to the new world, there remained one way of emphatically rejecting a reimagined Dutch society.[33]

In reflecting his own location in this range of possibilities, Herman Bavinck would later offer equally strong criticism, on the one hand, of Seceders who remained in the Netherlands but whose exercise of religious freedom was limited to worship services and evangelistic outreach *and*, on the other, of those émigrés who wished no further involvement in the cultural development of their fatherland: "Satisfied with the ability to worship God in their own houses of worship or to engage in evangelism, many left nation, state and society, art and science to their own devices. Many withdrew completely from life, literally separated themselves from everything, and, in some cases, what was even worse, shipped off to America, abandoning the Fatherland as lost to unbelief."[34] In the case of some of those who chose to remain, it took decades before they accepted their new status as minority groups in a religiously diverse society, in place of the early view that they had simply reconstituted the old, true church.[35] Others were far more enthusiastic in affirming the new social terrain. The Dutch Seceder Scholte, for example, was inspired by the practice of religious freedom in America and argued early on that the Afgescheidenen should embrace their new freedom in the Netherlands' new context.[36]

Prior to the 1848 constitutional revision, Scholte publicly called for the separation of church and state in the Netherlands. In doing so, he simultaneously denied the rights of the state to exercise authority over the church and the right of the church to involve itself in the political realm. When the government minister for religious affairs encouraged Reformed ministers to offer prayers of thanksgiving for William II on his birthday in 1841, Scholte, as editor of the Seceder publication *De Reformatie*,[37] set forth how one might pray for the king while believing in the separation of church and state.[38] In accordance with Scripture, he argued, Christians should pray for all those in authority. However, praying for William II as a person did not require a believer to pray in support of his particular regime—and in reality, Christians of different persuasions would invariably pray for different outcomes. To follow Scholte's reasoning, why would Dutch Roman Catholics not pray for the king to join their church and submit to their pope? And why would liberal Dutch Reformed Christians not pray for the king to act swiftly in dealing with the Seceders? Should the Seceders not pray for the king to follow their movement?[39] In any case, Scholte encouraged his own readers to pray that William II would experience conversion and grant freedom of religion to the Dutch people. Four years on from this, in 1845, Scholte published the full text of the *Virginia Statute for Religious Freedom of 1786* in *De Reformatie*, further encouraging his Seceder readership with this American example of religious pluriformity.[40]

Both van Raalte and Scholte encouraged Seceders to emigrate in view of what Scholte described (in an 1846 letter to the Dutch Calvinist statesman Guillaume Groen van Prinsterer) as "the government's obstinate opposition to the freedom of religion."[41] The pre-1848 Secession church became increasingly marked by what Hans Krabbendam has called "the spread of emigration-fever"[42] precisely because increasing numbers of Seceders were calling for a different kind of social state within which freedom of religion would be guaranteed.

In making this call for religious freedom, Scholte and those who followed him were not arguing for a godless, secular state. He believed that the House of Orange had been appointed by God to rule over the Dutch people and that the Dutch monarch had to be a Christian (though not a Mennonite, which would require pacifism and render the king unable to fulfill the role assigned in Romans 13:4, and not a Roman Catholic, which would make him subordinate to the pope).[43] In Scholte's view, the Dutch monarch should be a Reformed Christian who defended the freedom of his subjects' religious expression.[44]

In this context, interestingly, both van Raalte and Scholte did nonetheless emigrate to America despite the eventual implementation of religious freedom in the Netherlands. Attempts to explain why they chose emigration over the new social order for which they had campaigned quickly become mired in intra-Secessionist politics. The Seceder Simon van Velzen, for example, argued that Scholte's influence in the movement had waned and that he emigrated in search of greater personal appreciation and importance.[45] However, as Hans Krabbendam has helpfully acknowledged, this verdict probably tells us more about van Velzen than it does about Scholte, bearing in mind that their visions for the relationship between the Seceder church and the state were considerably different.[46]

Whatever truly motivated the likes of Scholte and van Raalte to emigrate, their stories, before and after 1848, demonstrate the ongoing nonstatic, non-homogenous nature of Seceder identity and theological vision. Clearly, the Seceders' path through the modern world was a complicated one.

Herman Bavinck as a Son of the Secession

What, however, does the history of theological diversity among the Afgescheidenen contribute to our biography of Herman Bavinck?

Bavinck has often been described not simply as the son of a Secession preacher, which he was quite literally, but also as a "son of the Secession" himself. This title predates by some time the development of the "two Bavincks" hermeneutic mentioned in this book's introductory comments.[47] Indeed, the "child of the Secession" label was invoked by Bavinck himself during his own lifetime. Nonetheless, in the heyday of more recent "two Bavincks" scholarship, the "son of the Secession" label was applied to the parts of his oeuvre deemed the work of the "orthodox Bavinck." As an epithet, "son of the Secession" was thus employed in sharp contrast to its antithesis, the "modern Bavinck,"[48] with the assumed implication that the Seceders were not modern and that fidelity to his Seceder legacy somehow should have directed him away from rather than into the modern world. While the problems with this reading of Bavinck's own thought are now well documented, a related flaw in its assumptions about his Seceder forebears should also be acknowledged—namely, that it assumes a certain degree of (negative) univocity among the Afgescheidenen regarding their posture toward their new, modernizing society.

From its inception onward, however, the Secession movement's theological vision was far from homogenous.[49] Such should hardly be surprising, given the movement's rapid growth and the manner in which its theological input came from a small original group of Seceder ministers and a larger number of untrained preachers. In that light, a new reading of Bavinck's identity as a "son of the Secession" would do well to heed J. van den Berg's reminder that speaking generically of "*the* Seceders" is highly problematic.[50] The Afgescheidenen were diverse. Unless we further nuance which stream of secessionist thought and tradition Bavinck followed, "son of the Secession" becomes a general, and not particularly useful, identifier.

As the Secession church grew rapidly in the first few decades of its existence, Seceder emigration began to tail off, and that branch of the church reached a generally settled view of its place as a tolerated minority group in late nineteenth-century Dutch society. Bavinck's life demonstrates a noteworthy development within this acceptance, whereby Seceders became increasingly ambitious in their own attempts to carve out a space within late nineteenth- and early twentieth-century Dutch society.

I continue to describe Bavinck as a "son of the Secession," but do so aiming to give the label a richer texture. Certainly, Herman Bavinck was the son of the Seceder Jan Bavinck and an inheritor of the movement instigated by Hendrik de Cock. But he was also a son in (at least parts of) the tradition of Hendrik Pieter Scholte and Albertus van Raalte, and this, of course, is to say nothing of his proximity to the many rank-and-file Seceders whose unchronicled lives sought a greater degree of integration in their revised post-1848 society. It is in this sense that I invoke the title "son of the Secession"—not as a symptom of division in his outlook but rather to identify the beginnings of Bavinck's trajectory within the primordial core of the Secessionist movement and to see him as a critical figure in carrying that trajectory forward. The book locates Herman Bavinck within Jasper Vree's characterization of the Seceder move-ment as walking "the path from separation to integration"[51] and functions as a recovery of G. M. den Hartogh's deployment of the term ("een echt 'kind der Scheiding'") precisely as a descriptor for Bavinck's commitment to orthodox particpation in the modern world.[52]

One of the core assertions in this biography is that the central concerns of Bavinck's life are framed by several important dates: the Dutch Afscheiding of 1834, the formation of the Old Reformed Church in Bentheim in 1838, and the Spring of Nations in 1848. Only against this backdrop can we begin to make sense of a life tasked with the reimagining of both Dutch culture and the orthodox Reformed tradition within it.

For the Afgescheidenen and the Old Reformed, little rest could be found on either side of the Spring of Nations. The first decade of their respective existences, pre-1848, was taken up with an existentially difficult question—namely, How should orthodox Reformed Christians inhabit an *early modern* society that (because of its restricted view of religious freedom) persecuted them and hindered the realization of some of their key ideals? Post-1848, the question shifted to ask how orthodox Reformed Christians should inhabit a *late modern* society that (because of its religious pluralism) tolerated them while rendering some of their original ideals obsolete and unachievable. The ground beneath them kept on shifting. This is the context within which Jan Bavinck came to the fore, and it required him to engage with the questions his son Herman would continue to answer throughout his own life.

2

Jan Bavinck and
Geziena Magdalena Holland

"At that time, we were still pariahs."

A Short and Modern Sketch

Jan Bavinck was pious and ambitious in equal measure, with each trait spurring on *and* frustrating the other. More still, he was every inch a man of his century's petite bourgeoisie, albeit of the religiously awakened sort. He witnessed the fall of rationalistic Enlightenment-led Christianity and the strongmen monarchs who favored it, and he shed no tears for the demise of either. Rather, Jan embraced the new alternatives—experiential Calvinism and liberal democracy—with open arms. Whatever great social changes his children could recount, Jan's stories were better still.

Toward the end of his colorful life, he bequeathed to his children an unpublished, handwritten autobiography entitled "A Short Sketch of My Life."[1] An undated piece of writing, it was composed after fifty-four years in the ministry and shortly before its author's eightieth birthday.[2] At some point between the end of 1905 and 1906, "in the evening of [his] life," Jan set out to ensure that his memories would not be lost. In addition to these private family reflections, written while the elderly Jan lived in Amsterdam with Herman and his family, Jan had previously published a set of autobiographical reflections in *Salvation Only in the Name of Jesus*, a sermon published in booklet form in 1888 to mark the fortieth anniversary of his ordination.[3] Ostensibly a sermon on Acts 4:12, it offers a biblical exposition interwoven with memories of his life thus far. Those recollections were made during his years as the Christian Reformed Church's *pastor loci* in Kampen.

In this readiness to chronicle his own experiences at the peak of his powers, and once again in old age, we see Jan as a modern figure. That the elderly Jan Bavinck penned an unpublished autobiography, intended to be read by his own family, is in itself laden with historical meaning. The practice of writing such an account of one's own life was by no means novel. The writing of such "egodocuments" had been commonplace in German and Dutch cultures for centuries before Jan Bavinck ever put pen to paper.[4] However, the particular emphases, details, and purposes of autobiographical writing changed significantly during those centuries.

For the most part, such private autobiography was intended for the author's immediate family. The earliest (medieval and post-Reformation) autobiographies were motivated by a desire to continue a family's collective memory, which later developed into a more individualistic impulse: the person writing did not want to be forgotten by his children. From 1800 onward—the period into which Jan Bavinck was born—two significant changes took place in the writing of family autobiography. In the first place, authors began to use the genre as an outlet for disseminating information that had proven too difficult to discuss more directly; and second, the authors began to use the genre to reflect more introspectively on their experiences of childhood. Seventeenth- and eighteenth-century autobiographies, in comparison, regarded childhood as largely irrelevant to one's adult formation. In his extensive study of the place of childhood in Dutch autobiographies, Rudolf Dekker describes these developments in a way that also frames "A Short Sketch of My Life" perfectly.

Historians of literature have made a distinction between two models of autobi-ography. In the traditional model the author tells a great deal about his family background, and less about his own youth. He sees himself in the first place as a link in a family lineage. In the modern model the author is brief about his forefathers, but dwells at great length on his early years. From the beginning the author is the central figure. This change took place in the second half of the eighteenth century, and was a consequence of a growing sense of individuality. The development of Dutch autobiographical writing fits into this scheme. Most authors from the sixteenth and seventeenth centuries do not spend more than a few words on their childhood. They usually limit themselves to mentioning their schools and teachers, and often start their story only when they have established a position of their own in society.[5]

Jan Bavinck's autobiography bespeaks his own location as a typical late modern European. He was interested in his forefathers and their influence on his life, albeit to a limited degree. Far more significant, he believed, was the impact of his own childhood and upbringing. In telling his children about his adult life, he turned to events that had been too difficult to discuss in conversation: the deaths of four of their siblings and of their mother, his acquaintance with religious persecution (which his children had never experienced), and his sense of failed ambition. Nineteenth-century Europeans, Jan Bavinck included, perceived the passing of time differently than their own forebears did. They paid more attention to its passing, which seemed to be occurring quickly, as their own century hurtled toward (and then beyond) revolutionary upheaval.[6] Jan's sketch is peppered with references to this awareness—this is an autobiography in which something as mundane as a house clock and as world-changing as the 1848 Spring of Nations play key roles. For that reason, Jan Bavinck's generation set about chronicling their experiences with remarkable enthusiasm. As a product of its time, Jan's autobiography is the tale of a life spent looking, desiring, and moving forward. It is modern through and through.

Piety in the Bentheimer Wald

A "short sketch" in name only—his account of his own life is over forty-two thousand words in length—Jan's recollections begin with a brief prologue reflecting on the promises of God to his people in Isaiah 42:16:

> And I will lead the blind
> in a way that they do not know,
> in paths that they have not known
> I will guide them.
> I will turn the darkness before them into light,
> the rough places into level ground.
> These are the things I do,
> and I do not forsake them. (ESV)

Jan Bavinck's deep personal piety is evident in this prologue: his journey through this world has depended on the promises of Isaiah's God, who shows mercy to sinners and redirects the paths of the blind. At the outset of the autobiography proper, he introduces himself as having been born in Bentheim on February 5, 1826—a recollection that immediately turns into appreciation of modernity's impact on his hometown during his lifetime. "In my youth, one did not know of railways, but now the line runs from Arnhem to Salzbergen via Bentheim, and it is a beautiful sight when the train steams through the wood like a snake."[7] This new train, making its way through the forest around Bentheim en route from Lower Saxony to the Netherlands, forms a striking symbol of the transition lived through during Jan's lifetime: the shift from the preindustrial to the industrial era. Wood, the prime material of preindustrial society, had now been surpassed by coal and iron, and with that, European life had changed forever. Indeed, the forest in question, the Bentheimer Wald, had been an important local source of fuel in preindustrial times. As this new mechanical wonder sped between the trees, it rendered the resources derived from them largely obsolete. And with this, it redefined how these newly industrialized Europeans, Jan Bavinck included, inhabited their world.

The cultural critic Wolfgang Schivelbusch has described this effect of railway travel on Europeans of Jan Bavinck's generation as the "annihilation of space and time."[8] Because of the steam train, Jan had learned to rethink how (and how quickly) he could move around his world. The advent of the steam train was perhaps the ultimate symbol of modernization in nineteenth-century Europe—and for Jan, it was a thing of beauty. In that regard, his birth in Bentheim had positioned him well to appreciate this shrinking modern world: because this particular train route linked the Netherlands to Europe more widely, his hometown played a prominent role in the travel literature of the day.[9]

Hermanus Bavinck and Fenna Niehaus

Jan Bavinck's parents, Hermanus and Fenna (née Niehaus), were members of the Reformirte Kirche in Bentheim. They had six children—five daughters and one son—with Jan being their fifth child. Hermanus, after whom Jan would name one of his own sons, was a carpenter who came from a family of carpenters. In 1829, when his children ranged from twelve years to a few months old, Hermanus died. He was forty-nine, and Jan only three.[10] "Although I was still so young, I have always been able to remember, in the distance, that Father lived, that he, for example, came home from work in the evenings, he went to sit by the fire, and that I had to stand on his lap to warm myself. Above all, this [memory] has remained vivid to me, that at Father's burial a neighbor took me and my four sisters by the hand, led us to the coffin in which Father lay, and that we all then began to weep bitterly."[11] Jan's mother mourned Hermanus's passing until her own death (in 1850) and never remarried, despite more than one opportunity to do so. Rather, she devoted herself to raising her children as a single mother. Until he was twelve, Jan Bavinck attended the Reformirte Schule, where he received a bilingual (German and Dutch) education. Jan's branch of the Bavinck family attended the Reformirte Kirche, where church services were also held in both German and Dutch, while he also attended a catechism class taught in German by the local minister, A. L. van Nes.[12]

Bentheim, at least in Jan Bavinck's memories, was a prosperous but spiritually slumberous place. There, Jan grew up in a home typical of the religious middle class, in which the Bible was occasionally read, but—to Jan's disappointment—its consequences for one's own life were never discussed. Although public and family prayers were the norm, Jan was drawn to stories of Christians who practiced private, fervent prayer. The Reformirte Kirche strongly emphasized moral behavior but shied away from accenting the transformative effects of the gospel on the Christian's life. (The sole book written by his pastor in the Reformirte Kirche, van Nes, was a moralistic work written to warn Christians against the consumption of alcohol in general and of Dutch gin in particular.)[13] As a teenager, Jan began to encounter Christians who discussed a different set of emphases within the Reformed faith—the "second birth" (*wedergeboorte*), "faith" (*geloof*), and "conversion" (*bekeering*). These terms were alien to Jan, who wanted to understand them as experiences. He began uttering emotional prayers of confession, all the while being unsure of whether God would hear or answer favorably.

Jan Bavinck's Spiritual Awakening

While Jan was still a teenager, his maternal uncle Harm Niehaus came under the influence of Jan Barend Sundag, the pious Reformed preacher introduced in the previous chapter. In Jan Bavinck's account, Harm had been drawn by Sundag's movement and, along with his daughter, had been converted to the same orthodox, experiential faith. This news attracted Jan, who—like many young northern Europeans in that period—experienced a longing for a faith more vital and orthodox than could be found in the established churches at that time.

In 1842, at age sixteen, he heard Sundag preach. This experience, a sermon delivered in a farmhouse in Schüttorf, was a "turning point" in his life. After this, he attended meetings of both the Dutch Seceders and the Old Reformed Church, regularly crossing the Bentheimer Wald on foot with his uncle and cousin to attend Old Reformed services in a farmhouse. In context, the choice to attend illegal church services held outside the auspices of the established Reformirte Kirche was both exhilarating and difficult for Jan. He felt a sense of loyalty to van Nes, who had taught him the Heidelberg Catechism. Significantly, though, the teenage Jan began to contrast Reformed doctrine and the Reformirte Kirche: the mere fact that a church styled itself Reformed, he now believed, was no guarantee that its doctrine was in line with the historic Reformed tradition. With that conclusion, it seemed inevitable that he would eventually leave the Reformirte Kirche. However, pre-1848, if he were to look for his favored doctrine beyond the established church, the personal cost would be considerable. In view of these consequences, he was "afraid of all sectarianism and separatism and wanted to remain in the Reformed line."[14]

As he walked through the Bentheimer Wald to Seceder meetings,[15] his affections and loyalties were being pulled between the illicit and the approved, between the farmhouse gathering and the Reformirte Kirche's seventeenth-century building, between his different loyalties to Sundag and van Nes, and between Reformed doctrine and the Reformirte Kirche. In that light, the contrast drawn in "A Short Sketch of My Life" between the Bentheimer Wald of his childhood, that of his teenage years, and his eventual view of it in the early twentieth century is conspicuous. To the young Jan Bavinck it was as a place of freedom and adventure[16] before it became the route between two conflicting worlds in a conflicted phase of his teenage life. Eventually, in a more tolerant age, the forest became the natural stage for a mechanical wonder. It is a subtle but important motif in "A Short Sketch of My Life."

> Could I indeed leave the Reformirte Kirche and join myself to those who had already and totally broken with her and who had set up an independent church alongside her? I deliberated on and thought about this question for a long time; I spoke about it with Sundag and with others; I went on my knees [in prayer] about it many times and sought the Lord's countenance, humbly and earnestly beseeching him that he would show me the way in this weighty matter that I had to take up and follow through. I hesitated and doubted for some time, but finally I reached the conclusion that I should join the Old Reformed Church as a member.[17]

Having discussed his newfound beliefs and experiential faith with the Reformed Church minister van Nes, he reached a conclusion: "Frankly, I can and may bear witness that in order to stay Reformed, I separated myself from the Reformirte Kirche and joined the Old Reformed Church."[18]

Jan Bavinck's Path toward Ministry

Having aligned himself with the Old Reformed, Jan Bavinck then took up an apprenticeship in wood turning. In his 1888 public recollections, he claimed, "[I] chose a profession, thinking that it was not the will of the Lord to send me to the ministry of the Word."[19] Privately, however, he gave his children a different story. Apparently, the teenage Jan Bavinck chose wood turning because it would mean moving to Gildehaus, where he would study under (and live with) J. B. Krabbe, a wheel turner who was a committed member of the Old Reformed Church. Residence in the Krabbe household carried a further attraction to Jan: at that time, Sundag also lived with the Krabbe family. This period offered Bavinck an extended exposure to Sundag's ideas: "I had the opportunity," he recalled, "to meet and talk with him every day."[20]

In exploring Jan Bavinck's life and its influence on Herman, paying special attention to Jan's eventual location in the diverse Secession movement, this early and formative interaction with Sundag is significant. Sundag strongly opposed the emigrationist tendencies of van Raalte and argued instead that Seceders should stay in their own land and contend for their faith there.[21] In coming into contact with the ideas of van Raalte and Sundag, Jan Bavinck entered a complex (and diverse) theological movement. Sundag was far more culturally conservative than van Raalte and opposed both the latter's emigrationist impulse and his openness to modern culture.[22] In their own Seceder circles, the Bavincks—Herman included—would become noted for their own particular take on these issues, combining openness to modern culture with a strongly antiemigrationist stance. Those views, it seems, were first shaped in a wheel-turning workshop in Gildehaus.

In 1845, when Jan Bavinck was nineteen, Sundag petitioned the Old Reformed Church classis for help in his work. Feeling overburdened by the demands of his ministry, he was keen to see another man enter ministerial training. The precise details of the classis's response to Sundag vary across sources, although the thrust of the story remains the same. According to "A Short Sketch of My Life," five Old Reformed members—"J. H. Reurik, F. Huisken, B. H. Kaptein, G. J. Dalink and J. Bavinck"—had expressed an interest in this undertaking and were present at the meeting. (H. Beuker's *Tubantiana*, however, says that only three were under consideration: Bavinck, Huisken, and Reurik.)[23] The twenty-two members of the classis, a mixture of elders and deacons, however, were divided on whether to grant Sundag's request: eleven were for, and eleven against. Jan Bavinck's own portrayal of the situation is dramatic. In order to ascertain the Lord's will, the chairman suggested that lots be drawn.[24] Bavinck's own account says that two letters were written, one *for* and the other *against*, and a housemaid was called to draw one. She drew *for*. (H. Beuker claims that three letters were written, two against and one for).[25] One of the young men would be trained for ministry. Following this, the classis voted on which man would become the candidate. Once again, the vote was evenly tied: eleven had chosen Frederik Huisken, and eleven, Jan Bavinck. Lots were cast, with the same housemaid this time drawing Jan Bavinck's letter. In this particular experience, divine providence and personal desire seemed to coincide neatly: Jan Bavinck received his heart's desire, with the validation of the lot. He would train for ministry.

As the Old Reformed Church looked to the Dutch Seceders for theological leadership, it was an unsurprising choice that Jan Bavinck's theological training should take place in the Netherlands. However, "A Short Sketch of My Life" makes plain that the Old Reformed were well aware of the non-homogenous nature of the Seceder movement over the border. At that time, Dutch Seceder ministerial training was provided in three locations—in Arnhem under Anthony Brummelkamp, in Groningen under Tamme Foppens de Haan, and in Ruinerwold under W. A. Kok. The classis decided that Bavinck should train in Ruinerwold, because "one judged that during the controversies between the sons of the Secession in Holland, Drenthe [Ruinerwold] had remained by the truth most purely."[26] The Old Reformed perceived various streams within the Secession movement and were intentional in their effort to direct their candidate into one of them in particular. Jan would need to find his own way among the sons of the Dutch Secession.

Theological Studies in the Netherlands

During Jan Bavinck's student years (1845–48), the theological school at which he studied was moved from Ruinerwold to Hoogeveen. There, the school met in a single room in a hired house—a situation that prompted ridicule from the locals. "I still remember very well how I was laughed at and mocked when going to the school for the first time. At that time, we were still always considered the pariahs of the society."[27]

Later accounts of Jan Bavinck's performance in Ruinerwold and Hoogeveen generally emphasize that he was an outstanding and accomplished student.[28] His autobiography, however, seems to emphasize more strongly that his own preseminary education had not prepared him well for this level of study. He recalls having to begin his studies by improving his Dutch, alongside learning geography and general history—a transition that proved challenging to him, at least initially. (Over the course of his own lifetime, Jan Bavinck sought a much higher level of schooling for his own children—no doubt motivated by his own awareness of the limitations of the Reformirte Schule in Bentheim.)[29]

He was also candid in acknowledging the shortcomings of his own seminary education, where two men were responsible for teaching theology, biblical and church history, exegesis, homiletics, Dutch history and language, Latin, Greek, and Hebrew. "Many subjects for only two men! It hardly needs saying that the education could be nothing other than deficient, very deficient, and inadequate."[30] This frank admission was tempered by his praise for the Seceder tradition insofar as its ideal, if not its early reality, had always been scientific training in theology. In any case, when considering Jan's support—decades later—of Herman's decision to pursue a rigorous scientific training in theology at Leiden, in preference to the education offered at the Theological School in Kampen, we must remember his openness about the limitations he felt at the small theological school in Hoogeveen.

Jan's studies and preparation for ordination concluded in the summer of 1848—a year that would prove pivotal for our understanding of the particularly modern Reformed heritage brought forward by his son. In Easter of that year, with Europe in the throes of revolution, Hanover went to war with Schleswig-Holstein. The young Hanoverian Jan Bavinck, then twenty-three, was called up to fight.

Privately, he despaired at this news, which came just as he was expecting to enter pastoral ministry. Having traveled back to Bentheim, he joined a group of reservists awaiting assessment by an officer and a doctor. "I can never forget that night," he wrote in 1888, "which I spent in the midst of cursing and drinking young men."[31] However, when they reached Jan Bavinck, he was told, "Put your clothes back on; we have enough men. . . . You are free; you can go."[32] If modern Europeans were indeed marked by the belief that the "ground was moving beneath their feet," in 1848—the year in which his personal circumstances took a string of dramatic twists—the ground under Jan Bavinck's feet was struck by an earthquake.

Under this pressure [of a busy study program] the days went by, and the year 1848 dawned, that year of troubles, revolts, and reversals. The revolution had broken out afresh in France and quickly affected other lands, also as far as Germany. The revolutionary movements were sometimes so strong and intense that they made the kings and princes tremble on their thrones. *Although the revolution caused all kinds of destruction and filled the hearts of thousands with terror and fear, for the "Separatists" or the Old Reformed in the Graafschap [Bentheim] it was the thing that brought relief and refreshment,* because not only did the persecutions stop in 1848—which they had been subjected to until then—but from that year on they [the Separatists] were also tolerated and could gather unhindered to serve the Lord according to their hearts' conviction. . . . The Old Reformed in the *Graafschap* were thus no longer opposed by the government; rather they were released and tolerated. *That they seized this, that they were happy about it and made use of it, goes without saying.*[33]

The Old Reformed had not sought or expected religious freedom. When their "enemies" began to celebrate and bells rang out, the Old Reformed asked what the celebration meant. The response surprised them: "because freedom of religion has arrived!"[34]

The Old Reformed in Late Modern Culture

Evidently, the Old Reformed embraced one aspect of their late modern period—a freedom fought for, as has been noted, by the likes of Kant and Lessing. What kind of posture did they adopt toward modern theology (as distinct from modern culture)? In *Tubantiana*, Beuker describes how the degree of separation between the Old Reformed and the Reformed Church only grew greater in this period. The former focused on the Dutch Seceders and their theology, whereas the latter "received only teachers and principles as they took shape in the rationalistic universities in Germany."[35] This division also developed along linguistic lines: the Old Reformed were free to hold services in German but preferred instead to worship in Dutch. In response, Reformed ministers who sided with Enlightenment-inspired theology made a concerted effort to strengthen German-language church services. Most younger preachers in Bentheim were more fluent in German than in Dutch, which gave German ideas a considerable advantage. (Prior to leaving Bentheim, Jan Bavinck was also more comfortable in German than in Dutch: when he arrived in Ruinerwold, his own Dutch was not yet good enough for further education.)[36]

The Reformirte Kirche published a monthly magazine and regular pamphlets criticizing Old Reformed doctrine—particularly its Augustinian account of election—and promoting the likes of Albrecht Ritschl and the *Vermittlungstheologen* (mediation theologians). In response, the Old Reformed disseminated their doctrine in pamphlets and monthly magazines (*De Vrije Presbyteriaan* and the *Graafschap Bentheimsche en Oostfriesche Grensbode*).[37] Although the Old Reformed were happy to accept the freedom offered by modern culture, they maintained a firm stance against modern theology—opposing and being opposed by it at every turn. Persecution had been replaced by a new struggle. They had been thrust into a battleground of ideas, where the combatants contended for the validity of their place in late modern society. To borrow Jan Bavinck's own turn of phrase, the Old Reformed had "moved from the farmhouse to the town."[38]

Ordination in Lower Saxony

Against that backdrop, on August 9, 1848, Jan Bavinck was ordained as minister of the Old Reformed Church. Now that the church was suddenly liberated from state persecution, he was set to work in the villages of Weldhausen, Uelsen, Wilsum, and Emlichheim, where Old Reformed services were held. In these villages, Old Reformed Church services were held on farms and in barns, with Jan Bavinck's ordination service taking place in the open air. A new manse was built in Uelsen, and the settled pattern of his ministry came to focus on Uelsen and Wilsum. In this phase of life, Jan's elders strongly encouraged him to marry. Soon after, Harm Hindrik Schoemaker—one of the most prominent early Seceders in Lower Saxony—introduced him to Geziena Magdalena Holland.

Geziena, the oldest daughter of Coenraad Bernardus Holland and Berendina Johanna Jonkman, was born on April 15, 1827, in Vriezenveen—a small town on the Dutch side of the border. There were links between the Old Reformed Church and a small Seceder group in Vriezenveen, where Jan had occasionally preached. However, Geziena's family belonged to the Dutch Reformed Church (Hervormde Kerk). The Hollands had not seceded. In writing of his wife's early life, however, Jan wrote that "she definitively chose to serve the Lord [and] . . . joined herself to the Lord's people to walk the narrow path to heaven with them."[39]

They married in Vriezenveen on April 27, 1850. Geziena was twenty-three, and Jan twenty-four. Although they were married after the Spring of Nations, at that time Old Reformed couples wishing to marry in Bentheim still had to seek the permission of the local Reformirte Kirche minister—a potential ignominy avoided by marriage in the more tolerant Netherlands.

After their wedding, Jan and Geziena were gifted a house clock (*huisklok*) by his students. (When Jan had left the theological school in Hoogeveen to begin his own ministry, he had agreed to teach the school's students in classical languages; during his years as a pastor in the Evangelical Old Reformed Church, eleven students traveled from Hoogeveen to Lower Saxony to study under him.) "My students also greeted us with joy; they honored us for this occasion with a house clock, which has served our family well for many years.

The Lord was good to us!"[40] S. J. Hofkamp's *A History of Civilization*, a cultural guide published six years after the Bavincks' wedding, noted that such timepieces were thoroughly à la mode in 1850s Dutch society.[41] In the early modern period, elaborate clocks were made fashionable by royal families, symbolizing a fusion of art and technology and demonstrating their owners' wealth. By the time Jan and Geziena married, this aspect of material and temporal culture had filtered down to the rapidly civilizing middle class. In the Bavinck home, the passing of time was constant and rapid and was to be observed in style.[42] Their first child, a daughter—Berendina Johanna—was born into this typically petit-bourgeois home in the following year.

Jan's early ministry in Bentheim was warmly appreciated. In 1853 he was called to pastor the Christian Reformed Church in Smilde, a small village in the northern Netherlands, but declined this call. This would not be his last call from a Dutch congregation. In the same year, he received—and accepted—an offer to work alongside his former mentor, W. A. Kok, in Hoogeveen. Jan's original intention was to combine roles as a minister and teacher at the theological school there. To his surprise, however, he had hardly arrived in Hoogeveen before the local theological school departed. On June 15, 1854, the synod moved to consolidate its efforts toward theological education—which until that point had taken place in several locations, reflecting a series of theological disputes among the Afgescheidenen—in a single school, to be opened later that year in Kampen.

Casting Lots and Writing Letters

The Seceders' new Theological School needed a full complement of teaching staff. Alongside Simon van Velzen, Anthony Brummelkamp, and Tamme Foppens de Haan—all prominent sons of the Dutch Secession—Jan Bavinck, then aged twenty-eight, was nominated. Once again, Jan felt himself hindered by the weakness of his own previous schooling: "How could I stand and work alongside men all three of whom had enjoyed an academic education?"[43] Because of this sense of inadequacy, he almost declined the nomination immediately. (The only commentary offered in *Salvation Only in the Name of Jesus* is, "I did not dare accept this nomination. By my own judgment, the task was too weighty for my capabilities.")[44]

After the synod, he spent time in Vriezenveen discussing the nomination with his wife and parents-in-law, who encouraged him to remain open to the possibility. As was relatively commonplace in his milieu, Jan entrusted his decision to God's will: once again, lots would be cast. He returned to Hoogeveen, penned two letters—one of acceptance, the other rejection—and sealed them in envelopes. He gave both to a local student, asking him to post one and discard the other.[45] "And which letter did he post? *The rejection letter.* No! I will not say anything about what I felt and what went on inside me at the moment I learned about this outcome! I only want to say this, that I had no peace about it, not then or for a long time afterward."[46] Why did Jan, the pious young Seceder, feel so disappointed in (and find no peace in) the outcome of a decisive lot? Jan's autobiography admitted that he was only reconciled to the outcome of the lot much later in life, because of Herman's own appointment at the Theological School. However, that appointment took place twenty-eight years after an unwitting student chose (in Jan's eyes, at least) the wrong envelope. For the time being, Jan remained ill at ease with the outcome of the lot—a discomfort made all the more acute in comparison to his earlier experience of casting lots in Bentheim. On that occasion, his own desire had converged neatly with the lot's expression of God's sovereignty. In his readiness to cast lots once again, it seems to be that Jan expected the same to happen: the student would send the letter of acceptance, and Jan would willingly take up his place in Kampen happy in the knowledge that the Lord had signaled his approval.

Events, however, had transpired somewhat differently: his trust in divine omnipotence had certainly not yielded the result he had expected. His displeasure at the lot's verdict became widely known. (Much later, interestingly, Herman would write that "casting lots and losing often makes one cantankerous.")[47] In the edition of the Seceder newspaper *De Bazuin* published on Friday, August 18, 1854, for example, the "Church News" carried a note detailing Jan's situation and calling for it to be reassessed: "We are informed that Rev. J. Bavinck, who declined a nomination as teacher at the to-be-established Theological School in Kampen, has had no peace [with this situation]. Would the trustees, when they gather, not call the honorable reverend anew, or preferably, urge the honorable reverend to accept the nomination?"[48] Jan's own later account of this episode also reflected on the apparent public clamor to overcome his refusal.

> When it had become generally known in the church that I had declined the nomination to be a teacher, I received many letters in which regret over my decision was pronounced. Among these letters there were even some that advised me to revisit my decision and to take it back. I did not dare to do that. I had already entrusted the decision once to the lot, and by this, I thought, I must remain. Although I had not been required to use the lot, the whole outcome of the lot belongs to the Lord. Could he not turn my refusal to a good end, make it work for good? Did I know what he in his high wisdom had intended for it

and what [purpose] it could and had to serve? Therefore, I did not revisit my refusal, and rather let it stand.[49]

However, this recollection sits awkwardly alongside the contents of his letters to the trustees of the Theological School following his refusal of their nomination. His initial rejection letter (July 18, 1854) offered no reasoning for his decision. Following this, he penned an angst-ridden letter to the trustees (July 25, 1854), explaining his lack of peace at the situation. In this letter, he posed hypothetical questions on whether he could rescind his decision, but found himself nonetheless faced with the now public knowledge (particularly in his own congregation) that he had already declined the nomination. A third letter followed (August 9, 1854), outlining the same dilemma, albeit in a calmer tone. The fourth and final letter (August 22, 1854), however, is the most significant. Referring explicitly to the aforementioned piece in *De Bazuin*, Jan wrote to express regret that this had become a public affair, and he set his future at the mercy of the trustees. If they were prepared to overlook his first refusal, he would be willing to accept the nomination.[50] Jan was now willing to see the lot's outcome as suggestive rather than definitive.

The trustees now had to respond. It was agreed that a vote would be held, for or against reconsideration of his nomination. Unlike his experience as a teenager at the classis in Bentheim, where a lot was cast because of an indecisive vote, a vote would now be held despite (or rather, because of) a decisive lot. The trustees voted seven to two against his appeal for reconsideration.[51] His chance had already come and gone. By this point, his pursuit of this position was met with an equally public rejection. At the end of September, *De Bazuin* reported that another minister, P. J. Oggel, the Seceder pastor in Utrecht, would receive the nomination.[52] Gallingly for Bavinck, Oggel also declined the nomination, and another man—Helenius de Cock—was eventually appointed.

One of Herman Bavinck's previous biographers, A. B. W. M. Kok, described Jan Bavinck as someone who was "*so* humble and who thought *so* little of himself and his gifts that he did not dare accept the nomination" to teach in Kampen.[53] Such a picture is hard to reconcile with Jan's efforts to overcome the lot's unwanted outcome: rather, the lot incident typifies the curious mixture of piety and ambition that shaped Jan's life. Another of Herman's biographers, Valentijn Hepp, had offered a slightly more muted, but similar, account, which leans on a report in *De Heraut* that notes that "through the lot he appealed to the Lord God [in this] decision, and was of the opinion that he had received an indication through it that he had to decline this nomination."[54] Jan's conduct in the aftermath of his (seemingly accidental) rejection of the nomination suggests a more complex picture—one in which he had tried to channel a sense of personal ambition through orthodox, experiential piety, learning (to his great surprise) that the lot did not always confirm the longings of a pious heart.

The Births and Deaths of Children

The Theological School in Kampen was opened—without Jan Bavinck among its faculty—on December 6, 1854. Exactly one week after this, Jan and Geziena's second child, a son, Herman, was born. The Bavincks, now a family a four, would spend another three years in Hoogeveen before Jan accepted a call to the Christian Reformed Church in Bunschoten. (Their daughter Femia was born in this period, in 1858.) They remained in Bunschoten until 1862, when Jan was called to pastor in Almkerk.

Their years in Almkerk (1862–73) were marked deeply by personal tragedy. In the year after their arrival, their fourth child, a son named Karel Bernhard, was born. This infant son died within two weeks of his birth. In 1864, their oldest child, Berendina Johanna (Dina) died at the age of thirteen. And four years on from this, their daughter Femia died aged only eight. The sense of loss he and Geziena felt at the deaths of Karel, Dina, and Femia was profound. (As was mentioned earlier, this style of unpublished autobiography was intended to tell its readers about things the writer had found too difficult to express verbally.) Their only comfort lay in the covenant of grace: God had promised to be faithful to their children in life and death. "That is how things were for us in Almkerk and Emmikhoven. We experienced love and distress there. The Lord, however, was with us in everything."[55]

Educating Seceder Children

The Seceder congregation in Almkerk included L. W. Hasselman,[56] who ran a private boarding school largely attended by children from the Christian Reformed Church. This school, in nearby Nieuwendijk, grew considerably in the 1860s. It quickly became important to the Bavincks: the Bavinck children attended its adjoining primary school, and Jan taught Greek and Latin. (In "A Short Sketch of My Life," Jan notes with pleasure that two of his former pupils in the Hasselman Institute had gone on to ministerial training in Kampen.) The school's curriculum was comprehensive and modern: its pupils learned Dutch, French, English, German, Latin, Greek, arithmetic, algebra, geometry, accounting, piano, art, and gymnastics.[57] It was a far cry from Jan's own piecemeal education in the Reformirte Schule in Bentheim, which had left him ill equipped for further study. For that reason, Jan was certainly glad to minister in the vicinity of such a school. (Indeed, in a 1923 obituary for Herman Bavinck, Hepp noted that due to their father's "love of science," the Bavinck children "enjoyed a far broader education than most ministers' children in their circles.")[58]

Pre-1848, of course, the Seceders had engaged in a considerable struggle with the state with regard to schooling. Convinced that the state should not exercise a monopoly on education and that Christian parents should assume the foremost responsibility in their children's education, some Seceders had begun their own clandestine schools, which were small in scale and limited in potential. While studying in Ruinerwold and Hoogeveen, for example, Jan Bavinck would likely have been familiar with the (illegal) Seceder schools in Hoogeveen and nearby Weerwille that had been run in the early 1840s— usually held in homes and often taught by people with little formal training— and that were eventually shut down by the government.[59] Post-1848, Seceder education improved considerably, with the Hasselman Institute as a particularly excellent example of the kind of schooling available to some Seceder children—in this case, the young Bavincks—in the 1860s.

As was mentioned at the outset of this chapter, Jan Bavinck's father, Hermanus, was both a carpenter and the son of a carpenter. In Hermanus Bavinck's preindustrial world, a father's occupational status had a direct and obvious impact on that of his son. His own son Jan, however, lived through the onset of industrialization—a process in which the labor market was transformed, rendering some occupations obsolete and others essential. As work became mechanized and highly specialized, trades largely ceased to be passed from fathers to their sons. Newly created education-dependent occupations proliferated, facilitated by the new reality that children's future prospects would be determined by their own attainments rather than by a professional status inherited from their parents. Although he was a carpenter's son, Jan Bavinck never became a carpenter. Rather, his brief foray into wheel turning aside, his working life was spent in a knowledge-based economy.

Jan Bavinck was well aware of this cultural shift. In "A Short Sketch of My Life," his awareness of the importance of education for participation in modern culture pulses through his own longings for a better education in Bentheim and Hoogeveen. Its echoes can be heard in his reluctance to accept a position (alongside better-educated colleagues) in Kampen. And it comes to the fore in the education he sought for his own children, with a view to their eventual role in Dutch society. The sense of ambition passed on between Jan and his children was also typical of their place as the petite bourgeoisie in the throes of industrialization: no longer assuming that their sons would follow their fathers' professions, Jan and Geziena were typical of that generation's parents, who directed their children toward longer, more rigorous educational streams.[60] The Bavinck children's schooling in Nieuwendijk was far removed from the small and struggling clandestine Seceder schools before 1848, just as it was also much better than Jan's own childhood experience in Bentheim. (And, as will be seen in the next chapter, Jan's ambition will also be evident in his support of his own children's ambitions to study at state universities.) The trajectory of his own life and that of the Seceder movement, and now that of his children, was moving along, its arc curving from its pre-1848 location at the periphery toward the center of Dutch society. Jan did not want his children to be pariahs.[61]

Jan Bavinck's Writings

The Almkerk years marked Jan's emergence as a writer. His first book, *Stemmen des heils* (Voices of salvation), a collection of published sermons, was released in 1863.[62] When that book was reprinted in 1870, it was noted in the cultural magazine *Onze Tolk: Centraalblad voor Kunst- en Letternieuws* (Our interpreter: Magazine for news on art and literature).[63] In the overview of that month's new book releases, Jan Bavinck's work is mentioned alongside books by Jules Verne[64] and Charles Haddon Spurgeon,[65] as well as a new Dutch translation of Martin Luther's Galatians commentary.[66] As a writer, the Seceder Jan Bavinck had joined the ranks of "new religious forces [who had] to contend for their own place in society."[67]

In 1866, his son Coenraad Bernardus (Bernard) was born. During the 1860s–70s, Jan would publish six more volumes of sermons.[68] In that period, he also became the editor of a new monthly magazine, *De Getuigenis* (The witness)—an outlet that showed a side to Jan's thought and relationship to modern culture not found in his volumes of printed sermons. Those were heavily focused on biblical exposition. In *De Getuigenis*, Jan addressed cultural themes far more directly. In the opening editorial of the magazine's first edition (coauthored with Helenius de Cock)—written when Herman was fourteen—Jan set out the case for a new Christian magazine written to address the needs of the day:

> In the present day, the intellectual climate is all-pervasive. Our church also experiences the influence of the age in which it finds itself. Our young people in particular can only be minimally held back from the influence of the *Zeitgeist*, as though that could somehow protect them from it. Therefore, we see the need that we should issue our own publication, in which the truths of the gospel

are declared and defended, and the truth and divinity of Scripture might be maintained against the attacks of both faithlessness and half-hearted faith, in greater depth than is possible in a weekly publication.[69]

The Bavincks' Move to Kampen

In the 1870s, Jan and Geziena welcomed two more sons—Berendinus Johannes Femia (Dinus) in 1870 and Johannes Gerrit (Johan) in 1872.[70] Shortly after this, in 1873, the Bavincks moved to Kampen, where Jan became the pastor of the town's Christian Reformed congregation. There, Jan's life was heavily invested in his preaching ministry: "On the Lord's Day there were three occasions to preach to be fulfilled, and in the winter there was also one occasion added in the week."[71] Although a faculty member from the Theological School preached one of these sermons, Jan was responsible for the rest. They were fulfilling years: "Oh, I still vividly remember some occasions especially in the evenings by gaslight, how quietly and attentively a great crowd could listen to the preaching and seemed to devour the words of the preacher! There was hunger and thirst for the Word of God, and the words of life were food and drink for hungry and thirsty souls. I may believe that my work in those days was not without fruit and blessing."[72]

Earlier in his life, Jan had hoped to labor in Kampen, albeit as a teacher in the Theological School rather than as *pastor loci*. Although those hopes had remained unfulfilled, his later reflections on his eventual move to Kampen include a remark by Simon van Velzen—a faculty member at the Theological School—that a greater good was served in that particular providence. "'Your influence on the students,' Prof. van Velzen once said to me, 'is still greater than that of the professors.' I shall allow this to be said by the professor, but this, I think, I might say, that both the professors *and* the students have more than once declared to me that they were edified through my preaching."[73] During these Kampen years, Jan and Geziena celebrated their twenty-fifth anniversary—a milestone announced in the advertisements section of *De Standaard* on April 29, 1875, with a further note in the same newspaper on May 8, 1875, thanking those who had congratulated them.[74]

Jan, Herman, and Scientific Theology

In 1882, Jan Bavinck was chairman of the Theological School's trustees when his son Herman—alongside Lucas Lindeboom and Douwe Klazes Wielenga—

was appointed to teach there. In this role, Jan was asked to give one of the lectures to mark the appointment. His lecture, alongside an address given by W. H. Gispen, was published in 1883.[75] This lecture is one of the most useful texts in understanding his support of Herman's own theological course, and also in viewing his own ambitions for the development of Seceder theology.

According to Jan's lecture, the purpose of the Theological School was to provide the Christian Reformed Church with "God-fearing, reliable, scientifically [*wetenschappelijk*] educated servants of the gospel."[76] When making such a claim, Jan anticipated the likely objections among some Seceders that the scientific element of this training was unnecessary: "I know well that there are some who will regard such scientific knowledge as unnecessary in a servant of the gospel and who will therefore reject all scientific education."[77] His reply centered on their particular historical context: "The nineteenth century legitimately sets high demands on the servant of the gospel, which he will not be able to meet without rigorous study."[78] For Jan Bavinck, the Theological School existed for the church and the world, training ministers and, in its own scientific practice, having a sanctifying presence in Dutch culture. In that light, he directly addressed the new professors, saying, "The Lord, the King of the church, is watching you; the Christian Reformed Church is watching you; the Netherlands is watching you; yes, the eyes of thousands, of friends and foes, are upon you."[79] His challenge to the faculty, as orthodox, scientific theologians, was to contend for their place in the world. This address was a statement of deep commitment to his son's task. It was a public affirmation of his son's strivings. (Read together, the addresses given in Kampen by Jan, in 1882, and Herman, in 1883—"The Science of Sacred Theology"—make a striking pair.)[80]

In the context of Seceder history, Jan Bavinck's contribution to this public attempt to reclaim *wetenschap* for orthodox theology should not be ignored. In its early history, after all, the Seceder movement certainly knew what it was to be rejected by those (in their case, theologians in the established Dutch Reformed Church) who used the notion of *wetenschap* against them. The Seceder C. J. van Hoeken's *Answer to the Writer of "A Word to the Seceders from the Reformed,"* for example, written in 1841, engages with the accusation that the content of Seceder theology had been "left behind by the progress of science."[81] In that light, Jan's address in support of Herman's approach to scientific theology should be seen within the context of the Seceders trying, over decades, to improve the "scientific" content of their in-house theological education. It was a concern broader than either Bavinck.

Such a drive had been integral to the purpose of the Kampen School from its inception. The address at the school's official opening, on December 6,

1854—a week before Herman's birth—was given by Carel Godefroy de Moen, the Seceder pastor in Den Ham.[82] De Moen's lecture offered an exegesis of Solomon's prayer in 2 Chronicles 1:10 ("Give me now wisdom and knowledge") as the basis for the Theological School's own brand of Christian scholarship.[83] His attempt to do so, however, fell flat. The Bible used by de Moen, the 1637 *Statenvertaling*, renders the verse in question "geef mij wijsheid en wetenschap" (literally, "give me wisdom and science") and reflects the meaning of *wetenschap* in a seventeenth- rather than nineteenth-century context. The nineteenth-century use of *wetenschap*, with its commitment to scholarly guilds, formal accreditation, and industry-wide standards, had come a long way from the seventeenth-century equivalent, which concerned insight and understanding of a more personal kind. In asserting that Christian ministers should seek both *wijsheid* (wisdom) and *wetenschap* (science) from the Lord, de Moen glossed over those centuries of linguistic development too easily. As a further example of godly scientific practice, he pointed his listeners to Daniel 2:21 ("The Lord is the God of *wetenschappen*, 'He gives wisdom to the wise and *wetenschap* to those who have understanding.'")[84] The new school's students, he believed, should dare to be the Daniels of the modern scientific academy.

Although the Theological School's opening public lecture tried to portray this new school as a scientific institute fit for its modern setting, it was a crude effort. By trying to force the overlap of seventeenth- and nineteenth-century (divergent) uses of the same Dutch term, with a shared anchor in the vocabulary of the Hebrew Bible, it produced an underwhelming impact.[85] De Moen's argument for the scientific calling of the Theological School was unconvincing. The report of his speech in *De Bazuin* reduced his chosen text to "Give me wisdom!" ("Geef mij wijsheid!"). The lecture, the reader was told, was a "powerful, stirring, and encouraging address."[86] However, the appeal to *wetenschap* was entirely missing from *De Bazuin*'s summary. Therefore, we are left to wonder whether *De Bazuin*'s writers thought it more opportune not to draw attention to de Moen's argument on that point. That the lecture itself did not go well is suggested in an article published the following week in *De Bazuin* by de Moen, in which he apologized for its underwhelming delivery.[87] The Theological School's first public attempt to identify itself as a place of scientific theological learning, it seems, was less than convincing.

Jan Bavinck's lecture, delivered twenty-eight years after this, represents a more mature stage of the Seceder narrative's appropriation of *wetenschap*. Indeed, his charge to the students, that "the Lord, the King of the church, is watching you; the Christian Reformed Church is watching you; the Netherlands is watching you; yes, the eyes of thousands, of friends and foes, are upon you,"[88] appears to be a direct play on de Moen's lecture, which was structured around a highly similar set of assertions: "The Lord Jesus is watching you! God's church is watching you! The apprentices in this school are watching you! The trustees of this school are watching you! *The Netherlands* is watching you! The father of lies is watching you!"[89]

In that light, the aforementioned lectures by de Moen (1854), Jan Bavinck (1882), and Herman Bavinck (1883) represent a range of attempts within one tradition to reconcile their own orthodox tradition with the scientifically oriented academy of their late modern culture.[90] Among the sons of the Secession, such a task predated Herman Bavinck by a long way. It was a significant part of Jan Bavinck's contribution to his tradition.

The Deaths of Johannes Gerrit and Geziena

To mark the fortieth (1888) and then fiftieth (1898) anniversaries of his ordination, Jan Bavinck published *Salvation Only in the Name of Jesus* and then *David's Prayer in Old Age*.[91] Between those anniversaries, however, Jan and Geziena dealt with the loss of another child: Johan.

Johannes Gerrit Bavinck had arrived at the close of the Bavincks' time in Almkerk. He was less than a year old when the family moved to Kampen. There, he had attended a Christian primary school, following which he (along with his brother Dinus) had been admitted to the town's gymnasium—a school where lessons were taught in Latin and where students were prepared for university-level education. Johan spent six years attending this school and passed his final exam cum laude. With the approval of his parents, he moved to Amsterdam, where he registered to study law at both the University of Amsterdam and the Free University of Amsterdam. His older brothers Herman and Dinus had already entered the world of higher education at state universities, Herman having studied theology at the University of Leiden and Dinus being a medical student at the University of Amsterdam when Johan began his own studies. These three were the grandsons of the carpenter Hermanus Bavinck, himself the son of a carpenter; they now worked in theology, medicine, and law. Bridging these generations stood Jan and Geziena Bavinck, who steered their family's course through industrialization into a new knowledge-based economy.

In Amsterdam, Johan progressed toward doctoral study in law and social science[92] and was writing a dissertation entitled "De Calvinistische Beginselen der Staatsleer" (The Calvinistic principles of the doctrine of the state) when he died of tuberculosis on December 26, 1896, aged twenty-four. (The story of Johan's death and its impact on the family will be discussed in more detail in chapter 8.) The title of Johan's incomplete thesis suggests that, like his father and oldest brother, he wrestled with the questions surrounding orthodox Reformed participation in modern society. His death was a bitter blow to Jan and Geziena, whose only consolation was his Christian profession.

In 1900, Geziena also passed away. "In her," Jan would recall, "I lost a loving and faithful spouse, one I would not call learned, but a wise housewife who paid good attention to her household and cared for her family faithfully. Next to God the Lord, my children and I have much for which to thank her. For around fifty years I was in an enjoyable and blessed marriage with her, and now she had been snatched from my side. As a result of her loss, I now felt so lonely and despondent in mood."[93] Following Geziena's death, Jan Bavinck moved into Herman's home.[94] "I left the manse and was received in my son's family. My son is married to the oldest daughter of Mr. A. W. Schippers of Vlaardingen. The Lord has given them one child, a daughter. This child, already a few years old, is the darling of the house."[95]

Having reached the last few years of his ministry in Kampen, Jan seems to have channeled this sense of loneliness into publishing, releasing two more books of written sermons in 1900 and 1901[96] and preparing two voluminous books expounding the Heidelberg Catechism, which appeared in 1903 and 1904.[97] Following his retirement from ministry[98] and Herman's appointment to a chair at the Free University of Amsterdam, he relocated to Amsterdam—where he wrote "A Short Sketch of My Life." The trajectory of his life, as portrayed in his own account, had taken him from the periphery of Lower Saxon society to his son's house in the Grachtengordel—one of the most prominent neighborhoods in Amsterdam.[99] The significance of these vastly different places was not lost on the elder (and now elderly) Bavinck: "When my son was later nominated professor at the Free University of Amsterdam and accepted the nomination, I moved to Amsterdam with him and his family, and in my old age have become a resident of this great world city."[100] The Bavincks' living situation bore the hallmarks of its time: Jan lived with Herman along with Herman's wife, Johanna Adriana, and daughter, Johanna Geziena, who was nine when her grandfather joined their household. Thanks to industrialization and economic modernization, the elderly were living longer, which often led to them taking up residence in their adult children's nuclear families. The Bavinck home in Amsterdam was typical of the Dutch "three-generation household" that arose in that setting.[101]

In 1909, having spent the final six years of his life in Amsterdam, Jan Bavinck died and was buried—beside Geziena and Johan—in Kampen.[102]

Through the influence of Hepp's biography, Jan and Geziena Bavinck have often been considered as otherworldly, anticulture (*Kulturfeindlich*), and in some sense antimodern people.[103] In reality, they were more modern than Hepp's account might suggest; indeed, Hepp himself began his biography by acknowledging that while he had known Bavinck in person, they had never discussed Bavinck's early years (a fact picked up on by at least one early review of his work).[104]

For that reason, Hepp overlooked the fact that in navigating a sudden cultural shift from classical to late modernity, Jan and Geziena were nonnatives in a new liberal democratic social terrain and chose to raise their children in that unfamiliar context. In that regard, Jan's particular influence on Herman—and lifelong support for his son's efforts to be an orthodox Calvinist in late modern culture—was of far greater significance than has previously been recognized. In contrast to Henry Dosker's description of Herman as both "so like and yet so absolutely unlike his parents,"[105] I assert that Jan and Geziena, on the one hand, and Herman (alongside his siblings), on the other, should be seen as sharing greater continuity: within one family, the Bavincks are a striking example of the Seceder impulse to find one's own place in the modern world. The key difference is that Herman, like his siblings, was born a cultural native in the late modern era, while Jan and Geziena had come of age in an earlier form of modern culture.

3

Herman's Childhood and Schooling

1854–72

"The modern youth has come under the
influence of the modern society."

Advertisements:
Today, by the goodness of God, GEZIENA MAGDALENA HOLLAND,
the warmly beloved wife of J. BAVINCK, v.d.m., very successfully gave
birth to a son,
HOOGEVEEN,
13 December 1854[1]

With this advertisement, taken out by Jan and Geziena Bavinck in *De Bazuin*
on Friday, December 22, 1854, Herman Bavinck's birth was chronicled in the
printed press. Like the tellingly modern (unpublished and private) autobiography mentioned in the previous chapter, this short piece of (published and
public) writing is rich with historical significance. When this advertisement
was placed, the Seceder newspaper *De Bazuin* had been in print for a little over
a year and did not have a dedicated "birth announcements" section. Rather,
Seceder parents who wished to publicize the births of their children had to pay

for space among the classified advertisements—a normal practice for Seceder pastors from the newspaper's earliest days.[2] That these announcements were made among the classifieds provides a useful setting against which to view Herman's early years: his birth was published above an advertisement by a copper- and tinsmith looking to find "a helper of moral conduct, and with good references."[3]

In chapter 2, I described Bavinck's place within a movement of rank-and-file Seceders whose lives—rarely intentionally documented by historians—sought a greater degree of integration within their newly constituted, late modern society. The advertisements section in *De Bazuin* provides us with fleeting glimpses of some of their stories. In addition to birth announcements, the ads in these years refer, for example, to Seceders running a vinegar export business,[4] a bread and rusk baker,[5] a family offering lodgings to fashion students,[6] and a list of vendors selling a range of medicinal pills.[7] Theirs were lives marked by simultaneous commitment to ecclesiastical separation and cultural integration. Indeed, the ad section in the early years of *De Bazuin* is typical of the post-1848 upwardly mobile middle class (*kleine burgerij*), whose sense of social aspiration was evident through such practices. The son whose birth was announced in *De Bazuin* on December 22, 1854, was a son of Seceders like these.

Jan and Herman Bavinck

Jan Bavinck was twenty-eight when Herman was born, and Herman only lived for twelve years beyond his father's death. In Herman's childhood, Jan Bavinck was both his father and his pastor. As will be seen in this chapter, Herman's journal entries from his time at the Zwolle Gymnasium—a classical high school—clearly show that he remained close to his father and involved in his ministry at that time. Letters from Herman's student days in Leiden make plain that he maintained a close connection to his parents throughout those years.[8] As was noted in the previous chapter, the elderly Jan lived with Herman and his family in Kampen (following Geziena's death), and then in Amsterdam during some of Herman's most intellectually fruitful years. Their lives overlapped to the extent that Jan Bavinck's role in our account of Herman Bavinck's life and times cannot merely be that of a background figure who is noted in an introductory chapter and plays no further role.

Therefore, this chapter, which deals with Herman Bavinck's childhood years, is necessarily framed against the backdrop of Jan Bavinck's lifetime as outlined in chapter 2. Jan's career and outlook set the course of Herman's early life. His ministry would define the towns in which Herman would grow up and the schools he would attend, and his influence would eventually extend to the bold choices Herman would make during his own student years.

In that light, though, the present chapter does not aim simply to repeat or expand on the bare chronological details of Herman's childhood relocations from Hoogeveen to Bunschoten, and onward to Almkerk and then Zwolle, and so on. Instead, it sets out to provide a more richly textured account of his early years by exploring his own recollections of them. These recollections, in turn, will be framed in relation to broader social-historical questions on the experience of childhood in the Netherlands of the mid-to-late nineteenth century. Its driving questions, then, are intertwined but distinct: What were the details of Herman's childhood? And what kind of childhood (compared to other Dutch children in the 1850s–70s) did Herman have?

Herman Bavinck's Autobiography

Beyond the birth announcement in *De Bazuin*, a small number of primary sources offer notable insights into Bavinck's childhood. In 1908, aged fifty-four, he published a short autobiographical piece, "An Autobiographical Sketch of Dr. H. Bavinck," in *De Grondwet*, a Dutch-language American newspaper.[9] (At the time, he was in the United States to deliver lectures and was asked by the newspaper to submit an overview of his life. This particular source has remained hitherto unknown in Bavinck studies. An English translation of this sketch has been included in the appendices to this biography.)

The autobiographical sketches of the senior and junior Bavinck make for fascinating comparison. In contrast to Jan's 42,000-word "short sketch,"[10] Herman's runs to a mere 360 words. As a piece of literature, Jan's autobiography conformed to the genre-specific categories of its time: it was unpublished, private, intended for his immediate family, and used to convey information too sensitive for public consumption. Herman's autobiography is typical of a later subgenre of autobiography: it was concise, written at the behest of a newspaper editor, and intended for the public domain. As autobiographies, however, both "A Short Sketch of My Life" and Herman's brief sketch in *De Grondwet* are nonetheless inherently selective pieces of writing, and it is precisely for that reason that the exercise of authorial discretion in their production is often telling. In that context, then, what information about his childhood—if any—did Herman find necessary in order to describe his life thus far? "Born 13 Dec. 1854, in Hoogeveen, where my father, Rev. Jan Bavinck, was a minister. Later my father moved to Bunschoten, and later again to Almkerk in North Brabant. There, I received an education at Mr. Hasselman's Institute. After that, I attended *gymnasium* (high school) in Zwolle. There, I became acquainted with the Dosker family and entered into a friendship with one of their sons, Henry Dosker, above all—a friendship that has lasted to the present day."[11] As was outlined in the previous chapter, Herman was the second child of an eventual seven; his older sister, Dina, had been born three years before him. As typical preacher's children, they spent their childhood between several towns. Herman was named after his own grandfather, Hermanus, who had died while Jan Bavinck was a small child. As the son of a minister, Herman was baptized by his own father in Hoogeveen four days after his birth.[12]

Beyond this, the details Herman presented in his autobiography—nodding toward the Hasselman Institute and the émigré Dosker family—were raised with an eye to his Dutch American audience, which would have been familiar with both.

Early Years in Bunschoten and Almkerk: The Mythical "Diamond in the Rough"

When the Bavinck children were seven and three, they left Hoogeveen for Bunschoten, where they would remain until Herman was eight. Although Jan's autobiography offers extended commentary on the history of the Seceder congregation in Bunschoten and his own ministry there, it says nothing of Herman's years there, which would likely have included his first experience of primary school. Herman's own autobiography is similarly muted in this regard, in contrast to the explicit mentions of the Hasselman Institute in Almkerk and the gymnasium in Zwolle.[13]

Hepp's biography, written shortly after Herman's death and heavily reliant on verbal reports from the Bavincks and their acquaintances, suggests that during his early childhood in Bunschoten, Herman had simply failed to demonstrate any obvious academic potential.

> Somewhere, I read the following: "There was a moment where this rough diamond (namely, the young Bavinck) would be cast to the side as though it were a normal stone. Back then—as was recalled to us shortly after his appointment as professor by someone in a position to know it—when Rev. Bavinck Snr. had taken up office in Almkerk and was welcomed by 'Monsieur' de Boer, the man from the Hasselman Institute, the father spoke about his children and their education thus far. In Bunschoten, one had not seen much academic strength in 'our Herman,'

although the opposite was true of the younger son. That one would become one of 'Monsieur's' pupils. But what the older son should become was as yet unknown to father Bavinck. 'Now!' said Mr. de Boer, 'let me test him nonetheless.' And that happened. When, after a couple of weeks, Rev. Bavinck asked the teacher whether anything could be expected of his older son, he gave the answer: 'Minister, he is a diamond, but he has not been cut well and needs to be smoothed.'"[14]

The factual difficulty with this story—as acknowledged by Hepp—concerns Jan Bavinck's apparently brighter younger son. According to the report, this younger son had also been schooled in Bunschoten and would likely attend the Hasselman Institute. However, when the Bavincks moved from Bunschoten to Almkerk, they were a family of four: Jan, Geziena, Dina, and Herman. None of their younger sons (or daughters) had been born by this point. Unfortunately for an otherwise charming story, the younger son central to its plot did not exist.[15] Bremmer's biography also includes a redacted version of this story in which the younger son has been removed and the focus is fixed on the claim attributed to "Monsieur" de Boer that the seven-year-old Herman was a rough diamond.[16] And following this, the chapter on Herman's childhood in Gleason's biography, entitled "Bavinck's Youth: A Diamond in the Rough," makes a range of dubious assertions about both Jan and Herman that depend entirely on Hepp's unverifiable and problematic story:

> According to father Jan's assessment, Herman was not a particularly precocious child. Jan was more than a little concerned about his son academically. At the early stages of his life—remember, he was only seven years old!—Herman did not seem to show too much promise as a thinker, according to Jan, and he wondered if Herman even qualified for further study. . . . Would Herman excel [at the Hasselman Institute], or would he not be able to keep up and fold under the pressure? These were questions that plagued Jan in the early stages of his son's development.[17]

The extent to which any of these assertions were truly "according to Jan" is highly doubtful. His own writings on the decision to send Herman to the institute convey no sense of anxiety about his capabilities and make no reference to any conversations with teaching staff about Herman's academic performance in Bunschoten. Rather, the assertions in the above quote are inferences made in a recent book, based on a recollection in 1921 of a story (told "by someone in a position to know it") at Herman's appointment as professor in Kampen in 1882, which was itself a recounting of an alleged conversation between Jan Bavinck and Monsieur de Boer in Almkerk in 1862.

Early biographies of Bavinck's eventual colleague Abraham Kuyper often shrouded Kuyper's early years in Romantic folklore.[18] In the case of Bavinck's childhood, the "rough diamond" narrative is perhaps an example of the same fantasy—based on the Romantic search for the first signs of genius in a young life—developing in subsequent biographical accounts of Bavinck's childhood. Although Hepp claims that such instances were common in *oral* Seceder tradition in the aftermath of Bavinck's death, his own biographical inclusion of one such "apocryphal" story about Bavinck's early years—despite Hepp's clear admission that the story is far from watertight—eventually normalized the "rough diamond" version of Bavinck's early education in subsequent *written* tradition. (As will also be seen, the folklore surrounding his early years also extends to descriptions of the Hasselman Institute, the secondary school attended by the Bavinck children in Almkerk.) On the Bavincks' own part, we find a general lack of interest in these early years—a neglect perhaps reflecting the fact that mid-nineteenth-century Dutch culture, for the most part, had yet to develop a romanticized notion of childhood or of the behavior specific to it.[19]

Regardless of the tale of Herman's fabled brighter younger brother, it is clear that the Hasselman Institute, which Herman attended between the ages of seven and sixteen, profoundly influenced his life: that particular school received considerable attention in Jan Bavinck's account of Herman's childhood and is similarly referenced in Herman's own shorter autobiographical sketch.

We should not gloss over the fact that Herman enjoyed a relatively privileged education. Although Dutch literacy and school attendance rates improved dramatically over the nineteenth century (in 1826, 62 percent of boys and 47 percent of girls attended school, whereas in 1888, those figures had risen to 73 percent and 65 percent, respectively), in the middle of the century, a quarter of the population was still illiterate, and school attendance would only became compulsory in 1901.[20] Despite the considerable advances in wealth creation and educational attainment during Herman's childhood, the majority of Dutch children in that period nonetheless lived in some form of poverty. The early years of a Dutch child in the mid-nineteenth century typically involved labor in factories or on farms, rather than lessons in Latin, English, music, and accountancy.[21] In that regard, Bavinck's childhood was somewhat atypical.

The Hasselman Institute and Herman's Teenage Years

Herman enjoyed a well-rounded and privileged education at the Hasselman Institute. Nonetheless, it is worth remembering C. Smits's warning against overstating that school's uniqueness and excellence, or even the importance of Herman Bavinck among its former pupils. Referring specifically to Hepp,[22]

H. Bouma,[23] and W. de Graaff,[24] Smits offers the critique that description of the institute is often "surrounded by a light Romantic mist that has been invented because . . . Herman Bavinck was educated there from seven to sixteen."[25]

As a corrective to the hazy picture that Bavinck was by far the best pupil at a unique school exclusively attended by the outstandingly gifted,[26] Smits offers a more realistic picture. The Hasselman Institute was excellent in many regards. It offered a challenging, broad, modern curriculum; it was an intentionally Christian school and—advantageously, from the Bavincks' perspective—was headed by a Seceder; it employed native English, French, and German speakers as teachers; and so on. (However, it was relatively normal for Dutch boarding schools to employ native speakers to teach modern languages in that era. The 1864 book *An English Lad at a Dutch School* describes the experience of an English boy sent to study at a Dutch boarding school for a multilingual education with native-speaker teachers.)[27] A number of its pupils would go on to distinguished careers. The noted theologian and pedagogue Isaäc van Dijk (1847–1922), who held a professorship in Groningen from 1883 to 1917,[28] was also a former pupil.

The assumption that the pupils at this school were always academically gifted is also likely part of the aforementioned "Romantic mist." The institute, which received no financial support from the government, was nonetheless sustainable because of monies generated by students whose families paid for them to board there.[29] The institute's boarders were there, in large part, because of their families' financial resources rather than on strict academic merit. Nonetheless, the Hasselman Institute did provide Herman with a strong education. It was excellent and atypical, but perhaps less unique than has been conveyed in some previous scholarship.

Hepp portrays these years at the Hasselman Institute as a period of introspection and inner conflict for the teenage Bavinck, alleging that he was torn between the "anticultural" atmosphere generated by his own parents and the more open, worldly environment of the institute.[30] However, as is typical of his biography, Hepp offers no sources through which this assertion might be verified. In any case, the portrayal of Jan Bavinck and his beloved Hasselman Institute as anti- and pro-culture, respectively, is puzzling to say the least. Although it is consistent with Hepp's characterization of the early Seceders as typified by *Kulturfeindlichkeit*—which is to say, maintaining a general disdain for modern culture as "worldly"—on this point, Hepp's portrayal of the Seceders succumbs to the problems inherent within homogenizing talk of "*the* Seceders."[31] When we bear Jan's consistently positive posture toward modern culture in mind, this contrast reads as somewhat strained.[32]

However, if Herman had indeed become withdrawn at some point during his time in Almkerk (1862–70), we ought to recall that these years (between the ages of seven and sixteen) were personally demanding for him. When he was nine, he gained and lost an infant brother, Karel, within the space of a fortnight. In the following year, his older sister, Dina, died. And five years on from that, his younger sister Femia also passed away. When Karel was born, on February 22, 1863, Herman became the second-oldest of four children. Two weeks later, he was the second-oldest of three. And in the year after that, he was the older of two. They were certainly hard years.

In his later (1911) reflections on the experience of puberty—which he understood as a phase of critical self-awareness wherein a childish dependence on parents lessens en route to full adulthood—in the late modern world, Bavinck would write,

> The modern youth demonstrates characteristics that in former times either were not present or not to the same extent. The modern youth has itself come under the influence of the modern society. It is certainly true that youth in every era and place have had to strive for independence, to wrest themselves free from respect for the past and to forge their own path into the future. There is nothing wrong with this, per se; it is a natural process of development that makes progress possible; it should not be suppressed with violence, but one must know how to direct it, so that the past and the future remain in harmony for the growing youth.[33]

Bavinck's mature thought on being a teenager was offered in general, rather than personal, terms. At its core is the humane assertion that being a teenager is inherently difficult and laden with awkwardness—both physical and social—regardless of one's era or culture. In that publication, however, Bavinck acknowledged that many modern Dutch teenagers raised in Christian homes nonetheless found the conflict between faith and unbelief unbearable and failed to progress toward a mature Christian profession.[34] Against that backdrop, we recall Jan Bavinck's opening editorial comments in the first edition of De Getuigenis, written when Herman was fourteen: "Our young people in particular can only be minimally held back from the influence of the Zeitgeist, as though that could somehow protect them from it."[35]

Gymnasium or Higher Burgher School?

In 1870, aged sixteen, Bavinck completed his education at the Hasselman Institute. Two years of study at the Zwolle Gymnasium now followed. Gymnasia, alongside Latin and French schools, and athenaea belonged to a special class of secondary schools that prepared Dutch teenagers for university-level education.

Pre-1848, they were few and were intended for the sons of the elite.[36] In 1860, for example, there were thirty such schools in the Netherlands, where around 1,300 pupils received a classical education (and only five of those schools had more than 50 pupils). In the whole of the Netherlands in 1860, among a population of 3.3 million people, there were approximately 1,400 university students.[37]

This hegemony was also shaken up in the liberalization of Dutch society.[38] In 1863, for example, Johan Rudolf Thorbecke, the prime minister and principal framer of the 1848 constitution, passed a Secondary Education Act that established fifty "higher burgher schools" (*hogere burgerscholen*). This initiative was designed to produce the professional class needed by the new, knowledge-based economy. Students at the higher burgher schools were taught a modern curriculum emphasizing the natural sciences and modern languages and would go on to populate a modern, professional class within society. They would become the clerks, accountants, and business managers of the late nineteenth-century Netherlands. Despite the new opportunities presented by the creation of these professional schools, Jan and Geziena nonetheless chose to send their son to a gymnasium. Herman's trajectory, at least as envisioned by his parents, was not well suited to a higher burgher school.

The mass expansion of these new burgher schools coincided with notable change in Dutch academic culture. By the time Herman came of age, Dutch was rapidly replacing Latin as the lingua franca of the Dutch academy—a shift made official in 1876.[39] Alongside this, the general consensus that Latin was no longer useful began to permeate the expanding middle classes. Despite this, the gymnasia—bulwarks of Latin-based education—retained their place in the Dutch educational system. Some parents, in this case Jan and Geziena Bavinck, still chose a gymnasium education for their children.

According to P. Th. F. M. Boekholt and Engelina Petronella de Booy, such a choice should be viewed as a manner of contending for space in a new society. In their argument, although Dutch society was undergoing liberalization, it retained a strong awareness of itself as hierarchical. A classical education, which conferred knowledge of Greek and Latin, marked one out as civilized, and it functioned to distinguish the elite from the middle class.[40] Such a general view of the choice for gymnasia as inherently elitist, however, requires greater nuance when discussing the choice of orthodox Reformed ministers to pursue a classical education for their children. Herman Bavinck was not the only son of a Seceder manse to be sent to a gymnasium: two of his closest friends, for example—Henry Dosker and Geerhardus Vos—also received the same kind of education.

At that time, of course, a limited number of subjects could be studied at Dutch universities: theology, literature, medicine, the natural sciences, and philosophy. Knowledge of Greek, Hebrew, and Latin was highly valued among

Reformed ministers and was itself a prerequisite to ministerial training. If a late nineteenth-century Dutch Reformed minister thought it likely that one of his sons would follow the same path, that son would almost certainly have been sent to a gymnasium as a preparatory school for eventual theological study. For that particular class of student, a gymnasium was essential, more for educational development than for upward social mobility.

Therefore, the distinct motivations that led Jan and Geziena to send Herman to the Gymnasium in Zwolle are difficult to identify with much certainty. In any case, their son was sent to an outstanding school. The Zwolle Gymnasium had grown out of the Modern Devotion movement in the Middle Ages and had a considerable and long-standing reputation.[41] Indeed, its former pupils included the then prime minister, Johan Rudolf Thorbecke,[42] and, albeit some time before this, Pope Adrian VI (1459–1523), the only Dutchman to have been appointed to the papal office.[43] Studying there certainly conferred social benefits upon Herman: it created the possibility that he could associate with the elite—regardless of whether this was his parents' intention in sending him to Zwolle—and qualified him to progress to university.

Herman's First *Dagboek*

In this period, Bavinck began to keep a journal (*dagboek*), which offers a fascinating window into his life and experience immediately before university.[44] In terms of literary genre, the late modern dagboek—a fragmentary style of autobiographical writing—is also a species of egodocument. The practice of keeping a dagboek emerged for very modern reasons, as people perceived time as passing rapidly, creating individuals who felt the need to chronicle their lives in a constantly changing world.[45] The dagboeken kept by Bavinck between 1872 and 1891 have been preserved in the Bavinck Archive. The last complete extant dagboek, "From 1896 to 1891," also includes several pages from a (presumably lost) dagboek written in 1901. (The biographies of Hepp and Bremmer, published in 1921 and 1966, both cite material from now-missing dagboeken that covered the remainder of his life.)[46] As a source of constant autobiographical reflection between the ages of seventeen and thirty-seven, and once again fleetingly at the age of forty-seven, the extant dagboeken will play an invaluable role in allowing us to follow Bavinck throughout his life—as will the fragments of the lost dagboeken that echo through Hepp and Bremmer.

Which life events did the teenage Bavinck chronicle? His dagboek's opening page contains a list of biblical texts, all of which concern either maintaining distance from an errant Christian brother or encouragements to stand fast in the faith. He added no comment on their significance, although their thematic pattern is suggestive: the seventeen-year-old Bavinck was wrestling with how to follow Jesus faithfully in his relationships. Following this, we find notes (in Latin) about a girl, *Amelia Dekkerana*. These first notes are undated, although chronologically they must precede the first dated note (June 20, 1871). By way of content, they were written at the very end of his time in Almkerk and provide a rare glimpse into his life at that time: "*Three days before the first day of May, I asked Amelia Dekker if we could write letters to each other, should we ever leave this place.*"[47] Amelia Josina den Dekker (1849–1933) was the daughter of Arie den Dekker (1813–94), a farmer, and Anna Middelkoop (1819–54), who were members of the Seceder congregation in Emmikhoven, adjacent to Almkerk.[48] Aged seventeen, Bavinck was enamored with a twenty-two-year-old.

Beyond that, his early journal entries were largely written in Latin, noting his entrance exam for the Zwolle Gymnasium (August 14, 1871) and successful admission thereunto, followed by a string of class prizes in Dutch history and algebra there and the engagements of acquaintances. He notes one further letter from Amelia den Dekker, on September 6, 1871. As his entries progress into 1872, the entries become more personal, slightly more expansive (although still concise), and are generally written in Dutch. They focus on visits from his parents, travel by rail, journeys back to the parental home, and his meetings with Henry Dosker.

The significance of his connection to the Dosker family is evident in this journal. Henry's father, Nikolaas, like Bavinck's, was a Seceder minister whose career had been intertwined with that of Jan Bavinck: Nikolaas Dosker had preceded Jan Bavinck as minister in Bunschoten, where Henry had been born. Like the Bavincks, the Doskers had also immigrated to the Netherlands from Germany.[49] As classmates in the Zwolle Gymnasium,[50] the teenagers Herman and Henry had a great deal in common. While their lives (and theological outlooks) would eventually move in different directions, it is hardly surprising that they struck up a close friendship in these early years.

Amelia den Dekker

Bavinck's feelings toward Amelia den Dekker seem to have continued through his time at the gymnasium. In the last few pages of his dagboek from 1872 to 1874, Bavinck includes a section of handwritten, romantic poetry dated to those years. These poems range in intensity and were not all original creations. One poem (meant to be read in columns from top to bottom and then bottom to top), written by Bavinck in English and dated "Leiden, 1874" (still likely referring to Amelia), for example, reads,

Read	C	that	me	If	you	No	2
down	will	I	love	U	love	knife	in
and	U	love	U	love	I	will	love
up	and	U	as	me	as	cut	our

The selection of poems written in Dutch and French and dated "Zwolle, 1872, H. Bavinck" also refer to this early period in which he was enamored with Amelia, albeit without referring to her by name. One of these poems— uneven in structure and intense in content—is clearly written as a marriage proposal, although it does not appear that Amelia ever read it. This particular poem (written in Dutch) offers a unique glimpse into the then eighteen-year-old Bavinck's love for the twenty-three-year-old Amelia.

> Beloved! For you my heart has striven
> To gain a helpmeet, in love given
> Grasp, my love, this declaration.
> Does your heart know ardor for mine?
> May this, my prayer, be also thine.
> Let love not withhold approbation.
>
> Thine eye's pure spark
> Engulfing, burning, coruscating
> Its pow'r hidden and stark
> My torchlit heart ne'ermore abating
> Speak out, speak out, lest I be lost
> Breathe out the spark, all fast and fleet,
> Born of thy face, and reckon this cost,
> As moon and sun thine eyes defeat.[51]

His involvement with and love for Amelia would carry on into—and beyond—his Leiden years, eventually leading to the trauma of an unsuccessful marriage proposal in 1877. For now, though, he remained besotted.

The Seceder's Son Becomes a Son of the Secession

On March 19, 1873, Bavinck formally joined the Christian Reformed Church as a member by profession of faith: "Profession of faith completed with

Rev. Dosker in the Christian Reformed Church in Zwolle." The entry for Sunday, March 30, notes that he was confirmed as a member of that church by Rev. Dosker.[52] Herman had formally identified himself with the Christian Reformed Church, and with that, the son of a Seceder had declared himself a son of the Secession. The particular flavor of the Seceder movement tasted by Bavinck in Zwolle under Nikolaas Dosker's ministry, however, is significant in identifying precisely what kind of Seceder the teenage Bavinck had become: Dosker encouraged integration and involvement within Dutch society. From the dagboek at least, it appears that Bavinck was keenly involved in the life of the congregation—he chronicles the details of congregational votes for the appointment of new deacons (June 8, 1873), an election in which he would have participated as a member, as well as meetings with other members of the congregation. Henry Dosker also became a member of the congregation at the same time.[53]

Shortly after Bavinck's profession of faith, however, Nikolaas Dosker received and accepted a call to pastor the Second Reformed Church of Grand Rapids, in Michigan. Two entries on from the note on his confirmation by Dosker, Bavinck noted Dosker's final address in Zwolle, on April 11, 1873. What was the young Bavinck to make of his pastor's decision to leave the Netherlands and its liberalized, late modern culture, *and* the Dutch Seceder church? Harinck has suggested that Nikolaas Dosker grew frustrated with the parts of the Christian Reformed Church that were content with a more peripheral place in Dutch society and that Dosker, who was not a particularly combative personality, chose emigration as a more straightforward way to realize his ideals.[54] A letter from Henry Dosker in the spring of 1874 suggests another reason—that they had emigrated for reasons of social mobility. Explaining the general shape of his American education—Dosker enrolled at Hope College, in Holland, Michigan, before studying at several American seminaries—he would tell Bavinck,

> For you it is wholly different. From your youth your studies were better funded than ours. Your father has the means to get you a university degree. A thousand paths are open before you that were always closed to us. With God's help, you can and shall become something, the shadow of which I could not have reached in the Netherlands. It is true, our educations are now becoming very different.[55]

Faced with the impending departure of his pastor and closest teenage friend, Bavinck remained in good spirits. Despite his fervent desire to marry Amelia den Dekker as expressed in the aforementioned 1872 poem, an entry written in the spring of 1873 noted his interest in Aaltje Klinkert (1857–1934).[56]

> *10 April '73. Sale of Rev. Dosker's furniture (sum of ± f. 1100). At this occasion I met* Ααλτιε Κλινκερτ *cum sororibus.*[57]

For reasons of secrecy, Bavinck saw it as needful to transcribe her name in Greek and mention that he met her with her sisters (*cum sororibus*) in Latin. Nothing, however, seems to have come of this interest. Rather, Amelia would remain the object of his affection for years to come.

Jan Bavinck's Call to Kampen

Family events feature prominently in this period's dagboek entries. He notes the birth of a younger brother (Johannes Gerrit) on September 25, 1872, mentioning that he received this news the day after the birth.[58] Entries in the following year chronicle his father's call to Kampen:

> *19 May. Father came to Zwolle because of the call to Kampen.*
> *20 May. Went to Kampen with father.*
> *22 May. Ascension Day. Father went home again. What shall the outcome of the call be? This was especially the question that kept us occupied.*
> *24 May. Received a telegram . . . that father had* <u>accepted</u> *the call from Kampen.*
> *27 May. The* <u>acceptance of call</u> *took place officially.*[59]

The dagboek entries from this period make plain that Herman was close to his parents, visited them regularly, and was involved in and supportive of his father's ministry. In noting that, I side with Bremmer and Gleason in their rejection of Hepp's view that at this point in his life, Bavinck's relationship with his parents was one of distance and tension.[60] Rather, the opposite was true. The Bavincks were a close family.

At the completion of his final exams at the gymnasium, he had won the class prizes in Latin, Greek, French, and Dutch. Academically, the gymnasium years had been a resounding success. His rival for the Dutch language prize, Gerrit Kalff (1856–1923), would go on to become professor of Dutch and rector at the University of Leiden. Bavinck's dagboek compared their final scores in an essay writing test: he was judged to have made one minor grammatical error to Kalff's three.[61] Like Bavinck, Kalff then studied at the University of Leiden. Both would eventually become members of the Royal Dutch Academy of the Sciences (Koninklijke Nederlandse Akademie van Wetenschappen) and be appointed to the Order of the Lion of the Netherlands.

That Bavinck had studied alongside (and in this case, ranked more highly than) this caliber of classmate will be important at several points in the remainder of this biography: it provides us with a greater degree of clarity in understanding why his short period as a resident student at the Theological School in Kampen failed to satisfy him (in that few of his fellow students there had enjoyed the same kind of secondary schooling), and it sheds light on the high professional ambitions he later harbored, particularly in his early adulthood. Like Kalff, Bavinck hoped not only to study at Leiden but later also to teach there.[62] His experience in this kind of environment gave him a heightened degree of social ambition.

The central thrust in the first section of this biography ("Roots") is that Bavinck's life ought to be perceived against the wider social trajectory of the Afgescheidenen. Their trajectory, as has been argued, was one that had moved from a clandestine pre-1848 existence (with limited opportunities for participation in society) to a place of toleration and freedom in late modern Dutch culture. By virtue of his birth on this side of the Spring of Nations, Bavinck was a late modern cultural native. This much is shown in gymnasium-era Bavinck's interest, for example, in Dutch political life: following the note on his victory over Kalff, his dagboek also mentions the election of members for the Second Chamber of the Dutch Parliament. It is unfortunate that further indicators of his constructive intellectual development in this period are limited by the lack of extant sources from the teenage Bavinck's own hand. Aside from the dagboek, the only known piece of writing by Bavinck from that period is a manuscript for a speech on the history of ancient Greek comedy, written in Latin, in an elegant hand, and with red ink.[63]

At this point, the first section of this biography draws to a close. Against the backdrop of twin ecclesiastical secessions in 1830s Lower Saxony and the Netherlands, a social movement gained rapid momentum. Its participants, the Old Reformed and the Seceders, emerged as the balance of powers in their societies was restructured and new possibilities for social mobility came into view. In that setting, one man, the Old Reformed German Jan Bavinck, migrated into Dutch culture, joining the Seceder church and assuming a place in an increasingly ambitious and upwardly mobile *kleine burgerij*. By this point, in 1873, his son Herman—who had self-identified with the Seceder church—had been afforded an outstanding education and, like his classmate Gerrit Kalff, stood on the cusp of university admission.

A surprising development, as this story moves toward its second part ("Student"), is that unlike Kalff, who moved from the Zwolle Gymnasium to the athenaeum in Amsterdam, and then the University of Leiden, Herman Bavinck—for a short while, at least—chose an altogether different educational path.

PART 2

Student

4

Kampen

1873–80

"The education there did not satisfy me."

L ate in his Amsterdam years, Bavinck penned an unpublished, undated
notebook entitled "Lijst mijner geschriften" (List of my publications).[1]
As a preface to this list, he wrote a time line of his educational and
professional development thus far.

Born	13 Dec. 1854	Hoogeveen	
Candid[ate] Theol.	Leiden	1 April 1878	
〃 Semit[ic languages]	〃	20 Sept. 1878	
Doct. exam	〃	4 Aug. 1879	
Doctorate	〃	10 June 1880	
Cand. Theol.	Kampen	20 July 1880	
Ordained in Franeker		13 March 1881	
Called,	Zwolle Synod	24 Aug. 1882	
Departure	Franeker	8 Oct. 1882	
Assumed office	Kampen	10 Jan. 1883	
〃 〃	Amsterdam	17 Dec. 1902.[2]	

In the early part of this time line, a fairly unsurprising progression is outlined. The young man who was born in Hoogeveen goes to study at the University of Leiden—the Netherlands' oldest and most prestigious university—and gains the present-day equivalent of a double-major degree in theology and Semitic languages (1878–79). Following this, he becomes a doctoral candidate (1879) and is then awarded a doctorate (1880). Shortly after this, his university education now complete, he passes ecclesiastical candidature exams in Kampen (1880), en route to his eventual ordination in Franeker (1881).

Dutch universities of that era served as a training ground for future careers in the church, the legal profession, and the academy itself—although theologians trained at Leiden who then ministered in the Christian Reformed Church were far less common.[3] However, insofar as this time line concerns his education, the smooth progression charted by the mature Bavinck would not look unusual compared, for example, to that of his gymnasium peer Gerrit Kalff, who moved from Zwolle to study in Amsterdam and then Leiden before taking teaching positions in Haarlem and Amsterdam and eventually assuming professorships in Utrecht and Leiden.

In reality, the first phase of Bavinck's postgymnasium education was more complicated than the progression sketched out in "Lijst mijner geschriften" might convey. That time line only records the successful completion of study programs and makes no mention of programs begun but then interrupted. Although his eventual degree at Leiden in theology and Semitic languages was an unsurprising path for a gymnasium graduate like Bavinck—as was a degree in Dutch language at Leiden for Kalff—this, somewhat more surprisingly, was not his next step. Rather than progress directly from gymnasium to university, the nineteen-year-old Bavinck made a decision perhaps at odds with his educational path thus far. His dagboek entry on September 18, 1873, makes the short statement "*[I] have become a student.*"[4] However, he had not become so in Leiden, Amsterdam, Groningen, or Utrecht. Rather, Herman Bavinck had enrolled at the Theological School in Kampen.[5]

The Theological School in the 1870s

Shortly before Herman enrolled in Kampen, where the Seceder Theological School had been located since 1854, his father had accepted a call to pastor the town's Christian Reformed congregation. However, while Jan had long since hoped to work in Kampen, the same could hardly be said of his teenage son. Although Gleason's repeated emphases on Kampen in that period as "bucolic," a "near idyllic . . . insular" place, and as a "small rural village"[6] are exaggerated, it was certainly far smaller and more culturally conservative than any of the aforementioned university cities. With its population sitting just over 15,000, Kampen was a small, albeit industrious, town.[7] In comparison, Amsterdam's population had just passed 280,000. To a culturally curious teen like Bavinck, the Netherlands' university cities were windows into the wider world. For all its own distinctive charms, Kampen could hardly compete.

The town's Theological School also faced an uphill struggle to capture his imagination. In its early years, the school's professors had held classes in their own homes. These classes eventually moved to a hall in a former primary school, before the Theological School purchased the home of one of its own professors, Helenius de Cock, in 1870, which was to be used for classes and would eventually be expanded into a larger building at the southern end of Oudestraat.[8] By the time Herman Bavinck enrolled there, it had been in development for nineteen years. It now had a dedicated building and four faculty members: Simon van Velzen (1809–96) and Anthony Brummelkamp (1811–88), both Leiden graduates; Helenius de Cock (1824–94), who had trained for ministry under the tutelage of his father, Hendrik de Cock; and Adriaan Steketee (1846–1913), who had formerly been a student at the Theological School. Steketee held a distinctive appeal for the young Bavinck. Appointed to teach classical and ancient languages the year before Bavinck's arrival, he was noted for his broad intellectual (and particularly literary, artistic, and philosophical) interests. Since he was the first lecturer to be appointed to teach ancient languages, Steketee's appointment had been important in the Theological School's efforts, begun in the 1860s, to modernize.[9]

Although the Theological School had made considerable progress between its establishment in 1854 and its form in 1873, its history in the early 1870s was nonetheless marked by debate on institutional identity, direction, and location, as well as the school's posture toward Abraham Kuyper, the brilliant young Calvinist theologian and pastor making waves within the Dutch Reformed Church (Nederlands Hervormde Kerk).

In this phase of its existence, the Theological School had a distinctly churchly character. Decisions on student admission and examination were taken by its trustees—pastors like Jan Bavinck, who had often received a piecemeal education—rather than its academic staff. In noting examples of failed entrance exams being excused by the trustees because of the applicants' "advanced age" and "weakness of body," den Hartogh has described the school's executive-level functioning in the 1870s as "primitive in character."[10] As has already been mentioned, the teaching staff had diverse educational backgrounds (the University of Leiden, study under a Seceder pastor, and the Theological School itself) and also represented generational differences within the Secession movement.

In addition to this, by the 1870s, subsequent waves of Seceder emigration to North America had led to Dutch American communities that either had established theological institutions in need of teaching staff or were in the process of setting up theological seminaries. In that regard, the Kampen school was (in theory, at least) vulnerable to its own teachers emigrating. In 1871, for example, Simon van Velzen received and declined a call to emigrate to Holland, Michigan, to teach at Hope College (which had been established three years before the Kampen school)[11] before refusing a further opportunity to establish a new theological college in Grand Rapids, Michigan, in 1874.[12] A report on the progress of the Kampen Theological School's exams in *De Bazuin*, on Friday, July 24, of that year, notes publicly the school's plea to van Velzen not to emigrate.[13] Kampen was vulnerable to losing its staff as well as its students.

The early 1870s also saw an ongoing debate within the Christian Reformed Church on how fully the Theological School should aim to integrate within the wider world of Dutch higher education. In 1875, for example, this debate became focused on whether the school's teachers, who until that point had used the title "lecturer" (*docent*), should be retitled "professor." The school's trustees were divided on the issue. The synod's deliberations also showed a lack of agreement, before the majority opinion was aired: the school's faculty were to remain "lecturers."[14] When Bavinck arrived at the Theological School, its relationship to the wider academy was ambiguous: although it had long cherished the ideals of science, its teaching staff were not clearly identified as practitioners of scientific theology.

These years also saw continued discussion among the trustees on whether the school itself should remain in Kampen. During Bavinck's year there, Amsterdam, Utrecht, and Leiden were discussed as potential alternative venues. The 1875 synod, which had decided against the *professor* title for the school's teaching staff, also considered an impassioned motion to relocate the school to Leiden. The reasons given for this possible move are interesting insofar as they shed light on Kampen as a cultural environment during Bavinck's year there as a resident student: "Above all, the opportunity for students to become more universally civilized and developed came to the fore."[15] The synod, however, ultimately decided against the relocation. Unlike Bavinck, the Theological School would remain in Kampen.

The school's student society (*studentencorps*) had been set up in 1863. Student societies were already a well-established feature of Dutch university life. Through their emphases on drama, music, sports, and literature, they functioned to reinforce the civilized social identity of the elite. The development of a student society at the Theological School in Kampen, which was not a university and was not attended by the sons of the elite, marked the spread of this "civilizing impulse" in the post-1848 process of social mobility. The student society provided Kampen students with the opportunity to familiarize themselves with modern culture, empowering an upward social climb in the process. Initially, however, the Kampen students were in no great hurry to become civilized.[16] Indeed, for the first decade of its existence, the society was nameless. This was to change on February 13, 1873, seven months before Bavinck enrolled at the school, when it became Fides Quaerit Intellectum (Faith Seeks Understanding).[17]

Evidently, the young Bavinck arrived in Kampen at a time of ongoing institutional self-reflection, generational shift, and, in a certain sense, instability.

Kuyper and Kampen

In 1871, two years before Bavinck enrolled in Kampen, the Theological School invited Abraham Kuyper—with whom Bavinck's own life story would become intertwined—to give a lecture. Kuyper had studied theology at Leiden, emerging as a classical liberal who then experienced a pietistic conversion during his first pastoral charge. By the time Bavinck entered the Theological School, Kuyper had begun to make waves as a leading reformist voice within the Dutch Reformed Church. Reflecting this somewhat unsettled period in the Theological School's history, Kuyper's first visit was occasioned by a conflict between the Theological School and the police regarding the imposition of smallpox vaccinations upon all Dutch schools. The first generation of Afgescheidenen was strongly opposed to vaccinating their children, which they saw as an act of unbelief in God's providence, although by 1871, the second generation of Seceders had begun to embrace preventive medicine.[18] In this context, Kuyper had already taken a publicly provaccination stance since 1865, and he addressed the Theological School as one who advocated both religious freedom *and* modern medicine, while also encouraging the Seceders to reject the imposition.[19] The acts of the Christian Reformed Church's synod for this year highlight that the school had received Kuyper warmly.[20]

By the time Kuyper made a second visit to Kampen, on March 24, 1874, Bavinck had become a student there, and Kuyper had recently been elected to parliament on an "Independent Protestant" ticket.[21] This visit was part of a lecturing tour taken by Kuyper to mark the twenty-fifth anniversary of the 1848 Constitution. The same lecture, entitled "Calvinism: Source and

Stronghold of Our Constitutional Liberties,"[22] was given at several Dutch universities, as well as at the Theological School at Kampen.[23] In essence, the lecture argued that among the fruits of Calvinism is a liberal state in which freedom (in general and, specifically in this case, as applied to religion) is protected. Kuyper attempted to convince the Kampen students that this distinctly modern social vision was nonetheless rooted in the historic Reformed faith, arguing that "Calvinism is not a rigid, unalterable power that had reached its final conclusions, its definitive shape, already in Calvin's time. On the contrary, it is a principle that only gradually reveals its power, that has a unique insight for every age, that assumes a form suitable for every country. Precisely in this metamorphosis its development continues."[24] Although James Bratt has described Kuyper's speech as having faced an uphill struggle insofar as "orthodox Calvinists had hardly been enthusiastic for [the 1848 Constitution] in the first place,"[25] many Seceders and Old Reformed, pre-1848, had actively campaigned for freedom of religion and rejoiced because of the new constitution. This was certainly true of the Bavinck family. Kuyper's reception among the school's academic staff was warm. Although his lecture provoked protests from some students in Kampen, the general impression surrounding this event was highly positive.[26] The report on the lecture in *De Bazuin* by Ph. W. Eskes (1851–1929), the secretary of the student society, is instructive in offering a glimpse into this lecture as a public event, as well as providing the consensus of the student society regarding Kuyper's vision.

Kampen. Last Tuesday evening, the student society, together with the teachers of the Theol. School and other invited guests, among whom were most ministers and the teachers of the higher burgher school in this city, were served a welcome and useful hour. At the invitation of the aforementioned society, Dr. A. Kuyper arose in their midst to hold his lecture on "Calvinism, source and stronghold of our constitutional liberties." With unusual skill, the speaker led us into the deep treasure troves of history, showing us Calvin's line there, along which the true freedom of the peoples, from Geneva to the Netherlands and England and America, had moved forward. The style of presentation was exciting, the way he made the facts speak for themselves was impressive, later generating insights and impulses. God's sovereignty was maintained powerfully in its honor, and in the recognition of this sovereignty, the path to freedom for church and society was pointed out. Reformation and Revolution were strikingly contrasted as branches that are sometimes wholly similar to each other but that have shot up from different trees and thus are distinguished in essence and vitality and in freedom and arbitrariness, the lots from which each of these branches must sprout.

What we have heard we hope to be able to read soon, and will not elaborate on it at greater length. But we do say:

Our sympathy for the principles of true freedom!

Not for reaction, but for the right development of these principles!

Our sympathy for the esteemed speaker, who presented [true freedom] so faithfully and truly!

Our thanks and blessings are thus also offered to him.

On behalf of the student society,

The Senate,
Ph. Eskes, Secr.[27]

Kuyper's address was noted by one Kampen student whose Old Reformed forebears had rejoiced at the freedom of religion gained in 1848. After hearing the lecture, Bavinck turned to his dagboek: "*24 March 1874*. *Saw Dr. Kuyper. He spoke about Calvinism as the source and stronghold of our constitutional freedoms.*"[28] Although Bavinck makes no further comment on Kuyper's argument, this entry is nonetheless significant. Thus far, Kuyper's political efforts were as an independent candidate, rather than on behalf of a party. He hoped to change that through this lecture tour and had gone in search of future leaders for his emerging antirevolutionary political movement. (Kuyper's efforts in these years would lead to the formation of the Netherlands' first modern political party, the Antirevolutionary Party, in 1879.) In Bavinck, whose Zwolle-era dagboek had already shown his early interest in national political affairs, Kuyper found one such future leader. Indeed, between 1905 and 1907, Bavinck would take over from Kuyper—albeit not with tremendous success—as chairman of the Antirevolutionary Party.[29]

This dagboek entry provides the first source in which the young Bavinck directly references Kuyper, and it seems to be the first time he heard Kuyper speak. Given the details provided by the dagboek and Eskes's report in *De Bazuin*, it appears unlikely that Kuyper and Bavinck had any substantial personal engagement at this event. Nonetheless, this lecture, on March 24, 1874, when Bavinck was nineteen and Kuyper thirty-four, marked the beginning of a considerable change in Bavinck's life. Soon after this, he would follow in Kuyper's footsteps by going to study theology at Leiden, where a poster of Kuyper would adorn his bedroom wall. Kuyper had captured his imagination.

Bavinck in Kampen

Other than noting that he had heard Kuyper give this lecture, Bavinck's early dagboek entries during this year in Kampen were infrequent and only concerned visits to friends in other parts of the country. Amersfoort, Baarn, and Bunschoten were more interesting to him than Kampen at that time. Only one set of his lecture notes from this year, a jotter of notes from Adriaan Steketee's philosophy class, has been preserved.[30]

Bavinck remained enamored with Amelia in this period. That spring, Henry Dosker wrote to him, saying that he hoped to have a photograph of himself taken that summer, which he would send to his friend, along with a picture of his own girlfriend: "If you have one of Amelia, send it to me, so that in considering her allure I will be able to imagine your happiness."[31]

Although the records of the Theological School's college of professors from that year only make two references to Bavinck's presence as a student there, the second reference is important.[32] The first reference regards his registration as a student, which is noted in the entry by Anthony Brummelkamp on September 17, 1873. The second concerns Bavinck's request for eligibility to take the school's literary exam. At that time, the school required new students to take classes in general humanities subjects prior to embarking upon concentrated theological study. After taking these general classes, students had to pass the literary exam in order to be recognized as theological students. For a gymnasium graduate like Bavinck, however, this general study was redundant. The college's notes for 1873 include a minute taken on March 19 by Brummelkamp describing how several students—including Bavinck—had requested permission to be excused from these classes and be declared eligible to take the literary exam. Although the professors expressed reservations about the requests of two of Bavinck's fellow students on account of physical infirmity, these requests were granted. By this point, then, Bavinck was no longer required to attend classes in Kampen. His official status had changed. He was now a student with permission to take the literary exam at the next available opportunity.

While many letters between the Theological School's lecturers and students from this year have been preserved, it does not seem that Bavinck engaged with the Kampen faculty in this way. His apparent lack of enthusiasm for most of the Theological School's teaching staff provides an instructive context for his later autobiographical summary of his time in Kampen, which contrasted the Theological School and the allure of the celebrated professors at Leiden. "After completing gymnasium, I spent one year at the Theol. School in Kampen, where my father was now a minister. But the education there did not satisfy me. So in 1874, I went to Leiden to study theology under the famous professors Scholten and Kuenen."[33]

Bavinck offered a more expansive comment on this time in a later publication (1914) on Adriaan Steketee, with whom he enjoyed a good relationship and whose intellectual breadth captured his students' imaginations.[34]

It was during the years 1873/74. I had completed my gymnasium education and harbored a strong desire to continue my studies at Leiden and become acquainted with Modern theology at close quarters. But my parents had only just moved to Kampen and were urging me to come home for at least a year and register as a student at the Theological School. Although I complied with this fully, I nonetheless held on to the desire to take part in a more scientific education than the Theological School could offer at that time; and so it was agreed that I would go to Leiden in Sept. 1874.[35]

This recollection, of course, was made by Bavinck in later life, as part of a publication posthumously celebrating Steketee's life and work. Steketee receives no mention in Bavinck's dagboek during his year in Kampen; it may be that his appreciation for his former teacher grew in retrospect.

As an academic environment, the Theological School was an awkward fit for the young Bavinck, who claimed (albeit in later life) that his true desire had been to progress from Zwolle directly to Leiden but who consented to spending a year in Kampen in order to satisfy his parents' wishes. He was also something of a misfit among the school's student body. In the summer of 1873, a list of incoming students was prepared for Jan Bavinck, who would soon be installed there as the Christian Reformed Church's *pastor loci*.[36] In this list, the students' ages, previous education, and former occupations are charted. While two of the incoming students had attended either a gymnasium or a Latin school and one had attended a higher burgher school, the majority either had no previous education or had spent a short period studying under a Seceder minister. The incoming cohort included a baker, a gardener, a number of farm workers, a cooper, a salesman, and one student listed simply as having "no profession." Only one incoming student was roughly the same age as Herman. All the others were older, with half being between their late twenties and late thirties. For the most part, the incoming students came from the lower social class—a group described by one historian as "more or less impecunious and [who] politically counted for nothing."[37] By contrast, Bavinck—like his father—was very much a part of the ascendant *kleine burgerij*. Although the other students had come to Kampen in order to train for pastoral ministry, Bavinck's teenage desire (according to the aforementioned statement in 1914) was to study the "Modern theology" movement in a purely academic context. While he would eventually spend one year in pastoral ministry, it does not seem that his choice to study theology was originally motivated by a sense of calling toward the pastorate. His early interest was in theology as a scholarly discipline, and despite the Seceder school's efforts—from de Moen's

1854 speech onward—to provide their pastors with a scientific education in theology, the product on offer in 1873 was not yet attractive enough to convince Bavinck to stay.

As this incoming student list was compiled in July 1873, two months before Herman registered as a student, his name and details were not included. Had they been written up alongside his soon-to-be classmates, he would certainly have appeared an irregular candidate: he was the youngest, had received an education far superior to that of his fellow students, was from a higher social class, and hitherto had spent his life in education rather than employment. Jan had asked for this list to be compiled on June 12, 1873. The day before had been Herman's last at the Zwolle Gymnasium. Had he been keen to find out what kind of student cohort could be expected were he to continue his studies in Kampen rather than go on to university, the information would have been easy to come by. In a number of regards, then, the choice to enroll in Kampen at the Theological School was a surprising one for a gymnasium graduate like Bavinck. His old rival Gerrit Kalff was now studying at the Athenaeum Illustre in Amsterdam in a cohort that included the future University of Amsterdam professors Ursul Philip Boissevain and Koenraad Kuiper.[38] The Zwolle Gymnasium had hardly prepared Bavinck for a new peer group composed, in large part, of uneducated farmhands.

The Bavincks' Motivation

Knowing that their son wanted to study under the leaders of the Modern theology movement at Leiden, why did Jan and Geziena first ask him to spend a year at the Theological School? Jan Bavinck's autobiography does recall that at the same time as his move to Kampen, his oldest son had completed a gymnasium education in Zwolle and had come to live with them. Interestingly, though, he does not mention that Herman had done so in order to study at the Theological School.[39] In fact, "A Short Sketch of My Life" makes no mention of Herman's year at the school. Herman's own writings on this particular parental wish also offer no hints as to their reasoning.

Hepp's account of the criticism directed toward Jan and Geziena by the Kampen lecturer Anthony Brummelkamp because of Herman's move to Leiden—namely, that they had sent their son into "the lion's den" of unbelief[40]—might suggest the idea that if he were indeed to progress to Leiden, a yearlong grounding in the Seceders' own theological tradition might help him remain true to his orthodox profession. Such, however, is speculation. Jan Bavinck's own writings express no anxiety about Herman's educational path or resilience of faith. The Bavincks did not explain their desire that Herman go to the Theological School prior to beginning in Leiden.

Perhaps the most plausible explanation stems from the fact that in order to attend a gymnasium in Zwolle, Herman had left the parental home (then in Almkerk) as a seventeen-year-old. After this, he had spent two years lodging with the Bosch family—long-standing Seceders and proprietors of *De zoete inval*, a bakery in the heart of the old city.[41] The Bavincks were a close family. Herman's younger brothers Bernard and Dinus were only five and one when Herman moved to Zwolle (with Johan yet to be born). Given the proximity of Jan and Geziena's new home to the Theological School, it may be that they saw Herman's first-year postgymnasium as a good opportunity for their sons to live together for a year, at least, before Herman embarked on his university studies.

J. H. Donner and the Pull of Leiden

His interactions with Steketee aside, Bavinck found his time in Kampen intellectually uninteresting. In comparison to the frequent notes on his years in the Zwolle Gymnasium and the abundant journal entries found in his subsequent Leiden years, he wrote almost nothing about his experiences at the Theological School in his dagboek. Aside from describing his first exposure to Kuyper (March 24, 1874), the only other event he described was having heard Rev. J. H. Donner speak at a missions event (June 5, 1874). The significance of this meeting with Donner, one of two Christian Reformed pastors in Leiden, is that it marked Bavinck's own decision to leave Kampen. "*5 June 1874. Decided, while Rev. Donner was here, occasioned by the missions meeting, that I should go to Leiden and that Rev. D. would hire a house.*"[42] Following this decision, he spent time with his parents and brothers in Vriezenveen and, having returned to Kampen, made a visit to Leiden in order to view possible accommodation there. "*23 June. Tuesday. To Leiden and back in one day. Saw the room at Ms. Smit's house, Haarlemmerstraat. I liked it. After I had hired it for one year, Rev. Donner received me very amicably.*"[43]

After the decision that he would indeed move to Leiden, the next round of literary and theological (oral) exams was held at the Theological School. Bavinck had attended these public exams. However, despite his own eligibility and his professors' likely expectation that he would take them, he came simply to observe his fellow students' performance. "*14–18 July '74. Exams in Kampen. Of the 13 litteratores 12 passed (Vonk, Impela) and 1 fell away.*

Of the 16 theologians, all passed. I enjoyed both exams very much, also the theological. They weren't brilliant though, neither were Eskes and Linden."[44]

At this point, Bavinck's official status at the Theological School was still that of a registered student with permission to take the literary exam, following which he would move onward into theological studies. This remained his status as he moved to Leiden and, as will be described in the following chapter, makes sense of his somewhat surprising return to Kampen after his second year in Leiden—when he finally took the literary exam (and passed with some style). Nothing is said in the notes of the college of professors when he moved to Leiden, because Bavinck had not actually left the Theological School at Kampen in so doing.

Shortly after Herman's decision to move to Leiden, Jan Bavinck would announce to his congregation that he had received a call to pastor the Christian Reformed Church in 's Gravenhage. Carel de Moen, by this time secretary to the Kampen congregation's church council, noted this call in the next edition of *De Bazuin* and made a public declaration of the congregation's desire that Rev. Bavinck remain in Kampen.[45] Although this call was one of many received and declined by Jan Bavinck, it is symbolic of the climate of rootlessness that pervaded Herman's year in Kampen. This was a year where Herman, Jan, and the Theological School itself were all faced with the choice to leave Kampen.

As that summer came to a close, Herman was still in Kampen at the opening of the 1874–75 academic year. However, his plans for the coming year had now been firmed up: on September 23, he traveled to Amsterdam by boat, and from there by train to Leiden, in order to engage with Modern theology face-to-face.

In moving from his year at Kampen toward his further studies at Leiden, we should bear in mind two points. The first concerns whether he cut all of his ties to the Theological School and made a clean break in changing institutions. As has already been seen in this chapter and as will be developed in the next, Herman's move to Leiden did not spell the end for his student involvement with Kampen. Within two years, and in intriguing circumstances, he would be back in Kampen to take the Theological School's literary exam. Several years after that, he would again be examined by the school's trustees en route to recognition as a ministerial candidate in the Christian Reformed Church. As was the case in the earlier handling of Jan's story vis-à-vis the narrative of his son's life, a strong degree of overlap can also be seen when we consider Herman's links to Kampen and Leiden. In J. van Gelderen and F. Rozemond's historical account of the Kampen School, which does not include interruptions in study programs (which were not unknown in the mid-nineteenth century), Bavinck is recorded as student number 281, who enrolled on September 17, 1873 and completed his studies in July 1880. In that list of students, those whose studies in Kampen were never completed are noted as *v* (*vertrokken*—"departed"), whereas those who successfully completed their studies are noted as *p* (*predikant geworden*—"became a minister"). In this list, Bavinck's student career in Kampen is listed as having been successfully completed rather than abandoned.[46] Although the close of this chapter marks a move into Bavinck's years as a student in Leiden, Kampen will continue to be an important location in the progression of our story. Indeed, after two years in Leiden, some within the Seceder Church and the Theological School made a concerted effort to bring him back to Kampen for the remainder of his studies. It is true that in 1874, Bavinck left Kampen for Leiden—but only in a qualified sense.

The second point to bear in mind deals with the extent to which some of his contemporaries saw his decision to enroll at Leiden as controversial. Bavinck was the first in his generation of Seceders to undertake theological studies at the University of Leiden, the bulwark of modern Dutch theology *post-Secession*. How large an impact did this particular choice have in the Christian Reformed Church? Bremmer's biography notes that Herman's move to Leiden was the center of a notable controversy in Kampen, within both the Christian Reformed congregation and the Theological School.[47] This debate centered on the Kampen professor Anthony Brummelkamp's strong criticism of Jan Bavinck's willingness to support his son's aspirations.[48]

In previous biographical accounts, a tendency to sensationalize the sense of controversy surrounding the young Bavinck's move to Leiden has been evident. Such can be seen, for example, in Gleason's portrayal of Bavinck's enrollment in Leiden as "the shot heard throughout Holland,"[49] which, we are told, "felt like a bomb in the Separatist churches and caused ripple effects that lasted for quite a long time."[50] Henry Dosker's eulogy (1922) also describes Bavinck "obeying an irresistible impulse, despite universal and bitter opposition," in moving to Leiden.[51] Whereas Bremmer's biography notes the gravity of Bavinck's decision, it correctly limits the ensuing controversy "to Kampen circles."[52] Anthony Brummelkamp was deeply unhappy with the Bavincks on this issue (as will be seen in the following chapter). This much was evident when Herman returned to take the literary exam at the Theological School in 1876. That Seceder churches across the Netherlands were truly shocked by the decision of a twenty-year-old (who was as yet unknown except as a member of the Bavinck family) to enroll at Leiden is hard to sustain. His move to Leiden received no attention in *De Bazuin*. Indeed, his first appearance in an orthodox Christian newspaper after his move to Leiden, in *De Standaard* on January 29, 1879—which recorded that he had preached in a Christian Reformed congregation in Leiden—incorrectly listed his name as "Mr. F. Bavinck."[53] It seems that even by then, he was not notable enough to ensure that his name would be correctly spelled in the press.

Although two Kampen faculty members—Brummelkamp and Mulder—opposed Bavinck's decision, he found support from his parents, as well as Helenius de Cock, Adriaan Steketee, and Maarten Noordtzij (1840–1915), who joined the Theological School shortly after Bavinck's departure.[54] Bavinck was not the first Seceder student to enroll at Leiden, which was itself the location of two Seceder congregations. While some within the Christian Reformed Church did not support the idea of a young Seceder student choosing Leiden over their own theological school, talk of a denomination-wide "Seceder reaction" to Bavinck's move to Leiden is almost certainly an exaggeration. Any such negative reaction was primarily local rather than universal. His choice was in no sense "bitterly opposed" by his parents, most of the Kampen faculty, the Kampen students who would then go to visit him in Leiden, or the Seceder pastor J. H. Donner, who welcomed him to Leiden warmly.[55]

At this point, Bavinck's trajectory had been set in motion early in his father's ministry. Like his father, Herman was moving from the periphery to the center, from the clandestine to the authorized. He was now a student at the University of Leiden.

5

Leiden

1874–80

"O God, protect me in Leiden!"

Ex animo et corpore. H. Bavinck.
"Alles Vergängliche ist nur ein Gleichnis."
Goethe[1]

The relocation to Leiden was marked in Bavinck's own autobiographical writings with the beginning of a new dagboek, introduced by the words above, *"From soul and body. H. Bavinck,"* followed by a line from the closing chorus in Goethe's *Faust* that *"all transience is only a likeness."* Goethe's tale, of course, concerns a scholar who had sold his soul to the devil in pursuit of higher knowledge and pleasures. The reader is left to speculate as to whether Bavinck's new dagboek began with a reminder to its author that he was not in Leiden to do likewise.[2]

Although he had begun to chronicle his Leiden experience in this new dagboek, he would continue to write in the Kampen-era dagboek until the middle of 1875—and would often describe the same events (sometimes differently) in both. The likely reason for this double-entry journaling concerns the physical size of the respective dagboeken. The Kampen-era dagboek was a small, pocket-sized book, whereas the Leiden-era dagboek was much larger. In his first year at Leiden, it appears that Bavinck kept this older dagboek on his person and used it to make short, immediate notes of events. These notes, which became steadily more untidy as that year progressed, would then be written up more carefully—in script and in content—in the larger Leiden-era dagboek. The differences between entries in these two dagboeken offer a window into Bavinck's own ruminations on his own daily life in a period marked first by culture shock and then by acclimatization to life as a Christian Reformed student in Leiden.

Early Days in Leiden

Thus far, Bavinck's experience of Seceder life in generally smaller, culturally conservative towns—Hoogeveen, Bunschoten, Almkerk, Zwolle, and Kampen—had not prepared him for the culture shock that would await him in Leiden. His awareness of this cultural shift does not come across in the Kampen-era dagboek's account of his journey from Kampen to Leiden. There, he simply noted the names of two friends who had traveled with him and the bare facts of their journey itself.[3] Later that day, in the new dagboek, he wrote down a far more personal insight into this moment of transition.

> 1874. 23 Sept. Traveled by boat to Amsterdam with van Deventer, Persille, v.d. Zwaan, and Linpers, and from there went by train to Leiden. Enjoyable journey, but still . . . boring at the end. Beautiful weather, until we arrived in Leiden under a rain cloud. I found saying goodbye to my parents hard, especially because of this, that I was going to Leiden. Shall I remain standing? May God grant it![4]

The starkness of the cultural contrast between the Theological School and the University of Leiden was immediately apparent: Bavinck's first full day in Leiden was also the beginning of freshers' week (*ontgroenings week*), a weeklong party where students joined the university student society (*studentencorps*) and were encouraged to drink excessive amounts of alcohol and "swear like true sailors."[5] His first introduction to student life in Leiden was a jarring one. Throughout the previous year, Bavinck was fairly indifferent toward participation in the Theological School's student culture. There, if anything, he was too highly educated and culturally refined to enjoy taking part in student life. In Leiden, the precluding factors were quite different.

What role, if any, could a member of the Christian Reformed Church play in this particular student culture?

Before he had left Kampen, it seems that Bavinck thought he would indeed be able to join the Leiden *studentencorps*. The new dagboek records a long conversation with Paulus Johannes Oostveen (1831–1909), the university's academic registrar,[6] following which Bavinck paid 284 guilders—a sizable sum—to be admitted to theological study. (As will be explained in this chapter, although Bavinck was registered as a theological student, he would not begin to take theological classes until he had completed a two-year program in the humanities.) The Kampen-era dagboek records that Bavinck "*began taking part in freshers' week [but] decided not to become a member of the Corps for reasons of conscience.*"[7] The Leiden-era dagboek, however, paints a fuller picture of this first experience of Leiden student culture: "*After this [meeting with Oostveen] I started taking part in freshers' week. . . . May I become a member of the Leiden student society as a Christian, I wondered? Rev. Donner came to me in the evening, at half past ten, advised me against it, and—I will not become a member, I decided. Often I ask myself whether it was indeed only and purely because of conscience that I did not become a member.*"[8] His Kampen-era dagboek shows that he had intended to join the student society after his move to Leiden. Among the miscellaneous notes at the end of that dagboek, he had sketched out "Leiden Costs," including 270 guilders for tuition, 14 guilders for society membership, and 5 guilders for beer.[9] Thanks to J. H. Donner's intervention, 14 of those guilders could now be spent on something else; the plans Bavinck had made to become a member of the Leiden *studentencorps* would not materialize.

Whatever reasons lay behind Bavinck's decision not to join the student society—conscience, submission to his pastor's will, or the possibility that non-Seceder students rejected him—his choice not to join was somewhat odd, but not uncommon. In 1874 there were 830 students at the University of Leiden, of whom 723 were members of the society.[10] This awkward first day's outcome meant that Bavinck was part of approximately one-eighth of the student body who did not take up society membership. Although he was certainly not the only student who refrained from joining, his move toward the center of the Dutch academy had now met a significant obstacle. By not joining the society, he had been left on the periphery of student culture: students who did not join the *corps* were referred to by its members as "the piglets" (*de biggen*).[11]

However much he had previously desired to come to Leiden, his first few weeks there were difficult. At the end of his second week, the three-hundredth anniversary of the city's liberation from Spanish occupation was commemorated. The celebration itself was a major international event. A cosmopolitan host of professors represented universities in Germany, Switzerland, the United Kingdom, Russia, Belgium, Denmark, France, Austria-Hungary, and Portugal.[12] (Alongside representatives from the other Dutch universities, the Kampen Theological School also received an official invitation. Adriaan Steketee, Helenius de Cock, Anthony Brummelkamp, and Simon van Velzen came to Leiden on their school's behalf.)[13]

This was exactly the sort of event that had attracted the teenage Bavinck to Leiden. Significantly, though, he now found himself unable to enjoy it. In that day's reflections in the Kampen-era dagboek, he described a keen awareness of his calling to follow Jesus well in Leiden. Thus far, the academy had been a dissatisfying place: "*3 Oct '74. I continue to be struck by the duties that I, as a Christian in the academy, have to fulfill here. May God grant me the strength to do this! Strength to show not only through words but also in deeds that I am a follower of Jesus.*"[14] Later that day, in the Leiden-era dagboek, he described the nature of his dissatisfaction more fully. "*3 Oct. Three-hundredth anniversary of foundation of Leiden; I was not in a festive mood and thus didn't enjoy it much: I saw the teeming crowd, that only uses this day as a reason for excess and debauchery, and then I thought, how little God is recognized for what He gives us.*"[15] In these early student days, Bavinck found it hard to feel at home in a city where few felt any need to live *coram Deo*. Life in Leiden was jarringly secular.

The Sermons of J. H. Donner

Although he noted his first lectures from several professors and even wrote "*I couldn't quite believe that I was a Leiden student*" after his first lecture from the famous mathematician David Bierens de Haan (1822–95),[16] the early dagboek entries from his time in Leiden devote far more attention to J. H. Donner's sermons, which were the most formative influence in this phase of his life. As far as can be seen in Bavinck's notes of them, these sermons captured his imagination in their combination of compelling exegesis and explicit engagement with themes relevant to his situation at that time—modernism and its fruits, the difference between faith and unbelief, and the contrast of sin and grace.[17] Donner's preaching was ideally pitched to a student like Bavinck.

Although Bavinck was clearly impressed by Donner's preaching, he was not wholly uncritical of it. His comment on Donner's sermon on Sunday, October 18, 1874, remarks that while Donner's thoughts were "*oh so beautiful*," the sermon was let down by language and style that failed to match his content.[18] The teenage Bavinck had high expectations. Despite this, Donner's ministry affected him deeply—regardless of its stylistic inadequacies. On the same date, Bavinck wrote in response to Donner's sermon on the comfort offered by the resurrection (delivered on Donner's fiftieth birthday), *"How was my mood today? For a brief moment, I only felt the delight of [living in] service to Jesus. And my wish was to live for him, but—that sin, that sin. I did want to live for Jesus, but [this] was more to place myself on the throne, than [out of] sincere concern for God's kingdom. I don't know precisely how to express myself, as though living for Jesus must also be 'rewarded' with honor and fame and regard. And that is not good! No!"*[19] In these years, Donner's preaching and example inspired and provoked a reaction within him. After all, it had drawn him from Kampen to Leiden and became the focal point of his theological formation in the first two years of general studies there. Over the course of these Leiden years, Bavinck watched closely as Donner followed the path from "separation to integration."

Seceder Diversity in Leiden

At that time, there were two Seceder congregations in Leiden: the congregation on the Hooigracht, pastored by Donner, and another on the Heerengracht, pastored by Rev. J. Holster.[20] These congregations also represented the diversity found in the Seceder movement at that time. In contrast to Donner, Holster was far from intellectual. The social classes who attended these congregations also reflected the kinds of ministry exercised by their respective pastors. The Hooigracht congregation, for example, included a number of aristocrats: the families of Cornelis Herman Baron Pallandt of Duinrel (1807–90) and Schelto van Heemstra (1842–1911), whose wife would become nanny to Princess Wilhelmina;[21] and the ladies of the Willinks of Bennebroek and Poelgeest were in regular attendance. The Hooigracht church's particular demographic was conspicuous in that it was surrounded by parked carriages during Sunday morning services.[22] The same could not be said of the Heerengracht congregation.

It is worth noting, of course, that even the upwardly mobile, socially integrated Seceders in the Hooigracht congregation were looked down on by the city's old establishment. J. H. Landwehr, a Seceder who grew up in Leiden under Donner's ministry, recounts one example of this. In 1879, Donner was appointed to the Leiden City Council (an appointment dependent on the support of local Roman Catholics) and served in that role until 1890. In one council meeting, Donner asked why an education report made no mention of the city's Christian Reformed schools, to which Joël Emanuel Goudsmid, a fellow council member—and, incidentally, the university's professor of law and rector magnificus from 1870 to 1871—offered the patronizing reply, "This was done in order not to compromise you and yours," implying both that Seceder education was poor (and was best withheld from further scrutiny) and that Donner and his congregation had sought isolation rather than integration.[23]

Landwehr's account has described the strength of Donner's preaching as having been located in its combination of compelling biblical exegesis and knowledge of psychology, rather than eloquence or the possession of a pleasant voice.[24] A similar account comes across clearly in Bavinck's dagboek, which makes plain that he viewed Holster's preaching as unimpressive in comparison and found early social interaction with members of the Heerengracht congregation somewhat awkward. "*4 Oct . . . afternoon, Rev. Holster on: Praise God in the congregation, you who are of the fountain of Israel. Ps. 68:27. Quid dicam? Went to Rev. Holster's after church. Many people, little enjoyment. . . . It didn't stir me very much. A slight feeling of mockery even came upon me from time to time. I must watch out for this, because it is very dangerous. Temptation comes clothed in many forms. May God expose them to me and deliver me from them!*"[25] His response to Holster's sermon ("Quid dicam?" [What can I say?]) stands in sharp contrast to the detailed notes on Donner's incisive sermons. These experiences of Seceder diversity in Leiden helped the young Bavinck perceive that he was a particular kind of Seceder: he was naturally drawn to Donner and the Hooigracht, but not to Holster and the Heerengracht. This pattern would be repeated in different settings across his life.

Multatuli and Kuyper in Leiden

His initial appraisals of his new professors were mixed: Huygens (*average*), Cobet (*perfect*), Dozij (*good*), Land (*bad*), de Vries (*perfect*), and Rutgers (*quite good*).[26] Attention to the professors in question sheds important light on Bavinck's early years at Leiden. At this point he was taking classes with, among others, the classicist Carel Gabriel Cobet (1813–89), the Arabist Reinhart Dozij (1820–83), the linguist Matthias de Vries (1820–92), the Semitic languages scholar Antonie Rutgers (1805–84), and the philosopher of logic Jan Pieter Nicolaas Land (1834–97). As was already mentioned, although Bavinck had gone to Leiden with the ultimate intention of engaging with

Modern theology, he was first required to follow a general humanities course for two years—the propaedeutic study period (during this period the student was called a *propedeuse*). Only when he had completed this period successfully would he be entitled to embark upon theological study.

Over the course of his first year in Leiden, Bavinck fluctuated between feeling at home and feeling foreign in his new environment. On November 3, 1874, for example, his view of the future was bleak and showed a view of his calling as a Christian as that of being a light in the darkness. On the following day, however, he described a meeting of the University Debating Society, where Theo Heemskerk—who was a son of the then prime minister Jan Heemskerk and who later became a neo-Calvinist—debated Abraham Kuyper on his "Calvinism: Source and Stronghold" lecture, which Bavinck had already heard in Kampen. Evidently, Bavinck relished such an event: "*Kuyper was there as well. O, I enjoyed it so much in K's . . .*"[27] While the remainder of this entry has been removed from the dagboek, it is likely that Bavinck was describing his enjoyment at an evening in Kuyper's company. Bavinck would meet Kuyper again two weeks later, on November 16, when both attended another meeting of the Debating Society. Until the spring of 1875, a pattern of convivial visits home, contrasted with a general lack of ease in Leiden's student culture, is evident. That he was struggling to find motivation to study is clear in a note from April 12: "*Back to Leiden. [Feeling] relatively relaxed. Prayer for the desire to study.*"[28]

The week after his return, he heard a lecture by Eduard Douwes Dekker (1820–87), an atheist novelist who wrote under the nom de plume Multatuli: "*20 April. Heard Multatuli for the first time, on the relationship of the attempts made at the perfection of the person in the school and family, with regard to spiritual, moral, and material issues.*"[29] Multatuli's breakthrough work, *Max Havelaar*,[30] a devastating exposé of Dutch oppression and injustice in the East Indies, had been released when Bavinck was six. By the time he had become a student in Leiden, Multatuli's anticolonial, anti-Christian, and anti-Calvinist work was contributing powerfully to the dechristianization of Dutch culture. In going to hear Multatuli, Bavinck had come into the presence of "the first openly non-Christian Dutch literary great."[31]

Bavinck's receipts record includes having spent *f*1.50 on a Multatuli book on the same day.[32] This attempt to understand an atheist of such stature carried on into Bavinck's mature work, where Multatuli often came into discussion.[33] While addressing parliament in 1913, Bavinck would go on to describe the extent of Multatuli's impact on society during his student years. Those recollections suggest that when faced with Multatuli's atheism, the student-era Bavinck could not imagine himself as anything other than Christian. Multatuli's call to atheism had no hold on his imagination. Despite this, these later parliamentary remarks point to his own struggle to process an acclaimed, revolutionary novel that highlighted oppression, exploitation, and injustice while also denouncing the faith tradition that had reared him.

> In my youth I witnessed that half of the youth of the Netherlands bowed down at the feet of Multatuli and looked up at him with amazement. I never shared in this amazement to the same degree, but there was one thing that strongly attracted me to Multatuli, and that is that his soul, according to his conviction, thought to perceive untruth and injustice in diverse contexts, here and in the East Indies; [that his soul] could smoulder with righteous indignation. We often need such a righteous indignation in the face of circumstances that are in themselves untruthful and unjust, and which one must not strengthen, but rather must set right as quickly as possible.[34]

In the face of Multatuli's powerful call to dechristianize Dutch society, Bavinck was drawn instead to another figure whose "soul could smoulder with righteous indignation": Abraham Kuyper. Unlike the young Bavinck, the student-era Kuyper had been a Multatuli fan, and in 1860 had even given a copy of *Max Havelaar* to his fiancée's parents in an effort to "civilize" them.[35] His relationship to Multatuli had been irreparably soured in 1874, however, when Kuyper's younger brother Herman—who had rejected Christianity and was influenced by *Max Havelaar*—was killed while fighting in the Dutch East Indies. Transfixed by Multatuli, Kuyper's thirty-four-year-old brother had died an unbeliever on a distant battlefield. Having blamed Multatuli for "robbing [his] brother of his faith,"[36] Kuyper would go on to present himself to the Dutch public as Multatuli's public nemesis.[37] By bringing Bavinck into the presence of Multatuli and Kuyper, Leiden had afforded Bavinck the chance to interact with two of the great human spirits of his day.

Confronted with the increasingly prominent voices of Multatuli and Kuyper in the public domain, the young Bavinck heard two visions of the future: one post-Christian, secularized, and atheistic and the other a renewal of Dutch culture through a revival of Calvinism. An undated dagboek entry (made at some point between April and June 1875) notes that Bavinck had *"bought Kuyper's portrait on that day."*[38] This purchase, for the sum of *f*1, is also noted in Bavinck's receipts book.[39] While his fellow students bowed down at Multatuli's feet, Bavinck instead looked to the rising star of Dutch Calvinism, whose poster now hung on his wall on Haarlemmerstraat.

Christiaan Snouck Hurgronje

At the same time, a fragment attached to the dagboek, dated June 8, 1875, provides the first mention of a fellow student who would go on to become one of Bavinck's most important lifelong friends: Christiaan Snouck Hurgronje (1857–1936), a theologically liberal student who would become his generation's most important Dutch scholar of Islam.[40]

Together, Bavinck and Snouck Hurgronje formed an unlikely pair. Although both were sons of the manse, their respective backgrounds were otherwise extremely different. The Snouck Hurgronje family belonged to the Dutch nobility. Christiaan was the son of the Dutch Reformed pastor Rev. Dr. Jacob Julianus Snouck Hurgronje (1812–70) and his second wife, Anna Maria Snouck Hurgronje-de Visser (1819–92). Father Snouck Hurgronje had left his first wife in 1849, fleeing to England with Anna Maria de Visser in an act of "unfaithful abandonment of service with aggravating circumstances," for which he was deposed from the ministry.[41]

As the son of a defrocked minister from his scandalous second marriage, to say nothing of the prominence granted by his aristocratic family associations, Christiaan Snouck Hurgronje bore a heavy existential burden. While Bavinck and Snouck Hurgronje were worlds apart in theological and ethical convictions, worldview, and family backgrounds, they shared a degree of social isolation at Leiden—Herman and Christiaan were the sons, respectively, of ecclesiastical secession and ecclesiastical scandal. In the 1870s, the university's student culture was dominated by a large group of aristocratic students who were interrelated by blood and marriage and who rarely associated with their nonaristocratic peers.[42] Ordinarily, a double-barreled student like Snouck Hurgronje would not associate with a petit bourgeois parvenu like Bavinck. That they became close friends says a great deal about both young men and their place in Leiden's student culture.

By mid-1875, Bavinck had begun to feel more at home among his fellow students. A dagboek note on June 15, 1875, for example, gives his approval to the university's Masquerade celebration—a historical annual event organized in that year by his friend E. Baak.[43] The Masquerade in that year was centered on the three-hundredth anniversary of the founding of the University of Leiden and presented the history of the city's most famous intellectual heroes. Prince William of Orange was present.[44] Something had changed. Bavinck was now in his element. *"It was beautiful to watch."*[45]

By this time, the older Kampen-era dagboek had lain untouched for months, its last entry being on October 3, 1874—when Bavinck had noted how little he had enjoyed Leiden's three-hundredth anniversary celebrations.

He returned to add an entry, however, on June 21, 1875: "*Wouterina died.*"[46] (The same two-word note is found in a fragment tucked into the Leiden-era dagboek.) Wouterina Arnolda den Dekker (1851–75), Amelia's younger sister, had passed away at the age of twenty-three.[47] Bavinck still followed the affairs of the den Dekkers with interest.

The earliest extant letter between Bavinck and Snouck Hurgronje also dates from this period—June 28, 1875.[48] Their correspondence from this period deals largely with academic matters, with their early letters being written while they were away from Leiden during holidays. In contrast to the dagboek entries, which devote more attention to Bavinck's church life and the exercise of his own Christian faith, these letters offer more insight into his course of study. This first extant letter refers to Bavinck and Snouck Hurgronje having started taking Arabic classes earlier than normal, following the advice of their professor Michael Jan de Goeje (1836–1909), who did not believe the standard one-year course in Arabic was long enough for students to learn the language adequately.[49] As their friendship developed over the years, their letters would become more personal. They are unique in our primary sources, in that they provide a window into the development of Bavinck's own character from his Leiden years onward. For that reason, they will be referred to often throughout the remainder of this book.

Returning from Kampen: "O God, Protect Me in Leiden!"

Soon after this, Bavinck's first year as a student in Leiden drew to a close. He returned to Kampen for the summer holidays and went to the Theological School to watch, but once again not to take, its public exams.[50] During those summer months, he returned to the Leiden-era dagboek often, chronicling visits to friends in different parts of the Netherlands before he returned to his propaedeutic studies with the prayer, "*O God, protect me in Leiden!*"[51]

The last diary entries in the Kampen-era dagboek, describing a visit to Nieuwendijk—where Amelia lived—are found in this period: "*14 Aug. Went home. I had stayed with W. Did not speak to Melia.*"[52] His entry in the Leiden-era dagboek clarifies that Bavinck had gone to Nieuwendijk on August 2, where he had stayed with the Seceder pastor Douwe Klazes Wielenga (1841–1902). Although Wielenga and Bavinck were friends, it was a nonetheless disappointing holiday: "*14 Aug Went back home again. Apart from with Rev. Wielenga, I didn't enjoy myself much in Nieuwendijk.*"[53] Although the Leiden-era dagboek does not elaborate on why this twelve-day visit was so unenjoyable, it is clear from the older dagboek that his disappointment centered on Amelia: he had spent the best part of two weeks in Nieuwendijk, but for undisclosed reasons, he *"did not speak to Melia."*

Haarlemmerstraat

As young men who were not expected to care for their own domestic affairs, Leiden students in 1870s typically lodged with a *hospita*—a landlady who kept them fed and in clean clothes.[54] A letter to Snouck Hurgronje dated September 16, 1875, points to Bavinck's frustration at learning that his *hospita* was moving her residence (albeit while remaining on the same street):

> At present I am pressed by a great difficulty. Namely, my landlady is going to move this coming November. [As] I rented a room from her and received meals there, I also have to move. Now she has rented another apartment on the same street, on one side of Bakkersteeg, with a beautiful drawing room (according to Rev. Donner, who has seen it for me) and a bedroom next to it, and she has asked me if I want to move with her to the new house. I didn't have anything against this, other than that it is further still from the Academy and in a less pleasant part of Haarlemmerstraat. Therefore, I have asked for more time with my decision, until I get to Leiden.[55]

In the midst of such mundane affairs, he wrote an extended entry in the dagboek in early October 1875 to describe a more significant experience—his first public profession of faith as a participant in the Lord's Supper.

> *10 October Sunday. Rev. Donner spoke about Ps. 34:9. It was the Lord's Supper. For the first time in my life I openly declared my public confession at the Lord's Table, that I am dead in sins and transgressions, but my only hope is in the righteousness of Christ. O, may I not have eaten and drunk judgment upon myself! O God, let the wish to serve you be in my case a true one, and not to be regretted.*[56]

Although Bavinck had become a member of the Christian Reformed Church in Zwolle during his time at the gymnasium (on March 30, 1873), it seems that his interpretation of the apostle Paul's teaching on unworthy participation in the Lord's Supper (1 Cor. 11:27–32) held him back from participating in it until late 1875. His decision to partake of the Supper was a significant step in his young life. Following this, normal life resumed. He moved the short distance along Haarlemmerstraat, from number 224 to 167A—a house, he remarked, that was *"better in many respects."*[57]

Kampen as Seen from Leiden

Two months on from this, Bavinck traveled home unannounced to surprise his parents by spending his twenty-first birthday with them. "*13 Dec. It was my birthday, I received a box of 250 cigars from Albert Gunnink.*"[58] During the same visit to Kampen, he attended the Theological School's own birthday celebrations and was clearly impressed: "*15 Dec. School celebration in Kampen, opened with a beautiful lecture on Plato by Steketee.*"[59] The lecture in question was on "the study of Plato, with a focus on theological formation."[60] As a window into the theological environment found in Kampen at that time, Steketee's lecture was fascinating. In it, he condemned Christian Aristotelianism and argued instead for a revived form of Christian Platonism, citing Friedrich Schleiermacher—the unorthodox German who had set modern theology on its head—as a prime example of a Protestant theologian who had rediscovered the superiority of Plato to Aristotle. In contrast to assumptions that the Theological School of the early 1870s was intellectually staid, Steketee's example suggests a different reality: in him, Kampen was caught up in a broad resurgence of Romantic Platonism emanating from the likes of Schelling, Schlegel, and Schleiermacher.[61] To the young Bavinck, this was quite an attraction.

His ongoing connections to the Kampen student body are also evident in the dagboek: having returned to Leiden, he was visited by two students from the Theological School, Cornelis Stadig and Cornelis Johannes Wessels (March 1, 1876), and took them to see the National Museum of Antiquities in Leiden.[62] His continued interaction with the Theological School in Kampen (as well as with its students), where he remained a registered student with permission to sit for the literary exam, does not appear to have been entirely negative in this period. Whatever suspicion toward him might have lingered in Kampen, it was not universal.

A Crisis of Doubt and a Return to Kampen

At the beginning of May 1876 Bavinck recorded returning to Leiden from a visit to Kampen in the throes of a crisis of doubt. "*1 May Back to Leiden. Continuation of study under an attack of doubt, but also with feeling of the inner truth revealed through Christ.*"[63] The exact nature of this doubt is not explained in this entry, though the circumstances seen in the coming months suggest that it refers either to a crisis regarding his own Christian faith (presumably in the context of his studies in Leiden) or to doubt that he should continue his studies there. If it did concern a crisis of personal faith, it would certainly shed interesting light on comments made in a later publication (1902) on the difficulties faced by the children of conservative Christian parents who go on to study at modern scientific universities and who there experience "the painful conflict . . . between religion and theology, between life and knowledge, . . . between the [common] people and the highly educated, between church and school." Writing of the experience of orthodox Christian students at secular universities, he claimed that "to the extent that faith has put down deeper roots in his impressionable conscience and has formed a seriousness about life and ideal character there, the conflict becomes heavier that he will later be exposed to within and outside of the lecture halls of the university. Many have succumbed in this dangerous crisis. They did not only become prey to doubt but also gave themselves over to skepticism and despair."[64]

It is also possible, of course, that this "attack of doubt" concerned Bavinck's own immediate future. The impending completion of his general humanities courses brought Leiden's famed Modern theologians ever closer. Bavinck's status in Kampen remained the same: there, he was still a student with permission to take the literary exam in order to progress toward theological study. By now, though, his *propedeuse* status in Leiden was all but outgrown. He was due to take the exams that would qualify him to sit under Scholten, Kuenen, and others.

The Leiden-era dagboek notes that he (alongside Snouck Hurgronje) had passed the propaedeutic exams summa cum laude (May 26), which cleared the path for progression into the scientific training in theology that had first drawn him to Leiden. However, the following entries portray a defining moment in Bavinck's story—his decision also to take the literary exam in Kampen, which created the possibility that he might give up on his studies in Leiden altogether: "27 May. *Went home, where they were very happy. Also decided to take exam in Kampen.*"[65]

Between those dates, Bavinck wrote two letters to Snouck Hurgronje. The first of these (June 6) states that he is preparing for the literary exam in Kampen, and it describes how he longs for the holiday to be over because "such a completely new and unknown terrain is opening up before us." He admits that while he previously found his (propaedeutic) lectures in Leiden to be "annoying," he has latterly begun to enjoy them. The conclusion of this letter is, "I will probably return to Leiden."[66] What did he mean by this? The mention of "new and unknown terrain . . . opening up before us" refers to the next phase of study that awaited Bavinck and Snouck Hurgronje in Leiden. For Bavinck, this would mean scientific training in theology, although Snouck Hurgronje was also unsure of his future path and eventually chose to study Semitic languages rather than theology. Having completed this period as a *propedeuse*, Bavinck now had two options open to him: to stay in Leiden, and with that, to come into close quarters with Modern theology, or to return to the Theological School in Kampen, take the literary exam, and progress onward to theological study within his own Seceder tradition.

In the second letter (June 29), Bavinck shared various pieces of news: "Last week, I—and you will be amazed at this—had my photograph taken. If it's OK with you, I will send you a portrait next time, if I have them by then." (A copy of this portrait, a typical nineteenth-century *carte de visite*, has been included in the gallery, plate 3.) He admitted to struggling for motivation regarding "all those arid subjects—history, linguistics, etc."—studied in the propaedeutic phase in Leiden, and he confirmed his plans to travel for two weeks after taking the literary exam in Kampen. His reasons for doing so suggest that by this point he still leaned toward a return to Leiden: "I think I will go traveling . . . to do some catching up and, in a certain sense, to prepare myself for the new study that awaits us."[67]

At some point prior to the exam, Bavinck had requested an attestation from Donner, required for progression within the Theological School, to show that he had remained a member in good standing of the Hooigracht Christian Reformed Church during his two years in Leiden. Donner granted this request on July 8.[68] Bavinck was now ready to face the Theological School's trustees.

The Literary Exam

Students taking the literary exam were required to devise their own essay topic in order to demonstrate their readiness for theological study. In tackling his chosen subject—"the origin and worth of mythology"—Bavinck advanced a nuanced argument that mythology finds its origins in the human capacities for religion and imagination and expresses the human longing for what can only be found in Christ. "*11 and 12 July. Literary Exam in Kampen completed: with high praise. Soli Deo gloria—et gratia! My essay was on the origin and worth of mythology, which I enjoyed indeed, and even led to discussion.*"[69] That Bavinck passed the literary exam in some style is also clear from the minutes of the Theological School's trustees' gathering for that year. "After the opening prayer by the president, one moves in the usual manner to judge the competence of those who have completed exams, with the result that, although a marked difference in ability has been perceived among those examined, they will all be advanced to further study, with the distinction that the brothers H. BAVINCK and H. SIJPKENS shall receive a diploma with noted praise; the remaining seven shall only receive a normal attestation."[70]

The other student to receive high praise, H. Sijpkens, wrote "Physiognomy." Aside from one candidate who wrote "Germanism in the Dutch language," the remaining essays had less intellectually ambitious themes: "The Six Weeks before the Exam," "A Conversation between Three Literary Students, after Hearing a Sermon," and the intriguingly titled essay "Nobody Helped Me with My Essay."[71] Having returned to Kampen after two years in Leiden, Bavinck continued to stand out. The question of whether (and if so, when) he would take the literary exam, which had remained unresolved for the last two years, had now been settled. Bavinck had a new status in Kampen—that of a student qualified to embark on the remainder of his theological studies.

In the months that followed, Bavinck reconnected with his roots—familial and ecclesiastical—visiting his maternal family in Vriezenveen (July 28) and then traveling onward with an uncle to Bentheim, where he met Jan Barend Sundag, the Old Reformed preacher so influential in his father's conversion and journey toward Christian ministry (Aug. 7).[72] At their only known meeting, Sundag was sixty-six and (Herman) Bavinck was twenty-two. Unfortunately, Bavinck did not record what he and Sundag had discussed or what his particular impressions of his father's old mentor were. The only additional detail that can be gleaned from our sources is a note in his student receipts book that he received twenty-five guilders on this short visit to his father's *Heimat*. This son of the Dutch Secession had received a welcome and favorable return to the German Old Reformed Church.[73] When this visit is viewed in the light of Bavinck's letter to Snouck Hurgronje on June 29, it appears that in going to meet Sundag—a man who had been imprisoned numerous times on account of his religious disobedience—Bavinck was somehow galvanizing himself for what was to come in Leiden. The day after this, he returned to his parents' home in Kampen, from where he visited friends until late September.

A Definitive Return to Leiden

Despite having taken all the necessary steps to resume his studies in Kampen, Bavinck did indeed return to face the Modern theologians in Leiden. "25 *Sept*. *Under much external opposition, [I] went back to Leiden*."[74] What was the source of this external opposition? Nothing in Bavinck's own writings would seem to suggest that his parents pressured him on this point. The Leiden-era dagboek makes plain that Jan Bavinck came to see Herman in Leiden and that his father enjoyed being there.[75] Rather, the opposition in question seems to have centered on the Kampen professor Anthony Brummelkamp, who strongly opposed Christian Reformed parents sending their sons to state universities and had also refused to let his own sons follow that path.[76] Brummelkamp, it seems, thought it likely that Bavinck was about to return to the Theological School and was particularly disappointed when it became clear that Herman intended to carry on his studies in Leiden despite having passed the literary exam in Kampen.

In that context, Brummelkamp became highly critical of Jan Bavinck's parenting, regarding his behavior as an orthodox Christian father as "inappropriate and outrageous."[77] He initiated a debate on Herman's plans in the Kampen Theological School's College of Professors, proposing that they issue a unanimous statement of disapproval. He was opposed, however, by Simon van Velzen, who defended Bavinck's decision on the typically late modern ground that to place such a restriction on him would be an intrusion into his "personal freedom."[78] Only one member of the Kampen faculty, Mulder, sided with Brummelkamp. The rest supported Bavinck's return to Leiden.

One further opposing voice came from North America. In a letter dated December 23, 1876, Bavinck's friend Henry Dosker—by this time a student at Hope College, in Michigan[79]—expressed reservations on his friend's choice to remain in Leiden as a theological student.

> I thank God that you have remained standing, among all the attacks of unbelief around you. What motivates Herman to study theology *there* was the question which, perforce, arose in my mind. Leiden, the focal point of modernism. The names of Kuenen, Scholten, etc. are, alas, only too well known. What can you seek there . . . ? Only this, in my opinion, a thorough knowledge of the plan of attack, the weaponry, and the enemy's strength. May God help you, Herman, to remain steadfast in your choice and to choose the clear truth of faith of our historic Christianity above all the flickering light rays of an enemy science. And yet, *you risk a lot*. We are both susceptible to the influence of seemingly logical arguments. We are growing, tender plants that are bent in the storm and easily keep a misshapen form; there [i.e., in Leiden] you will, I think, have to withdraw within the narrow walls of your own opinions; you will have to be on the defensive too much, and as a result *have to* adopt a somewhat terse opinion of the truth, while you can grow and develop *only* by attack. These are just a few points that I would like to see cleared up in your next letter. What motivates you to study in Leiden? What do you expect from it? What is the general opinion on this question?[80]

While Dosker's predictions on the likely reality that awaited Bavinck as a theological student in Leiden—an intellectual withdrawal into the "narrow walls of his own opinions" as a means of guarding his own conservative faith and piety—would prove to be accurate in some respects, this letter's closing question is also telling. As a young émigré, Dosker was unsure of whether most Seceders in the old country shared his anxieties for the young Herman, or of how much Seceder culture had changed since his own departure for the New World.

Brummelkamp's displeasure at Jan Bavinck's parenting—which was probably synonymous with the "general opinion" sought by Dosker—would resurface in 1878, when Jan Bavinck received a call from the Christian Reformed congregation in Harderwijk and sought the advice of the Theological School's faculty. In response, Brummelkamp suggested to his colleagues that they oblige Jan to accept the call, as his decision to allow Herman to study theology in Leiden had fundamentally compromised the integrity of the Theological School. In this instance, as before, van Velzen would intervene in order to contain Brummelkamp's anger.[81] Regardless of this, Jan Bavinck decided to stay in Kampen.

The Higher Education Act (1876)

The particular point at which Bavinck moved from the propaedeutic phase into concentrated theological study was overshadowed by the Dutch government's continued wrestling with the consequences of the 1848 constitutional revisions for the academy. The Higher Education Act, passed midway through 1876, attempted to resolve a (by then) long-standing debate on whether theology, as it had been taught until then in Dutch universities, should be replaced by religious studies (as an apparently neutral approach to the study of human religious behavior). That this disagreement could not be satisfactorily resolved is evident in the result of this act, which required faculties of theology to retain the name "theology" (*godgeleerdheid*) but to teach a de facto religious studies program. Bavinck's own later recollection of the act's effect on his student experience was that it made university-level theological study somewhat intellectually chaotic: "The result was a strange mixture of incompatibles lacking all integration and unity of conception. Some of the subjects taught remind one of the old theology programs; others clearly belong to the field of religious studies."[82]

Thus, Bavinck's Leiden years progressed into their theological phase just as academic theology itself entered a period of crisis and instability.

The Social Life of a Theological Student

That the course of Bavinck's studies in Leiden had changed is evident in the Leiden-era dagboek entries from this point on. New names—the likes of

Johannes Henricus Scholten (1811–58) and Johannes Jacobus Prins (1814–98)—begin to appear. In contrast to the lack of academic enthusiasm seen in the earlier entries, a newfound earnestness would come to the fore: "*26 Sept. Theol. Lectures opened, in my ongoing attendance [these lectures] strengthen me in my faith. 'Establishment of Theologico Sacrum,' propositions from Bruining about the Reformation, responded to by Daubanton, me, Wildeboer and de Hoogh. For myself, I did not find much satisfaction, which was perhaps a good thing. O God! Let me fight for your honor!*"[83] In the months that followed, Bavinck's notes focused on his social, rather than academic, engagement with his professors. "*3 March Dined with Prof. de Vries. Very nice. 18 March Sunday—supper at Prof. Prins's house. Average. 21 March Supper at Prof. de Goeje's.*"[84] However, this first period as a theological student would be dominated by a traumatic episode in his relationship with Amelia den Dekker rather than by his interaction with Leiden's Modern theologians. On April 16, 1876, Bavinck traveled from Kampen to Leiden with his fellow Seceder student Nieuwhuis. His dagboek entry for this date notes, "*[Nieuwhuis] shared with me that he is engaged to Miss H. Ravenshorst.*"[85] Evidently, marriage proposals were on Bavinck's mind.

Despite his previous disappointing stay in Nieuwendijk (in 1875), Bavinck returned there in the summer of 1877. The intent of his visit is clear from his dagboek entries. The day after his arrival, he made the Latin note *Ameliam rogavi*: "*I asked Amelia.*"[86] The nature of his question is spelled out in the entries that follow: he had gone to Almkerk to seek her hand in marriage. Her response to his proposal is not recorded, although the next three entries—largely composed in Latin—give some insight into the events that would follow.

> *8 Sept Saturday. Spoke with Miss Melia, Amelia is my love, I am intoxicated with her.*
> *9 Sept Went to church with Am. I noticed a few problems.*
> *10 Sept The wife of a minister must be a Christian, it was said to me. A great help, it was said to me. To you, Lord, I give thanks and pray that you will show us favor.*[87]

Although the exact nature of the problems perceived by Bavinck when he went to church with Amelia are unknown, it appears that he was nonetheless hopeful they would marry. That she had not accepted his proposal and that Bavinck himself might have felt a degree of reservation about marrying her can be seen in a dagboek entry written in the following April (1878). "*30 April. Received a letter from Mons[ieur]. [de] Boer, who shared his conversation with A. with me and gave me hope that A. will answer the question posed on 1 Sept. 1877 with 'yes.' O God, may this happen, and grant that no reservations might arise on my part.*"[88] Monsieur de Boer was Bavinck's former teacher at the Hasselman Institute, and as such was connected to both the Bavincks and the den Dekkers. Despite this hopeful message for Bavinck, however, Amelia did not accept his proposal. Tellingly, the latter half of this entry has been scribbled over in pencil—presumably by Bavinck himself—although the text underneath is still visible. Despite this, Amelia would feature in his next dagboek (begun in late 1879), when the reason for this failed proposal would become clear.

Interestingly, the following entry describes how another friend had also gone to Almkerk to propose to a young woman. This particular friend "*received an unsure response (after her first answer had been yes) when her mother strongly opposed it.*"[89] As would become clear in the 1879 dagboek, Bavinck had good reason to sympathize with his friend's plight. Almkerk was fast becoming a foreboding place for young men in search of fiancées.

In the midst of the trauma of frustrated romance, Bavinck's interaction with Leiden's Modern theologians would nonetheless emerge. The university's two most celebrated theologians at that time, Johannes Henricus Scholten and Abraham Kuenen (1828–91), both feature in Bavinck's entries in this period. Having begun as a New Testament scholar, Scholten had become the Leiden school's foremost systematician in that era. Through an earlier debate with the philosopher Cornelis Willem Opzoomer (1821–92), Scholten had become convinced of the principle of absolute material determinism, which his dogmatic work tried to wed to the Calvinistic doctrine of predestination.[90] By the late 1870s, however, Scholten's period of great intellectual development was long gone. His deterministic modern account of Reformed theology, novel in the 1850s, was now well known, with his resolute adherence to it rendering him intellectually predictable to his students. Abraham Kuenen was a modernist Old Testament scholar who made great strides in advancing the higher-critical reading of the Bible. When Bavinck became his student, Kuenen was reaching the height of his powers and was a figure of some international reputation.[91] Bavinck records having been invited to dinner by Scholten in 1877. "*6 June. Dined at Prof. Scholten's, seated at his right hand, I utterly enjoyed it.*"[92] On a personal level, he enjoyed contact with Scholten. Bavinck knew, however, that intellectually, Scholten was a spent force—a view shared widely among theological students in Leiden in the 1870s.

The familiar pattern of close contact with Donner and agreeable visits to his parental home in Kampen (which coincided with the public exams at the Theological School) continued through this period, as did his increasingly public involvement with the wider Christian Reformed Church. "*21 July. Sunday. This morning I preached my first sermon, in Enschede. It went well. My*

text was 1 John 5:4b. Thanks be to Your name, O God."[93] A letter to Snouck
Hurgronje from August 3, 1878, describes the twenty-four-year-old Bavinck's
reflections on this first experience of preparing and preaching a sermon, as
well as explaining the surrounding circumstances.

> On Sunday, eight days ago in Enschede, I preached for the first time. I would have
> rather delayed it a bit, but my parents were enthusiastic and an aunt and uncle of
> mine, who live in Enschede, were invited specially. I had already promised them
> long before that I would preach my first sermon there, and because my aunt's
> health situation might well be that she doesn't have long to live, there was all
> the more reason to fulfill my promise. There was obviously much difficulty, and
> a lot of time lost before our exam. Writing a sermon was no small thing for me,
> but in the end it worked out. My text was 1 John 5:4b, "This is the victory that
> has overcome the world, our faith." I very much enjoyed preaching it. I was very
> calm and collected. Because of that, I am happy just to have done it, and the
> greatest difficulty with [preaching] has already been conquered. However, I was
> still somehow unfulfilled, in that it had inspired me less than I had expected. I
> didn't speak with that feeling for myself as I had hoped and that I should; while
> the thought of always standing so far beneath the ideal was constantly with me.
> But overall it went well and I have an overabundance of reasons to be thankful.[94]

In the following month, he would also preach for the first time in Kampen,
to a congregation that included various members of the Theological School's
faculty. *"It went quite well. For this also, O God, my innermost thanks."*[95]
The successful completion of his studies in Semitic languages is recorded on
September 20, 1878, with Snouck Hurgronje having also come through the
same exam—albeit with a higher mark—the following day. An insight into
Bavinck's parents' interaction with their son's liberal friends is seen in his
congratulatory letter to Snouck Hurgronje: "On Saturday evening I arrived
here safely and, as you would think, my parents were very happy, also about
your exam, for which they asked me to congratulate you on their behalf."[96]

Doctoral Study: Pragmatism and Failed Romance

Having become a recognized candidate in both theology and Semitic languages, Bavinck now turned his thoughts toward his doctoral dissertation.
His letters to Snouck Hurgronje in 1879 show that his first plan was to write a
thesis on the Secession of 1834. This topic was suggested to him—incidentally,
on Bavinck's twenty-fifth birthday—by the recently appointed church history
lecturer J. G. R. Acquoy.[97] Having voiced this plan to his doctoral supervisor,

Scholten, Bavinck quickly learned that another student was also planning to write on the same topic. "Scholten . . . told me that, *nota bene*, Proost was also thinking about writing a dissertation on the Secession. Scholten, however, had asked him to leave that to me, and he might well do that."[98] That both Bavinck and Snouck Hurgronje harbored ambitions to follow their doctoral studies by moving on to German universities is also suggested in their correspondence from this time. Bavinck wrote to his friend, "I still see you going to Strasbourg as *litteris Semiticis doctor*," and also described his own plan—with his parents' blessing—to visit a number of German universities.[99]

A letter from Snouck Hurgronje later that year would also recount Bavinck as having met the Scottish Hebraist Andrew Bruce Davidson (1831–1902) of the Free Church University in Edinburgh (now New College, the Divinity School of the University of Edinburgh), who inquired of Bavinck: "Are you still thinking of going to visit that university? And how are your German plans coming along?"[100] In many respects Davidson and Bavinck were kindred spirits: Davidson had also reacted against moderate Christianity in a Scottish context, striven for a scientific articulation of evangelical theology, and learned Arabic and Dutch.[101] Strahan's biography of Davidson mentions a visit to Leiden, where, "as far as languages went he was . . . at home . . . taking up the morning newspaper . . . and reading it like a native."[102] Strahan's work offers no further information on this visit, when Davidson (then aged forty) met Bavinck (then aged twenty-five).

Although Snouck Hurgronje would indeed progress into a notable academic career, Bavinck's own plans to visit Germany (and possibly Scotland) would come to naught. Instead, he busied himself in Kampen with gathering sources for his dissertation and continued to preach there and in Zwolle. Prior to embarking on the dissertation itself, Bavinck first had to take doctoral exams, which would come in the following March and April.

> *28 March.* 1st part doctoral, afternoon, 3 o'clock. It went well. As subject for 2nd part, Prof. Prins gave me "short summary of the influence of Schleiermacher on the explanation of H. Scripture."

> *4 April.* 2nd part doctoral, everything was done by quarter to three. . . . I got a cum laude, but had the feeling that it was less well deserved than at my candidate's exam. S.D.G.[103]

Having passed these exams, Bavinck returned on vacation (April 5) to Kampen, where he preached to the local Christian Reformed congregation on the following Easter Monday and was given as a gift both a copy of Isaak Dorner's

The History of the Development of the Doctrine of the Person of Christ[104] and thirteen guilders.[105] The Kampen Seceder congregation's choice of gift—the christological writings of Dorner, a German Lutheran who wrote in response to the antisupernatural Christology advanced in Strauss's *The Life of Jesus*[106]— was certainly one intended to encourage Bavinck, given his Leiden context. The financial gift given by the congregation's elders was generous indeed: a large, uneven sum, it suggests that a collection was taken in support of his studies. After passing his doctoral exams he faced another move—again within the same street—in Leiden: for the remainder of his time there, his address would be Haarlemmerstraat 216. Despite his initial intention to write a doctoral dissertation on the Secession, a dagboek entry in the following month shows that Abraham Kuyper tried to steer him toward writing an Old Testament thesis:

> <u>30 May</u>. *Friday. 1 o'clock in the afternoon, went to The Hague to make acquaintance with Dr. A. Kuyper. He had just gone out for a walk, as Fabins, who was staying with Kuyper, told us (Lucasse and me). We decided to stay in The Hague, walked to Scheveningen, ate there, and returned to Kuyper (who was now at home) once again at quarter to seven. We stayed with him until half past eight, speaking with him about my dissertation (he advised me [to write on] a minor Old Testament subject), about the Free University with its confession, about the inspiration of Scripture. It gave me little light. The reception was hearty, though.*[107]

Kuyper, of course, had his own reasons in trying to steer Bavinck's doctoral study toward the Old Testament: as Bavinck's dagboek entry noted, Kuyper had grand plans for the establishment of a new Christian university, for which he would need faculty members. This direction was given because Kuyper was on the lookout for an Old Testament scholar.

Unsure of what to write on, Bavinck carried on with a by-now-familiar pattern of social engagements—in this case, centered on an unexpected visit from Henry Dosker (June 3)—and continued preaching in Christian Reformed congregations throughout the final phase of his doctoral studies. In these early years, Bavinck would preach on two particular biblical texts—1 John 5:4b and Galatians 2:20—over and over, and he seems to have developed the skill of preaching with minimal (or no) notes in so doing.[108]

Leaving Leiden

That summer marked the end of Bavinck's time as a resident of Leiden. Although he would not complete his doctorate for another year, on July 3, 1879, he returned to Kampen, where he would write his dissertation. With this move, another new dagboek (entitled "From 1879 to 1886") was begun.[109]

In October of that year, Bavinck would once again return to Almkerk. He first visited Amelia's father—an awkward encounter he described as "*very stiff*"—before visiting Amelia's aunt, Melia,[110] and giving her a letter to be passed to Amelia (October 4). The 1879 dagboek notes that Amelia was present when he preached there on the following Sunday: "*I was strengthened and inspired by the presence of A.*"[111] An entry made in the following week finally clarifies why Bavinck and Amelia had not become engaged two years before and why their relationship had no future. "*8 Oct. In the morning I said goodbye to Miss Melia and Mr. d. Dekker. In the afternoon I come under the impression that Mr. d. Dekker is alone at home with [Aunt] Melia. I go there. Miss Melia was there, but left the room right away with [Aunt] Melia. I began to speak with Mr. d. Dekker, told him the whole story, asked why he was against it, etc. His only answer was: I cannot give permission.*"[112] The story of Herman and Amelia was definitively ended by her father's will. Under the law of the day, Dutch citizens aged twenty-three or under could not marry without a formal statement of parental permission. Those aged between twenty-four and thirty were legally required to seek parental approval three times, with parents being granted the legal right to refuse such a request on each occasion. Only after a third refusal could those in this age group marry regardless of parental disapproval. By this point, Herman was still only twenty-four, had a limited number of opportunities to seek Arie den Dekker's approval (before leaving himself with only the socially controversial option of marrying without parental permission), and therefore was more or less powerless before him. For that reason, a sympathetic aunt could serve as a useful broker in such approaches—as Bavinck seems to have known.

The circumstances behind Arie den Dekker's refusal to grant consent, however, remain unknown. It may well have been that Arie den Dekker saw little value in acquiring a son-in-law who had no interest in joining the family farming business.[113] It is also possible that he deemed Bavinck's piety or doctrine to be inadequate—Arie den Dekker was strongly influenced by the experiential piety and doctrine of the Further Reformation (Nadere Reformatie) and had been noted for his insistence that Seceder pastors adhere to "hard, strict, strong, orthodox Truth."[114] Indeed, his earliest efforts to organize a Seceder congregation in Almkerk have been described elsewhere as impulsive and careless.[115] In 1836, aged twenty-three, he was sentenced to "between three and five years in prison" in addition to a fine of $f120$ for his role in establishing the local Seceder church.[116] And without extant writings from Amelia's own perspective on Herman, of course, it also remains possible that his love was unrequited and that she hid behind her father's strong decision. Whatever the reason, Arie consistently refused to allow his daughter to marry Herman Bavinck. Despite this, Amelia would feature again in his writings. However, this particular exchange marked the definitive end of their prospects of marriage.

Although he makes no mention of her in his correspondence with Snouck Hurgronje, a letter written one month after his definitive rejection by den Dekker makes plain the sense of ennui felt by Bavinck at that time, and also sheds some light on why he chose to spend a year with his immediate family after the completion of his doctorate (rather than pursue a pastoral call immediately): "Anyway, there is no news. For me, each day is more or less the same. But the joy of being at home is something I had never valued as much as now. It wouldn't amaze me if I spent a year at home after this one, or at least didn't take on a congregation yet."[117] His hopes of marriage to Amelia, with all that their prospective future had meant to him, had been ended. And with that, Bavinck sought solace among his parents and siblings.

Researching Zwingli in Kampen

Despite the promptings of Acquoy and Kuyper to write his doctoral thesis on the Secession or the Old Testament, Bavinck eventually settled on an altogether different topic: the ethics of the Swiss Reformer Ulrich Zwingli (1484–1531). In a letter to Snouck Hurgronje on November 11, 1879, he laid out the reasons for this choice. Congratulating his friend on passing the doctoral candidature exam, he wrote:

> And now I hope that you, after a few days or weeks of relaxation (which you will indeed need), might be happier than I am in choosing a dissertation subject. I have thought about it a great deal, with much to-ing and fro-ing. And after much hesitation I have finally chosen, as you will have heard, to deal with Zwingli's ethics. I have chosen this not so much because it was particularly attractive to me but because it seemed the best of all the things I had considered and because I finally had to make a decision. Thankfully, I am enjoying the preparation; it had a definite attractive side, it yields more fruit than the "Secession," and—which is very important for me now—it doesn't bring those objections that would make another subject almost impossible at the present time. Thus, I shall keep to this subject and am happy that I finally have certainty.[118]

His dissertation topic seems—in part, at least—to have been strategically chosen. He does not spell out the specific obstacles faced by other options, leaving us to wonder whether Bavinck would have felt unable to defend an

Old Testament thesis (per Kuyper's prompting) before the scriptural critic Kuenen, or whether the prospect of a "son of the Secession" writing on that movement at Leiden was simply too fraught with problems to be academically worthwhile. A historical-theological dissertation on Ulrich Zwingli was no doubt a relatively safe choice, with a view to Bavinck's own theological and ecclesiastical commitments *and* his relationship to Scholten, his *Doktorvater*.

In any case, Bavinck was not impressed with Scholten's contribution as supervisor. Commenting to Snouck Hurgronje on the difficulty of working out how to structure his dissertation, Bavinck wrote:

> If I had another supervisor, I would certainly have spoken about it with him by now; but I don't think Prof. Scholten will bring me much further along. When I wrote to him recently that I would deal with Zwingli's ethics if he would grant his approval, he gave a very typical answer: "It is a nice subject, especially to demonstrate the connection between Zwingli's doctrine of *election* and his ethics. Consult my *Doctrine of the Reformed Church* and another couple of works," which he then named. This is enough proof that a supervisor like that doesn't invest much [in his students].[119]

While he had been personally impressed by Scholten in his early days in Leiden, by this point Bavinck seems to have found him intellectually dull: in the dagboeken and letters, Scholten comes across as a now elderly scholar living off the glories of his own dogmatic writings (penned some thirty years before this), who was uninterested in further constructive theological engagement with his students and who had a tendency to focus theological discussion on the doctrine of election (due to his own rigid material determinism). Hepp cites an example from the 1876 Leiden student almanac that shows that these sentiments were common among the university's theological students, who valued the theological system advocated by Scholten but nonetheless longed for a more expansive and creative theological education.[120]

In that light, the letter providing Scholten's response to Bavinck's choice of topic, dated November 30, 1879, makes for instructive reading. In what appears to have been a hastily written letter, Scholten expressed support for Bavinck's choice on the grounds that Zwingli's ethics (à la those of Scholten himself) were grounded in a "complete determinism."[121] In addition to telling Bavinck to read his own *Doctrine of the Reformed Church*,[122] he recommended two works on Zwingli: Eduard Zeller's *Zwingli's Theological System* (1853)[123] and Jacob Tichler's *Ulrich Zwingli, the Church Reformer* (1858).[124]

Although Scholten was Bavinck's supervisor, the most significant constructive interaction with Bavinck's developing doctoral thesis came from Abraham

Kuenen, the Old Testament scholar, rather than Scholten (whose comments on Bavinck's doctoral writings only covered grammar and typographical errors). Crucially for Bavinck, although Kuenen had made his name as an Old Testament scholar, his remarkable intellectual breadth and depth also covered Christian ethics and theological encyclopedia, both of which he had also taught at Leiden for many years. While Scholten had ultimately proved underwhelming to Bavinck, his experience of Kuenen was fast becoming the opposite.

> A few weeks ago I sent my manuscript to Prof. Kuenen for him to have a look at it; he had offered to do this; and after a few days, four or five, he had already sent it back. That is how quickly he finished this tedious work. Thankfully there weren't many comments, so that after some revisions here and there, I could have it printed and set things in motion. The introduction was the only thing that Kuenen didn't like, and neither did I; and even after extra work on it, I am happy with everything apart from [the introduction]. But it has been printed, and you'll soon be able to judge it for yourself. I always send a sample sheet to Scholten—upon Kuenen's advice (who has spoken with him about it)—for his inspection. He sends it back quickly, without any comments (thus far) other than language and printing corrections, to which he pays close attention.[125]

A long and carefully crafted letter from Kuenen, dated October 14, 1879, serves as a conspicuous example of how much more interested he was than Scholten in Bavinck's project. With a striking degree of humility, Kuenen prefaced his advice to Bavinck with a recognition that he was not a specialist in Zwingli's thought, before recommending study of Zwingli on the grounds that while Zwingli was not the most gifted of the Reformers, he pursued the greatest degree of harmony between the religious scholar and the common man. For that reason, Kuenen wrote, his ethics are worthy of further study. On that basis, he then offered Bavinck a careful set of observations on how to go about writing on this topic—noting that Bavinck would have to read Zwingli's corpus widely rather than restrict his study to a small number of sources and that his interaction with sources would have to develop with a view to Zwingli's own life context for each source. Kuenen advised Bavinck to read an extended list of later works on Zwingli, offering his own critiques of their relative merits and prefixing a number of their titles with "(†)." The letter—which began by addressing Bavinck as a friend (*Amice!*)—closes as follows: "The books marked with † are in my possession and are at your service. . . . T. T. A. Kuenen."[126] The letter, from a modernist professor to a theologically conservative student, is a model of grace.

If the move to study theology at Leiden was indeed the choice to enter "the lion's den," in the case of Scholten at least—whose attempts to impose his theological outlook on Bavinck quickly petered out—the modernist lion had little desire to consume the young Seceder.[127] From the Leiden-era writings, it does not appear that Bavinck saw himself as having been particularly challenged or influenced by Scholten. (While serving as a pastor in Franeker, Bavinck seems to have undergone a post-Leiden realization that he had indeed been influenced by Scholten in his student years—a realization that will be explored in the next chapter.) In a very specific sense, however, Bavinck was profoundly influenced by Kuenen's example: the latter modeled a theological intellect that was both capacious and generous and exemplified careful historical-theological scholarship to his de facto doctoral student. In both style and rigor, Bavinck's own work would come to resemble Kuenen's scholarship closely.[128]

As Bavinck was based in Kampen while writing his dissertation, he regularly attended the Theological School's events and continued to wrestle with the long-standing Seceder ambition (as mentioned in previous chapters) to practice scientific theology in a confessional institution. In a letter to Snouck Hurgronje from this period, he wrote:

> In comparison to twenty-five years ago, our school has made great strides forward. But if it can ever be what I sometimes wish, I have my doubts. Financially and morally supported by the congregations, it is dependent on them in every sense and, it seems to me, cannot acquire and maintain much more than a practical purpose. Obviously, it can never become pure science. However much I sometimes regret this, I am comforted—and can be well comforted—by the thought that it can still exercise a mighty impact on life. And that finally settles the matter.[129]

The Close of Bavinck's Doctoral Studies

In the middle of May 1880, Bavinck had traveled to Leiden to ascertain when he would be allowed to defend his dissertation. On May 21, a message reached him via Scholten. "*In the afternoon a telegram was sent to Prof. Scholten's for me. The telegraph conveyed that a telegram from Dr. Kuyper had come to my address in Kampen, saying, come for an urgent meeting on Saturday, May 22, at one o'clock in the afternoon at the home of Dr. Rutgers.*"[130] Kuyper's intention was clear to Bavinck: Bavinck was being summoned to a meeting regarding a position at Kuyper's new Reformed university—which had yet to open and had no students. "*I spoke about this with Rev. Wielenga, who happened to be in Leiden and advised me not to accept a professorship at Kuyper's Free University.*"[131] On the following day, Bavinck traveled to Amsterdam, where he spent three hours discussing Kuyper's offer of a chair in Semitic Languages as well as his own concerns regarding the church (at this point Bavinck was moving toward ordination in the Christian Reformed Church, whereas Kuyper was still a minister in the Dutch Reformed Church, and the Free University was not to be affiliated with any denomination) and Scripture.[132]

Bavinck was told to return the following Tuesday and did so. At that meeting, Kuyper and Rutgers strongly encouraged him to accept the position. "*I will take it, then,' I said.*"[133] That evening, however, Bavinck began to question his own judgment. "*At eight o'clock I should have departed, but I had no peace with the decision. I went back on it.*"[134] Stranded in indecision, Bavinck missed his train and ended up staying with Rutgers. What caused him to go back on his decision? "*I couldn't accept it. I felt absolutely no sense of calling to it. And if I had accepted it, I would [only] have done all of this because of Kuyper's will and glorious study.*"[135] Before returning to Kampen, Bavinck told Rutgers that he could not accept their offer. "*It was a cool parting. I was shy.*"[136]

Echoes of his father are painfully evident in Herman's own uncertainly about this decision. "*Did I handle this well? Should I have accepted it? Grant, O God, that the calling might be repeated if I had done wrongly, and let me enjoy peace and desire in the decision taken! My parents thought it was good, in a way.*"[137] In a letter from this period, dated March 27, 1880, Bavinck's friend Henry Dosker sent a letter inquiring about his future plans. By way of primary source materials, this appears to be the first letter (albeit one written *to*, rather than *by*, Bavinck) that might indicate an ambition to teach at the Theological School in Kampen. After mentioning his belief that Kuyper was likely to "cozy up" to Bavinck in order to recruit him for the Free University, Dosker wrote: "How is it going with your Kampen plans? What are your prospects there? What do you say of intentions from the church's viewpoint?"[138] While this letter has been interpreted by George Harinck and Wouter Kroese to refer to Bavinck's plans to take ecclesiastical candidature exams in Kampen,[139] the letter's content—particularly regarding Kuyper's approach and the question of "prospects" in Kampen—also leaves open the possibility that Bavinck had disclosed a desire to teach at Kampen. If that is true, it would shed new light on the first extant source from Bavinck's own pen, written in 1882, that made his "Kampen plans" explicit.

Dogmatics and Ethics

Bremmer has described Bavinck's doctoral thesis as reading like a necessary university assignment rather than an outpouring of his own theological voice.[140] It is true that in this piece of writing, Bavinck was still a student who was trying to develop skills as an interpreter of a noted figure in the Reformation—and therefore his dissertation was typical of its time in general and of Herman's development during this phase of his life. However, on the occasions where his own voice can be heard—notably in the introduction and conclusion—some ideas that would later become important, and even life defining, were voiced for the first time.

While Bavinck was aware that ethics was a trendier field than dogmatics, he began his thesis by setting out the importance of their reciprocal relationship.[141] (Later, Bavinck would spend decades writing his own works in dogmatics *and* ethics.) Zwingli's neglected ethics was worth studying because, perhaps more than his fellow Reformers, the "ordinary citizen" Zwingli grasped that the Reformation was a rediscovery of the sovereignty of God, which necessitated the reformation of every sphere of life.[142] (Although Bavinck would later attribute this to the Reformation more generally, it remained a key insight that profoundly shaped his attraction to Kuyper's newly emergent modern Calvinism.) Within this, Zwingli's reformation of all of life allowed the individual to flourish by grounding individuality in community—thus preventing the collapse of the individual via individualism.[143] (Bavinck would draw on this insight at various points in later life, albeit then tracing it to Calvin, rather than Zwingli.) Bavinck argued that in Zwingli's acute awareness that he occupied a particular point in history and in his willingness to connect his present-day articulation of ethics with the past and the future, Zwingli was both unusual in his time and a model to theologians in the present.[144] (Throughout his own life, Bavinck would consistently argue that theology needs precisely this "historical sense.")

At the conclusion of his thesis, Bavinck even argued, "Zwingli is closer to our own times than any of the other Reformers" because of his "respectful" posture toward "differing convictions."[145] Without getting into the question of how accurately Bavinck had interpreted Zwingli as a personality in history— which on the last point may have been colored by his experience of Kuenen's gracious interactions on Zwingli—this was certainly a statement that matched Bavinck's aspiration for his own theological development.

The Young Doctor

Bavinck was awarded a doctorate in theology on June 10, 1880. He faced no awkward questions from his professors and was awarded a cum laude. "*Soli Deo gloria!*" he wrote. "*I went home. All the theological professors came to my house, also Groszen, Acquoy, and Oort. Scholten and Kuen[en] stayed until after half past five. Lucasse, Snouck, Wildeboer, Cramer and I dined in the Place Royale. For dessert, we rode to Endegeest. We parted at one in the morning.*"[146] Before taking the train back to Kampen, Bavinck spent the next day visiting Professors Kuenen and Scholten and the local Christian Reformed pastors Donner and Holster. His parents had arranged a party to mark his return home to Kampen as a Leiden doctor. However, despite the successful completion of his doctorate, the final dagboek entry made in his Leiden years reveals a sense of purposelessness. He had gone to Leiden with the intention of marrying Amelia den Dekker and in the thrall of Abraham Kuyper. Six years on, marriage to Amelia had proven impossible, and in a moment of uncertainty he had spurned the chance to work with his hero. Painfully for Bavinck, Kuyper even published the details of their conversation in *De Heraut*.[147] That Bavinck did not enjoy that particular publicity is clear in a letter from Snouck Hurgronje: "How extensively *De Heraut* shared the state of affairs regarding the appointment of a professor of Hebrew! You certainly found that fullness of detail less than welcome, especially as all that is now doing the rounds in all the daily newspapers."[148] Bavinck's immediate postdoctorate outlook was one of listlessness and uncertainty over the future. The dagboek that began with Goethe's "*All transience is only a likeness*" was concluded in a similar vein: "*And so everything comes to an end, and the student years—in their entirety—lie behind me. And what now? What is there for me to do?*"[149]

This sense of purposelessness, however, was not unique to Bavinck. Rather, his doctoral degree was awarded at a time when young Dutchmen with doctorates in theology began to increase in number but thereafter found inadequate social structures—ecclesiastical or academic—to receive them. The struggle for purpose common to these "young doctors in theology" came about because Dutch culture, in its church and universities, had historically recognized theological expertise as something accrued over decades rather than proven by doctoral certification in young adulthood. (As has been demonstrated by Bos, the "young doctor in theology" was essentially a nineteenth-century invention.)[150] Although this began to change as a result of the nineteenth century's drive toward clerical professionalization, by the time Bavinck was awarded his doctorate, his immediate role in society was still unclear. He was a certified expert twentysomething entering a society where many—including some Seceders—were more or less oblivious to his claims of expertise.

Unlike many at that time, Abraham Kuyper did recognize the value in the young Doctor Bavinck's education, although Bavinck had declined his (first) job offer. Despite this, he would not have to wait long for confirmation that

Kuyper intended to keep their lines of communication open. Soon after, he sent the young doctor a congratulatory letter prefaced by a reminder of their shared confession and principles.

> Worthy Doctor,
>   I received your book, and it moved me to praise and thanksgiving, that by God's goodness such a skillful advocate of our shared holy principles has come forth. I had wished for a closer connection to you, and I continue to wish for it.[151]

As will be seen in subsequent chapters, the lives of Kuyper and Bavinck would become closely intertwined. This was not the last time Kuyper would try to bring Bavinck to the Free University.

News of Bavinck's completed doctoral degree was reported in mixed tones by *De Bazuin*. The appearance of Bavinck's first book—the published version of his doctoral dissertation—was greeted warmly, as was Bavinck's own emergence as a scientific theologian. However, the view offered of his alma mater was less glowing.

> We note with much satisfaction: *THE ETHICS OF ULRICH ZWINGLI*, in which our youthful friend Dr. H. Bavinck has provided proof that his voice may resound among the men of science. The theol. faculty in Leiden has conferred its doctoral degree upon him on the basis of that dissertation. That he pursued this doctorate at an institution that adorns itself with the ancient title of "theol. faculty," but that has removed what is actually called theology—that is, dogmatics and ethics—on the basis of the sciences, which it teaches—we cannot fail to say that this is a cause of great sorrow for us. In pursuing this degree from such a faculty, one emphasizes strongly, a falsehood is concealed within us. A faculty that does not teach theology, but only the sciences (which stand in relation to it), cannot bear that name according to its ancient meaning and also cannot award this degree. We understand that this youthful doctor has been offered a professorship at the Free Reformed University but that he has declined it. Meanwhile, he has joined the number of those who have registered for the final exam at the Theol. School in Kampen.[152]

By this point, *De Bazuin* was explicitly styled as a newspaper offering a Christian Reformed perspective to the benefit of the Theological School in Kampen. As such, it held to an editorial policy that left no room for praise for the Leiden theological faculty, particularly given the Leiden faculty's willingness to conform to the 1876 Higher Education Act. The narrative presented to *De Bazuin*'s Christian Reformed readership was that Bavinck—youthful,

energetic, and scientific—had finally left Leiden for Kampen. As will be seen
in the following chapter, upon the completion of his doctorate, Bavinck had
now registered to take his final exams in theology in Kampen.

A Horizontal and Vertical Trajectory into Dutch Society

Thus far, this biography has charted the trajectory of Bavinck's life against the
backdrop of the new (late modern) social landscape created in the Netherlands
by the 1848 constitutional revision and all that it meant for the Christian Reformed Church. Among those who chose not to emigrate and who sought to
carve out a space for their group in Dutch society, Herman Bavinck had joined
a group of socially ambitious Seceders—alongside the likes of the Leiden
pastor J. H. Donner (and various members of the Hooigracht congregation)
and his fellow Leiden students Christiaan Lucasse and Willem Nieuwhuis—in
exploring the possibilities and limits found in their new terrain. In so doing,
they moved through society along both a horizontal course toward its center
and a vertical course toward its upper echelons. In less than fifty years, the
Seceder movement had progressed from persecuted, clandestine origins to
produce a Leiden-educated doctor in theology. This certainly bespeaks the
degree of tolerance and opportunity afforded across denominational lines in
post-1848 Dutch society. However, the particular case of Bavinck's experience
at Leiden (that of an orthodox student in a modernist school, who generally
experienced toleration, rather than fierce opposition, from his professors)
also serves as a striking example of the setting within which these orthodox
Calvinists now found themselves as they followed "the path from separation to integration."[153] For the most part, they were tolerated and allowed to
participate in a long-standing social institution like the University of Leiden.
However, the question of the extent to which their tradition's still distinctively
orthodox voice could speak into their late modern culture remained unclear.
For this reason, among others, what the newly minted Leiden doctor should
do with the rest of his life was not immediately apparent.

PART 3

Pastor

6

Franeker

1881–82

---

*"It is quite a big and, for an inexperienced
candidate, fairly difficult congregation."*

By the time he was awarded his doctoral degree from Leiden, Bavinck
had already been living in Kampen for a year. Unsure of how to use
his life, he would remain in his parental home until March 1881. This
period, in which he busied himself with visits to friends and preaching engagements, was marked by a profound loneliness following his failed romance
with Amelia. A dagboek entry dated July 29 (1880), for example, notes that
he had to accompany an ill friend on a journey back to Almkerk—a stone's
thrown from Nieuwendijk, Amelia's hometown—where he stayed for five
days without contacting her or her family: *"I brought him home. Stayed at
the school [i.e., the Hasselman Institute]. No news. Visited nobody from the
family d. D."*[1]

Of the various friends mentioned in that period's dagboek entries, one
would quickly become important: Jan Hendrik Unink (1858–83), a Christian
Reformed theological student four years younger. Bavinck and Unink do not
seem to have been close prior to Bavinck's relocation from Leiden to Kampen.

Unink's first mention in the dagboek comes in an entry on the "small house party" organized by Jan and Geziena Bavinck on the night of Herman's return from the Leiden doctoral defense. Despite this, Unink's friendship became important during Bavinck's impending year in the pastorate, following which Unink's untimely death would affect him deeply.

The Path toward Ordination

In the following month, Bavinck underwent a two-part public theological examination in Kampen. These exams, taken en route to ordination, were administered by the Theological School's trustees—a group that included Herman's own father, Jan, and Christiaan Steketee, the father of Adriaan—rather than its own teachers.[2] As open events, they were attended by friends and family, Christian Reformed pastors, and members of the public. (George Harinck and Wim Berkelaar have noted that these exams were even attended by members of the town's Jewish community.)[3] Ordinarily, students would take the first exam (*examen A*) at the end of the second year of theological study, with the second (*examen B*) coming at the end of the following year.[4] Doctor Bavinck, however, took both exams in quick succession. Importantly, two pastors who were actively promoting his increasing prominence within the denomination—Henricus Beuker and Douwe Klazes Wielenga—were present in Kampen during these exams.

> *13 July Exams began here in Kampen. It was very poor. Many failed.*

> *16 July Began theol. exam A. Taking part: me, Unink, Munnik, Proosdy, v. d. Hoogt, etc. It went quite well. Some difficulties regarding criticism, etc. arose; nothing else.*

> *18 July Sunday. Beuker spoke here in the morning, Wielenga in the afternoon.*

> *19 July Theol. exam B. I preached first, on Matt. 15:14a. The exam went well.*

> *20 July Tuesday afternoon result at 5 o'clock. Balhuizen, Dee, Romein, Steketee failed. I, Foppens ten Hoor Snr and Jnr, Kok, Nijenhuis, Elzenga went through.*[5]

Although Bavinck's own diary does not elaborate on the "difficulties" that arose around "criticism" in this exam, it most likely concerns his views on the biblical criticism taught by the Leiden school. Such seems to be the case given the choice of text upon which he was asked to preach: in Dutch, Matthew

15:14a, "Let them go, they are blind leaders" (Laat hen varen; zij zijn blinde leidslieden), is clearly a play on words directed at his former professors in Leiden. (In Dutch, *Leidsche lieden*, men of Leiden, and *leidslieden*, leaders, are near homophones.) For this reason, Hepp and Bremmer have both portrayed this trial sermon as a public test intended to show whether the young Bavinck would openly distance himself from Scholten, Kuenen, and their heterodox followers.[6]

Hepp's biography provides an extended account of the circumstances—without offering any traceable sources, unfortunately. According to his biography, Bavinck was "furious" at the choice of text, refused to preach on it, was prepared to give up his candidature in protest, and had to be talked into preaching by his father and friends. Hepp claims that Bavinck's sermon began by refusing to preach against the Leiden professors, while also chiding Reverend Bulens for assigning only part of the verse (Matt. 15:14a) and rendering Scripture a polemical plaything in the process. These, Hepp writes, were "approximately" his opening words: "Why one has given this text to *me*, we can easily imagine. The words 'of the blind' [Matt. 15:4b] have been left out intentionally. The only thing we're waiting for is for them to be added. However, they dare not do that."[7] One eyewitness account of Bavinck's sermon—provided by his early biographer Landwehr—acknowledged Bulens's habit of assigning sermon texts tendentiously but made no mention of any such wild reaction. Rather, his account claimed that Bavinck preached "with beautiful diction" and that the "old Bulens" was impressed by the sermon "even though he did not get what he wanted."[8]

Although Hepp's 1921 recollection offers little to corroborate the citation in question, his account has been influential: Bavinck's trial sermon and his apparently enraged reaction to the assigned text were repeated in various sources, Dutch and foreign, throughout the twentieth century.[9] By contrast, the various "Church News" reports in newspapers from 1880 simply report that Dr. H. Bavinck had passed the exams in question and was now available to be called by a congregation.[10] Among these, one newspaper, the *Leeuwaarder Courant*, noted that although Bavinck had passed the relevant exams, he had declared himself "not available for a call at present"[11]—something, curiously, that Bavinck's own dagboek does not note. Whether or not he was indeed temporarily unavailable for a call, Bavinck nonetheless began preaching regularly in Seceder congregations around the country.

The dagboek entry on one of these preaching trips—to Zwartsluis—points to the increasing importance of his friendship with Unink in this period. On August 14, Bavinck traveled to Zwolle en route to this preaching engagement. "*To Zwolle, ate at Unink's, [went] together to Zwartsluis in the evening.*"[12] Having preached there on the Sunday—accompanied by his friend—Bavinck returned to Kampen via Zwolle, where he notes having spent the day with Unink before returning to his parental home.[13] This friendship blossomed quickly. Over the course of the following year, in which Bavinck entered the busy and isolating world of pastoral ministry, Unink became a regular visitor and close companion.

Franeker or Broek op Langedijk?

Of the regular preaching trips in these months, Bavinck's visit to Franeker—a town in the northwestern province of Friesland—receives the most detailed dagboek entry.

> *18 Sept. Went to Franeker in the morning, arrived at half past two, stayed with L. Hofstra Jr. In the afternoon looked around the planetarium, city hall, portraits, etc.*
>
> *19 Sept. Preached in Franeker on Jn. 17:19 & Rom. 8:28. The church session discussed issuing a call to me.*[14]

Bavinck would eventually receive calls from two congregations: Franeker and Broek op Langedijk. While the visit to Franeker allowed the local Christian Reformed congregation to hear and consider Bavinck, from the dagboek's details it also appears that Bavinck was assessing the town's own credentials. Both Broek op Langedijk and Franeker had long histories. However, whereas Broek op Langedijk was a small farming village, Franeker had some of the trappings—albeit faded—of a university town,[15] as noted by Bavinck: among other things, it had a planetarium and an architecturally striking sixteenth-century city hall.[16] Its sixteenth-century university, however, had been disbanded by Napoleon in 1811. Following the demise of the French regime, the University of Franeker was not reinstated. Rather, it was reinvented as an athenaeum—a small-scale educational institution with degree-awarding powers intended by the Department of Home Affairs to promote "taste, civilization, and learnedness" in its local area.[17] As such, the Franeker Athenaeum was provincial in scope, and it closed in 1843 due to lack of students.[18] Visiting the town's best offerings in the early 1880s, Bavinck was sampling the remains of a bygone era. Clearly, he was not in Leiden any more.

The contrast between Leiden and Franeker could scarcely have been lost on Bavinck. Between the sixteenth and nineteenth centuries, Franeker's history was one of ongoing rivalry with Leiden. At the start of that period, the same grand ambition saw universities established in both cities. As the centuries went on, however, Franeker fell further and further behind its Hollander neighbor. By the nineteenth century, Bavinck's alma mater had long since been a university of international significance; the University of Franeker simply had not been able to compete. In comparison to Leiden, Franeker had "no academic hospital, no observatory, no noteworthy collection of instruments for practical science (it was only well equipped for optical instruments), there was no satisfactory collection of botanical rarities, the anatomical theater in one of the upper rooms contained almost nothing at all."[19] In their three-hundred-year race to become the Netherlands' leading university city, there had long since been only one winner. When he visited Franeker's cultural highlights—impressive in their own right, but nonetheless artifacts of a failed marathon attempt—Bavinck was no doubt aware of this. While Franeker was more like Leiden than was Broek op Langedijk, it certainly could not be mistaken for Leiden.

After this visit to Franeker, Bavinck traveled south, preaching in Rotterdam before visiting friends (and his former professors Scholten and Rauwenhoff) in Leiden, shortly after which he received significant news: "*5 Oct. Left Leiden again, half past three. At half past eight arrived in Kampen, where I found out that a call had been issued to me on the previous day by the Franeker congregation.*"[20]

Three days later, in the Friday edition of *De Bazuin* (Oct. 8), the Franeker congregation issued a public appeal to Bavinck to accept their call.

> FRANEKER, October 3, '80. Today, under the leading of Rev. K. Kuiper of Ferwerd, three Ministers were presented in alphabetical order to the congregation, comprising Dr. H. Bavinck, candidate at the Theol. School in Kampen; L. van Dellen of Koudum; and J. Wessels of Bedum. Dr. H. Bavinck was chosen by the male members. That the Lord may incline the heart of this brother to accept the calling with full boldness is the wish of the church session and congregation. On behalf of the church session, J. F. TUINSTRA.[21]

A Twofold Decision

Later that month, Bavinck preached to and promptly received a call from the Christian Reformed congregation in Broek op Langedijk. Immediately thereafter he made two important decisions, each in its own way bespeaking his ambitions.

> *1 Nov. Morning, 9 o'clock, to Leiden again, to speak with D. Donner about the publication of the "Synopsis." This edition shall appear under my direction;*

honorarium 150 guilders and 20% for each copy from 300–500. Afternoon, to
Kampen again.

2 Nov. <u>Accepted</u> the call to Franeker & declined that of Broek op Langendijk.[22]

Bavinck had chosen the city—albeit one less lustrous than Leiden—over the village. High culture, even of the faded sort, drew him in a way that agriculture could not. However, it does not seem that he intended to stay in Franeker, or even in the pastoral ministry, for the long haul. Just as he had accepted the call to Franeker, he met with Dirk Donner (1858–94), his former pastor's son, who had begun to emerge as an important Seceder publisher. The day before he accepted the call, he had committed himself to the publication of a new edition of the *Synopsis purioris theologiae*, a Latin summary of early Reformed orthodox theology published by four Leiden professors—Johannes Polyander, Andreas Rivetus, Antonius Walaeus, and Anthonius Thysius—in 1625.[23]

By this twofold choice, Bavinck had acted decisively in setting a clear trajectory for the coming years. Although he was going to Franeker, his ambition was to become something that had not been found there for some decades: a scientific theologian. (Incidentally, the last systematic theologian to have taught at the University of Franeker prior to its closure in 1843 was Bavinck's own *Doktorvater*, J. H. Scholten.) Clearly, Franeker could only be a stepping-stone, and never a final destination, on this route. In choosing Franeker, he had set his sights on another terminus.

In order to keep this step in motion and prevent himself from coming to a standstill in Friesland, Bavinck needed to generate scholarly motion sufficient to carry him beyond it. In that light, by choosing to release a new edition of the *Synopsis*, he acted astutely. From the vantage point of his Christian Reformed public, where some—though by no means all—viewed his connection to the University of Leiden with a degree of dubiety, this particular publication would cast his own theological pedigree and relationship to Leiden's theologians in a new light. It meant Bavinck's name would now be heard alongside that of the orthodox Johannes Polyander rather than the modernist Johannes Scholten. In generating this association, the publication had considerable potential to boost his appeal as a prospective teacher at the Theological School in Kampen.[24]

Alongside this, the *Synopsis* represented an important opportunity for him to study his own theological tradition: his education at Leiden had familiarized him with modern theological trends, biblical criticism, and Arabic, but it had not given him a deep knowledge of the kind of theology that animated

Seceder piety. And while he had remained a registered student in Kampen throughout those years and had passed his final candidature exams at the Theological School, he had done so without taking any of the school's classes in theology. By working on the *Synopsis*, he could kill many birds with one stone.

That Bavinck accepted the call to Franeker with an eye to an eventual appointment in Kampen seems clear from his choice to work on the *Synopsis* and from his appointment during the year in Franeker as editor (alongside the noted Seceder pastors Henricus Beuker and his friend D. K. Wielenga) of the Seceder theological journal *De Vrije Kerk*—a publication that was also acquired by Dirk Donner at the same time.[25] While Bavinck was in Franeker, *De Vrije Kerk* would play a useful role in allowing him to position himself as a key thinker on the future of scientific theology in the Seceder church.

Anticipating the Difficulties of Ministry

After accepting the call from Franeker, he received a letter from Henry Dosker (Feb. 12, 1881), whose life in America had become a tale of love and loss. As a newly married pastor, Dosker had suddenly lost his wife (who was carrying their first child) and found himself bereft and lonely in the pastorate: "Your own intended solitary life reminds you of my desolate condition. . . . I live with an aged couple and a hired girl. In company and yet <u>severely alone</u>. Alone, with my great, undiminishing sorrow."[26] In the coming months, Dosker's own sense of domestic isolation would be echoed in Bavinck's experience. Later in this letter, Dosker expressed considerable surprise that Bavinck had indeed accepted a call within the Christian Reformed Church. "I was astonished to read in the papers of your acceptance of the call of Franeker. Why? Because of the struggles, through which you past [*sic*] according to your last letter. Have the 37 Articles become plainer[,] or more acceptable, than before? Knowing your character, I must accept that as the most plausible explanation, and I do thank the Lord for this victory of faith."[27] Unfortunately, whatever doctrinal uncertainty Bavinck might have entertained toward his orthodox confessional heritage, even in the early 1880s, remains unknown. If these doctrinal issues did indeed exist, they did not prevent him from preaching regularly in Christian Reformed congregations in that period.

It is possible, of course, that Dosker's letter is not a reliable guide to Bavinck's outlook at that time. As Harinck has noted, while Dosker was Bavinck's friend, he was never a neo-Calvinist. He left the Netherlands before Kuyper's rise to prominence and before Bavinck's effort to balance orthodoxy and modernity had begun to mature.[28] In that light, it is hardly surprising that Bavinck's theological moves were increasingly surprising to him. Furthermore, in general, Dosker's letters to Bavinck are lengthy, emotional, and introspective. In them, he complains regularly that Bavinck's replies are too short. This leaves open the possibility that Dosker was reading too much into, or had misunderstood, whatever brief point Bavinck had communicated to him. In this particular letter, for example, Dosker's complaint about Bavinck's brevity suggests that he was a reader given to drawing inferences: "Your note was short yet full of reminiscences that seemed to spring up from between the lines." (Another example of the same is found in a later letter, when Dosker asks him, "Am I wrong when I was reading between the lines and felt and thought with you?")[29] In any case, it is less obvious from Bavinck's own writings that his decision to move to Franeker was marked by any degree of surprise.

Although Bavinck had accepted the call to Franeker early in November of 1880, his work there did not begin until the following March. In the intervening months, he seems to have busied himself with preparations for the pastorate and beyond. In response to two letters from Snouck Hurgronje regarding newspaper notes on Bavinck's ecclesiastical exams[30] and call to Franeker,[31] Bavinck replied (Nov. 13) with confirmation of his impending move to Franeker and an indication of the struggles he anticipated there.

> Just as you have read, I have accepted the call to Franeker. It is quite a big and, for an inexperienced candidate, fairly difficult congregation. Trembling [at the thought of] going into practice, I would gladly have declined, but I didn't think I could hold back any longer and sacrifice duty to desire. The installation has been set in advance for Sunday, March 6, 1881. Thus, I have some time to prepare myself in one way or another. I am indeed sorry that Franeker is so far out of the way, but when you have returned from your stay abroad, I still hope to see you soon in the manse. I am counting on it. It shall not be so often that we meet each other; and yet I hope and wish that the opportunity to do so will present itself often. I am very happy that you are so far on with your dissertation. I am expecting [a copy] soon and am curious about the content. I don't think I can accept your invitation to attend the defense. I am very busy, with an eye to the impending departure to Franeker, and am gradually being taken up in all sorts of ecclesiastical affairs, which are quite difficult at first.[32]

At this time, Snouck Hurgronje was about to defend his doctorate before moving on to further studies at the (then German) University of Strasbourg. For him, this would be the first step in a glittering, controversial career in the academy and public life.[33] Bavinck, however, was steeling himself to work in the "big and . . . fairly difficult" Christian Reformed Church in Franeker. The local Seceder pastor from 1851 to 1875, Rev. K. J. Pieters, was theologically combative[34] and struggled with excessive drinking.[35] When he was eventually deposed by the church, Pieters was followed by a section of the congregation and began to preach and administer the sacraments in a barn, before eventually becoming pastor of the local Free Evangelical Church.[36] In Hepp's account, the following minister, Rev. P. W. H. Eskes, drew the ire of many by preaching too often on the doctrine of predestination and was criticized for his sympathies toward Kuyper.[37] Regardless of whether Bavinck was indeed about to minister to a congregation suspicious, in part at least, of Kuyper— bearing in mind his own proximity to Kuyper—it is beyond doubt that he was moving to a community riven by division.

In another letter written to Snouck Hurgronje in the same month (Nov. 24), Bavinck wrote to congratulate his friend on the successful completion of his doctorate. Reflecting on the end of their student years at Leiden, he focused on the ongoing divergence in their theological outlooks and likely futures.

> And so, we have both reached the end of our academic studies. I can only regret that we have gone so far, so immensely far, from each other in principle and view of life. And yet my sincere friendship and warm interest will remain with you despite such great difference in insight and conviction. I hope that this difference will become smaller, but I do not yet see this [happening]. Now that I have left Leiden and look at modern theology and the modern worldview differently than when I stood so strongly under the influence of Scholten and Kuenen, many things seem different to me than they did at that time. I learned a great deal in Leiden but also unlearned much. This latter part could have been harmful to me, and more and more I am beginning to see the harm in it. The period in which the old convictions that we brought with us [to Leiden] were thrown into the melting pot of criticism has passed. It is time to be faithful to the convictions that we now have and to defend them with the weapons at our disposal. But if we both always earnestly and sincerely seek the truth, we shall also find it. Because I regard this as undoubtedly true, [the truth] is there, it must be there, and reveals itself to the eyes of those who truly seek it. Forgive me for this digression. It spilled involuntarily from my pen. It is such an immensely important thing, to see [one's] academic studies conclude. But once again, also on behalf of my father, [I] wish you happiness with the doctor's title. May you carry it for many years, and with ever increasing benefit. *t. t.* H. Bavinck.[38]

This particular correspondence occasioned a moment of self-reflection in which Bavinck claimed to have realized retrospectively, after sufficient time away from Leiden, that he had indeed been strongly influenced by Scholten and Kuenen during his student years.

Snouck Hurgronje's response (Dec. 22, 1880), however, quickly poured cold water on this recollection. "In the time of our daily interactions I never discovered such a strong influence from Scholten and Kuenen in you, other than in formal questions, which is to say, I understood that your stay in Leiden consistently left you unshocked in the area of dogmatics, but had given you a clearer insight than [you] formerly [had] on the critical objections to the old view of Scripture."[39] Snouck Hurgronje's incredulity on this point accords with the general tenor of Bavinck's own entries from the Leiden-era dagboek (and his later claim, in 1914, that he had gone to Leiden to become acquainted with Modern theology at close quarters).[40] This denial of the Leiden school's influence on his thought prompted further self-reflection in reply (Jan. 13, 1881). In the following letter, it becomes clear that he was struggling to transition between two worlds. He had learned to speak convincingly as an academic theologian in the Leiden circle but now found himself quite unprepared to do the same as a pastor in a Christian Reformed congregation.

The time to begin in my post is coming quickly. My installation and first service have been set for the second Sunday in March. To the extent that the moment draws near, I am increasingly dreading it. There is such a colossal amount that I still wanted to study and make my own in order to be able to speak about it with confidence, with inspiration, with belief. But it is possible that I might never finish [such a task]. Perhaps interaction with the congregation, with simple, pious people, will give me what the study cannot. No, it is true, Kuenen and Scholten have not had much influence on me (apart from in the contemplations of Scripture), if by that you mean the loss of the truths of faith and the adoption of others, of theirs. But they have (how could it be otherwise?) had an influence on the power and manner with which I embrace these truths. The naïveté of childlike faith, of unbounded confidence in the truth instilled within me, you see, that I have lost, and that is a lot, such a lot; in this way, that influence was great and strong.

And now I know it, that I will never get that back. I even find this good, and I am truly and sincerely thankful that I have lost it. There was also much in that naïveté that was untrue and needed to be purified. But still, there is in that naïveté (I know no better word), something that is good, that is a consolation; something that must remain, if the truth is to be sweet and precious to us. And if I then sometimes—very occasionally, because oh, where is the rock-solid faith of yesteryear in our age?—meet people in the congregation who have this, and do well by it and are so happy, now, I cannot help but wish that I believed again as they do, so happy and jolly; and then I feel that if I had that, and could preach like that, inspired, warm, always fully convinced of what I say, yes, as one of them, oh I think, then I would be strong, mighty, then I could be useful; myself alive, I could live for others.[41]

Moving to Franeker While Looking to Kampen

After traveling to Franeker to be examined by the local classis—a regional gathering attended by representatives of local congregations—a process that involved a short trial sermon on Colossians 1:27–28 (Dec. 16), he preached there the following Sunday (Dec. 17), before making a number of visible contributions to the ecclesiastical and academic communities in Kampen. In contrast to the sense of foreboding that darkened his gaze to the northwest, Kampen seems to have been a place of comparative lightness and ease. After all, it was the home of his parents, Adriaan Steketee, and a growing theological community.

> *18 Dec. Back to Kampen again. The Christmas vacation began the previous day. A. Steketee held a lecture on the mean[ing] of art [for Christian ministers] on Thursday Dec. 16.*
>
> *26 Dec. Preached in Kampen in the morning, 2nd Christmas Day on 1 Tim. 1:15 ([sermon no.] 57).*
>
> *3 Feb. Thursday eve., half past seven to ten o'clock, held a lecture for the students about "The Kingdom of God, the Highest Good."*
>
> *6 March (Sunday) morning, preached in Kampen on Isa. 53:4–6 for the last [time] before my departure to Franeker ([sermon no.] 58).*[42]

By this time, Bavinck was prominently invested in the life of the Christian Reformed Church in Kampen, in both its Theological School and its congregation. Due to the timing of his classis examination, he had missed one of the intellectual highlights of the Theological School's year: a public lecture by his beloved Adriaan Steketee, "The Meaning of Art for the Future Servant of the Gospel."[43] At the same time, Maarten Noordtzij (1840–1915) was appointed rector. A third-generation Seceder, Noordtzij was a politically engaged Old Testament scholar who was active in the fields of Egyptology and Assyriology—and like Bavinck, Noordtzij's son Arie would also study theology in Leiden and Kampen.[44] Noordtzij's installation as the Theological School's rector goes some way in explaining the allure of Kampen to Bavinck in this period. There, a new generation of Seceders continued to follow the path "from separation to integration." Bavinck was keen to join their number.

The lecture "The Kingdom of God, the Highest Good," given by Bavinck to the Kampen student society Fides Quaerit Intellectum in February 1881, is important in this regard. The lecture itself was published in serial form in *De Vrije Kerk*,[45] which provided a wider Christian Reformed audience with the opportunity to become familiar with his abilities and distinctive theological voice.[46] By way of content, "The Kingdom of God, the Highest Good" serves as a manifesto for Bavinck's early intellectual commitments. Opening with a critical but cautiously positive comment on Schleiermacher's contribution to modern theology (à la Steketee's 1875 lecture on Plato),[47] it makes constant recourse to Scripture and presents its author as an exponent of Calvin's thought[48] who is drawing from the emergent Kuyperian tradition.[49] It is infused with a commitment to organicism as a means of holding diverse things in unity and uses an Augustinian account of creation and sin—wherein the latter has no right of existence in the former—to argue that the kingdom of God is both *in* and not *of* this world. In short, it is a smorgasbord of what will become typically neo-Calvinistic ideas.

The report on the lecture given in *De Bazuin* mentions that it was attended by the students, the rector, the professors, and the *pastor loci* Jan Bavinck, and their wives. "May the Lord make this doctor in theology a rich blessing," it closes, "as much in the practice of science as in the ministry of the Word!"[50] When Bavinck became a candidate for ordination, it seems there was uncertainty in some quarters of his church as to the particulars of his theological makeup. After the delivery of this lecture to the Theological School in 1881 and its wider, serialized dissemination over the coming year, that uncertainty had dissipated. Bavinck's distinctive voice had now been heard.

Onward to Franeker

Bavinck's activities in Kampen at this time would seem to suggest that he was positioning himself for an eventual appointment at the Theological School. In the immediate backdrop, this effort was also supported by a number of strategically positioned campaigners: most prominently, his father, as the local Christian Reformed pastor and a trustee of the Theological School; Dirk Donner, as the leading Seceder publisher; and the editors of *De Vrije Kerk*. However, a Leiden doctor with no ministerial experience could not be called to the Theological School. Although he had begun to make waves as a theologian-at-large, Bavinck could only arrive in Kampen via Franeker. For a time at least, he had no choice but to stand still on the stepping-stone. The next month's dagboek entries portray this step, as if in slow motion, as the dreaded moment drew near.

*11 March. After all my books etc. were sent to Franeker by train on Tuesday,
I myself went on Friday afternoon. I arrived in Franeker in the evening at half
past five, was received with love, and stayed with L. Hofstra Jnr.*

*12 March. My parents came at half past five in the afternoon. I was in a somber
mood.*[51]

Initially, at least, the congregation's love for their new pastor was unrequited. This gloomy mood, however, was lifted on the following day.

*13 March Sunday. In the morning I was installed by father, at the direction
of Isa. 52:7. Stirring occasion. In the afternoon at half past five I began with
1 Thess. 2:4. Many, many people ([sermon no.] 59).*[52]

At his son's induction, Jan Bavinck preached on the text, "How beautiful
upon the mountains are the feet of him who brings good news, who publishes
peace, who brings good news of happiness, who publishes salvation, who
says to Zion, 'Your God reigns.'" And with that, Herman, who had thus far
preached fifty-eight times, usually on the same small pool of biblical texts,
was set to work as a pastor.

The Loneliness of Ministry

Following the departure of his parents, who *"took with them a good impression of Franeker,"*[53] Bavinck's time soon became filled. He was now busy with
the work of a pastor, delivering exegetical sermons on Sunday mornings and
preaching through the Heidelberg Catechism on Sunday evenings. On the first
Sunday after his installation, he noted: *"20 March. Preached in Franeker on
Isaiah 53:4–6 and Catech. Question 1 (wholly improvised for the first time,
went well)."*[54] From then on, it appears that Bavinck's sermons were extemporaneous, and they were certainly delivered without the use of manuscripts.[55]
Dagboek entries in the following weeks record a first marriage service (April
3) and receipt of wages: *f*108.42 for his first month (April 10). Shortly after
this, Unink visited Franeker for ten days (April 16–26).

As was the case between the Leiden years and his arrival in Franeker, when
he lived with family and busied himself with friends, a deep and heavy loneliness lay under this surface of social activity. Franeker, however, was different
from Leiden and Kampen in that it confronted him with this loneliness in a
new way. There, the camaraderie of friends and companionship of parents

and siblings had become occasional events rather than a constant feature. After each visit, Bavinck was painfully aware of his isolation.

24 April. In the morning Unink preached for me on 2 Cor 5:17a. It went well. In the afternoon I preached again on Catech. Q. 7 and 8 (72nd time [preaching]).

26 April. Tuesday. Unink went on his way back to Zwolle. I am alone again.[56]

More than he had in the past, Bavinck began to deal with loneliness by focusing on his work. His next recorded social engagement (May 16) was a visit to a local book club. For a character stimulated by ideas and close friendships, the Franeker book club was an obvious attraction: the typical reading group in Dutch towns of that era discussed belles lettres and provided its members with high-culture conviviality.[57] However, he made no comment on his visit and did not return. In context, it is easy to imagine why. Reflecting on these early months to Snouck Hurgronje, he complained that to the locals he was "always the 'minister'" and could not speak "in a familiar way" with them.[58] He had gone to the local reading group in search of like-minded friendship, only to find that its members saw him as intractably "other." Herman had become Reverend Doctor Bavinck—a formal identity not easily overlooked in a small town.

That his congregation was growing is evident in his notes on the monies taken in during the annual renting of pews. (In the nineteenth-century Netherlands, families paid an annual sum to rent their seats in the church building, which contributed to the upkeep of the building and the minister's stipend.) Bavinck's ministry was bearing fruit: that year's sum was "*300 gld. more than the last time.*"[59] At a time when pew rental was decreasing in most places, any such increase was no doubt encouraging to a young pastor.[60]

The pattern of his lonely early work—two sermons on Sundays, interspersed with ecclesiastical and pastoral duties throughout the week, including his first two funerals (June 2 and 6) and his appointment as clerk to his classis (June 9)—was interrupted by a visit from Albert Gunnink, the friend who had given him 250 cigars upon his twenty-first birthday. "*6 June. Pentecost Monday. Morning, preached on Eph. 2:19–22 ([sermon no.] 86). Midday, buried Nanta, father of Mrs. Stekelenburg. Morning, 10 o'clock, Albert Gunnink came to me in the church and stayed with me until 7 o'clock in the evening. It was pouring.*"[61] That Bavinck was overwhelmed by these duties is hinted at in his choice of sermon text for the following Sunday morning (June 12): Galatians 2:20, the homiletical security blanket relied upon dozens of times before coming to Franeker. While this might have been too subtle for his congregation to notice, a letter to Snouck Hurgronje from that week (June 16) explains in some detail his private struggles with his new calling. In response to Snouck Hurgronje's questions on whether he had been able to maintain his scholarly interests in the pastorate, Bavinck wrote, "If you think for a moment that I must preach twice every Sunday, teach the catechism four times through the week, must also devote much time to visiting homes and the sick, and then sometimes have to lead a Frisian funeral, you won't have to ask further whether any time or opportunity remains for my own study."[62]

In the same letter, he discusses frankly his struggle with singleness. Thus far, ministry had been a crushingly lonely experience. Its reality was far different from the hopes he had entertained while still enamored with Amelia. Sudden and full immersion in the demands of congregational life had even led Bavinck to question his own sincerity as he carried out his pastoral tasks.

> The most difficult part of my work is always to have to lift myself up to, and to stay at, the ideal level in my faith and confession. Oh, to have to deal with the holy constantly, always to be called to prayer, to thanksgiving, to exhortation or comforting. And then often to be able to project myself so little into those ever-changing circumstances: that is hard, it creates a feeling of dissatisfaction and often of numbness. I now understand better than before how in the guise of the spiritual, a deeply unholy, unfeeling, and insincere heart can reside. Apart from this serious and onerous difficulty in the office of the preacher, a shadow side is attached, and I feel this deeply. And that is, that one is always "the minister" and can never more speak in a properly familiar way. That's how it is for me, anyway. Thus far, I haven't found anyone here with whom I can (or might dare to) enjoy that familiarity. And I find that difficult. At home I am alone, in my room, and outside I am always "the minister." If I ever longed for a wife who could understand me and in whom I could confide fully, it is in these recent days.[63]

In that setting, it was assumed that an unmarried young man would not take care of his own cooking or cleaning. Whereas Bavinck had hoped to live with Amelia, he was expected, instead, to live with a *hospita*, Mrs. Stekelenburg, who resided on the ground floor of the manse with her husband.[64] In the Leiden years, of course, he had also been looked after by a *hospita*, Ms. Smit. There, however, Bavinck had lived the carefree life of a student. His societal place in Franeker was altogether different. To the Stekelenburgs, Herman was Reverend Bavinck. Even in his own home, he could only escape his congregants' formal expectations by retreating to his own room, where isolation served as informality's poor substitute. Like Dosker in Michigan, "in company and yet severely alone," Bavinck was now a young, unmarried pastor who lived with an elderly couple by necessity rather than choice.

Despite this personal struggle, his congregation continued to grow. Indeed, following this letter's bleak opening, he would describe the congregation itself to Snouck Hurgronje in more positive terms, before explaining its fractured history.

> The congregation, however, is generally good. Only, there are still some less welcome after-effects from earlier times. For a few years, there was a minister here who was certainly an exception in the whole of our church. Unusually sharp in intellect, he could not be satisfied with our confession, didn't bother himself with it, and preached what he himself found good. Alongside this, he was guilty of a very great misuse of strong drink—all of this together meant he was eventually deposed. My predecessor, Eskes, had much conflict with the friends of this deposed minister. And there are still those who condemn the sin of the former minister Pieters, but still entertain his doctrine. From that, there is here—which in our church otherwise never arises—much confusion and difference of opinions. In particular, Pieters's faithful followers are quite prominent and imagine and regard themselves to be quite clever. So far, however, they have been satisfied by my preaching. Particularly when I disapprove of their feelings, I try, through conversations here and there, to correct them. A lot can be done with patience and love.[65]

Coming Up for Air

By July 11, Bavinck had preached thirty-eight times in Franeker. On the next morning, he took a train to Kampen, and he would not return to Friesland for two and a half weeks.

He had taken a holiday that coincided with the next round of public exams in Kampen. Given his own hopes to be appointed at the Theological School, his father's pulpit was a strategically important location on the Sunday between *examen A* and *examen B*. Needless to say, Herman was given the occasion and preached on John 5:17, *"where trustees, profs. & students were all present."*[66] His dagboek entries on these exams also follow Unink's progress: evidently, Unink did not take part in the preaching exams and was told he *"had to wait another year."*[67]

Following more holiday travels with Unink, Bavinck traveled to preach in Amsterdam (July 23–24)—an engagement that would soon result in a call to leave Franeker. In Amsterdam, a large Christian Reformed congregation was interested in him. He was becoming a man in demand. Despite this, other forces within the denomination saw his future in theological education rather than the pastoral ministry. Two weeks after his return to Franeker,

D. K. Wielenga visited Bavinck in order to discuss changes to *De Vrije Kerk*, the theological journal to which both contributed.

> *8 Aug. Rev. Wielenga came to mine at 10 o'clock in the morning . . . in order to talk with me about how things needed to go with the "Vrije Kerk." Decided . . . to change publisher and to take a different format. Final editing, from now on, by me.*[68]

De Vrije Kerk was widely read in Christian Reformed circles and was heavily promoted in *De Bazuin*, the Seceder newspaper. Bavinck was now its editor-in-chief. Although he had been forced to counter some suspicion because of his Leiden connections in order to be ordained in Franeker, he had now received a considerable demonstration of trust from the denomination's theological journal. This was an appointment that added to the scholarly motion that had carried Bavinck onto his stepping-stone and would soon take him beyond it.

Countering Loneliness

In the months that followed, Bavinck became more at ease in his ministerial work. Initially, this seems to have depended on the increasing efforts of others—primarily Unink and Bavinck's own family—in spending time with him. In mid-August, he spent two days with his parents before traveling with Unink to Utrecht to attend a pastoral conference. When Bavinck was struck midconference by toothache and a swollen face, Unink accompanied him on the journey back to his parental home. Two days later, Bavinck returned to Franeker accompanied by his younger brother Bernard (Coenraad Bernardus), who holidayed with him for several days.

Alongside this, Bavinck also began to develop friendships within his congregation, as well as with Seceders in the surrounding area (who, crucially, were not members of his own congregation). A dagboek entry on September 8 records an outing with one of his elders to Sexberium, where they dined with one of the local Christian Reformed deacons. The pastor's life was becoming more pleasant: *"Beautiful weather. Much enjoyment."*[69]

As the year progressed, his increasingly positive outlook continued to develop. The installation of his friend Munnik as pastor in Monster (Oct. 16), at which Bavinck had also preached, was a *"welcome day."*[70] Later that week, he spent two days with Unink in Kampen and Zwolle (Oct. 20–21). A month later (Nov. 21), his friend C. van Proosdy[71]—another young Christian Reformed pastor with scholarly interests—arrived in Franeker unannounced:

"an enjoyable day."[72] Against a backdrop of loneliness as an unmarried minister, these friendships mattered a great deal.

First Birthday as a Pastor

Any impression that this period's dagboek entries show Bavinck as surviving in Franeker by focusing on friendships and activities beyond it is dispelled by the lengthy note made on his first (and only) birthday in the pastorate.

> *13 Dec. Birthday. I received many proofs of esteem from the congregation. From Kamstra, Pars, J. Tamminga, Jule Draaisma, each 1 box of cigars. From the Women's Union a cigar set, from some of the young ladies (Anne Brouwer et al.) a silk bookmark, from the church session a chair. From the young girls (catechism class, Wednesday evenings, 8 o'clock) a silver spoon, fork & napkin. In the evening the church session came over with their wives. A welcome day, an overabundance of reasons to offer thanks to God.*[73]

Indeed, a lot can be done with patience and love. Bavinck was now twenty-seven years old and—perhaps to his own surprise—was much loved by his flock.

He spent the remainder of December with Unink. Shortly before Christmas, they attended a *"convincing lecture from Rev. Noordtzij on Assyriology & Egyptology"* in Kampen together,[74] followed by a *"convivial gathering"* with friends.[75] After this, Unink also traveled to Franeker to provide his friend with pulpit cover on New Year's Day.

Opportunities in Amsterdam

Bavinck's activities in Franeker maintained a dual focus: he was working hard at ministering to his congregation while also making moves that kept up a public, scholarly profile. These two foci, of course, were interlinked. By excelling in both, he sent a clear message to the Christian Reformed Church and its Theological School—the obvious import of his activities was that he was a scholar who had done well in the pastorate and who would do well in forming others for pastoral ministry. The Theological School, however, was not the only one to pick up his scent. On February 14, his dagboek noted, *"I received a letter from Rev. J. W. Felix, president trustee of the Free University, [asking] whether I had objections in principle to the acceptance of an eventual appointment as prof. in hermeneutics & New Testament exegesis and whether I would earnestly consider such an appointment.*"[76] Kuyper had not ceased pursuing the young doctor. Despite the awkwardness of Bavinck's earlier acceptance-turned-rejection of a chair in Semitic languages at the Free University, the opportunity to work with the hero of his youth had come around again. If he so wished, he could now move off the stepping-stone and swap Franeker—difficult congregation, planetarium, and all—for the Keizersgracht in Amsterdam. "*16 Feb. To the first question I answered: no. To the second, yes; but that I would still very probably decline, because of the importance of our School, at which I would very much like to be appointed at the forthcoming synod in Aug.*"[77]

While the dagboek does not elaborate on these comments or dwell on the "principle objections" that Bavinck might have had toward the Free University, the letter sent to Rev. Felix in response says a great deal. Indeed, this letter shows that Bavinck had *not* decisively declined the Free University. Rather, he had declared Kampen to be his first love: to her, the first refusal.

Your honored letter of the 13th of this [month] was no small surprise to me. I am thankful for the good thoughts that you wish to entertain toward me. In response to the questions posed, after earnest deliberation I give you the following honest reply. I have no objections in principle which a priori would already make the acceptance of an eventual appointment impossible for me. The Free University is, rather, something that I greet with happiness in many regards. In its establishment, I honor a work of faith. Thus, an eventual appointment would be the subject of my earnest and prayerful consideration. To a certain extent, I could stop [my response] at this. However, my conscience would not feel itself wholly free were I not to share with you in particular confidence why I would as yet most likely decline such an appointment. I love my church. I prefer to work in building it up. The flourishing of its Theol. School is a deep concern to me. There is, however, a great deal in that establishment that needs immediate improvement. The Christ. Ref. Church is for the most part convinced of this and shall be alert to improvement at the next synod in August. Speaking honestly, I now have a quiet longing and hope (the right to both has not only been derived from my ambition, has it?) that the synod will offer me a place at its school. That place certainly does not have much charm, but it attracts me in the importance of the church that I serve. I also know well that this hope that I entertain can be disappointed and that, judged by some details, it also *shall* be disappointed. But as long as our church has not yet openly declared, by not appointing me at the coming synod, that it does not want to be served by me at its school, *for as long as that* I feel no freedom to withdraw from it the abilities that I might have and to commit myself to another establishment for higher education. To it, then, the first choice; after this, I am free. With

this, in keeping with your wish and the urge of my own heart, I have shared
my response with you confidentially and fraternally. On account of the nature
of the matter, I would have preferred to keep this last [section] to myself; but
I could not do this without taking upon myself the appearance of dishonesty.
Please receive again my cordial thanks for your favorable feelings toward me.[78]

Although the Theological School had yet to choose Bavinck, he had nonetheless chosen it over Kuyper's new Free University. (Indeed, this is the first extant
source in which we find Bavinck writing explicitly of his hopes regarding an
appointment in Kampen at the 1882 synod.) For the time being, our romantic
pragmatist would remain on the stepping-stone.

Another opportunity to relocate to Amsterdam—this time, in the form
of a call from the Christian Reformed congregation there—presented itself
within a matter of days. His dagboek entry notes that he was the congregation's overwhelming choice ("*I got 307 votes. Nederhoed 58. Van Minnen 28*")
and that his salary would be much higher than in Franeker: *f*2,400 per annum,
over his then current (approximate) *f*1,300. Despite this, he declined the call;
his sights were now set firmly on the Theological School. Indeed, when his
mother fell ill later that month, prompting him to return to his parental home
to visit her, he also used this opportunity to give a lecture to the Theological
School's students on "*the character, basis, content of unbelief.*"[79] While he
was clearly doing whatever he could to position himself carefully in view
of a potential appointment there, he spent the coming months preaching in
Franeker and increasing his portfolio of ecclesiastical responsibilities more
widely. Having only preached fifty-eight times prior to his ordination, by June
4, 1882, he had delivered two hundred sermons.

Later that summer, his interactions with Abraham Kuyper continued in
July when he (accompanied by van Proosdy) heard him give a lecture in Leeuwarden on the future prospects that awaited graduates of the Free University.[80]
The employability of his new university's students was a significant issue for
Kuyper at this time, most notably with regard to graduates in theology: the
Free University was founded on "Reformed principles" but was not affiliated
with (or recognized by) any particular Reformed church, and therefore its
theological students could not yet become ministers. In that light, the extended
dagboek commentary provides a rare private glimpse into Bavinck's view of
Kuyper's university project at that time.

*Summary: Two observations at the outset: a) he spoke entirely on his own
behalf, not at the behest of anyone else, b) the University is the abode of science, it does not take care of jobs and posts for the students. Three parts: 1st*

prospects in the immediate context: for doctors, good; for philos. literature, law, almost alright, for theologians bad, because of the church. 2nd on the horizon of expectations—in the state more freedom is coming; in the church, though, [it is] not: the synod must suppress freedom in order to remain in existence. 3rd according to the prophecy of faith—bearing a cross, suffering etc., believers, is what the Teacher expects of us, but the reward is in heaven. Conclusion was: there are no future prospects. There was no debate of any significance.[81]

Bearing in mind the content of Bavinck's letter to Rev. Felix shortly before this, in which he pleaded love for his church, it does appear that the Theological School held a considerable advantage over the Free University in the race for his affections. In crudely pragmatic terms, Kampen's graduates were employable. Restated in terms closer to Bavinck's own: for a Kampen student, the lecture hall was a training ground for the pulpit. In the young Bavinck's thoughts on his own contribution as a theological educator, that distinction gave Kampen the upper hand. (In 1883, Kampen also had more theological students than the Free University: forty-eight to thirty-one.)[82]

Approaching the Synod

As the 1882 synod drew near—and having already given Kampen the first option on his services—whatever Bavinck thought about the Free University's students' future prospects became a more distant concern. The moment for which he had positioned himself carefully (and had been positioned carefully by the likes of D. K. Wielenga and Dirk Donner) was fast approaching. In the month before, he once again found himself in the Kampen pulpit, preaching on the Sunday of the Theological School's examination week. Happily, for Bavinck, Unink's examination went well: *"He passed."*[83]

The synod itself was momentous for Bavinck in two respects. Most obviously, it would be the moment of truth regarding his own calling as a theologian. More ominously, however, it was also the scene of Adriaan Steketee's sudden dismissal as a member of the Theological School's faculty. That decision was made by the school's trustees, meeting in camera, who made no initial public statement on the reasons for his dismissal. The minutes from that committee meeting, however, portray a wide-ranging dissatisfaction with the direction and quality of theological education offered in Kampen at that time. "In general," the minute begins, "the trustees have not received a favorable impression."[84] Student performance in the literary and theological examinations was deemed poor (a verdict also shared at various points in

Bavinck's dagboek), the quality of teaching on offer was deemed inadequate, and the older teachers were judged too physically weak to improve in their performance.

Of the younger teachers, two received explicit attention: the Old Testament scholar Maarten Noordtzij, positively; and Adriaan Steketee, negatively. "Steketee is not the right fit. We are disappointed in him."[85] Particular displeasure was voiced regarding his gifts as a teacher and his "one-sided fondness for [biblical] criticism." The trustees also criticized Noordtzij's study of "critical theology," chided the dogmatician Helenius de Cock for his failure to keep abreast of developments in his field, and reproved the teaching staff in general for their collective failure to integrate their disciplines better. More gravely than all of this, the blame for the Theological School's apparently frivolous, ill-disciplined student culture came to rest at Steketee's feet.

According to these minutes, an attempt was made to elicit his resignation, but to no avail. And so, Steketee was pushed when he refused to jump. (Harinck and Berkelaar have noted that irritation from the trustees toward Adriaan Steketee was nothing new. Until this point, though, his father, Christiaan Steketee, had been the Theological School's longest-serving trustee and had shielded his son from their criticism. Crucially for Adriaan, however, his father had passed away two months before the 1882 synod. Bereft of this paternal protection, the younger Steketee soon found himself out of a job.)[86]

The trustees' view of the Theological School as an underperforming institution, of course, was shared by Bavinck. In his letter to Felix earlier that year, written to decline the Free University's approach, he had observed that "there is . . . a great deal in that establishment [the Theological School] that needs immediate improvement. The Christ. Ref. Church is for the most part convinced of this and shall be alert to improvement at the next synod in August."[87] The trustees certainly were alert to the school's failings. De Cock was relieved of dogmatics and directed instead to teach liturgy and symbolics. More starkly, Steketee was dismissed and would be replaced by new appointments who met the trustees' aspirations for the school: more rigorous in dogmatics, at the forefront of scientific theology, more academically demanding of their students, and with a more coherent collective direction. In short, Herman Bavinck was cast as the antidote to Steketee's failings.

Bavinck's writings from this time make almost no mention of Steketee's dismissal—a silence that might seem unusual, given his admiration (in writings public and private) for him over a number of years. He said nothing of Steketee, for example, when discussing his own appointment in correspondence with Snouck Hurgronje. The sole relevant reference in his dagboek notes that Steketee had requested a public confirmation from the trustees that he had not been dismissed on moral grounds, a request granted by the synod. (Steketee's supporters, including Bavinck, would only go on to speak publicly of his dismissal after his death, in 1914.) That immediate silence, though, perhaps bespeaks the strange reality of the circumstances around Bavinck's own appointment: he was hired, in part at least, because Steketee was fired. It is a silence of the existential sort, borne of an attention divided between his former teacher's plight and his own future.

The synod made known its intention to nominate three new teachers for the Theological School. Forty-five voters were asked to bring their nominations. Of the nineteen names to be mentioned in the first round of votes, Herman Bavinck (40), D. K. Wielenga (44), and Lucas Lindeboom (33) were the clear front-runners. (Jan Bavinck received 8 votes.) A second round followed, this time excluding all those who had received fewer than four votes. In this round, the results were more even: Wielenga (39), Beuker (32), Doorn (11), Brummelkamp Jr. (23), Lindeboom (33), Hessels (22), Nieuwhuis (8), Jan Bavinck (10), van Andel (8), and Herman Bavinck (31), with 4 votes spoiled by their nomination of an unspecified Bavinck. From this round, the top six candidates were then subject to a final vote. Herman recorded,

> *These six had to excuse themselves.*
> *In this vote [the following names] had*
>
> <u>*Wielinga*</u> *[sic] 39. Beuker 4*
> <u>*Bavinck*</u> *39 Hessels 2.*
> <u>*Lindeboom*</u> *32. Brummelk. 4.*
>
> *A striking moment for me and my father.*[88]

In his own autobiography, Jan Bavinck also recalled this moment and provided an extended comment on its personal significance to father and son alike. Noting a range of strange coincidences between their respective experiences of nomination to teach in Kampen—both were twenty-eight, both nominations took place at synods held in Zwolle, and both were nominated to the same position—he turned to reflect on their great difference. He had declined his nomination, whereas his son had accepted it boldly, telling the synod that "he had prayed to God for this post." After many years of private doubt and difficulty following a lot cast in error, Jan was finally at peace:

> Now, I know well that there is nothing extraordinary behind these peculiar circumstances, and therefore I do not announce that, but I did see the finger of the Lord before me in this, and I thanked him for it, that my son, I would

not say succeeded me, but that he would take the place that I had not dared to take through lack of faith. Could it be that I was led to decline so that an opportunity for my son would remain open? I do not know, but I know well that since that time I have been able to rest better in my refusal.[89]

The Bavincks' dream had come true: Herman had moved beyond his stepping-stone, and Jan had finally been reconciled to his own past. On the selfsame day, however, Steketee's scholarly career had been dealt a death blow. Emotionally exhausted by this dual outcome, Herman sought solace in his family home and declared himself unfit to tell his congregation of his departure. "*26 Aug. To Kampen again with father. I was too exhausted to go to Franeker. Rev. Eerdmans went for me and made my appointment known there.*"[90]

At the close of the synod, it was decided by the trustees that Bavinck would teach dogmatics, ethics, encyclopedia, philosophy, and third-year Latin. After intimating his formal acceptance of this lectureship (Sept. 8), Bavinck set his departure from Franeker in motion. Once again, Jan and Geziena came to vacation with their son (Sept. 12–15). His books and furniture were packed up, following which he left the manse to stay with Mr. and Mrs. Hofstra (Oct. 2). "*In this week I visited the members of the congregation in the town.*"[91] The same sequence of events, of course, had been played out in reverse order in March 1881, when he arrived in Franeker in a somber mood, dreading what lay ahead. A year and a half later, his mood had lifted somewhat. He left in much finer fettle. "*8 Oct. Morning. Preached on 2 Tim. 3:14, 15. Midday, 2 o'clock departure on Jn. 17:17. Incredible number of people. Tuinstra addressed me. An unforgettable day! [sermon numbers] 232. 233.*"[92]

PART 4

Professor in Kampen

7

Gathering Materials

1883–89

"My books are my true company."

News of Bavinck's nomination at the Theological School quickly spread far and wide. Perhaps the most interesting reportage of his appointment was run in the *Java-Bode*, a daily Dutch-language newspaper published in the East Indies. On Saturday, October 14, 1882, the *Java-Bode* published an article explaining the significance of Bavinck's appointment.

> In our land, there is still independent study. A notable example of this was provided in the most recent nomination of three teachers at the Theological School in Kampen, the educational school—as it is known to you—for the teachers of the Christian Reformed (Seceded) Church. One of the three was Dr. H. Bavinck, minister of the congregation of that denomination in Franeker. This young man first gained a doctorate a couple of years before with a learned Latin dissertation at the University of Leiden, where he had also studied. During the entirety of his study time he was known as an ultraconfessional man, and immediately after gaining his doctoral degree he submitted himself to the Seceders' candidature exam. It hardly needs to be said that they joyfully received the man who had

remained standing through the trial-by-fire of the Leiden faculty. Let me add to this that the Leiden professors always spoke of him with high praise. But this phenomenon is noteworthy enough—a short while ago theological student in Leiden, now teacher at the Theological School in Kampen.[1]

The *Java-Bode* account of Bavinck's student years might have benefited from more careful fact-checking: his dissertation, for example, was written in Dutch, rather than Latin,[2] and the "trial-by-fire" view of the Leiden faculty bears little resemblance to Bavinck's own experience as a student there. Regardless of this, for a newspaper like the *Java-Bode*—traditionally an elitist, liberal title that had been shaped by the editorship of the former Leiden theological-student-turned-journalist Conrad Busken Huet in the early 1870s[3]—the story of a young Seceder forging a new path through Dutch society by moving from Leiden to Kampen was inherently newsworthy. At the outset, this biography noted that the first Seceders lived out a difficult existence, finding their feet reactively, as the ground beneath their feet shifted beyond their control. Half a century later, a son of the Secession had made that same ground move: not only had it become possible for a Seceder theologian to gain a doctorate at Leiden; it had also become possible for a Leiden-educated theologian to be appointed at the Seceder Theological School. On both fronts, history (and news) had been made.

Post-Franeker Reflections

Although Bavinck had intimated acceptance of his nomination to the Theological School in September 1882 and had left Franeker within a matter of weeks, his installation in Kampen would not take place until January 1883. While the dagboek entries in this intervening period show that his life had returned to its pre-Franeker pattern of activities—trips to visit friends and preach across the country, an enjoyable trip to see the Panopticum in Amsterdam, followed by a visit to Kuyper—the extended reflections on his year in the pastorate found in a letter to Snouck Hurgronje (Nov. 10) suggest that while his time as a pastor was short, its impact upon him had been profound. Post-Franeker, Bavinck was different.

> I am now in Kampen, at home with my parents. The newspapers have informed you that the synod of our church, held in August in Zwolle, by unanimous vote nominated me as a teacher in its Theological School. I had half expected this; still, before that time I was often fearful that it would not happen. You

understand that I had longed for it in silence. I was up in the north. The congregation that I served was agreeable to me; the love and esteem that I received in and beyond it were great. On Sundays, many, very many people came to hear me, so that the church soon became too small. And the most important thing is—I worked there not without fruit, blessing was enjoyed under the ministry of the Word. Still, it was a difficult post. It was a large congregation. And preaching alone is not enough; house visits had to be done, to comfort those in mourning, to encourage the sick, to prepare the dying, to raise up the weak and lowly, and to exhort the strong to humility. I did this with love, with fruit and also for my own heart and life, but not without self-denial and giving over what was close to my heart. . . . Despite all that good, for which I cannot be thankful enough, I longed for something different, where I thought I would possess more calling and desire and suitability. And that longing has been fulfilled. I was nominated by a general vote. I write this to you to show you the great trust that I, against all thought and expectation, possess in our church and that truly brings me to deep humility.

After the nomination I stayed in the congregation for a few weeks. These last weeks were heavy in many regards. The congregation was so attached to me. Old and young, rich and poor, in and beyond the congregation—all were sorry that I was leaving. It affected me sometimes and made me ask whether my longing had been good and pure. . . . I learned a lot in those last few weeks; my life has been enriched by them. I am happy that I have worked in a congregation for around a year and a half and have gotten to know the people in their various imperfections yes, but also in their deep piety and noble sense of what is good and true. And now I have already been in Kampen for a few weeks, at home with my parents. Things can turn out wonderfully; when I formerly left my parental home, I never thought of returning for more than a few days. And now I will stay at home, perhaps for a long time, because I am not yet engaged, and it doesn't look like that will happen in a hurry. Still, I would have nothing against getting married; it's because of circumstances, not my will or in principle, that I am still single.[4]

Although the return to his family home provided valued companionship and made his singleness more bearable, Bavinck still held out hope that he might indeed marry Amelia.[5] His more pressing concerns, however, were the inaugural lecture that would follow his induction at the Theological School and the heavy teaching load that would begin shortly thereafter. In the same letter, he continues: "I tremble sometimes at the thought of what has been placed on my shoulders, but on the other side I hope to begin this work with desire and courage. The subject of my oration is not yet wholly certain. Probably: the character (essence) of theology. . . . If my oration is published (which is not yet sure), I will send [a copy] to you; you can then see where I now stand. Thankfully, I now know that *a bit* better than [I did] at the time in Leiden."[6] Shortly before his installation and inaugural lecture, Bavinck advised Snouck Hurgronje not to attend the event, claiming that as his parents regularly provided accommodation to lodgers, they had no space to host any more guests, and that with such a great number of other visitors, they would have little time to spend together. After promising to send on a copy of the printed lecture,[7] he observed that while they differed in starting points and, by necessity, conclusions, he would welcome Snouck Hurgronje's critique of it: "To receive it sharpens and is of great importance."[8] His friend would certainly oblige.

Installation in Kampen

Alongside his fellow new appointments Douwe Klazes Wielenga and Lucas Lindeboom, Bavinck was installed at the Theological School on January 9, 1883.[9] This was the occasion for Jan Bavinck's lecture on the importance of scientific theological training in the Christian Reformed Church,[10] as described in chapter 2: at his induction, Herman received a public show of support from his father, who spoke as chairman of the Theological School's trustees.

Wielenga (1841–1902), an experienced pastor with whom Herman Bavinck had long since been closely acquainted, was appointed to teach church history and ecclesiastical law. Like Bavinck, Wielenga was an irenic figure who sympathized with Kuyper. They would go on to become close friends and confidants in the Kampen years. Lindeboom (1845–1933) was an altogether different breed. Far closer than Wielenga to Bavinck's intellectual gifts, Lindeboom was a self-assured, often surprising, and fearless thinker. Prior to his appointment in Kampen, for example, he had spent a decade pastoring in Zaandam. In that time, the ninety-strong congregation had grown to three hundred, while also seeing one hundred members leave for other churches.[11] As a character, he could attract and repel in equal measure. Unlike Bavinck, Wielenga, or the recently installed rector, Maarten Noordtzij, Lindeboom had no love for Kuyper or the Free University and showed him no public deference—an open antipathy shared, quite naturally, by Kuyper himself.[12]

Since Bavinck was the youngest of three new teachers, his inaugural lecture was scheduled last. Wielenga's oration, which lasted two and a half hours, was given after their induction. Lindeboom and Bavinck were scheduled to speak on the following day. "*10 Jan. Midday 12 o'clock Lindeboom spoke on biblical history, 3½ hours. Evening 6 o'clock Bavinck on the science of sacred theology 1 hour.*"[13]

As is typical of his account, Hepp's retelling of this event is dramatic. According to him, these orations were given in the Burgwalkerk on a particularly cold day. Lindeboom's speech was long and laborious, infuriating the young Bavinck, who thought it outrageous that a congregation should be expected to sit in the cold for so long. In response to Lindeboom's long oration, Bavinck apparently told his father that he would not deliver his own because the people could soon read it in print form. Having been convinced by his father and closest friends to give his lecture, Bavinck "spoke at such a fast tempo that everything had finished within an hour and fifteen minutes. This lecture could not count as a demonstration of eloquence."[14] As is also typical of Hepp's account, he offers no sources to verify this story, which does not correspond to Landwehr's own eyewitness recollection of an apparently "majestic" lecture: "As students, we had held great expectations, but everything that we heard exceeded those expectations. . . . We students were captivated by that lecture."[15]

Puzzlingly, Bremmer's otherwise careful biography claims that the dagboek entry on the length of Lindeboom's lecture was marked with a "thick underline" (a claim repeated, but developed into a "thick double stripe," in Gleason's biography),[16] which is used to illustrate Bavinck's early antagonism toward his new colleague. Regardless of Bavinck's feelings toward Lindeboom—which certainly would turn cold over time—the dagboek entry in question contains no such marking.

Defining Theology Theologically

If his earlier lecture "The Kingdom of God, the Highest Good"[17] functioned as a manifesto for the theological enterprise that would later be recognized as neo-Calvinism, "The Science of Sacred Theology" had followed it with a precise definition of *theology* itself.[18] Opening with the Leiden professor Lodewijk Rauwenhoff's claim that "theology must be secularized,"[19] Bavinck presented a counterclaim: theology must rather be *theologized*. As the knowledge of God, he argued, theology is its own avenue of inquiry. It is a science possessing its own object, animating principle, content, and goal. In this lecture, each of these points was construed theocentrically: theology comes from God, is concerned with God (and all else in relation to God), and finds its end in God. Precisely as such, theology can only live by its own agenda. It exists sui generis. Although Bavinck's definition of theology was classical, with strong shades of Augustine and Aquinas, his effort to restate this ancient idea depended on his engagement with a more recent conversation partner:

Friedrich Schleiermacher.[20] As he locked horns with the Leiden school, Bavinck fought modern with modern.

In its bold implicit claims on the self-governing nature of theology and on the inherent difference between theology (as the queen of the sciences) and religious studies, Bavinck's inaugural lecture had rejected the Higher Education Act (1876), to which the Leiden school had, at least in part, conformed. Indeed, in a move reminiscent of the German philosopher Ludwig Feuerbach, who argued that God is a projection of human needs and desires, Bavinck argued that to accept the limitations of the Act was to make theology *anthropological*, rather than *theological*, in character: "Theology simply becomes anthropology; God [becomes] an ideal, an image, formed by the human— that is, an idol."[21] While he had stated his case carefully, he also did so with astonishing boldness: the Leiden school's theology, he had claimed, was a temple in which idols of the mind were fashioned and served.

This critique goes some way in explaining why in a letter from this period he told Snouck Hurgronje that he did not intend to send a copy of his oration to any of his Leiden professors.[22] It appears that he was unsure of their likely reactions to the sound of his own constructive theological voice, particularly given the starkness of his argument vis-à-vis their own history and intellectual commitments. Eventually, however, Bavinck did send copies to two of his most irenic former professors, his de facto doctoral supervisor Abraham Kuenen and Cornelis Petrus Tiele. Kuenen's response is typical of his earlier interactions with Bavinck. "*Am*[ice]! Receive my hearty thanks for sending your oration, which I have read with great interest. Not with agreement, as you understand. But my dissent does not hinder me in reading from remarking that you have set out and defended your view clearly, consistently, and worthily."[23] Tiele's reaction was similar: "Although my viewpoint is extremely different from yours, this does not hinder me in congratulating you for the manner in which you have defended your own."[24] Both were happy to see him gain employment in Kampen and restated their already good terms with their former student (with Kuenen's letter also giving Bavinck news on his wife's ailing health), but neither showed much willingness to enter theological dialogue with their former student. Even when making essentially absolute theological claims, the young Seceder doctor of theology was met with an unengaging kind of toleration.

Thankfully, the same does not hold true of Snouck Hurgronje. Having received a copy of Bavinck's lecture, he sent a detailed and critical engagement that centered on Bavinck's reliance on the authority of Scripture (given his own knowledge of higher-critical views of biblical texts) and how the absolute nature of his claims related to non-Christians.[25] Snouck Hurgronje's assessment of the lecture's apparent weakness—"Your lecture was directed to people who agree with you, among whom these issues, named with such hard words, do not have to be fought"—would almost certainly have been received as an incisive criticism.[26] While Bavinck's lecture had been intended as a critique of the Leiden school, his faithful Leiden-era friend had immediately responded by probing whether the move to a confessionally homogenous environment had already caused his previously high standards to slip.

Bavinck's response is equally fascinating—both in viewing his theological development at this stage and in understanding the friendship that existed between these two drastically different thinkers. While admitting the limited scope afforded by a single lecture, we can observe that he claimed that his task had never been to deal with the mechanics of biblical criticism. "My goal was wholly different. That goal was to show what theology is and wants to be, according to its own character. Theology is, I think, knowing God. It provides the answer to the very simple and very practical, and for every person, also the least learned, most important question: *How do I know God?* and *How may I have eternal life?* When the matter is considered this way, there is no possible answer other than, 'Only from the Holy Scriptures.'"[27] Having argued that the theologian's relationship to Scripture is akin to that of the natural scientist's dependence on nature itself—as one who assumes a priori that nature *is*—he then tried to account for why Snouck Hurgronje found his use of Scripture's authority to be so problematic. "This is the difference between you and me (let me speak personally for a moment): you want, through and after research, to reach this viewpoint [i.e., a judgment on Scripture reached a posteriori]; I move forward from it [i.e., a view of Scripture asserted a priori] and go on researching. I think that the latter is necessary if there is ever to be talk of theology in the actual sense."[28] At this point, Bavinck's a priori commitment to the authority of Scripture and the role played by Scripture in the task of theology rendered the higher-critical concerns voiced (and given a central role) by Snouck Hurgronje of secondary importance. Most notably, however, this particular letter ends with the following frank admission: "I must add something else: I am thus in no way finished with my view of Scripture."[29] Beyond his long-standing prior commitment that God is revealed in Scripture, his settled opinion on the doctrine of Scripture was still far from its final form.

A more positive reaction to the lecture came from Abraham Kuyper. Writing in *De Heraut*, Kuyper objected to Bavinck's use of Schleiermacher but gave him an otherwise sparkling assessment: "Now, this is truly Reformed scientific theology. This has been thought through, the first principles have been laid down correctly, a path has been defined that can lead to an excellent development."[30] Of course, it is hardly surprising that Kuyper was thrilled to read a young Leiden doctor not only openly criticizing the Leiden school's secularized theology but also complimenting Kuyper (who shared this criticism) in the process.[31]

Recognition in the Academy, Rejection in Romance

Perhaps unsurprisingly, Bavinck's early days at the Theological School were intensely focused on the preparation and delivery of lectures. He complained in letters to Snouck Hurgronje from this period—the summer and autumn of 1883—that he was too busy to take a planned holiday to Germany or produce much of his own writing.[32] Despite his circumstances as an overworked new appointment at a relatively unglamorous institution, Bavinck soon received the considerable honor of being appointed a member of the Society of Dutch Literature (Maatschappij der Nederlandse Letterkunde). Membership of this exclusive Leiden-based society depended on nomination from one of the society's existing members. While the relevant dagboek entry simply notes that he had been nominated by the society on June 21 and that he had been informed of this nomination three days later, a letter to Snouck Hurgronje on June 26 shows that he had not expected the nomination and was unsure who had proposed his name.

> Perhaps you have read that I was nominated as a member of the Society of Dutch Literature. I do not know whom I have the honor of thanking; I suppose, Prof. Kuenen. If this supposition was correct, I would thank him warmly for it. But as long as nothing of this has been made known to me and the whole nomination is a pure surprise, I cannot do so easily. The secretary of the Society is called J. J. A. A. Frantzen. That name is wholly unknown to me. If it is not asking too much of you, could you, would you, enlighten me *this week* as to who and what this secretary is. He seems to live in Leiden, and you surely know him, at least by name. It is difficult to write a letter to someone if one does not know precisely who that "someone" is, especially with regard to titles, and so on. You can do me a great service in this regard.[33]

In 1883, Kuenen was serving in his final year as chairman of the society's executive committee. If one of his final acts in this role had indeed been to nominate Bavinck for society membership, it would have been a kind public gesture toward his former student, particularly given the implicit (and explicit) criticisms of the Leiden school aired in Bavinck's inaugural lecture in Kampen. It is also possible that J. G. R. Acquoy, professor of church history at Leiden and also a member of the executive committee, had nominated him. In any case, nominations by society members were subject to a general vote, which was also cast in Bavinck's favor.

Alongside the unsurprising cast of establishment figures in the society's 1883 intake (for example, the Utrecht law professor J. Baron d'Aulnis de Bourouill, his Leiden counterpart H. B. Greven, and their Amsterdam equivalent J. P. Moltzer, alongside the Dutch Infantry's First Lieutenant H. T. Chappuis), their number also included Frederik Lodewijk Rutgers and Jan Woltjer, both professors at Kuyper's Free University of Amsterdam. Bavinck had already interacted with the Kuyperian Rutgers (whose father, Antonie Rutgers, was professor of Old Testament in Leiden) in his first approach from the Free University and would later be influenced by Woltjer's ideas. At this point, then, the Calvinist revivals in Amsterdam and Kampen had overlapped in the country's most prestigious learned society.[34]

Membership in this society gave Bavinck and his ideas a more prominent position in the Dutch academy and extended his reach beyond Seceder circles.[35] In a letter to Snouck Hurgronje later that year, for example, Bavinck noted that Frantzen had asked him for copies of his dissertation and inaugural lecture for the society's library.[36] His early scholarship and bold constructive writings had now found their place there, received in that year by the society alongside his former gymnasium rival Gerrit Kalff's latest book, *The Song in the Middle Ages*.[37] The society gave him a foothold in Leiden, in a setting more glamorous than that of the Theological School. As will be seen, in the early Kampen years, Bavinck experienced a sense of his own inferiority toward Leiden and its scholars and believed he had found his place at the Theological School. Against that backdrop, this early affirmation from Leiden is significant: after six years in Kampen, he would gain enough self-confidence to hope to be appointed to a chair in Leiden to replace Lodewijk Rauwenhoff, the very figure criticized in his inaugural lecture. The gradual emergence of such an aspiration would be hard to imagine without this particular development.

By this point, four years had passed since Bavinck's previous ill-fated conversation with Amelia's father. Now a person of some gravitas in church and academy, rather than an unproven student, Bavinck, it seems, hoped that Arie den Dekker's evaluation of him might have changed. In August 1883, he reopened their lines of communication: "*24 Aug. Friday. Afternoon. Sent a letter to A[rie]. den Dekker, with a letter included to A. J. [Amelia Josina].*"[38] Having written to father den Dekker, Bavinck traveled northwest to preach to his former congregation in Franeker (Aug. 26: "*In the afternoon I spoke with great difficulty for myself*").[39] His return to Kampen, however, was disappointing: "*29 Aug . . . Evening at 8 o'clock I came to Kampen. At*

*home there was a letter for me, containing nothing but my enclosed letter to
A. J., still unopened.*"[40] Despite this, Amelia would still feature in Bavinck's
dagboek into 1885.

The Death of a Friend

Bavinck's friendship with Unink had continued to develop during his first year
in Kampen. At the beginning of 1883, Unink had been ordained to serve the
Christian Reformed congregation in Almelo. The guest preacher at Unink's
induction, of course, was Herman Bavinck, who preached on Ezekiel 3:17–21:
"Son of Man, I have made you a watchman for the house of Israel."[41] Over the
coming months, however, Unink's health declined rapidly. Bavinck's dagboek
records another visit to his friend on August 11: "*Morning to Almelo, Unink
was very weak and of little cheer.*"[42] Having provided his friend with preaching cover on the following Sunday, Bavinck had only just returned home before
Unink's decline brought him back to Almelo—this time, accompanied by his
younger brothers. "*I had little enjoyment in this trip.*"[43] Unink was dying and
would pass away barely a month after this visit. "*21 Sept. 1883. Jan Hendrik
Unink died, 25 y. old. buried 25 Sept. 1883. Father led the ceremony.*"[44] His
only subsequent written recollection of Unink's death would come in 1886,
when he was writing to Johan van Haselen (1865–87), a terminally ill Kampen
student. There, he recalled how upon his deathbed Unink had declared himself
ready to die: "He had been prepared for some time and had given himself
over to the Lord."[45] Bavinck's visits to Almelo in 1883 prompted some hard
self-examination: his friend's readiness to let go of this life posed deep and
unsettling questions of his own Christian faith. In that situation, while Unink
realized he was theologically and existentially prepared for death, Bavinck
found that he was an unprepared onlooker.

A report of Unink's funeral and Jan Bavinck's sermon—an "appropriate,
comforting, and encouraging word"—was carried in *De Bazuin* later that
week (Sept. 28). By way of chronology, Unink's death occurred within weeks
of Arie den Dekker's most recent (wordless) rejection of Bavinck's suitorship
for his daughter. These were lonely and difficult days for Bavinck: at twenty-
nine years old he lived with his parents, saw no immediate prospect of marriage, and, following Unink's untimely death, had few friends close at hand.

These circumstances set the scene for a comment made in a subsequent
letter to the dying Johan van Haselen that typifies the phase into which his
life was moving: "My books are my true company."[46] Barred from pursuing
Amelia, bereft of Unink, and with the likes of Snouck Hurgronje and Henry

Dosker only accessible by letter, Bavinck surrounded himself with new conversation partners. In the prime of life, his closest companions became a group of long-dead theologians.

The Beginnings of the *Reformed Dogmatics* and *Ethics*

Having found himself doubly isolated by Arie den Dekker's resolute will and Unink's cruel fate, Bavinck threw himself into his work at the Theological School. In the July 1883 round of exams, the first to be held after his arrival, he had recorded that *"the exam in dogmatics was bad."*[47] By the following summer, his appraisal of his students' performance had changed: *"17 July. Exam and the trustees' gathering have finished. The investigation in dogmatics went quite well. Trustees were happy."*[48] Evidently, his teaching during the first year had gone well. However, the trustees' satisfaction with his students' attainment was discordant with Bavinck's own view of his work. Writing to Snouck Hurgronje on October 23, 1883, he contrasted his friend's burgeoning portfolio of publications with his own struggle to write while preparing his new courses in dogmatics, ethics, theological encyclopedia, and philosophy.[49]

> I wish that I could also get writing. But it is not yet possible for me. I must first come to grips with the subjects I have. And that costs time and study. Above all, in these subjects it is so difficult for me to say something, as nothing stands in isolation, but [each subject] is indissolubly connected to the other, and the formal issues—truly not the easiest—control everything. Often I feel dispirited under this. So many questions of the greatest importance remain unsolved. And the distance between the ideal and my capabilities is so astonishingly great, and seems to become greater still through continued study. One could quickly decide to say nothing, and just to maintain a shy distance.[50]

Over the course of 1883, Bavinck's writing—beyond the booklet version of his inaugural lecture—would be limited to short articles and book reviews in *De Vrije Kerk*.[51] In December of that year, Dirk Donner placed a notice in *De Standaard* to announce that the journal's editorial team was to change: Bavinck and Wielenga would continue to support *De Vrije Kerk* as contributors, but their editorial responsibilities were to be passed on to others.[52] The reason for Bavinck's decision to relinquish this responsibility is suggested in a letter to Snouck Hurgronje in February 1884. "I myself am still busy gathering the building materials for my own dogmatics and ethics. This is to say, at the moment I summarize these in lectures largely from a historical angle and attempt to orient myself and my students in the historical information, obviously, especially in Reformed dogmatics. A historical foundation must first be laid before [one] can think of erecting one's own building."[53] One particularly important line at the end of this letter offers a clear insight into his intention to produce twin volumes of Reformed dogmatics and Reformed ethics. Describing the kind of scientific theology increasingly published by the journal *Theologisch Tijdschrift*—the prestigious scholarly publication favored by the Dutch theological academy—as "more and more incomprehensible," he wrote, "It strikes me that at present in that area [i.e., scientific theology] a certain standstill can be perceived and that one can neither go forward, while the path is being ever more closed off, nor backward, where this is much more difficult."[54] In view of (unspecified) "terrible occurrences taking place in the natural and moral world,"[55] Bavinck believed that the "critical direction" taken by modern Dutch theology was "far too weak" to meet the needs of the day. Unwilling to return to the theology of yesteryear but unable and unwilling to craft a theology for the future, the likes of Scholten and Rauwenhoff had ground to a halt.

Given Bavinck's commitment to orthodox Calvinism, of course, such a critique is not surprising. More interesting is his own insistence that the orthodox solution could not simply be a restatement of the theology of a bygone era. In the *Synopsis purioris theologiae*, Bavinck had already published a new edition of the sixteenth century's seminal Dutch Reformed text. However, his own (Latin) foreword to that edition had ended on a striking, albeit fleeting, note: "The times are changing."[56] For all the *Synopsis*'s importance in a previous century, Bavinck did not think it could be the last word in his own day. Reformed theology needed progress more than it needed to be repristinated. A new age required a new articulation of dogmatics and ethics.

Like Scholten and Rauwenhoff, Bavinck could not move backward, although his reasons for this were quite different from theirs. His professors' rejection of pre-Enlightenment theology was revolutionary and wholesale, a sharp break with an apparently irrational older mode of thought. Bavinck's own unwillingness to depend on the past was in no sense an outright rejection of it. Rather, Bavinck favored ongoing reformation over revolution. Paleo-Calvinism stood in need of a late nineteenth-century update.

For that reason, Bavinck believed that, unlike his former teachers, *he* could move theology forward—a belief that would lead to his magnum opus, the *Reformed Dogmatics*, a four-volume work of remarkable lucidity and depth, and a never-finished manuscript on Reformed ethics. Once he began to gather building materials for the *Reformed Dogmatics* in 1884, the construction of this theological edifice would cast an ever-enlarging shadow over his work for the next eleven years. Something similar can be said of his *Reformed Ethics* manuscript. That text, however, seems to have been abandoned and remained incomplete, like an unfinished painting in a crowded *atelier*, following Bavinck's eventual move to the Free University of Amsterdam in 1902. For that reason, it will be revisited in chapter 9.

Snouck Hurgronje's Journey to Mecca

In June 1884, Bavinck wrote again to Snouck Hurgronje prior to the latter's famed and controversial yearlong *séjour* in Arabia. Following six months in the Dutch Consulate in Jeddah, Snouck Hurgronje then spent five months living in Mecca, taking a Muslim name ('Abd al-Ghaffār) and living as a practicing Muslim while conducting research for his own magnum opus, the two-volume German-language *Mekka* (1888–89).[57] News of Snouck Hurgronje's impending departure and the purpose of his visit—to conduct scientific research on Islam in general and the Muslim population of the Dutch East Indies in particular—had already been announced in the *Algemeen Handelsblad* (June 14), which prompted a letter from Bavinck.

> I had hoped that [a meeting in person] would soon take place. On Sunday, July 27, I have to preach in Delft, and I was intending to pay you a visit on that Monday. But this won't work due to your journey. Also, I had thought to attend the Meeting of the Society of Dutch Literature. But that is very difficult for me. I have to deliver a paper on the theology of Chantepie de la Saussaye and am thus occupied with his writings. This lecture will probably expand into a short book on Saussaye's theology. . . . You will certainly have no time to write to me before your departure. I also do not dare ask you to. But whether from Arabia, or after your return, let me hear something from you. I sincerely wish you and your study a successful journey. But also, I hope that you are kept from valuing Islam as Mr. van Bemmelen (according to a message in the *Handelsblad*) recently declared.[58]

Here, Bavinck referred to Pieter van Bemmelen (1828–92), a Dutch jurist who had worked in an Egyptian Mixed Court from 1874 to 1880 and whose book *Egypt and Europe*[59] had been reviewed in the *Algemeen Handelsblad* the month before. According to the review read by Bavinck, which was entitled "A Defender of Islam," "Mr. van Bemmelen thinks that Islam has not been well understood in Europe, [which is] the fault of orthodox and modern Protestants as much as of unbelievers. Islam is pure monotheism. . . . The writer thus ranks Islam very high among religions, especially when one returns to the doctrine of the Koran; he believes in the future of Islam and encourages Christians to honor it, to win [both] its trust and also the respect of Muslims."[60] Van Bemmelen had returned to the Netherlands arguing that the most common European criticisms of Islamic cultures as uncivilized—particularly regarding human rights and a fatalistic determinism—dealt with phenomena that were not truly Islamic, and these criticisms, he contended, could be countered by a return to the Qur'an. While Bavinck was concerned that his friend would return from Arabia in similar style, Snouck Hurgronje's own eventual scathing criticisms of van Bemmelen's work would suggest that Bavinck's fears were misjudged: to Snouck Hurgronje, van Bemmelen represented a colonial impulse to "civilize" Islamic cultures, with the implication that any such praise for Islam was more profoundly in praise of the West.[61]

At that time, advocates of Dutch Modern theology who went on to abandon Christianity altogether were not uncommon. The Leiden-educated journalist Conrad Busken Huet (mentioned earlier as the editor of the *Java-Bode*) and the celebrated art historian Allard Pierson (1831–96)[62] were high-profile examples of this pattern. In raising this specific concern with Snouck Hurgronje immediately prior to his journey to Arabia, Bavinck, it seems, was concerned his friend's path would lead him to Islam rather than the secularized post-Christianity of Pierson and Busken Huet. However, while Snouck Hurgronje would flit in and out of Islam during this journey, Bavinck's particular fears suggest that at this point at least, he had misunderstood his friend's motivations. In their correspondence in the early 1880s, Bavinck assumed that they both lived in search of a grand narrative and unifying worldview.[63] And from this, then, the fear arose that his friend would return from Mecca as another "defender of Islam" over the superiority of the Christian religion and worldview. In reality, while Snouck Hurgronje had adopted Islam while living in Mecca, he had no problems with relinquishing it once the *Dar al-Islam* (the "abode of Islam") lay far enough in the distance, and he had little interest in defending or critiquing Islam as a religion.[64] Jan Just Witman's note captures Snouck Hurgronje's outlook well and points out what seems to have eluded Bavinck at that time: "[Snouck Hurgronje was] a keen and cynical observer of human nature, without much esteem of human idealism, often detecting ulterior, usually materialistic motives behind religious acts."[65]

At this stage of their lives, however, Bavinck's failure to foresee his friend's conduct in Mecca was reasonable. The rationale behind Snouck Hurgronje's "outward Islamic behavior" would only emerge more clearly later in his life—Snouck Hurgronje would later live for sixteen years as a Muslim in Java; take Muslim wives, one of whom was thirteen at their marriage; and father numerous Muslim children there. Before Snouck Hurgronje had ever left Europe, however, Bavinck had no frame of reference with which to imagine his friend as ʿAbd al-Ghaffār, the *hajji* who bought and lived with a young Ethiopian slave girl in Mecca.[66]

The dagboek records that Bavinck did indeed travel to Leiden to see Snouck Hurgronje prior to his departure to Jeddah (July 28). From their following letter (Aug. 3, 1884), however, it is clear that during that visit, Bavinck found it hard to engage with his friend, whose worldview was so inscrutably alien to his own. Strangely, Bavinck attributed that lack of comprehension to a sense of intellectual inferiority, which in turn fed into a view that the Theological School at Kampen was an appropriate context for someone of his own caliber. At this point, an appointment at the University of Leiden was far above the scale of Bavinck's personal ambitions: "I have been directed to a more modest path, entrusted to a more humble working environment. Perhaps I am not active there in a wholly fruitless way. A higher calling would go above my abilities; I remain vividly convinced of this and therefore [am] very happy in my setting."[67] He aired similar sentiments of incomprehension in his next letter to Snouck Hurgronje (Dec. 23, 1884). Nonetheless, that particular engagement ended with the desire to remain friends: "We can still learn a great deal from each other and be useful to each other. And precisely because I live among kindred spirits, the correction of opponents who are still friends is all the more indispensable to me."[68]

The Future of Theology in the Modern World

Despite his sense of inferiority toward Leiden at this point, Bavinck nonetheless believed that he had sensed the limitations of the Leiden school's theological Modernism, and for that reason he had begun to prepare his own dogmatics and ethics. Early in that process, however, we find a sustained engagement with another emergent school of thought—namely, the Ethical theology of Daniël Chantepie de la Saussaye (1818–74). A fellow Leiden alumnus, Chantepie de la Saussaye—a pastor in Leeuwarden, Leiden, and Rotterdam, and latterly professor of theology at the University of Groningen—led the Dutch equivalent of the German mediation theology (*Vermittlungstheologie*). Like its German counterpart, Chantepie de la Saussaye's movement attempted to ease the tension felt between the scientific theology of the academy and the church that gave it birth. In context, this tension had created a rift between academic theology and the church, where the former had become increasingly estranged from the latter.

In response to this, Chantepie de la Saussaye's movement offered sustained criticism of Bavinck's *Doktorvater*, Scholten, and the theologian-turned-art-historian Allard Pierson.[69] Like the Modern theologians, their Ethical critics accepted historical-critical approaches to Scripture. Their great difference, though, lay in their views of Christianity's future prospects. The likes of Scholten and Rauwenhoff believed that Christianity's shelf life had all but expired on the ground that its doctrine had been debunked, while its only useful social contribution, diaconal care for the poor, could be better provided by the secular state.[70] By contrast, the Ethical theologians made a constructive effort to rearticulate Christian doctrines for the present day, particularly with regard to the immanence of God in human moral agency, alongside Christocentric recastings of old theological formulations. (In this regard, their doctrinal reformulations sat somewhere between Schleiermacher in the early nineteenth century and Karl Barth in the mid-twentieth.)[71] Through all this, the Ethical theologians attempted to create a future for Christian theology in the light of the advancements of modern science.

In a letter to Snouck Hurgronje on June 6, 1884, Bavinck mentioned that he had engaged with Chantepie de la Saussaye's thought[72] in order to present a short paper at a pastors' conference in Utrecht in that summer. To his disappointment, however, that conference paper generated no discussion.[73] As indicated in the aforementioned letter, that paper would grow into a short book, *The Theology of Prof. Dr. Daniël Chantepie de la Saussaye: A Contribution to Knowledge of Ethical Theology* (1884).[74] While this book was ultimately critical of Chantepie de la Saussaye and his school, telling Bavinck's Seceder constituency that "his theology cannot be ours,"[75] it was for the most part a summary of Chantepie de la Saussaye's works framed as a corrective to common misunderstandings of his views.

Among Bavinck's first sustained critical interactions with a rival theological tradition, the book ends with a brief conclusion that typifies the blend of irenicism and critique found throughout his later works. Chantepie de la Saussaye, he argued, was "one of the outstanding theologians of this century," whose resistance to theological liberalism "brought no shame on the name of Christ." Nonetheless, Bavinck judged the alternative offered in his writings to be theologically unworkable. He gladly recognized Chantepie de la Saussaye's primary goal—the reconciliation of that century's tension between the church and the theological academy—as noble. He argued, however, that his doctrine of Scripture and overemphasis on divine immanence (at the cost of the transcendence of God) would nonetheless eventually lead to the reconciliation of *all* theological tensions, even between "Athanasius and Arius, Augustine and Pelagius."[76] In short, Bavinck argued that the future course projected by the

Ethical school was one in which Christian theology would be reimagined as a loose-limbed discipline whose content was pliable enough to play catch-up with the authoritative leading now provided by modern science.[77] To Bavinck, this was no future at all. This was not Christian theology living sui generis.

As has been noted, Bavinck's initial efforts to engage with Chantepie de la Saussaye provoked no response from an audience of orthodox Reformed pastors. The publication of his short criticisms, however, did succeed in piquing the interest of the Ethical theologians themselves. Over the course of 1884, he engaged in a lively debate with Johannes Hermanus Gunning Jr. (1829–1905), the ecclesiastical professor at the University of Amsterdam, in *De Vrije Kerk*.[78] As the leading exponent of Chantepie de la Saussaye's vision of a reinvigorated theology for the new age, Gunning Jr. had already been engaged in fairly combative debate with Kuyper for some years. The engagement that developed between Bavinck and Gunning Jr. at this point, however, was brotherly and warm in tone and set in motion what would be a meaningful friendship between the two.

At this early stage in their relationship, both had perceived the inadequacies of the Leiden school but were trying to work out the sense in which their alternatives to it were different. Clearly, the Ethical school and Bavinck's Calvinism had much in common. Unlike the Modern theologians, who rejected the supranatural in favor of a strict materialism, both Bavinck and Gunning Jr. affirmed that reality needs metaphysics, alongside which both regarded the kind of doctrine advanced by Scholten and his school as unacceptably revisionist. Although the sense in which Bavinck and Gunning Jr. belonged to separate schools of thought was perhaps unclear to the untrained eye, it was something that occupied both men. At this point, Bavinck believed that at heart, the differences in their views on "the principle, the source, and the method of theology" were subtle but significant. Because "principles are mightier than the humans who hold them," he told Gunning Jr. that "there is a great danger that the difference will only increase, also on many points of belief where there is currently agreement [between us]."[79]

Rather than being repulsed by doctrinal positions taken by the Ethical theologians at that time, Bavinck found himself unable to side with them because of the eventual conclusion pointed to by their views. While Gunning Jr. did not relativize the differences between Arius and Athanasius or between Augustine and Pelagius, Bavinck believed his theological offspring eventually would. And for that reason, this particular interaction pushed Bavinck further into Kuyper's orbit.

Discussing Gunning Jr.'s response to his book[80] in a letter to Snouck Hurgronje (Dec. 23, 1884), Bavinck discussed Kuyper's increasing theological appeal, while frankly admitting that his growing proximity to Kuyper left him feeling increasingly alone in the Christian Reformed Church. By this point, his critique of the Ethical school was that its mediation between Christianity and modern culture failed by subjecting the former to the latter: to have a future in the modern age, the Ethical theologians insisted, Christianity had to be *modernized*. Bavinck's instinct, however, was to invert that claim: to have a future, modern culture had to be *Christianized*. Western culture, he thought, was too deeply rooted in the Christian worldview to survive without it. To save Western culture from its eventual post-Christian demise, Bavinck insisted that Christ's lordship had to be brought to bear on every area of modern life. Bavinck was beginning to sound more like Kuyper by the day. "I wish to apply this to the whole of human life, in all the breadth it allows. And this is precisely where I differ from many in the Christian Reformed Church. . . . I am beginning to see all that is disadvantageous in a seminary and then also in Kampen. A Christian university would be my ideal; and [despite] how very much I object to a lot about Dr. Kuyper, I wish his greatest foundation [the Free University] blessing and success."[81] That Bavinck now felt intellectually constrained by his seminary environment was striking: only months before, he had told Snouck Hurgronje the very same was his (happy) lot in life. In that light, the eventual emergence of Bavinck's neo-Calvinism owed a great deal to the Ethical school: its exponents would provide him and his neo-Calvinist project with lifelong critical conversation partners, helped him see his sympathy for Kuyper's project, and, in a strange way, played a part in his eventual move to the Free University.[82]

In the background to the public polemics between Bavinck and Gunning Jr., of course, we find an open, personal engagement. In the spring of 1885, when in Amsterdam to see the aquarium and give a lecture, "The Meaning of Tragedy," for a Christian youth association, Bavinck made a point of visiting his sparring partner in person.[83] In 1888, when Gunning Jr. was in Kampen on other business, he came to the Theological School to attend Bavinck's morning lecture. Bavinck, however, did not merely welcome his friend as a member of the audience. Rather, he told his students, "We have the rare privilege of having Prof. Gunning of Amsterdam in our midst. I dare ask the highly esteemed brother whether he would take my place for this hour."[84] Gunning Jr. gladly obliged.

Final Meeting with Amelia

Bavinck's final mention of Amelia would come in a dagboek entry in August 1885. In between a preaching tour of the south of the Netherlands and a holiday to Belgium with Monsieur de Boer (his former teacher at the Hasselman Institute), he stopped in Nieuwendijk. "*6 Aug. Afternoon, met and spoke with Am. alone. A.d.D [Arie den Dekker] had gone to Tilburg with Rev. van Goor.*"[85] A great deal had happened since the first dagboek writings to and about Amelia thirteen years before. The besotted mediocre teenage poet ("Read—down—and—up—and—U—will—C . . .") had been replaced by a careful and respected scholar, but to no avail in the game of love. The final meeting between Herman and Amelia was only made possible because her father was elsewhere for the day. After this—as far as extant sources show—he would write nothing more of her, and he never preached again in her congregation. Amelia would outlive Herman by twelve years, remaining unmarried in Almkerk until her death in 1933 at the age of eighty-four.

Snouck Hurgronje's Return from Mecca

By the close of 1885, following a political controversy with the French vice consul in Jeddah, Snouck Hurgronje had fled Mecca and returned home. His story attracted considerable media attention and provided the opportunity to publicize his work on the hajj in the *Nieuwe Rotterdamsche Courant.*[86] Having read of his friend's success in entering and spending a number of months in Mecca—a forbidden city for non-Muslims—Bavinck wrote to express his (naïve) amazement at this feat. It does not seem to have occurred to him that his friend had temporarily adopted Islam in order to do this. After all, Snouck Hurgronje was now back in the Netherlands, did not identify as a Muslim, was not going by an Arabic name, and dressed in Western clothes. By the laws of Bavinck's imagination, this certainly meant that his friend had proven himself impervious to the allure of Islam (despite which, he had somehow gained entry to the Muslim-only Mecca).

Why had he so misunderstood this particular situation? For Bavinck, religion had a unique power in the lives of believers. In its grand narrative, each religion exerted a matchless gravitational pull that reordered the lives of those receptive to it. In Snouck Hurgronje's outlook, as has been noted, a religion was more like a piece of clothing to be put on and taken off as required. Blind to this, Bavinck wrote, "Happily, in any case, your journey didn't go wholly wrong, and you were able to spend some time in Mecca. This especially has utterly amazed me. When I was with you before your departure, you said to me that unbelievers may not enter Mecca; I am now all the more curious to know how you succeeded in entering the holy city."[87] At this point, he had yet to grasp his friend's view of religion as powerless—an oversight that would be corrected in coming years as Bavinck responded to his friend's new publications on Islam[88] and discussed his views on the "defender of Islam" Pieter van Bemmelen.[89] Bavinck's grasp of Snouck Hurgronje's inability to imagine the power of religion would only come to a climax in the later years of his life, when he challenged his friend's belief that the Islamic faith would be unable to match the pull of secularization.[90] For the time being, though, Bavinck's high view of religion left him oblivious to his friend's conversion of convenience. He only knew his friend as Christiaan Snouck Hurgronje. Likewise, the Ethiopian slave girl purchased in Mecca for 150 Maria Theresa dollars and left behind there within a matter of months had only known him as ʿAbd al-Ghaffār.[91] In reality, it seems, neither knew him as well as they perhaps thought.

National Drama and International Contacts

Toward the close of 1885, Bavinck's view on the Netherlands, its culture, and even its illustrious academy had become fairly gloomy—a feeling of European *Weltschmerz* no doubt informed by Snouck Hurgronje's return from exotic and more exciting distant shores. "It strikes me," he wrote, "that we, in every area, also in the realm of science, live in a time of malaise."[92] In this regard, Bavinck's impressions are typical of the spirit of the age: like young Europeans of his generation, he felt the *mal du siècle* keenly.

Despite this general sense of dullness, the history of the Dutch Reformed Church (Nederlands Hervormde Kerk) in the mid-1880s was tumultuous to say the least. In 1885, Kuyper led an Amsterdam-based movement in formally complaining about the toleration of heterodox theology in the denomination. Within these circles, a new insistence on strict subscription to the Reformed confessions as a condition for church membership arose, an insistence that led to the suspension of those in question—including Kuyper—from the church in December of that year. Shortly after this suspension had begun, congregations sympathetic to Kuyper responded by ordaining ministers trained at the Free University (whose education had no formal ecclesiastical recognition). By July 1886, Kuyper would be stripped of his ecclesiastical office, following which he occupied the historic *Nieuwe Kerk* in Amsterdam in protest.

From this conflict—the *Doleantie* (from the Latin *dolere*, "to lament")— a new denomination would emerge: the Nederduitse Gereformeerde Kerk (Dolerende). The time of malaise had quickly given way to a time of high drama: within two years, some 200 congregations and 76 pastors had followed Kuyper out of the mother church, along with approximately 181,000 people.

Despite the national impact of the ecclesiastical earthquake in 1886, Bavinck's immediate focus seemed to fall predominantly on his growing international contacts. His dagboek records that the Theological School's public exams in July 1886 were attended by a Free Church of Scotland minister, Rev. James Hunter, who had encouraged him to contact a number of Reformed theologians on the other side of the North Sea. (Led by the brilliant Christian social visionary Thomas Chalmers,[93] the Free Church of Scotland had seceded from the Church of Scotland in 1843, nine years after the Christian Reformed Church had broken away from the Dutch Reformed Church. Due to the historical proximity of their respective secessions, the churches of Chalmers and de Cock were of considerable interest to each other.)

14 July. The exams in these days are attended by Rev. James Hunter . . . Laurieston Manse, (in) Falkirk (between Glasgow and Edinburgh). He gave me the following addresses:

Rev. John Laidlaw D. D.,   prof. of Syst. Theol,   Free Church College Edinburgh.

Rev. Salmond DD   *id.*   *id.*   *in Aberdeen.*

Rev. Candlich [sic] DD   *id.*   *id.*   *in Glasgow.*

Rev. Wm. Binnie DD, Prof. of Church History, Free Church College, in Aberdeen.[94]

In his earlier student years, Bavinck had planned to visit Edinburgh in order to view the Free Church of Scotland's own fledgling Christian university, although nothing would come of those particular plans. At this stage in his life, the Edinburgh-based Free Church University had not grown beyond its founding theological department.[95] It was, however, the scene of increasing integration between Scotland's own seceder theologians and its ancient universities. The Free Church theologians noted above are prime examples of this. Robert Smith Candlish (1806–73) had been awarded an honorary doctorate of divinity (DD) by the University of Edinburgh in 1865.[96] (Oddly, however, Candlish had been dead for thirteen years before Hunter's visit to Kampen, and he had worked in Edinburgh rather than Glasgow.) Of the remainder of the Free Church theologians on Bavinck's list, Stewart Salmond (1838–1905) had studied both at the Free Church College in Aberdeen and in Germany at the University of Erlangen, before teaching at the University of Aberdeen and then the Aberdeen Free Church College.[97] John Laidlaw (1832–1906) had studied at the Free Church College in Edinburgh and the University of Heidelberg, and in 1880, while professor of systematic theology at the Free Church College in Edinburgh, was awarded an honorary doctorate (DD) by the University of Edinburgh. William Binnie (1823–86) had been awarded the same by the University of Glasgow in 1866. It is hardly surprising that these Scottish seceder theologians were of interest to Bavinck. They were able to move with ease between their own Free Church, its theological institutions, and the aforementioned Scottish and German universities, and even gain accolades from the mainstream academy. The sons of the Scottish secession were well along the path from separation to integration.

Shortly before Rev. Hunter's visit, however, Bavinck had made other plans to travel abroad. "*8 July. Formed a plan to go to Berlin, where Geerh. Vos currently is.*"[98] The person in question, Geerhardus Vos (1862–1949), was a Seceder émigré of similar vintage and outlook. Indeed, the Vos and Bavinck families had an unusual degree of shared history.[99] Both found their roots in the Evangelisch-altreformierte Kirche in Bentheim. Beyond this, Herman and Geerhardus were both sons of Old Reformed pastors who had been educated in Hoogeveen before returning to Germany to minister in Uelsen and who then moved to the Christian Reformed Church in the Netherlands.[100] Geerhardus's father, Rev. Jan Hendrik Vos, had also placed his son in an ambitious educational stream, sending him to a French-language school before enrolling him at the Municipal Gymnasium in Amsterdam. Unlike the Bavincks, however, the Vos family was not opposed to emigration. In 1881, Rev. Vos accepted a call to pastor in Grand Rapids, which led Geerhardus to redirect his own projected plans from theological study in Kampen to Grand Rapids, and then Princeton.

The issue of emigration aside, the lives and personalities of Herman and Geerhardus were strikingly similar. We might say that while Bavinck's other émigré friend, Henry Dosker, liked to imagine that he and Herman were soul mates who lived "parallel lives" on either side of the Atlantic,[101] Geerhardus Vos was unquestionably far closer to Bavinck in every respect: personality, intellect, theological sympathies and imagination, love for poetry, and concerns regarding theology's place in the academy. Unlike Dosker, Vos understood Bavinck and would become a public advocate for his thought in North America.

By 1886, Vos had graduated from Princeton Theological Seminary and returned to Europe to pursue postgraduate education in biblical studies in Berlin. Evidently, his presence in Germany had not gone unnoticed in the Netherlands: over the course of 1886, Kuyper courted Vos with a view to his appointment to teach oriental languages and Old Testament at the Free University. (As Bavinck had, Vos would decline Kuyper's approach.)[102]

Vos's own consideration of Kuyper's approach also closely resembled Bavinck's experience in 1880. Although Geerhardus was sympathetic to

Kuyper, his father was not. In that regard, Jan Vos's attitude toward Kuyper was shared by many Seceders, who saw Kuyper as tainted by virtue of his ties to the Dutch Reformed Church. In such eyes, Kuyper's verve for orthodoxy, and even his recent ejection from the church, counted for little.

Against that backdrop, Bavinck and his younger brother Dinus first traveled to Hannover (July 23, 1886), before going onward to meet Geerhardus Vos in Berlin. On the following Sunday (July 25), after attending a local church with Vos, according to Bavinck's dagboek he visited the Berlin Zoo and attended a concert. These were far from the normal ways he would spend Sundays on home turf, where organizations such as the Dutch Society for the Christian Setting Apart of the Sunday (established in 1869) and the Dutch Union for the Advancement of Sunday Rest (established in 1882) kept alive the historic Dutch Calvinist commitment to a shared weekly Sabbath as an important element in the Dutch Protestant *folk*'s collective identity.[103]

While this holiday in Berlin allowed Bavinck to become better acquainted with Vos, it also afforded him the opportunity to step into a world, albeit momentarily, that he had previously known only through books: while Dinus visited the Grunewald, Herman attended two lectures by Julius Kaftan (1848–1926), a German dogmatician with whose work Bavinck's own *Reformed Dogmatics* and *Philosophy of Revelation* would later wrestle. On the same trip, he heard the famous Hegel scholar Eduard Zeller (1814–1908) lecture in Hegel's former lecture hall but was unimpressed ("*humdrum & dry*"),[104] and listened to Zeller's eventual successor, the neo-Kantian philosopher Friedrich Paulsen (1846–1908), who was also lecturing on Hegel. After two days spent enjoying the trappings of modern culture with his brother—the Kaiser and Sedan Panoramas, an art exhibition, the Panopticum, the Berlin Aquarium, and, perhaps unsurprisingly given their indelible Calvinism, Giacomo Meyerbeer's opera on the Huguenots—Bavinck returned for another lecture by Paulsen, "*who spoke on the history of the life of the mind, rejected Gen. 1, warned against disdaining the doctrine of human descent from [the] animal, [and] claimed that this theory [would] cast much more light in the future, when there is otherwise depravation.*"[105]

In the same holiday, Bavinck had sought face-to-face contact with Vos, on the one hand, and the likes of Kaftan, Zeller, and Paulsen, on the other. Of these four, of course, only one was a kindred spirit. Nonetheless, the works of all four would feature regularly in Bavinck's *Reformed Dogmatics*.[106] Despite his considerable fundamental differences with Kaftan, Zeller, and Paulsen, his interactions with them in print made constructive, and often appreciative, use of their work.[107] As was the case with his public opponent J. H. Gunning Jr., Bavinck prized human contact with conversation partners—even those driven by radically different convictions—and took pains to understand them on their own strongest terms. The above notes on Paulsen's lecture on human descent were the last entry in the "From 1878 to 1886" dagboek. Following this—on the same holiday—Bavinck immediately began a new dagboek, "From 1886–1891,"[108] the first entry in which is an extended copy of Vos's own notes on a (seemingly different) lecture by Paulsen. He did not want to waste this opportunity to learn. Arriving back in Kampen on August 14, Bavinck noted that *the whole journey had cost the both of us less than 400 gulden.*[109] In every respect, this particular trip had been good value for the money.

Tension in the Theological School

On January 1, 1887, Bavinck wrote to Snouck Hurgronje of his increasing unhappiness in Kampen. Commenting on an article titled "Philosophy in the Dutch Universities" in the English-language journal *Mind*,[110] which was unavailable to him in the Theological School's library, he wrote, "I would so gladly want to read it, but cannot get it here in this unhappy little city. How often I long for the Leiden library! And how gladly I would immediately move from Kampen to Leiden or Amsterdam. Here, we live so far away and are becoming so provincial!"[111] In the following summer, it would become clear that Bavinck's dissatisfaction with life there concerned more than the paucity of new library acquisitions. In July of that year the simmering tension between Bavinck and Lucas Lindeboom, his anti-Kuyperian colleague at the Theological School, came to a head. When Bavinck, Wielenga, and Lindeboom were appointed in 1883, the trustees had been highly critical of the culture of informality that existed in Kampen in the era of Steketee and his contemporaries. Lindeboom shared their view and did not believe his colleagues—and in particular, Bavinck—had made sufficient progress in that regard.[112]

Lindeboom was also increasingly unhappy with his colleagues on theological grounds. In 1885, a committee composed of Kampen lecturers, local pastors, and teachers from the town's higher burgher school had invited Herman Schaepman (1844–1903), a Roman Catholic theologian and member of parliament who also supported Kuyper's political project, to give a public lecture in the town.[113] (Elsewhere, Schaepman has been memorably described as Kuyper's "Catholic twin.")[114] Bearing in mind Lindeboom's frustrations with Bavinck and intense public dislike of Kuyper, one will not be surprised that the sight of Bavinck publicly welcoming a Roman Catholic Kuyper-sympathizer to lecture in Kampen—the Mecca of Seceder theology—was too much to bear. By 1887, Lindeboom's wide grievances had reached boiling point. He initiated a formal complaint against his colleagues, which led to a daylong sitting of the Theological School's trustees in camera. "*21 July. Thursday. The trustees' gathering has spent almost the entire day in secret! They are speaking about the relationship of Lindeboom to the other lecturers. In the morning Van Velzen and Brummelkamp were called in separately, and then Lindeboom. In the afternoon Cock, Wiel., Noordtzij, and I had to come in. We were asked about our relationship to Lindeboom etc. Afterward L. was called in again on his own.*"[115] Although Bavinck and Lindeboom remained in their respective posts at the Theological School following this meeting, Lindeboom's anger at this shared platform between a Seceder and a Roman Catholic continued to grow: in 1890, he published a booklet arguing that the Reformed church's calling in the world is to work against the Roman Catholic Church.[116] The distance between Lindeboom and Bavinck was growing steadily.

Bavinck among the Neo-Calvinists

As has been mentioned at various points of this biography thus far, Bavinck's name is inextricably linked to the neo-Calvinist theological stable. Despite this, it was only in 1887, when he was thirty-two, that this term was coined. As Harinck has noted, "Bavinck grew up with the words 'Anti-Revolutionary' and 'Reformed' instead of 'neo-Calvinist.'"[117] As the product, rather than the starting point, of his life's strivings, the neo-Calvinism now synonymous with Bavinck's name simply did not exist in his youth.

As a movement, neo-Calvinism took shape during his lifetime as the result of different Calvinist revivals in Amsterdam and Kampen. In the mid-to-late 1880s, it was clear that these localized revivals were moving in ever closer proximity to one another. In the autumn of 1887, the Free University ethicist Willem Geesink's book *Calvinists in the Netherlands*[118] was the subject of a critical review in which Geesink and his ilk were described variously as "new-fashioned Calvinists," "reborn Calvinists," "modern Calvinists," and "neo-Calvinist[s]."[119] Although Kuyper's own creative energies would focus on the idea of "Calvinism" throughout the 1890s,[120] the initially pejorative "neo-Calvinist" label would not be used positively by those within that movement until an article in *De Bazuin* in 1896,[121] following which the Kuyperian jurist Anne Anema (1872–1966) set out a positive claim on the label in 1897[122] and 1900,[123] which preceded the wide currency it would gain in the early 1900s.[124] Nonetheless, as of 1887, they had been subjected to theological taxonomy: their species had been spotted, classified, and named. Whether they liked it or not, Bavinck, Kuyper, and his Free University colleagues had become the "neo-Calvinists." With these circumstances in view, it is hardly surprising that Bavinck would become increasingly drawn to his comrades over the course of the 1880s.

In this period, he also corresponded with Vos on their shared feelings of institutional rootlessness.[125] In terms of possibilities for Bavinck's professional relocation, of course, Amsterdam had a certain gravitational pull. His brother Dinus was a student there, as his youngest brother, Johan, would soon be. It was the epicenter of Kuyper's grand project, which was now well under way and which also led to Bavinck's growing involvement in talks regarding the possible union of the Christian Reformed Church and Kuyper's Dolerenden. Although these were still Bavinck's Kampen years, their significant events often took place in Amsterdam.

In 1889, somewhat unexpectedly, his longing glances would also be fleetingly directed toward the University of Leiden. In the same period, however, his attention would come to rest most decisively on an altogether different location—Vlaardingen, a small town to the west of Rotterdam, the home of Ms. Johanna Adriana Schippers (1868–1942) and the location of Bavinck's own eventual burial.

First Meeting with Mr. and Mrs. Schippers

In the summer of 1888, both of Bavinck's émigré friends, Geerhardus Vos and Henry Dosker, visited him in Kampen. Vos had been awarded his doctorate in Strasbourg and had come to see Bavinck en route back to America, while Dosker had returned to attend the synod of the Christian Reformed Church. Having been widowed early in his first marriage (in 1880), Dosker had married Minnie Doornink in 1882. Vos and Bavinck, however, were still single. As Harinck has noted, "Both were unmarried, they lived with their parents, and studied day and night."[126]

Later that year, however, each would come into contact with the woman he would eventually marry—Vos, while studying in a public library in Grand Rapids (where he first met Catherine Francis Smith, a volunteer librarian), and Bavinck, while on a preaching trip to Schiedam. Having spoken alongside his father at the funeral (June 7) of his colleague Anthony Brummelkamp—the Kampen theologian who had vociferously opposed Jan and Herman Bavinck with regard to Herman's move to Leiden in 1874—Bavinck traveled south on a preaching trip to Vlaardingen, a trip that marked a turning point in his life. "*17 June. Preached in Vlaardingen on Ez. 16:14, Rom. 8:14–17 ([sermon numbers] 365, 366). Stayed with A. W. Schippers.*"[127] In the dagboek, for reasons that soon become apparent, he wrote his host's name with particular care. Andries Willem Schippers (1843–1924) was the kind of Seceder to whom Bavinck was naturally drawn: a wealthy shipowner, he was active within Kuyper's Antirevolutionary Party,[128] played a leading role in the local burgher school,[129] and would later cofound the Marnix Gymnasium in Rotterdam.[130] That he would quickly and enthusiastically greet Bavinck's pursuit of his daughter is no surprise: in almost every respect, Andries Schippers could scarcely have been more unlike Arie den Dekker. As different kinds of Seceder families, the Bavincks and the conservative den Dekkers were chronically mismatched: the Bavincks' openness to modern culture had always been far removed from the rural conservatism that marked the den Dekkers. The Bavincks and the Schippers, by contrast, were a much better fit.

In the following September, Bavinck traveled to Schiedam, the town adjacent to Vlaardingen, to preach. On this trip, he stayed with another host—incidentally, Andries Schipper's sister-in-law—who had invited her sister and brother-in-law to join their company for the evening.

15 Sept. To Schiedam. Stayed with Mrs. (Widow) Vrijland. Mr. and Mrs. Schippers from Vlaardingen [were there] in the evening also.

16 Sept. Preached on Jn. 1:16–18 and Col. 3:23 ([sermon numbers] 369, 370), in the evening, Ms. Johanna Schippers also came from Vlaardingen, along with her lodgers Ms. Jantine Bos from Wildervank and Ms. Geertje Wieringa from Adnard.[131]

Before returning to Kampen, Bavinck recorded having "*spoken with Mrs. Vrijland about J.*"[132] Once again, he had approached an aunt to inquire about her niece. On this occasion, the eventual outcome would be much happier for all concerned.

The Seceders and the Dolerenden

In August 1888, the Christian Reformed Church's synod, which met every three years, was in Assen. The most important issue under discussion was the prospect of an ecclesiastical union between that century's two secession churches: the Christian Reformed Church, birthed by the Afscheiding of 1834, and the more recently separated Nederduitse Gereformeerde Kerk of 1886. Across the various meetings of the synod over that year, and into 1889, Bavinck argued passionately for the union of the Reformed churches. Despite his best efforts, there was to be no chance of an immediate ecclesiastical merger. For all that many in the Christian Reformed Church admired the Dolerenden, numerous points of difference remained unresolved: some in the Christian Reformed Church struggled to reconcile their own conservative, experimental piety with the optimistic openness to modern culture that marked Kuyper's movement. Alongside this, to them Kuyper remained tainted by his association with the church from which they had seceded decades before.[133]

To Bavinck's great frustration, the differences between the two churches came to focus on their respective centers for theological education: the Theological School in Kampen and the Free University in Amsterdam. As a bastion of Seceder heritage, Bavinck's institutional base became the thing (some) Seceders clung to as a reason not to unite with the Dolerenden.

In 1887–88, Bavinck had served as rector of the Theological School—a position he also used to promote unity between the Seceders and the Dolerenden. As that year in office came to a close, his outgoing rectorial lecture, later published in book form as *The Catholicity of Christianity and the Church*,[134] addressed the division between the Seceders and the Dolerenden directly. Although this lecture did not mention Kuyper by name, his influence was palpable throughout. In Bavinck's criticisms of pietism and biblicism, his reminder that the Seceders of 1888 were children of their historical era (and thus necessarily affected by modern culture), his support for the pluriformity of the church, and his argument that "art, science, philosophy, political and social life" required ongoing reformation, Bavinck was siding firmly with Kuyper, over against the anti-Kuyperian wing of his own church. Unlike Bavinck, the anti-Kuyperian wing did not share Kuyper's optimism toward modern culture or see it as the church's task to address or redeem it. Bavinck, however, had taken his stand. "The gospel," he argued, "is a joyful tiding not only for the individual person but also for humanity, for the family, for society, for the state, for art and science, for the entire cosmos, for the whole groaning creation."[135] Two months before, Kuyper's own rectorial address at the Free University—a lecture held in the Scots Kirk and attended by Bavinck at Kuyper's behest—was on "Calvinism and art."[136]

For those with ears to hear, Bavinck's time as rector of the Theological School had ended with an unambiguous message. Its general theological thrust had an obvious real-world application: the Seceders and Dolerenden should unite. Kuyper's public response, published in *De Heraut*, was equally clear: "This oration is a masterpiece."[137] Having later read the printed version of this address, Henry Dosker wrote to Bavinck imagining the responses of his colleagues: "I saw the pensive Noord, the restless Wielenga, the *clever* Lindeboom, the cynical Cock, the fat Mulder, the worthy Van Velzen. I saw the students and studied their expressions as you did your best to set out your train of thought and your *ideal* for Christianity and its mission on earth."[138] Bavinck would not be surprised that Dosker, knowing something of the Theological School's characters, was keen to know how they responded to Bavinck's argument.

As was the case with "The Science of Sacred Theology," Bavinck sent copies of this lecture to his critical friends Snouck Hurgronje and Gunning Jr.[139] Unlike Kuyper, Gunning Jr. responded to Bavinck's plea for ecclesiastical union with cynicism, claiming that Bavinck's view of catholicity was a hopelessly ideal abstraction that could never become reality in the harsh, separatist Christian Reformed Church. "Why do they tolerate you?" he asked, before offering his own answer: "Because you are an outstanding scholar and godly teacher, because they cannot do without you . . . [, because of] worldly utility."[140] If Snouck Hurgronje offered a response to Bavinck's lecture, it has not been preserved. Bavinck's comments to him on the lecture, however, show Bavinck as having delivered the lecture in a more hopeful frame of mind.

> You have surely received my oration. Imagine with this lecture that it is primarily intended as a medicine for the separatist and sectarian tendencies that sometimes appear in our church. There is so much narrow-mindedness, so much pettiness among us, and the worst thing is that this is regarded as piety. I know well that the ideal for which I strive is unreachable here, but to be a human in the fullest natural sense of that word, and then as a human, a child of God in all things—that seems to be the most beautiful of all. That is what I strive for.[141]

In a further meeting of synod in Kampen in January 1889, Bavinck's ongoing lively argumentation for ecclesiastical union clearly drew from the rectorial address given in the previous month. Landwehr's eyewitness account of that particular moment at synod is striking in this regard: "I still see Prof. BAVINCK standing in the middle of the brothers. His short sentences shot out into the soul like arrows. He was so caught up with enthusiasm that he even stamped on the ground with his foot, something that was otherwise entirely foreign to him. It was a mighty, compelling plea to move the synod to accept the proposed act."[142] Despite Bavinck's enthusiasm, the churches would not unite until 1892. Stamp as he might, he had not yet made this ground move far enough.

Unexpected Opportunities in Amsterdam and Leiden

While his actions in 1889 had spelled out the latent support for Kuyper found in the previous year's rectorial address, Bavinck had already been quite explicit in his pro-Kuyper and pro-union stance in private correspondence earlier in 1888. In a letter to Snouck Hurgronje immediately before the synod began, for example, he portrayed Dutch theology in general as a discipline that had lost itself in a frenzy of critical deconstruction, forgetting its own essence and purpose in the process. Although Snouck Hurgronje was underwhelmed by Kuyper, Bavinck looked to him as a rare example of someone who shared his views on the essence of theology and was trying to develop theology constructively in that light. "Theology in general must make such a poor impression on those who look in on it. Certainly, because most [theologians] know approximately how [theology] should *not* be, and only a single person like Dr. Kuyper thinks he knows how it must indeed be."[143] In the midst of these frustrated ecclesiastical strivings, Bavinck's stock continued to rise in Dutch society. In the spring of 1889, he was appointed a member of the Royal Netherlands Institute for South East Asian Studies (Koninklijk Instituut voor Land- en Volkenstudie van Nederlands Oost-Indië),[144] an appointment arranged by Snouck Hurgronje, who hoped that his friend would contribute to the institute's conversations on the Dutch colonies in the East Indies.[145] Later that month, and with no immediate prospect of the Reformed churches uniting, Bavinck received another nomination for a chair at the Free University. Although his dagboek offers no further comment on this particular approach other than that he waited almost three weeks before declining, the events between nomination and decision were highly charged.

This (third) nomination was to take the place of Philippus Jacobus Hoedemaker (1839–1910), a Free University professor who had refused to leave the Dutch Reformed Church in the Doleantie and whose working relationship with Kuyper had proven impossible as a result.[146] The Free University's most recent approach had come unexpectedly. Although Bavinck's dagboek entry only notes the nomination on March 26, his correspondence with Kuyper in January of that year shows that he had first been asked to consider an appointment in Amsterdam alongside his position in Kampen. This approach was rebuffed for ecclesiastical and practical reasons,[147] following which the Free University offered Bavinck its vacant chair outright (Mar. 26).

Bavinck's response to the first approach from the Free University, in 1879, when he accepted a position only to withdraw the next day, had been painfully awkward. It had laid bare his youthful tendency toward indecision. The second overture, addressed to him while he was ministering in Franeker in 1882, had been more decisively handled. It allowed him to state his admiration for Kuyper's University but also to prioritize his duty toward his own church. To this third approach he again responded with private indecision, which he channelled into a surprisingly frank public stance toward both the Free University and the Theological School at Kampen.

In a letter to F. L. Rutgers, Bavinck wrote, "I am standing at a fork in the road, and I don't know which way is the right one."[148] The Free University offered him a more intellectually sophisticated set of colleagues, greater freedom to write, and a more attractive degree of choice as to his own teaching responsibilities. (At this time, Bavinck still carried the same heavy teaching load in Kampen, which would not be reduced until September 1890.) To leave Kampen, though, would be to move away from a place where, Lindeboom aside, he was widely loved and popular. The autobiography of Idzerd van Dellen (1871–1965), who studied under Bavinck at the Theological School from 1889 to 1894, describes how, particularly in his single years, Bavinck gave himself to and was loved by his students.

> For three years we studied dogmatics with Bavinck. His classes met in the morning. Before he began his lecture, usually at 9 a.m., he stood near the stove and we gathered around him and asked him questions. We touched upon all kinds of subjects—an article by Dr. Kuyper, a novel that had appeared recently in one of the modern languages, socialism, psychology—anything. And when he answered us he proved to be well informed, and usually he placed the subject in the light of the great principles of the Word of God. Then we were treated to a brief improvisation and learned much. After that, glancing at his watch, he would say, "Gentlemen, it is time to begin." Then he led us in prayer and lectured on dogmatics. He spoke in such a way that we often forgot to take notes as we were supposed to do—he had not published his dogmatics as yet—and just listened to his enthusiastic presentation of the subject.[149]

A range of provincial newspapers, as well as the widely read liberal (and anti-Kuyperian) daily *Algemeen Handelsblad*, covered Bavinck's latest quandary.[150] When this news reached the Theological School's students, they began a campaign to persuade Bavinck to stay. On March 29, he received an elegantly drafted letter signed by eighty-nine of the Theological School's students, congratulating him on the nomination but asking him to decline for the good of the school and the Christian Reformed Church.[151] Three days after this, he also received a similar letter on behalf of the Free University's student body, encouraging him to accept the nomination.[152]

Bavinck's response to the Free University—a strikingly frank letter—expressed a clear admiration for the Free University alongside a sense of personal reservation about working with a superior class of scholars in Amsterdam (which was likely an expression of politeness). Despite this, he could see no clear indication that this was the obvious time to leave Kampen: his teaching was going well, he loved his students and (for the most part) his colleagues, and he thought a move to Amsterdam might damage the prospects of a future union with the Dolerenden. "To decline your nomination causes me sorrow," he wrote, "especially because opponents . . . naturally ascribe it to motivations that are not mine."[153]

When he announced his decision to stay in Kampen—which was also reported on by the national press[154]—the local paper, the *Kamper Courant*, noted that the town's students had greeted the news by hanging flags from their windows.[155] The reasoning behind Bavinck's decision was also circulated in the media. In the same issue of *De Bazuin* (April 19, 1889), the Theological School's trustees placed an article calling the Christian Reformed Church to thanksgiving for his decision, alongside an article by Bavinck himself thanking the Christian Reformed public for its encouragement toward him and explaining his outlook on the Free University and the Theological School at that time. "It is perhaps puzzling to many that I considered the nomination for so long and so earnestly. But it struck me that I could not do otherwise. Knowing the circumstances in which it had taken place, I saw it in a different light than many others. Alongside this, the Free University, however little it matches up to its name and goal, is nonetheless a representative and bearer of a great thought. It sets itself a goal that every Reformed [Christian] must be holy, . . . maintaining God's honor also in the domain of science."[156]

While Bavinck had confirmed that he had declined the Free University's approach, his explanation also sounded an ominous tone for his long-term future in Kampen. His preference for a university over a seminary, aired privately to Snouck Hurgronje in 1884, had now been made public. "Despite its shadow side," he wrote, "a university therefore always has preference over a theol. school, because it seeks to bring the truth of God, revealed in Christ, to mastery over *every* domain of the human life."[157] In contemplating a move to the Free University, Bavinck had not considered joining the Nederduitse Gereformeerde Kerk (a rumor that likely grew from Hoedemaker's demise). The son of the Secession would stay in the church of the (1834) Secession. However, he had now stated his open disagreement with the decision reached by that church's 1888 synod. He had made plain that the decisive factor in his decision had been the sheer volume of love and esteem shown by friends and students across the Christian Reformed Church rather than the merits of the Theological School as an environment for theology.[158]

Following this, the chairman of the Free University's committee of trustees, Willem Hovy (1840–1915), would echo Bavinck's response as a note of praise for the Free University in several newspaper articles on Bavinck's decision. Although Bavinck had rejected the Free University, Hovy wrote, "the university character of the Free University brings with it a much more extensive circle of faculty than that of a theological school, however admirable that is."[159] By leaving this reminder to hang in full public view, the Free University's pursuit of Bavinck had changed tactics: for the time being, it would play a waiting game.

Although Bavinck had chosen not to leave Kampen for Amsterdam, in the same period rumors began to circulate that he was on the cusp of an appointment at his alma mater. Lodewijk Rauwenhoff—his former professor of the history of dogma at Leiden and the entry point of his critique of the Leiden school in "The Science of Sacred Theology"—had died on January 26, 1889. Three days after Rauwenhoff's death, Bavinck wrote to Snouck Hurgronje (in response to a letter that has not been preserved) to discuss the prospect of an appointment as Rauwenhoff's replacement.

> You write on another matter. That you first raised it gives me boldness to tell you my opinion. Honestly, I admit that a chair like the one Rauwenhoff held is very attractive to me. I don't hide the [associated] concerns, especially not that of working with *my* manner of thinking among men who *all* occupy a different standpoint, which many also entertain and defend with great scientific power. Nonetheless, such a post would attract me by the freedom and rich opportunity that it offers to confirm [one's] own convictions scientifically and share them with others. Still, I would not have thought of occupying such a post if you had not *fixed* my thoughts on it. For the rest, I believe that ruminating and speaking about it further would not be worth it.[160]

Snouck Hurgronje, who at this time was a lecturer at Leiden, had been keen to find out whether his friend would consider joining him there. That Bavinck would readily have swapped Kampen for Leiden is a significant private admission, given that he still could not be persuaded to leave Kampen for Amsterdam despite his explicit sympathy for the ideals of a Christian university. Earlier, I described Bavinck's particular Seceder and family background as characterized by a powerful drive toward the center and upper echelons of society. This was the sense of ambition that had taken him as a student from Kampen to Leiden. While that impulse had become more muted in the early 1880s, it had certainly been reawakened as that decade came to a close.

In a subsequent letter to Snouck Hurgronje (March 15), it became clear that his friend had been promoting him in the corridors of power: "I must give you a word of thanks from the heart for the recommendation of my person at the Royal Institute [for South East Asian Studies] and for the vacancy in Leiden with Minister Keuchenius."[161] The government minister in question, Levinus Keuchenius (1822–93), was minister for the Dutch Colonies, and as such worked closely with both Snouck Hurgronje and the then prime minister, Baron Aeneas Mackay (1838–1909). Crucially, Keuchenius was the only serving minister in Mackay's cabinet who was, in Kuyper's estimations at least, a "true-blue Antirevolutionary."[162] (Kuyper and Keuchenius enjoyed a long-term friendship—Kuyper's youngest son, Levinus Willem Christiaan [1882–93], was named after Keuchenius, who served as his godfather.)[163] Given the necessity of political support for any hypothetical appointment at Leiden, Bavinck needed friends in high places. Clearly, Snouck Hurgronje had identified Keuchenius as one such ally.

However, despite his friend's advocacy, the same letter shows that Bavinck had yet to be contacted about Rauwenhoff's chair. "I did not want to give the appearance that I was to a certain extent pushing myself [for the appointment], and I have sometimes regretted what little I had written to you about it. I have heard nothing more about this whole affair than a few uncertain rumors about the people who were proposed by the faculty and [that] I was among them, which seemed quite unlikely to me. One thing has truly heartened me, however, that *you* judged me worthy of filling this vacancy."[164] This silence on the part of the university and the government (which was ultimately responsible for professorial appointments at state universities) quickly became awkward for Bavinck. Within days of this letter, rumors began to circulate in the press that his name was on a four-person list of candidates for the Leiden chair: following an initial claim in the *Oranjevaan* (an Antirevolutionary publication), reports of Bavinck's place on the Leiden short list quickly featured between March 15 and 19 in the *Zwolsche Courant*, the *Haagsche Courant*, the *Leeuwarder Courant*, and even the *Algemeen Handelsblad*.[165] These rumors would stay in the news cycle for another month: they were mentioned again, for example, in the education section of *De Wakker* on April 27.[166] Crucially, and wholly differently from his handling of the Free University's latest approach, Bavinck made no public statements on the Leiden chair. Publicly, the rumors were left as rumors.

At the end of May, he would find out—secondhand, in a letter from one of his younger brothers—that the chair would be filled by his long-standing rival (and friend) J. H. Gunning Jr. "*20 May. From a letter from Dinus I found out that Prof. Gunning has been appointed in Leiden in place of Rauwenhoff. It had been said that I was on the short list with him.*"[167] Evidently, Bavinck still had not received any official communication regarding this position.[168] Indeed, the theological faculty's own discussion on this appointment eventually emphasized that the new appointment should teach "neutrally" and not on the basis of "a foundation in religious dogma."[169] Had Snouck Hurgronje been promoting Bavinck's candidature among his colleagues, this particular emphasis—given Bavinck's own public criticisms of neutral scholarship on religion—would have promptly suffocated any chance of serious consideration.

Touching the Glass Ceiling

At the outset, I portrayed the Afgescheidenen as orthodox Reformed Christians whose early experience—between the Secession of 1834 and the Spring of Nations in 1848—had been hard. In that period, their adherence to a contraband church meant a cripplingly limited set of social possibilities. For the early Seceders, a glass ceiling did not so much hang slightly above as press down upon them. In the aftermath of 1848, of course, the world had become a different place. The onset of late modernity had thrust the next generation of Seceders into an open-ended experiment in pluralistic liberal democracy. Under those new social conditions, the Seceders had grown considerably in number. The 40,000 souls who belonged to the Seceder church in 1849 had increased to 189,000 by 1889, and now represented 4.2 percent of the Dutch population.[170] As a member of that expanding and ambitious generation (and a participant in said social experiment) during his early life, Bavinck had viewed the glass ceiling from a great distance indeed, if he thought it existed at all. As a young Seceder, he had been able to attend the Zwolle Gymnasium, gain degrees from the most prestigious university in the land, and—by invitation—join an elite, learned society. In all of this, it might well have seemed that the old limitations had been definitively shattered by the events of 1848 and had now been consigned to memory. This impression changed during the awkward turn of events in 1889, when it appears Bavinck's discreet efforts to pursue an appointment at Leiden were rejected. After thirty-five years of unhindered exploration in his native liberal democratic domain, Bavinck found himself looking at, but unable to rise beyond, a glass ceiling. Overlooked for an appointment at the University of Leiden on ideological grounds and rapidly outgrowing the Theological School in Kampen, his theological project needed a new home.

Plate 2.
Jan Bavinck

Plate 1.
Geziena Bavinck-Holland

Plate 3.
Student-era portrait
of Herman Bavinck,
1874

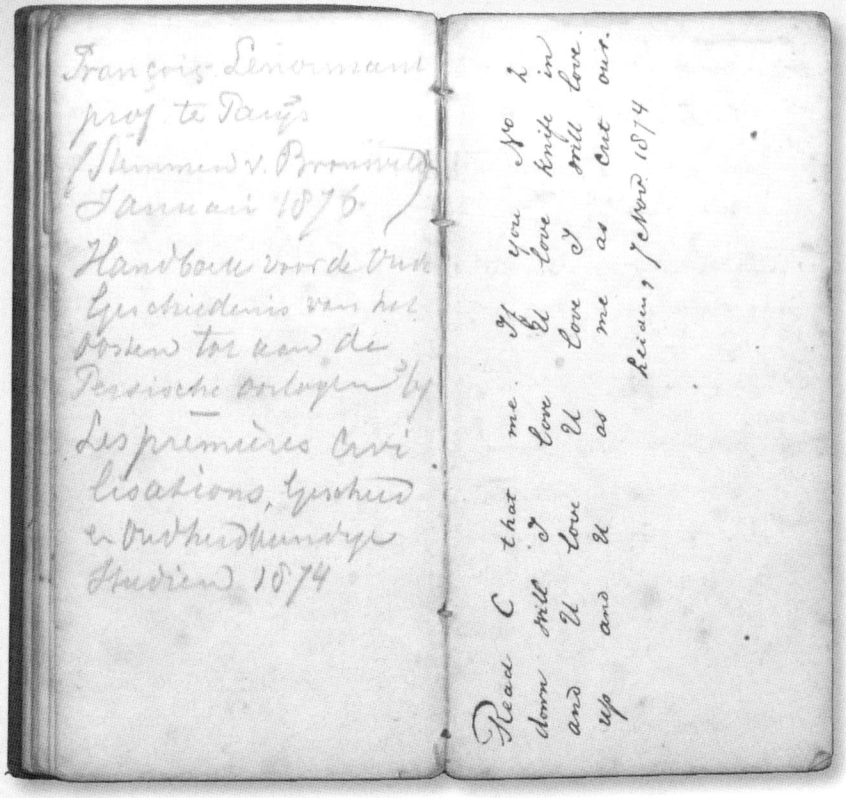

Plate 4.
Kampen-era *dagboek*,
1874

Plate 5.
Abraham Kuyper,
1875

Plate 6.
Adriaan Steketee

A. STEKETEE

Plate 7. Cover of Leiden-era *dagboek* "Ex animo et corpore [From soul and body]. H. Bavinck, Theol Stud."

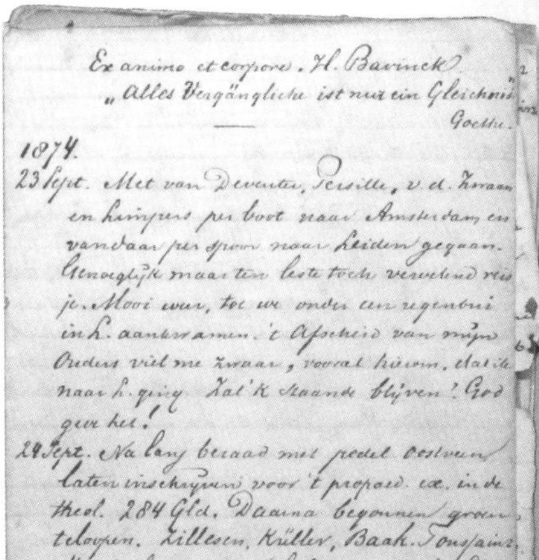

Plate 8. First page of "Ex animo et corpore. H. Bavinck, Theol Stud."

Plate 9.
Christiaan Snouck Hurgronje,
student-era portrait, ca. 1880

Plate 10.
Johannes Henricus Scholten

Plate 11.
Abraham Kuenen

Plate 12.
C. P. Tiele

J. H. DONNER.
Anti-revolutionair.
Afgevaardigde voor het Kiesdistrict *Katwijk.*

Plate 13.
J. H. Donner

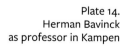

Plate 14.
Herman Bavinck
as professor in Kampen

Plate 15.
Herman Bavinck
as professor in Amsterdam

H. Bavinck.

Plate 16.
Johanna Bavinck-Schippers

Den Heer Dr. H. Bavinck

te

KAMPEN.

ALGEMEENE BELANGEN.

VERGADERING

op **Maandag 23 Januari 1893**, des avonds te **8** uren

in de zaal boven de Societeit „Het Collegie" alhier.

Spreker: Dr. **H. BAVINCK**,
over: „Indrukken van Amerika".

Ieder Lid heeft het recht *de Dames behoorende tot zijn gezin* in deze Vergadering te introduceeren.
Als nieuwe leden worden voorgesteld de H.H.: A. S. Russer, 1ste Luit. en W. F. Privé, Mil. Apoth.

Kampen, 18 Januari 1893.

De Secretaris,
LEIGNES BAKHOVEN.

Plate 17. Announcement of Bavinck's society
lecture "Impressions of America," 1893

Plate 18. Notes made during 1908
journey to America (page 1)

Plate 19. Notes made during 1908
journey to America (page 2)

Plate 23. Singel 62, Amsterdam (*first house on the left*)

Vrije Universiteit (Keizersgr.) Amsterdam

Plate 24. Vrije Universiteit, Keizersgracht, Amsterdam, ca. 1900

Plate 25. Letter to Bavinck with "Do not deliver on Sunday" sticker, 1918

CBG, Centrum voor familiegeschiedenis, Fotocollectie Veenhuijzen

Plate 26.
Portrait of Herman Bavinck,
1916

Plate 27.
Abraham Kuyper,
1906

HIS MASTER'S VOICE.

Plate 28. Satirical cartoon mocking Abraham Kuyper, 1913

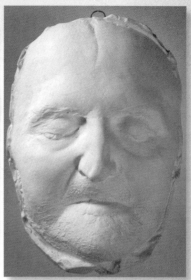

Plate 29. Abraham Kuyper's death mask

Plate 30. Last known portrait of Bavinck, in Bussum, 1920, following the baptism of grandson Theodorus Ruys (*Left to right*: Hannie, Johanna, Theodorus, Herman, and Gerrit)

Plate 31. Bavinck's coffin is carried from Singel 62, 1921

Plate 32. Jan Woltjer's address at Bavinck's graveside, 1921

CHRISTENDOM EN VROUWENBEWEGING

ONDER REDACTIE VAN

J. A. BAVINCK—Schippers,   Mr C. FRIDA KATZ,

A. C. DIEPENHORST—De Gaay Fortman

INLEIDING

DOOR

Mr C. FRIDA KATZ.

UTRECHT - G. J. A. RUYS - 1923.

Plate 33. First issue of *Christendom en Vrouwenbeweging* (Christianity and the women's movement), coedited by Johanna Bavinck-Schippers, 1923

Plate 34. Letter to Johanna Bavinck-Schippers from Wm. B. Eerdmans Publishing Co., 1930

Plate 35.
Johanna Geziena (Hannie) Ruys-Bavinck,
1937

Plate 36.
Gerrit Ruys

Plate 37.
Theodorus Ruys

Plate 38.
Hugo Floris Ruys

Plate 39.
Herman Ruys

8

Writing a Modern Reformation

1889–1902

"It is the theology needed by our age."

Through the experience of being overlooked for Rauwenhoff's former chair at Leiden, Bavinck had been reminded that regardless of his own willingness to take his modern Calvinist project to a state university, there was no guarantee that a theologian of his convictions would be deemed appointable there. While Leiden had been glad to receive him as a student, it was not willing to add him to its faculty. Alongside this, he was increasingly aware of Abraham Kuyper's influence on his view of theology as it related to every sphere of life, and also toward other academic disciplines. That particular influence had complicated his life in Kampen somewhat. While he was not the only theologian there to sympathize with Kuyper, Bavinck's willingness to nod in Kuyper's direction had set him at odds with the likes of Lucas Lindeboom from the outset. And furthermore, Bavinck was now well aware that a theological school offered limited prospects for the realization of his growing desire to apply Christ's lordship across the entirety of the *universitas scientiarum* (the university of the sciences).

During the 1880s, he had carefully articulated his view of theology as a modern, servant-hearted "queen of the sciences."[1] By the time of the Leiden incident, Bavinck saw the *regina scientiarum* as the avenue of inquiry needed to satisfy her disciplinary neighbors' deep doxological longings. Therefore, he had primed theology to serve the other sciences as a modern integrative discipline, without which they would be doomed to an unfulfilling future of arbitrary coexistence. The sciences needed theology, just as theology—albeit in a different sense—yearned for the other sciences. By arguing this, however, Bavinck had now pushed himself into a difficult location: on the one hand, the state universities had little desire to submit to his servant queen, while on the other, the private theological seminary could offer his queen no other sciences to serve. While his location at a seminary was no hindrance to writing the beautiful and capacious *Eloquence*[2] at the close of 1889—a work on art, history, literature, linguistics, and philosophy as they relate to preaching—he now believed that a Christian university offered something that a seminary could not.

Taken Up with Johan and Johanna

By this point his younger brothers Dinus and Johan were students (and housemates) in Amsterdam. (Their other brother Bernard was a student at the Theological School in Kampen.) Having traveled in late October to visit them in Amsterdam, where he would note that "*Johan was not all that well*,"[3] Bavinck then went to Utrecht to lecture on Judaism at a missionary conference. Later that day, he traveled with Mrs. Vrijland—Johanna Schippers's aunt—to Schiedam. "*25 Oct. Morning, visited Mrs. Vrijland Snr., Johanna Schippers had stayed there and had also attended the lecture. Afternoon, after a welcome morning drink and dinner, left for Kampen at half past four*."[4] In his earlier writings on Amelia, it is hard to discern whether his feelings for her were requited. By contrast, his early dagboek entries on Johanna suggest that their interest in each other was mutual. In the early months of 1890, however, Johan's health was fast becoming a cause for concern. For that reason, Bavinck soon found himself traveling regularly to Amsterdam to visit his brother.

4 Feb. Morning, [went] to Amsterdam. Johan was reasonably well [and] didn't want to come along.

20 Feb. Afternoon, home to Kampen [from Amsterdam]. Johan was not well and came with me.[5]

On the same day (Feb. 20, 1890), Bavinck learned that his antagonist Lucas Lindeboom had declined a call to leave the Theological School for the Christian Reformed congregation in Rotterdam. In an unusually wry moment, he noted that "*the students were not imploring him [to stay].*"[6] Just as Bavinck's own emotional energies were becoming increasingly directed away from the Theological School—particularly toward Johanna and his ill younger brother—Lindeboom had dug in his heels. In response to Bavinck's underwhelming public statements about the Theological School in the previous year, Lindeboom had made a more resolute declaration: unlike Bavinck, he was going nowhere.

Wedding Season

On April 20, 1890, the Bavinck brothers placed a note in *De Bazuin.*

Our beloved parents,
JAN BAVINCK
AND
[GEZIENA] MAGDALENA HOLLAND
hope to commemorate their **40th anniversary**
on this 28th April.
Their thankful sons,
H. BAVINCK
C. B. BAVINCK
B. J. [F.] BAVINCK
J. G. BAVINCK,
Kampen[7]

This particular milestone was soon followed by a number of marriages in Bavinck's circle—Herman to Johanna, his brother Bernard to Grietje Bouwes, and, in altogether more controversial circumstances, his friend Snouck Hurgronje to Sangkana, a Muslim teenager.

By this time, Bernard was a twenty-four-year-old who stood on the cusp of ordination in the Christian Reformed Church. Although the dagboek entry on Jan and Geziena's ruby anniversary (April 28) introduced Bernard's new girlfriend without giving her name, she would become Grietje Bavinck-Bouwes in the coming November.

The circumstances around Snouck Hurgronje's (first) marriage were considerably less conventional. In 1889, he had moved to the Dutch East Indies and resumed his "outward Islamic conduct." Soon after his arrival, as ʿAbd al-Ghaffār, he married the first of his Muslim wives, the seventeen-year-old Sangkana, who would bear him four (Muslim) children.[8] Rumors of Snouck Hurgronje's marriage to a local provoked controversy in the Netherlands and led him to deny—both privately and publicly—that he was married. Indeed, in July 1890, writing in response to a now lost letter from Bavinck, Snouck Hurgronje denied outright that he was married and blamed any such rumors on gossipmongers.[9]

In reality, his reply was less than truthful. The Dutch East Indies operated a dual legal system whereby indigenes and colonists were governed by separate Islamic and Dutch legal codes. By the letter of the Dutch law, Snouck Hurgronje's union with Sangkana had no formal recognition. The indigenous community in Java, however, which regarded Snouck Hurgronje as a bona fide Muslim, certainly treated the union as legitimate. Following this interaction, Bavinck and Snouck Hurgronje would not correspond for five years.

Herman's path toward marriage was less complicated. Until this point, as far as extant sources show, he had only been in Johanna's company on two occasions: during a preaching trip to Schiedam in the autumn of 1888 and following his lecture in Utrecht toward the close of 1889. In June 1890, he would return to her hometown once again.

> 1 June. Preached in Vlaardingen on Jn. 8:23, 24 and Jn. 9:4, 5 ([sermon numbers] 411 & 412). I stayed with A. W. Schippers. . . . On the Monday I stayed in Vlaardingen until three o'clock. Much enjoyment. Johanna.

> 4 June 1890. Wednesday. By letter requested permission from Mr. and Mrs. Schippers to ask for their daughter Johanna's heart and hand.

> 8 June. I received permission and wrote [to Johanna] immediately.

> 12 June. Thursday evening, I received a message from Johanna that she had accepted my request.[10]

Following the conventions of the day, Herman and Johanna had become engaged by letter. He quickly returned in person to Vlaardingen (having preached in Goes en route) to meet his new fiancée in person—a meeting recorded in an uncharacteristically messy script. As he wrote these words, his hand was shaking.

> 16 June. Morning, on the train at 8 o'clock over Moerdijk to Rotterdam. From there to Vlaardingen. I arrived here at 2 o'clock and was heartily received by

all. Got better acquainted with Johanna. . . . Made an agreement with Johanna on the manner of publicizing our engagement.[11]

(On the same day, *De Standaard* also reported that the youngest Bavinck, Johan, had passed his propaedeutic exams at the Free University and would now progress toward further legal study.)[12] Stylish folded engagement cards were soon printed by Faddegon & Co., a celebrated Amsterdam-based lithography company.[13] On the following Sunday (June 20), they attended church together for the first time as fiancés. That afternoon, a steady stream of well-wishers caused them to miss the evening service. Having done so, Bavinck noted, he "*read Gerok in the summer house with Joh.*"[14] Their poet of choice, Karl Gerok (1815–90), was a German religious writer whose *Palm Leaves* (1857)—released in a Dutch edition in 1865—was a work styled explicitly as a poetic promotion of the "Christian faith and Christian worldview."[15] As they bonded over his poetry, it was clear that Herman and Johanna shared aesthetic and religious sensibilities. Theirs was a promising match.

In that light, Gleason's claim that in Johanna "Herman was not looking for someone with whom he could discuss theology" gives a misleading impression.[16] While she was not an academic theologian, Johanna had enjoyed a privileged upbringing and was evidently a cultured and intelligent person: she had learned English and French while growing up and enjoyed reading, writing, and speaking English throughout their married life. At this early stage of their relationship, she had heard him lecture in Utrecht and shared his interest in theologically rich poetry. As will be seen in later chapters, Johanna would form her own opinions on Herman's theological debates. After his eventual death, she would found and coedit the periodical *Christianity and the Women's Movement* (1923), which interacted with his later publications and ideas.[17] In the years after his passing, she would collect publications on his life and thought.[18] In those years, she was also closely involved in early attempts to turn his *Gereformeerde Dogmatiek* into the *Reformed Dogmatics* and *Reformierte Dogmatik*.[19] Although the German edition she discussed for publication with Vandenhoeck & Ruprecht in 1927 never came to fruition,[20] her negotiations with the William B. Eerdmans Publishing Company show her concerns for the theological accuracy of any eventual English rendering.[21] In Johanna, it seems, Herman found someone with whom he would indeed discuss theology—and who would busy herself with his theology for many years after his death.

Following an engagement party thrown by Johanna's parents and attended by Jan and Johan Bavinck (July 23) and the purchase of an engagement ring (July 29), Herman and Johanna spent the next few weeks visiting friends and reading poetry together. (On Aug. 4, for example, he noted that together they had been reading Isaac da Costa, the Messianic Jew whose poetry animated the Calvinistic Réveil movement.) Their wedding had been planned for July 1891. Before that, in November 1890, Bernard and Grietje were married by Jan Bavinck, an occasion described by Herman as "*not very convivial*" in the dagboek.[22]

New Bible, New Workload

By this point, six years had passed since the first admission to Snouck Hurgronje that he had begun to prepare his own dogmatics and ethics. Beyond that remark, Bavinck does not seem to have commented on his progress in dagboek notes or private correspondence until this point. From these years, his own lecture notes show an early airing of some material that would eventually appear in *Reformed Dogmatics*: unpublished lecture notes between 1883 and 1890 include headings such as "Theological Method," "Theological Directions in Germany," "The Agnostic (Antimetaphysical) Direction in Theology," "The Doctrine of the Covenants," "Theological Encyclopedia," and "The Marrow of Theology: Dogmatics."[23] Alongside these, dated unpublished manuscripts from those years also provide glimpses into early dogmatic formulations: "The Human Being, God's Image," "The Knowability of God," and "Theology as a Science in the Present Day."[24] Between 1883 and 1887, Bavinck made substantial progress in writing a first draft of a Reformed ethics—a text that was never finished. Although the *Reformed Dogmatics* would be completed, at this point he was still some way from that goal.[25]

If his grand plans were to come to fruition, something would have to change: his classroom responsibilities were now holding back his plans to meet the new age's great need for dogmatics and ethics. Alongside this, in mid-1890—a season otherwise taken up with engagements and wedding planning—it was also widely announced in the Dutch press that Bavinck had joined forces with Kuyper, F. L. Rutgers, and Jan Woltjer to produce a new version of the Dutch Bible.

Across the nineteenth century, the 1637 *Statenvertaling* had remained the dominant biblical translation among Dutch Protestants of every stripe. However, there was a growing frustration with its readability. To the average Dutch speaker at that time, the *Statenvertaling* was an increasingly arcane text. Several attempts had been made to produce a new nineteenth-century translation prior to the efforts of Kuyper and his associates. The *Palmbijbel* (1822–30) had set out to update the *Statenvertaling*'s archaisms gently, following which

Gerbrand Visschering had provided a fresh translation of the New Testament (1854–59) that gained currency among Dutch Mennonites. The *Voorhoeve-vertaling* (1877) had followed the work of John Nelson Darby—the founder of the Plymouth Brethren—who had produced an English translation of the New Testament in 1867. In 1899, a group of Leiden professors, including Bavinck's de facto doctoral supervisor, Abraham Kuenen, would also begin a new translation of Scripture under the influence of biblical criticism and liberal theology. (Their text, the *Leidse Vertaling*, would not be completed until 1912.)

Kuyper and his coworkers, however, were not Brethren or Mennonites. Furthermore, Johannes van der Palm (1763–1840), the poet responsible for the *Palmbijbel*, was the great public rival of Willem Bilderdijk (1756–1831), the bard beloved by Bavinck and Kuyper.[26] And the eventual *Leidse Vertaling* would hardly be to their taste. For obvious reasons, they were unsatisfied by the range of available alternatives.

The initial wave of newspaper advertisements for their own new rendering of the Bible—placed in *De Standaard*[27] and *Het Nieuws van de Dag*,[28] among others, alongside a host of local newspapers—noted that it would update the spelling and diction of the seventeenth-century *Statenvertaling*. Alongside a new Reformed university, a new political party, and new Reformed dogmatics and ethics, Kuyper's movement needed a new rendering of the Bible itself. The project, these advertisements noted, would take three years. (In reality, it took five.) Just as his progress toward *Reformed Dogmatics* and *Reformed Ethics* was grinding along ever more slowly, Bavinck had committed himself to another major, multiyear book project: *Biblia*.

Until this point, the scope of Bavinck's work had been shaped by the teaching responsibilities given to him upon his appointment at the Theological School in 1883. At that time, his appointment had depended on a delicate balance of powers. In the buildup to the 1882 synod, he had exerted considerable energy in a short time to make his candidature competitive. More important still, he had depended on the support of those more influential in the denomination who made space for him in strategically important pulpits and publications in the early 1880s. For those reasons, while a new appointee, he was in no strong position to negotiate his teaching load: the Theological School's trustees held all the aces and determined his responsibilities accordingly. By 1890, that power dynamic had changed considerably. He had become a theologian publicly coveted by both the Theological School (where he now served as rector) and the Free University.

When declining the Free University's latest approach, he had gone public on his views of the Theological School's limited horizons *and* his ideological sympathies for the Free University. He had stated his frustrations quite openly. If he were to stay in Kampen for much longer, it would have to be on something closer to his own terms. He now held the stronger hand—a comment in the *Algemeen Handelsblad* from this period read, for example, that "the Theological School in Kampen will soon have to yield Bavinck to the 'Free University.'"[29] In terms of satisfying Bavinck as a faculty member, the ball was in the Theological School's court.

Therefore, it is unsurprising that we find him recording a significant change in circumstances in the autumn of 1890: "*16 Sept. Faculty meeting with Mr. Kapteyn. I was given much less teaching.*"[30] The figure mentioned, Johannes Kapteyn (1862–1906), was a new appointment hired to take over a great deal of the literary (pretheological) classes, reducing the teaching load borne by Bavinck, among others, in the process.[31] (Idzerd van Dellen's autobiographical account notes that when he arrived as a student in Kampen in 1889, Bavinck was still heavily involved in teaching the Theological School's literary classes.)[32] Further appointments were soon made to cover the remainder of the literary subjects: Jacob van der Valk and Hendrik Reinink.[33] The Theological School's new appointments in 1890 and 1891 meant a different kind of working life for Bavinck—and with that, all would change. At both lectern and writing desk, his life was about to become engrossed in dogmatics.

Ending a Modest Record

Although Bavinck's publications record in the 1880s had shown moments of great promise and had already given his readers a clear impression of his distinctive theological traits, it was nonetheless modest. To date, he had yet to produce anything like a magnum opus. His work on the *Synopsis purioris theologiae* had been strategically useful but had only fleetingly demonstrated his own theological voice (in the introductory comment that the present day needed its own theology). Beyond his published doctoral thesis, his book on Chantepie de la Saussaye had been primarily descriptive, and his other short books (*The Science of Sacred Theology*, *The Catholicity of Christianity and Church*, and *Eloquence*) had been derived from lectures, rather than a longer-term writing agenda. Beyond a piece on Albrecht Ritschl in *Theologische Studieën*,[34] his articles had only ever been published in *De Vrije Kerk*, the Christian Reformed Church's in-house journal.

Had his written output carried on at this level for the remainder of his life, Bavinck would almost certainly have become a figure of minor significance to nineteenth- and twentieth-century theology, perhaps earning him a place among the footnotes of works on seminal figures like Kuyper and Kuenen. Such, however, was not to be his fate. The change in his personal and professional circumstances in 1890 set him on a different course and marked out a new phase in his life. Enlivened by Johanna and less encumbered by wide-ranging classroom responsibilities, he was soon to produce writings of outstanding intellectual ambition and lasting international impact. The four volumes of *Reformed Dogmatics*, begun tentatively in 1884, would finally emerge in print across the coming decade, appearing in 1895, 1897, 1898, and 1901, by which point his work on the *Reformed Ethics* would also progress to a substantial (but never finished) manuscript.[35]

The 1890s would be years of remarkable literary output. After Bavinck's death, an obituary by his former student Idzerd van Dellen recalled how for the first half of that decade, his classroom material and writing were both consumed by the same project: "Bavinck spoke quickly. We could only make short notes. . . . How much easier it must have been [for his students] later, when his *Dogmatics* was published."[36]

Marriage

Herman and Johanna spent the close of 1890 in each other's company. Their December began with a day trip to Rotterdam to buy *Sinterklaas* gifts (Dec. 5) and ended with Bavinck preaching in Bernard's congregation in Hazerswoude, at Christmas, before traveling onward to Vlaardingen to holiday with Johanna's family (Dec. 26). In the same week, an awkward note on his relationship status featured in *De Grondwet*, a Dutch American newspaper, to announce that he was to visit America in the following summer *and* to correct local reports (in Holland, Michigan) that he was engaged. "The *NEWS* understands from a reliable source that Dr. Bavinck of the Theol. School in Kampen will visit this land in the coming summer and at that time will be accompanied by his spouse. People in a position to know assure us that Dr. Bavinck has no spouse."[37] News travels fast. One week later, the same newspaper issued a correction: "We have received more information from the *NEWS* that Dr. Bavinck intends to marry, before he shall visit our land in the summer."[38] While (Dutch) America had yet to hear about Johanna, she had already heard about this prospective journey: a dagboek entry three months before (Sept. 15) had noted, "*In the morning I had a conversation with Joh. about America.*"[39] Having read descriptions of America in the letters of his émigré friends for many years, he was now planning to see it for himself. However, these plans would have to wait: first would come marriage, and shortly thereafter, the union of the Seceders and Dolerenden.

Bavinck's transatlantic contacts in 1891, particularly during the summer prior to his journey to America, were fairly significant. In those months, he approached Geerhardus Vos, who was teaching at the theological school in Grand Rapids (now Calvin Theological Seminary), where Vos was the first faculty member to hold a PhD. Bavinck had contacted Vos regarding a possible appointment in Kampen (with a view to Maarten Noordtzij's impending move into Antirevolutionary politics), which Vos declined two days before Bavinck's wedding.[40] Like Bavinck, Vos continued to struggle to find an institutional home, telling his friend,

> I will honestly answer your question concerning the vacancy of Noordtzij. I am well acquainted with the civic and social life in America. I cannot say that of the ecclesiastical and religious life. Lately, I have more and more come to the conclusion that in the long run I do not want to stay in my present position. Then the question arises: What then? More than once I have been approached concerning how I feel about accepting a chair in a seminary of the Presbyterian Church. Lately I like the idea more than before. However, there is much in those churches that I am uncomfortable with. Looking at the matter from a *theological* point of view, I would say: I would rather work in the Christian Reformed Church than in a Presbyterian church here. There are two more considerations: (1) my parents are here; (2) there is a certain charm in American life from which it is hard to withdraw after first having been under the influence of it. It is impossible for me to say to which side the scale would turn if I had to make a decision. But you did not ask me for that. Your question was, If I would decline a priori a possible call. To this I have to answer: No.[41]

Although Vos was reluctant to leave America to work with Bavinck in Kampen, he was nonetheless enthusiastic about promoting Bavinck's work in American theological circles. At Vos's suggestion, for example, Bavinck was contacted by Princeton professor B. B. Warfield (1851–1921), for whom Bavinck would write an article, "Recent Dogmatic Thought in the Netherlands," for the *Presbyterian and Reformed Review*.[42] In this period, the idea of America offered a valuable relief from his feelings of claustrophobia in Kampen.[43]

Herman and Johanna were married in the summer of 1891. After they registered their intention to marry on June 15, a pre-wedding feast was held in Kampen. That evening's menu (June 17) has been preserved in the Bavinck Archive: vermicelli soup, hors d'oeuvres, beef tenderloin, haricots, braised veal, carrots, roast chicken, pears, salmon, salad, compote, pudding, cake, and dessert.[44] (Such extravagant, multiple-course dinners were typical of the early neo-Calvinists, whose religion was one of feasting more than of fasting.)[45] Their wedding took place in Vlaardingen on July 2.[46] An entry preserved in Hepp's biography from the lost dagboek offers Bavinck's own summary of the day, when the couple were legally married in a civil ceremony (as per Dutch law) before their church wedding service.

> *2 June. Wedding day. Glorious weather. Sunny and yet fresh. My parents, B. and G. [Bernard and Grietje] had come over. At 12 o'clock I traveled from Rev. Sieders to Mr. Schippers. At 12.45 the 14 carriages arrived. At around one o'clock [we went to] the city hall. Married by van der Brugge. After, at 1.45 until ± 3 o'clock [we were] married in the church by Rev. Sieders, with the text Ps. 25:6–7. Home afterward, and at 6 o'clock, with the carriages, to the "Vriendschap" in Schiedam. Glorious dinner until 4 a.m.*[47]

Idzerd van Dellen, his former student, was present at the wedding and later recalled the event in his own autobiography.

> Bavinck married during the time I was at school, and since I happened to be a member of the "Senaat" (Council) at the time, I was invited to be present at the wedding. I remember well that I did not feel at ease on the occasion. We boys, hailing from the country, were not accustomed to mingle with the elite, and the bride, Mejuffrouw Schippers, was the daughter of a rich reeder (shipowner) in the city of Vlaardingen. We wore kid gloves (*glacé handschoenen*), and when candy was presented to us, it slipped from my trembling fingers, and rolled directly to the bride to whom we were introduced by Prof. Noordtzy. Fortunately I had the presence of mind to act as if nothing had happened. At the dinner which followed I noticed with a measure of satisfaction that old Dominee and Juffrouw Bavinck, the father and mother of the bridegroom, knew just as much about table manners as we did.[48]

Following a honeymoon in Paris and Geneva,[49] the newlywed couple moved into their first home: 32 De la Sablonièrekade, an elegant Kampen villa by the IJssel River that was built in 1880 and designated as a national monument (*rijksmonument*) by the Dutch state in 1972.[50]

Christian Politics and Church Politics

Bavinck had expressed the desire to develop an expansive Christian account of each sphere of life at various points in the 1880s: we recall his letter to Snouck Hurgronje on this impulse in 1884,[51] his public comments on "social life" needing ongoing reformation in 1888,[52] and his support for the Free University's calling "to bring the truth of God, revealed in Christ, to mastery over *every* domain of the human life"[53] in 1889.

In that decade, both Kuyper and Bavinck felt the impulse toward Christian social activism strongly. The 1880s had begun, of course, with Kuyper's most famous utterance, that there is "not a square inch in the whole domain of our human existence over which Christ, who is Sovereign over *all*, does not cry: 'Mine!'"[54] As that decade rolled on, this drive was ever present in Bavinck's world. It was felt in the increasingly prominent notion of worldview—in context, the idea of "worldview" presupposed pluralistic liberal democracy and required the participation of the masses, without which it would remain an abstraction. It gained mass traction in Kuyper's transformation of Antirevolutionary politics from an essentially elite concern (as in the time of Groen van Prinsterer) into a popular movement centered on the ordinary citizen (*de kleine luyden*). In Bavinck's world at that time, this capacious push for the Christianization of culture was anything but an abstraction. During the 1880s, he had watched the transformation of real-world social institutions. At the outset of the following decade, in 1891, he would take his own first public steps toward the application of that ideal in the political realm by addressing the living and working conditions of industrial laborers.

The nineteenth century knew two great industrial revolutions. The first had begun its sweep across northern Europe at the end of the previous century. That revolution came to a close in the 1840s, bequeathing to the day's young Europeans newly mechanized professions (in Jan Bavinck's case, his brief foray into wheel turning) and producing the likes of Charles Dickens's *Hard Times* (1854) and Elizabeth Gaskell's *North and South* (1855). The second industrial revolution—a period in which mechanization leapt forward both in scientific advancement and in the vast scale of industry it generated—took place toward the end of the nineteenth century and left its subjects, like Herman Bavinck, to grapple with profound social and existential questions on the life of the industrial worker. These issues, known as the "social question" (*sociale kwestie*), concerned how entrepreneurs should treat their industrial workers, what those workers' living conditions should be, whether child labor was acceptable, and whether the state should involve itself in these issues.[55] (In that year, the same questions prompted Pope Leo XIII's encyclical *Rerum Novarum*.)[56]

Following similar events held by German Protestants and Belgian Catholics, Kuyper set to work energizing Dutch Calvinists to respond to the "social question" via the inaugural Christian Social Congress, a conference organized by

Kuyper and the Nederlandsch Werkliedenverbond Patrimonium labor union in Amsterdam on November 9–12. This conference was the scene of Kuyper's lecture "The Social Question and the Christian Religion."[57] Bavinck was invited to take part and was asked to identify general principles—derived from Scripture and with particular focus on the Ten Commandments—that could answer the "social question."

His lecture centered on the notions of work as an aspect of God's common grace and of the human being as the image of God (a topic already covered in his earlier, unpublished dogmatic writings).[58] On account of that unique status, he argued, all humans—factory owners and workers alike—share the same basic human dignity and have the right to an "unburdened life." Unending toil on a production line, day and night, was not appropriate for the *imago Dei*.[59] Following a careful theological argument, Bavinck offered a small number of succinct practical assertions: he stood against poverty and the accumulation of capital and landed property, and he was for the introduction of a "living wage" for every person.

Although this event marked their first shared social platform, their speeches demonstrated a quality that would forever mark Kuyper and Bavinck as different. Kuyper's vantage point was the big picture. Zeus-like, he looked down on the world of human beings and their ideas, supremely confident in his own abilities to intervene in and reorder their efforts. His lecture was a swashbuckling engagement with the French Revolution and socialism and ended—to rapturous applause from the thousand-strong audience—with a call for specific political action on the part of Christian industrial workers.[60]

Bavinck, as typified in his lecture at the Social Congress, was more reserved and conservative. An Odysseus to Kuyper's Zeus, he assumed a *starting* rather than a *vantage* point. For Bavinck, the starting point was always the source text or basic idea, which would be explored and—subject to the results of his investigation—built upon. Needless to say, while Bavinck's approach lent itself well to careful scholarship, it was less well suited to the production of big pictures. By all accounts, he failed to make a strong impression at the Social Congress—a letter to *De Standaard* shortly afterward pointed out that he had been wrongly presented to the audience as "Pastor Bavinck" and that his working-class audience should have heard that their speaker was the more authoritative sounding "Prof. Dr. Bavinck."[61] This effort had been underwhelming and unfortunate.

This difference has led to a long-standing (and accurate) description of Kuyper and Bavinck, respectively, as essentially deductive and inductive thinkers—a claim first made in 1921 by the Kampen theologian Tjeerd Hoekstra and popularized shortly thereafter by Landwehr:

Corresponding to his disposition and perhaps also in connection to his dogmatic
convictions, BAVINCK felt more for Aristotle than for Plato. Herein lies, in
part, his difference with Kuyper. In the future these two great minds will repeatedly be compared to each other. Here, posterity will have a fruitful field for
research. It seems to me that an important point of distinction between these
two men is that BAVINCK was an Aristotelian spirit, and Kuyper, a Platonic
spirit. BAVINCK was the man of the clear concept; Kuyper was the man with
the brilliant idea. BAVINCK built upon and out from the historical fact; Kuyper
speculated with intuitively grasped thoughts. BAVINCK was primarily inductive; Kuyper was primarily deductive.[62]

That particular difference, so evident at their first shared social contribution,
would not go away. Indeed, it would be the source of much tension in their
relationship during Bavinck's Amsterdam years.

For the time being, however, the intensification of their shared labors was
about to bear fruit, albeit in the realm of ecclesiastical, rather than civil,
politics. In 1892, their longed-for ecclesiastical union became a reality. In
that year, a new denomination, the Reformed Churches in the Netherlands
(Gereformeerde Kerken in Nederland), was born. And with that, Kuyper
and Bavinck found themselves in positions of great influence over the 700
congregations, 425 pastors, and 370,000 members now affiliated with it.[63]
Once again, the ground had been moved.

What Has Kampen to Do with Amsterdam?

Although their churches had united, the practicalities of union—for the most
part—remained to be resolved. Many towns and villages had well-established
Seceder and Dolerende congregations that, despite their new packaging as Reformed Churches in the Netherlands, continued to perpetuate older theological
and cultural differences (and tensions) between their preunion traditions. In
many places, neighboring Reformed Church congregations would continue
to function as "A-churches" (Seceder) and "B-churches" (Doleantie)—and in
some cases, this continued until the 1930s.[64] More pressing, for Bavinck, was
the future of the theological institutions inherited in the union: How could the
Theological School at Kampen, which had always been strictly accountable
to the church, function in the same denomination as the Free University of
Amsterdam, which thus far had hardly craved the recognition of the Dutch
Reformed Church?

From 1892 onward, Bavinck's ideal was for the unification of the new
denomination's two centers of theological education in a single institution.

However, ongoing debate on the nature and place of theology made plain that the newly united church was far from univocal. Postunion, many former Seceders—led by Lucas Lindeboom—maintained a principled objection to the theological training provided by the Free University because of Kuyper's belief that theology was a science that could be practiced independently of the church.[65] This branch of the new denomination carried on another strain of Seceder thought that looked on the secularized Dutch state universities with disdain. Finding themselves in the newly united Reformed Church, the likes of Lindeboom became strongly protective of the Theological School and increasingly critical of the Free University.

Between 1892 and 1902, the questions around the relationship of the Theological School and the Free University would form a constant backdrop to Bavinck's life and efforts. At the end of that period, having become exhausted by repeated failed attempts to bring out their institutional unity, Bavinck would depart from Kampen. Before then, however, his life would be eventful personally and professionally.

To America in a Hop and a Skip

Bavinck's plans to travel to America, first mentioned in an 1890 dagboek entry, were finally realized in 1892. Despite the aforementioned speculation in *De Grondwet* regarding his rumored travel companion, he was joined by D. K. Wielenga, rather than Johanna: in light of the recent ecclesiastical union in the Netherlands, Bavinck's American *séjour* took on a distinctly ecclesiastical character.

By this time, the North American Dutch diaspora had formed two Reformed denominations: the Reformed Church in America, established in 1628 by early Dutch émigrés, and the Christian Reformed Church, which had been formed in 1857 in a wave of more recent Seceder immigration.[66] Encouraged by the new ecclesiastical union in their own locale, the Kampen colleagues traveled as emissaries for unity in the Dutch American churches—a historically novel piece of transatlantic churchmanship made possible in the age of the steam engine.[67]

Back at home, their voyage was chronicled for the public in *De Bazuin*. The commentary found there points to another motivation undergirding the journey: alongside his mission to the divided Dutch American Reformed denominations, Bavinck intended to visit the Presbyterian Council, an interdenominational gathering of (primarily anglophone) orthodox Reformed denominations held that year in Toronto. There, he planned to speak as an ambassador for the resurgent (neo-)Calvinism that had made such waves in the Netherlands. To borrow the language of one report in *De Bazuin*, Bavinck was going to America "to defend Calvinism" (literally, "to break a lance for Calvinism"!) beyond the confines of the Dutch world.[68] His writings in this period show a keen and clear awareness that "Reformed" and "Calvinist" were no mere synonyms. His trip to America was intended to highlight and promote this difference.

> Reformed expresses merely a religious and ecclesiastical distinction; it is a purely theological conception. The term Calvinism is of wider application and denotes a specific type in the political, social and civil spheres. It stands for that characteristic view of life and the world as a whole, which was born from the powerful mind of the French Reformer. Calvinist is the name of a Reformed Christian in so far as he reveals a specific character and a distinct physiognomy, not merely in his church and theology, but also in social and political life, in science and art.[69]

This trip to the Presbyterian Council, then, was an effort to spread Calvinism among the merely Reformed—an audience that included the famed missionary to the New Hebrides John G. Paton (1824–1907) and the Scottish theologian James Orr (1844–1913) as well as missionary delegates from China, Japan, Persia, and southern Africa.

These two motivations were tightly interwoven. In June 1892, immediately prior to the (Dutch) Christian Reformed Church's fusion with the Dolerenden, Rev. George D. Mathews addressed its final synod. An active leader in ecumenical discussions between orthodox Reformed denominations, Mathews spoke in favor of the prospective Dutch church union. (Incidentally, Bavinck translated Mathews's English-language address for the synod's members.)[70] Mathews was also responsible for organizing that year's Presbyterian Council in Toronto, and he edited the published version of the proceedings—Bavinck's paper included.[71] In Mathews, Bavinck found an influential non-Dutch ally for both his ecclesiastical efforts at home and his theological ambitions further afield.

Bavinck's own reflections on his journey across the Atlantic were preserved in an extended series of notes entitled "My Journey to America" ("Mijne reis naar Amerika").[72] Unpublished in his own lifetime, they are unique among our sources as a piece of extended autobiographical travel writing and formed the basis of public lectures on his journey following his return to the Netherlands. On account of their richness and elegance, these particular notes have since received significant recognition: they were published in 1998 and in 2010 were honored with the Dutch Royal Library's Award for Outstanding Travel Writing. (A complete English translation of these notes is found in appendix 1 of this biography.)[73] In their express commitment to viewing travel as an "art that one must learn" and in their reluctance to judge the foreign, his travel memoirs are a striking example of how the *ars apodemica* (the "art of travel") of the Renaissance has influenced late modern travel writing.

Bavinck and Wielenga left Rotterdam on July 22, spending several days in London before traveling onward to Liverpool, whence they set sail. Whereas the public recollections of the sea in "My Journey to America" focus on its vastness and restless power, Hepp's biography preserves a more private note from the lost dagboek on a danger common to that crossing: iceberg collision. "*At three thirty we saw an iceberg. Boat went at half speed. Cheerfulness at dinner was gone. Just after dinner we saw another one of them, now on the south side. Boat stayed still and stopped entirely. May the Lord protect us!*"[74] After twelve days at sea, they landed in Quebec City before moving on to Montreal, and then to Michigan. There, Bavinck stayed with Geerhardus Vos in Grand Rapids and with Henry Dosker in Holland (where Dosker was a professor at Hope College). Echoes of the lost dagboek in Hepp's biography point to long conversations with Vos on dogmatics and to lessons in English pronunciation with Dosker's wife.[75] From these bases, Bavinck visited emigrant Seceder communities in Pella, Iowa, and Overisel, Michigan. From there, they returned to Canada, where Bavinck was due to speak at the Presbyterian Alliance (Sept. 22). This particular address, "The Influence of the Protestant Reformation on the Moral and Religious Condition of Communities and Nations,"[76] followed the Free Church of Scotland theologian Thomas Lindsay's morning lecture entitled "The Protestant Reformation: Its Spiritual Character and Its Fruits in the Individual Life."[77]

The species of Calvinism defended by Bavinck was clearly Kuyperian in character. As alternative iterations of Protestantism, he argued, Lutheranism and Anabaptism failed to promote the moral and religious flourishing of communities and nations: Lutheranism prioritized the individual believer's religious change and neglected the reformation of that believer's cultural location, whereas Anabaptism held culture at arm's length in an effort not to be corrupted by it. Calvinism, by contrast, was holistic and reformed the individual and the community. (In that regard, his comment that "the family and the school, the Church and Church government, the State and society, art and science, are all fields which he has to work and to develop for the glory of God" echoes his earlier Kuyperesque arguments in the 1888 rectorial address, "The Catholicity of Christianity and the Church.")[78]

Calvinism, he put forward, produces cultures that "distinguish themselves by extraordinary activity, clearness of thought, religious spirit, love of liberty, and by a treasure of civic virtues, which are not found, to that extent, among Catholic nations."[79] Bavinck's vision of a faith capable of promoting individual and social reformation is conceptually close to the view of Calvinism as a "life system" raised by Kuyper in his 1898 Stone Lectures—with both men standing somewhere in the long shadow of Hegel's integrative *Volksreligion*.

The report on this lecture carried in *De Grondwet* noted that "Dr. Bavinck apologized for his poor English, saying that this was his first attempt [to lecture in it], but needed no such apology, [as] his language was just as clear and correct as it was powerful."[80] In the lost dagboek, Bavinck's lack of self-assurance is evident: "*At 3.20 I read my paper at the meeting. At first I was a bit nervous, later it went better.*"[81] Following the lecture at the previous year's Social Congress, which had fizzled, Bavinck had made another effort at producing a rousing, big-picture address. Although this lecture was not the finished article, it seems he had made progress.

While "My Journey to America" primarily provides (intentionally nonjudgmental) impressions of America's landscape, culture, and religious life, the chronicle of Bavinck and Wielenga's journey found in *De Bazuin* offers a more critical account. An article on the Toronto conference includes an extended report from Wielenga that details the city's pride in hosting such a noteworthy ecumenical gathering of Presbyterian dignitaries: they were hosted for meals by locals, provided with travel to Niagara Falls, invited to restaurants, and introduced to the city's governors—all of which Wielenga contrasted with the city of Amsterdam's public indifference to notable ecclesiastical gatherings held there in the same period.[82] From their perspective, Christianity seemed to be faring better in North America than in Europe.

Following Toronto, Bavinck and Wielenga moved onward to New York. In the lost dagboek, Bavinck recorded traveling from there

> to New Brunswick . . . saw the College. Then to the Seminary. . . . First saw the library, which is very good. The librarian is very friendly. We saw a lot of books. . . . Saw the chapel. Visited Prof. Lansing . . . went to the train at one o'clock. Then on to Princeton. To Prof. B. Warfield. Saw the buildings with him and visited Profs. Patton and McCosh. The Seminary has 200 students, the College 1100. . . . Had supper at Warfield's. At 7 o'clock on the train to Philadelphia, where we arrived at 8.13.[83]

On the following day, they visited Washington, DC, before returning to New York, where they heard the famous preacher Thomas De Witt Talmage

(1832–1902).[84] Despite De Witt Talmage's celebrity status—he preached to an eight-thousand-strong congregation, and his sermons were estimated to have been read by twenty-five million people—Bavinck was not impressed: "spirited but shallow."[85]

They set sail from New York on October 5, traveling home via Liverpool and reaching Dutch shores on the 16th. By the end of the nineteenth century, the world had become a smaller place—small enough for a young theologian to leave his new bride in the Port of Rotterdam, cross the Atlantic on church business, and return home within a matter of months. As Gispen concluded in *De Bazuin*, "One can now go to America in a hop and a skip, but still, a lot can happen in four months."[86]

A report on the success of Bavinck and Wielenga's mission was carried in the same newspaper in the following month. Evidently, it was important to *De Bazuin*'s readership that their vision of Calvinism had gained international admirers: "Dr. Bavinck defended Calvinism. . . . It cheers the heart to hear that Calvinism had many friends among the members of the council. Did they only recognize the scientific quality of Dr. Bavinck's work, without being convinced of the position that he defended? It is possible that there were some who [merely] put up with the Calvinistic character of his lecture, while praising it as a literary product. But this cannot and absolutely must not be thought [true] of all present."[87]

"Not the Only Truth": Challenging Calvinism at Home

Although ostensibly Bavinck had undertaken his journey to America to promote and defend (neo-)Calvinism before an anglophone audience, and certainly did praise the movement in lofty terms, the public lectures he gave upon his return to the Netherlands ("Impressions of America") are remarkable for the directness with which he critiqued the same Calvinism on home ground. These addresses were delivered first in Kampen, where he spoke to a local society,[88] and then in Amsterdam, where he held a ticketed event at the Maison Stroucken (in the present day, the Theater Bellevue). Tickets for an evening with Bavinck and the chance to hear his views on America cost 25 cents at the door or could be reserved in advance for 50 cents.[89]

Beginning with his philosophy of travel ("Travel is an art that one must learn"; "moving oneself easily, opening one's eyes, preferring observation [to judgment]"; "observing, perceiving, and valuing"),[90] Bavinck's impressions of America were that it was a young country busy with its own invention. Viewed through his eyes, America was a precocious teenager on the international stage: all progress and ambition, boisterous, but still some way off from maturity. "The American spirit is all 'go-ahead,' everything is 'in a hurry,' everything is restless, everything is drive and pursuit. Boston sleeps, New York dreams, Chicago is awake."[91]

For all that his impressions of America were flattering and open, Bavinck held out little hope for Calvinism's future prospects there. Arminianism, rather than Calvinism, would more readily take root in American soil. "As Calvinism has found little acceptance there, Arminianism (through Methodism) has gained mastery over the American spirit. The American is too aware of himself, he is too much conscious of his power, his will is too strong, to be a Calvinist."[92] (From the responses to a lecture on America given by Bavinck at the 1893 Union of Reformed Youth conference, it appears that his description of America's religious terrain as "flooded with Methodist water" was used as a reason to discourage young Seceders from moving there. Ever the anti-emigrationist, Bavinck seemed to want his listeners to take home the message "Do not become American.")[93]

When comparing European and American cultures, and particularly in explaining Calvinism's bleak prospects in America, Bavinck traced out a cultural shift that had taken place in Europe but that had not been followed by his Dutch audiences' American cousins. Thanks to the buffering powers of the Atlantic, the horrors of the nineteenth century felt so closely in Europe—bloody revolution, tyrannical monarchs, tumult, and famine—had barely touched the American psyche.

A further layer in this divergence concerned widely held assumptions about God in popular culture: while deism was still the philosophy du jour in America, European culture had since moved over to pantheism. In its assumptions regarding a distant deity who can be satisfied by human virtue, Bavinck believed, deism tended toward optimism and moralism—both qualities he found in abundance in the unscarred American spirit. The European *Geist*, however, had become deeply pessimistic about human nature and the future of European culture. As was mentioned earlier, he lived in a Europe of *Weltschmerz* and *mal du siècle*. For Bavinck, these were the inevitable outcomes of pantheism against the backdrop of a brutal and exhausting century: if God *is* the world itself (unlike deism's uninvolved *deus otiosus*) and that world is a place of unyielding suffering and disappointment, its inhabitants will be given to hopelessness and indifference toward religion and morality.

For these reasons, Bavinck's audiences in Kampen and Amsterdam were told that Americans and Europeans were different. Calvinism had a distinct promise in Europe: it directed morally apathetic, culturally despairing Europeans to utter dependence on a divine grace powerful enough to reform individuals and transform their societies. To Americans—already optimistic, convinced of their capacity for virtue, and looking wholly to the future—this antidote seemed unnecessary. The Calvinist missionary had come home with disappointing news about unresponsive natives on distant shores: America was, and would likely remain, the land of moralistic deism.

This pessimistic forecast became Bavinck's settled view and would even work its way into a memorable line in his *Dogmatics*: "There is clearly no rosy future awaiting Calvinism in America."[94] Remarkably, however, Bavinck used these lectures to argue that American unreceptivity to Calvinism was no obstacle to the Christian faith's progress there: God would build his church, and the gates of do-gooder optimism would not prevail against it. America's Christianity would not be Calvinistic, but—for Bavinck, at least—this was no cause for despair. Each of these public lectures closed with a staggering admission to the contrary. "Having seen so much that is good, one shrinks back from critique. May American Christianity develop according to its own law. God has entrusted America with its own high and great calling. [May America] strive for it, in its own way. Calvinism, after all, is not the only truth!"[95] The lecture that had begun with a preference for observation over judgment ended on the same note: neither America nor its Christianity should be looked down on for this unreceptivity to Calvinism. Such a message was unexpected by a Dutch Reformed public buoyed by the success of (neo-)Calvinism in meeting their own needs. Commenting on this line, Harinck has noted that "Bavinck regularly caught his public unawares by choosing the outsider's perspective as an insider. This led to irritations: with Bavinck, you never know where exactly you stand."[96]

Whether to Abandon Dogmatics and Ethics for Old Testament Exegesis

Prior to the 1892 union, Bavinck's ecclesiastical location in the Christian Reformed Church had provided a constant reason to decline the Free University's repeated advances. In those years, his memorable declaration to Rev. Felix in 1882—"I love my church"—was itself an acceptable and noble reason to choose Kampen over Amsterdam. Ten years on, however, that argument no longer held water. Formally, at least, the Seceders and Dolerenden were now members of the same denomination—and therefore, Bavinck could move from the Theological School at Kampen to the Free University of Amsterdam with no inherent lack of fidelity to the Reformed Churches in the Netherlands.

In that light, it is hardly surprising that postunion, Kuyper wasted little time in trying to draw Bavinck to Amsterdam: by the end of October 1893,

Bavinck had once again been offered a chair at the Free University. More remarkable than this was the position now offered to him—Old Testament exegesis, rather than dogmatics—and the fact that he came within a whisker of taking the job (and giving up on his long-standing project in dogmatics and ethics in the process). The Old Testament post previously declined by Geerhardus Vos had fallen uncomfortably into his friend's lap.

By late 1893, Bavinck had been preparing to write volumes of dogmatics and ethics for almost a decade. His teaching load had been lightened in 1890 to allow him to invest himself more fully in that task. At the time of Kuyper's most recent approach, the first volume of the *Reformed Dogmatics* was close to completion, and with that, his quest to meet the great needs of the day was finally on the cusp of tangible results. Nonetheless, his initial answer to Kuyper showed a willingness to move away from dogmatics altogether, on the grounds that, "on our part, the study of the Old Testament must be taken up with power, and I know of no-one who would be the appropriate and currently available person. If there were such a person, I would immediately withdraw."[97]

He was about to make a breathtaking change in direction. Privately, he signaled to Kuyper that he was willing to accept the post but that he would not take it up immediately: the Bavincks' lease on their house in Kampen had to run until the following summer, by which time he had planned to finish the first volume—the *Prolegomena*—of his *Reformed Dogmatics*. That first volume, he decided, would be repurposed as a handbook of dogmatics—a single introductory work rather than the first of four volumes.[98] And with that, his contribution to dogmatic theology would come to an end. In his own words, this change was an act of "self-denial."[99] In private correspondence with Kuyper, he wrote,

> However, I lack courage more than self-denial. I tremble at the weight of the task that I am taking upon myself. I only draw the necessary courage to invest my strength in this work from now on from the conviction that this subject must be taken up as quickly as possible on our part, that there is no other suitable person for it at this moment, and that something good might be done through me in this area. Obviously, in the first year I will not be able to do much other than resume my study [of Old Testament exegesis], which I have not done since my arrival here. Thus, I will have to begin very small and humble on the path.[100]

At this point, Bavinck was thirty-eight. Although he had invested many years in the study of dogmatics and ethics, his status as a dogmatician had not yet been anchored in a completed magnum opus. If ever he were to reinvent himself as something other than a dogmatician, this was perhaps his last chance. His willingness to leave the work of dogmatics to other scholars may also have been influenced by Kuyper's own intended tour de force, the mammoth *Encyclopedia of Sacred Theology*—a three-volume work on the essence, history, method, and future of Reformed theology, published in 1894 and based on fourteen years of lectures at the Free University.[101]

The relative proximity of the almost complete first volume of Bavinck's *Dogmatics* and Kuyper's *Encyclopedia* was striking. Bavinck certainly became familiar with the contents of Kuyper's work in 1893: in a letter to Bavinck discussing his move to Amsterdam (dated Jan. 24, 1894), Kuyper mentioned that Bavinck had read the *Encyclopedia*'s first volume, and Kuyper thanked him for his approval of it.[102] (In reality, while Bavinck never publicly criticized the *Encyclopedia*, his classroom lectures in the coming years would engage with it rigorously, often expressing his dissatisfaction with Kuyper's methodology, tendency toward speculative conclusions, and sharp statements of antithesis between Christian and non-Christian scholarship.)[103]

In his correspondence with Kuyper, Bavinck's own willingness to move into Old Testament exegesis was expressed in fairly pious terms: the study of the Bible "on our side" (which is to say, on the basis of neo-Calvinistic principles) was important enough to warrant his move away from dogmatics, particularly as the Free University had no other likely candidates for the post. However, it is also possible that this motivation was affected by basic market factors. Initially at least, Kuyper had beaten him in an uncoordinated race to publish a substantial work in dogmatic theology.[104] Bavinck could hardly have been oblivious to public perceptions of their similarity. An article in *De Heraut* (entitled "Waste of labor," no less) from this period noted, for example, that "in Kampen Dr. Bavinck teaches *Dogmatics* and in Amsterdam Dr. Kuyper *Encyclopedia*, and [they] have to give both their time and labor to the selfsame task."[105] The *Encyclopedia* had crowded Bavinck's chosen field. Given this development, the move into Old Testament studies may have been a disappointing but otherwise viable consolation for a man young enough to restart in a new discipline.

Although Bavinck had decided to move to Amsterdam, his discussions with Kuyper had thus far remained almost entirely private.[106] He shared his decision with Geerhardus Vos, whose reply (March 28, 1894) reveals Bavinck's lack of certainty about his choice, even after intimating acceptance to Kuyper.

> You asked me what I think about your move to Amsterdam. It is very difficult for me to give an opinion, since I cannot judge the situation in the Netherlands very well. Also you have already made your decision. I do not doubt that you

will do an excellent job in the field of Old Testament studies as well. You are still young enough to get thoroughly acquainted. But would it not be a pity if your position in Kampen were handed over to one of the extreme secessionists? Last week I read the address of your colleague Lindeboom, and the lecture displeased me so much that I said to myself: if the training at Kampen has to be directed totally in this spirit, then it is a sad situation for the scholarly prospects of the Reformed Churches in the Netherlands. It seems to me as if your work is the only counterweight to that direction. On the other side, it is true that the Free University is in urgent need of you. Certainly it needs to have a more solid foundation. If Kuyper would be taken from us, it would be doubtful if the Free University could maintain itself.[107]

Vos's letter pointed out the obvious consequences Bavinck's departure for Amsterdam would have for the Theological School. The denomination was already strongly divided on Kuyper and his views of theology and theological education: without Bavinck in Kampen, Lindeboom's anti-Kuyperian influence there would only grow stronger, and the prospects of union between the Theological School and the Free University would certainly fade. The other factor identified by Vos—the Free University's reliance on Kuyper and its unsustainability were he to die—was no mere conjecture. In the early 1890s, Kuyper was an active combatant in a bruising political realm, central to all the affairs of the Free University, and the writer of constant journalistic output. Not for the first time in his life, he was running himself into the ground. The winter of 1893 saw Kuyper badly stricken by influenza. The following summer, while holidaying in Belgium, he came close to death. (To allow his lungs to recover, a period of enforced rest in France and Tunisia came after this.)[108] The Free University depended on a single person who had a track record of burning himself out. Bavinck's ideal institution was vulnerable.

His eventual course of action was indeed swayed by a death—albeit not that of Kuyper. At the beginning of 1894, the elderly Kampen professor Helenius de Cock passed away and was replaced by Petrus Biesterveld (1863–1908). A highly regarded young preacher who was strongly influenced by Kuyperian thought, Biesterveld was a promising ally for Bavinck.[109] Indeed, his presence at the Theological School—alongside the supportive voices of Noordtzij and Wielenga—had potential to change the school's internal dynamics considerably. From Bavinck's perspective, the long struggle with Lindeboom now looked different: prior to Biesterveld's arrival, the practical theology taught in Kampen had distinguished itself from the Free University by emphasizing that it prepared men of the cloth rather than men of science. Biesterveld, however, intended to reimagine practical theology along the lines of Kuyper's

Encyclopedia.[110] Together, Bavinck and Biesterveld could change the school's culture and produce a different kind of graduate.

Alongside this, Kuyper had expressed the desire to see Bavinck's move receive formal ecclesiastical approval. The prospect of being thrust into the center of a denomination-wide debate, however, was particularly unappealing to Bavinck, who began to reconsider his position. He first tried to delay his appointment, which led Kuyper to pressure him to commit quickly. In an awkward turn of events, Bavinck eventually rescinded, writing, "I cannot see that I am called to the self-denial that is demanded in order to break away in the middle of the work and to go over to a wholly different group of subjects. . . . And the chair that I have here would, I believe, in no way easily be filled by another. . . . It is better to stop half way than carry on in an error."[111] In typically indecisive fashion, he had chosen—once again—for Kampen. More crucially still, he had chosen not to make his name in Old Testament exegesis. Rather, his commitment to his own work in dogmatics had just passed the point of no return. There would be no *Handbook of Dogmatics* from Bavinck's pen.

Fatherhood

Later that year, on November 25, Herman and Johanna became parents for the first (and only) time: their daughter, Johanna Geziena (1894–1971), was born. She was named after Herman's own mother and father, but known to her parents as Hannie (sometimes spelled by them as Hanny). Her arrival was announced in the *Nieuwe Vlaardingsche Courant*,[112] the local paper in Johanna's hometown, with more widely read birth notices being placed in the Kuyperian paper *De Standaard* and the historical Seceder title *De Bazuin*.[113] Even in announcing his daughter's birth, Bavinck was navigating the complexities of divided ecclesiastical subcultures. The lost dagboek recorded Hannie's baptism on the first Sunday following her birth: "*In the afternoon I held our Johanna Geziena at her baptism.*"[114]

Calvinism and the Future

In 1894, Bavinck published an article in *The Presbyterian and Reformed Review*—an American theological journal—offering an extended reflection on his 1892 address in Toronto, with a specific focus on Calvinism's future prospects at home and abroad.[115] Although the Kuyperian movement had

experienced quite remarkable success in the Netherlands from the 1870s onward, Bavinck recognized that its adherents were nonetheless a minority group
in Dutch society. In addition, he recognized that the older (pre-1848) social
order was now long gone. Indeed, he admitted that

> a Calvinistic state, a favored church, an extension of the Reformed religion to
> the whole nation, are out of the question. The situation has totally changed
> since the time when these things were possible. Church and state, religion and
> citizenship, have been separated forever. Unbelief has permeated all classes and
> alienated a great part of the people from Christianity. To the alarming fact that
> unbelief is increasing on all hands, the Reformed do not close their eyes. They
> do not wish to repristinate and have no desire for the old conditions to return.
> They heartily accept the freedom of religion and conscience, the equality of all
> before the law. As children of their time they do not scorn the good things which
> God in this age also has given them; forgetting the things that are behind, they
> stretch forward to the things that are before. They strive to make progress, to
> escape from the deadly embrace of dead conservatism, and to take their place,
> as before, at the head of every movement.[116]

In the 1890s, Bavinck believed that the emergence of a secularizing, post-
Christian Europe was good for Christian theology. Christianity had never
before been challenged to account positively for its ongoing existence or faced
a call to justify its contribution to every sphere of life. This challenge had
highlighted the need for Christianity to do something new, which, in turn,
had set the stage for the next great period of its progress through history: if
Christianity had a future, he believed, it could only be as a faith made present in every domain of human life to the glory of God. Of all Christianity's
discrete traditions, Calvinism—holistic, democratic, and open to its own
reformation—was the best placed in meeting the needs of the day. For that
reason, Bavinck held out much hope for the future of Calvinism—despite
its minority status in relation to post-Christians, political liberals, Roman
Catholics, and rival schools of Protestant thought. After all, as he reminded
his readers, "David can conquer Goliath."[117]

As Harinck has previously suggested, in the mid-1890s Bavinck saw his
engagement with this pluralistic modern culture as a temporary necessity.[118]
He could not imagine that a public domain filled by mutually incompatible
worldviews would be existentially or intellectually satisfying enough to continue in the long term: while the Dutch state could not impose one favored
religion on the people, he was convinced that the Dutch people would soon
favor one particular religion. For that reason, the liberal pluralistic social experiment into which he had been born "seemed to him a kind of interregnum,

a period between two reigns."[119] In the mid-1890s, he expected that this hiatus would necessarily conclude as cacophony gave way to harmony, leaving Calvinism to rise from the ashes of the late modern social experiment. In the same year, his rectorial address at the Theological School, published as *Common Grace*, noted his belief that the rationalist, antisupranaturalist segment of modern Dutch culture had begun to collapse.[120] The Dutch were increasingly dissatisfied with the meaningless, cold, mechanical worldview imposed by rigid empiricism and materialism. Calvinism's most substantial opponent had failed to capture the Dutch cultural imagination and was now flagging. At that time, such an outcome was no surprise to Bavinck, who wrote that "Calvinism is the religion of the Dutch nation, and he that would take our Calvinism away from us, would rob us of the Christian religion and prepare the way among us for unbelief and revolution."[121]

Much like the twenty-first-century philosopher Charles Taylor, in this phase of life Bavinck sketched out a historical arc that curved back to a return to faith.[122] In a fractured, pluralistic age, Bavinck argued that Calvinism's longevity would far outstrip its modern competitors because it enabled a happier way of living in the world. Employing Augustine's distinction between use and enjoyment (according to which this life is best lived by *using* created things to *enjoy* their triune Creator, rather than expecting created things to bring ultimate satisfaction),[123] he claimed that by its holism, Calvinism heals the disorder of modern life by reordering it in relation to God, and that in so doing, it directs the believer to look beyond this world for true happiness. Calvinism had a future, he believed, because it cares even more for eternity than it does for the present.

> The Calvinist in all things recurs upon God, and does not rest satisfied before he has traced back everything to the sovereign good-pleasure of God as its ultimate and deepest cause. He never loses himself in the appearance of things, but penetrates to their realities. Behind the phenomena he searches for the noumena, the things that are not seen, from which the things visible have been born. He does not take his stand in the midst of history, but out of time ascends into the heights of eternity. . . . For his heart, his thinking, his life, the Calvinist cannot find rest in these terrestrial things, the sphere of what is becoming, changing, forever passing by. . . . He does not remain in the outer court of the temple, but seeks to enter into the innermost sanctuary. He views everything *sub specie aeternitatis.*[124]

(In the same article, Bavinck sets Calvinism's "deep vein of mysticism" in contrast with the "worldly Christianity" produced by liberal Protestantism in its failure to recast this life in light of the hereafter. On this point, the caricatures of the neo-Calvinist tradition, and of Bavinck in particular found in the writings of Michael Allen and Hans Boersma—as "this-worldly" and unspiritual, and having "sidelined the beatific vision," in contradistinction to the apparently more mystical Kuyper—do not suggest close familiarity with Bavinck's biography or oeuvre.)[125]

The alternative to Calvinism, then, was for Dutch culture to remain perpetually "lost in things"—an outcome so unsatisfying, he believed, that the Dutch would certainly avoid it. "The Dutch people will either be Calvinistic or will cease to be a Christian nation. They are by far too absolute, too resolute, to put up in the long run with anything that is of a hybridical or mediating character."[126] In a later phase of life, Bavinck would realize that the interregnum was indeed here to stay. His countrymen were far more willing to tolerate pluralism and cacophony than he had first assumed. The Dutch people remained a nation, albeit (perhaps unthinkably to Bavinck in the 1890s) no longer a Christian one. Once he realized this, his later public strivings would move from defending Calvinism to advocating more broadly for Christianity and would mark out (many of) his Amsterdam-era publications as substantially different from those of this earlier phase. For the time being, though, Calvinism was in the ascendancy, and Bavinck was fully engaged in its development.

Ongoing Intensity

In their views on the nature of theology, Lindeboom and Kuyper had long since occupied opposite extremes. For Lindeboom, theology was a churchly task and had no need of the scientific university.[127] In stark contrast, Kuyper saw scientific theology as an academic endeavor that was only indirectly related to the life of the church. By the mid-1890s, it seems, Bavinck was striving for a middle ground. By affirming that theology belonged with the other sciences and that these other sciences should be Christianized, he stood in agreement with Kuyper. Despite this, he was deeply uncomfortable with the distance between scientific theology and the church found in Kuyper's *Encyclopedia*.[128] Believing theology should be vitally connected to the academy and the church,[129] Bavinck aimed at an ideal according to which the Theological School would become a seminary attached to the theological faculty within the Free University.[130]

As was mentioned in the previous chapter, the Theological School had been engaged in a process of modernization, conscious of its need for improvement, for several decades. Following the Free University's most recent attempt to recruit Bavinck (in 1894), the school's trustees asked Bavinck and Lindeboom to provide proposals for the future of its education. Bavinck's vision saw the school's preparatory classes relocated to a new gymnasium and saw the responsibility for examining theological students being shifted from the school's trustees to its teaching staff. On both points, Lindeboom proposed the opposite: the sum total of theological education, he believed, should be delivered under one roof, and its results judged by churchmen rather than scholars.

As these proposals were being advanced, Kuyper enshrouded himself in further theological dispute. In his 1894 commentary on the Heidelberg Catechism, *E Voto Dordraceno*, he advocated the doctrine of eternal justification.[131] (According to this doctrine, the elect have been righteous with God since all eternity and are regarded as just by God throughout their earthly lives, even prior to repentance or conversion.) This view, which had hitherto been widely treated as eccentric in the history of Reformed theology, thickened the cloud of controversy that followed Kuyper: even Bavinck, his public ally, could not stand with him on it.[132] This would not be the last time that Kuyper adopted an unusual doctrinal position or that Bavinck would have to state his disagreement publicly.

Publications: *Dogmatics* and *Biblia*

In 1895, five years after the first public announcement that Bavinck had joined forces with Kuyper and Rutgers in preparing a new version of the Dutch Bible, their crowd-funded project, *Biblia*, finally saw the light of day.[133] Clearly, Kuyper had high hopes for their new Bible: in *De Heraut*, he recommended that it become the approved version in the Reformed Churches in the Netherlands.[134] This ambition, however, would not be realized. *Biblia*'s first run was in an oversized format that included intertextual study references and comments by Bavinck, Kuyper, and Rutgers on textual variants. Alongside this, the first edition included a selection of maps and biblical antiquities drawn by Jan Woltjer. These images, however, proved theologically contentious: while Dutch Calvinists of that era were certainly not image-averse in all circumstances, the inclusion of pictures among the pages of Holy Writ was a step too far for some. In Kuyper's strategy, this oversized edition was intended as a household and pulpit Bible, although it failed to gain widespread adoption.[135] A smaller, image-free edition (released in 1896) proved more popular. Despite this, *Biblia* failed to dislodge the *Statenvertaling* in the religious imagination of the Dutch Reformed public. (As late as 1904,

Kuyper was still trying to promote *Biblia* by selling copies by installment and subscription—again, without lasting success.)[136]

In the same year, another of Bavinck's long-term writing projects would come to completion: the first volume (531 pages) of his *Reformed Dogmatics*.[137] Unlike *Biblia*, this work would have a considerable impact. In a brief foreword,[138] Bavinck laid bare his intellectual commitments and goals: in line with his 1881 foreword to the *Synopsis purioris theologiae*, this new publication was a bold effort to meet the theological needs of his own day. "To praise the old simply because it is old," he wrote, "is neither Reformed nor Christian. And dogmatics does not describe what [used to] be the case, but [rather] what must be the case [now]. It is rooted in the past, but works for the future."[139] The time had come for something new.

In context, of course, Bavinck was not the only late nineteenth-century Dutch theologian to produce new work in dogmatic theology. Alongside Kuyper's mammoth *Encyclopedia*, the same era saw the release of new publications in dogmatics by G. H. Lamers,[140] J. J. van Oosterzee,[141] F. E. Daubanton,[142] and perhaps most significantly by P. J. Muller, whose *Guide to Dogmatics* was also released in 1895 and aimed to shore up the practice of dogmatics in the (mainstream) Dutch Reformed Church.[143] While Muller's work was influential in his own denomination and was reprinted in 1908, its ambition and eventual influence were dwarfed by Bavinck's accomplishment: in comparison to Muller's stand-alone handbook (covering theology, Christology, and pneumatology in 296 pages), Bavinck's four volumes would span an eventual 2,875 pages. (The revised and expanded edition, developed in his Amsterdam years, was longer still.) Bavinck's shoulder had been put to the wheel of Kuyper's modern reformation.

In this particular marketplace, Bavinck's sense of ambition for his *Dogmatics* was clear. Prior to agreeing to a deal for publication with Bos, he wrote to six different publishers asking what kind of honorarium they were prepared to pay for the rights to publish his work. A letter from the nephew of one of these publishers, written to a Kampen student, complained, "Our offer was actually too high; if I tell you all the conditions, you will be amazed at the large sum. The work won't be sold [to Bos]; it will be hired temporarily for a period of 5 years, during which people can buy one of 800 copies that are signed by the author. After 5 years, the author has the right to set new conditions, and to hire it out anew. *Voila! Enfin*, we hope we'll get along without the great professor."[144] Bavinck was quite aware that in his own day, his *Dogmatics* was peerless. He fully expected it to be a success.

Bavinck's *Dogmatics* vis-à-vis Kuyper's *Encyclopedia*

The appearance of Bavinck's first volume certainly had potential to make his relationship with Kuyper more awkward. After all, in choosing not to accept Kuyper's prompting to move from dogmatics into Old Testament exegesis, he had committed to entering a field within which the *Encyclopedia* loomed large: from within the same theological stable, he had now given Kuyper's intended magnum opus some stiff competition. Coupled to this, some of Kuyper's detractors quickly began to play Bavinck's work against the *Encyclopedia*: an article in *De Bazuin* published in June 1895 engaged one particular critic who praised the first volume of Bavinck's *Dogmatics* as properly *theological*, in contrast to Kuyper's seemingly speculative *philosophical* work. (For all that Kuyper strove to promote Christian philosophy, he would not have received this reading of his work as complimentary.) The same critic also praised the high literary quality of Bavinck's volume, as an original piece of writing, in contrast to the less fluent style of the *Encyclopedia*, which was based on lecture notes made by Kuyper's students.[145]

This challenge was not lost on Kuyper. Within two weeks of Bavinck's first volume appearing in print, an article in *De Heraut*—Kuyper's newspaper—argued that Bavinck's *Dogmatics* was complementary to the *Encyclopedia* in that both were thoroughly rooted in the same commitment to Reformed principles. (Interestingly, Bavinck's initial criticisms of the *Encyclopedia*, delivered in lectures to his own students in Kampen, critiqued Kuyper's work on this precise point.)[146] Noting that Bavinck's effort was "no less heroic" than that of Kuyper, it claimed that whoever reads both works will conclude that "these two men are in agreement."[147] It seems that Kuyper, rather than Bavinck, now felt his chosen field had become crowded: "Like the *Encyclopedia*," the article closes, "this *Dogmatics* is also the work of a fallible person; human shortcoming clings to it. But still, we shall not go into that."[148] That Bavinck maintained a degree of intellectual independence from Kuyper was clear to both men. Equally obvious to Kuyper was that in Bavinck he had found an important ally in church and academy. It was not in his interests to accent their distinctives in full public view.[149]

Conflicts in Kampen and Amsterdam

At the close of 1895, Lindeboom's public lecture at the Theological School's *dies natalis* celebrations offered a blistering dismissal of Kuyper and his

supporters. In his eyes, Kuyper and Bavinck were guilty of the very charge
they had previously laid at the feet of the Leiden theologians: by viewing
theology as an independent science they were secularizing it and would eventually leave it a hollowed-out shell. Lindeboom's cry was a preemptive *Ichabod*:
Kampen's glory was soon to depart. "How is it possible," he argued, "that
men like Dr. KUYPER and RUTGERS do not see that Sacred Theology has
left 'its own home'? Even worse is that men of the Secession, who originated
in the free church and school, also seem to be blind to this sin and danger. Is
it also the influence of the worldly, ungodly gymnasia and universities on the
church and her seed? Or can this university idea be ingrafted into a *Reformed
root*?"[150] Between 1895 and 1896, their debate spilled over into the pages of
De Bazuin. Lindeboom's tone became increasingly aggressive: in a column
published in the spring of 1896, he publicly decried Bavinck's proposal as the
"bastardization" (*verbastering*), rather than the improvement (*verbetering*),
of the Theological School's work.[151]

At the same time, Bavinck became closely involved in an internecine feud
at the Free University. There, tensions had long simmered between Kuyper and
his jurist Alexander de Savornin Lohman (1837–1924). While Lohman had
been an indispensable ally to Kuyper in the early days of the Antirevolutionary
Party, the Free University, and *De Standaard*, by the 1890s their friendship had
become strained. Like Bavinck, Lohman was a carefully inductive thinker who
held critical views on Kuyper. At this stage in his life, though, Bavinck's public
posture toward Kuyper was fairly submissive: he criticized Kuyper in private,
and did so in public only reluctantly.[152] Lohman was different: he was Kuyper's
equal in both age and self-assurance, and his intellectual independence set
the two on an inevitable collision course. His critiques were public and, for
Kuyper, politically and theologically problematic. For all that Kuyper's grand
project had sought to Christianize the Free University's academic departments
(including the School of Law) by applying "Reformed principles" to them,
Lohman expressed doubt that these principles were clearly identifiable in
relation to Scripture or that they made the study of law at the Free University
distinctive.[153]

Behind this theological divergence, Kuyper and Lohman had come into
public dispute on politics. At that time, voting rights were only granted to
a section of the male population (in 1890, for example, 14 percent of men
aged twenty-three or older could vote). While Kuyper supported the efforts
of the Liberal Union politician Johannes Tak van Poortvliet to expand voting
rights across a wider section of the population, Lohman was less enthusiastic about mass democracy and modern political parties. His ideals, rather,
centered on political rule by a benevolent expert class—a view that could

not be reconciled to Kuyper's own democratic values. By appealing to the "little people," Kuyper set himself against men like de Savornin Lohman, "the men with the double names."[154] This divergence in political vision also threatened Kuyper's leadership in the Antirevolutionary Party: Kuyper was party chairman, and Lohman was chairman of the Antirevolutionary Club in the Second Chamber of Parliament. Alongside this, Lohman had also assumed the editorship of *De Nederlander*, a Christian newspaper that rivaled *De Standaard*.[155]

For these reasons, Lohman's ongoing employment at the Free University had become an intolerable problem for Kuyper. Indeed, the question of how a professor with such convictions might carry on teaching at the Free University captured the public imagination: the Lohman question drew a crowd of two thousand to the 1895 Annual Meeting of the Union for Reformed Higher Education (*Vereeniging voor Hooger Onderwijs op Gereformeerden Grondslag*). At that meeting, held in the Seinpost restaurant in Scheveningen, a commission of inquiry was set up with the express intention of exploring Lohman's critiques of the Free University. The chair of this commission, a choice approved by Lohman, was the famously even-handed Herman Bavinck.[156] Kuyper's desire, however, was for a far less open-ended conversation. To him, the commission represented an opportunity to relieve Lohman of his duties. Although Lohman trusted Bavinck to chair the commission professionally, Kuyper had approached Bavinck beforehand, and Bavinck kept Kuyper informed of the commission's inner workings throughout.[157] Aided by Bavinck, Kuyper outmaneuvered Lohman, who received an "honorable discharge" from his professorship.[158] (Remarkably, Bavinck and Lohman kept up amicable correspondence after the Seinpost scandal. Indeed, it appears that Lohman was never aware that Bavinck had failed to act neutrally as chairman.)

The wider consequences of Lohman's dismissal were considerable: his son Witius Hendrik (1864–1932), who also taught law at the Free University, left his post, and Witius Hendrik's father-in-law, Willem Hovy—the head of a major brewery and a Christian philanthropist—resigned as director.[159] Beyond this, the Seinpost scandal would eventually lead to the fracturing of Antirevolutionary Christian politics in the Netherlands: Lohman left the Antirevolutionary Party, a departure that led to the formation of a breakaway party, the Christian Historical Union (*Christelijk-Historische Unie*). Only in 1980 would these groups reunite in the creation of the Christian Democratic Appeal (*Christen-Democratisch Appèl*). For less than glorious reasons, then, Bavinck's role in the Seinpost scandal would help to shape Dutch national politics for the best part of the coming century.

In pondering this notable example of underhanded action, Gleason has described Bavinck's conduct as "incomprehensible."[160] Although his breach of trust is not defensible, it may at least be somewhat explicable in the light of Kuyper's influence in the 1890s. Interpretations of Kuyper's life in these years follow two trends: some have read these years as showing a ruthless ascendant opportunist who eliminated his rivals en route to assuming the premiership, while others have more positively described his Calvinistic empowerment of the ordinary people and simultaneous assault on the aristocratic elite.[161] These threads are not easily disentangled, not least because each one contains an element of truth. In both readings, Lohman was a problem to Kuyper: either as a public rival in the political realm or as a Christian intellectual who tied Calvinism to aristocracy.

During this period in Kuyper's ascendancy, Bavinck's life was profoundly invested in his grand project: for more than a decade, Bavinck's energies and talents had been animated by Kuyper's vision of the church, theology, and politics. His eggs were delicately balanced in a decidedly Kuyperian basket. And, as has already been described, Bavinck and Kuyper believed that the Netherlands' future as a Christian nation depended on the progress of neo-Calvinism. Ostensibly, Lohman posed an existential threat to neo-Calvinism (and the modern Christian university at its core), to the grassroots anti-elitist politics relied upon to bring about modern reformation, and even to the future of the Netherlands as a Christian nation—and for those reasons, Bavinck allowed himself to become complicit in Kuyper's scheme to depose him. For good and ill, Bavinck was much in Kuyper's thrall.

The Death of a Brother

From dagboek entries in 1890 onward, it is clear that Bavinck's youngest brother, Johan, struggled with poor health. In 1895, while working on his doctoral thesis (on "the Calvinistic doctrine of the state"), he developed tuberculosis. Jan Bavinck's autobiography recounted the first time Johan coughed up blood and the subsequent failure of his health: "On a certain evening, coming home, he brought up a little blood, and from that time on he began to ail and salivate. Whatever we did to look after him, and whatever means we directed toward his recovery, nothing helped."[162] In an entry in the lost dagboek, written during the Christmas of 1896, Herman recorded his brother's death. "*26 Dec., 2nd Christmas day, Saturday. Our dear Johan, who vomited blood at Biesterveld's house on the evening of*

Sunday 8 September, died this morning at 1.30am, 24 years and 3 months old (25 Sept. '72–26 Dec. '96)."[163]

On the same day, the Bavinck family prepared his death notice for the newspapers.

> This morning, after long and patient suffering, our beloved youngest son and brother, JOHANNES GERRIT BAVINCK, Doctoral candidate in the Science of Law and the State, died in the hope of eternal life, at the age of 24 years.
>
> J. BAVINCK.
> G. M. BAVINCK-HOLLAND.
> H. BAVINCK.
> J. A. BAVINCK-SCHIPPERS.
> C. B. BAVINCK.
> G. BAVINCK-BOUWES.
> B. J. F. BAVINCK.
> *Kampen*, 26 Dec. 1896.[164]

Johannes's death was a bitter blow to the Bavinck family. "In him," his father wrote, "we lost a dear and very promising son and a deeply loved brother. We were all bitterly distressed; we had so wanted to keep him."[165] Shortly after this, Herman shared the news of Johan's death with Kuyper.

> Johan was our youngest brother; we all loved him so much and had such high hopes for him, for the church and fatherland. He had such a modest, simple character and also such precious gifts of understanding and mind that we thought the Lord had given us and our parents a glorious gift in him. But the Lord has given, and he has also taken away, and in both may his name be praised. . . . He was not fully assured [of his salvation] for himself; he was subjected to much challenge, and sometimes it was dark in his soul. But still, his heart was directed toward the Lord, and he gave himself over to God's free grace; he wanted to know nothing but Jesus Christ and him crucified; and so he has gone, ahead of us, to a better fatherland.[166]

At the age of forty-one, Herman had lived through the loss of two sisters, Dina (1851–64) and Femia (1858–66), and two brothers, Karel (1862–62) and Johan (1872–96). He was now the eldest of three siblings—one of whom, Dinus, would go on to write a doctoral thesis on the mortality rates of tuberculosis in the Netherlands in the two decades leading up to Johan's death.[167] In strange and distinct ways, the Bavinck brothers' doctoral dissertations in theology, law, and medicine—two finished, and one forever incomplete—were closely intertwined.

Productive Years: Dogmatics, Psychology, and Ethics

The period that followed, from 1897 to 1901, formed an exceptionally prolific phase in Bavinck's career. The second volume of his *Reformed Dogmatics* (571 pages) appeared in 1897, with volumes 3 (572 pages) and 4 (590 pages) being published, respectively, in 1898 and 1901.[168] When the second volume was released, Kuyper's review offered praise for Bavinck and criticism of the mainstream Dutch Reformed Church's best efforts—P. J. Muller's *Guide to Dogmatics*—in the same breath: "After the appearance [of Bavinck's work], what the former professor Muller published as a dogmatics immediately crawled away [to hide] under the couch in shame. This is a *real* dogmatics, ripe and mature, clear in form and devoid of all bitterness toward different viewpoints."[169] In these years, among other things, Bavinck also contributed to highly regarded journals at home and abroad,[170] wrote the foreword for the Dutch translation of Matthew Henry's *Commentary on the Bible*,[171] and penned numerous articles in local and national newspapers. Indeed, in the late 1890s his journalistic output was such that in 1900, shortly before the completion of his *Dogmatics*, he was appointed editor of *De Bazuin*.

In 1897, while preparing the second volume of his *Dogmatics*, he also published a substantial book, *The Principles of Psychology* (208 pages).[172] That Bavinck prioritized a book on psychology in the midst of a multiyear writing project in dogmatics and ethics—even completing this book midway through the volumes of his *Dogmatics*—is perhaps surprising. In an intensely busy phase of theological writing, why make this early foray away from dogmatics and into the life of the mind? A significant clue is offered early in the *Reformed Dogmatics*. In Bavinck's eyes, the theology of the nineteenth century—in its entirety—had been recast in light of Friedrich Schleiermacher's efforts to base theology in human self-consciousness. Schleiermacher popularized the view that the theologian's knowledge of God is categorically different from God's own self-knowledge. The former is subjective and inexhaustive, and the latter, objective and full. One occurs in the human mind, and the other, in the mind of God. In promoting this distinction, Schleiermacher had entrenched the view that despite its focus on God, theology was an endeavor of the human mind—a development that, for Bavinck, had been universally accepted across nineteenth-century theologians. "Through and after Schleiermacher," Bavinck wrote, "theology in its entirety, as much among the orthodox as the moderns, is a theology of consciousness."[173]

For that reason, post-Schleiermacher, one could not simply reissue older theological texts. Rather, in Bavinck's eyes, the breadth and depth of Schleiermacher's impact was such that no new dogmatics could meet the needs of his day without an accompanying work that took this Schleiermacherian shift into account.[174] For that reason, then, a reissue of the *Synopsis purioris theologiae* would not meet the needs of his day—while that work's early modern authors also engaged with the inner life of the soul, they had not engaged with Schleiermacher's specific and modern concerns. (Throughout his career Bavinck felt driven to balance dogmatics with the study of psychology. In his later work *Philosophy of Revelation*, he would reassert that "dogmatics . . . must become more psychological, and must deal with religious experience." And later still, two years after his death, *Principles of Psychology* would be reissued in a new edition based on Bavinck's continued work.)[175]

The original release of *Principles of Psychology* hints at Bavinck's allure across the constellation of late nineteenth-century Christian thinkers. Under Schleiermacher's influence, that era's changing priorities in higher education had replaced the polymath of previous centuries with academic specialists who kept firmly within the narrow boundaries of their scholarly disciplines: by and large, the late nineteenth century produced intradisciplinary experts rather than renaissance men. In precisely that period, spurred on by the holism of Kuyper's Calvinism and having long since desired to be "a human in the fullest natural sense of that word" and "a child of God in all things,"[176] Bavinck had begun to emerge as an intellectual who combined the precision and nuance of the late modern world and the polymathic dream of the medieval and early modern eras. His publications record was no longer modest. More importantly, his life had become marked by a rich diversity and depth: he was now a husband and father, churchman, dogmatician and man of science, a modern Calvinist, and latterly, a newspaper editor.

Kuyper's Lectures on Calvinism

In 1898, Kuyper crossed the Atlantic—as Bavinck had done in 1892—to promote Calvinism. Unlike Bavinck's trip, however, Kuyper's was primarily focused on the academy rather than the church. In 1896, Princeton University had offered Kuyper an honorary Doctor of Law degree in recognition of his work in writing the Christian political manifesto *Our Program*.[177] Kuyper was then also invited to hold the Stone Lectures at the adjacent Princeton Theological Seminary, where Geerhardus Vos was now teaching. In 1898 he traveled to Princeton and received his doctorate and delivered the Stone Lectures.

In Kuyper's eyes, this occasion had been divinely ordained and would serve as a key moment in Calvinism's march into the future. Although Kuyper's cultural impressions of America were similar to Bavinck's on some points,[178] his assessment of Calvinism's prospects there could hardly have been more different. To Kuyper, America was ideally suited to embrace Calvinism. This was so, he thought, because America's newness required an intentionality toward each sphere of life. More than any other Christian tradition, he believed, Calvinism could provide this. In addition to this, the place of religion in American society matched Kuyper's ideals beautifully. There, he found a society that encouraged public religious expression while also maintaining a strict separation of church and state. America had avoided the antireligious core of French republicanism and the (to Kuyper) arbitrary denominational privileges maintained in Lutheran and Roman Catholic European nations. To the wide-eyed Kuyper, America was already great, but it would become greater still by embracing Calvinism. Such was Kuyper's belief in the importance of Calvinism to America (and vice versa) that he extended his stay from three to five months, writing to his wife, "My journey was commanded [by God], was necessary, it was meant to be in my life, it is a part of my task."[179]

His lectures in Princeton set out perhaps his clearest articulation of Calvinism as a "life-system" encompassing history, religion, politics, science, art, and the future.[180] Although Kuyper had intended the *Encyclopedia* to be his magnum opus, in the longer term that work was far less widely read than his Princeton lectures would be. Having received a copy of the *Lectures on Calvinism* from Kuyper, however, Bavinck replied somewhat cryptically and critically. "I do doubt whether the listeners in Princeton, for whom this world of thought is wholly foreign, were immediately able to grasp your lofty and broad proportions. You give so much in condensed form that only those who are to some degree acquainted [with your thought] can value what it contains."[181] That Bavinck was critical of Kuyper's *Lectures on Calvinism*, given their eventual importance to the development of neo-Calvinism, is itself significant. Bavinck was certainly convinced of its need in the Netherlands. After all, Calvinism was deeply rooted in Dutch cultural soil. Indeed, he believed those roots to be so extensive that without them, the soil would not hold together. Throughout the 1890s, however, Bavinck was unwilling to assert that the same might be true of other cultures, on the grounds that "Calvinism wishes no cessation of progress and promotes multiformity. It . . . honors every gift and different calling of the Churches. It does not demand for itself the same development in America and England which it has found in Holland. This only must be insisted upon, that in each country and in every Reformed Church it should develop itself in accordance with its own nature and should not permit itself to be supplanted or corrupted by foreign ideas."[182] For that reason, he argued that while Calvinism is "a specific and the richest and most beautiful form of Christianity," it is "not coextensive with Christianity."[183] Although he believed strongly that the Dutch future needed Calvinism, his views on the movement's international prospects flatly contradicted those of Kuyper: "Nobody," he wrote, "can tell whether Dutch Calvinism is still destined to exert influence on the future of Calvinism in other countries."[184]

Considering Alternative Locations: Amsterdam, Amersfoort, Haarlem, or Hilversum?

By 1899, Bavinck was not far off completing a major scholarly achievement. The first three volumes of his *Dogmatics* were now in print. Although he had previously been overlooked for a chair at the University of Leiden (as well as having declined the Free University on three separate occasions), his stock had continued to rise in the Dutch academy. One unsympathetic newspaper report in that year remarked, "At this time, neo-Calvinism must be taken into account. . . . The *Reformed Dogmatics* of Dr. Bavinck is very influential among many young theologians."[185]

Indeed, by 1899 his influence had increased to the point that he came into consideration for another appointment in Amsterdam. This chair, however, was at the University of Amsterdam. He was now being cautiously courted by the Municipal University, rather than Kuyper's Free University. There, a chair in the history of dogma held by Pierre Daniel Chantepie de la Saussaye (1848–1920)—whose father, Daniël, had been the subject of Bavinck's critique in 1883—had been vacated following de la Saussaye's move to the University of Leiden. In view of Bavinck's work on the *Dogmatics*, the liberal Remonstrant professor Izaak De Bussy (1846–1920) wrote to inquire of his interest in this post:

> Dear colleague!
>
> As a consequence of de la Saussaye's departure for Leiden and the reshuffling of classes among our faculty, we shall have to appoint a professor in the history of dogma, in the history of the doctrine of God, and in encyclopedia.
>
> There are few who deserve to come into consideration for this professorship, and when it comes to naming them, in my opinion, your name may not be held back.
>
> But in this, a great difficulty arises for me. I certainly have every reason to assume that you would not accept an eventual nomination, and you perhaps would not welcome a nomination. And so I find myself between my scientific conscience and the demands of the practical! The faculty has to make up a proposed list of persons who we, without directly asking them,

can guess would be prepared to accept a nomination. . . . Of the few whom I have named in the faculty until now, yours is the only name I don't dare to mention, for this reason, and to whom I am therefore writing. I wish to say to the faculty that I do not desire to see your name added to the list because I am certain that you would not be inclined [to accept it] and that you would simply shrug your shoulders in response. But I also wish to share this with you.

I ask that you keep the content of my letter secret until the trustees' proposal has been made public, which shall probably be in fourteen days. The faculty is not yet ready, so, before we reach the end of this process, we still have time to catch our breath.

> Yours faithfully, remembering the
> approach I made to you in May, and
> with polite greetings, obligingly,
> De Bussy[186]

Had Bavinck been prepared to put himself forward, he now had the opportunity to do what seemed impossible in 1889—be appointed to a professorship at a state university. While he had previously been eager to move to Leiden (even shortly after declining a nomination at the Free University), a decade on, he had no such enthusiasm for the University of Amsterdam. There was no public speculation that Bavinck might move there, and it does not seem that Bavinck himself did anything to encourage De Bussy's overture. De Bussy's instincts were correct: by this point in Bavinck's life, it was not a welcome approach. The time for moving to a state university had passed.

This apparent lack of interest in the University of Amsterdam was certainly not caused by a peaceful set of circumstances in Kampen. There, Bavinck remained locked in conflict with Lindeboom regarding the relationship of the Theological School to the Free University. Over the course of 1899, Bavinck prepared and submitted a proposal to the church's general synod, held that year in Groningen (Aug. 15–30), to have the Theological School relocated from Kampen to Haarlem or Amersfoort or Hilversum—all small cities within shouting distance of Amsterdam but far enough away to make clear to his opponents that the Theological School could maintain its own location and identity.

While Bavinck presented his argument in Groningen, Kuyper was struck by tragedy further afield. At various points in his life, the chronically overworked Kuyper was prescribed holidays as a form of medicine. In August 1899, one such vacation took him and his wife, Johanna, to Meiringen, a Swiss village made famous by Arthur Conan Doyle as the setting for Sherlock Holmes's final duel with Moriarty. There, midholiday, Johanna—whose physical and mental health had never recovered from the death of their eight-year-old son, Willy, in 1893—became ill, died, and was buried.[187] The proposals on missions submitted to the synod by Kuyper, to be discussed in his absence, were put on hold.[188] Bavinck, though, was left to carry on making his arguments on the relocation of the Theological School and failed to gather sufficient support.[189] It had been a low and difficult week.

In this context, his efforts to defend the future of scientific theology in Kampen, contra Lindeboom, dominated his writing schedule. In *Theological School and Free University: A Proposal for Unity*,[190] he further developed his argument that the denomination's two centers of theological education belonged together and could be united while assuring the Theological School of its ongoing distinct identity. (He restated his compromise solution to move the Theological School without placing it in Amsterdam—i.e., to move it to his preferred city, Haarlem.) His short book *The Right of the Church and the Freedom of Science* made painfully clear his deep frustrations with the anti-Kuyperian wing of his church.[191] (That summer, the opposition of Lindeboom and his allies to the Free University was hardly helped by the appointment of Kuyper's son Herman H. Kuyper [1864–1945] to a professorship in Amsterdam.) At the close of 1899, he passed on the Theological School's rectorship to his ally Petrus Biesterveld, publishing his rectorial address in expanded form as *The Office of the Doctor*.[192] There, he argued that the stark tension asserted by Lindeboom between churchly and scientific theology was out of step with the history of the Christian faith. Over the centuries, he argued, Christianity had developed the theologian's vocation as a distinct and holy calling—a development that was inextricably linked to the emergence of the university itself. Contra Lindeboom, Bavinck's reasoning was that this history allowed the same practitioner to serve the church *and* move in the scientific academy. The two need not be in conflict.

Taken together, these three books represented a substantial investment of time: the final volume of his *Dogmatics* was still somewhere on the path toward completion but was being held back by his efforts to bring Kampen and Amsterdam together. (And this is to say nothing of the still incomplete *Reformed Ethics* manuscript, which had now lain untouched for some time.) As those pleas fell on increasingly deaf ears, Bavinck began to cut a frustrated figure. In an undated letter from this period, he wrote to Kuyper, "I still always wish with my whole heart that the union of both schools of education might come. But my hope of a favorable outcome has not been strengthened this year. Perhaps it is best, for the time being, to remain

standing next to each other in friendship, and for each [of us] to work
in his own setting for the growth of the churches and the development of
theological science."[193]

Editorship of *De Bazuin*

Bavinck continued to work on his *Dogmatics*, with the fourth and final volume
appearing in print in 1901. Before this, however, in January 1900, he assumed
the editorship of *De Bazuin*. This role gave him a distinctive position of influence in shaping views on the Theological School and its relationship to the
Free University. Since 1856, its full title had been "*De Bazuin: Ten voordeel
van de Theologische School te Kampen*" ("For the benefit of the Theological
School in Kampen"). For the most part, its readership in 1900 had roots in the
Seceder Church and was certainly more skeptical of the Free University than
the average reader of *De Standaard* or *De Heraut*. A new editor sympathetic
to the Free University could shift that bias somewhat.

Bavinck's opening editorial—a survey of the editorial policies of his
predecessors—acknowledged this piece of history while setting out that
under his editorship the paper would reflect the diversity of views now held
throughout the denomination. "In unity," he reminded readers, "God loves
diversity."[194] Under the new editor's watch, *De Bazuin* would no longer be
for the benefit of only one of the denomination's theological institutions.

Over the coming three years Bavinck poured himself into his journalistic
work, writing hundreds of articles covering an array of topics—among others, modern art,[195] politics,[196] war,[197] John Calvin,[198] baptism,[199] feminism,[200]
women's voting rights,[201] liturgy,[202] and the art of travel,[203] alongside numerous
short pieces on the struggles regarding Kampen and Amsterdam. The eventual
release of the final volume of his *Dogmatics* was described in one such article.
The article did not mention the author's heavy engagement in church politics
as a reason for the delay. Rather, the volume's publication was apparently held
back by (unspecified) difficulties on the part of his publisher and by the time
taken to prepare the final indexes (which Bavinck's younger brother Bernard,
now a pastor in Rotterdam, had compiled). In the midst of this busy journalistic
phase, "the theology needed by our age" was finally completed.[204]

In 1901, alongside the final volume of the *Reformed Dogmatics*, a slew of
significant shorter books also saw the light of day—many of which were first
developed as lectures in the 1890s. In that year, he published an extended pastoral meditation on participation in the Lord's Supper (*The Sacrifice of Praise*),[205]
a book exploring the widespread sense of religious doubt that plagued the

late nineteenth century (*The Certainty of Faith*),[206] a commentary on the role of parents and witnesses in infant baptism (*Parents or Witnesses?*),[207] and a work on evolution (*Creation or Development?*).[208] The previous two decades of research had finally turned into a flood of published work.

The only remaining detailed example of Bavinck's preaching also dates from this period. Although he had preached regularly since his student years, the only records of these sermons—preached with no (or minimal) notes—are the sermon texts themselves, as noted in his dagboeken. Our sole full example of a sermon as preached by Bavinck was delivered on July 30, 1901, in the Burgwalkerk in Kampen. The text, 1 John 5:4b, was a familiar one: it was the first text from which he had preached as a student and the one to which his sermons regularly returned over the years. (Given this fact, this print sermon was probably quite representative of his preaching in general.) A widespread public clamor for access to this particular sermon, delivered extemporaneously, grew because it had been attended by Paul Kruger (1825–1904)—the president of the South African Republic (Transvaal) and the face of Afrikaner resistance against the British in the Second Boer War (1899–1902). Bavinck's sermon was explicitly political, praising the Christian faith of the Boer farmers in their fight against their British oppressors and noting the same battle of faith in the recent Dutch parliamentary elections, in which the Antirevolutionary Party had come a close second to the Liberals. In response to public demand, Bavinck tried to recall his content, which was then released as a booklet.[209]

While he had been preaching more or less the same sermon for decades—that faith is strong enough to overcome the world—in 1901, in the Netherlands at least, the world now looked close to being overcome: in the aftermath of the national elections, Kuyper was asked to form a coalition government. In August he became prime minister. The dreams of a Calvinistic future that had sustained Bavinck throughout the previous decade seemed to be coming true. (Somewhat confusingly, Gleason's biography claims that in this period of political success for the neo-Calvinists, Queen Wilhelmina appointed Bavinck "to be the president of the Council of Ministries"—a distinguished appointment that brought him "a number of weighty political responsibilities."[210] That honor, however, was actually given to Abraham Kuyper, who carried far more political heft than Bavinck.)

A Hidden Dagboek Fragment

Although Bavinck's dagboek entries from the years 1891 onward appear to have been lost and are only preserved in echoes found in the works of Hepp and Bremmer, several pages of diary material dated from July 13, 1900, to April 8, 1901, remain tucked into the back cover of the "From 1886 to 1891" dagboek in the Bavinck Archive. In these, we glimpse the Bavincks' family life in the midst of this intense period. In June 1900, Herman and Johanna traveled to Germany and Austria, leaving Hannie—now aged six—with Johanna's parents. After visiting Cologne and Heidelberg, they met Petrus and Martha Biesterveld in Stuttgart, before traveling together to Innsbruck. The two couples traveled together until July 31, when the Biestervelds moved on to Frankfurt. What is perhaps most remarkable about Bavinck's notes on their holiday together—sightseeing excursions, fine dining in hotels, train trips, attending local church services in the Evangelische Kirche—is their ordinariness: their embattled situation at home was no obstacle to a very agreeable holiday. Typically, his approach to travel was theologically imbued. In a column in *De Bazuin* from this period, he wrote, "The time for relaxation that regularly replaces the work of the mind is a rich blessing and precious gift that comes down from the Father of Lights. The heart is opened up and the chest expands, the eye becomes clearer, the forehead loses its wrinkles, when you may set your work to the side for a time, and freely, to your heart's content, enjoy the glory that God's creation offers to us. . . . Travel remains a delight and a rich pleasure."[211] Having enjoyed the general revelation of God in the splendor of the Alps, the Bavincks journeyed home via Frankfurt, Mainz, and Cologne, with Herman and Johanna parting ways in Arnhem: she traveled south to collect Hannie while he went onward to Kampen. After a month apart, the family reunited: "*Saturday, 18 Aug.: Johanna, Hannie came home again.*"[212] Another significant change in the Bavinck family was recorded in this fragment: Herman had to cancel a scheduled lecture in Utrecht on November 16, 1900, "*because of mother's illness.*"[213] Herman, Bernard, and Dinus traveled home, knowing that their mother was gravely ill. Ten days later, she passed away: "*26 Nov. Monday. Mother died at 3.45 in the afternoon and was buried on Friday 30 Nov.*"[214]

As was mentioned in an earlier chapter, following Geziena's death, the elderly widower Jan Bavinck moved into Herman's household—a situation that perhaps explains the fragment's final entry: "*April 8. Back to Kampen, arrival in the new house, Vloeddijk.*"[215] In Jan Bavinck's own autobiography, he recalled consulting with his sons following the death of his wife and concluding that he should live with Herman's family, as they were also resident in Kampen (where Jan was a pastor). To accommodate Jan, then, they moved to a more suitable house.

Until this point, Jan's publications had been books of sermons. Now, like Herman, he became consumed by writing new material. Faced with the loneliness of widowerhood, he threw himself into the production of a vast commentary (943 pages) on the Heidelberg Catechism, which was released in two volumes between 1903 and 1904.[216] During what would be a short stay in this house on the Vloeddijk, the Bavinck home was a hive of theological industry: a review of Jan's work in *De Heraut* described him as "having stayed young and fresh in spirit, despite his old age," before adding that "whoever looks through the first volume will notice how outstandingly well informed Rev. Bavinck is in what is being written in the field of dogmatics in our time. For the connoisseur of dogmatics, these sermons promise to be a treat."[217] Given the Bavincks' living situation, it is hard to imagine that Jan would have been anything other than thoroughly engaged with the cutting edge of dogmatics.

This fragment of the lost dagboek also provides a rare glimpse into Herman's preaching in this period: the fragment's last recorded sermons—three addresses delivered in Johanna's home congregation at Easter services in April 1901, on Matthew 28:1–8, John 20:11–17, and Colossians 3:2–3—were noted as sermon numbers 695, 696, and 697. The last noted sermon in the previous complete dagboek, preached in May 1891, was number 440: to the previous decade's constant activity, we can add 257 sermons. Little wonder that one of Bavinck's later translators would describe these years as the "period of great activity."[218]

Moving to Amsterdam: "The More Businesslike, the Better"

During his tenure at the helm of *De Bazuin*, Bavinck certainly tried to present a positive face toward the paper's readership. While the denomination was caught up in division between the "A-churches" and "B-churches," the paper's balance of content—led by editorial example—tried not to be eclipsed by these ongoing battles. Despite this, Bavinck's own irritations, usually against the anti-Kuyperians but also sometimes against the Free University itself, became increasingly evident.[219]

By 1902, he realized that no progress was being made on this particular issue, despite years of argumentation and attempted bridge building. The Free University made another (discreet) approach to Bavinck, and this time, also to his colleague Biesterveld. Against that backdrop, Bavinck made a proposal to that year's synod, held in Arnhem: the church-oriented Theological School and the Free University's theological faculty should be united into a single institution that would train theologians for the church *and* the academy.

The results of the Arnhem Synod were deeply frustrating for Bavinck. His proposal finally won the majority vote but was met with a prediction by its opponents that the merger would lead the denomination to split.[220] Faced with the prospect of ecclesiastical fracture, the synod backed down. Bavinck's reply came in a lengthy editorial accusing the church of giving itself over to the tyranny of the minority. The consequence of the synod's backtracking, he argued, was that the Theological School could no longer claim to represent the Reformed Churches in the Netherlands, but rather had become a niche institution catering only to a minority group within it.[221] It was a damning verdict.

Within a short space of time, Bavinck further responded with his own show of gunboat diplomacy, releasing a short book entitled, *Staying or Going? A Question and an Answer*.[222] "Now," he began, "after almost fifteen years of work, it seems we are still in the same place as at the beginning. In this affair, it is as though a judgment rests upon our church."[223] His conclusion was stark: if the impasse remained, he and Biesterveld would move to the Free University (in Bavinck's ideal, not to leave Kampen behind, but rather to tread a path that the Theological School might eventually follow). Naturally, Lindeboom was furious—as was Bavinck's long-term ally, Maarten Noordtzij. Together, Lindeboom and Noordtzij published a response in *De Bazuin* that criticized Bavinck and Biesterveld for their "aggressive intervention."[224] Having played their hand in *Staying or Going?* and also having risked their good relations with Noordtzij, Bavinck and Biesterveld quickly realized they had backed themselves into a corner: they had to leave the Theological School. In the midst of all this, on September 5, 1902, *De Bazuin* announced that "Dr. H. BAVINCK, *Professor at the Theol. School*, belongs in the number of those who, on the occasion of the birthday of H. M. our honorable Queen, have been added to the Knights of the Order of the Lion of the Netherlands."[225] A major civic honor, Bavinck's knighthood could not have come at a more stressful moment. He scarcely had time to enjoy this accolade in a period consumed by intensive private negotiations with the Free University, even as Maarten Noordtzij made moves to persuade him to stay in Kampen. Noordtzij's efforts, however, were in vain. Bavinck agreed to a salary and pension package with the Free University, writing to Kuyper in early October to ask for him to announce their move in strictly nonpolemical terms. "I have no objections," he wrote, "that *De Heraut* and *De Bazuin* announce the facts of [our] nomination and acceptance. But I ask you politely, for the time being, to leave it at the facts in the announcement, and not to add any words of praise or thanks. The more businesslike, the better."[226] His final editorial comment on the long-standing dispute on Kampen and Amsterdam, entitled "Cease-fire," ran on October

31, shortly before his departure to Amsterdam.[227] Thereafter, his contributions to the *De Bazuin* were minimal, with the editorship being passed over to Maarten Noordtzij at the close of the year.[228] On December 15, Bavinck and Biesterveld gave a parting address to the Kampen student body, formally accepting their new posts at the Free University later that week.[229]

In that address, an impassioned Bavinck stood with both hands on the table before him, telling his students, "I could not have imagined my time at the Theological School would end like this," and reassuring them that his departure should not be interpreted as "a lack of love for the Theological School" or, indeed, for them. He used this occasion to reveal that he had previously had several opportunities to leave Kampen but had not done so because he believed that his Calvinistic vision could be realized at his beloved seminary. Strangely, given his various earlier private comments to the contrary to Snouck Hurgronje, and also publicly in *De Bazuin*, he claimed, "According to my lifelong inclination, I worked and would still much rather work at a theol. school than at an institution that carries the name of a university."[230]

Before a crowd of students whose own roots were in the Secession church, Bavinck painted himself as one of them: he was leaving because of, rather than despite, his particular Seceder roots. He received rapturous applause when he told them, "I said before, and now I say it again, I am a child of the Secession, and I hope to remain so!"[231] In the surviving notes of this speech—which were not those of Bavinck himself—he is recorded as having pointed out that both of his parents grew up in Secession churches. (If he did indeed say this, it was not true: his mother had grown up in the mainstream Dutch Reformed Church.) His outlook, he recounted, was profoundly shaped by the influence of his open-minded Seceder parents and his education at Leiden, both of which had taught him to fear narrowness and sectarianism. In this, however, he recognized that he had grown up under the influence of only one discrete stream of Seceder thought.

In distinguishing his own upbringing in that context, he typified two poles in the Christian Reformed Church of his youth: one that prioritized an otherworldly holiness of life, and another that insisted that the catholic Christian faith necessarily addresses every aspect of life in this world. In describing these, he made a telling comment on the reasons for his own commitment to holding orthodoxy and modernity together—a commitment that he now believed had forced him out of the Theological School. "In that time in the church, there was the idea that we need to leave the world to its own fate, but precisely because I come from the circles that I do, I felt obliged to seek out an education at a university, because that church was in great danger of losing its catholicity in order to hold on to holiness of life. And then the thought arose within me: Is it possible to reconcile these? . . . My goal is to hold tightly to both, and not to let go of either."[232] Aware of the likelihood that some students would follow him to Amsterdam, he spoke frankly on his own uncertainty about the future of his new institutional home: "If you ask me whether the VU [Vrije Universiteit / Free University] shall become great, then I say, I do not know."[233] He was not openly encouraging students to move with them, and those who chose to certainly had not received a rose-tinted view of life as students in Amsterdam. In the lost dagboek, Bavinck wrote, "*Biesterveld and I said goodbye to the students: Rector Noordtzij led the gathering, Lindeboom was sitting there. Noordtzij addressed us [and] took a sideswipe at the [outcome] forced after the Synod.*"[234] For Bavinck, Biesterveld, Noordtzij, and many of the Theological School's students, the synod's outcome had been regrettable. Although it had become inevitable, it had never been necessary.

Of the students addressed that day, more than half moved to Amsterdam with their departing professors.[235] This mass departure was nothing less than a disaster for the school, which tried to compensate for Bavinck's loss by appointing a Kuyperian as his replacement—Anthonie Gerrit Honig (1864–1940), whose doctorate (on the Scottish theologian Alexander Comrie) had been supervised by Kuyper.[236] Bavinck, though, could not easily be replaced. Although Honig would later publish his own substantial *Guide to Reformed Dogmatics*,[237] he publicly described Bavinck's *Reformed Dogmatics* as "the very best that has appeared in the scientific realm."[238]

PART 5

Professor in Amsterdam

9

Christianity in the Age of Nietzsche

1902–9

"In reality there are only two worldviews."

In chapters 4 and 5, I challenged previous interpretations of the young Bavinck as having become a persona non grata in Kampen on account of his choice to study in Leiden. Although Bavinck had encountered a degree of suspicion from some Seceders in that phase of life, for the most part he continued to enjoy the good grace of the Kampen Theological School, its teachers, and its students. Although he was based in Leiden, Kampen's door was always open to him. In reality, it was in 1902, while he was in his late forties, that Bavinck's relationship to Kampen became deeply strained. Indeed, his resignation from the Theological School was made all the more awkward by the protracted nature of his departure from the town itself: unable to find a suitable home in Amsterdam at short notice, he continued to live in Kampen, a stone's throw from the Theological School, for almost two months after his appointment in Amsterdam.[1] During that time, his father, with whom he still lived, remained the *pastor loci*—albeit with a reduced preaching schedule—to the Theological School's faculty and students.[2] Shortly before his son's family left for Kampen, however, Jan became *pastor emeritus*. With the commentary on the Heidelberg Catechism as his swan song, his ministry ended.

A great deal had happened in the fifty-five years since Jan's ordination in the Evangelical Old Reformed Church in Bentheim. Over the course of those decades, he had imparted a distinct vision of scientific Reformed theology to his son, whose commitment to the same ideals now meant that Jan would become an Amsterdammer in old age. Before that, however, father and son had to endure one last moment of discomfiture at the hands of a theologian who did not share their outlook: at a special service to mark his retirement, held in Kampen on January 26, 1903, Jan was addressed on behalf of the Theological School by Lucas Lindeboom.[3] And with that, the Bavincks left Kampen. For the Theological School and the congregation on the Burgwal, it was the end of an era.

Certainty and Doubt at the Free University

Before this, in his last months as a resident of Kampen, Herman had already held his inaugural lecture at the Free University. On December 17, two days after his final words to the student body at the Theological School, he addressed the Free University's students—including many familiar faces who had transferred from the Theological School—in a lecture later published as *Religion and Theology*.[4] There, he framed this new phase of his working life in the light of his inaugural lecture in Kampen ("The Science of Sacred Theology")[5] twenty years before. Once again, he set out his case for theology as necessarily scientific and pious.

As a science concerned with knowing God, he argued, theology was different from but closely bound to Christian piety. "Religion and theology . . . are two sisters, each of whom has a special role and calling in the family of God's church. They are like Mary and Martha in Lazarus's household."[6] Like Mary, theology longs to look into the face of Christ, pondering the mystery of God made flesh. Like Martha, religion busies itself with serving Christ. In Bavinck's account of their difference, neither sister had reason to despise the other. After all, "Martha also served the Lord, and Jesus loved them both."[7] This opening lecture in Amsterdam sounded a clear, confident note: while it had proven impossible (for the time being, at least) to reconcile Mary and Martha in Kampen, Amsterdam offered better prospects. As the lecture drew to a close, he also directly addressed the university's trustees, offering public commentary on why he had finally left the Theological School.

In my earlier years, because of the moral obligations that I felt to the church in which I was born and to the school that was established by it, I lacked the freedom to take up one of the nominations that you brought to me. Now, however, I may say that the moral obligations that I bear in this issue have been fully and more than adequately met. Although I carry a deep sense of disappointment that I have not been appointed to your institution in another manner and along a different path, I nonetheless accepted your appointment with full boldness and show you my thanks openly, that you wished to issue this nomination to me and to my colleague Biesterveld.[8]

Claiming that his task at the Theological School had been fulfilled, he stated his intentions for the direction of his work in Amsterdam.

I have come here to work for the realization of a high ideal. It will bring me inner joy if I might contribute somewhat, to the extent of my abilities, so that under your prudent and energetic direction the connection between [religious] confession and science might be illuminated ever more clearly, in theory and practice; so that the relationship of the theological faculty to the Reformed churches in this land will be fully and sufficiently ordered; and so that by a rapid and powerful expansion of the number of lectureships held across the different faculties, this school may make a steadily more legitimate claim on the beautiful name that it received at its foundation.[9]

Bavinck's statement of public praise and personal ambition concealed a criticism toward the Free University—as an institution, it had not yet lived up to its name. It was a small school and lacked the capacious character of a true university. Privately, Bavinck was less than convinced of what might be accomplished there. In early January 1903, he wrote to Snouck Hurgronje,

I am no great enthusiast for the Free University and see its weaknesses and shortcomings. But here, I seem to have given the impression of [holding] a conviction that I do not have. Although I am very convinced that in the absence of a public Christian university the church might have a strong say over a theological faculty, I cannot accept the "principle of [the church's] own institution" as a dogma, and I find in it an immature and bitter product of separatism, which has also spread its roots in our Christian Reformed Church. It cost me a lot of combat to choose as I have. Many bands held me tightly. But finally, I could not and ought not to have done otherwise. I hope now that through this our people will to an extent become more sympathetic to the Free University and that through this its strength will also increase. I don't think it will ever become a more or less complete university. But if it can produce a certain number of ministers, men of literature, and jurists who stand at the cutting edge of their day and who are also men of conviction and character, then it still may be a blessing, to a modest degree. All parties have need of such men, ours especially.[10]

In part, his choice to switch institutions was influenced by Kuyper's own appointment as prime minister, which in effect meant the end of his close involvement at the Free University.[11] However, the choice was also forced because of an awkwardly played hand, more than because of a sure belief that the ideal time to take up Kuyper's offer had finally come. The contrast between his public and private statements on his new institutional home was striking. This was an (almost) accidental relocation, albeit one from which Bavinck hoped good might come.

The Saddest Experience in Life

That Bavinck was privately unsure about the Free University's eventual contribution to Dutch society is also significant, in view of the political context at that time. He had moved from Kampen to Amsterdam just as the rising neo-Calvinist sun was coming to its zenith. After all, his services as a dogmatician were needed in Amsterdam because Kuyper was otherwise occupied with his work as prime minister. Under their neo-Calvinist leader, members of the Antirevolutionary Party now held a host of influential political positions across the nation. Despite this, Bavinck had begun to sound jaded—in his sense of what might be achieved by the Free University in the long run, but more painfully, by his experience of people. Years of battle in the halls of the Theological School, on the pages of *De Bazuin*, on the floor of the synod, and in page after page of published argument had not come without cost. In a letter to Snouck Hurgronje from this period, he remarked that "the saddest experience in life is indeed the [sense of] disappointment that one acquires through people."[12] As his two decades in Kampen reached their final month, Bavinck was exhausted. For the time being, he had no more appetite for conflict. It was time to leave Kampen for good.

Reformed Ethics

Over the course of his years at the Theological School, Bavinck had taught a broad range of subjects. Although that range had narrowed somewhat in the 1890s, he had continued to teach ethics throughout his time there. By the time he moved to Amsterdam, however, his lengthy manuscript on Reformed ethics was still unfinished. One surviving set of notes from his classes on ethics in Kampen, by Jelle Michiels de Jong (1874–1927), was taken just as Bavinck's time there came to its abrupt end. De Jong's class notes finish in November 1902, with Bavinck midway through his ethics course. Notably, the handling of Christian ethics found in his lectures at that point differed from the class notes left by Bavinck's students earlier in the Kampen years, and also from the *Reformed Ethics* manuscript itself.[13] Clearly, by 1902, he had yet to settle on a final articulation of this area of his thought.

Within a month, de Jong had followed his professor to the Free University, where ethics had been taught since 1890 by the irenic Willem Geesink. Like Bavinck, Geesink was concerned about the "dearth in our time of specifically Reformed ethical studies"[14] and was also in the throes of preparing a major work in Reformed ethics. After joining Geesink as a colleague, it appears that Bavinck backed away from this particular writing task. Although he had been willing to press on with *Reformed Dogmatics* regardless of Kuyper's *Encyclopedia*, he would not do the same with *Reformed Ethics*. (Despite this, Geesink's *Reformed Ethics* was never actually completed in either man's lifetime: both of their ethics manuscripts were published posthumously.)[15]

In Amsterdam, Bavinck was to teach dogmatics. With that, the balance of his teaching and writing in the Kampen and Amsterdam periods took on a strangely inverted shape. At the Theological School, he had taught broadly but harbored the desire to focus his teaching and writing on dogmatics and ethics. At the Free University, he was now free to focus his teaching on dogmatics but began to write far more broadly.

Watergraafsmeer, London, and Amsterdam

In February 1903, the Bavincks finally moved to their new home: Linnaeus-parkweg 37, a newly built house in Watergraafsmeer, a town to the east of Amsterdam. (In a letter to Snouck Hurgronje, he explained that he "couldn't find a suitable house so quickly in Amsterdam itself.")[16] His initial impressions of life there were good. In the winter of that year, he would write, "It's going very well for us here. . . . Life is not as peaceful as in Kampen, but it is richer in diversity, and the intellectual circle is of higher standing."[17]

Shortly after his arrival in Watergraafsmeer, Herman and Johanna traveled together to London. In the year before, his old friend and colleague (and travel companion to North America) Douwe Klazes Wielenga had died. His son Douwe Klaas Wielenga (1880–1942) had recently moved to London to study at Livingstone College in preparation for missionary work in the

Dutch East Indies.[18] The Bavincks were keen to make the most of Wielenga Jr.'s presence there and had him lead them on a tour of the city's sights and sounds.[19] If this trip had been planned as a much-needed rest following the previous year's traumatic turn of events, Bavinck nonetheless quickly found himself pressed into service. While in London, he preached and administered the Lord's Supper in a Sailors' House (and noted in the lost dagboek his theological reservations about celebrating the sacrament there), preached in the Austin Friars Dutch Church, and lectured on "religion and science" to a largely Dutch audience in a Young Men's Christian Association building.[20] However this vacation began, it ended as a busman's holiday.

In Watergraafsmeer, a number of his new colleagues also became neighbors: Willem Geesink, Herman Kuyper, and Petrus Biesterveld—himself a native Amsterdammer—all lived nearby.[21] Despite this, and despite his positive earlier views on life in Watergraafsmeer, Bavinck quickly became unsettled there. Having spent two decades living a few minutes' walk from the Theological School, he soon perceived the consequences of the forty-five-minute commute into central Amsterdam, where he became that year's rector magnificus: a daily round trip of ninety minutes was not compatible with the level of productivity he had sustained for the previous twenty years.[22] To carry on writing, he would have to live far closer to the office. In 1904, then, they moved into the heart of the city, purchasing a house a short distance from the Free University. For the rest of his life, Bavinck lived at Singel 62, in the prestigious Grachtengordel. This house, originally dating to 1638 but rebuilt in a Neo-Renaissance style in the mid-1890s, was far more to his liking. There, the unsettling pangs of rootlessness he felt from time to time in Franeker, Kampen, and Watergraafsmeer quickly faded. The trajectory that had carried Jan and Herman from the periphery to the center had finally reached a more or less settled stop. In their case, the Seceder and the son of the Secession had come a long way in following the path from "separation to integration." Whatever they were, they were certainly no pariahs. And with that, Herman finally felt he belonged. In 1905, he wrote to Snouck Hurgronje,

> I really don't remember if I have already written to you from my new home here in Amsterdam. After our departure from Kampen, we had temporarily gone to Watergraafsmeer, because at that time we couldn't immediately find a suitable house. But we didn't like it there; it was about forty-five minutes removed from the Free University's building, and it was also a quiet, unconvivial neighborhood. After a lot of looking we found and bought a property in Amsterdam and took up residence there in September last year. It is a lovely little house, with a nice small garden, near Central Station and by the Free University's building,

and thus far, it has been terrific. But here it is an expensive house; the houses are very pricey and the taxes are high. One needs to have a fair bit [of money] to live in Amsterdam. But still, despite this, I don't waste so much time when [coming in and] giving lectures and don't live in such an isolated and lonely way. In general, I am happy that I am no longer in Kampen; it was nice there, but also very out-of-the-way and provincial.[23]

A New Long-Term Neighbor: The *Übermensch*

In the 1890s, Bavinck had believed that the secular social conditions of the day would soon give way to a new phase of Dutch history—a modern age in which the light of Christianity, refracted through a Calvinistic prism, would shine more beautifully than ever. For that reason, his work in those years had positioned him as a public apologist for Calvinism. That much seemed to be the need of the day because the Netherlands' future, like its past, was Calvinistic.

At some point in the close of his Kampen years or in the early days in Amsterdam, he revised that belief. It became clearer to him that for the most part, Dutch people found a secularized public domain—filled as it was with a cacophony of clashing truth claims—to be quite tolerable. In a book published in this period, *Christian Science* (1904), he noted that despite a cultural shift in which "many of the most excellent scientists are returning from atheism to theism,"[24] those dissatisfied scientists were not flocking toward orthodox Christianity in great numbers. If anything, the diverse range of broadly theistic viewpoints they assumed—among others, philosophical idealism, mysticism, theosophy, panpsychism, and teleologism—merely added to the disharmony.

Alongside this, while the particular species of scientifically focused atheism popular in the early 1890s (described by Bavinck as the "age of Renan") had lost much of its influence,[25] a new kind of atheism had come into fashion: that of the recently deceased German philosopher Friedrich Nietzsche (1844–1900).

Nietzsche's atheism was intended as a wholesale and radical departure from the theism it had rejected, and as such, it was unlike anything that had come before. If God was dead, Nietzsche had argued, all moral values should be revalued—and for that reason, atheists were under no obligation to carry over any of the moral trappings of theism. Therefore, his atheism was not intended to supersede a previous stage of Christianity's long history. Rather, it would shun Christianity entirely and create something utterly new in its place. Crucially to its appeal, Nietzschean thought decoupled atheism and nihilism by its focus on the *Übermensch*—a mighty, this-worldly human who prefers the concreteness of domination to the flighty pursuit of happiness. Nietzsche's was a purposeful atheism involving both subtraction *and* addition.

Among Nietzsche's Dutch sympathizers, led by the likes of Frederik van Eeden (1860–1932), this revaluation produced a general disinterest in Darwin's biological "survival of the fittest" (favoring domination to mere survival) and a particularly low view of Jesus's model of grace and servanthood.[26] (A noted Dutch literary figure in his day, van Eeden popularized the *Übermensch* in his fictional character Vico Muralto.)[27]

This new variety of atheism looked disdainfully on Bavinck *and* his theological adversaries, had no interest in the Netherlands' Christian past, and pointed to an unimaginable future wholly untethered from it. While Bavinck agreed with Nietzsche's assessment on the moral consequences of atheism,[28] the fact that some of his compatriots were willing to venture into Nietzsche's uncharted, dechristianized waters confounded his earlier expectations regarding Dutch cultural sensibilities. They were much less rooted in Calvinism than he had previously thought. In *Present Day Morality* (1902), Bavinck now recognized that "in his moral philosophy, Nietzsche has only given voice to what lived unconsciously in many hearts."[29]

Consequently, he found himself staring across this *Notgemeinschaft*—a society formed of necessity, in a state of emergency, rather than as a result of careful planning—at fellow citizens with whom he shared no theological or philosophical common ground, having to accept "a more or less permanent co-existence of different principles, principles that did not cross roads anymore."[30] His modern sparring partners would be around for the long haul and had been joined by an inscrutably foreign newcomer. The realization of this led Bavinck to look at his neighbors afresh: What threat did they pose to neo-Calvinism if this complex cohabitation were to remain for the foreseeable future?

Culture had changed. The "age of Renan" had given way to the "age of Nietzsche"—and with that, the theology of the day faced new questions, challenges, and needs. In their general relationship to Nietzschean atheism, discrete Dutch Christian traditions had something novel in common: Nietzsche's deathly shadow was cast upon Christians of every stripe and did not discriminate between Protestant and Catholic, orthodox and liberal, Kuyperian and Ethical, or modern and pietist. For that reason, Bavinck would soon argue that at the most basic level, "in reality, there are only two worldviews, the theistic and the atheistic."[31] In order to meet the needs of a new day, the focus of his public apologetics would have to change. While Bavinck did not set Calvinism and a more generic Christianity in tension—rather, he recognized their interdependence—it nonetheless became clear to him that the early twentieth century needed defenders of Christianity even more urgently than it did apostles for its idiosyncratic traditions.

In previous decades, Bavinck had not written a great deal on the notion of worldview: his contributions were limited to a short critique of the "contemporary worldview" in 1883[32] and a review of James Orr's *The Christian View of God and the World* in *De Vrije Kerk* in 1884.[33] If he were to meet the (new) needs of the day, the Amsterdam years would have to yield much more original material on the Christian worldview.

Gathering a Theistic Coalition

Harinck has argued that the emergence of this new species of atheism prompted two changes in Bavinck's outlook. On the one hand, because this atheism intentionally rejected both the roots and fruits of Christianity, it was a "part of modern culture he could not reach anymore."[34] In the 1870s–90s, Bavinck's conversations with Modern and Ethical theologians were facilitated by a high degree of mutual intelligibility: in such dialogue, Bavinck could call on common history, texts, concepts, and moral values and draw on primordial Christian instincts (particularly regarding the significance of the incarnation). For all of those reasons, Bavinck could recognize something of himself in his theological rivals. Despite their distance, Abraham Kuenen and Gunning Jr. were still close enough to him to serve as critical friends.

On the other hand, because he faced an uphill struggle in finding common ground with these new atheists, "he had to leave that part of modern culture to itself and concentrated instead on uniting Christians."[35] In these years, Bavinck would expend considerable effort in highlighting to his theological rivals that their historic opposition to Calvinist orthodoxy was fast becoming myopic: they were camped on the same side of the Valley of Elah and faced the same Goliath, and—in this moment, at least—they would stand or fall together.

The Struggle for Christian Education

In that light, Bavinck quickly set about publishing three substantial books, all of which appeared in 1904. In *Christian Worldview*, originally a rectorial address at the Free University, he argued that the modern age lacked a united world- and life-view. Instead, it gravitated toward extremes, privileging one aspect of reality—the heart, the head, the will, feeling, knowing, acting, the physical, the supranatural—at the expense of the others. Consequently, from Kant to Nietzsche and Marx, the modern age presented its inhabitants with a range of (ultimately) one-dimensional options—and for that reason, he argued, it failed to be intellectually or existentially satisfying. Bavinck argued for the Christian world- and life-view as an antidote, claiming that Christianity's explanatory power was capacious, rather than reductionistic, and could provide harmonious answers to a string of interconnected philosophical questions central to a satisfying human existence: Why is what exists that which exists? How can what exists be both constant and ever changing? And how do we know how to act well against that backdrop? (This piece of philosophical apologetics served as an early trial run for his later Stone Lectures in Princeton.)

In the same year, Bavinck published *Christian Science*—a book occasioned by a particular political issue. Since the late nineteenth century, Dutch politics had been caught up in the *schoolstrijd*—a national debate on whether the state should provide the same level of financial support to schools that taught on the basis of distinctive religious or worldview commitments as it provided to apparently "neutral" schools.[36]

Bavinck had been involved in debates on Christian education for many years. He had lectured on it while a pastor in Franeker[37] and while active within the Union for Reformed Higher Education during his time in Kampen, and he had enthusiastically cheered the development of new Christian schools while editor of *De Bazuin*.[38] By the time he arrived in Amsterdam, he was vice chairman of the Reformed School Union (Gereformeerd Schoolverband), a national organization dedicated to the promotion of Christian schooling.[39] Although he was a seasoned campaigner in the *schoolstrijd*, his inaugural lecture in Amsterdam—"Religion and Theology"—gave him a more central place in this national discussion. That lecture had tried to reconcile Mary and Martha, arguing, in essence, that there is no discord between personal Christian faith and the practice of theology in the academy. This claim provoked a response from the liberal Remonstrant theologian Herman Groenewegen (1862–1930) that thrust Bavinck, in turn, into the middle of a debate on the very academic legitimacy of the Free University.

In 1903, Groenewegen published an article that responded to "Religion and Theology" by arguing that theology could not be considered a science if its practitioners spoke as insiders within their theological traditions.[40] Religions, he claimed, should be studied on the basis of confessionally neutral, empirical observations—with Groenewegen believing that such a presuppositionless approach would objectively demonstrate Christianity as the superior religion, with modern liberal Christianity at its pinnacle. In his critique, Groenewegen also asked why the neo-Calvinists felt it necessary to circle their wagons at the Free University rather than pursue chairs at the state universities.[41] For those with ears to hear, the allegation implied by his question was clear: the Free University was a pseudo scientific echo-chamber, and its neo-Calvinist professors were too sectarian to be taken seriously in the realm of real science. If that were true, there was no question as to the outcome of the *schoolstrijd*: the state could not endorse such faux scholarship.

In *Christian Science*, Bavinck offered a response to the epistemological core of Groenewegen's criticism, arguing that all human knowledge is subjective and rests on a priori assumptions—and that, therefore, theology (practiced by Christian believers) is no less worthy of its place in the academy than any other avenue of inquiry.[42] This was an argument that Bavinck had been rehearsing for years—it was the same basic claim against the myth of neutrality that he had deployed against Snouck Hurgronje after his inaugural lecture in Kampen two decades before and had developed (at length) in the *Prolegomena* to his *Reformed Dogmatics*.

More novel, perhaps, was his reply to the aspersions that had been cast on the Free University as an institution. Central to Kuyper's vision of the Free University was the notion that the antithesis of faith and unbelief not only led to "two kinds of people" (the regenerate and the unregenerate) but also produced "two kinds of science."[43] To be sure, Kuyper also affirmed (and wrote extensively on) the notion of common grace—the belief that God also gives good gifts to unbelievers, including in the realm of scholarship.[44] In the Free University's earliest public raison d'être, however, common grace existed as a consequence of the antithesis. A Christian university was needed, the argument went, because unregenerate science is categorically not the same as regenerate science.

Bavinck wrote his *Christian Science* against that backdrop. Foregrounding his response to Groenewegen in the notion of common grace (rather than antithesis), Bavinck first argued that unbelievers should pay heed to the scholarship of Christians, then pointed out that Christians have always recognized the intellectual virtues of unbelievers. "Christians have never been so narrow-minded as to dismiss all scientific research advanced by unbelievers as false . . . because [Christians] believe that God, the same God, whom they confess as their Father in Christ, causes the sun to shine upon the evil and the good, and rain to fall on the righteous and the unrighteous."[45] In that year, he also released *Principles of Pedagogy* (178 pages), a book based on earlier lectures and promoted by Bavinck as an accompanying volume to *Christian Worldview*.[46] In this particular work, he tried to put flesh on the bare bones of a commitment to Christian education, arguing both that Christianity has its own account of human nature and that this distinct view of human nature has profound pedagogical consequences. Surveying the pedagogical trends of the day, he claimed that the optimistic view of the nature of the child found in Rousseau and the pessimistic equivalent aired by Tolstoy were equally imbalanced. By contrast, the Christian account of the nature of the child—created in the divine image but spoiled by sin, preserved by common grace in its capacity for knowledge, and made capable of great virtue when redeemed by saving grace—better explains the good and bad in children and enables their flourishing.

To that end, Bavinck argued that a life-affirming Christian school curriculum should educate children in religious knowledge, in skill in the use of language, and in the natural sciences, and that these should be taught in a way that engages the head, the heart, and the hands. In all of this, he mediated cutting-age developments in (primarily German) psychology and pedagogy to his Dutch audience.[47] It was a holistic, organicist vision of Christian education—and it resonated with many in his day. The twentieth century's leading Dutch Catholic pedagogue, Fr. Siegbertus Rombouts (1883–1962), reflected deeply on Bavinck's pedagogy, wrote extensively on it, and preferred for his own students to read Bavinck rather than the "monotone" neutral alternatives.[48] The liberal Remonstrant Rommert Casimir (1877–1957) and the anti-Kuyperian pedagogue Johannes Hermanus Gunning Willemszoon (1859–1951), the nephew of Bavinck's theological rival, both offered lofty public praise for Bavinck's *Principles of Pedagogy*.[49] Within Bavinck's own neo-Calvinist constituency, numerous commentaries on his pedagogy were published,[50] and primary schools were eventually named in his honor in towns across the country.[51]

Over the course of that century, Bavinck's distinctive articulation of educational theory along worldview lines played an important role in the Kuyperian side's eventual victory in the *schoolstrijd* in 1917—a result, in turn, that continues to shape the Dutch state's provision of equally funded education, from kindergarten to university, based on all kinds of worldviews, in the present day. Although Bavinck is perhaps best known to twenty-first-century audiences as a theologian, for much of the twentieth century, his international reputation was primarily as a leading pedagogue—a significance that has now largely been forgotten outside of the Netherlands.[52]

Moving on from *Unbelief and Revolution*

In 1904, Bavinck provided the foreword to a new edition of Guillaume Groen van Prinsterer's *Unbelief and Revolution*.[53] A text first published in 1847,

Unbelief and Revolution had portrayed the values of the French Revolution as a life system that systemically excluded the lordship of Christ from every sphere of human existence. Through that work, Groen van Prinsterer had inspired the tradition of antirevolutionary Dutch politics—a tradition that had been taken up and developed into the Antirevolutionary Party by Abraham Kuyper and that had defined neo-Calvinism's late nineteenth-century guise as the systematic response to a methodical foe. Just as the French Revolution's relentless de-Christianizing logic would progress predictably through society, the antirevolutionaries would fight it on every corner by asserting their own Calvinistic life system.

Although Bavinck had been receptive to those ideas in the 1870s–90s, by 1904 it was clear that he had become much more aware of their flaws. For all that he continued to appreciate Groen van Prinsterer, he was now critical of the predictability posited in *Unbelief and Revolution*—as though people will always live and act consistently with their (wrong or right) presuppositions. Groen van Prinsterer, Bavinck wrote, "believed not only in the laws of nature but also (without fatalism) in the laws of the moral world."[54] By this time, however, Bavinck believed differently and had accepted that life in a fallen creation was messier and more surprising. While he admitted that there is a certain force of logic in the events of nature and history, he also claimed that this force is always frustrated by "the gifts and needs of men" and "the ordinances of God."[55] Early in the Amsterdam years, he now perceived that sin was systemic rather than systematic and was seen in madness more than in method. As a counterpoint to this, the particular workings of God's grace were also harder to predict. The differences between Kuyper and Bavinck were increasingly evident: while one remained an idealist, the other was increasingly open as a realist.[56]

The Election of 1905: The Setting of the Neo-Calvinistic Sun?

These differences became more pronounced as Kuyper began to prepare for the 1905 national elections. Kuyper's first term in office had not been easy and had faced challenges from the outset. When extending his American *séjour* in 1898, Kuyper, at that time a sitting parliamentarian, had chosen to promote Calvinism abroad over attending the coronation of Queen Wilhelmina at home—a slight, Bratt claims, that she had not forgotten and that led her to harbor suspicions that Kuyper held republican sympathies.[57] Without the queen on his side, and working with a relatively inexperienced cabinet, Kuyper's premiership was caught up in the implementation of a complex system of healthcare provision set in motion by his Liberal Union predecessors and faced regular scrutiny regarding the sense in which a Christian political party could govern a country that recognized the separation of church and state. In the midst of this, his firm response to a railway workers' strike in 1903 had hardly helped his public image. Despite this, he expected to be reelected to another term as prime minister in 1905. In the run-up to that election, however, the political tactic he favored made plain that his cultural instincts were not well aligned with those of his younger colleague.

In his 1901 election campaign, Kuyper had sensed the mood of the time well, tying his political coalition to Christianity rather than Calvinism. For obvious reasons, this politics of "Christianity *beneath* theological differences" had also appealed to Bavinck. In 1904, however, the political terrain changed considerably. That election became the first in Dutch history to be centered on political personalities and sloganeering rather than parties and politics. On that front, Kuyper and his opponent Pieter Jelles Troelstra (1860–1930) were similarly adept. Meaningful nuance became impossible—a shift that produced, in effect, a return to a politics of antithesis.[58] Everything was for or against Kuyper. Political participation was forced into a package-deal choice between Christianity, which became tied to Kuyper's persona, and paganism for those not inclined to vote for him.

Since his election to the premiership, the Antirevolutionary Party had been trying to encourage Kuyper to give up his role as party chairman. It was only in the midst of his reelection campaign in 1904, though, that Kuyper announced his intention to stand down from that particular position, making plain that Bavinck was his preferred successor. Despite Bavinck's initial reservations, by late December he had agreed to proceed with the nomination. Kuyper set about promoting him among the party's members, who voted for him en masse at the party conference in Utrecht the following April.[59] Bavinck's speech at that conference tried to provide a constructive reply to criticisms of a Christian party governing a secular state, arguing that affirming the mutual relationship that exists between religion and politics should not be confused with a murkier mixing of the two. For that reason, he put forward, mixing religion and politics was no less objectionable to the Antirevolutionary Party than their enforced separation.[60] In that light, he argued that the Dutch public had nothing to fear from a Christian political party, but rather, that they should be concerned by the new alternatives: "Unbelief is a foreign import, and neutrality an invasive species" in the garden of Dutch culture.[61]

On this kind of rhetorical and theoretical ground, Bavinck spoke with confidence and clarity. When discussing the party's history and future, however, he clearly lacked self-assurance in the role he was about to assume: "We must be aware of the changes that are brought into our party by [Kuyper] in his resignation as chairman and installation as minister. There is no promise that we will be blessed with another leader after Groen and Kuyper who matches their talent and energy. But our party does not stand or fall with one person, because it lives upon principles that have stood the test of time. God can save through many or few, through great and small powers."[62] It was also clear to him that the stakes were high: an Antirevolutionary victory would be a watershed moment for the history of twentieth-century Dutch politics. Should the party lose, he argued, its political movement "would probably break up into smaller groups permanently."[63]

At this crucial point in Kuyper's political career, his campaign began to go badly. Dutch Christians were too diverse—theologically, and also in their views on his persona—to be herded into a single party and thus resisted this attempt to be gathered together in a "theistic coalition." Within the Antirevolutionary Party itself, it was soon apparent that Bavinck was not forceful enough to hold together the party's squabbling factions. His fears on the imminent fragmentation of the Antirevolutionary political bloc were quickly being realized, and he was ill equipped to stop it. Kuyper had lasted for twenty-six years as chairman. Bavinck's tenure would be over within two.

The 1905 elections were not good for Kuyper and the Antirevolutionary Party, which dropped nine seats and lost its parliamentary majority in the process. Gallingly for Kuyper, his own seat was lost to a progressive liberal candidate. Troelstra's slogan, "Get rid of Kuyper!" ("*Weg met Kuyper!*"), had been effective. Following his defeat, Kuyper retreated, leaving on an extended tour of the Mediterranean and the Arab world—the period in which he penned a great deal of the remarkable devotional work *To Be Near unto God*[64] and that provided the basis for his mammoth (1,075-page) travelogue and commentary on Islam, *Around the Old-World Sea*.[65]

Working in Kuyper's Absence

That May, Bavinck received a letter from Derk Rumpff (1878–1944), a student in Kampen, requesting a meeting with him on the basis of "a firm belief that you are aware of a certain movement among the Kampen students and that you sympathize with it."[66] Although three years had now passed since Bavinck's departure from the Theological School—along with Biesterveld and a large number of its students—there were still students there who were considering moving to the Free University. Following his correspondence with Bavinck over the coming months, Rumpff would be one of a number of Kampen students who relocated to Amsterdam.

Meanwhile, as Kuyper traveled far and wide, Bavinck struggled on in his ill-suited leadership of the Antirevolutionary Party. As was the case in much of northern Europe, public debate on universal voting rights became steadily more important in the Netherlands in the early 1900s, with a particular focus on female enfranchisement. Because of the onset of industrialization, young working-class women were now entering a centralized workforce and delaying both marriage and childbirth. As a consequence, some women—although by no means all—were increasingly active in Dutch society as independent citizens rather than participating as wives or daughters. In that context, although most Dutch women still opposed individual voting rights for all, the Free Women's Association (Vrije Vrouwen Vereeniging) and the Union for Women's Enfranchisement (Vereeniging voor Vrouwenkiesrecht) were active in promoting mass enfranchisement to all individual adults.

That development within mass democracy caused no shortage of problems for the Antirevolutionary Party. Ten years before, in the context of the Kuyper-Lohman conflict, Kuyper had supported a form of mass democracy centered on families rather than individuals. In that system of *huismanskiesrecht* (houseman's enfranchisement), each family—as a unit sharing a world- and life-view—was democratically empowered in the vote granted to its (male) head. In 1895, Kuyper saw this form of mass democracy as a happy union of Calvinism and modern culture, insofar as it empowered ordinary people without undermining the organic unity of the family unit. By contrast, he saw individual enfranchisement as reducing the family to an association of arbitrarily connected individuals, with no expectation that they will function together toward a common goal. A society that enfranchised an electorate of individuals, he believed, was one in which the family was holed below the waterline. (And it is worth noting that Kuyper's proposal won considerable support across Dutch society.)

By 1906, in Kuyper's ongoing absence, a range of different opinions on individual enfranchisement had become clear within the party. Some found Kuyper's "houseman's enfranchisement" to be in conflict with Groen van Prinsterer's writings, while others pondered why extending the vote to individuals was necessarily in conflict with antirevolutionary principles.[67] Bavinck's own view was that Kuyper's position in 1895 had been consistent with a Reformed worldview and had a "pedagogical value" in its own time but that it was no longer readily applicable.[68] Kuyper, however, was not present to respond—either to restate his ongoing support for his earlier position or to provide some new steer.

In these discussions, Chairman Bavinck spoke as one voice among many. His natural disposition was to provide nuance in furthering a conversation rather than to dominate it as leader. And this disposition made him poorly suited to this kind of political leadership: in 1954, one hundred years after the birth of her father, Hannie (then aged sixty) took part in a radio interview in which she was asked to describe her father in relation to his most famous colleague. "Kuyper," she claimed, "wanted to rule, my father wanted to serve."[69] Bavinck had none of Kuyper's chutzpah and floundered in this kind of political role.

Tellingly, when Kuyper returned in the summer of 1906, he immediately positioned himself at the center of this debate—remaining firmly committed to his earlier view—and took the party chairmanship back from Bavinck in 1907. Under his renewed leadership, the party continued to oppose universal individual voting rights, despite the presence of many doubters—the now-former chairman included—in their midst. This brief foray into party political leadership had been difficult and unsuccessful. Later, Bavinck would describe it to Snouck Hurgronje in fairly negative terms: "A demoralizing influence often reaches many from [politics]. . . . As far as I was involved, I only took it on because of a sense of responsibility, not because of an inclination or desire."[70]

The Conclusions of Utrecht 1905

In these early Amsterdam years, Bavinck and Kuyper had faced intensity on every side, with 1905 being particularly demanding: Bavinck stated it mildly when telling Snouck Hurgronje, "Time is flying by, life here is busier than in Kampen."[71] As well as that year's disastrous political outcome, he was heavily involved in a series of theological disputes stemming from older differences between the Seceders and Dolerenden that came to a head at that year's synod, held in Utrecht.

The denomination formed in the union of 1892 was not theologically univocal: a range of theological differences had long since been evident on issues like the logical ordering of God's decrees (supralapsarianism versus infralapsarianism), the question of whether the elect are justified from all eternity, the nature of God's work of regeneration as either immediate or mediated by means, and the relationship of infant baptism to the assumed regeneration of the child.[72] Within the scope of these debates, Lucas Lindeboom had mounted a sustained claim that Kuyper was advancing theological views that contradicted the denomination's confessional standards. Bavinck had already engaged with these particular debates in a series of articles in *De Bazuin* between 1901 and 1902, which had then been published in book format as *Calling and Regeneration* in 1903.[73] There, Bavinck tried to mediate between Kuyper and his critics, demonstrating that Kuyper's views could be accommodated within the denomination, even by those who did not share them—a group in which Bavinck carefully located himself. His arguments proved influential: the Synod of Utrecht published a series of doctrinal conclusions affirming a Bavinckian reading of Kuyper's theological eccentricities.[74] In contrast to the image of Bavinck as "Dr. Kuyper's loyal and learned henchman" popularized in the English-speaking world at that time, the reality was somewhat different: in their mature theological states, Bavinck's own thought had come to function as a discreet (but important) corrective of Kuyper's.[75] Clearly, while Bavinck was willing to critique Kuyper's theology, it was also invaluable to him. Part of his calling as a theologian, it seems, was to serve as the one who took it upon himself to work Kuyper's insights into a more carefully formed end result. (In that light, the deductive Kuyper and the inductive Bavinck began to look increasingly like the pairing of theological goldminer and goldsmith memorably depicted in the former's *Encyclopedia*.)[76]

In the background to this public theological controversy, of course, his teaching duties at the Free University went on as normal. He continued to hope that the remainder of the Theological School's faculty and students would join him in Amsterdam, writing to Snouck Hurgronje that this would mean "an end would come to petty contests and divisions in our Reformed churches."[77] To his disappointment, no such movement was forthcoming.

Women at the Free University

Bavinck's lecture at the opening of the 1905 academic year, later published as *Learnedness and Science*, left his audience in no doubt that the "age of Nietzsche" had arrived.

> If God falls, everything falls—truth, science and art, nature and history, the state, society, and the family. If there is no God, there is also no idea, no more thought in which things rest and by which they are knowable. . . . Everything that we receive from the past is old and outmoded, not only religion and Christianity but also morality and art, all the wisdom and civilization of antiquity. Everything must be reformulated on the basis of modern culture: school and science, marriage and the family, state and society, religion and morality. There is no shortage of reformers [in our day].[78]

The challenge of the day was considerable. In this new age, he argued, the Free University's distinct calling was to be a *conservatorium* of all the good bequeathed to modern culture through its Christian past; a *laboratorium* in which to test claims of truth, goodness, and beauty; and an *observatorium* from which to study the past and present and to look to the future. In Bavinck's estimations, though, the university was still some way from rising to that challenge. "My wish would be that it might become more and more a center of real scientific life and work, research and thought. It must be a union for men, and later also perhaps women, animated by one spirit, who distinguish themselves by firmness of principle, breadth of vision, and belief in the future."[79] Culture was changing in more ways than one. This particular lecture was a call for all hands on deck—including those of Christian women—in the university's fight against Nietzsche's frightening terra incognita.

Bavinck's public openness to the prospect of women coming to the Free University as students was notable. Since its inception, the Free University had allowed Reformed women to attend lectures, but it did not permit them to register as students—this being an extension of the antirevolutionary view that society's most basic building block was the (male-led) family rather than the individual. In 1905, Bavinck was not strongly opposed to the idea of female students coming to the Free University. Rather, he seems to have become fairly ambivalent on this point, viewing the shift to a "society of individuals" as having already passed the point of no return. Although he believed that this change had been occasioned by the French Revolution, he thought it was neither an obvious good worthy of uncritical celebration nor an evil to be opposed in principle. It was what it was, and nothing more.

In the same year, Biesterveld—the 1905 rector magnificus—admitted the Free University's first female student, Segrina 't Hooft, who had registered to study law. The decision to admit her was referred to the university's senate, whose members then voted, seven to two, in support of Biesterveld's decision.[80] Change was afoot on the Keizersgracht.

On this particular issue, while the newcomers Bavinck and Biesterveld were certainly not radical egalitarians or self-professed feminists, their ambivalence set them in tension with Abraham Kuyper and Willem Geesink. Indeed, Geesink had spoken at the Union for Reformed Higher Education in 1898 of his "heartfelt wish that the Free University might always be protected from the *defeminizing* of the woman and may never bear the shame of the symptoms of madness of the woman who thinks she has the intellect of a man."[81] In 1905, Bavinck and Biesterveld's collective action had challenged that position, and in the following year it provoked a reply from Herman Kuyper. At a conference chaired by Bavinck, Herman Kuyper attempted to nuance his father's position by arguing that while the doctrine of creation gave womankind a general purpose—namely, to be wives and mothers—there were nonetheless some exceptionally gifted women for whom these roles were inappropriate.[82] It was hardly a ringing endorsement of 't Hooft's presence at the Free University, where no other women would enroll until 1917—following which their numbers would steadily increase. (Remarkably, the second woman to be awarded a doctorate there, in 1937, was Fenna Lindeboom—a granddaughter of Lucas Lindeboom.)[83]

Although Bavinck's views on the changing role of women in society were more or less irresolute in his early years in Amsterdam, this issue would dominate his writing schedule in the coming years—particularly toward the close of his life, as he surveyed the societal consequences of the Great War. Before then, though, in 1905, he assumed distinct critical postures toward *both* Kuyper's insistence on a "society of families" *and* the French Revolution's individualistic alternative. He certainly sympathized with the Kuyperian bulwark now being overrun by the daughters of that revolution, but he did not see it as a hill on which to die. Rather, he regarded himself as a powerless onlooker as history took its course.

Trusting in, and Doubting, Scripture

Although Bavinck faced the Nietzschean challenge gallantly as a theologian in the public eye, one private admission of doubt in that year was striking. His correspondence with Snouck Hurgronje had returned to the same issue that divided them in their discussions of his inaugural lecture in Kampen in 1883 and that remained a point of contention: the authority of the Bible.

Snouck Hurgronje still held to the view that in Bavinck's thinking, Scripture was indulged with an arbitrary and unwarranted power, and he continued to challenge his friend on this point. Two decades before, Bavinck had replied by pointing out that the natural scientist believes a priori that nature exists—just as the Christian theologian proceeds a priori from the belief that God has spoken in Scripture. In 1883, Bavinck had presented his friend as the one whose view was deeply problematic: it was Snouck Hurgronje, rather than Bavinck, who naïvely claimed he was a veritable tabula rasa. Now, in 1905, Bavinck admitted the difficulties with his own view, all the while remaining committed to it.

> For my part I agree that the presupposition on which my life-view is based—namely, the truth of Holy Scripture—contains a difficult problem. I can only

say this about it: to the extent that I live longer and more deeply, I notice that I cannot detach myself from the authority of the Scriptures, in more or less the same way that I cannot uproot myself from the authority of the laws of thinking and of morality. Sometimes I am inclined to break away from it, but when I take a good look at myself, [I see that this inclination] goes together with the evil in my human nature, and then there is something in it that is not good and that cannot exist before God. And to the contrary, to the extent that I am, let me say, in a more pious frame of mind and am going through better times, I feel completely ready and inclined to accept and submit to the Bible, and I have peace in my heart. That is quite mystical, but it seems to me that every world- and life-view wrestles with such an experience of the soul that precedes conscious thinking and acting.[84]

It had been an exhausting year for Bavinck and Kuyper. As 1905 drew to a close, it was little wonder that Kuyper procured doctor's orders requiring a long break elsewhere. (That year, his son, the theosophist Jan Frederik [1866–1933], observing that his father had reached the pinnacle of Dutch politics, urged him, "Let it go, dear father.")[85] There was no such extended respite for Bavinck. Other than a short holiday in nearby Soestdijk with his family and father, he carried on in his work at the Free University, in his writing projects, and—until Kuyper resumed the party leadership in 1907—in his unenjoyable political role.[86]

A Renaissance Man at Work

From his youth onward, Bavinck had cherished a love for poetry: we recall his own grandiose efforts at romantic poetry for Amelia in his teenage years and the time spent reading Gerok and da Costa with Johanna. By 1906, though, he had moved to writing about, rather than producing, poetry. In that year, he published the book *Bilderdijk as Thinker and Poet*—a substantial (221 pages) work on the early nineteenth-century Calvinist poet Willem Bilderdijk, occasioned by the one hundred and fiftieth anniversary of his birth.[87]

For Bavinck and Kuyper, Bilderdijk epitomized the organically connected, holistic world- and life-view also prized by the neo-Calvinist movement, and he was beloved by both for that reason. In Bavinck's eyes, he was no less than Rembrandt's poetic counterpart: "Above all, in both, a longing for light and harmony was born from the hardships of life. They looked upward for the light that fell in golden beams into the somber depths of earthly existence. They received it first in the revelation of God in his Word; each in his own way, Rembrandt and Bilderdijk were both students of the Bible and translators of impressions and thoughts from Scripture."[88] Having previously written critically acclaimed works in dogmatics, psychology, and pedagogy, Bavinck had now turned his hand to biography and literary analysis. Once again, his reputation as a renaissance man had been further established: the *Algemeen Handelsblad*'s recently appointed chief cultural critic, the Jewish novelist Israël Querido (1872–1932),[89] reviewed *Bilderdijk as Thinker and Poet*, comparing his dislike of a series of other works on Bilderdijk with Bavinck's "important book."

> Dr. Bavinck has provided more than a one-sided or dull biography of Bilderdijk, the man, poet, and thinker. Therefore, I can recommend this book with enthusiasm. He presents us with Bilderdijk in the family, the state, and society, in his view of history, his personality, his view of nature, his manner of thinking on religion, morality, and law. And although I differ so very much from the opinions, considerations, and especially declarations of Bilderdijk's intellectual life [as presented] by Bavinck, he has produced what is in many ways an important and lucid book on this giant.[90]

To receive this praise from one of the nation's most celebrated non-Christian literary figures was no small feat. Bavinck's star was continuing to rise. (In the same year, awkwardly, Kuyper published a book on Bilderdijk that then became embroiled in a newspaper spat—also in the *Algemeen Handelsblad*—on the question of whether unbelievers could produce poetry worthy of that name.[91] Although Kuyper affirmed that they could, on the grounds of common grace, it was certainly the case that his earlier penchant for antithesis had come back to haunt him.)[92]

Influence beyond the Free University

In addition to his contact with the likes of Derk Rumpff—a student in Kampen who intended to move to Amsterdam—Bavinck also remained in contact with students there who had no plans to leave. In 1906, for example, he wrote on behalf of his father and his wife to Tjeerd Hoekstra and Fenna Lucasina Lindeboom—the daughter of his former colleague—in advance of their wedding. A future faculty member at the Theological School at Kampen, Hoekstra had scholarly interests in both theology and philosophy. In the midst of his congratulations, Bavinck noted his own joy at seeing Hoekstra's academic interests develop and encouraged him to "make the name of the Lord great in the field of science."[93] (Bavinck continued to correspond with Hoekstra in the years that would follow, with their last exchange coming in 1918.)

As the "age of Nietzsche" continued to unfold, the extent of Bavinck's influence on Dutch intellectual life became steadily more evident: in December 1906, one of his former students at the Theological School, Tjitze de Boer (1866–1942), was appointed professor of philosophy at the University of Amsterdam. At the close of de Boer's studies in Kampen, Bavinck had recommended that he move on to a doctorate in Semitic languages at the University of Bonn. De Boer, however, moved to Strasbourg, where he completed a doctorate in Islamic philosophy.[94] Although de Boer's own glittering career would see his intellectual contributions focus fairly evenly between a range of Islamic and European philosophies,[95] in 1906 his gaze was firmly focused on Friedrich Nietzsche. In an inaugural lecture later published as *Nietzsche and Science*,[96] de Boer interacted with Nietzsche in a way that echoed his former teacher's example. Having presented a nuanced account of Nietzsche's works and biography, de Boer also tempered his criticism of him with questions on how he might be read profitably. His conclusion, above all, was both empathetic and incisive: Nietzsche's lot in life, he argued, was that of an Icarus who soared upward until the godless sun to which he ascended became his undoing.[97]

At the close of his lecture, the new professor turned to one particular member of the audience in a show of thanks: "Before all others, [I thank] you, Prof. Bavinck, formerly of Kampen, and now of this city, who awoke in me the love of philosophy."[98] At both the Free University and the University of Amsterdam, the early reception of Nietzschean thought was inextricably linked to Herman Bavinck.

Conscious that a profound cultural shift was unfolding around him, Bavinck spent much of these early Amsterdam years revising his *Reformed Dogmatics*. An updated version of his first volume, more expansive and more precisely formulated—and taking into account both the responses to his work from the Ethical theologians and developments in European intellectual life in the decade since it had first appeared—was released late in 1906.[99]

The revision of all four volumes would occupy him until 1911 and formed the backdrop to his ongoing efforts to gather a theistic coalition. Indeed, to his mind, these two tasks were intimately linked. In an essay titled "The Essence of Christianity," published in the Free University's 1906 student almanac,[100] he argued that the question of the essence of Christianity stood paramount among the challenges of the day and that striving for the true essence of the faith was itself "the point of a complete dogmatics and the whole history of Christianity, of which dogma is, after all, but a part."[101] Although this essay had been written for a neo-Calvinist audience, it was a significant step forward in a bold new effort: Bavinck was now balancing an increasingly specific neo-Calvinism in the revised *Reformed Dogmatics* and a generalized notion of Christianity in the public domain. (As has been noted by Bruce Pass, this particular balancing act closely resembled C. S. Lewis's articulation of "mere Christianity" later in the same century.)[102]

At this point, Bavinck was approaching the peak of his powers. At the beginning of 1906, he had accepted an invitation from Princeton Theological Seminary to give the 1908 Stone Lectures.[103] Later in the same year, he was appointed as a member of the literary branch of the Royal Academy of Science (Koninklijke Akademie van Wetenschappen). "*9 April . . . On this day I was elected as a member of the Roy. Academy of Sci., with 28 of the 45 votes. Boer, Six, and Naber were also elected.*"[104] Bavinck had been elected alongside his former student Tjitze de Boer, now of the University of Amsterdam; the art historian Jan Six (1857–1926), whose eponymous ancestor had been immortalized in a famous seventeenth-century portrait by Rembrandt; and the jurist Jean Charles Naber (1858–1950), one of the last Dutch academics to teach and publish predominantly in Latin. Clearly, it was not lost on Bavinck that he was keeping illustrious company. (One familiar face, Snouck Hurgronje, was already a member of said branch.)[105]

In the midst of this growing public acclaim, of course, Bavinck was not without his critics. Shortly before the new edition of his *Prolegomena* was published, his *Dogmatics* was the subject of a lecture—entitled "On the Pagan Character of Contemporary Orthodoxy"—by the Leiden professor Bernardus Eerdmans (1868–1948) at the Modern Theologians' Assembly (Vergadering van Moderne Theologen) in 1905.[106] There, Eerdmans had attacked Bavinck's claim to have produced a dogmatics that was both orthodox *and* modern. Whatever orthodoxy remained in the *Reformed Dogmatics*, he argued, was superficial: in its substance, rather, Bavinck's work was a secularized mixture of psychology, antisupernaturalism, and higher criticism. Having produced a theology in which "a miracle is not actually a miracle," he put forward, Bavinck should own up to the impossibility of having a foot in both camps. It was time for him to admit defeat, Eerdmans claimed: neo-Calvinism had failed to usurp the tradition of Scholten and Kuenen.

Somewhat predictably, Eerdmans's lecture received a savage response in *De Heraut*, which portrayed him as a poor exponent of a once great tradition: "Prof. Eerdmans seems to know nothing of the earlier or the new *Reformed Dogmatics*. He speaks here as a blind man on colors. Kuenen and Scholten would never have expressed themselves so carelessly. But the generation of imitators seems to have a different approach to polemics. It is sad to see this decline."[107] Bavinck's own considered response would not come for some years and eventually appeared as *Modernism and Orthodoxy*—a publication that followed the completed revision of the final volume of the *Reformed Dogmatics* in 1911.[108] Before then, his two-pronged thrust into the future—further refining his own neo-Calvinist theology, on the one hand, while shoring up a broad Christian coalition, on the other—kept him fully occupied. For the time being, Eerdmans could wait. Bavinck was far more concerned with his impending return to North America, writing in the lost dagboek that while Johanna and Hannie had returned to Vlaardingen during the Christmas of 1907, he *"stayed at home to write [his] lectures for America."*[109] (In order to prepare for these lectures, Bavinck was also granted a one-year preaching sabbatical from the Amsterdam-based congregations of his denomination, where members of the Free University's theological faculty were otherwise expected to preach once per month.)[110]

"We Are . . . Cosmopolitan in Outlook"

The Reformed Churches in the Netherlands' general synod in 1908 heard speeches from two representatives of British Reformed denominations—Rev. Robert Morton (1847–1932) of the Original Secession Church in Scotland and Rev. Dr. Abraham de Vlieger (1868–1909), a Dutchman who pastored an English Presbyterian congregation in Chorton-cum-Hardy. In describing the circumstances surrounding the Reformed faith on their side of the North Sea, it seems both were enthusiastic about the development of neo-Calvinism in the Netherlands. Morton was familiar with Kuyper's *Encyclopedia*, part of which had already been translated into English. De Vlieger, though, as a Dutchman, had also read Bavinck's *Reformed Dogmatics*, and he appealed to the synod to make that work available to anglophones: "Works like Dr. Bavinck's *Dogmatics*," he argued, "need to be more widely known."[111] Called upon to respond in English, Bavinck admitted that his denomination recognized itself to be numerically small, then continued:

> We are also cosmopolitan in outlook and *very much value* the connection with our brothers [abroad]. The crisis that we are experiencing is moving in a downward direction. The foundations of truth are being given up on by many. Therefore, keep your guard, stand fast. As well as this, there are also good reasons for us to be happy at your visit. The conviction that materialism has disappointed is widespread; religion is in demand. The revivals thus have a certain value, for which we have to rejoice with you. Then there is the revival

of the social life, which we have to take part in powerfully. Finally, there is the powerful recovery of the practice of Foreign Missions. Along this line, we have to show more and more the truth of Christianity. In this, we can learn more from you than you from us.[112]

Returning to America

A few months after this, it was time for Bavinck, the self-professed cosmopolitan Calvinist, to return to America. A great deal had changed since Bavinck's first voyage across the Atlantic. He had swapped the Theological School for the Free University and was now a father. He had published (and begun to revise) the *Reformed Dogmatics*—to say nothing of his other achievements and accolades—and had moved into (and promptly out of) leadership roles in journalism and party politics. The world had also changed around him. The "age of Renan" had gone, and the "age of Nietzsche" had arrived—with all that this now meant for Bavinck's task as a modern Calvinist. Between his trip to the Presbyterian Council in Toronto in 1892—which he undertook, as has been noted, as something of an emissary for Calvinism—and his impending return in 1908, of course, was Kuyper's own American adventure, which had also been used for the public promotion of Calvinism. An article in *De Heraut* during Bavinck's second journey to North America certainly signaled the expectation that Bavinck's Stone Lectures would be a further boon for neo-Calvinism's prospects there. "Prof. Bavinck's journey to America, at the invitation of Princeton University [i.e., Princeton Theological Seminary] makes the bonds between America and our school [i.e., the Free University] even closer and shall certainly produce a good result for the application of Reformed principles in mighty and influential America."[113] Bavinck's second journey, however, would not quite follow suit. He had already "broken a lance" for Calvinism on American soil and concluded that America would not likely be the locus of a neo-Calvinistic revival. This time around, he intended to make a case for Christianity. He wanted to address unbelievers, rather than merely the Reformed.

Herman and Johanna set sail on *The Rotterdam* on August 28, 1908, leaving the now fourteen-year-old Hannie with her grandparents. Their departure was itself a notable enough event to be covered by *De Telegraaf*, which recounted a gathering of family and friends coming to the ship at 10 p.m. to wish them well, before the boat departed at 2:30 a.m. "Despite his old age (82 years)," the article noted, "Rev. J. Bavinck was present at their departure."[114] Johanna's father and brothers sailed ahead of *The Rotterdam* in their own ship until it reached Boulogne-sur-Mer. It was a grand send-off.

Their journey lasted almost two weeks. On their last day at sea, Herman wrote, "*On this ocean crossing we have experienced everything: rain, wind, storm, beautiful weather, fog, dark clouds, thunder, porpoises, the northern lights.*"[115] On September 7, they reached New York City, "*tired and despondent.*" In contrast to his arrival in North America in 1892, when he was overwhelmed by the grandeur of the Canadian landscape, their first impressions of an intensely pressured city were less relaxing: "*Enormous bustle (hurry)[;] . . . no time to repose. No place for sick people or the needy. The city is based on strong nerves. Over-the-top, screaming advertisements. The howling . . . is tiring; it wears you down.*"[116] While in New York, he also had to find a publisher to take on the English edition of his Stone Lectures. Hepp's biography recounts a letter from Johanna to her parents commenting, "How this works here is odd, because there is no mention of agreeing to a contract. Herman has to give the whole [manuscript] over in confidence, and will have to see whether anything is left in place. And then friends have to go out of their way to correct it."[117] During this part of the journey, Bavinck agreed to publish his lectures with Longmans, Green and Company. The eventual English edition, however, would not appear until 1909: although these were Bavinck's lectures, the editorial and translation process was taken over by Geerhardus Vos, B. B. Warfield, Nicholas Steffens, and Henry Dosker.[118] Bavinck was not used to his work being left in the hands of others.

From New York, Herman and Johanna traveled northwest, visiting Niagara Falls, Detroit, Grand Rapids, and Holland. By this time, however, both Geerhardus Vos and Henry Dosker had left Michigan—Vos was now in Princeton, and Dosker in Louisville. From Michigan the Bavincks traveled to Illinois, visiting Chicago before moving on to Louisville, Kentucky, where Johanna finally met Henry Dosker in person. In a letter to Hannie, Johanna wrote, "Mr. [Dosker] is a funny, convivial man who never seems to run out of humour." That he and her husband were hardly the doppelgängers Dosker had imagined was fairly obvious to Johanna: Dosker, she told Hannie, was "a very different kind of professor from Father."[119]

From Louisville, they made their way to Washington, DC, where they had a short audience with President Theodore Roosevelt—a meeting also recorded in Roosevelt's diary.[120] While this meeting certainly bespeaks Bavinck's international standing, it does not appear that their conversation was eventful. Roosevelt did not strike Bavinck as a particularly refined or remarkable man.[121]

From there, they continued on toward Princeton, where Bavinck was finally reunited with Geerhardus Vos. The time to deliver the Stone Lectures, which he had been busy preparing for well over a year, had arrived. In this phase of life, Bavinck's writing tried to hold his twofold aim—to further his own tradition while narrating a theistic coalition into existence—in equipoise. For every book on neo-Calvinism, it seems, a *Mere Christianity* also needed to be issued. The distinct focus of his Stone Lectures would be the latter: in them, the arguments rehearsed earlier in the likes of *Christian Worldview* (1904) were developed into the *Philosophy of Revelation*, a series of lectures on the reasonableness of belief in divine revelation. Without belief in revelation, he argued, it is impossible to have concepts of philosophy, nature, history, culture, or the future—for which reason, no atheist truly lives by his creed. Rather, in maintaining concepts like nature, history, or culture, the atheist constantly relies on theism.[122]

In alleging the practical impossibility of thoroughgoing atheism, Bavinck had followed his former student Tjitze de Boer, who had portrayed Nietzschean atheism in Icarus-like terms: its wings might well carry their wearer off Crete, but only until the godless wax melts and the free spirit crashes somewhere in the Aegean Sea. At Princeton, Bavinck had thrown down the gauntlet to this new breed of atheism. Indeed, Gordon Graham has noted memorably that although there are "just four or five express references to Nietzsche" in *Philosophy of Revelation*, "his spirit hovers over the whole text."[123]

When Bavinck had read Kuyper's 1898 Stone Lectures, he had criticized their level as being unreachably high for an American audience. A decade on, when giving the same lecture series, it seems that he also struggled to capture the Princeton crowd's attention. Johanna reflected Herman's frustrations when she wrote to her family that Americans "never tire of hearing sermons, but when it comes to scientific lectures, you cannot get an audience. Even though you do your best to be simple and clear, they are afraid of learnedness and having to make an effort to think about something."[124]

By this point in his life, the high ideals of "travel as an art that one must learn, preferring observation to judgment," espoused in his 1892 journey, were long gone: aged fifty-four, Bavinck was more socially conservative than he had been at thirty-eight. The otherness of America was now a challenge and an annoyance more than an exotic delight. The problems of racial hatred were overwhelming and struck him as almost impossible to resolve. Because of the strict separation of church and state, he now judged the American public-school system to be a training ground of unbelief. He was shocked that workers had few rights and that many older Americans retired without pensions. Although his short American autobiographical sketch publicly stated that he and Johanna were "particularly taken with America, its land and people," his private opinion was quite different. For the most part, he now found Americans to be superficial, ignorant, materialistic, and self-interested.

The behavior of American youngsters, above all, piqued his frustration: "*They act strangely, coming and going without greetings. The children are rude, unmannerly, for example, young men are not introduced, they walk out the door without a parting greeting. Girls do not offer greetings, ridicule each other, cross their legs in company, lean forward, etc. very free, independent, but coarsely uncivilized, careless.*"[125] This was, of course, the year in which he published *The Christian Family*.[126] Although that work was concerned with the notion of the family as part of a Christian worldview and is not a guide to etiquette, Herman clearly cared a great deal for mannerliness in the home. He was now middle aged, the father of one child—who was herself becoming a young woman—and a resident of a changing city.

A Sad Return: The Death of Petrus Biesterveld

Herman and Johanna arrived back in Rotterdam on December 11, 1908. Shortly before their departure from New York, they received word that Petrus Biesterveld was gravely ill. Bavinck wrote to Snouck Hurgronje, "[On] Saturday, Dec. 12, I visited him briefly and spoke a few words with him, not thinking that it would happen so quickly. But on Monday, Dec. 14, he had already died, at the age of fifty-four years."[127]

In Biesterveld's passing, Bavinck had lost a friend and ally. They had worked closely since 1894, when Biesterveld's arrival at the Theological School played an important role in Bavinck's decision to stay there (for the time being). More recently still, in their move to the Free University, their fates had become entwined. And between those moments of arrival and departure, of course, the Bavincks and Biestervelds had shared in joys and sorrows. Johan had first coughed up blood in the Biesterveld home. Herman and Johanna had holidayed together with Petrus and Martha in the midst of stressful days at the Theological School. This was a major loss.

Tales of a Racist Disaster: A Warning to Would-Be Émigrés

As he had done following his previous journey to America, after returning home, Bavinck held public lectures on his impressions of his journey.[128] The report of one such "Impressions of America" talk, given to a Christian youth organization in Rotterdam, was covered in the *Rotterdamsch Nieuwsblad*. In an auditorium so full that listeners were also seated on the stage around the speaker, Bavinck went through the usual motions, discussing the majesty of the ocean and Niagara Falls and the historic influence of the Dutch on American society before speaking in apocalyptic tones of the unfolding disaster that was racialized hatred in America. In the lost dagboek, he had recorded being told by "a Southerner" that "negroes are not humans. Canaan went to Lod and took a wife. That wife was an ape."[129] (Bavinck disagreed, profoundly.)[130] In handwritten notes for this lecture series, he had observed, "Whites accuse negroes of all sorts of bad qualities (of stealing chickens . . . [;] of sensuality, lynching; alcoholism, laziness). I don't know whether whites are any better, with their prostitution and alcohol and mammonism [i.e., love of money]."[131] "Yes, in the future," the *Rotterdamsch Nieuwsblad* reported, "there truly lurks a danger, the speaker said, and in the future a struggle will doubtless be fought between black and white, a heated struggle, fanned into flame by the strong antipathy on both sides."[132]

In his own study notes from this journey, it is clear that Bavinck made a considerable effort to understand race relations in America: these notes cover a lecture by Booker T. Washington (1856–1915), the progress of African Americans in the world of business, rising literacy rates among African Americans, and their place in projected demographic trends. While this particular document is now in poor condition and is illegible in parts, one author's name remains clearly visible on the page: that of the civil rights activist W. E. B. Du Bois (1868–1963), whose work Bavinck had referenced.[133]

In both his "Impressions of America" lectures and the lost dagboek, Bavinck discussed one "solution" to the race issue presented to him by white Americans, the back-to-Africa idea, as unworkable. In the lost dagboek, he also recorded finding the way forward offered in Harriet Beecher Stowe's *Uncle Tom's Cabin* to be simplistic, in view of the complex problems at hand.[134] In the newspaper report of another "Impressions of America" lecture, this time held in Assen, he was recorded saying this division could only be overcome by "the way of religion."[135] Even then, though, he was struck by the segregated reality of American church attendance. Unless it also underwent a profound transformation, the American church could not offer a solution to the problem of race.

All in all, his impressions were bleak. Bavinck had returned to the Netherlands pondering the possibility that the American experiment might fail. For that reason, he warned an audience of young Dutch Christians of "a great danger hidden in today's emigration to America."[136] In lectures to Dutch youngsters following his 1892 journey to America, we recall, he had warned them, "Do not become American," because of the likelihood that they would then become Methodists. Now, the dangers of emigration were much graver. His lifelong aversion to emigration continued, but for new reasons. Not only was there "no rosy future for Calvinism" in America. By 1909, Bavinck doubted whether there was a rosy future for America itself.

America and the Task of Evangelism

Bavinck's parting impressions of America, of course, were not entirely negative. Nations and peoples remained in the palm of a sovereign God, whose ordinances often thwarted the evil intentions of the human heart. Although he left America in a pessimistic frame of mind, it was still too early to predict the certain failure of the New World experiment. For the time being, he still found reason to appreciate it. "Is America a model country and people? We do not know. No single circumstance there is settled. We do not know what will become of it or how it will develop. It is entirely in the making. There is the glory of the imperfect, the charm of the impossible."[137]

Perhaps the most significant change to enter Bavinck's thinking as a result of this trip was his encounter with American attitudes toward evangelism. The American cultural melting pot had fairly obvious consequences for the global diffusion of Christianity in the early twentieth century. Bavinck had encountered American Christians who were well aware of this and who saw their own young nation as both a target for mission and a great production line of missionaries. "Just like the English," he wrote, "the Americans see themselves as a world-people. 'Save America and you save the world.' Through immigration the United States has become in a wholly unique way 'the most foreign country and the greatest mission field on the globe.' People of every nationality have compatriots in America, and from them missionaries go out to every part of the world. 'Evangelization of the world in this generation, in this century.'"[138] Bavinck had been exposed to the fervor for global evangelization that had swept the English-speaking Protestant world from the 1890s onward. Indeed, by this point "the evangelization of the world in this generation"—a slogan recorded in Bavinck's Dutch notes in English—had come to function as a catchphrase for the world missionary movement as a whole. Writing of this phrase, Brian Stanley has described how "the Americans loved it . . . ; the Germans hated it . . . ; while the British were, as always, somewhere in the middle."[139] At that point, Bavinck's Dutch verdict was left unstated: these particular notes were observations of things seen and heard in American company. It is undeniable, however, that when he left America and stepped back into the shadow of Nietzsche, evangelism would become a more noticeable part of Bavinck's vocabulary. Within a few short years, his realization of the importance of evangelism in the Netherlands would even lead him to share a public platform with Lucas Lindeboom.

A Skeptical Reaction to the Philosophy of Revelation

One of Bavinck's great frustrations during the second American voyage concerned his struggle to provoke reactions to his Stone Lectures within the
Princeton community. No such difficulty arose from Snouck Hurgronje, who
had earlier received them in written (Dutch) form. As always, he was happy
to provide critical feedback.

> Your critique of the different systems, world- and life-views seems to me to be
> particularly sharp and powerful. . . . I am skeptical, without wanting to make
> a system out of skepticism or agnosticism. As always, your standpoint seems
> weak with regard to Scripture, in part because the enormous concerns provided
> by the most conservative and careful historical criticism are more or less denied
> and fade away; and in part because the objective character of revelations that
> are spoken by human mouths, written by human hands, canonized by human
> declaration, finally becomes subjective again. . . . Receive this confession for
> what it is intended to be: an open-hearted declaration regarding a fundamental
> difference from someone who values your work like no other.[140]

For all Bavinck's efforts at careful public apologetics for the Christian faith, his
friend remained unconvinced. The Bible continued to divide them. Bavinck's
reply, interestingly, hinted at his awareness of this—and signaled his attempt
to overcome Snouck Hurgronje's doubt without engaging directly with ap-
peals to scriptural authority.

> I understand your skepticism. But although my lectures are also intended for
> people who are not kindred spirits, nowhere did I call, as such, on the author-
> ity of Holy Scripture. I only said, (a) this is how human beings and the world
> seem to be. Without a higher, almighty and gracious power, it cannot exist, and
> (b) that now, the central issue comes from the mouths of prophets, Christ, and
> the apostles: such an almighty and gracious will *does* exist. . . . To accept that
> and to recognize it as truth is certainly an act of faith, [but it is] one to which
> the whole world and especially our own hearts compel us.[141]

Defending Calvin and Calvinism in a Changing Society

Over the course of 1909, Reformed Christians across Europe and North America marked the four-hundredth anniversary of John Calvin's birth—celebrations
that culminated in the inauguration of the Reformation Wall in Geneva that
summer.[142] However, as Christians from across the Protestant world reflected,
often in lavish terms, on the impact of Calvin and Calvinism on their societies—

precisely the impact praised by Bavinck in earlier years, particularly in his 1892 Toronto address—the Dutch Reformed fell strangely quiet. For the most part, Dutch Protestants were fairly muted in their praise of the Reformer, who did not enjoy a good public image in the Netherlands at that time.

Led by Bavinck's *Doktorvater* Johannes Scholten, the first generation of Modern theologians were well disposed toward Calvin on account of his assertion of predestination and divine sovereignty: to them, he was the theological forerunner to modern scientific determinism. Their early twentieth-century inheritors, however, were no fans of Calvin. To the likes of Allard Pierson, Willem Klinkenberg (1838–1921), and Isaäc Hoog (1858–1928), Calvin's character—deemed lifeless, loveless, and tragic—mattered more than his ideas.[143] At around the same time, in some Dutch circles, Michael Servetus (1511–53), an antitrinitarian burned at the stake in sixteenth-century Geneva, became something of a patron saint to intellectual freedom.[144]

In a setting in which Servetus had become the hero and Calvin the heretic, it became important to Bavinck that Calvin's public image be defended: alongside an article (translated into English by Vos) entitled "Calvin and Common Grace,"[145] Bavinck's contributions to that year's *Calviniana* were public lectures on Calvin in London ("The Leading Articles of Calvin's *Institutes*") and across the Netherlands[146] and a short written biography in which he emphasized Calvin's character—not warm and hearty like Luther, but nonetheless sincere, thoughtful, and pious.[147] This particular publication was modest in tone—perhaps intentionally so. While a review in *De Bazuin* noted that "Dr. Bavinck has not produced anything new" on Calvin's life,[148] his book's lack of pomp was received appreciatively by Snouck Hurgronje, who praised it precisely because it was "less sensational" than that year's Calvin celebrations in Geneva.[149]

Bavinck's correspondence before and after his trip to speak on Calvin in London, where he was joined by Johanna, suggests a growing fondness for that city: they had already visited it together in 1903 and would do so again. They had friends in both London and Birmingham—in 1906, a young woman from Birmingham, Ada Corah, had spent three months living with them in Amsterdam[150]—and by this point were well known enough in English Presbyterian circles to receive an invitation there as part of their own Calvin celebrations. Indeed, by this time his international connections were developing considerably: he was corresponding with James Orr in Glasgow, was consulted by Potchefstroom University in South Africa in their search for a professor of theology (Bavinck recommended Lindeboom's son-in-law Tjeerd Hoekstra), and was in regular contact with A. T. Robertson of the Southern Baptist Theological Seminary in Louisville, Kentucky, who had sought his help in preparing a Dutch version of his *A Short Grammar of the Greek New Testament*.[151] Bavinck's Calvinism had become thoroughly international in character.

On home turf, Bavinck's presentation of Calvin's character emphasized the historic (and beneficial) impact of Calvinism on the Dutch psyche. Subtly, this was a return to the claims made in Toronto years before. Even if some of his countrymen had shown themselves willing to follow Nietzsche in rejecting their Christian past, Bavinck continued to argue that the Dutch character was indelibly Calvinistic—with atheism and unbelief as the foreign imports. (Kuyper particularly appreciated this aspect of Bavinck's defense of Calvin.)[152]

Bavinck remained invested in both Calvin and Calvinism and was keen (in appropriate ways) to defend both. In that vein, the task of revising the *Reformed Dogmatics* also continued apace. The new version of the second volume, *God and Creation*, had already been released in 1908, with volumes 3 and 4 seeing the light of day in 1910 and 1911, respectively.[153] Significantly, while he worked hard at expanding the original text of the *Reformed Dogmatics*, he also began to invest time in the production of a shorter book in theology. Although he believed the expanded *Reformed Dogmatics* met the great intellectual needs of the day, the Christian faith faced a more pragmatic challenge: the professionalization of society had left young professionals with little time or energy to read lengthy tomes produced by theologians in previous generations, however worthy their content might be. More strikingly, Bavinck reasoned,

> Those old works are no longer of our time. The difference of language and style, of thought process and manner of expression make them strange to us. The questions that one formerly thought the most important have lost their meaning to us, either entirely or in large part. Other concerns, not named by them, now push themselves to the fore. . . . We are children of a new time and in a new era. . . . However much Franken's *Kern*, Marck's *Merg*, and Brakel's *Reasonable Religion* were applied in days gone by, they are no longer capable of being brought to life, do not speak to the younger generation, and unintentionally create the impression that Christianity is no longer applicable in this age. Therefore, there is an urgent need for a work that can take the place of these works of the fathers and can carry forward the old truth in a form that responds to the demands of this time.[154]

In that light, in 1909, he published *Magnalia Dei*—a more succinct (658 pages!) and, he hoped, accessible statement of his theology for "all those young men and women" for whom even the best theology of yesteryear was increasingly distant.[155] At the same time, then, he was trying to write distinct theological works that were *more* and *less* expansive. True to his form as a renaissance man, *Magnalia Dei* was released in the same period in which

Bavinck's article "On the Psychology of the Child" was published in a scholarly pedagogical journal.[156] The grand striving to think Christianly about all of life showed no signs of abating.

New Contact with Lindeboom

At the end of 1909, Lucas Lindeboom celebrated a quarter century as chairman of the Association for the Christian Care of the Mentally Ill in the Netherlands (Vereniging voor de Christelijke Verzorging van Krankzinningen in Nederland)—an organization that he had established in 1884. For all that Lindeboom had made himself a thorn in the Free University's flesh in its earlier years, his own insistence on the importance of distinctively Reformed care for those suffering mental illness had played an indispensable role in the creation of a chair in psychiatry there in 1907.[157] Two years on from that, and having worked tirelessly to support a series of newly opened Christian psychiatric clinics across the country, Lindeboom held a commemorative lecture which he then sent on to Bavinck, who soon wrote in reply.[158]

> Esteemed Chairman, I send you a most friendly word of thanks for sending the memorial lecture on behalf of the board, delivered on the occasion of the twenty-fifth anniversary of the Union. It provides a precious overview of its history and can make known many blessings. May it be used in the advancement of the Union's goals, and through the Lord's favor, may these become an increasing blessing to our people, just as it has already been, to such a great extent, for the last twenty-five years. With best regards, at your service, H. Bavinck.[159]

The year before this, of course, both men had been reminded afresh of their shared history: 1908 had marked the twenty-fifth anniversary of their appointments at the Theological School. The Christian press had commented widely on that milestone, with the general tenor being a call to thanksgiving for the "eloquent" Bavinck and the "practical" Lindeboom—both of whom (according to the *Gereformeerd Jongelingsblad*, at least) "work on the basis of the same faith and the same principles."[160]

The Parting of Jan and Herman

Despite this example of renewed contact with his old antagonist in 1909, in the years since Bavinck's move to Amsterdam, the Kampen Theological School's leadership had faced regular criticism regarding the fact and circumstances of his departure. In 1904, an article in *De Bazuin* responded to the claim that his move to the Free University had been a "justified punishment for the onesidedness and shortsightedness" of those who had conceded to the minority at the synod in Arnhem. This criticism closed with "the observation that Dr. Bavinck left in order to flourish at the Free [University] in a rich and glorious scientific center and to give his beautiful lectures to packed lecture rooms, while the brothers in the minority now have a fairly empty school. We know this, and our soul is sorrowful about it. We would have wished to see it otherwise."[161]

Given the extent of his achievements since moving to Amsterdam, it seems some within the Theological School had come to rue his move as a missed opportunity. An article on the history of the Theological School in *De Bazuin* in 1908 noted, for example, "How blessedly did he not work through his many publications? We do not have space to name them all. To mention his *Ref. Dogmatics* already says enough. . . . God spare him for many more years for the rich blessing of church and science!"[162] In those years, however, Bavinck did not look back toward Kampen, wondering what might have become had he remained there. Kampen was a part of his past rather than his future. His only ongoing connection to the town continued because his favored publishers—Kok, Bos, and Zalsman—were all based there.

Late in November 1909, however, Herman—together with his brothers and their respective families—had reason to return to Kampen. That month, on a Sunday morning at their home on the Singel, the eighty-three-year-old Jan Bavinck passed away. In the months before this, it seems that Herman and Jan both knew that the evening of Jan's life was almost over. We recall that several months before Jan's death, he and Herman had spent time retracing the Bavinck family's religious history in Bentheim, and further back still—reminiscences that were eventually published in the Mennonite newspaper *De Zondagsbode*.[163] Now, Jan's time had come. He too had become a part of that family history.

Jan's death (Nov. 28) was reported on in newspapers across the Netherlands— from *De Bazuin* to the *Algemeen Handelsblad*—and Dutch America.[164] On the Tuesday that followed, Jan's body was taken by train to Kampen, where Geziena and Johan had already been buried. His coffin sat on a catafalque in the Burgwalkerk overnight, underneath his former pulpit, which was now draped in black mourning cloths.[165] His surviving sons—Herman, Dinus, and Bernard—and their families reassembled in Kampen on the following day for Jan's funeral, at which Herman and Bernard spoke. Writing in the lost dagboek, Herman noted that it had been "*a sad and welcome day. The concern was moving.*"[166]

At the age of fifty-five, Bavinck found himself shorn of his father's supportive presence.

10

Showing His Colors

1910-20

---

*"Mr Chairman! Our modern culture
and Christianity are inseparable."*

Prior to his father's death, Herman had taken stock of his forefathers—Roman Catholic, then Lutheran (with Mennonite offshoots), and finally Reformed—in their own meandering path through German and Dutch church history. The story of the Reformed churches in the Netherlands was etched into his ancestry.

In 1910, in an article for the *Princeton Theological Review*, Bavinck retold that national religious history—from the sixteenth-century Reformation to twentieth-century neo-Calvinism—in a way that closely mirrored the sojourn of the diverse Bauingas, Bavingas, and Bavincks across the centuries.[1] That historical account ended with the Netherlands' current religious condition from the vantage point of an early twentieth-century neo-Calvinist: despite the successes of both Afscheiding and Doleantie and their union in 1892, Bavinck's constituency was still a small minority group in the religious demographics of the day. They were dwarfed by both the mainline Dutch Reformed and Roman Catholic churches and now found themselves in a rapidly dechristianizing culture. "In general," he wrote, "the current of the times is away from Christ and His cross."[2] It was fast becoming clear to him that the missionary outlook he had been struck by in America two years before— namely, to see one's own nation as a mission field, as well as a supplier of missionaries—was also needed in the Netherlands.

Although this realization seems to have struck Bavinck with some power only through his experiences among mission enthusiasts in 1908, interest in foreign mission had increased markedly in the Netherlands since the turn of the century. In 1900, his successor at the Theological School, Anthonie Honig, had published a book entitled *Missions and Schools*,[3] which was itself an attempt to further Kuyper's contributions to the debate on the task of missionaries in the Dutch East Indies from the 1870s onward. At its 1902 synod, held in Arnhem, the Reformed Churches in the Netherlands had formalized a revised polity with regard to foreign missions—a development that promoted, across the denomination, a sense of responsibility for the spread of the gospel in the East Indies.[4]

Although particular denominations were increasingly active in promoting foreign missions, the interdenominational spirit of the evangelical movement had also affected the Netherlands. The country's first dedicated missionary college, the Dutch School of Mission (Nederlandsche Zendingsschool), established by missionary societies (De Nederlandsche Zendelinggenootschap and De Utrechtsche Zendingvereeniging) rather than a church, had opened in Rotterdam in 1905. There, future missionaries proceeded through a course of general studies, following which they were taught modern languages, missiology, and theology, before taking general classes in medicine, Eastern languages, the history of non-Israelite and non-Christian religions, and the religious, civil, and economic history of the Indies. The goal of that comprehensive in-house education was the formation of Christians "who can and want to be a Javan to the Javans, a Papuan to the Papuans, an Alfur to the Alfurs."[5]

From 1910 onward, Bavinck began to invest himself in promoting evangelism—internationally, as well as domestically. Alongside his article in the *Princeton Theological Review* (which had concluded by stating, "It is of small consolation over against this apostasy in the civilized world, that in the heathen world missionary work is advancing"),[6] in that year he also published a piece on foreign missions in a South African theological journal.[7]

At the same time, a considerable debate arose within the Reformed Churches in the Netherlands regarding its own provision of training to overseas missionaries. The denomination was about to send its fourth missionary, Rev. Aart Merkelijn (1878–1943), to the East Indies.[8] In order to prepare for his new work, Merkelijn had registered as a student at the Dutch School of

Mission. His presence there provoked criticism from Rev. Johannes Cornelis
Sikkel (1855–1920), an Amsterdam-based pastor, who argued that insofar as
a denomination has a distinct theological identity, it should not outsource its
missiological training to parachurch institutions. "In this, especially regarding
the study of Islam and paganism in the Indies," he argued, "the Reformed
principle is of such great importance."[9] Bavinck agreed. That summer, at the
Free University's annual "University Day," he gave a lecture that argued the
university should create a new post for a professor of missions and evangelistic
work.[10] (Until his recent death, Petrus Biesterveld had taught New Testament
and practical theology, which included missiology. Bavinck's proposal was for
missiology to become the exclusive focus of a new professorship and, as such,
to be detached from both New Testament and practical theology.)

Writing in *De Bazuin*, one pastor noted that while Bavinck had highlighted
that "the missionary spirit, the love for mission, and the desire for mission
has also been awoken in our circles," the denomination was still "lacking
a man who lives entirely for mission, who directs all his energies toward
it, advises pastors-in-training, and inspires them with love for mission."[11]
Another missionary periodical, *De Macedoniër*, expressed confidence that
Bavinck's vision would soon become a reality: "That Prof. Bavinck wields
great influence is beyond doubt. . . . I do not doubt that within a couple of
years we will have a chair, perhaps even two, because the churches will not
leave Kampen behind."[12]

Bavinck's plea quickly gained traction. It was publicly announced that the
Free University would establish a chair for mission in the East Indies (and that
Rev. Merkelijn would receive the rest of his training within his own denomination),[13] shortly after which plans were announced to petition the synod for a
similar appointment at the Theological School.[14] Despite this initial enthusiasm, however, Bavinck's plan was not implemented quite as he had hoped.

In 1912, Biesterveld's former position was divided into two separate chairs,
one in New Testament, filled by Frederik Grosheide (1881–1972), and another in practical theology, filled by Petrus Sillevis Smitt (1867–1918). Sillevis
Smitt's teaching remit included classes on the theory of mission and the theory
of evangelism—two subjects in which he had little previous experience—
alongside homiletics, liturgy, and catechesis.[15] Although missiology continued
to be taught at the Free University, Bavinck's ideal had not been achieved: Sillevis Smitt was not the man called for in his 1910 appeal, the "man who lives
entirely for mission." Rather, he was a practical theologian whose job description included some theoretical missiology. Biesterveld's workload had been
divided, but not as radically as Bavinck had hoped. In any case, Sillevis Smitt

was plagued by health problems that led to an untimely death in 1918. The ideal outlined by Bavinck in 1910 would remain unfulfilled for some time.

Separating Foreign Missions and Colonial Expansion

Early in 1911, Bavinck held a public lecture in Amsterdam—advertised "for women as much as for men"—"The Meaning of Mission in our Time," in which he tried to disentangle foreign missions from colonial expansion.[16] Describing the geopolitics of the day, he observed that the increase of European cultural influence in the non-Western world was inevitable. For the most part, though, he believed that this influence promoted a rationalistic, antisupernatural, consumerist worldview quite alien to the non-Western world: colonialism's evangel was that of capitalism and the Enlightenment, rather than the cross and the empty tomb, and its motivation was sheer economic dominance. Because of this, he argued, its influence unraveled a rich and ancient tapestry of native non-Western beliefs about this world and the next—and offered nothing more to take its place than the already threadbare chintz of secular consumerism. For that reason, "European culture can be a blessing to the peoples of the world, but it can also be a curse. If, as is actually the case, it undermines the heathen's indigenous religion and gives them no other and better faith in its place, it impoverishes them internally more than it enriches them."[17]

Bavinck believed that if Western culture was bereft of Christianity's leavening influence, it could only teach the rest of the world a model of exploitation, domination, and war. Thanks to Multatuli's *Max Havelaar*, it had long since been argued among the Dutch that colonialism robbed the colonized of precious natural resources. To this, however, Bavinck added its effects in depriving the colonized of the richness and power of religious belief, leaving only the meager offerings of Western consumerism as a replacement—a sleight of hand that would likely lead non-Westerners to regroup around their ancestral religions in intensified, anti-Western forms. In view of this, he told his audience that the presence or absence of a strong missionary impulse in the West's contact with the non-Western world would have major repercussions long into the future. "If these mighty peoples [i.e., the East Indies, China, and Japan] acquire our civilization without Christianity, of which it is the fruit, they borrow from us the weapons with which they will fight us in the future. And this danger grows all the more earnest while Buddhism and Mohammedanism [i.e., Islam] have recently been awoken into a new life and secretly equip themselves for a struggle with the Christian faith."[18]

If the Christians of 1911—"whatever their tradition"—failed to take foreign mission seriously, their descendants would face "a global struggle between Buddha, Muhammad, and Christ."[19] For Bavinck, failure to spread the gospel had stark consequences in this world *and* the next. He feared religious violence on a global scale.

The Completion of *Reformed Dogmatics*

In 1911, the fourth and final volume of the revised *Reformed Dogmatics*—a work that he had begun tentatively in 1884—was published. When he had completed the final installment of the first edition in 1901, the four volumes totalled 2,265 pages. Now, after another ten years' labor, his revised edition had been expanded to almost 3,000 pages—an increase equivalent in length to each of the four original volumes.

A comment in *De Heraut* that the *Dogmatics*, now in its fullest form, was "not a devotional book, but rather a study book that has only been written for the scientifically educated" and that "the price of such a work means that it is certainly not within reach of everyone's budget" perhaps sheds light on why he had no sooner finished the expanded version than he set about restating its contents more concisely.[20] Although he had already tried to provide a shorter (albeit still lengthy) overview of Christian doctrine for busy young professionals in *Magnalia Dei* (1909), he followed the completion of his magnum opus by setting to work on the still more concise (251 pages) *Guidebook for Instruction in the Christian Religion* (1913), a work aimed at older high school pupils and lower-level college students: this was a book for "all those who want to become acquainted with the chief content of our Christian, Reformed confession of faith through the means of a book that is not too long or too expensive."[21]

Modernism and Orthodoxy

Earlier that decade, in 1905—just before the revised version of volume 1 of Bavinck's *Reformed Dogmatics* was released—his neo-Calvinistic project had been critiqued by the Modern theologian Bernardus Eerdmans as liberal theology deceptively cloaked in pious language. Alleging that it was impossible to be both orthodox *and* modern, Eerdmans had called him to show his true colors by abandoning his claim to orthodoxy and giving himself over to the Modernist cause of his Leiden professors.

In the years that followed, while the *Reformed Dogmatics* was in the process of revision, Eerdmans had continued to define "orthodox" and "modern" as mutually incompatible, claiming that the former was tied up in the superstition of a prescientific age and had been superseded by the latter. For that reason, he still viewed Bavinck and Kuyper—in their claims to be epistemologically and culturally modern people who also insisted that they held on to the beating heart of premodern Christianity—as charlatans. Eerdmans insisted that while Calvin himself was "orthodox," Kuyper and Bavinck were not. He argued that, as those who caused many to believe that oil and water could indeed be mixed, the neo-Calvinists were wreaking havoc on their intellectual, cultural, and ecclesiastical environs.[22]

Now, in 1911, having completed the revision of all four volumes, Bavinck returned to Eerdmans's critique in an important lecture given at the Free University, later published as *Modernism and Orthodoxy*.[23] There, Bavinck subverted Eerdmans's claim that modernity had superseded orthodoxy, arguing instead that the development of both "modernity" and "orthodoxy" through history is more complicated than this. For all its claims to have broken definitively with its orthodox predecessor, he reasoned, "modern theology in general thinks and lives from the Christian tradition much more than it presumes to do."[24] Unlike the Nietzscheans, the moderns did not reject pre-Enlightenment Christian tradition utterly. They still spoke the language of Christian theology (albeit with revised definitions) and maintained a broadly Christian set of social values. In all of this, Bavinck argued, they remained a new branch that extended from and depended on a deeply rooted Christian tree.

After challenging the Moderns' self-presentation as bluff and bluster, he moved on to the notion of orthodoxy, which, "unless it totally cuts itself off from its environment, stands to a greater or lesser degree under the influence of the intellectual currents of this century."[25] In Christian history, he argued, "orthodox" had never functioned as a static concept that was hermetically sealed from the host cultures in which it was invoked. Rather, it put down roots in diverse historical locations, just as it was now doing in twentieth-century Dutch culture. Far from being like oil and water—a portrayal of these terms that Bavinck deemed "petty and narrow-minded"—neither "modernity" nor "orthodoxy" precluded the other. Indeed, both notions had evolved in meaning throughout the course of history and continued to do so in the early twentieth century.

Bavinck believed that as a tale of progress, history was better served by careful reformation, rather than the intellectual revolution purported to have taken place in the works of Scholten, Kuenen, and Rauwenhoff. In his criticisms of the neo-Calvinists, Eerdmans had tinkered with whether their movement was best defined as "modern orthodoxy" or "orthodox modernism" and questioned whether those semantics made any difference. In response, Bavinck refused to nail his colors to any of these masts. Rather, the "Reformed" label suited his purposes more effectively: "This name deserves preference far above orthodox and also that of Calvinistic or neo-Calvinistic."[26]

Bavinck was comfortable with the "Reformed" label, rather than "orthodox" or "modern," because it expressed a particular view of how Christians should participate in the onward march of history. He claimed that, in their dim view of the world before Kant, the Moderns underestimated history. The opposite, a paralyzing overvaluation of the past, of course, was also quite possible: indeed, such stood at the heart of Bavinck's criticisms of the Roman Catholic Church on account of its rejection of the Reformation.[27] The better model, he believed, was one that simultaneously looked backward and forward, enabling both development and a sense of rootedness in history. While Bavinck had set some critical distance between his own thought and that of Groen van Prinsterer earlier in the Amsterdam years, by this point the antirevolutionary father's voice came roaring back: in *Modernism and Orthodoxy*, Bavinck had argued passionately for reformation over revolution. His life's project had been based on nothing less.

Leaving Dogmatics Behind?

Having remained in conversation with his Modern critics throughout the revision of his *Dogmatics*,[28] Bavinck had followed the completion of that work by offering one final, rousing interaction with their criticisms. Accordingly, Bremmer has described *Modernism and Orthodoxy* as Bavinck's "dogmatic-theological swan song."[29] From then on, in that account, Bavinck's life moved into a new phase—a shift portrayed under the heading "Departure from Theology."[30] Hepp's biography claimed the same: this particular publication marked the end of his efforts to formulate dogmatic theology.

One detail included at this point in Hepp's account—that "a couple of years before his death, [Bavinck] gave away the most important dogmatic works, especially including old Reformed theology, 'because,' he told me, 'I don't do that anymore'"[31]—has given rise to a popular impression that following the completion of his *Dogmatics*, the last decade of Bavinck's life was overshadowed by despair that even extended to the dogmatic work that he had produced.[32] (Hepp mistakenly argued that during this period of disappointment and despair, Bavinck's theological identity shifted as he was less convinced of Reformed theology than in his early years and increasingly sought to define himself in contradistinction to Kuyper.)[33] Somewhat obliquely, in describing this phase of Bavinck's life, Hepp also mentions public suspicion that the increasing prominence of Christianity in his public discourse meant that he "might have exchanged the specifically Reformed, for the most part, for the generically Christian."[34]

Clearly, the completion of the revised *Dogmatics* marked the close of one chapter of Bavinck's life and the beginning of another. However, how he was navigating that change and what effect it had on him were perhaps less well understood by those around him. It was certainly not the case that in these years he had begun to accent the importance of Christianity because of some crisis of confidence in his own Reformed heritage. Rather, as has been seen, he advocated Christianity in an increasingly public way as he attempted to gather a theistic coalition under the shadow of Nietzsche. As the Amsterdam years progressed, those writings on Christianity were also closely linked to his support of evangelism at home and abroad, because public apologetics for Christianity had become a necessary first step in publicly defending his own brand of Reformed theology.

Furthermore, thus far in the Amsterdam years at least, his pattern of writing had been to balance his publications fairly evenly between works on the Reformed tradition and works on Christianity construed more generally. Indeed, the most indicative statement of how closely related those tasks were had been made in his (1906) argument that in plumbing the depths of his own theological tradition, the dogmatician must recognize that his task was always to identify the true essence of the catholic Christian faith.[35] He set up the pattern of his publications in a way that would demonstrate the vital connection that existed between his own Reformed tradition and the catholic Christian faith.

It seems hard to sustain that during the first decade in Amsterdam, Bavinck had gone through any dramatic internal shift akin, for example, to the about-face in the young Karl Barth's thinking in the run-up to the *Römerbrief*. Rather, Bavinck in this period developed gradually, always clinging to reformation over revolution, even of the personal intellectual sort—a development that had been poorly understood by the general public, perhaps, because he had grasped the consequences of the "age of Nietzsche" more than most and had altered his course subtly, but significantly, in response.

It is true that in the decade of life after he completed the revised *Reformed Dogmatics* in 1911, no further revisions of that text were ever published. We might say, then, that as a public defense of that project against Eerdmans, *Modernism and Orthodoxy* functioned as a fairly public dénouement

intended to end his long-running competition with Modern theology. However, claims that quickly thereafter he lost interest in the construction of Christian doctrine—or even despaired in the years that he had previously invested in
it—are simply untrue. His personal copy of the revised second edition of the
Dogmatics contains handwritten notes and revisions throughout—questions,
corrections for typographical errors, changes in biblical texts cited, and ad-
ditions to the literature cited. This personal copy also includes twenty-three
new pages of his own notes on material for further expansion—among other
things, these pages cover teleology, the Trinity, the logos doctrine, the interpretation of Genesis 1–3, and geological periods.[36] That developments in
geology in particular would prompt subsequent revision to his *Dogmatics* is
unsurprising. In the second edition, Bavinck had written of this new science
in glowing terms: "The facts advanced by geology . . . are just as much words
of God as the content of Holy Scripture and must therefore be believingly
accepted by everyone."[37] In that edition, however, he had also recognized that
this emergent science would quickly make rapid progress, and therefore, he
had left an open door for further revision in response to it. While many of
the notes made by Bavinck in this copy of his *Dogmatics* are undated, those
that can be dated range between 1911 and 1918. While these revisions went
unpublished, it is certainly not the case that he gave up on dogmatics after
1911 or that he lost interest in it.

Alongside this, Bavinck never expressed the expectation that his dogmatics would be a lifelong endeavor—as it would later become, for example, for
Barth, who died six million words into the unfinished *Church Dogmatics*.
Rather, Bavinck had set to work on this task in response to the needs of the
day (and then made the revisions he deemed necessary when the needs of the
day changed). However, as he had already stated publicly, even "a complete
dogmatics" was "but a part" of something far bigger: Christianity.[38]

Although he never published his ongoing revisions of the *Reformed Dogmatics*, he spent the next two years preparing the *Guidebook for Instruction
in the Christian Religion* (1913)—a summary of theology that follows the
same structure as his *Dogmatics*—precisely because he wanted his dogmatic
project to reach those whose previous education or financial resources would
otherwise have prevented them from accessing his scientific work.[39]

While it was not disclosed within Bavinck's own lifetime, in the last decade
of his life he also prepared—albeit without publishing—revisions to *Magnalia Dei*. Following his death, these particular revisions were found by his
brother Bernard "in an envelope marked 'intended for an eventual new edition of *Magnalia*.'"[40] These revisions—which added sections on the means of
grace, Word and sacrament, and ecclesiastical offices—were then added to the

original text by Bernard in a new edition (1931) that was later made available in English as *Our Reasonable Faith*.[41] Clearly, Bavinck retained some interest in the revision of his constructive publications, although not on any grand scale: a third edition of the *Reformed Dogmatics* was printed in his lifetime, in 1918, but was materially identical to its final form in 1911. And in any case, by the time he had completed his own revised *Dogmatics*, his former student Abraham Kuyper Jr. (1872–1941) had already published his first book, *Of the Knowledge of God*,[42] which was itself an accomplished piece of dogmatic theology—to the point that in some circles, at least, he was being tentatively positioned as the new Bavinck.[43] Younger voices, who were themselves natives of this new age, were emerging and could carry dogmatics forward.

Following Bavinck's death, that lack of desire for further wholesale revision or expansion was explained by his colleague Willem Jan Aalders (1870–1945), who commented on Bavinck's "ineradicable need for atonement, for harmony, for synthesis, for which the phrase could have been coined, if it hadn't already existed: 'I am a human, and I think nothing human to be foreign to me [homo sum et nihil humanum a me alienum puto].'"[44] According to his (Calvinistic) views on Christianity as a catholic faith that brings every square inch of this disordered existence into harmony, Bavinck regarded the Christian as one in whom flashes of true, restored humanity could be seen. In Bavinck's own life, he had long since articulated the desire for a rediscovery of all of life lived *coram Deo*—or to reprise his language from 1888, "to be a human in the fullest natural sense of that word, and then as a human, a child of God in all things."[45] In his early Kampen years, he cherished that aspiration as "the most beautiful thing of all."

As the Amsterdam years went on, he certainly was bruised, tired, and no stranger to deep disappointment. By 1911, for example, it was clear that he had given up on the hope that the Theological School and the Free University would unite: while he had been asked to draft a new plan for a prospective union in 1910, he did not attend the 1911 synod, at which a possible union was discussed.[46] Despite these factors, though, he was still animated by the same "unattainable ideal." For distinctly Christian reasons, he still longed to be a polymath.

For that reason, having spent decades producing (and then extending) a magnum opus in dogmatic theology—with which he seems to have been fundamentally satisfied[47]—Bavinck moved into a new phase of life. The intense workload that had prevented him from taking holidays as a young theologian in Kampen had now been completed. As that long effort drew to a close, he had the resources and time to travel more extensively—an aspiration that had proved impossible at an earlier stage of his career. In his holiday travels during these years, he sailed the Rhine (1909), traveled to Venice (1910), and returned to London (1912). In the following year, he made a longer journey, visiting Rome, before making his way home via San Remo, Monte Carlo, Nice, and Paris (1913).[48]

The season of dogmatic writing had now passed. As he approached his sixth decade, his urgent task became the ongoing realization of his Christian worldview in concrete, human terms. And given the change that was about to come upon him—a change in social role, rather than intellectual commitments—we could hardly expect the last decade of his life to have been otherwise.

Reentering Politics: The Parliamentarian

Few years in Bavinck's life were as significant as 1911. As has been noted, it marked the completion of a magnum opus and the delivery of a particularly important public lecture. Alongside this, it brought one development that he had not expected: that August, he was elected as a member of the First Chamber of Parliament to represent the Antirevolutionary Party. When describing this election to Snouck Hurgronje, Bavinck wrote of it as "a total surprise to me, because for a couple of years I had withdrawn entirely from the world of politics."[49]

Bavinck's previous experience in a notable political role, as chairman of the Antirevolutionary Party between 1905 and 1907, had not been a resounding success. His conciliatory nature and constant concern for nuance had made him a poor fit for party leadership. Since then, Antirevolutionary politics had gone through a challenging period. Kuyper had returned from his tour of the Mediterranean with renewed enthusiasm and had set himself up, once again, as the life and soul of the party. In these years, during which Bavinck served as a member of the party's Central Committee, little progress had been made toward identifying a suitable long-term successor to Kuyper. Internally, the party lacked discipline, became increasingly divided, and struggled to keep its focus. Kuyper's early biographer Petrus Kasteel described this as a period in which "the lion had grown old, and the cubs chose their own paths."[50]

By this point, the relationship between Bavinck and Kuyper had lost a great deal of the energy and excitement shared between them in the 1880s and 1890s. A lot had changed since the days when Kuyper's poster hung on the wall of Bavinck's student room on the Haarlemmerstraat in Leiden.

Since then, their stories had become thoroughly intertwined in times of joy and sorrow. In 1907, just as his time as chairman came to a close, Bavinck had played a central role in Kuyper's seventieth birthday celebrations, presenting him with a book in his honor, alongside an old Dutch-style chest, and giving one of the many speeches—following which, at a dinner in Kuyper's honor, Bavinck was seated at the head table.[51] On that day, Bavinck's birthday address to Kuyper was almost pastoral in character, talking directly to an old man whose life had known glittering success, crushing disappointments, and not a little heartache. In all of that, Bavinck portrayed his colleague as a man of strong principles and as one whose life was a powerful example of the outworking of faith, through which Kuyper's Calvinistic revival had changed the nation: "Although you went back to the time of the Reformation," he told Kuyper, "that was never simply to repristinate the past. The past was taken up within you, but in order to make it a part of the present and the future."[52] Kuyper's life had been an exhausting effort, and it had not been perfect, but it was a life that had been lived "for others, for the whole of our nation."[53]

The general tenor of Bavinck's address was summed up in another contribution to the *Gedenkboek* presented to Kuyper on that occasion: "Dr. Bavinck has rightly noted that only the one who does *nothing* makes no mistakes."[54] This speech, then, had been a *laudatio* in response to a lifetime of achievements. While it ended with the wish that God would grant Kuyper "many more years" to carry on in his diverse public roles, Bavinck's address had reflected on the past and the present but had invested little in the future. (And clearly, it was an appropriately pitched address with a view to the occasion: Bavinck closed his speech by leading the company in "resounding applause," for which Kuyper "rejoiced inwardly.")[55]

In that regard, as Bremmer has observed, this speech had been strikingly different from an earlier address given by Bavinck in 1897 to commemorate the twenty-fifth anniversary of *De Standaard*.[56] In that jubilant speech, the script of which includes prompts to allow laughter from the audience at key moments, an energetic young Bavinck clearly saw Kuyper as the future: "As long as Dr. Kuyper is editor of *De Standaard*—and God grant that this will be for a long time!—for as long as that, the Antirevolutionary Party's concern for principle is safe in the hands of *De Standaard*."[57] In those halcyon days, Bavinck was forty-two, and Kuyper, fifty-nine. By 1907, in only ten years, both men had aged considerably. Looking at the seventy-year-old Kuyper, Bavinck now saw the past rather than the future.

Despite his declining health, however, Kuyper would continue to fight tooth and nail for his place in the present for some time yet—a reality that would cause their relationship to cool somewhat, particularly in the political realm. In 1908, for example, Bavinck wrote to Kuyper to express disbelief at his willingness to strike (what were to Bavinck) questionable political alliances and turn a blind eye to proper process, in order to outflank his opponents: "I cannot believe that you are prompting and supporting these efforts. . . . Maybe [these new allies] will serve the control of the party for a time; but they will do incalculable damage to its moral content."[58]

By 1908, Bavinck's place within the party was vulnerable: this was the autumn in which he had disembarked from *The Rotterdam*, stressed and tired, in New York, before returning home with dire visions of the future. By 1909, he had taken leave of the Central Committee and had more or less withdrawn from politics. For that reason, he was surprised to be elected to the First Chamber in 1911. Having received a note of congratulations from Kuyper, Bavinck wrote back, expressing a degree of reservation toward his new post. "I have accepted [the appointment], trusting in the God of my life, and pray to him that I can do something in the Senate, small as it may be, to the honor of his name and to the blessing of our people. If that is not the case and the task is too heavy for my shoulders, then I hope to receive the courage to leave a place where I do not belong."[59]

By this point, Kuyper, a (full-time) member of parliament in the Second Chamber, was suffering from hearing loss—among a host of medical complaints—to the point that he could not follow debates there. Fairly soon after Bavinck took his place in the chamber, Kuyper gave up his seat in the Second Chamber and joined Bavinck in the Senate.[60] (The Dutch Parliament is divided into two chambers: the First Chamber, also known as the Senate, meets once a week and is attended by part-time members of Parliament; the Second Chamber is attended by full-time politicians.)

As a member of the First Chamber, Bavinck was committed to parliament part-time: for the rest, he remained an active participant within his own community. Alongside his normal work at the Free University, Bavinck had been given an outlet for public speech as a politician-theologian, but without the responsibility of party leadership. It was a role that he valued deeply and that he would occupy for the last decade of his life. To an extent, the parliamentary chamber had become his pulpit, from which his voice reached the general public through reports in the *Algemeen Handelsblad* and *De Telegraaf*.

Christianity and Culture

Bavinck's first speech as a parliamentarian, in the context of a debate on Dutch educational provision in the East Indies, was a reprisal of his lecture "The Meaning of Mission in our Time," given earlier that year. Beginning with the claim that Dutch "modern culture and Christianity are inseparable,"[61] he argued that those who thought the Dutch should educate Javans in every area of Western thought bar Christianity had failed to grasp that Western culture is itself the fruit of Christianity. If colonists provide animal-worshiping locals with education in modern Western biological science, he argued, but do not also teach them that Western science is the product of the Christian religion, the colonists will have necessarily disabused the locals of their ancestral religion, on the grounds that modern biological science invalidates animism. However, the colonists will not have filled that void with anything else. Better then, Bavinck thought, to export Dutch culture and Christianity hand in hand.

Bavinck, of course, was not against the expansion of Western culture in principle: to him, these were "our Indies." As a European of his era, he believed in the superiority of Western culture, albeit not on the grounds of ethnicity. Rather, he was convinced that Christianity had been responsible for the elevation of the West and that the combination of Christianity and Christianized culture was worth sharing, particularly in the case of Dutch culture. Even toward the end of the Amsterdam years, he believed Dutch culture to have been abundantly blessed by Calvinism: it had created a national character that was hardworking, honest, and unpretentious, and a society characterized by freedom and democracy. That culture, he believed, was well worth sharing and was certainly an improvement on the unchristian cultures of the East Indies. The conclusion of this particular speech, for example, told the paternalistic tale of a Javan who had received this combination of Christianity and culture and now worshiped Christ *and* revered the Dutch queen.

As has been seen, however, in the Dutch politics of his day, he was perhaps the fiercest critic of secularized colonial expansion. In this first parliamentary speech, it was clear that such a prospect filled him with a sense of apocalyptic dread. Indeed, he used this speech to disagree publicly with Snouck Hurgronje's expectation that the spread of Dutch culture without Christianity would lead Javans to leave Islam, stating instead, "I believe that he will find himself disappointed in this expectation, the further we go into the future."[62] Bavinck and Snouck Hurgronje were still divided on their impressions of the power of religion. Unlike his friend, Bavinck thought that a thin, irreligious secularism was no match for the compelling world- and life-view that was Islam.

According to his own testimony, Bavinck had not intended to make a speech that day but had rather felt compelled to in view of the debate at hand. This is not implausible, given his own nerves in this new setting—and the fact that the contents of his speech drew on recent lecture material that was still churning in his mind, as well as arguments already practiced in earlier forms

in *Christian Science, Christian Worldview*, and *Philosophy of Revelation*.
That he was able to pull together such a speech with some skill was noted
in *De Telegraaf*, which commented, "Prof. Bavinck surprised us with a very
special ease in speaking, so that in this regard he is much more likeable than
his colleage Dr. Woltjer, who always stands to speak in a miserable, somber,
plaintive tone and is often *very* unclear."[63] Perhaps more significantly for this
particular topic, his speech also received attention in widely read newspapers
in the Dutch East Indies.[64] Evidently, a voice spoken in The Hague could be
heard around the world. From then on, Bavinck made the most of his position
in the First Chamber, giving speeches every year until 1920.

Private Moments in a Public Life

By this stage in his life, Bavinck was an established figure in Dutch public life.
Unlike Kuyper, who recognized no meaningful distinction between the categories of private and public—and whose very existence was always intended for
public consumption—Bavinck's private life was now closely guarded: much
of his correspondence from these years was businesslike and gave away little
about his own home life. However, one draft letter from this period, written in
late 1912 to a Swiss friend (whose name is unclear) by both Herman in French
and Johanna in English does provide an important glimpse into their family
life at that time. While Herman's section of the letter is fairly unremarkable
and deals with the French-language literature he had recently been reading,
Johanna's portion showed that both she and Hannie were anglophiles: "Because we had no opportunity to speak French, and I am occupied to-day with
reading English books, I fear I have forgotten nearly all my French and it is
very necessary that I later begin anew. Hanny is in Birmingham and enjoys
herself very much. Every Sunday I write her a long letter on the events of the
week, and every Thursday we receive an answer that is full of joy and happiness. So we have many reasons to thank the Lord our God."[65] Hannie, now
aged eighteen, was in Birmingham, England—the hometown of their family
friend Ada Corah, who had lived with them in Amsterdam six years before.

The Vine, the Branches, and the Ax

Following his appointment in the First Chamber, the general writing pattern
employed by Bavinck thus far in the Amsterdam years continued apace. In *Christianity* (1912), he tried to provide an answer to the question of the "essence of

Christianity," a question that had loomed large over European thought since the beginning of the nineteenth century.[66] That issue had arisen in conjunction with the development of modern critical history as a discrete science.[67] The nineteenth century's "historical turn" had heightened awareness that over the course of its long past, Christianity had been subject to constant change—an awareness that birthed a growing concern for how one should account for whatever it was about Christianity that remained constant throughout.

Bavinck's contribution to this debate was the argument that Christianity's *essence* was reflected in its *phenomena*. While Christianity has birthed many diverse groups across its history, he argued, no single group has claimed to have remained identical to the first Christians (and, on that basis, to have stayed coterminous with the first Christians, regardless of historical distance); for this reason these diverse groups of Christians, each in its own way, have oriented their faith back toward the New Testament, and more profoundly still, toward Jesus himself. From these *phenomena*, he claimed, the true *essence* of Christianity becomes clear: it is Jesus Christ. Accordingly, Christianity makes the question "Who do you say the Christ is?" central to its essence.[68]

This attempt to contribute to one of the major historical questions of his day dovetailed with his efforts in gathering a theistic coalition. Claiming that "there are indeed innumerably many formulations of the essence of Christianity," Bavinck noted the division of major ecclesiastical traditions before highlighting a strikingly diverse range of individual thinkers: alongside the Eastern Orthodox, Roman Catholic, Lutheran, and Reformed Churches, his list gave room to Kant, Hegel, Schleiermacher, Ritschl, and von Harnack.

Surveying this array of rival traditions and (heterodox) individuals, Bavinck noted that "thankfully, on different points, a recognizable agreement still exists."[69] Each tradition and individual tried to make sense of Jesus, even if their answers to the question of Christ were profoundly different. And importantly for Bavinck's purposes, their common christological concern—however differently articulated or concluded—meant that they all faced the same Nietzschean threat. In this book, Bavinck argued that those who reject Christianity's *phenomena* must ultimately also reject its *essence*: the denial of the Christian religion requires the dismissal of Jesus himself.[70] Implicitly, this was Bavinck's reminder to his theological rivals that Nietzsche's New Testament hero was Pontius Pilate, rather than Jesus of Nazareth. If Christ was the vine and Christianity's diverse traditions were the branches, Bavinck's warning was that the *Übermensch* had come bearing an ax rather than pruning shears. Nietzsche's new man had no reason to discriminate between Kant's moral teacher, Schleiermacher's supremely God-conscious human, and Bavinck's God incarnate. These would stand or fall together.

Importantly, Kuyper strongly agreed: shortly after this book was published, he wrote to Bavinck praising it as "a masterpiece."[71]

A Man in Full Flow

In that year, Bavinck continued to contribute in parliament, giving a rousing speech against the state assuming the responsibility to care for the poor (on the grounds that the state is responsible for deeds of justice, but the church is responsible for acts of love).[72] He lectured in support of Kuyper's vision of state-funded, worldview-oriented schools,[73] gave public support to the Dutch translation of Matthew Henry's biblical commentaries,[74] and corresponded with Albertus Pieters (1869–1955), an American Calvinist missionary in Japan. Indeed, in order to promote awareness of Pieters's work there, Bavinck published their correspondence.[75]

His work in 1913 carried on in the same vein. His *Guidebook for Instruction in the Christian Religion* was completed—thus making his dogmatic project accessible to a new group of readers. A revised version of *Christian Worldview* appeared in print,[76] as did articles on Christianity and natural science[77] and on social inequality.[78] He addressed the National Christian School Congress on pedagogy[79] and spoke at the Modern Theologians' Assembly, at which he interacted with Modernist reactions to *Modernism and Orthodoxy*.[80] In March of that year, he gave an outstanding speech in parliament in which he recounted the effects of the 1876 Higher Education Act on his theological studies in Leiden (that particular legislation had required the university to teach religious studies under the name "theology") and argued that the place of theology in Dutch universities needed to be better protected. (This was the speech in which he described witnessing how in his teenage years "half of the youth of the Netherlands bowed down at the feet of Multatuli and looked up at him with amazement.")[81]

That April, he also gave the opening plenary address at the Congress for Reformed Evangelization, held in Amsterdam—a conference chaired by Lucas Lindeboom, who also introduced Bavinck's address.[82] In a series of eight propositions entitled "The Concept and Necessity of Evangelization" (included in the appendices of this biography),[83] Bavinck outlined the Christian gospel against the backdrop of the New Testament before describing the significance of the Reformation as a rediscovery of the gospel and noting the church's calling to reevangelize Europeans, whose culture had been birthed by Christianity but who had grown estranged from it. The full text of his lecture, published in *De Bazuin*, sketched out the early twentieth-century

Netherlands in a way that Bavinck had been unable to imagine in his Kampen years: it had become a nation in which "professional atheists call God the last and greatest enemy of the human race," while others live out precisely the "hybridical" life—agnostic, superstitious, and indifferent—upon which he had previously poured cold water.[84] Theologically, it was now a context that could be responded to appropriately only with evangelism.

Significantly, Bavinck's portrayal of the Reformation as a rediscovery of the gospel also included the sense in which the Reformation was a fresh realization that the gospel's power extends to every area of life; in that regard, he insisted that the Reformed should evangelize in a distinctively Reformed way. The gospel was not simply good news for one's soul, an experience that passed in a moment, or a private decision that only aimed to affect quiet religious practices. As Bavinck and Kuyper had insisted for decades, the gospel was good news for body *and* soul, for art, science, and society.

In that regard, the conference followed Bavinck's lead in responding to the growing influence in the Netherlands of the American revivalists Ira Sankey and D. L. Moody: Bavinck had encountered that branch of evangelicalism in America and was now warning his countrymen against it.[85] The Reformed, he insisted, should not compromise on the fullness of the gospel by evangelizing like Methodist revivalists.

Thirty years had now passed since Lindeboom and Bavinck had been appointed together at the Theological School—a fact of which they were reminded afresh earlier that year when the Theological School called for a day of thanksgiving in honor of both men.[86] Several months later, faced with the dire decline of Christianity in their nation, Bavinck and Lindeboom had found a reason to share a platform. Lindeboom, of course, remained opposed to the Kuyperian veins that ran deep through Bavinck's view of the gospel. Following his lecture, Lindeboom disputed Bavinck's choice to include "works of mercy" within the definition of evangelism.[87] While they agreed on the necessity of the gospel, their views on its meaning still differed. In the end, the conference's findings sided with Lindeboom: "Evangelization," it concluded, "is the work by which the church approaches those who are estranged from the faith, with the intention that they will be brought back to faith in Christ. This work is deemed necessary."[88] Bavinck's neo-Calvinistic expansion, by implication, was not.

Interrupted by War

At the beginning of 1914, the almost-sixty-year-old Bavinck's effort to bring every sphere of life under Christ's lordship was in full flight. By the end of

March, he had given three speeches in parliament on education in the East Indies—speeches that continued his earlier argument that dechristianized Western cultural expansion would be disastrous for East and West alike.[89] In the same period, he published reflections on the now-deceased Adriaan Steketee (and his own experiences as a student in Kampen),[90] following which he produced new material on psychology,[91] mission in the New Testament,[92] and aesthetics.[93] His tremendous momentum, which simultaneously extended in so many directions, showed no signs of slowing down.

That July, however, all would change. The assassination of Archduke Franz Ferdinand in Sarajevo on June 28 prompted the Austro-Hungarian Empire to declare war on the Kingdom of Serbia a month later, plunging Europe—and with it, the world—into war. On July 30, the Netherlands declared itself neutral, as it would remain until the close of hostilities four years later. Together, the shot that ignited the powder keg of Europe and the (centrist Liberal) Dutch government's preference for neutrality had pushed Bavinck and his grand intellectual plans into a strange no-man's-land. In these years, while surrounding nations waged war around him, Bavinck, for the most part, was able to go about his daily business as usual, and—if he so desired—could carry on writing about the wide array of subjects that had animated him thus far in the Amsterdam years.

And this he did, to an extent. While he continued to ruminate on revisions to his *Dogmatics*, he did not publish another major work in that vein (and never resumed writing his *Reformed Ethics*). That said, these were not unfruitful years. He continued to give public lectures throughout the war years. In 1915, a public audience in The Hague heard him speak on "individuality and individualism"—in which he presented Calvin as a thinker who preserved individuality better than the modern individualists.[94] Audiences in Bussum (1916) and Amsterdam (1917) heard lectures on "Christianity in the twentieth century."[95]

His involvement in the Antirevolutionary Party also carried on: in 1915, he coauthored a short book entitled *Leader and Leadership in the Anti-Revolutionary Party*,[96] which reflected appreciatively but critically on Kuyper's leadership and called for a restructuring of the party that would break its dependence on its now seventy-eight-year-old leader. (Although Bavinck is officially listed as one of several authors, his coauthor Pieter Diepenhorst later claimed that the book was Bavinck's work.) In the same year, he contributed entries to the *International Standard Bible Encyclopedia*[97] and engaged directly with Snouck Hurgronje on his friend's belief that when presented with secular Western culture, Javan Muslims would readily give up their Islam. (Bavinck's retort was that "religion can only be conquered and replaced by religion.")[98]

In 1916, and perhaps reflecting the needs of his own family in these years—Hannie was nineteen when war broke out—his interest in psychology led to the production of an article entitled "Individualism and the Individuality of the Child,"[99] alongside the remarkably comprehensive and original work *On Raising Teenagers*.[100] New material on the "unconscious" appeared in 1917,[101] as did a book chapter reaffirming the historic impact of the Reformation on the Dutch character[102] and a short book, *The New Education*,[103] that critiqued the influence of Darwin and Nietzsche's *Übermensch* on modern pedagogy. (In that particular book, he criticized a dangerous cocktail of Darwinian and Nietzschean thought for teaching children that they are only their bodies and that powerful bodies are better than weak bodies—Bavinck was troubled by the increasingly common view that epileptics and others whose bodies were deemed "less worthy" should be sterilized.)[104] And although he made no changes to it, a third edition of *Reformed Dogmatics* was released just as the war came to a close.

Intellectually, Bavinck remained active and continued to push the same broad writing agenda forward. However, despite the strange buffer provided by the country's neutral status, he could not ignore the war. Neutrality changed everyday life throughout the Netherlands. In 1914, an estimated one million Belgians crossed the border in search of refuge among their northern neighbors. The Dutch stock exchange had closed soon after the war began. Contact with the colonies became more difficult, and food became much more expensive. While Bavinck busied himself with *On Raising Teenagers* at his home on the Grachtengordel, 57,470 men lost their lives in a single day at the Battle of the Somme. In 1917, while Bavinck was publishing "The Unconscious," basic foods were becoming harder to come by, and rationing was introduced. In that year, nine people were killed in a riot over potatoes a short distance from his home.

Bavinck certainly believed in his ongoing theological project, and yet there was a certain unreality about life in this eerie and increasingly difficult neutral environment. By the end of the war, millions upon millions of people had lost their lives. For a theologian like Bavinck, whose own thought proceeded along a gentler path of perpetual reformation and who eschewed the sudden chaos of revolution—intellectual and political—the effects of the war were jarring and not easily ignored. While the numerous shorter works mentioned above kept up his broad project of modern reformation, the war focused his attention on two particular interrelated issues, which dominated his thought for the rest of his life: the problem of war and the role of women in society.

The Problem of War

Three months after the outbreak of war, Bavinck published a short article that was quickly reissued as a booklet entitled *The Problem of War*.[105] In this, he argued that as the religion of the Prince of Peace, Christianity naturally leaned toward mercy rather than violence. For that reason, declarations of war do not form part of the church's remit. In this world, that is the calling of the state. However, as a religion called to promote righteousness and defend the oppressed, he claimed, "Christian ethics indeed allows no other conclusion than this, that good and justified wars *are possible*."[106] In making this admission, however, Bavinck openly doubted whether any of the wars of history had truly been just. After all, every previous war contained elements that were deplorable to both "Christianity and humanity." In his eyes, there was no justification for war on the basis of "the rights of the strongest, the virtues of patriotism, bravery, courage, patience, steadfastness, the consensus of the majority, sacrifice, etc., that it can cultivate; . . . and less still for the beneficial [financial] consequences, the extension of territory, the expansion of culture, or even of the [spread of] Christianity that might accompany it."[107] However, having supported "just war" theory, he struggled to imagine how conflict between any of the countries in Europe could be unequivocally just. After all, this was now a continent in which Christianity's influence had been replaced by the pursuit of economic and nationalistic dominance. He feared that in a godless world, all wars would be unjust. As will be seen in the postscript, Bavinck's descendants certainly did see the anti-Nazi resistance during the Second World War as a just cause, for which they paid a high price. For the time being, though, Herman struggled to make sense of the First World War. "Who can tell us what the reason is for this war, why it is being waged, and what purpose it serves? From whatever angle one looks at it, no light shines on it. It is surrounded by darkness."[108] In Bavinck's judgment, it was no surprise that a growing rejection of the way of the Prince of Peace, which was deemed "no longer to apply to our age," had plunged Europe into violence. This turn of events, he believed, was inextricably linked to the new atheism of the age. Bavinck laid the blame for this nihilistic war at Nietzsche's feet.[109]

Serving Reformed Youth in the War

Prior to the First World War, the provision of chaplaincy to Dutch soldiers was fairly unsystematic, with spiritual care being largely dependent on whatever local clergy might be present.[110] Although the Netherlands had taken a neutral stance in this war, the Dutch army had nonetheless been mobilized shortly after war had been declared: in order to guard the country's neutrality, some two hundred thousand men were stationed at key locations around the country. That deployment now meant that many Protestant soldiers from the north had been stationed in the predominantly Roman Catholic south, and vice versa. Young Dutch Catholics, Protestants, and socialists—groups that generally had little direct exposure to one another prior to their deployment, apart from those resident in the big cities—now spent their time together as comrades, and often with little to do. Given the sparsity of Protestant churches in the south, Dutch Protestants grew increasingly nervous about how the lack of supportive Protestant infrastructure would affect their young men while they were stationed in primarily Catholic areas.[111] (Bavinck shared that concern, believing that a generation of young Reformed men was at risk of spiritual and moral degradation.) For that reason, Dutch Protestants began to establish their own soldiers' rest houses, for which they received no funding from the state.

In 1915, Bavinck led a movement in the First Chamber arguing that the spiritual care of these soldiers should continue to be provided by their own churches but that the financial costs thereof should be borne by the state.[112] Throughout this effort, he remained unsure of whether this was a just war or whether the policy of neutrality was the right one. His arguments in parliament focused rather on mitigating the effects of the war on a future generation—a generation of men whose lives had been put on hold at a crucial stage of their adult formation. The government consented. In Bavinck's judgment, this was a successful campaign insofar as it sent Protestant ministers to those stationed on the frontiers and brought young soldiers back to their villages with their commitment to the Protestant faith—in doctrine and life—intact.

This attention to how young Protestant soldiers were navigating the war formed part of a broader concern for the impact of the war on Dutch young people and what their role in society might be if peace were to return. In 1917, he gave a talk at the annual meeting of the Dutch Bond of Reformed Youth Associations (Nederlandschen Bond van Jongelingsvereenigingen op Gereformeerden Grondslag) to address that particular audience. Speaking to seventeen- and eighteen-year-olds, he soon shifted from introductory light-hearted self-deprecation to seriousness: "The times in which we live are perilous."[113] When he had written *The Problem of War* three months after the war had begun, he had wondered whether the war might pass quickly, leaving relatively little damage in its wake. Three years on, it had become a global conflict, leading to the deaths of millions. How should these young men face this ongoing terrible reality and understand their future role in relation to it?

In the first place, using the "great lines of Scripture," he sketched out a fundamental model of social order: God creates man and woman in the divine image; these come together in marriage as the first protosociety; and from that protosociety comes all subsequent human culture. All relationships within culture, he argued, fall into four categories: man and woman, parents and children, masters and servants, and government and the governed. "All social questions," he claimed, "however complicated they may be, ultimately lead back to these four."[114] Under the dispensation of sin, these four categories of relationships had been disordered—as was seen all around them. He continued to insist, however, that Christianity provided the necessary resources to restore their original harmony. For this reason, he encouraged these teenagers to see themselves as those called to draw on their tradition's resources to rebuild a devastated society: they were to be peacemakers in a world of broken relationships. In closing, he speculated that the future might indeed be different.

> I will not make an attempt at prophecy, because nobody knows which circumstances will arrive after the war. But I dare to assure you of this, that if one thing will be necessary, it will be this: that [people] will need to work harder than ever to restore the damage suffered, to make right the wrong that has been done, to survive financially and economically, and to prepare all the energies of men and women for the struggle that will no longer be on battlefields, but that will certainly have to be fought in the realm of economics and politics. . . . Make yourselves ready for the work to which the future will call you, and understand particularly the calling that rests on you as Reformed men.[115]

Ending the *Schoolstrijd* and Expanding Voting Rights

In the same year, a constitutional revision brought the long-term struggle over whether the state should assume equal financial responsibility for Christian schools—the *schoolstrijd*—to a conclusion. From 1917 onward, the state would support both neutral and Christian schools equally—a system that remains to the present in the Netherlands. Over decades, throughout the Franeker, Kampen, and Amsterdam periods, Bavinck had worked tirelessly in support of Christian schools.[116] Notably, however, his response to this outcome was one of caution: "The *schoolstrijd* is not over; rather it has been relocated, and for the sake of the future of our people, it must be relocated from political to pedagogical terrain." This was a warning that the Reformed community should not rest on its laurels, simply on account of its newfound financial stability. Its ongoing challenge, rather, was to keep up the process of "restless, perpetual, inner reformation" in its development of Christian pedagogy. If it failed to do so, "then this year it could be that the *schoolstrijd* was *won financially*, but *lost spiritually*."[117] Access to the state's purse did not come without dangers—a warning that would continue to echo in the halls of Dutch Christian pedagogy for years to come.[118]

The same constitutional revision expanded voting rights to all men aged twenty-three or above. (Prior to this, the men who could vote had that right only on account of their socioeconomic status.) Because this revision did not include votes for women, it was criticized by many as a halfhearted increase that fell some way from the ideal of universal suffrage (*algemeen kiesrecht*). In mid-May, Bavinck responded with a long and nuanced parliamentary speech setting out his criticisms of universal suffrage and the feminist movement, while also arguing that the possibility of equal voting rights for women *should* be considered.[119]

In the politics of the day, Bavinck believed, the notion of "universal suffrage" was bandied about glibly, as though it had no history and was a self-evident social good. In his estimations, however, the term did not have a promising historical pedigree: it was rooted in a revolutionary individualism that rejected the facts of history in favor of an idealized, abstract notion of the human as an individual who had been mythically untied from the bonds of kith and kin. (Two years before, Bavinck had given a lecture that claimed Calvinism preserved individuality by refusing to elevate it to an "-ism.") Furthermore, he argued that the notion of universal suffrage was riddled with arbitrary limitations regarding age and social status: why, he asked, was suffrage not being extended to those younger than twenty-three, or those in prison? "It is purely arbitrary. . . . Universal suffrage is not universal, but its supporters have accepted this slogan because it sounds good and makes it attractive to the people. It is, however, not universal."[120]

Clearly, Bavinck had no desire to tether himself to the shoddy reasoning of others, even if they would nonetheless arrive at the same conclusion. The same was true in his view of the feminist movement, which he believed argued for women's enfranchisement on a foundation of Darwinian and Marxist thought: "The man is always bourgeois, the woman is always proletariat."[121] While Bavinck certainly thought that sin had corrupted the relationship of man to woman, he was also convinced that neither Darwin nor Marx was able to heal their division. Rather than fixing men and women on opposite sides of an eternal class struggle, Bavinck's insistence was that men and women together were the *imago Dei*.

In this debate, Bavinck's sympathies lay, instead, with the women's suffrage campaigner Aletta Jacobs (1854–1929), the first Dutch woman to attend

university and one of the first Dutch female doctors. Crucially in winning
Bavinck's support, Jacobs "demanded universal suffrage precisely on the
grounds of the *inequality* and the *difference* between men and women."[122] A
lifelong realist, Bavinck appreciated Jacobs's insistence that the differences
between men and women should be affirmed rather than denied. And to this,
she had added a call for fairness: accepting men and women for what they
are, also including their differences, she had asked whether it was fair that
only men received the vote. Bavinck answered that it was not.

The theological content of Bavinck's answer was fairly light: "When the
Son of God has deemed a virgin worthy of being his mother," he argued,
"when he has been carried under the heart of a woman, and when he has
nursed at the breast of a woman, there can be no more talk of contempt toward
women in Christianity."[123] Beyond this, his support for women's enfranchisement came from observations on profound and irreversible changes in the
world around him. Mass industry had changed the nature of a woman's role in
society. Declining rates of marriage and births meant that many young women
who had been raised with the expectations of marriage and motherhood now
found themselves at a loss for purpose. "You only need to have spoken with
young girls these days, or have heard them talking together, to know what is
happening in the hearts of these young women. It boils down to this: we actually have nothing to do, and we have ended up in a miserable position where
we have to sit waiting for a husband who might never come along, because
the chances of marriage have gone down so incredibly. I think that is a terrible
position."[124] Having entered the newly industrialized workforce en masse, and
now receiving more and more often a level of education equal to that which
men received, women, he believed, would inevitably desire equal political
participation. Such, of course, was hardly surprising: when the first woman
student had enrolled at the Free University twelve years before, he already
thought that this particular social development had generated unstoppable
momentum. Now, though, he stood in the First Chamber, asking his fellow
members: "In the future, shall it be that women are excluded from the right to
vote purely and simply because they are *women*? That is the question before
us. And I dare, Bible in hand, to give nothing but an answer that confirms
[the following]: that possibility should be opened up to women."[125] While
some antirevolutionaries, including even Herman Kuyper, praised Bavinck's
speech, Kuyper Sr. was not pleased. In a series of three articles in *De Standaard*, he critiqued Bavinck's position—calling it a "principled attack" on his
own party—and continued to insist that women's suffrage was incompatible
with Reformed principles.[126] For all that Bavinck had continued to advance the
neo-Calvinist cause throughout the Amsterdam years, the difference between

his realism and Kuyper's idealism was more obvious than ever. Bavinck had decided to roll with the times, "Bible in hand," but—from Kuyper's perspective, at least—not with antirevolutionary principles at heart.

With this speech, Bavinck had put himself in an awkward position: he now had to demonstrate how his support of women's voting rights was indeed compatible with his party's heritage. Publicly, he did so in *The Woman in Contemporary Society*, a substantial defense (186 pages) of his view as in line with the Antirevolutionary Party's tradition.[127] Privately, Kuyper pursued a rapprochement with Bavinck, telling him that he did not want this to develop into a longer public spat.[128] In the face of Kuyper's public criticisms of him, Bavinck did not appreciate an exclusively private offer of forgiveness. Frustrated with Kuyper's effort to save face and lack of readiness to affirm him in public, Bavinck soon gave a lecture at a party meeting in which he claimed that the foundations of his parliamentary speech had in fact been laid long ago "by the 'honored' leader of our party."[129] Was it not Kuyper, after all, who had first blazed an antirevolutionary trail in support of mass democracy? As van Driel has observed, "Bavinck's use of quotation marks here reveals a great deal about his attitude toward Kuyper at this time."[130]

Rebuilding after the War

As 1918 progressed and the First World War approached its conclusion, Hannie married the lawyer Gerrit Ruys[131] (1888–1945) in a ceremony conducted by her father in the Keizergrachtskerk in Amsterdam.[132] Bavinck's new son-in-law had studied at the Free University and had defended his doctoral thesis shortly before the wedding.

Alongside this, Bavinck tried to continue in his normal work schedule. In that year, he presented a paper entitled the "Philosophy of Faith" in Leiden (once again returning to Calvin in answering modern questions),[133] wrote the short work *The Imitation of Christ and the Modern Life*,[134] and continued to produce material on Christian education.[135] By mid-November, the war was over, leaving Bavinck deeply troubled by the state of a Christendom that had grown utterly estranged from Christianity. Why had Europe's long Christian history not prevented historically Christian nations from marching into (what he still believed to have been) a needless and meaningless war—dragging the rest of the world with them? The answer, he argued in "Christianity, War, and the Bond of Nations,"[136] was that toward the end of the nineteenth century, Darwin's notion of the "survival of the fittest" and Nietzsche's anti-Christian "philosophy of domination" had migrated from the realms of biology and philosophy into the world of nationalist politics. As a result, international politics had been transformed into a race for domination at all costs, with no regard for Christianity as a restraining factor—a development that occurred just as the dominant liberal theology of the day realized it was no match for an *Übermensch* intoxicated with its sense of evolutionary superiority.[137]

In the middle of the war, Bavinck had told a group of teenagers that their calling would one day be to rebuild their nation as peacemakers. Spared to see the return of peace himself, Bavinck set about following his own advice. By the end of the war, he had concluded that neither nationalism nor internationalism was inherently evil, but he was convinced that both will quickly metastasize in the absence of a higher, universal community. In the aftermath of a world war, he saw the Christian faith as more necessary than ever: "Christianity is universal; it teaches that the whole human race is of one blood and the gospel is intended for all peoples."[138]

11

Bavinck's Final Years

1920–21

---

*"Do not put it in the newspaper;
that does not befit me!"*

By the time peace had returned, Kuyper's health—which had been precarious for many years—had taken a notable turn for the worse. Although he managed to avoid lung surgery during a full-blown chest infection in 1917, by the following year he faced periods of bed rest due to chronic bronchitis. He participated in society less and less often, and he did so increasingly by writing rather than in person. By the autumn of 1920, the recurrent bouts of dizziness that developed after an earlier nasty fall spelled the end of his working life.[1] In September he could no longer write and had to dictate his political resignation letter to one of his daughters.[2] He was now eighty-two, in obvious terminal decline, and would pass away shortly after his eighty-third birthday.

By contrast, Bavinck was sixty-three at the close of the war—still energetic enough, it seems, to have applied himself to the task of rebuilding shattered European Christendom. In a parliamentary speech in March 1919, for example, he argued (drawing on Kuyper in support) that even politicians who profess no personal Christian faith should recognize that present-day Dutch society had been developing along Christian lines for centuries and was still organized by "Christian principles"—for which reason even unbelieving politicians should adopt a positive, supportive posture toward Christianity.[3] This was a public plea for reformation over revolution in the political domain, and it was made with an eye to the public calls for a Dutch socialist revolution months before by Kuyper's old adversary Pieter Jelles Troelstra.[4]

Throughout the following year, Bavinck published a collection of essays entitled *Biblical and Religious Psychology*, in which he argued—perhaps presciently, with regard to the history of the mid-twentieth century—that a terrible change had been introduced to popular Western psychology through "the emergence of Friedrich Nietzsche," who "with deep disdain for the masses glorified only a few great men who came forth from humanity, and vindicated for them that 'might is right.'"[5] In response to the *Übermenschen* who would surely arise in the coming decades, Bavinck posed Christ's own question: "What does it profit a man to gain the whole world and forfeit his soul?" (Mark 8:36).

He continued to write on evangelism[6] and education[7] and spoke regularly at Christian women's societies across the country.[8] His contributions to public debate on the role of women in society remained important. In 1919, he gave the opening lecture, "The Professional Work of the Married Woman," at the Second Christian Social Congress in Rotterdam.[9] As a result of these efforts, he had become a high-profile champion of girls' education. His colleague J. C. Rullmann (1876–1936) later recalled an afternoon in that year in which Professor and Mrs. Bavinck had joined his family for coffee and Herman spoke to Rullmann's young daughters at length on these issues: "In the afternoon— and nobody who has heard this will ever forget it!—how heartily and simply, how compellingly and comprehensibly, he, the famous professor, spoke to our girls about women's education."[10] And of course, he remained a public campaigner for Calvinism, writing the foreword to the Dutch translation of B. B. Warfield's *Calvin as a Theologian and Calvinism Today* (1919)—a work that ended on the line, "Calvinism is nothing more, and nothing less, than the hope of the world."[11]

As it had been for many years, life was still in full swing. In May 1920, Herman and Johanna became grandparents to Theodorus Ruys (1920–86), the firstborn of Hannie and Gerrit's three sons. In the midst of this relentless activity, however, Herman had aged. In his last known portrait, taken after he had baptized his new grandson, he certainly looked every one of his sixty-six years. The wild hair of his first student portrait had receded, and a deep groove had been worn into each of his cheeks. His shoulders now sagged. It was the picture of a tired man. Finding his feet on ever-shifting terrain for so many years had taken its toll. Indeed, in this period, Bavinck—like Kuyper—made a different impression in person than he did in print. After his death, his friend W. J. Aalders recalled him attending a Christian student retreat as speaker in 1919:

> Dr. Bavinck was one of the old guard and had a great influence on the flow of conversations and decisions. I can still see the last Sunday evening in the front room. There was an intimate conversation about faith; how much pertained to it; how much of a degree of certainty there needed to be. At first, Dr. Bavinck didn't say much. His sturdy frame didn't naturally invite you to come close—it bore the hallmarks of gathered strength and reserve. But when he finally started to speak, it was to say this, that one should not imagine that faith is something so businesslike and perfect. In any case, he felt that as he became older, more and more, very little remained: [he saw himself as] a sinful person who continually and ever more deeply needs to entrust himself to God's grace. Although a man, he spoke like a child: stirred, and stirring.[12]

The Leeuwarden Synod

In August 1920, Bavinck traveled north to Leeuwarden to take part in that year's synod. An array of potential conflicts were due to be discussed: alongside a list of proposed changes to the denomination's liturgy and confessional documents, his replacement at the Theological School, Anthonie Honig, was pushing for the church to formalize its opposition to the theater, dancing, and cards (problems Bavinck deemed to be fairly unimportant, given the scale of the challenge faced by Christianity in the wider world).[13] More urgently for him, one of his former students, Rev. J. B. Netelenbos (1879–1934), came into conflict with the synod on account of his views on the authority of Scripture.

A highly regarded figure among the Free University's student body, Netelenbos had attracted critical scrutiny from the university faculty while still a student for frequenting Dutch Reformed Church services.[14] In 1917, while the pastor of a Reformed Churches in the Netherlands congregation in Middelburg, he had courted controversy by preaching in a Dutch Reformed Church congregation in The Hague and was by this point widely suspected of holding a fairly liberal view of biblical authority—although Netelenbos believed that his views fell within a nuanced reading of the church's doctrinal standards. (Netelenbos was associated with a new development in the Reformed Churches in the Netherlands, the "movement of the younger generation" [*beweging der jongeren*].)

Importantly for Bavinck, Netelenbos defended his positions by linking his views to those of his former professor. In a formulation resembling the notion of Jesus as the perfect union of divine and human natures, Bavinck had taught him that Scripture was organically inspired in a way that preserved and united its authentic humanity *and* divinity—for which reason Netelenbos now claimed that as a truly human text, Scripture's form and content were fallible. The synod's debate soon came to focus on the historicity of Eden's cunning and articulate serpent, which Netelenbos argued was mythological, and for which reason he was deposed.

His deposition was deeply painful for Bavinck, whose notes on his former student's views and private correspondence with him show that he took Netelenbos's arguments seriously. Indeed, he recognized that Netelenbos did not stand alone; rather, his views represented a generational shift within their church. In these notes, Bavinck described Scripture's human form as "weak" and "totally human from beginning to end."[15] Alongside this, however, he still insisted that Scripture was also divine through and through. Akin to Christ, who was fully God and fully human—and thus physically weak and vulnerable while also remaining God of God—Bavinck's Bible was God's word in human form. By building on this, Netelenbos had raised possible consequences stemming from that view on Scripture's fragile, servant form: to err is human, after all. Bavinck feared those consequences, which struck him as compromising Scripture's divine authority, and for that reason he was unwilling to follow Netelenbos's steps forward. Rather, he would have to hold his ground, or retrace his own steps back further still.

In a strange way, Netelenbos's tactic was reminiscent of the move played against Kuyper by Bavinck himself following his parliamentary speech on women's voting rights in 1919: although Kuyper was utterly unwilling to endorse Bavinck's position, Bavinck had nonetheless given him a painful public reminder that he had supported an earlier form of mass democracy long before, without which Bavinck's position would not have been possible. Now, though, Bavinck was in Kuyper's position, looking on as a young upstart developed his ideas beyond his control. When push came to shove, Bavinck would cling to Scripture's divine authority just as Kuyper had held to his view of Reformed principles, and for the same reason: to concede on this point was to lose everything. For all that Netelenbos had made Bavinck's position much more difficult to maintain, in their private correspondence, the real issue for Bavinck was not whether snakes or donkeys could have spoken. It was, rather, "Has God spoken?" The real issue was *Deus dixit*.[16] Bavinck had never been willing to make doctrinal moves that risked compromising God's ability to speak as God—and the Netelenbos affair was no exception. To his mind, for all the problems that might be solved in the acceptance of Scripture not simply as human, but also as errant, far more fundamental theological problems would immediately arise.

In that regard, the authority of Scripture had always been a problem for Bavinck. In a decades-long conversation with Snouck Hurgronje, his skeptical friend had repeatedly pushed him on this, arguing that he indulged the Bible with an unwarranted, arbitrary authority. While Bavinck preferred to present his view as a priori rather than arbitrary, he had long since recognized that in practice, there was little real difference. However it was packaged, his insistence remained that everyone needs a starting point somewhere. Time and time again, he had shown himself unwilling to let go of his own. However sharp his inner conflict, here he stood and could do no other: *Deus dixit*.[17]

Regardless of his private sympathies with Netelenbos and the difficulties that he recognized had been presented for his view of scriptural inspiration, his public response—albeit delivered through the committee that he directed—to questions on whether the denomination's confessional standards should be revised or minimized was unequivocal: the confessional standards, he believed, should retain their existing content *and* be expanded, particularly with regard to "the divine inspiration and authority of Holy Scripture, the doctrine of the true and false church, and that of the office of government over church and state."[18]

The Netelenbos affair had prompted Bavinck to step forward on the basis of his belief in the weak human form of Scripture. Now, however, he chose to step back, retracing his steps until he stood upon the terra firma that was its divine authority. As always, he was an orthodox Calvinist trying to find his feet in the modern world. The admission made to Snouck Hurgronje in 1883 that he was "in no way finished with [his] doctrine of Scripture" was still true in 1920.[19] Having taken part in the synod for a week, he left for Amsterdam, writing in the lost dagboek on Saturday, August 20, that he was "*exhausted*" at walking the short distance from Central Station to his house.[20] The next day, he suffered a heart attack. Although he survived that day, it was the beginning of the end.

At some point in these final years—Bremmer suspects it to have been after the heart attack—Bavinck selected a list of his shorter writings (from 1892 onward) that he believed would "continue to be of interest to future generations because they dealt with important subjects that remain the order of the day."[21] Whether it was before or after the heart attack, he was now consciously curating his legacy. Although that particular book, *Essays on Religion, Science, and Society*,[22] was published fairly quickly, its author was gone before it had been released. Edited by his brother Bernard, it would be Herman's first posthumous release.

Dying in Public, Dying in Private: Abraham Kuyper (1837–1920) and Herman Bavinck (1854–1921)

Following the heart attack, Bavinck wrote in the lost dagboek, "*The doctors all say, as they visit me during the week, to keep on resting.*"[23] The synod continued in its business, but Bavinck never returned. In the meantime, Kuyper's relentlessly public "life for the Dutch people" merged into a death for the same: he was dying, intentionally, in the public eye.

During one visit to Kuyper's deathbed, the Antirevolutionary politician Alexander Idenburg (1861–1935) had asked for permission to share their conversation with the people. Kuyper gladly agreed. His daughters Henriëtte (1870–1933) and Johanna (1875–1948) chronicled their father's experiences in awaiting and preparing for his end in their vivid and detailed book, *The Last Days of Dr. Abraham Kuyper.*[24] Prior to his death, Kuyper even arranged for a plaster deathmask to be made and was among the last generation of Dutchmen to preserve the memory of his image in this way.[25] For decades, cartoon satirists in Dutch newspapers had lampooned his face. By arranging a deathmask, however, Kuyper had given himself the last word in reminding the world how he really looked. Shortly after his passing, an illustrated book of the Kuypers' home, *The Kuyper House*, was released.[26] In death, as in life, Kuyper held nothing back.

His passing, on November 8, 1920, was noted in Bavinck's dagboek. In a series of chronicles of Bavinck's own experiences dating to 1872, the note on Kuyper's death was the last event he would record.[27] It was a striking way to finish what had been a near lifelong habit of journaling, within which their lives had become intertwined until the very last.

Before Kuyper died, Bavinck's own health had made some small improvements. Newspaper reports throughout September were fairly positive about his prognosis.

Prof. Dr. H. Bavinck is seriously ill. The situation, however, is not perilous.[28]

There has been some improvement in Prof. Bavinck's condition; his life does not seem to be in danger.[29]

Prof. Dr. Bavinck's health situation is progressing slowly. There is hope of a full recovery.[30]

By mid-October, he had been able to go downstairs and eat and had started reading newspapers again. His decline, however, was irreversible. He had begun to show signs of uremia. His body was shutting down. When Alexander Idenburg had visited the dying Kuyper, he asked him—quoting Psalm 46—whether the Lord was "a refuge and strength to him in times of trouble" and found that Kuyper wanted his affirmative response to be shared widely. Now, he came to visit the ailing Bavinck and posed the same twofold question: was the Lord also *his* refuge and strength, and could he tell the world of Bavinck's answer? He replied, "Yes, but do not put it in the newspaper; that does not befit me!"[31]

Bavinck shared Kuyper's faith but had none of his desire to die in full public view. Although this wish not to report on his thoughts on dying was respected, his decline continued to be followed in the press: he was, after all, a person of national significance. Newspaper reports in November reported, "In recent days, there has been no noticeable improvement in Prof. Dr. Bavinck's condition."[32] By December, the tone had started to shift. Clearly, his heart had sustained serious damage.

"Prof. Dr. H. Bavinck's situation is grave."[33]

"The First Chamber member Prof. Bavinck's condition has improved slightly. The tightness of chest has not returned. The patient is very weak, but his heart is a little better."[34]

Within weeks, *De Telegraaf* had reported that his condition was "very concerning" and that his "tightness of chest" was now coming and going.[35] By early February 1921, worse news was being reported: "In the last few days, Prof. Dr. H. Bavinck's condition has rapidly deteriorated. Hope of a recovery is no longer being entertained."[36] Within days, other newspapers wrote that he was "suffering terrible pain" and was no longer eating.[37] A week later, a cardiologist had confirmed that he would not recover. Palliative care had now begun.[38] By March, it was being widely reported—even in papers as far flung as *De Sumatra post*—that he was close to death.[39]

Despite this expectation, death approached Bavinck slowly. He was still alive in May. Indeed, he was lively enough to dictate a telegram—presumably sent by Johanna—to the newly named Bavinckschool in The Hague, expressing his approval.[40] In June, he had even made plans to spend part of the summer in Bussum with Hannie, Gerrit, and Theo. Those plans, however, came to naught. Once again, his condition deteriorated rapidly, with the *Rotterdamsch Nieuwsblad* noting, "There is no more discussion of going to Bussum."[41]

While it would not be possible for him to leave Amsterdam, his condition once again picked up to the point that he was able to sleep normally—after which he began to receive short visits in the afternoons.[42] Some records of his comments on these visits—in which he moved between lucidity and sleep—have been preserved in the early biographies of Hepp and Landwehr. During one such visit, the latter recalled Bavinck expressing the wish that having entered heaven, he could momentarily return to earth "to bear witness to all of God's people, and even to the world, of that glory."[43] Hepp recounted visiting Bavinck toward the very end of this period. By this point, he had difficulty speaking and had to draw breath between his words, telling his young visitor, "Living . . . is . . . strange . . . , dying . . . is . . . stranger . . . still."[44] Decades before, at the bedside of his dying friend Jan Hendrik Unink, Bavinck had been perplexed by death. Now, it seems, the same was still the case.

At the close of that month (June 28), Snouck Hurgronje wrote to Johanna referring to his own visit to his ailing friend: "I am still deeply affected by my last visit: despondent, but also edified. I have never known my good friend to be anything other than pious: 1874–1921."[45] Snouck Hurgronje was himself about to undergo surgery and had written to Johanna to ask whether she thought her husband would still be alive by the time he was mobile again. "The situation is still exactly the same," she replied, "as when you saw him last. His capacities are declining slowly. Now that the situation has remained the same for so long, I have hope that the end will not come soon."[46] By this time, his speech had become unclear—Johanna was always present during visits and had to interpret his words for visitors.[47]

In this period, of course, Bavinck had expressed the wish to keep his own reflections on his decline from public view. In a sense, he was trying to die differently than his always-visible colleague did. This wish was respected by the press, which dealt with news on his health situation but betrayed no confidences on his own thoughts about dying. Those he wanted to hold more closely. At the close of July, however, a piece in *De Telegraaf* finally broke this media silence: "According to reports, Professor Bavinck is becoming extremely weak. Although he is very patient, he continually expresses the longing that the Lord would have mercy on him and take him quickly to himself."[48] Bavinck now felt ready to pass on.

He would not have to wait much longer. Early the next morning, at 4:30, July 29, 1921, he died quietly at home.

A Final Resting Place

The family requested that no flowers be brought to Bavinck's funeral, which took place in the Nieuwe Oosterbegraafplaats in Amsterdam at 1:45 p.m., on August 2.[49] There, Tjeerd Hoekstra, Lucas Lindeboom's son-in-law, with whom Bavinck had long corresponded (and who was by now the rector of the Theological School), described him as having followed the path of his own particular Seceder roots over the course of his lifetime: "For some [Seceders]," the attendees heard, "life even had an anticultural tone, but not so for Bavinck."[50] At the close of his life, it was clear to those with eyes to see that in his efforts to be an orthodox Christian in the modern world, Bavinck had been a son of the Secession from first to last. Like his father before him, he had followed the path that led from "separation to integration."

Surrounded by representatives from the Free University, the Theological School, his former congregation in Franeker, the First Chamber of Parliament, and the various Reformed student societies with which he had long been involved, his body was lowered into the ground—at which, the crowd spontaneously burst into a jubilant psalm of praise to Christ.

> Yea, all the mighty kings on earth
> before him down shall fall;
> and all the nations of the world
> do service to him shall. (Ps. 72:11)[51]

Although Bavinck was buried in Amsterdam, this was not to be his final resting place—a fact acknowledged in passing by Hepp but not mentioned by Bremmer or Gleason.[52] Shortly after his burial there, his coffin was taken up and transported to the Emaus cemetery in Vlaardingen. There, he was laid to rest among Johanna's family—where she would eventually join him (1942). While his gravestone there is large, it carries only the most minimal of detail: *Dr. H. Bavinck, b. 13 Dec. 1854, d. 29 July 1921.*

Shortly after his death, a group of former friends and colleagues formed a group (the Bavinck-Comité) in order to promote and curate his legacy. On their behalf, Abraham Kuyper Jr. quickly began a fundraising effort in order to commemorate him with their own gravestone.[53] Nothing, however, came of that initiative. Rather, the original memorial still stands. Much might be added to it: here lies a dogmatician, an ethicist, an educational reformer, a pioneer in Christian psychology, a politician, a biographer, a journalist, a Bible translator, a campaigner for women's education, and eventually, the father, father-in-law, and grandfather of heroes and martyrs in the anti-Nazi resistance movement.

Under that heavy slab lie the earthly remains of Herman Bavinck—an orthodox Calvinist, a modern European, and a man of science.

Postscript

In the months that followed her husband's death, Johanna busied herself by compiling newspaper articles on his life and work.[1] That August, she received a letter of condolence from Henry Dosker, informing her, "I loved him so deeply. We went to school together, we fought for the same prizes in the gymnasium in Zwolle, as young lads we were in love with the same girl"; then he asked her to write back immediately with the details of "what he died of, and how Herman died."[2] Closer to hand, of course, was a steady stream of well-wishers. By October, their visits began to tail off, as did the printed reflections on Herman's life and work. As autumn turned to winter, Johanna placed her own note of thanks to friend and stranger alike in *De Bazuin* for their support during her "unforgettable" husband's illness and death.[3]

Within a year of his passing, Valentijn Hepp, a pastor whose doctoral studies had been supervised by Bavinck, had produced a full and dramatic account of his life—an account that also prompted Dosker to write to Johanna to complain that Hepp had not written enough about the things Herman had enjoyed during his 1908 American journey.[4] This letter was perhaps awkward for Johanna, whose own critical remarks on America (and description of Dosker himself) Hepp had also included.

Johanna and the Christian Women's Movement

By this time, Johanna was moving into her midfifties and possessed considerable energies and intelligence of her own. As was mentioned in chapter 8, she channeled these by carrying on Herman's work in two directions: in furthering his work on the women's movement and in the international dissemination of his *Reformed Dogmatics*.

Before Herman had died, Johanna was already active as president of the Dutch Christian Women's Bond and took particular responsibility for providing young women with help in choosing a profession.[5] In 1919, she had become a member of the Dutch Women's Bond for Moral Improvement,[6] and also served as a member of the Women's Committee at the Christian Social Congress—at which Herman had spoken alongside Ms. H. M. Crommelin in a session entitled "The Woman's Professional Life."[7]

After Herman's death, Johanna moved to Bussum, where Hannie, Gerrit, and their growing family lived: two more grandsons were born in quick succession, Herman (1923–43) and Hugo Floris (1924–45). At the same time, Johanna became one of the editors of a new periodical, *Christendom en Vrouwenbeweging* (Christianity and the women's movement)—a publication intended to address the women's movement in relation to the family, education, society, law, art, science, social work, and the church. A typically neo-Calvinistic endeavor, it was set up because of the belief that Christianity should live by its own terms as it rose to meet the needs of the day. The first issue, authored by the famed Dutch Protestant activist Cornelia Frida Katz (1885–1963), was itself a significant engagement with Herman's writings on that topic.[8] When the periodical was set up, Johanna agreed to contribute a volume on "halfway houses." Although it does not seem that her own intended volume was ever published, those that were released followed Katz's example in wrestling with Herman's legacy.[9] At the same time, Johanna was involved in raising support for a medical mission among girls on Java.[10] These were busy years.

In the midst of these activities, a considerable controversy arose around another of Herman's former students: Rev. Johannes Geelkerken (1879–1960). The question "Did the snake speak?" arose, and in 1926—as had been the case with Netelenbos in 1920—a deposition case ensued. And once again, Bavinck's name was invoked by Geelkerken and his supporters, who claimed that if he were still alive, he would have supported them. Prior to Geelkerken's deposition, Herman's irenic brother Bernard coauthored a short book, *"The Mother of Us All,"*[11] which pushed both sides for greater nuance in setting out their own positions (as well as in their readings of Herman's work). In response, Herman Kuyper published the details of private conversations with Bavinck following Netelenbos's dismissal in 1920, saying that "Prof. Bavinck had no hesitation in declaring that the Leeuwarden Synod couldn't have acted differently. However much personal sympathy he had for Rev. Netelenbos, he said 'Rev. Netelenbos is not to be supported.'"[12] His argument was that as Bavinck had rejected Netelenbos's attempts to tie his program to the *Reformed Dogmatics*, the same would now happen in relation to Geelkerken.

In any case, Geelkerken soon found himself expelled from his office. Unlike Netelenbos, who joined the Dutch Reformed Church after his own deposition, Geelkerken was soon thrust into the center of a newly formed denomination—the Reformed Churches in Restored Association (Gereformeerde Kerken in Hersteld Verband). Although this new denomination was relatively small—in 1928 comprising some fifty-eight hundred members in twenty-three congregations—it soon gained three particularly notable members: Gerrit Ruys, Hannie Ruys-Bavinck, and Johanna Bavinck-Schippers.

Johanna's choice to join Geelkerken's church in 1928, two years after its formation, was newsworthy enough to be highlighted in the *Algemeen Handelsblad*.[13] In that regard, the three formed a striking contrast with Herman, who had not sided with Netelenbos in 1920 (and also with Herman's brother Bernard, who did not join Geelkerken's church). Evidently, Johanna and Hannie knew their own minds. Although Johanna never commented publicly on her reasons for this (controversial) choice, the fact that her new denomination was more open to women's participation in the work of the church certainly seems significant: in 1923, she had coedited an issue of *Christendom en Vrouwenbeweging* that had argued women should be given voting rights equal to those enjoyed by men within the church (a position that her late husband *had* clearly supported)[14] and should be allowed to serve as deacons.[15] In 1927, shortly before Johanna left the Reformed Churches in the Netherlands, the denominational synod had published a report advising *against* women's voting rights within the church, arguing instead that Scripture grants authority in the church only to men and that "at the present moment in time," the extension of ecclesiastical voting rights to women "would not be without danger, with regard to the unchristian emancipation movement that goes against the ordinances of God."[16] Whatever her (unknown) views on the early chapters of Genesis, it is hard to imagine that Johanna would not have felt unsettled in the Reformed Churches in the Netherlands after 1927—and so it is perhaps unsurprising that she quickly moved to a denomination that (by 1936) had published a new church order that allowed for women to serve as deacons and to vote in church elections.[17] In so doing, she had remained close to Herman's views—in one part, at least.

Negotiating with Publishers

From the late 1920s onward, Johanna began to explore possible outlets through which the *Gereformeerde dogmatiek* might be translated into German and English. In her correspondence with the publisher J. H. Kok in 1927, it is clear that the plan to have the *Dogmatics* translated into German was her own initiative. She then entered discussions with Vandenhoeck & Ruprecht (a German academic press) to that end, although nothing eventually came of that plan. In 1930, she also began discussing an English translation with the Smitter Book Company, which then bought the rights to the *Gereformeerde dogmatiek*. Despite this, the plans for this English-language *Reformed Dogmatics* soon ran into difficulty. The first publisher to buy the rights went out of business. While another publisher, Eerdmans, had long since shown an interest in publishing a major work by either Kuyper or Bavinck, confusion arose on both sides—between Johanna and Eerdmans—as to whether an eventual project would be a full and accurate translation of Bavinck's own work or a looser, incomplete rendering of his *Dogmatiek*.

Johanna's insistence was for a full, carefully translated project—a view perhaps colored by the patchy paraphrase of *Het christendom*—released under the title "Christ and Christianity"—that had appeared in English in 1916 and that was some way from conveying the contents of Bavinck's original text.[18] The *Dogmatiek*'s originally intended translator, William Hendriksen (1900–1982), had planned rather to produce an abridged version that did not include the first volume.[19] The cost and time implications of producing the full translation that Johanna desired, however, were not inconsiderable. In the end, the circumstances of history conspired against her plans: the conditions of the Great Depression were not favorable to a major project like this.

Instead, part of Bavinck's second volume would eventually be published in translation in 1951 under the title *The Doctrine of God*,[20] with *Magnalia Dei* appearing in English as *Our Reasonable Faith* five years later. The full translation of his *Dogmatiek* in English would not be completed until 2008—following which it would appear in Korean, Portuguese, and (thus far, only in abridged form) Chinese. While Johanna did not live to see any of this, she remained involved in the promotion of scholarship on Calvinism—a role she occupied conspicuously as a woman in mid-twentieth-century Dutch theological circles. In 1934, for example, she was the only woman on the organizing committee for the Second International Conference of Calvinists, held that year in Amsterdam.[21]

As had been the case for her late husband, however, Johanna's energetic activity was also interrupted by the outbreak of war. In 1939, at the beginning of World War II, she was seventy-one. Nothing is known of her own activities during the war years, during which the Netherlands came under Nazi occupation from 1940 onward, despite its neutral status. Her family, though, quickly devoted themselves to an underground struggle against the Nazis:

these were not days to work in full view. (In a striking contrast, the elderly Herman Kuyper wrote in *De Heraut* to describe the very same occupiers as "the leaders whom God has given us" who "have not been idle these summer months, but have shown us the way that has become necessary for our people through the upheaval in Europe.")[22]

In the final years of Johanna's life, her nephew Johan Herman Bavinck (1895–1964)—a pastor who had served as a missionary in Indonesia and who was himself a distinguished intellectual—emerged as the most prominent public member of the clan. In 1939, Johan Herman was appointed to teach missiology at both the Theological School and the Free University, finally fulfilling his late uncle's call for the appointment of a man who "lives solely for missions."[23] Three years after this, on May 31, 1942, Johanna Bavinck-Schippers passed away at the age of seventy-four. As the wider world was in the throes of war, Johanna's death notice—placed by Hannie and Gerrit, interestingly, in *De Telegraaf*, rather than the antirevolutionary *De Standaard*—announced that she had "fallen asleep in Jesus."[24] In the following week, she was laid to rest with Herman in her native Vlaardingen.

Heroes and Martyrs of the Resistance

By the time their grandmother died, Theo, Herman, and Hugo Ruys were twenty-two, nineteen, and eighteen. Theo had finished his studies at the Christian Lyceum in Bussum,[25] where their father was chairman of the school's board of trustees. His younger brothers were still in education. Like their parents, they were supporters of the anti-Nazi resistance movement. Gerrit, a lawyer and president of the Amsterdam Life Insurance Company, worked discreetly to protect Jewish property from falling into Nazi hands. Hugo and Herman were among the first to join *Het Parool*, an illegal anti-Nazi newspaper (and now a national daily title)—printing copies that were then distributed under cover of darkness—and actively helped Jews in hiding. Nothing is known of the specific involvement of Hannie or Theo, although it would soon become clear that they were regarded by the Nazis as a "terrorist family."

Throughout 1943, Herman worked with a number of resistance groups, covertly taking photographs of Nazi defenses, army transports, and troop locations. That August, he was involved in the attempted assassination of E. J. Woerts, the local police commandant and a member of the Dutch National Socialist Movement. Shortly after this, on September 9, Herman was betrayed and arrested at an illegal meeting in the Jeugdkapel—a church venue built to hold youth evangelistic events—minutes from his parental home. From there, he was taken to Amsterdam, where he was held in the Weteringschans House of Detention—the prison in which Anne Frank and her family would also be held in the following year. Toward the close of the following month, on October 22, he was sentenced to death and faced the firing squad the next day.

On the night that Herman was arrested at the Jeugdkapel, Hugo went to the adjacent manse in search of information about his brother, where he was also arrested: on the same night, both brothers were taken to Amsterdam. Hugo, however, was released after three weeks. He never saw his brother again.

At the same time, the war divided the next generation of Kuypers. Herman Kuyper's son Elisa Willem (1896–1944) renounced Christianity altogether, leaving his wife for a younger mistress before enthusiastically joining the Waffen SS on the Eastern Front, where he soon died working as a wartime reporter for the Nazi press.[26] Elisa's cousin Johanna (Johtje) Vos, née Kuyper (1909–2007), chose the opposite. In their three-bedroom house, Johtje and her husband, Aart (1905–90), sheltered thirty-six Jews during the war, eight of whom lived in their home for a number of years. A sympathetic local policeman would call their house whenever Nazis were in the vicinity, allowing the phone to ring twice before hanging up—after which their Jewish friends would escape through a concealed tunnel that led directly from their coal shed into the woods behind their house.[27] (In 1982, Johtje and Aart received a Righteous Among the Nations Award from the State of Israel. Her story could scarcely have been further from that of her cousin.)

In the first half of 1944, while Johtje and Aart shared their rations with their hidden guests and Elisa lost his life in the Crimea, Hugo Floris Ruys was involved in the production of a local edition of *Het Parool*, which he delivered after nightfall on a bicycle with no lights. During his delivery run on the night of January 12, 1945, he was caught by Wehrmacht soldiers and taken to Weteringschans. The Ruys home was promptly searched. Theo hid in the attic and was not found. Gerrit and Hannie, however, were unable to avoid capture. Both were arrested. Although Gerrit was initially sentenced to death, he was sent rather to the Neuengamme concentration camp, following which he was scheduled to be taken to Stalag X–B, a prisoner-of-war camp in northern Germany. On April 5, 1945, while being transported from Neuengamme, he died of dysentery.

One month before, members of the resistance had tried—and failed—to assassinate Hanns Albin Rauter, the highest-ranking member of the SS in the Netherlands. On March 7, in response, hundreds of captive Dutch resistance members were executed by firing squad. Among them stood Hugo Floris Ruys—in whose honor a street in Amsterdam is now named.[28] In the meantime, Theo survived in hiding, protected by another resistance family.

Hannie was released on April 22. As was the case for many resistance families, theirs was a story of unimaginable loss, trauma, and faith.[29] The bodies of Herman and Hugo were eventually relocated to the Honorary Cemetery in Bloemendaal.[30] There, Psalm 18:2 is carved into Herman's gravestone: "You, O God, my Lord, are my shield and protector!"[31] Hugo's stone cites Christ's own commandment to those who are imprisoned and suffering (Rev. 2:10): "Be faithful unto death, and I will give you the crown of life."

APPENDIX ONE

"My Journey to America"

(1. Travel is an art that one must learn.

2. Moving oneself easily, opening one's eyes, preferring observation [to judgment].

3. Observing, perceiving, and valuing.)

Whenever one travels far, one gains stories to tell. That is especially the case when one travels to America—distant, great, and powerful. The impressions [gained there] are so overwhelmingly numerous and rich that study is needed should one wish to sort and present them in an orderly fashion. I have endeavored to do so and, following an initial overview of our[1] journey, offer the following outline: (1) land and nature, (2) culture from the bottom, (3) towns and cities, (4) houses and home life, (5) character of the inhabitants, (6) social, (7) moral, and (8) religious life.

Mijne reis naar Amerika, ed. George Harinck (Barneveld: De Vuurbaak, 1998). An earlier version of this translation was originally published in James Eglinton, "Herman Bavinck's 'My Journey to America,'" *Dutch Crossing: Journal of Low Countries Studies* 41, no. 2 (2017): 180–93. Thanks are due to the Uitgeverij de Vuurbaak for granting permission to publish an English translation of this work.

The journey. However long a journey of three months may seem to be, and really is, it is not long enough when traveling from England to America. On July 22, we went to Rotterdam en route via Harwich to London, and stayed there until July 27. Then, we went to Liverpool and set out on the new and beautiful Dominion Line steamboat the *Labrador* to Quebec and Montreal in Canada. The journey across the sea was pleasant in many regards, as far as our two journeys are concerned. We did not meet the sea in its rage; we did not see its anger. (Seasickness—weak, slothful, listless, sickly, bleak, bored, miserable, irritated.) Only once have we felt how she can grow angry and furious when she is goaded by the wind and throws up her waves. Now our only impressions of her are twofold: concerning her endless magnitude and width and her ceaseless turning. The journey from Liverpool to Quebec is 2,600 [miles], [from Liverpool] to New York—2,812 miles long, which is approximately 130 hours. That is quick to say, but one feels the length and the cost first, when one sees nothing but water—infinitely wide, everywhere—day after day, night after night. And with that the commotion, no single moment of stillness, always in motion, vigorous but never still, looking for peace, chasing it, but finding it nowhere—a picture of the disquiet of the human heart. The journey is so long that one grows bored in the last days, and one gasps for land. It is an event, *ein Ereignis des Tages* [an "Event of the Day"], when a ship, a bird, a whale, an iceberg is seen; and joy beams from all [on board] when, after days at sea, land finally comes into sight. *Overigens ist die ganze Sache etwas langweilig* ["Anyway, the whole thing is a bit boring"] (Dr. Goebel);[2] and no comfort from the boat, no pleasure from food or drink, no friendly treatment from the staff, no warm conversation between passengers can keep us from that monotony and irritation. It is so overwhelming, to have no firm ground beneath one's feet, always to be rocking back and forth. We are not marine animals. Quite simply, we were created [as] land animals. We need a firm base upon which to stand and cannot live in the air. Thus at sea one learns to understand the beauty of the promise: "For the mountains may depart, and the hills be moved, but God's covenant is for ever fixed."[3]

[1.] For us it was a joy to set foot on dry land again. And what we first saw was a marvel. Between Labrador and Newfoundland we traveled through the Strait of Belle Isle into the Gulf of St. Lawrence. It is called a gulf, but it is more than a sea, it is so large. Gradually, the gulf becomes smaller and takes us onto the St. Lawrence River. A stunning river, broad, great, mighty, hemmed in on both sides by high banks and hills with very friendly villages here and there. (French origins and names of churches.) The rivers of America are exceptionally beautiful. Everything is great and grand, graceful and noteworthy; it is all colossal. And there are also beautiful views, beautiful beyond description. The sunset, on the evening of Friday, August 5, was astounding. On the following day, Saturday, August 6, we arrived in Quebec by midday. The location is exceptional. The city is built on a protruding, sharp rock in the middle of the river. The boat stayed there for a few hours. We wandered around and beheld beauty as never before seen. We made our way to the easterly side of the St. Lawrence River and had, on the one side, the view of the elevated Quebec. Behind that, on the other side, in the west, the sun set slowly. A shroud of cloud, now heavier, then lighter, hung before her. And through the shroud the sun threw her beams at the beautiful and electronically lit Quebec in a thousand tints and colors and forms. Indescribably beautiful, unapproachable with the pen, that it might be turned into poetry; it is only to be enjoyed in unspoken wonder and silent worship. We have beautiful skies, but Canada's are more beautiful still.

From Montreal we traveled with the American Great Trunk Railway, through the tunnel of Port Huron (train travel in America), which goes on for more than half an hour under the sea, to Michigan, to the colony of Dutch [*Hollandsche*] settlers. The part of Michigan that we saw is good and beautiful land, but in terms of virtue pales in comparison to Pella, the colony of Scholte;[4] and this also falls short of Orange City, the settlement of Rev. Bolks[5] and Mr. Hospers.[6] Michigan was all forest; in Orange City everything was prairie, endless grasslands, but nonetheless a fruitful, rich, and beautiful foundation, with few trees, but still beautiful in its immense undulation.

We did not go farther than Orange City, which is approximately halfway across the United States. That was the furthest point to the west. From there, we turned toward Milwaukee and Lake Michigan, moving slowly eastward. Our journey led us back to Toronto, where the council was held.[7] Together with the delegates we visited Niagara Falls on Saturday, September 24, around three hours' journey from Toronto. A mental image of this waterfall cannot be given. At first it takes some effort, but the more and longer one sees it, the more it increases in greatness and grandeur. The Niagara gathers all the water from the four great Lakes of America (Superior, Michigan, Hudson, and Erie) and leads over to Lake Ontario. It is colossally broad before the waterfall and is very shallow (and comes to an end half a mile before the falls). The ground is rocky; it is as though the water itself is nervous, to bore through the rock it is forced over and along it. And that is where the current comes, tumbling (playing, frolicking), springing, greeting, sparkling over the thousands of rocks and along the many (rocky) islets (especially the [Three] Sisters [Islands]). One can go or travel to these islands, and then there, for the first time, behold the waterfall.[8] Beyond this, the bottom immediately breaks off, and one sees a depth of . . .[9] feet. The water, as though it had been enraged by the rocks and islands, does not fall, but rather crashes into the deep with violence, furious, boiling, tumbling, and falls away in the water beneath, so deeply that the surface of the water below remains calm, so much so that one can take a boat very near the waterfall itself. The water forced under first comes back to the surface half an hour later (by the strong curve of the river, formed by the whirlpool) and has such power that it is unnavigable. The beauty is increased by the waterfall itself being broken into two great sections, the American part at . . .[10] feet wide, and the Canadian part, which is shaped like a horseshoe and is . . .[11] feet long. When we had seen the waterfall from above, we then finally viewed it from the other side. The Rhine Falls are beautiful, but Niagara is majestic beyond description.[12] It was unfortunate that we did not have more time there.

At five o'clock we traveled by train to Albany, and after passing Sunday, September 25, there we left on Monday by steamer for New York, following the Hudson. The Hudson is the American Rhine but broader; it passes along hilly banks (the Catskill Mountains), with cities and towns on both sides, its winding curves propelling it, pushing it through the rocks. But here there are no days like those on the Rhine;[13] romance is absent. America is too young. At six o'clock we arrived in New York, which is also beautifully located. To the east it is divided from Brooklyn by the East River, to the west from Jersey by the Hudson. And then both of these areas, Brooklyn and Jersey City, leap out in a great bend before us and form a cordon around the actual New York, making up the New York Bay, while different islets (Long Island to the north, Staten Island to the south, and between them Ellis and Governors Islands) in the bay have taken root, as it were, like faithful sentries around New York. That sight was especially beautiful, on October 5 when we left the American coast from Jersey and set off by New York through the bay into the ocean. Europe, yes, but also America has its beautiful and stirring natural scenes. God is great, also in America.

2. In terms of culture, this land, wide in a dizzying sense, is only four centuries old. It was precisely four hundred years ago that Columbus, having left the Spanish haven on July 12, arrived in Columbia on October 14. The Columbian Celebration is held everywhere in America and was prepared in the last days of our stay. And since that time America has been a place for refugees and pilgrims, for thousands from Europe. While South America was populated from Spain and Portugal, the North was populated primarily by the Germanic and Anglo-Saxon race. And once again, the north of [the] Americas' United States [was populated] by Puritans, democrats, men of the people, and in the south especially by Episcopalians, aristocrats, monarchists. The power of the United States lies in New England (Yankee [Maine, Vermont,

New Hampshire, Massachusetts, Rhode Island, Connecticut]): the throne of power and energy. Reformed Puritans have left their mark on America. Our people and land have had their part in this. Hollanders, who were the first settlers there, founded New York. Numerous names were originally Dutch and still call this to remembrance (Harlem in New York, see Cohen Stuart[14]). Many families treat their descent from these old Dutchmen as a badge of honor. In many families Dutch [*Hollandsch*] was still spoken until recently, or it was used for reading and prayer. "Grandfather or grandmother still knew Dutch," many told me. In Iowa I traveled with someone, Mr. A. van Stout, whose forefathers left the Netherlands for New Amsterdam in 1627. The Dutch Bible and Dutch books are still kept as heirlooms in many families. The descendants of these old settlers are now becoming the current-day nobility, the aristocracy of America.

But the influence of the Hollanders is greater still. New research has brought this to the fore. Griffis[15] and Douglas Campbell[16] in particular have invested their strength in this. The founding of the monument to Robinson[17] in Leiden is a prior reason for this. Earlier historians have traced the making of America in politics (social, religious) to England. However, [the reality] seems to be wholly different. England was never an example for America. Rather, first, many Hollanders were exiled to the eastern parts of England during the time of persecution, precisely the land from which most immigrants under the Stuarts left for America. And secondly, the Pilgrim Fathers sojourned in the Netherlands for fifteen years, sailing from Delfshaven to America in 1620. The oldest inhabitants of New England seem to have learned their industry, politics, freedom of religion, social establishment, and diligence from the Dutch.

And finally, America has also been a refuge to thousands of Hollanders in this century. Michigan was purchased in 1847 by Van Raalte.[18] One hundred thousand Hollanders still live in America: twenty thousand in Grand Rapids, with twenty-two churches; farmers within a twenty-mile radius of Pella and Orange City, with a great number in Paterson [NJ] and Roseland [NJ], Holland [MI] and the surrounding area (the united states of the Netherlands). For all of these immigrants, the earliest history was one of suffering. I recall only those of Van Raalte: They arrived in the winter. Everything was forest, [long] hours and the expanse of miles. Everyone had to work. Wood had no worth; rather, it was the enemy. And when a section of forest had been cut down, the [sun's] rays shone through [and the clearing] became an oven. Numerous gasses arose. Many suffered and died, but Van Raalte inspired bravery. He preached on Sundays, after which everyone went back to work with renewed courage. And so they suffered and battled on, year after year. In time it became a flourishing colony. Many towns were begun. In the surrounding area Dutch is spoken and understood: New Zeeland [Zeeland, MI], Overissel [Overisel Township, MI], Drente [Drenthe, MI], Groningen [Holland Charter Township, MI]—the united states of Holland. America has been developed like this throughout, by Hollanders, the English, Germans, by all manner of European nations. Deserts, forests, and prairies are transformed into blooming and fruitful fields, upon which cities and towns are laid. In many places it is holy ground: the blood, tears, suffering, and prayers of the forefathers have made it holy. And still the culture goes on. Immigration continues. America is so wondrously large. One can travel through it for days and nights on end. We do not understand its expanse. It is . . .[19] miles wide, and . . .[20] miles long (approximately as large as Europe, sixty times larger than England and Wales). A single province is far larger than the Netherlands. And it is a fruitful, rich land. It has everything, can provide for itself, and can exist independently. It has grain, meat, bread, gold, silver, iron, tin, coal, gas, petroleum, everything necessary for human existence. For one who is willing to work, there is bread in abundance. There is indeed poverty, but it does not need to be there. The people there are all thankful. They press on. They see a bright future. They have renewed faith and hope, the courage to face life, and the strength to live life. Not everyone there becomes rich. That only happens to a few, and that more by the increase of the price of land than by normal work. But everyone there has a piece of bread. Many there have bread, and many have also found faith in Christ.

3. This cultivation still carries on. There, everything is unpolished, a work in progress: nothing looks tidy, finished, or ready. And in everything there is the impulse to work. Meadows, houses, cities, towns—everything is marked by its newness, by its state of becoming. A city like New York, old, and European, is more or less an exception in that regard. The farther one travels westward, the more one encounters that newness and incompletion. Idle hands are ne'er to be found, but nothing is complete. The meadows are often covered in weeds—there is no time for weeding, and not enough hands to cover endless fields. [The fields] are divided by rows of rough tree stumps, upturned tree roots, pieces of wood angled against each other, and for the first time more recently by iron wire fences. The houses, first made of logs in the settlers' time, are still made of wood, even in the large cities. The pavements are wooden and coarse. Even in the middle of the city the roads are still often rough, gritty, sandy, or made of clay and cannot be crossed in the rain. However, to the extent that the residents of the street become wealthier (as they must pay for the roads in the form of taxation), these are making way for beautiful roads of cedar wood, of gravel and stones, and especially of asphalt. The more recent cities and towns are all planned in the same square shape. The streets form straight lines and crisscross in equally straight lines.

They have no names other than First, Second, or Third Street. This is not so in the older cities and the oldest parts of New York, but the newer cities are (almost) all planned in this way. One can feel at home there very easily. The streets are broad and spacious, but there is something monotonous about it all. The cities are all systematically, methodically developed, then constructed. Nothing has grown; rather, everything is made. All the cities are the same in build and design. Chicago, New York, Philadelphia, Washington—everything is the same. They have no history or poetry. Further to this, all the cities have in common that the area for business and the area where the businessmen live are separate. It is completely the norm that the businessmen do not live in or above their stores. The houses [buildings] in the business area are only for business, intended as shops, stores, offices. But the people live outside these areas in individual houses. And these boulevards are beautifully laid out. Every day, in the mornings at six or seven or eight o'clock, the gentlemen go to their businesses; and they return in the evenings at six o'clock, and then the majority of the shops are closed, and there is nothing more to be done. The residential houses are beautifully built. In the business area the houses [buildings] stand close to each other, but on the boulevards each house stands separately; each has its own yard and, before and behind and on both sides, is surrounded by a well-maintained, clean, fresh patch of grass (lawn), and sometimes also by flower beds (cemeteries). The houses are very different from ours in terms of interior design and build. First, they all resemble villas and all have larger or smaller verandas. Following this, they are all, accordingly, lighter, happier, livelier, and more varied than our houses. And finally the division and design of rooms is wholly different from our own. Hallways running through the entire house are unknown. Sometimes one does have a hall (vestibule) with the stairway leading up, and the parlor next to it. After this there are always two rooms, a sitting room and a bedroom; and after this another two, a dining room and a bedroom; and after this a kitchen, a maid's room, and so on. The houses are very comfortable and practically designed. One can also enter the sitting room from outside, and immediately one is in the house. The outside corresponds to the inside: furniture is usually far lighter in color than ours; carpet, chairs, tables, ceiling, and walls are all light yellow. It is striking and less somber, chic, simple in style, compared to our own. Comfort is catered for, particularly so by the chairs. In each room there are rocking chairs, upon which one can place oneself in a free and easy manner, women included. Sometimes an entire company can sit in ceaseless rocking back and forth, a symbol of the restless and nervous American nature: certainly comfortable, but not gracious or charming. The bedrooms are outstanding, with large and wide bedframes, superbly set out and covered. Only the pillows disappoint.

4. The people who live in the west are indeed remarkable. People are always the most important thing. "The study of mankind is man."[21] And among the peoples, the American people are assuming a greater and greater place. They are already noteworthy because of their background. The Anglo-Saxon, and thus Germanic, element forms the foundation and chief ingredient of this. But how many other peoples have exercised influence, and what number of other elements has been taken in! Not to speak of the blacks, emancipated since 1865 and currently increasing in number and strength, and of the Chinese, who are becoming wealthy in America: the Americans themselves are a mixture. English, Scots, Irish, Dutch, French, Germans, Italians, Swedes, Norwegians—all the peoples of Europe have added something of themselves to the American character. The first thing to catch one's eye in this character is certainly the activity, the energy, the youth and freshness, which stands as a wonderful contrast to the old and more sedate Europe. The American people does not yet have a past—it is only four centuries since its discovery, and only one century since its independence—but everything bears witness to this: it has a future. In this regard it is the exact opposite to Europe, living off the past and despairing of the future. It is young, fiery, brave, full of verve, full of enthusiasm and vivacity, full of optimism and enterprise. It knows no concerns or limitations. It conquers everything. An example says more than a multitude of assertions. After the Great Chicago Fire of 1871, several days after the fire, someone set this notice on the heap of rubble that had been his building: "Wife and energy safed [sic], office continued." The American spirit is all "go-ahead," everything is "in a hurry," everything is restless, everything is drive and pursuit. Boston sleeps, New York dreams, Chicago is awake. Chicago is *the* wonder city, two million inhabitants, a wilderness for fifty years, burned down in 1871 and rebuilt shortly after. Under the influence of the climate and the work, the men there are all more or less gaunt, thin, taller than they are wide, dry skinned, quick to gray, angular, but muscular. There are few handsome men, but more and more beautiful women. America is the land of the woman. Here, the cause of emancipation was first advanced. Not only do they enjoy every possible freedom and distinction; they also enjoy the first place everywhere, always have priority when traveling, in the street and at home. In order to be respected in America, it is enough simply to be a woman. A woman's word counts in a court of law. They can charge their tempters and compel them to marriage or payment of damages. The law cares for her after the death of her husband. They have the right to vote in school affairs, sometimes also for the mayor and [city] council. And this process seems only to have begun. Perhaps later the right to vote for Senate and Congress and president will also follow. They wield the most influence in societies. The movements against smoking

and drinking are largely led by women. Numerous posts—in the telegraph service, the post, the education system—are filled by women. They enjoy a freedom that is unknown here. They travel, cycle, practice gymnastics, hold meetings, make public addresses, preside, administrate, and govern to a high degree. They distinguish themselves from the men by their beauty. Of a slim, high stature, well formed (and elegant), free in their movements, with a white color, dark brown hair, dark eyes and eyebrows, they make—in contrast to the men—a striking impression. They also do not do much. They often have no understanding of housework. Raising children is not their work. The writer[22] of *Our Country*, the second edition, page . . .[23] (Boissevain I, 113),[24] says: "There is little reverence, and therefore little authority, in many American homes, except that which is exercised by children over their parents."[25] American children often distinguish themselves by a freedom that differs little from rudeness. And therefore, women can live for their bodies or their souls, for the societies and unions of which they are glad members. They love this all the more because American servants have a bad name. They are not all dressed as ladies, but wish to be treated as such. A high salary, good food, regularly going out, and doing little work are their demands. Many families eat in restaurants or allow themselves to be served so.

5. However much the American is industrious, he is not indifferent to food and drink. He eats three times a day, but also [does so] well and more than well. Even the most modest man can live well there. The daily and normal provisions are good and cheap. Meat, milk, eggs, cake in all variety of forms are within everyone's reach. All the immigrants who suffer poverty [despite] hard work here live plentifully there. Wine (beer) and strong drink are not used at all in the gentlemanly circles of the west, [where] it is seen as something base. But the consumption of candy is increasing. A hot meal is eaten three times a day. Each meal consists of meat, vegetables, potatoes, all sorts of fruits, and sometimes six or seven kinds of tart (cakes, pies) from a variety of desserts, coffee, tea, chocolate, and many kinds of cooled drinks. The most wonderful shops in America are the drugstores—the pharmacies, where not only medicines but also cigars, sweets, candy, pies, soda water, ice cream, vanilla ice, and so on, and so forth, can be found. Going there is gentlemanly, but a saloon is stigmatized. The saloons are also shunned. They are not inns where one can rest. [Rather,] they are counters where one can only stand, drink, and leave again. The entire notion of visiting, sitting in convivial [*gezellige*] company,[26] is unknown there. Just sit at the counter on your (office) stool, and then move on!

6. Social life also lacks the convivial intimacy [*gezelligheid*][27] that we possess here. Many, having come here, mourn that momentous loss. (Women,

however, feel more at home than men. The men complain about the . . .[28] Women had more money to idle away, and found it pleasant [*gezellig*].) Work, eat, sleep—this is the substance of American life. There is no time left over for convivial friendship [*gezellige omgang*] and conversation. The rich have their parties, of course; resplendent in abundance and opulence. Americans particularly love the theater, visiting it in great numbers. Dancing and playing are also very much enjoyed, and are also found in Christian, Presbyterian circles—even among ministers. But the middle classes have few convivial [*gezellige*] pleasures. However, hospitality is a virtue practiced by Americans in the widest sense. A stranger is welcome everywhere. The best is always set before him. A bedroom is made available to him for weeks on end. The most glorious recreation and excursions are prepared for him. It is as though everyone does his best to give a stranger a favorable impression of the people and land, the nature and culture. The Americans feel that although much coarseness and lack of refinement clings to them, they are trying, as it were, to cast this off and to conquer [it]. The transition from barbarity to the highest culture is thus amazing. The Americans can, in a certain sense, make this transition because they have neither traditions nor prejudices, no default condition, no conservatism to overcome. Electric light and electric trams, an exception here, are there already normal—and notable, more so in the west than in the east. New York and Chicago still have horses, but Grand Rapids has its electric cars. One even finds electric light in Pella and Orange City. Everywhere nature is suddenly giving way to the highest culture. Both limits thus often converge: dirt roads in the most proper neighborhoods, electric light in the simple houses of Pella, and so on. And this is also so with regard to education. [Education] is highly regarded: in America they feel that they are behind in this regard, and now they want (by force) to place themselves on par with Europe. The school buildings look beautiful. No expense is spared. Rich people regard it as an honor to establish colleges. The educational system comprises the grammar school, the high school (*Hoogere Burgerschool* with some Latin), the colleges (preparatory study for university), and the universities with four faculties and the theological seminaries. In general, education is carried out more [widely] than in our own country. The natural sciences play a greater role. The years of study are no less numerous, but nonetheless one has the impression that the breadth [of study] is greater than the depth and thoroughness and that the *multa* [many] falls short of the *multum* [much]. The building of knowledge there is [erected] more hastily than deeply; it is broader than it is high. There is something forced about it, something inflated, a kind of so-called learning. A traveling companion in Iowa made me aware of the important role of the state in education and said: "Therefore we

Americans can talk about everything and understand you when you discuss issues in your own field as a theologian, and so on." The interest in education is strengthened by the desire for freedom and independence: every American wants to be free, independent, researching and seeing for himself. The reading of newspapers is wondrous (Boissevain, 183):[29] here, most people do not read a newspaper, or only (for example) *Gideon*,[30] or some read a newspaper in a group of five, whereas in America everyone reads his own newspaper, and the newspapers, majestic in size, love everything up-to-date, share everything (sensational stories, interviews, everything public), from the most banal to the most important; they keep the people informed. The libraries, the public libraries, also contribute to the development of the people. Every place of any importance has its own library, which was sometimes established and maintained by particular gifts, or sometimes by the city council, and which is available to all (without distinction), free of charge. Science and knowledge are popularized in every way possible. An abundant precocity is the consequence of this. The honoring of strict scientific research is not advanced by this. There is a democracy that even denounces the aristocracy of geniuses and [great human] minds. That said, it bears witness to a force of will to work on one's own self, to a mighty striving for the highest [standard], to an exceptional initiative and energy.

7. This striving is underpinned by a powerful moral feeling. Obviously, in America not all that glitters is gold. New York and Chicago (the city of scoundrels, rogues, and knaves) are, in their slums, cesspools of unrighteousness and are in no way inferior to London, Paris, Vienna, and Berlin in that regard. But nonetheless, a mighty moral feeling lives in the American people, a high ethical consciousness. The puritanical sense of the first settlers continues to have effect. As Calvinism has found little acceptance there, Arminianism (through Methodism) has gained mastery over the American spirit. The American is too aware of himself, he is too much conscious of his power, his will is too strong, for him to be a Calvinist. In addition to this, he has been too successful. He succeeds at whatever he does. He sees no limit to his might. Calvinism finds acceptance among a people who have been saved by [God's] council and action, [a people] that despairing in itself can only be saved by God's grace. But the Americans know no suffering; their struggle for independence against England, the war of the North against the South, were times of bravery, triumph, and the unfolding of power. Americans are not pantheistic; they are far more deistic, intellectualistic, and moralistic, and all of that through experience [as the source of knowledge]. That moral consciousness is powerful and inherently strong. In America there is a strong longing to improve the [individual] human, humanity, the world, and destiny.

They do not think much about the past, but far more about the future. There is faith, hope, a wonderful optimism, a strong altruism. They believe that things can be better, different, that every person on earth can have a reasonably good life. The issues facing Europe are not known there: there is no overpopulation, there is enough space, the land is fruitful and can supply with abundance, poverty is not necessary, whoever wants to work can eat and live, there is no high taxation, there is no army or navy that devours wealth, there is no established church living off a bursary, there are no monopolies or privileges for a certain social class, there is the greatest possible freedom and equality. The door is open to all for an existence that is both civil and worthy of a human. However, many are self-defeating. Evil fancies and desires block the way. Now, far more strongly than in Europe, a battle is waged against these, and all particular sins. There is no shortage of unions that endeavor to combat a special sin or misery. Tobacco and drink are fought against with particular vigor. In many circles both are forbidden in the strongest possible terms; their use is placed on par with a non-Christian life. But however excessive that is, it does not stop there. Other sins are also opposed. All powers are called upon, mobilized, and armed against the enemy. Everyone is a member of a union, sometimes of different unions simultaneously. Every union has its orders, ribbons, distinctions, titles. How democratic: the Americans attach a lot to this. In Illinois there is a group of men who call themselves the University of Illinois and who, for a couple of dollars, will award a degree in a particular science.

Secret societies in particular play a large role. The age of publicity is also the age of secrecy. There are dozens of these [societies]. The Freemasons is only one example. There are also the Odd Fellows, the Knights of Labor, and so on, and these societies wield enormous power. Many workers' unions are affiliated to them and do not buy, for example, wares or cigars (and so on) from certain vendors, do not work past eight o'clock, do not work for an employer who rejects certain conditions, and so forth. All of these [societies] intend the betterment of society. Sin and misery are combated against mightily. Works of mercy are many. Every state takes outstanding care of its poor, its wretched, its mentally ill. The psychiatric institutions look magnificent. The poor in America have a better life than here. They receive exactly what other citizens receive, not only bread but also meat and cake.

8. And as regards religious life—it is beyond doubt that [all this] leads to great superficiality. The contrast of sin and grace is weakened. The new birth and the work of the Holy Spirit are shoved into the background. The preaching mostly deals with morals. Election and justification—the entire religious element either falls short or is altogether missing. Preaching is not the

unfolding and ministering of the word of God; rather it is a speech, and the text is simply a hook. The religious life, in its entirety, has a different character from our own. Religion does not master the people; the people master religion, just as they also master art and science. Religion is a matter of amusement, of relaxation. The church buildings make this clear. The churches have much that is better than ours: they are cozy [*gezellig*], welcoming, warmed in the winter, without a pulpit; but it is also the case that they could be used as theaters without a single alteration. Light in color, with red carpets, light-hearted, lively, clear, fresh—precisely the opposite of that solemn, dignified, somber, serious [character] found in our European churches. And as the church is, so is the religion. Religion there is an amusement. The preacher is the most in-demand [person], who knows how to speak in the most exciting way (short, varied, lively, theatrical: Rev. Parker,[31] Rev. Pankhurst,[32] Talmage[33]): spirited but shallow, enjoyable, peppered with humor. And this preaching is interspersed by songs, by choirs, by solos, by vocal and instrumental music. Through this, the idea of church has almost entirely been lost. Churches are religious societies. Membership by birth and death is not counted. The number of those participating in the Lord's Supper is counted. There are so many sects and unions of churches that the idea of church is totally gone. *The church does not exist there.* There is no established church. All [churches] are equal. Individualism thus also reigns on ecclesiastical terrain.

But against this, one can say: what American religious life lacks in depth, it wins in breadth. The distinction between faith and unbelief, as we have here, is unknown there. (We are so astoundingly [focused on] principle that we forget the practice thereof.) There are indeed unbelievers, but they are not organized; they do not make themselves known in their own party. The Democratic and Republican Parties deal with issues wholly outside of belief and unbelief. The fundamental, the spiteful [element] in this battle is lacking. They do not deny each other salvation or heaven. To be against the Antirevolutionary Party (against Dr. Kuyper), against Groen [van Prinsterer], against the free Christian school—here that is taken immediately as opposition to God, Christ, and the Bible. This is not so in America. There are Christians who are Republican and Christians who are Democrats. There are those who are for, and against, the common school. Some are for, and against, free trade. All of that is outside of "Christian." The "Christian" [approach] is, to a certain extent and in a dualistic manner (theology is not taught at the university; science is separate from faith) next to all the other terrains of this world. All more or less come under the influence of, and are shaped by, the Christian faith. The state is still vaguely Christian. Prayer remains customary in the primary schools, where the Bible is also still read. The Sabbath and holidays are celebrated nationally and recognized in the busy cities. Days of prayer and thanksgiving are issued by the government. The Columbian Celebration from October 9 to 12 is opened with a demonstration of gratitude in the churches. There is no liberal party that systematically follows the principles of the [French] Revolution and fights the faith. An orthodox [Christian] is a pariah here, an outsider, unenlightened; but in America this is not so. Gospel preaching on the streets is heard with deep silence. There, one does not think of mockery, of ridicule, such as that of the common riffraff here. The delegates of the Presbyterian Alliance in Toronto were not only received with distinction; they were also hosted by the city mayor and the governor. The interest in churchly and religious matters is exceptional. Sunday schools, home and foreign mission, and all sorts of work in God's kingdom enjoy a level of interest that is unknown here. They are issues alive in the heart and mouth. The meetings of the Alliance were attended by great numbers of people for eight days. When mission was dealt with, the speakers had to speak in two churches. And the women's union for mission was attended by a crowd of twelve hundred women. It is held as an honor by the richest families if their son becomes a missionary. A very significant lady wished that her only son would dedicate himself to this. Young men and women are no less interested [in missions]. At present there is a union, the Christian Endeavor Society, which began as small, but has now spread through the entire English-speaking world and requires its members to be Christian always and everywhere and to attend the prayer meetings it organizes. The English-speaking world lives for the heathen and sympathizes with its missionaries. It carries the whole heathen world in its heart. Arminianism and Methodism are no less committed in this regard. There is much twaddle in this. But we would do better to carry over the good found therein and to imitate it than simply to judge everything. The students in particular, in their morality, stand far above those of Europe's universities. This is consistent with the whole principle of formation. The universities are not in the big cities; rather, they are in small, remote places. They form scientific colonies. The students live there in one or more great buildings and are under supervision. A chapel is attached to every school. There is a daily gathering, prayer meeting, the reading of the Bible, singing, prayer, a short address. They are treated as students, not as lords, and receive a particularly practical formation. Religious and moral sensibility is cultivated. Drunkenness and lust are unknown. The manner of living is sober and healthy.

Having seen so much that is good, one shrinks back from critique. May American Christianity develop according to its own law. God has entrusted America with its own high and great calling. [May America] strive for it, in its own way. Calvinism, after all, is not the only truth!

TWO

"An Autobiographical Sketch of Dr. H. Bavinck"

The editor of *De Grondwet* requested that Dr. Bavinck trace out a line, in a few points, that would enable him to provide a sketch of the life of our equally welcome and honored guest, and behold![1] The doctor has enlivened his heart with a life portrait from his own hand. His heart? Yes, but also yours. Yours, where it beats in Holland, Zeeland, Muskegon, Grand Rapids, yes! in Chicago, wherever your heart encounters him.

When the editor hereby openly acknowledges its thanks to the *dea[r] Doctor* for what he so promptly and generously provided, [the editor] knows he is guilty of no presumption by doing so in the name of the entire *Grondwet* readership.

[J. B. Mulder]

Born 13 Dec. 1854, in Hoogeveen, where my father Rev. Jan Bavinck was a minister. Later my father moved to Bunschoten, and later again to Almkerk in

---

"Autobiographische schets van Dr. H. Bavinck," in *De Grondwet*, no. 9, October 6, 1908, 3.

North Brabant. There, I received an education at Mr. Hasselman's Institute. After that, I attended gymnasium (high school) in Zwolle. There, I became acquainted with the Dosker family and entered into a friendship with one of their sons, Henry Dosker, above all—a friendship that has lasted to the present day.

After completing gymnasium, I spent one year at the Theological School in Kampen, where my father was now a minister. But the education there did not satisfy me. So in 1874, I went to Leiden to study theology under the famous professors Scholten and Kuenen. I completed my studies in five years and was awarded the title of doctor of theology in 1880, with a dissertation entitled "The Ethics of H. Zwingli."

After spending one year as a minister in Franeker, I was called as professor at the Theological School in Kampen, in 1882. There, I was charged with teaching dogmatics as my central subject, and also having moved to the Free University in 1902, I retained this as central subject. Alongside this, I also published an extensive work in four volumes, 1895–1900, that has now appeared in a second, revised and enhanced edition. But besides this, many other writings have come from my hand, of which I will name only *Present Day Morality* [*De Hededaagsche Moraal*], *Creation and Development* [*Schepping en Ontwikkeling*], *The Certainty of Faith* [*De Zekerheid des Geloofs*], *Principles of Psychology* [*Beginselen der Psychologie*], *Principles of Pedagogy* [*Paedagogische Beginselen*], *Bilderdijk as Thinker and Poet* [*Bilderdijk als denker en dichter*], and many more.

Several years ago, I was appointed to the Order of the Lion of the Netherlands by the queen. In addition to many societies (for example, the Society of Dutch Literature in Leiden), I am also a member of the Royal Academy of Science in Amsterdam. I am present in America to hold my lectures in Princeton but am also using this opportunity to visit old friends again and become better acquainted with America than was possible sixteen years ago. Mrs. Bavinck and I are enjoying it very much here and are particularly taken with America, its land and people.

THREE

"Propositions: The Concept and the Necessity of Evangelization"

I.

Evangel is a Greek word that had already received the meaning of "good news" before the New Testament.

II.

In Scripture, this word became the fixed term for the good news of salvation in Christ.

III.

In the New Testament, the verb *to evangelize* indicates the proclamation of the evangel to Jews and gentiles.

Herman Bavinck, "Stellingen: het begrip en de noodzakelijkheid der evangelisatie," *Congres voor Gereformeerde Evangelisatie op dinsdag 8 en woensdag 9 april 1913 te Amsterdam* (n.p., 1913), 8–9.

IV.

The church was called both to this work of mission and to work continually toward its own edification and completion.

V.

In the history of the Christian church, because of its digression and decline, another work arose between these activities, which strove to bring restoration through a return to the original evangel and which thus at times received the name of *evangelization*.

VI.

In relation to the decline of the church, the first duty that rests upon believers is to reform it according to the Word of God.

VII.

This reformation, as a consequence, by means of the church, school, science, art, and so on, is to be spread out as far as possible through the entirety of the life of the people.

VIII.

In our day, this work should accompany the activity that seeks to win over again a Christendom estranged from the faith and that, as part of the work of home missions—alongside works of mercy—bears the name of *evangelization* more specifically.

Abbreviations

BHD Harinck, George, and Wouter Kroese, eds. *"Men wil toch niet gaarne een masker dragen": Brieven van Henry Dosker aan Herman Bavinck, 1873–1921*. Amsterdam: Historisch Documentatiecentrum voor het Nederlands Protestantisme (1800–heden), 2018.

ELV Harinck, George, and Jan de Bruijn, eds. *Een Leidse vriendschap*. Baarn: Ten Have, 1999.

ET English translation

GD¹ Bavinck, Herman. *Gereformeerde dogmatiek*. 4 vols. 1st ed. Kampen: Bos, 1895–1901.

GD² Bavinck, Herman. *Gereformeerde dogmatiek*. 4 vols. 2nd ed. Kampen: Kok, 1906–11.

HBA Herman Bavinck Archive at the Historisch Documentatiecentrum voor het Nederlands Protestantisme (1800–heden), Vrije Universiteit Amsterdam

LGV Dennison, James T., Jr., ed. *The Letters of Geerhardus Vos*. Phillipsburg, NJ: P&R, 2005.

RD Bavinck, Herman. *Reformed Dogmatics*. Edited by John Bolt. Translated by John Vriend. 4 vols. Grand Rapids: Baker Academic, 2003–8.

Key Figures, Churches, Educational Institutions, and Newspapers

Figures

BERENDINUS JOHANNES FEMIA "DINUS" BAVINCK (1870–1954)   Herman Bavinck's younger brother, a medical doctor.

COENRAAD BERNARDUS "BERNARD" BAVINCK (1866–1941)   Herman Bavinck's younger brother, Bernard studied at the Theological School and served as a pastor.

JAN BAVINCK (1826–1909)   Herman Bavinck's father. A Hanoverian who immigrated to the Netherlands, he served as a pastor both in the Evangelical Old Reformed Church in Lower Saxony and in the Christian Reformed Church.

JOHAN HERMAN BAVINCK (1895–1964)   Herman Bavinck's nephew and a son of Bernard Bavinck. Johan Herman was a celebrated missiologist and served as a missionary in Indonesia.

JOHANNES GERRIT "JOHAN" BAVINCK (1872–96)   Herman Bavinck's younger brother. He died of tuberculosis while a doctoral student in law.

GEZIENA BAVINCK-HOLLAND (1827–1900)   Herman Bavinck's mother, a native Dutchwoman, she grew up in the Dutch Reformed Church but chose to join the Seceders.

JOHANNA ADRIANA BAVINCK-SCHIPPERS (1868–1942)   Herman Bavinck's wife and a prominent figure in the Christian women's movement.

AMELIA DEN DEKKER (1849–1933)   The object of the young Bavinck's romantic affections.

321

JOHANNES HENDRIKUS DONNER (1824–1903)   Seceder pastor in Leiden. His preaching was highly influential in Herman Bavinck's early formation. Starting in 1880, he served as a member of parliament in the Second Chamber.

HENRY ELIAS DOSKER (1855–1926)   Theologian who immigrated to the United States as a teen alongside his pastor father. Dosker and Bavinck were students together at the Zwolle Gymnasium and corresponded (albeit not always frequently) throughout their lives.

GUILLAUME GROEN VAN PRINSTERER (1801–76)   Calvinist statesman who served as secretary to Willem II and whose work *Unbelief and Revolution* (1847) provided key early inspiration to the Dutch antirevolutionary political movement.

J. H. GUNNING JR. (1829–1905)   Ecclesiastical professor at the University of Amsterdam. Gunning Jr. was his generation's leading exponent of the Ethical theology movement. He maintained a long-standing, critical friendship with Bavinck.

ABRAHAM KUENEN (1828–91)   Professor of Old Testament at the University of Leiden, who taught—among other subjects—ethics. Kuenen served as the de facto supervisor of Bavinck's doctoral thesis.

ABRAHAM KUYPER (1837–1920)   Liberal Reformed pastor who experienced a pietistic conversion during his first pastorate. Kuyper spearheaded a renewal movement within the Dutch Reformed Church, eventually seceding in the Doleantie (1886). He founded both the Antirevolutionary Party (1879) and the Free University of Amsterdam (1880) and served as Prime Minister of the Netherlands between 1901 and 1905.

ABRAHAM KUYPER JR. (1872–1941)   One of Abraham Kuyper's sons, a former student of Herman Bavinck who showed early promise as a dogmatician.

HERMAN KUYPER (1864–1945)   Abraham Kuyper's oldest son, a professor at the Free University of Amsterdam, and a longtime colleague of Herman Bavinck.

LUCAS LINDEBOOM (1845–1933)   Pastor and theologian within the Christian Reformed Church and noted long-term theological antagonist of Abraham Kuyper, Herman Bavinck, and the Free University of Amsterdam. Lindeboom was appointed to teach at the Theological School in Kampen at the same time as Herman Bavinck.

FRIEDRICH NIETZSCHE (1844–1900)   Nineteenth-century German philosopher. Nietzsche argued for a novel variety of atheism that freed itself from the moral trappings of theism and pursued a "revaluation of all values" on the basis of the "death of God."

GERRIT RUYS (1888–1945)   Herman Bavinck's son-in-law; husband of Hannie. A lawyer in Amsterdam, he served in the anti-Nazi resistance movement and died while being transported to a prisoner-of-war camp.

HERMAN RUYS (1923–43)   Herman Bavinck's grandson. An active member of the anti-Nazi resistance movement, he was held at the Weteringschans House of Detention and later executed by firing squad in Overveen.

HUGO FLORIS RUYS (1924–45)   Herman Bavinck's grandson. An active member of the anti-Nazi resistance movement, he was executed by firing squad in Haarlem.

JOHANNA GEZIENA RUYS-BAVINCK (1894–1971)   Daughter of Herman and Johanna, she and her family were active in the anti-Nazi resistance movement during World War II. She was known to her parents as Hannie.

ALEXANDER DE SAVORNIN LOHMAN (1837–1924)   Jurist at the Free University of Amsterdam, he first served in the Antirevolutionary Party before coming into conflict with Abraham Kuyper.

ANDRIES WILLEM SCHIPPERS (1843–1924)   Herman Bavinck's father-in-law, a wealthy shipowner and Kuyperian.

FRIEDRICH SCHLEIERMACHER (1786–1834)   Nineteenth-century German theologian whose redefinition of religion as a "feeling of absolute dependence" on God was profoundly influential throughout Bavinck's lifetime.

JOHANNES HENRICUS SCHOLTEN (1811–85)   Theologian who had taught in both Franeker and Leiden. In Leiden, where he taught from 1843 to 1881, his classes covered New Testament, natural theology, dogmatics, and the philosophy of religion. Alongside Abraham Kuenen, Scholten stood at the forefront of the Modern theology movement. He was Bavinck's doctoral supervisor.

CHRISTIAAN SNOUCK HURGRONJE (1857–1936)   The most celebrated Dutch Orientalist of his age. Snouck Hurgronje and Herman Bavinck became friends while students at Leiden.

ADRIAAN STEKETEE (1846–1913)   Teacher at the Theological School during Bavinck's year as a resident student there, Steketee was relieved of his duties in close connection to Bavinck's own appointment at Kampen.

GEERHARDUS VOS (1862–1949)   Old Princetonian theologian who had moved from the Netherlands to the United States at a young age. Vos and Bavinck were kindred spirits and corresponded over many years.

DOUWE KLAZES WIELENGA (1841–1902)   Pastor and theologian within the Christian Reformed Church and long-standing friend of Herman Bavinck. Wielenga was appointed to teach at the Theological School at the same time as Herman Bavinck.

Churches

CHRISTIAN REFORMED CHURCH (Christelijke Gereformeerde Kerk)   Denomination that departed from the Dutch Reformed Church in the Secession (Afscheiding) of 1834. Jan, Herman, and Bernard Bavinck were pastors within this denomination. Originally known as the Seceders (Afgescheidenen), its members styled their church as the Christian Reformed Church from 1869 onward. It merged with the Dutch Reformed Church (Dolerende) to form the Reformed Churches in the Netherlands in 1892.

DUTCH REFORMED CHURCH (Nederlands Hervormde Kerk)   Mainstream denomination from which both the Christian Reformed Church and later the Dutch Reformed Church (Dolerende) seceded.

DUTCH REFORMED CHURCH (DOLERENDE) (Nederduitse Gereformeerde Kerk [Dolerende])   Denomination led by Abraham Kuyper that seceded from the Dutch Reformed Church in 1886. It merged with the Christian Reformed Church to form the Reformed Churches in the Netherlands in 1892.

EVANGELICAL OLD REFORMED CHURCH IN LOWER SAXONY (Evangelisch-altreformierte Kirche in Niedersachsen)   Denomination formed in Bentheim, Lower Saxony (Germany), in 1838 following a secession from the Reformed Church of Bentheim. Jan Bavinck joined this church as a teenager and served as a pastor within it.

REFORMED CHURCHES IN RESTORED ASSOCIATION (Gereformeerde Kerken in Hersteld Verband)   Denomination formed in 1926 following a controversy surrounding Johannes Geelkerken, one of Bavinck's former students. Johanna Bavinck-Schippers, Hannie Ruys-Bavinck, and Gerrit Ruys joined this denomination.

REFORMED CHURCHES IN THE NETHERLANDS (Gereformeerde Kerken in Nederland)   Denomination formed in 1892 by the merger of the Christian Reformed Church and the Dutch Reformed Church (Dolerende).

Educational Institutions

FREE UNIVERSITY OF AMSTERDAM (Vrije Universiteit Amsterdam)   Originally
a private university established by Abraham Kuyper in 1880, intended
to be run along Reformed principles, but without recognition from any
particular church. It is now known as the VU University Amsterdam.

KAMPEN THEOLOGICAL SCHOOL (Theologische School Kampen)   Originally
the seminary of the Christian Reformed Church; it was established in
1854. It is now known as the Theologische Universiteit Kampen.

PRINCETON THEOLOGICAL SEMINARY   Historically Presbyterian seminary in
Princeton, New Jersey. Both Bavinck and Kuyper maintained close contact
with the Princeton professors Geerhardus Vos and B. B. Warfield and gave
the seminary's annual Stone Lectures.

Newspapers

ALGEMEEN HANDELSBLAD   First published in 1828. It was the most important
liberal (and anti-Kuyperian) Dutch newspaper at that time. In 1970, it
merged with the *Nieuwe Rotterdamsche Courant* to become the *NRC
Handelsblad*—one of the most important left-liberal daily Dutch newspapers in the present day.

DE BAZUIN   Produced by the Seceder Church (later the Christian Reformed
Church) from 1853 onward.

DE HERAUT   First published by the Scots Kirk in Amsterdam in 1850. Originally intended to promote missionary work among Jews, it was taken
over by Abraham Kuyper in 1870 and became an important outlet in the
promotion of his own theological and political projects.

DE STANDAARD   First published in 1872. It was the official newspaper of the
Antirevolutionary Party—a Christian democratic political party also
founded by Abraham Kuyper.

Notes

A Note on Sources

1. George Harinck and Jan de Bruijn, eds., *Een Leidse vriendschap* (Baarn: Ten Have, 1999). This book includes letters both to and from Bavinck.

2. George Harinck and Wouter Kroese, eds., *'Men wil toch niet gaarne een masker dragen': Brieven van Henry Dosker aan Herman Bavinck, 1873–1921* (Amsterdam: Historisch Documentatiecentrum voor het Nederlands Protestantisme [1800–heden], 2018). This book includes only letters from Dosker.

3. James T. Dennison Jr., ed., *The Letters of Geerhardus Vos* (Phillipsburg, NJ: P&R, 2005). This book includes only letters from Vos.

4. Michael Wintle, *An Economic and Social History of the Netherlands, 1800–1920: Demographic, Economic and Social Transition* (Cambridge: Cambridge University Press, 2000), 315.

Introduction: Prolegomena

1. Jan Veenhof, *Revelatie en Inspiratie: De Openbarings- en Schriftbeschouwing van Herman Bavinck in vergelijking met die van de ethische theologie* (Amsterdam: Buijten & Schipperheijn, 1968), 108–11.

2. Malcolm Yarnell, *The Formation of Christian Doctrine* (Nashville: B&H, 2007), 51.

3. Brian Mattson, *Restored to Our Destiny: Eschatology and the Image of God in Herman Bavinck's Reformed Dogmatics* (Leiden: Brill, 2011), 12; cf. Eugene Heideman, *The Relation of Revelation and Reason in E. Brunner and H. Bavinck* (Assen: Van Gorcum, 1959), 131–32, 138, 142, 144, 156–57, 177–79, 183, 189n1.

4. James Eglinton, *Trinity and Organism: Towards a New Reading of Herman Bavinck's Organic Motif* (London: Bloomsbury T&T Clark, 2012).

5. Eglinton, *Trinity and Organism*, 209.

6. Eglinton, *Trinity and Organism*, 207.

7. J. H. Landwehr, *In Memoriam: Prof. Dr. H. Bavinck* (Kampen: Kok, 1921); Valentijn Hepp, *Dr. Herman Bavinck* (Amsterdam: Ten Have, 1921); Henry Elias Dosker, "Herman Bavinck," *Princeton Theological Review* 20 (1922): 448–64; reprinted as "Herman Bavinck: A Eulogy by Henry Elias Dosker," in *Essays on Religion, Science, and Society*, ed. John Bolt, trans. Harry Boonstra and Gerrit Sheeres (Grand Rapids: Baker Academic, 2008), 13–24. Dosker's biography is, in effect, an extended eulogy to a recently deceased friend.

8. A. B. W. M. Kok, *Dr Herman Bavinck* (Amsterdam: S. J. P. Bakker, 1945).

9. J. Geelhoed, *Dr. Herman Bavinck* (Goes: Oosterbaan & Le Cointre, 1958).

10. R. H. Bremmer, *Herman Bavinck en zijn tijdgenoten* (Kampen: Kok, 1966). Bremmer also published a short biography in Afrikaans: *Herman Bavinck (1854–1921): Portret van 'n Reformatoriese denker in Nederland* (Potchefstroom: Potchefstroomse Universiteit vir Christelike Hoër Onderwys, 1998).

11. Herman Bavinck, *Reformed Dogmatics*, 4 vols., ed. John Bolt, trans. John Vriend (Grand Rapids: Baker Academic, 2003–8).

12. See, for example, John Bolt, "Editor's Introduction," in Bavinck, *RD*, 1:12–13; Eglinton, *Trinity and Organism*, 1–26; "The Christian Family in the Twenty-First Century," in *The Christian Family*, by Herman Bavinck, trans. Nelson D. Kloosterman (Grand Rapids: Christian's Library Press, 2012), ix–x; J. Mark Beach, "Introductory Essay," in *Saved by Grace: The Holy Spirit's Work in Calling and Regeneration*, by Herman Bavinck, trans. Nelson Kloosterman (Grand Rapids: Reformation Heritage Books, 2008), ix–xi.

13. Ron Gleason, *Herman Bavinck: Pastor, Churchman, Statesman, and Theologian* (Phillipsburg, NJ: P&R, 2010). For reviews of this biography, see Harry van Dyke, review in *Calvin Theological Journal* 46, no. 1 (April 2011): 192–97; James Eglinton, review in *Scottish Bulletin of Evangelical Theology* 29, no. 1 (Spring 2011): 127; Guy Davies, review in *European Journal of Theology* 21, no. 2 (October 2012): 176; Russell Dykstra, review in *Protestant Reformed Theological Journal* 46, no. 1 (November 2012): 133–37.

14. Gleason, *Herman Bavinck*, 55.

15. Shmuel Noah Eisenstadt, "Multiple Modernities," in *Comparative Civilizations and Multiple Modernities* (Leiden: Brill, 2003), 2:535–60; Jacques Robert, *The European Territory: From Historical Roots to Global Challenges* (London: Routledge, 2014), 70–137.

16. Herman Bavinck, *Philosophy of Revelation: A New Annotated Edition*, ed. Cory Brock and Nathaniel Gray Sutanto (Peabody, MA: Hendrickson, 2018), 71.

Chapter 1 The Old Reformed Church in Bentheim

1. T. C. W. Blanning, introduction to *The Oxford Illustrated History of Modern Europe*, ed. T. C. W. Blanning (Oxford: Oxford University Press, 1996), 1.

2. For an overview of Dutch Modern theology (*de moderne theologie*) across the nineteenth century, see Eldred Vanderlaan, *Protestant Modernism in Holland* (Oxford: Oxford University Press, 1924).

3. "Oude Doopsgezinde Geslachten, III: Bavink," *De Zondagsbode*, September 5, 1909.

4. An earlier source, published in 1877, provides a largely similar story (and is based on the same map by Ubbo Emmius, the sixteenth-century German cartographer) and cites a fifteenth-century Frisian—Douwa Bawngha—as the earliest "son of Bavo" on record. See Johan Winkler, "Een en ander over Friesche Eigennamen," *De Vrije Vries* vol. 1, sections 3–4 (1877), 285; W. Eekhoff, ed., *Oorkonden der geschiedenis van het Sint Anthonij-Gasthuis te Leeuwarden, uit de 153 en 16e eeuw, Eerste deel, Van 1406–1562* (Leeuwarden: n.p., 1876), 133.

5. Eduard Visser, *God, het woord en de tering: Leven en werk van Simon Gorter (1838–1871), met een teksteditie van zijn brieven en een keuze uit zijn proza en preken* (Hilversum: Verloren, 2017), 28. Bavinck's lifelong friend Henry Elias Dosker, whose family roots were also in Lower Saxony, also retained an interest in the Dutch Mennonites, giving the Stone Lectures at Princeton Theological Seminary on this subject in 1918–19: Henry Elias Dosker, *The Dutch Anabaptists* (Philadelphia: Judson Press, 1921).

6. Swenna Harger and Loren Lemmen, *The County of Bentheim and Her Emigrants to North America* (Holland, MI: Swenna Harger, 1994), 4.

7. Swenna Harger and Loren Lemmen, *Beloved Family and Friends: Letters between Grafschaft Bentheim, Germany and America* (Holland, MI: Bentheimers International Society, 2007).

8. *Nota bene*: Jan Bavinck's writings use the older spelling *Reformirte* (rendered *Reformierte* in contemporary German). References to the German Reformed Church will follow the nineteenth-century rendering.

9. George Harinck and Lodewijk Winkler, "The Nineteenth Century," in *Handbook of Dutch Church History*, ed. Herman Selderhuis (Göttingen: Vandenhoeck & Ruprecht, 2015), 445.

10. J. Roegiers and N. C. F. van Sas, "Revolution in the North and South, 1780–1830," in *History of the Low Countries*, ed. J. C. H. Blom and Emiel Lamberts (New York: Berghahn Books, 1999), 308.

11. Harinck and Winkler, "Nineteenth Century," 450.

12. With the exception of a short-lived government between February and June 1866, every Dutch government between 1807 and 1871 had separate departments to regulate both Reformed and Roman Catholic worship. Amry Vandenbosch, *Dutch Foreign Policy since 1815: A Study in Small Power Politics* (The Hague: Martinus Nijhoff, 1959), 141.

13. Jacobus Klok and Hendrik de Cock, *De evangelische gezangen getoetst en gewogen en te ligt gevonden* (Groningen: J. H. Bolt, 1834).

14. Jasper Vree, *Enkele aspecten van de Afscheiding in Delfzijl: Gebeurtenissen van toen—een vraag aan ons* (n.p., 1985), 5.

15. Klok and de Cock, *De evangelische gezangen getoetst*, 74. "Het gezangboek in zijn geheel beschouwd, deze 192 gezangen zijn kortom mijns inziens Sirenische minneliederen, om de Gereformeerden al zingende van hun zaligmakende leer aftehelpen, en eene valsche en leugenleer intevoeren, en alle partijen, buiten de kerk overtehalen om tot ééne kerk of gemeente zich te vereenigen."

16. See H. van Veen, "De Afscheiding en de gezangenstrijd," in *Afscheiding—Wederkeer: Opstellen over de Afscheiding van 1834*, by D. Deddens and J. Kamphuis (Haarlem: Vijlbrief, 1984), 117–49.

17. Douwe Fokkema and Frans Grijzenhout, *Dutch Culture in a European Perspective: 1600–2000* (New York: Palgrave Macmillan, 2004), 331.

18. Gerrit Jan Beuker, *Umkehr und Erneuerung: Aus der Geschichte der Evangelisch-altreformierten Kirche in Niedersachsen 1838–1988* (Bad Bentheim: Hellendoorn KG, 1988).

19. J. Schoemaker, *Geschiedenis der Oud-Gereformeerde Kerk in het Graafschap Bentheim en het Vorstendom Ostfriesland* (Hardenberg: A. Kropveld, 1900), 28.

20. Beuker, *Umkehr und Erneuerung*, 288.

21. Beuker, *Umkehr und Erneuerung*, 259, 427–31.

22. Robert Schoone-Jongen, "Dutch and Dutch Americans, to 1870," in *Immigrants in American History: Arrival, Adaptation, and Integration*, ed. Elliott Robert Barkan (Oxford: ABC-CLIO, 2013), 1:63.

23. Gerrit Jan Beuker, "German Oldreformed Emigration: Catastrophe or Blessing?," in *Breaches and Bridges: Reformed Subcultures in the Netherlands, Germany, and the United States*, ed. George Harinck and Hans Krabbendam (Amsterdam: VU Uitgeverij, 2000), 102.

24. For example, Ron Gleason, *Herman Bavinck: Pastor, Churchman, Statesman, and Theologian* (Phillipsburg, NJ: P&R, 2010), 4; Valentijn Hepp, *Dr. Herman Bavinck* (Amsterdam: Ten Have, 1921), 7.

25. Schlüter's study of the place of lay exorcists and soothsayers in Bentheim from the Middle Ages to the nineteenth century provides a clear example of this process of social change. Dick Schlüter, "De grensoverschrijdende activiteiten van duivelbanners," in *Nederland en Bentheim: Vijf eeuwen kerk aan de grens / Die Niederlande und Bentheim: Fünf Jahrhunderte Kirche an der Grenze*, ed. P. H. A. M. Abels, G.-J. Beuker, and J. G. J. van Booma (Delft: Eburon, 2003), 131–46.

26. Jacques Robert, *The European Territory: From Historical Roots to Global Challenges* (London: Routledge, 2014), 70–137.

27. Matthew Lauzon, "Modernity," in *The Oxford Handbook of World History*, ed. Jerry H. Bentley (Oxford: Oxford University Press, 2011), 74.

28. Pieter R. D. Stokvis, "The Secession of 1834 and Dutch Emigration to the United States: Religious Aspects of Emigration in Comparative Perspective," in Harinck and Krabbendam, *Breaches and Bridges*, 22.

29. Harinck and Winkler, "Nineteenth Century," 468.

30. James Kennedy and Jan Zwemer, "Religion in the Modern Netherlands and the Problems of Pluralism," *BMGN—Low Countries Historical Review* 125, no. 2–3 (2010): 249.

31. Despite the virtual unattainability of this quest, it should be acknowledged that some Seceders and their later descendants continued to strive for the recognition that theirs was the true church. This can be seen, for example, in much of the history of the Dutch Reformed Churches (Liberated) (Gereformeerde Kerken vrijgemaakt), which historically asserted that it was the "only true church" (*de enige ware kerk*).

32. Kennedy and Zwemer, "Religion in the Modern Netherlands," 249.

33. As will be seen, in the case of a Seceder like Hendrik Pieter Scholte, the call to emigrate was not always motivated by a desire to reject modern society. Rather, Scholte argued for immigration to America because he believed it offered better conditions for the practice of religious freedom.

34. Herman Bavinck, *De katholiciteit van Christendom en kerk* (Kampen: G. Ph. Zalsman, 1888); ET: "*The Catholicity of Christianity and the Church*," trans. John Bolt, *Calvin Theological Journal* 27, no. 2 (1992): 246. For emigration from the Old Reformed Church, see Beuker, "German Oldreformed Emigration," 101–13.

35. Koert van Bekkum, "Verlangen naar tastbare genade: Achtergrond, geschiedenis en typologie van spiritualiteit in de Gereformeerde Kerken (vrijgemaakt)," in *Proeven van spiritualiteit: Bijdragen ter gelegenheid van 160 jaar Theologische Universiteit Kampen*, ed. Koert van Bekkum (Barneveld: Uitgeverij De Vuurbaak, 2014), 140.

36. In this context, Harinck has demonstrated that while the likes of Scholte were sympathetic to the concurrent secession movement (the Disruption of 1843) in the Church of Scotland, where Thomas Chalmers led the formation of the Free Church of Scotland, they rejected the church-state relationship affirmed therein. In the Scottish case, the Disruption saw both the Church of Scotland and the Free Church of Scotland assert, under the Establishment Principle, that they were the true Reformed Church in Scotland. Instead, Scholte favored an American-style separation of church and state. See George Harinck, "Groen van Prinsterer en Thomas Chalmers: 'Precious Ties of a Common Faith,'" in *Groen van Prinsterer in Europese context*, ed. George Harinck and Jan de Bruijn (Hilversum: Uitgeverij Verloren, 2004), 45.

37. On Scholte's editorship of *De Reformatie*, see Eugene P. Heideman, *Hendrik P. Scholte: His Legacy in the Netherlands and in America* (Grand Rapids: Eerdmans, 2015), 163–84.

38. Hendrik Pieter Scholte, "De zesde december," *De Reformatie* 2, no. 1 (1841): 291.

39. Heideman, *Hendrik P. Scholte*, 150.

40. Hendrik Pieter Scholte, "Wet op de Verdraagzaamheid opgesteld door Jefferson," *De Reformatie* 2, no. 8 (1845): 175.

41. Hans Krabbendam, *Vrijheid in het verschiet: Nederlandse emigratie naar Amerika 1840–1940* (Hilversum: Uitgeverij Verloren, 2006), 30: ". . . hardnekkige tegenstand der Regering tegen vrijheid van godsdienst."

42. Krabbendam, *Vrijheid in het verschiet*, 35: ". . . verspreiding van de emigratiekoorts."

43. Hendrik Pieter Scholte, "Moet in de Nederlandsche Staatsregeling de Bepaling worden Opgenomen, dat de Koning Behooren moet tot de Hervormde Godsdienst?," in *De Reformatie* 1, no. 7 (1840): 326–27.

44. For further discussion of this, see Heideman, *Hendrik P. Scholte*, 152–56.

45. Krabbendam, *Vrijheid in het verschiet*, 30.

46. Krabbendam, *Vrijheid in het verschiet*, 30.

47. See, for example, G. M. den Hartogh, *Onze Theologische School* (Kampen: Kok, 1953), 23. "Een echt 'kind der Scheiding,' bij zijn optreden en in zijn werk te Kampen de trots van School en kerken, 'onze doctor,' zoals men hem met liefde en met dank noemde."

48. See, for example, John Bolt, "Grand Rapids between Kampen and Amsterdam: Herman Bavinck's Reception and Influence in North America," *Calvin Theological Journal* 38, no. 2 (2003): 264–65.

49. J. van den Berg, "De Spiritualiteit van de Afgescheidenen," *Gereformeerd Theologisch Tijdschrift* 92 (1992): 172–88.

50. Van den Berg, "De Spiritualiteit van de Afgescheidenen," 174. "De Afscheiding was niet een homogene beweging, en ook al werden uiteindelijk binnen de hoofdstroom de tegenstellingen in een geleidelijk proces van samensmelting opgelost, toch kan men niet zonder meer van 'de' Afgescheidenen spreken."

51. Jasper Vree, "Van separatie naar integratie: De afgescheidenen en hun kerk in de Nederlandse samenleving (1834–1892)," in *Religies en (on)gelijkheid in een plurale samenleving*, ed. R. Kranenborg and W. Stoker (Leuven: Garant, 1995), 176.

52. Den Hartogh, *Onze Theologische School*, 23.

Chapter 2 Jan Bavinck and Geziena Magdalena Holland

1. Jan Bavinck, "Een korte schets van mijn leven," unpublished, handwritten autobiography, n.d., HBA, folder 445. See also G. A. Wumkes, "Bavinck (Jan)," in *Nieuw Nederlansch Biografisch Woordenboek*, ed. P. C. Molhuysen and P. J. Blok (Leiden: A. W. Sijthoff's Uitgevers-Maatschappij, 1911), 34–35.

2. Jan Bavinck, "Een korte schets van mijn leven," 75. "Hij heeft mij ruim 54 jaren in dien dienst doen arbeiden, mij steunende en sterkende, zoodat ik schier zonder onderbreking mijn werk kon verrichten," and, "Ik ben nu oud en grijs geworden. Nog enkele dagen en ik heb den leeftijd van *tachtig* jaren bereikt. Ik ben aan den avond, aan den laten avond van mijn leven."

3. Jan Bavinck, *De zaligheid alleen in den naam van Jezus* (Kampen: J. H. Bos, 1888).

4. For the history of this term, see Rudolf Dekker, introduction to *Egodocuments and History: Autobiographical Writing in Its Social Context since the Middle Ages*, ed. Rudolf Dekker (Hilversum: Verloren, 2002), 7–20.

5. Rudolf Dekker, "Childhood in Dutch Autobiographies, 1600–1850: Changing Memory Strategies," *Paedagogica Historica* 32 (1996): 69.

6. Arianne Baggerman, "Lost Time: Temporal Discipline and Historical Awareness in Nineteenth-Century Dutch Egodocuments," in *Controlling Time and Shaping the Self: Developments in Autobiographical Writing since the Sixteenth Century*, ed. Arianne Baggerman, Rudolf Dekker, and Michael James Mascuch (Leiden: Brill, 2011), 455–535.

7. Jan Bavinck, "Een korte schets van mijn leven," 3. "In mijne jeugd kende men nog geene spoorwegen, maar thans loopt de spoorlijn van Arnhem naar Salzbergen langs Bentheim heen, en het is een prachtig gezicht den spoortrein als een slang door het woud zien stoomen."

8. Wolfgang Schivelbusch, *The Railway Journey: The Industrialization of Time and Space in the 19th Century* (Berkeley: University of California Press, 1986), 33.

9. Daniël François van Alphen, *Reisverhalen en indrukken van een togt via Bentheim (Münster), Hannover, Hamburg, Kiel en Korsör naar Kopenhagen* ('s Gravenhage: J. M. van 't Haaff, 1874).

10. The use of autobiography as an effort to recall and maintain the distant memories of early childhood is also a nineteenth-century development. See Dekker, "Childhood in Dutch Autobiographies, 1600–1850," 72–76.

11. Jan Bavinck, "Een korte schets van mijn leven," 3. "Doch ofschoon ik nog zoo jong was, heb ik mij toch altoos als uit de verte kunnen herinneren, dat Vader leefde, dat hij bij voorbeeld des avonds van zijn werk tehuis kwam, bij het vuur ging zitten, en dat ik in zijn schoot moest komen staan om mij te verwarmen. Inzonderheid bleef mij dit steeds levendig voor den geest staan, dat

bij de begrafenis van Vader eene buurvrouw mij en mijne vier zusjes bij de hand nam, ons naar de kist geleide, waarin Vader lag, en dat wij toen alle bitterlijk begonnen te schreien."

12. See *Hof- und Staats-Handbuch für das Köningreich Hannover auf das Jahr 1844* (Hannover: E. Berenberg, n.d.), 431.

13. A. L. van Nes, *Woorden van broederlijke onderwijzing en waarschuwing ten opzigte van het gebruik der sterke dranken* (Groningen: J. Oomkens, 1841). See also *Hof- und Staats-Handbuch für das Köningreich Hannover auf das Jahr 1844*, 431.

14. Jan Bavinck, "Een korte schets van mijn leven," 12. "Ik was daarom bang voor alle sectarisme en seperatisme, en wilde op de Gereformeerde lijn blijven."

15. Jan Bavinck, "Een korte schets van mijn leven," 11. "Ik herinner mij nog levendig, dat wij, te weten, oom, zijne dochter en ik des Zondagmorgens vroeg ons opmaakten en dat wij bij schoon weêr door een gedeelte van het Bentheimsche woud gingen om ons te begeven naar de bijeenkomst der Afgescheidenen, die destijds in de woning van den landbouwer Sandfoort onder Gildehaus gehouden werd."

16. Jan Bavinck, "Een korte schets van mijn leven," 5. "Menigmalen heb ik het Bentheimsche woud doorkruist, op de bergen gedoold, de boerenplaatsen rondom Bentheim afgeloopen om er naar te zoeken en heb mij soms daarbij aan gevaren blootgesteld."

17. Jan Bavinck, "Een korte schets van mijn leven," 13. "Mocht ik mij nu wel van de 'Reformirte Kirche' scheiden, en mij voegen bij degenen, die geheel en al met haar hadden gebroken en voor zich eene zelfstandige Kerk nevens en naast haar hadden gesticht? Over deze vraag heb ik lang nagedacht en gepeinsd; ik heb met Sundag en met anderen er over gesproken; ik heb er meermalen mijne knieën voor gebogen en het aangezicht des Heeren gezocht, Hem ootmoedig en ernstig biddende, dat Hij mij in deze gewichtige zaak den weg mocht wijzen, dien ik had in te slaan en te bewandelen. Lang heb ik geaarzeld en getwijfeld, maar eindelijk ben ik er toe overgegaan om mij als lidmaat in de Oud-Gereformeerde Kerk te doen opnemen."

18. Jan Bavinck, "Een korte schets van mijn leven," 13. "Vrijmoedig kan en mag ik van mijzelven getuigen dat ik, om Gereformeerd te blijven, mij van de 'Reformirte Kirche' heb afgescheiden en mij bij de Oud-Gereformeerde Kerk heb gevoegd."

19. Jan Bavinck, *De zaligheid alleen in den naam van Jezus*, 19. "Ik koos een beroep, denkende, dat het de wil des Heeren niet was, mij in de bediening Zijns Woords te stellen."

20. Jan Bavinck, "Een korte schets van mijn leven," 20. "Ik was dus in de gelegenheid om hem dagelijks te ontmoeten en te spreken."

21. H. Beuker, *Tubantiana* (Kampen: Kok, 1897), 62.

22. Gerrit Jan Beuker, "'The Area beyond Hamse and Hardenberg': Van Raalte and Bentheim," in *The Enduring Legacy of Albertus C. Van Raalte as Leader and Liaison*, ed. Jacob E. Nyenhuis and George Harinck (Grand Rapids: Eerdmans, 2014), 26.

23. H. Beuker, *Tubantiana*, 64.

24. The casting of lots as a means of discerning the will of God in ordination choices was commonplace among pietistic Protestants in that era. See, for example, Heinrich Rimius, *The History of the Moravians* (London: J. Robinson, 1754), 13.

25. H. Beuker, *Tubantiana*, 64.

26. Jan Bavinck, "Een korte schets van mijn leven," 23. "Men oordeelde, dat Drente bij de twisten onder de zonen der Scheiding in Holland het zuiverst bij de waarheid was gebleven."

27. Jan Bavinck, "Een korte schets van mijn leven," 27. "Ik herinner mij nog zeer goed, dat ik in het eerst op den weg naar de School door sommigen uitgelachen en bespot werd. Wij werden toen nog altoos als de pariati's der maatschappij geacht."

28. For example, R. H. Bremmer wrote: "Jan Bavinck bleek een scherpzinnig student. . . . De leerling was spoedig verder dan de meester" (*Herman Bavinck en zijn tijdgenoten* [Kampen: Kok, 1966], 11). See also Ron Gleason: "Jan Bavinck was a dedicated and precocious student who was very bright and quickly grasped the subject matter." *Herman Bavinck: Pastor, Churchman, Statesman, and Theologian* (Phillipsburg, NJ: P&R, 2010), 12.

29. This contradicts the assumption in Henry Dosker's 1922 eulogy for Herman Bavinck that his father "must also have enjoyed earlier privileges" in his schooling in Bentheim. "Herman Bavinck: A Eulogy by Henry Elias Dosker," in *Essays on Religion, Science, and Society*, ed. John Bolt, trans. Harry Boonstra and Gerrit Sheeres (Grand Rapids: Baker Academic, 2008), 14.

30. Jan Bavinck, "Een korte schets van mijn leven," 24. "Vele vakken voor slechts twee mannen! Het spreekt vanzelf, dat het onderwijs niet anders dan gebrekkig, zeer gebrekkig en onvoldoende kon zijn."

31. Jan Bavinck, *De zaligheid alleen in den naam van Jezus*, 20. "Nooit kan ik dien nacht vergeten, die ik daar ten midden van tierende en drinkende jongelingen heb doorgebracht."

32. Jan Bavinck, "Een korte schets van mijn leven," 31. "Ziehen sie euch nun wieder an, wir haben schon Mannschaften genug. . . . Sie sind frei, sie können gehen."

33. Jan Bavinck, "Een korte schets van mijn leven," 28. "Onder die drukte vlogen de dagen voorbij en brak het jaar 1848 aan, dat jaar van beroeringen, opstanden en omkeeringen. De revolutie was bij vernieuwing uitgebroken in Frankrijk en sloeg weldra tot andere landen, ook tot Duitschland over. De bewegingen der revolutie waren soms zoo sterk en hevig, dat zij de Koningen en vorsten op hunne tronen deden beven. *Doch richtte de revolutie allerlei verwoestingen aan en vervulde zij de harten van duizenden met schrik en angst, zij was het die voor de 'Seperatisten' of de Oud-Gereformeerden in het Graafschap verademing en verkwikking aanbracht;* want niet alleen hielden de vervolgingen, waaraan zij tot dusver hadden blootgestaan, met het jaar 1848 op, maar zij werden van dat jaar af aan ook geduld, en mochten onverhinderd samenkomen om den Heere naar de overtuiging van hun hart te dienen. . . . De Oud-Gereformeerden in het Graafschap werden alzoo niet meer door de Regeering bemoeilijkt, maar zij werden vrijgelaten en geduld. *Dat zij hiermede ingenomen, dat zij er blijde mede waren en er gebruik van maakten, spreekt vanzelf.*" Emphasis added.

34. H. Beuker, *Tubantiana*, 62. "De Oud-Gereformeerden—zoo noemden zij zich—hadden geen vrijheid gevraagd, noch dezelve nu reeds verwacht, toen de vijanden, die hen vervolgd hadden, de vlaggen uitstaken en de klokken begonnen te luiden. Op de vraag van de onnoozele verdrukten: wat dit toch te beduiden had?—gaven de feestvierders ten antwoord: 'omdat er vrijheid van godsdienst is gekomen.'"

35. H. Beuker, *Tubantiana*, 67. "De klove tusschen de Oud-Gereformeerde en de dusgenaamde 'Groote Kerk' werd al gaandeweg grooter en de tegenstelling beslister. De eene leefde, in correspondentie met de Nederlandsche kerken, uit de Gereformeerde beginselen; de andere kreeg uitsluitend leeraren en beginselen, zoo als ze aan de rationalistische Universiteiten in Duitschland gevormd werden."

36. For the experiences of Old Reformed students in the Netherlands after Jan Bavinck's own student years, see Berthold Bloemendal, "Kerkelijke en nationale achtergronden van Duitse studenten in Kampen, 1854–1994," *Documentatieblad voor de Nederlandse Kerkgeschiedenis na 1800*, no. 85 (December 2016): 62–78.

37. H. Beuker, *Tubantiana*, 68–69.

38. Jan Bavinck, "Een korte schets van mijn leven," 35. "Wij waren alzoo met onze godsdienstoefeningen uit de boerschappen naar de dorpen zelve verhuisd."

39. Jan Bavinck, "Een korte schets van mijn leven," 72. "Reeds in de dagen van hare vroege jeugd was de Heere begonnen door Zijnen Geest het goede werk in haar te werken. Door dien Geest bewerkt deed zij in hare prille jeugd met beslistheid de keuze om den Heere te dienen en sloot zich bij het volk des Heeren, om met hen op den smallen weg naar den hemel te wandelen."

40. Jan Bavinck, "Een korte schets van mijn leven," 41. "Ook mijne Studenten begroetten ons met blijdschap; zij vereerden ons bij deze gelegenheid eene huisklok, die vele jaren hare goede diensten aan ons gezin heeft bewezen. De Heere was goed over ons!"

41. S. J. Hofkamp, *Geschiedenis der Beschaving: Een leesboek voor de hoogste klasse der lagere scholen* (Groningen: M. Smit, 1856), 121.

42. Elizabeth Sullivan, "A Brief History of the Collection," in *European Clocks and Watches in the Metropolitan Museum of Art*, ed. Clare Vincent, Jan Hendrik Leopold, and Elizabeth Sullivan (New York: Metropolitan Museum of Art, 2015), 3.

43. Jan Bavinck, "Een korte schets van mijn leven," 49. "Hoe zou ik kunnen staan en arbeiden nevens mannen, die alle drie eene academische opleiding hadden genoten!"

44. Jan Bavinck, *De zaligheid alleen in den naam van Jezus*, 24. "Ik durfde die roeping niet aanvaarden. Die taak was, naar ik toen oordeelde, te zwaar voor mijn krachten."

45. The rejection letter, penned in Hoogeveen, on July 18, 1854, notes that Jan Bavinck has given the nomination serious consideration but has decided to decline. It does not offer any explanation of the decision. Letters from Jan Bavinck to P. Dijksterhuis, July 18 and 25, August 9 and 22, 1854, inventory number I–9, 12772, Archives of the Trustees of the Theological School, Stadsarchief Kampen.

46. Jan Bavinck, "Een korte schets van mijn leven," 50. "En welke brief was door hem op de Post gedaan? *De bedankbrief*. Neen! ik zal er geen melding van maken van hetgeen ik gevoelde en in mij omging op het oogenblik, dat ik met dien uitslag bekend werd! Alleen dit wil ik ervan zeggen, dat ik er geen vrede mede had, noch toen noch langen tijd daarna."

47. Herman Bavinck, *Gereformeerde Ethiek*, ed. Dirk van Keulen (Utrecht: Uitgeverij Kok-Boekcentrum, 2019), 438. "Het lot maakt bij verlies dikwerf gemelijk." I am indebted to Dirk van Keulen for this observation.

48. "Kerknieuws," *De Bazuin*, August 18, 1854. "Ons wordt gemeld dat Ds. J. BAVINCK, die bedankt heeft voor de benoeming als leraar aan de op te rigten Theol. School te *Kampen*, daarbij geene rust heeft. Zouden de Curatoren, als zij samenkomen, ZEw. niet op nieuw mogen beroepen, of liever op de aanneming van het beroep bij ZEw. mogen aandringen?"

49. Jan Bavinck, "Een korte schets van mijn leven," 50. "Toen het algemeen in de Kerk bekend was geworden, dat ik voor de benoeming tot Docent had bedankt, ontving ik vele brieven, waarin leedwezen over mijn bedanken werd uitgesproken. Zelfs waren er enkele onder die brieven waarin mij aangeraden werd om op mijn bedanken terug te komen en het terug te nemen. Dit durfde ik ook niet te doen. Ik had eenmaal de beslissing aan het lot toevertrouwd, en hierbij, dacht ik, moest het ook blijven. Al had ik van het lot geen gebruik moeten maken, het gansche beleid van het lot is toch van den Heere. Kon Hij mijn bedanken niet ten beste doen keeren en doen medewerken ten goede? Wist ik wat Hij er in Zijne hooge wijsheid mede voorhad en waartoe het kon en moest dienen? Ik kwam daarom op mijn bedanken niet terug, maar liet het erbij blijven." He made a similar statement in *De zaligheid alleen in den naam van Jezus*, 24.

50. Letters from Jan Bavinck to P. Dijksterhuis.

51. G. M. den Hartogh, *De Afscheiding en de Theologische School* (Aalten: N.V. de Graafschap, 1934), 29; "De eerste halve eeuw," in *Sola Gratia: Schets van de geschiedenis en de werkzaamheid van de Theologische Hogeschool der Gereformeerde Kerken in Nederland*, ed. J. D. Boerkoel, Th. Delleman, and G. M. den Hartogh (Kampen: Kok, 1954), 26.

52. "Kerknieuws," *De Bazuin*, September 29, 1854.

53. A. B. W. M. Kok, *Dr Herman Bavinck* (Amsterdam: S. J. P. Bakker, 1945), 17. "Hij was echter zóó bescheiden en dacht zóó klein van zichzelf en zijn gaven, dat hij de benoeming tot docent aan de Theologische School niet durfde aannemen."

54. Quoted in Valentijn Hepp, *Dr. Herman Bavinck* (Amsterdam: Ten Have, 1921), 16. "Volgens *De Heraut*, 'riep hij door het lot de beslissing in van God den Heere en meende daarin een aanwijzing te ontvangen, dat hij voor deze roeping bedanken moest.'"

55. Jan Bavinck, "Een korte schets van mijn leven," 62. "Zoo is het ons gegaan in de gemeente te Almkerk en Emmikhoven. Wij hebben er lief en leed ondervonden. De Heere echter was met ons onder alles."

56. In "Een korte schets van mijn leven," Jan Bavinck refers to him as "P. Hasselman." In other sources, he is more commonly referred to as L. W. Hasselman. See, for example, Adriaan

Cornelis Rosendaal, *Naar een school voor de gereformeerde gezindte: Het christelijke onderwijsconcept van het Gereformeerd Schoolverband (1868–1971)* (Hilversum: Verloren, 2006), 20.

57. H. Hille and J. P. Neven, "Verheerlijkt en verguisd," *Oude Paden*, March 2001, 42–52.

58. Valentijn Hepp, *Levensbericht voor Herman Bavinck* (Leiden: Brill, 1923), 2. "Herman genoot van meet af breedere vorming dan de meeste domineeskinderen uit zijn kring. De omstandigheden werkten daartoe mede en niet het minst de wetenschappelijke liefde van den vader."

59. Emo Bos, *Souvereiniteit en religie: Godsdienstvrijheid onder de eerste Oranjevorsten* (Hilversum: Verloren, 2009), 399.

60. Richard Lindert Zijdeman, *Status Attainment in the Netherlands, 1811–1941: Spatial and Temporal Variation before and during Industrialisation* (Ede: Ponsen & Looijen, 2010), 92.

61. Herman would also reflect on this social development at length. See Herman Bavinck, *De opvoeding der rijpere jeugd* (Kampen: Kok, 1916), 174–88.

62. Jan Bavinck, *Stemmen des heils* (Gorinchem: Van Nas, 1863).

63. *Onze Tolk: Centraalblad voor kunst- en letternieuws* 1, no. 8 (January 5, 1870): 62.

64. Jules Verne, *De Noordpool-expeditie van kapitein Hatteras*, trans. Gerard Keller (Leiden: de Breuk & Smits, 1870; first published in French in 1864).

65. Charles Haddon Spurgeon, *Voor iederen morgen: Dagboek voor huisgezin of binnenkamer*, trans. P. Huët (Amsterdam: W. H. Kirberger, 1870; first published in English in 1866).

66. Martin Luther, *Het regtveerdigend geloof verklaart en bevestigt: In eene verhandeling over Paulus brief aan den Galaten*, trans. Theodorus van der Groe (Utrecht: A. Visscher, 1870; first published in Latin in 1519).

67. James Kennedy and Jan Zwemer, "Religion in the Modern Netherlands and the Problems of Pluralism," *BMGN—Low Countries Historical Review* 125 (2–3): 249.

68. Jan Bavinck, *De vriendschap der geloovigen met God: Leerrede over Jac. 2:23b* (Amsterdam: Van den Bor, 1866); *Het toebrengen van andere schapen tot de kudde van Jezus: Leerrede over Johannes X:16* (Amsterdam: Van den Bor, 1867); *Klachte van eene geloovige ziel over de verberging van Gods aanschijn: Leerrede over Psalm 88:15* (Kampen: G. Ph. Zalsman, 1868); *Wilt gijlieden ook niet weggaan? Leerrede over Joh. 6:66–69* (Amsterdam: Kröber, Heijbrock & Hötte, 1868); *"Houd wat gij hebt": Afscheidswoord aan de Gemeente van Almkerk en Emmikhoven, uitgesproken den 27 Juli 1873* (Kampen: G. Ph. Zalsman, 1873); *De bediening des Evangelies een schat, gelegd in aarden vaten: Intreêrede, uitgesproken te Kampen, den 3 Aug. 1873* (Kampen: G. Ph. Zalsman, 1873).

69. Jan Bavinck and Helenius de Cock, "Inleiding," in *De Getuigenis: Maandschrift in het belang van Waarheid en Godzaligheid* 1 (1869): 3–4. "Ook onze kerk ondervindt den invloed van den tijd waarin zij zich bevindt. Onze jongelingen vooral zijn het, die aan den invloed van den tijdgeest zoo min kunnen onttrokken kunnen worden, als dat zij er zich van kunnen vrijwaren. Daarom achten wij het behoefte, dat er ook van ons een orgaan uit mocht gaan, waarin de waarheden des Evangeliums breedvoeriger verklaard en verdedigd, en de waarheid en goddelijkheid van de Schrift tegen de aanvallen van het on- en het halfgeloof gehandhaafd worden, dan dit in weekbladen kan geschieden."

70. Berendinus Johannes Femia was named after his two sisters: Femia, who had died two years before his birth, and Berendina Johanna.

71. Jan Bavinck, "Een korte schets van mijn leven," 68. "Er waren drie predikbeurten op den Rustdag des Heeren te vervullen en des winters kwam er nog eene beurt in de week bij."

72. Jan Bavinck, "Een korte schets van mijn leven," 68. "O ik herinner mij nog levendig enkele beurten, vooral des avonds bij het gaslicht, hoe stil en aandachtig eene groote schare naar de prediking kon luisteren en de woorden van de prediker scheen op te eten! Er was honger en dorst naar het Woord Gods en de woorden des levens waren spijze en drank voor die hongerige en dorstige zielen. Ik mag gelooven dat mijn arbeid in die dagen niet zonder vrucht en zegen is geweest."

73. Jan Bavinck, "Een korte schets van mijn leven," 69. "'Uw invloed op de studenten,' zeide eens Prof. van Velzen tot mij, 'is nog grooter dan die van ons Professoren.' Ik laat dit door den Professor gezegd zijn, maar dit, dunkt mij, mag ik zeggen, dat èn Professoren èn Studenten mij meer dan eens betuigd hebben, dat zij door mijne prediking waren gesticht."

74. "Advertentien," *De Standaard*, April 29, 1875; "Advertentien," *De Standaard*, May 5, 1875.

75. Jan Bavinck and Willem Hendrik Gispen, *De Christ. Geref. Kerk en de Theologische School: Twee toespraken, gehouden den 9 Jan. 1883 bij de installatie van de drie leeraren aan de Theol. School* (Kampen: G. Ph. Zalsman, 1883).

76. Bavinck and Gispen, *De Christ. Geref. Kerk en de Theologische School*, 19. "Die Kerk heeft behoefte, groote behoefte aan godvruchtige, degelijke, wetenschappelijk-gevormde dienaren des Evangelies."

77. Bavinck and Gispen, *De Christ. Geref. Kerk en de Theologische School*, 20. "Ik weet wel, dat er zijn, die zulk eene wetenschappelijke kennis niet noodig achten in den dienaar des Evangelies, en daarom alle wetenschappelijke opleiding afkeuren."

78. Bavinck and Gispen, *De Christ. Geref. Kerk en de Theologische School*, 20. "Bovendien stelt de negentiende eeuw met recht groote eischen aan den dienaar des Evangelies, aan welke hij zonder degelijke studie niet voldoen zou."

79. Bavinck and Gispen, *De Christ. Geref. Kerk en de Theologische School*, 24. "De Heere, de Koning der Kerk ziet op U; de Chr. Geref. Kerk ziet op U; Nederland ziet op U; ja de oogen van duizenden, van vrienden en vijanden zijn op U geslagen."

80. Herman Bavinck, *De wetenschap der H. Godgeleerdheid: Rede ter aanvaarding van het leeraarsambt aan de Theologische School te Kampen* (Kampen: G. Ph. Zalsman, 1883); cf. James Eglinton, *Trinity and Organism: Towards a New Reading of Herman Bavinck's Organic Motif* (London: Bloomsbury T&T Clark, 2012), 38.

81. C. J. van Hoeken, *Antwoord aan den schrijver van: Een woord aan de afgescheidenen uit de hervormden, en aan allen die de waarheid lief hebben* ('s Gravenhage: J. van Golverdinge, 1841), 22. "Over den inhoud van ons geloof, kan er geen twijfel bestaan . . . dat men zelfs . . . ons beschuldigt van illiberaliteit, (stonden tegenover vrijheid van denken) begrompenheid, en, van, bij vooruitgang der wetenschap, achterlijk te blijven."

82. The de Moens were wealthy Afgescheidenen from Leiden. The leading Seceder pastors Anthony Brummelkamp, Albertus van Raalte, and Simon van Velzen were brothers-in-law through their de Moen wives. Gerrit Jan Beuker, *Abgeschiedenes Streben nach Einheit: Leben und Wirken Henricus Beukers 1834–1900* (Bad Bentheim: Hellendoorn KG, 1996), 43.

83. That de Moen would give this opening lecture was announced beforehand in *De Bazuin*. See "De Theologische School," *De Bazuin*, December 1, 1854. For the final published version of his lecture, see Carol Godefroy de Moen, *De Bede van Salomo om wijsheid en wetenschap: Een gepast voorbeeld voor allen, maar inzonderheid voor de dienaren in 's Heeren wijngaard, die met Gods hulp de hun opgelegde taak willen aanvaarden en volbrengen* (Kampen: S. van Velzen Jnr., 1854).

84. De Moen, *De Bede van Salomo om wijsheid en wetenschap*, 28. "De Heere toch is de God der wetenschappen, 'Hij geeft den wijzen wijsheid, en wetenschap dengenen die verstand hebben,' *Daniël* II : 21b."

85. It should be acknowledged that de Moen's book was favorably reviewed in the magazine *Vaderlandsche Letteroefeningen, of Tijdschrift van Kunsten en Wetenschappen* (Amsterdam: P. Ellerman, 1855), 322–24. This review describes the quality of early Seceder preaching unfavorably but celebrates the foundation of the new Theological School, noting that it is staffed largely by teachers "formed in our Fatherland's academies."

86. "Verslag van de Opening der Theologische School te Kampen, 6 December 1854," *De Bazuin*, December 16, 1854: ". . . eene krachtige, opwekkende en bemoedigende toespraak."

87. C. G. de Moen, "Toelichting," *De Bazuin*, December 22, 1854. In this article, de Moen responded to criticism that his address had not been an extemporaneous sermon, but had, rather, been written out in advance and read from a manuscript. The address had to be written beforehand, he claimed, for two reasons. In the first place, that it would be published had been agreed on before he had written it (which necessitated a manuscript), and in the second, he had been too busy to devote adequate time to planning and memorizing it. He also admitted that having to read his address (which, he notes, he had not done in thirteen years of pulpit ministry) meant that the quality of its delivery had not been to his own satisfaction.

88. Bavinck and Gispen, *De Christ. Geref. Kerk en de Theologische School*, 24. "De Heere, de Koning der Kerk ziet op U; de Chr. Geref. Kerk ziet op U; Nederland ziet op U; ja de oogen van duizenden, van vrienden en vijanden zijn op U geslagen."

89. De Moen, *De Bede van Salomo om wijsheid en wetenschap*, 21. "De Heere Jezus ziet op U! De Gemeente Gods ziet op U! De Kweekelingen dezer School zien op U! De Bezorgers (Curatoren) der School zien op U! *Nederland* ziet op U! De Vader der leugenen ziet op U!"

90. Incidentally, "A short sketch of my life" also notes that shortly after his arrival in Kampen as pastor, Jan Bavinck addressed the local theological students on the text Proverbs 1:7, rendered in Dutch as, "De vreeze des Heeren is het beginsel der wetenschap." Jan Bavinck, "Een korte schets van mijn leven," 67. This address was also noted in *De Bazuin*, September 26, 1873.

91. Jan Bavinck, *De zaligheid alleen in den naam van Jezus*; *Davids bede in den ouderdom: Eene overdenking bij gelegenheid van zijne vijftigjarige bediening van het Woord Gods* (Kampen: Ph. Zalsman, 1898).

92. University of Amsterdam, *Album academicum van het Athenaeum illustre en van de Universiteit van Amsterdam: Bevattende de namen der curatoren, hoogleeraren en leeraren van 1632 tot 1913, der rectores magnifici en secretarissen van den Senaat der universiteit van 1877 tot 1913, der leden van den Illustrissimus senatus studiosorum Amstelodamensium van 1851 tot 1913, en der studenten van 1799 tot 1913* (Amsterdam: R. W. P. de Vries, 1913), 21.

93. Jan Bavinck, "Een korte schets van mijn leven," 72. "Ik verloor in haar eene lieve en trouwe Gade, eene, ik zeg niet geleerde, maar verstandige huisvrouw die op hare huishouding goede acht gaf en haar huisgezin trouw verzorgde. Ik en ook mijne kinderen, wij hebben naast God den Heere, veel, zeer veel aan haar te danken. Ruim 50 jaren was ik in een genoeglijken en gezegenden echt met haar vereenigd geweest, en nu was zij van mijne zijde weggerukt. Ik gevoelde mij ten gevolge van haar verlies nu zoo eenzaam en mismoedig gestemd."

94. Jan Bavinck, "Een korte schets van mijn leven," 72.

95. Jan Bavinck, "Een korte schets van mijn leven," 72. "Ik verliet de pastorie en werd in het huisgezin van mijn zoon opgenomen. Mijn zoon is gehuwd met de oudste dochter van den heer A.W. Schippers te Vlaardingen. De Heere heeft hun één kind, eene dochter gegeven. Dit kind, reeds eenige jaren oud, is de lievelinge des huizes."

96. Jan Bavinck, *Feeststoffen (voor het Kerstfeest en voor het Oud- en Nieuwjaar)* (Kampen: Ph. Zalsman, 1900); *Feeststoffen (voor het Paaschfeest)* (Kampen: Ph. Zalsman, 1901).

97. Jan Bavinck, *De Heidelbergsche Catechismus in 60 leerredenen verklaard*, 2 vols. (Kampen: Kok, 1903–4).

98. His final address was also published: Jan Bavinck, *De algeheele heiliging van de geloovigen, de wensch van de dienaar des Evangelies: Afscheidswoord uitgesproken den 25 Januari 1903* (Kampen: Kok, 1903).

99. From 1902 to 1904, Herman Bavinck rented Linnaeusparkweg 37, in Watergraafsmeer, to the east of Amsterdam, following which he purchased Singel 62, in the Grachtengordel. Hepp, *Dr. Herman Bavinck*, 289.

100. Jan Bavinck, "Een korte schets van mijn leven," 72. "Toen mijn zoon later tot hoogleeraar aan de Vrije Universiteit te Amsterdam werd benoemd en die benoeming aannam, ben ik met hem en zijn gezin naar Amsterdam vertrokken en nog op mijn ouden dag een inwoner van die groote wereldstad geworden." While in ministry, he had more than one call from the

Seceder congregation in Amsterdam, although he declined these approaches. See, for example, "Kerknieuws," *De Bazuin*, June 8, 1855; "Kerknieuws," *De Bazuin*, July 30, 1855; "Kerknieuws," *De Bazuin*, August 31, 1855.

101. See, for example, Michael Wintle, *An Economic and Social History of the Netherlands, 1800–1920: Demographic, Economic and Social Transition* (Cambridge: Cambridge University Press, 2000), 332.

102. "Ds. J. Bavinck van de oud-gereformeerde kerk is overleden," *Kamper Courant*, December 31, 1909.

103. Hepp, *Dr. Herman Bavinck*, 14.

104. Hepp, *Dr. Herman Bavinck*, v; *De Bazuin*, December 17, 1921.

105. Dosker, "Herman Bavinck: A Eulogy by Henry Elias Dosker," 14.

Chapter 3 Herman's Childhood and Schooling: 1854–72

1. "Heden beviel, door Gods goedheid, zeer voorspoedig van een *Zoon* GEZIENA MAGDALENA HOLLAND, hartelijk Echtgenoot van J. BAVINCK, *v.d.m.*, HOOGEVEEN, 13 December 1854." "Advertentiën," *De Bazuin*, December 22, 1854. *Nota bene*: The abbreviation "*v.d.m.*" stands for the Latin *verbi divini minister*, meaning "minister of the divine word."

2. "Advertentie," *De Bazuin*, August 4, 1853. In this example, in the first edition of *De Bazuin*, the émigré Seceder Albertus van Raalte announced the birth of a "well-formed" daughter in Michigan.

3. "Advertentiën," *De Bazuin*, December 22, 1854.

4. "Advertentiën," *De Bazuin*, March 30, 1855.

5. "Advertentie," *De Bazuin*, December 1, 1853.

6. "Advertentie," *De Bazuin*, October 20, 1853.

7. "Advertentie," *De Bazuin*, May 16, 1855.

8. Bavinck to Snouck Hurgronje, Kampen, January 6, 1879, in *ELV*.

9. Herman Bavinck, "Autobiographische schets van Dr. H. Bavinck," *De Grondwet*, no. 9, October 6, 1908, 3.

10. Jan Bavinck, "Een korte schets van mijn leven," unpublished, handwritten autobiography, n.d., HBA, folder 445.

11. Bavinck, "Autobiographische schets van Dr. H. Bavinck," 3.

12. R. H. Bremmer, *Herman Bavinck en zijn tijdgenoten* (Kampen: Kok, 1966), 17.

13. Despite the Bavincks' own lack of focus on Herman's early education in Bunschoten, it is now the location of a Reformed primary school, the Gereformeerde Basisschool "Dr. H. Bavinckschool," named in his honor.

14. Valentijn Hepp, *Dr Herman Bavinck* (Amsterdam: Ten Have, 1921), 17. "Wel las ik ergens het volgende, 'Er is een oogenblik geweest, waarin deze diamant (n.l. de jonge Bavinck) ongeslepen zou zijn ter zijde gelegd als een gewone steen. Toen,—zoo is ons reeds kort na zijn optreden als professor door iemand, die het kon weten, verhaald,—toen Ds. Bavinck Sr. te Almkerk zijn intrede gedaan had, en door "Monsieur" de Boer, den man van het Instituut Hasselman, werd verwelkomd, sprak de vader over zijn kinderen en hun verder onderwijs. In "onzen Herman" had men te Bunschoten niet veel studiekracht gezien; wél in den jongeren zoon. Die zou wel een leerling van "Monsieur" worden. Maar wat de oudste zoon moest worden, dat wist vader Bavinck nog niet. Nu! zeide de heer de Boer: "geef hem mij toch maar eens op proef." En dat geschiedde. Toen na enkele weken Ds. Bavinck den onderwijzer vroeg: of er van zijn oudsten zoon nog iets te verwachten was, gaf deze hem ten antwoord: "Dominé, 't is een diamant, maar die is niet goed geslepen, die moet nog ontbolsterd worden.""'

15. Hepp, *Dr. Herman Bavinck*, 18.

16. Bremmer, *Herman Bavinck en zijn tijdgenoten*, 17–18.

17. Ron Gleason, *Herman Bavinck: Pastor, Churchman, Statesman, and Theologian* (Phillipsburg, NJ: P&R, 2010), 32–33.

18. For a critique of this tendency, see James Bratt, *Abraham Kuyper: Modern Calvinist, Christian Democrat* (Grand Rapids: Eerdmans, 2013), 3.

19. Michael Wintle, *An Economic and Social History of the Netherlands, 1800–1920: Demographic, Economic and Social Transition* (Cambridge: Cambridge University Press, 2000), 335.

20. Wintle, *Economic and Social History of the Netherlands*, 270.

21. Colin Heywood, "Children's Work in Countryside and City," in *The Routledge History of Childhood in the Western World*, by Paula S. Fass (London: Routledge, 2013), 133; cf. Wintle, *Economic and Social History of the Netherlands*, 335.

22. Hepp, *Dr. Herman Bavinck*, 17–20.

23. H. Bouma, *Een vergeten hoofdstuk* (Enschede: Boersma, 1959), 133–35.

24. W. de Graaff, "Een merkwaardige school in de vorige eeuw," *De Hoeksteen* 11 (1982): 105–12.

25. C. Smits, *De Afscheiding van 1834*, vol. 8, *Provincie Noord-Brabant* (Dordrecht: J. P. van den Tol, 1988), 165. "Het reilen en zeilen van deze onderwijs-inrichting—kostschool en lagere school—is in de literatuur omgeven met een lichte nevel van romantiek. En deze is enigszins verdicht doordat . . . Herman Bavinck er van zijn zevende tot zijn zestiende jaar onderwijs heeft genoten." To the list of sources Smits critiqued in 1988, we might add Gleason's account of the Hasselman Institute, which depends on Hepp and Bremmer. See Gleason, *Herman Bavinck*, 32–33.

26. See, for example, Hepp, *Dr. Herman Bavinck*, 19. "Want het instituut-Hasselman had een goeden naam. Het was eenig in het land."

27. P. J. Andriessen, *Een Engelsche jongen op eene Hollandsche school* (Amsterdam: P. N. van Kampen, 1864), 9.

28. Smits, *De Afscheiding van 1834*, 8:165. Isaäc van Dijk is also noted as a former pupil in Bremmer's account. Bremmer, *Herman Bavinck en zijn tijdgenoten*, 17.

29. Smits records that a boarder paid ƒ225 per year, which could be supplemented with ƒ26 for piano lessons and ƒ50 for instruction in Greek and Latin. See Smits, *De Afscheiding van 1834*, 8:168.

30. Hepp, *Dr. Herman Bavinck*, 20.

31. Hepp, *Dr. Herman Bavinck*, 14; van den Berg, "De Spiritualiteit van de Afgescheidenen," 174.

32. For a similar critique of Hepp's portrayal of Jan Bavinck, see John Bolt, *Bavinck on the Christian Life: Following Jesus in Faithful Service* (Wheaton: Crossway, 2015), 25. Henry Dosker's "Herman Bavinck: A Eulogy by Henry Elias Dosker" (in *Essays on Religion, Science, and Society*, ed. John Bolt, trans. Harry Boonstra and Gerrit Sheeres [Grand Rapids: Baker Academic, 2008]) also portrays Jan and Geziena as marked by *Kulturfeindlichkeit* (15).

33. Herman Bavinck, *De opvoeding der rijpere jeugd* (Kampen: Kok, 1916), 79: "De moderne jeugd karaktertrekken vertoont, die haar in vorige tijden niet of niet in die mate eigen waren. De moderne jeugd heeft zelve den invloed der moderne maatschappij ondergaan. Wel is waar is het aan de jeugd ten allen tijde en overal eigen, om naar zelfstandigheid te streven, aan het gezag van het verledene zich te ontworstelen, en in de toekomst zich een eigen weg te banen. Er ligt daarin op zichzelf ook niets verkeerds; het is een natuurlijk proces van ontwikkeling, dat vooruitgang mogelijk maakt; men mag het daar om ook niet met geweld onderdrukken, maar moet het weten te leiden, zoodat verleden en toekomst bij de opwassende jeugd in harmonie met elkander blijven."

34. Bavinck, *De opvoeding der rijpere jeugd*, 75.

35. Jan Bavinck and Helenius de Cock, "Inleiding," *De Getuigenis: Maandschrift in het belang van Waarheid en Godzaligheid* 1 (1869): 3–4. "Onze jongelingen vooral zijn het, die aan den invloed van den tijdgeest zoo min onttrokken kunnen worden, als dat zij er zich van kunnen vrijwaren."

36. Wintle, *Economic and Social History of the Netherlands*, 269.

37. P. Th. F. M. Boekholt and Engelina Petronella de Booy, *Geschiedenis van de school in Nederland vanaf de middeleeuwen tot aan de huidige tijd* (Assen: Van Gorcum, 1987), 197–98; Frederick Martin, *The Statesman's Year-Book: A Statistical, Genealogical, and Historical Account of the States and Sovereigns of the Civilised World for the Year 1886* (London: MacMillan and Co., 1866), 353.

38. For Bavinck's own mature thoughts on the liberalization of education and the creation of "higher burgher schools," see the manuscripts "Inrichting der gymnasia," "Gymnasiaal onderwijs," "Bezwaren tegen gymnasiaal onderwijs en hedendaagsche gymnasia," and "Hoogere burgerscholen" (1896, 1901, 1903, 1904, 1908), HBA, folder 122.

39. Boekholt and de Booy, *Geschiedenis van de school in Nederland*, 199.

40. Boekholt and de Booy, *Geschiedenis van de school in Nederland*, 199.

41. Boekholt and de Booy, *Geschiedenis van de school in Nederland*, 10.

42. Marius Buys, *Mr. Jan Rudolf Thorbecke herdacht* (Tiel: D. Mijs, 1872), 6.

43. Ross Fuller, *The Brotherhood of the Common Life and Its Influence* (New York: State University of New York Press, 1995), 195.

44. "H. Bavinck, 1872, Zwolle," HBA, folder 16.

45. Arianne Baggerman, "Lost Time: Temporal Discipline and Historical Awareness in Nineteenth-Century Dutch Egodocuments," in *Controlling Time and Shaping the Self: Developments in Autobiographical Writing since the Sixteenth Century*, ed. Arianne Baggerman, Rudolf Dekker, and Michael James Mascuch (Leiden: Brill, 2011), 455–535.

46. For example, Hepp, *Dr. Herman Bavinck*, 209; Bremmer, *Herman Bavinck en zijn tijdgenoten*, 108.

47. "H. Bavinck, 1872, Zwolle." "III dies ante Cal. Junias ego rogavi Ameliam Dekkeranam, alius alia litteras scribene, si hunc locum relinquam."

48. "Amelia Josina den Dekker," *Bevolkingsregister, Almkerk, 1910–1920*, 34:96; "Wouterina Arnolda den Dekker," *Bevolkingsregister, Emmikhoven en Waardhuizen, 1870–1879*, 14:103; Smits, *De Afscheiding van 1834*, 8:150; *Provinciale Noordbrabantsche en 's Hertogenbossche courant*, December 18, 1933.

49. George Harinck, "'The Tares in the Wheat': Henry E. Dosker's Calvinist Historiography of Dutch Anabaptism," in *Religious Minorities and Cultural Diversity in the Dutch Republic*, ed. August den Hollander, Mirjam van Veen, Anna Voolstra, and Alex Noord (Leiden: Brill, 2014), 269.

50. "Binnenland," *Provinciale Overijsselsche en Zwolsche courant*, August 19, 1872, 2. Herman's fellow students are recorded as E. S. Eisma, W. H. Roijer, J. H. Tobias, A. Fränkel, T. Brouwer, H. Kerbert, H. N. Dosker, A. H. van Deventer, B. Wartena, H. E. Dosker, G. Kortenbos van der Sluijs, S. Gratama, E. Damsté, G. Kalff, P. Sichterman, J. A. de Vos van Steenwijk, S. J. van Buuren, J. C. Roosenburg, H. Ferwerda, D. Z. van Duijl, and E. F. J. Heerspink.

51. "H. Bavinck, 1872, Zwolle." "Lief meisje! Dat ik u hartelijk min, / 'K zag gaarne u tot echtsvriendin / Ziedaar mijn declaratie / Voelt ge ook voor mij genegenheid / Zoo bid ik, lieve beste meid / Geef mij uw approbatie / Een vonk geschoten uit uw ogen / Veel schooner dan een diamant / Stak door een heimelijk vermogen / Mijn jeugdig hart in vollen brand / Spreek uit, spreek uit of ik ben verloren / Blaas met een vonk die mij verteert. / Een vonk uit uw gezicht geboren / 't Gezicht dat zon en maan braveert."

52. "H. Bavinck, 1872, Zwolle." "19 Maart 1873. Belijdenis des Geloofs afgelegd bij Ds. Dosker in de Chr. Geref. Kerk te Zwolle. 30 Maart '73. Zondag. Bevestigd door Ds. Dosker."

53. Bremmer, *Herman Bavinck en zijn tijdgenoten*, 19.

54. Harinck, "Tares in the Wheat," 269.

55. Dosker to Bavinck, Holland (Michigan), Spring 1874, in *BHD*. "Met u is het gansch anders. Van jongs af waren uwe studieën beter gebaseerd dan de onze. Uw vader bezit de middelen om u een academische graad te doen verkrijgen. Voor u staan duizend wegen open die

ons voor immer gesloten waren. Met Gods hulpe kunt en zult ge iets worden, waarvan ik in Nederland de schaduw zelfs niet had kunnen bereiken."

56. "Zwolle, Geboorteakte, Aaltje Klinkert, 18-11-1857, Zwolle," Historisch Centrum Overijssel, inventory no. 14445, article no. 556; "Zwolle, Registers van overlijden, 1811–1942, Aaltje Klinkert," Historisch Centrum Overijssel, inventory no. 15325, article no. 231.

57. "Notes, H. Bavinck, 1873, Zwolle." "10 April '73. Verkooping van Ds. Dosker inboedel (ten bedrage van ± ƒ. 1100). Bij die gelegenheid kwam ik in aanraking met Ααλτιε Κλινκερτ cum sororibus."

58. "H. Bavinck, 1872, Zwolle." "25 Sept. '72. Broertje gekregen. 26 Sept. kreeg ik er de tijding van."

59. "H. Bavinck, 1872, Zwolle." "19 Mei. Vader hier gekomen te Zwolle wegens de roeping naar Kampen. 20 Mei. Met vader naar Kampen gegaan. . . . 22 Mei. Vader weer naar huis gegaan. Wat zal de uitslag van diens roeping zijn? Dit was de vraag die ons vooral bezig hield. 24 Mei. Kreeg ik een telegraam . . . dat vader de roeping v. Kampen had <u>aangenomen</u>. 27 Mei. Had voor goed de <u>Aanneming der roeping</u> plaats."

60. Bremmer, *Herman Bavinck en zijn tijdgenoten*, 20; Gleason, *Herman Bavinck*, 35–37.

61. "Notes, H. Bavinck, 1873, Zwolle." "10 Juni. De uitslag der Hollandsche Prijsthemata was dat ik den prijs van Kalff had gewonnen. 't Laatste thema had ¼ fout voor mij en ¾ voor Kalff." The biography of Kalff written by his son omits to mention that his father lost this prize to Bavinck. Gerrit Kalff jnr., *Leven van Dr. G. Kalff (1856–1923)* (Groningen: Wolters, 1924), xiii–xiv.

62. Bavinck to Christiaan Snouck Hurgronje, Kampen, January 29, 1889, in *ELV*.

63. Manuscript "Oratio de Historia Atticae Comoediae Antiquae: Elocutus est H. Bavinck Jz. die III in. Sept. a. MDCCCLXXIII" (1873), HBA, folder 17.

Chapter 4 Kampen: 1873–80

1. Manuscript "Lijst mijner geschriften" (no publisher, no date), HBA, folder 99.
2. Lijst mijner geschriften.

Geb.	13 Dec. 1854	Hoogeveen.
Candid. Theol.	Leiden	1 April 1878.
" Semit.	"	20 Sept. 1878
Doct. exam	"	4 Aug. 1879
Doctorate	"	10 Juni 1880
Cand. Theol.	Kampen	20 Juni 1880
Intrede te Franeker		13 Maart 1881
Benoemd,	Syn. Zwolle	24 Aug. 1882
Afscheid	Franeker	8 Oct. 1882
Ambt Kampen aanvaard		10 Jan. 1883
" Amsterdam "		17 Dec. 1902.

3. Michael Wintle, *An Economic and Social History of the Netherlands, 1800–1920: Demographic, Economic and Social Transition* (Cambridge: Cambridge University Press, 2000), 271. The Kampen professors Simon van Velzen and Anthony Brummelkamp had studied theology at Leiden, albeit well before the 1834 Afscheiding. However, before Bavinck's move to Leiden, no post-1834 Seceder student had studied theology there. There were, however, other Seceder students—the physicist Willem Hillebrand Nieuwhuis and the legal student Christiaan Lucasse—who were already studying in Leiden upon Bavinck's arrival. F. L. Bos, "Velzen, Simon van," in *Biografisch lexicon voor de geschiedenis van het Nederlands protestantisme*, ed. D. Nauta, A. de Groot, J. van den Berg, O. J. de Jong, F. R. J. Knetsch, and G. H. M. Posthumus Meyjes, 2nd ed. (Kampen: Kok, 1983), 2:431–33; Melis te Velde, "Brummelkamp, Anthony," in *Biografisch*

lexicon voor de geschiedenis van het Nederlands protestantisme, ed. D. Nauta, A. de Groot, J. van den Berg, O. J. de Jong, F. R. J. Knetsch, and G. H. M. Posthumus Meyjes (Kampen: Kok, 1998), 4:74–77.

4. "Notes, H. Bavinck, 1873." "19 Sept. Student geworden."

5. His enrollment at the Theological School was noted in *De Bazuin*, September 26, 1873.

6. Ron Gleason, *Herman Bavinck: Pastor, Churchman, Statesman, and Theologian* (Phillipsburg, NJ: P&R, 2010), 136, 147, 307, 399.

7. *Verslag van den toestand der gemeente Kampen over het jaar 1873* (Kampen: n.p., 1874), 1. For an impression of the character of life in Kampen in that period, see, for example, *Handelingen van den raad der Gemeente Kampen, 1873* (Kampen: K. van Hulst, 1873).

8. G. M. den Hartogh, "Varia," in *Sola Gratia: Schets van de geschiedenis en de werkzaamheid van de Theologische Hogeschool der Gereformeerde Kerken in Nederland*, ed. J. D. Boerkoel, Th. Delleman, and G. M. den Hartogh (Kampen: Kok, 1954), 61.

9. George Harinck and Wim Berkelaar, *Domineesfabriek: Geschiedenis van de Theologische Universiteit Kampen* (Amsterdam: Prometheus, 2018), 61.

10. Den Hartogh, "Varia," 60.

11. *Handelingen der Zes-en-twintigste Vergadering van de kuratoren der Theologische School der Christelijke Gereformeerde Kerk in Nederland* (Kampen: S. van Velzen Jnr., 1871), 12.

12. *Handelingen der Dertigste Vergadering van de kuratoren der Theologische School der Christelijke Gereformeerde Kerk in Nederland* (Kampen: G. Ph. Zalsman, 1874), 16. In the years 1854–83, van Velzen taught French, the ancient languages, ethics, church history, natural theology, and homiletics. From 1883 onward, his teaching was limited to homiletics. Bos, "Velzen, Simon van," 431.

13. "Theologische School," *De Bazuin*, July 24, 1874.

14. Den Hartogh, "Varia," 61.

15. Den Hartogh, "Varia," 61. "Vooral de gelegenheid tot meer universele beschaving en ontwikkeling van de studenten werd naar voren gebracht."

16. Gerrit Roelof de Graaf, "Fides Quaerit Intellectum: 'Het geloof zoekt te verstaan'; Het Kamper studentencorps 'Fides Quaerit Intellectum' in zijn omgang met de 'moderne' cultuur (1863–1902)," in *Documentatieblad voor de Nederlandse kerkgeschiedenis na 1800* 28 (2005): 20–35.

17. Den Hartogh, "Varia," 68.

18. The disagreement on this between Hendrik de Cock, the father of the Afscheiding, and his son, the Kampen professor Helenius, typifies this generational shift. In his youth, Helenius de Cock was also opposed to vaccination, but he changed his opinion when he visited Scotland and discovered that Scottish Reformed Christians were mystified as to the position maintained by their Dutch cousins. See Helenius de Cock, *Waarom heb ik mijn kinderen laten vaccineren? Open brief aan de heer D. Wijnbeek* (Kampen: Simon van Velzen jnr., 1871), 11.

19. Jasper Vree, *Kuyper in de kiem: De precalvinistische periode van Abraham Kuyper, 1848–1874* (Hilversum: Verloren, 2006), 135.

20. *Handelingen der Zes-en-twintigste Vergadering van de kuratoren der Theologische School der Christelijke Gereformeerde Kerk in Nederland*, 20.

21. R. H. Bremmer, *Herman Bavinck en zijn tijdgenoten* (Kampen: Kok, 1966), 21.

22. Abraham Kuyper, *Het Calvinisme, oorsprong en waarborg onzer constitutioneele vrijheden* (Amsterdam: B. van der Land, 1874); ET: "Calvinism: Source and Stronghold of Our Constitutional Liberties," in *Abraham Kuyper: A Centennial Reader*, ed. James Bratt (Grand Rapids: Eerdmans, 1998), 279–322.

23. James Bratt, *Abraham Kuyper: Modern Calvinist, Christian Democrat* (Grand Rapids: Eerdmans, 2013), 78.

24. Kuyper, "Calvinism," 293.

25. James Bratt, introduction to "Calvinism: Source and Stronghold of Our Constitutional Liberties," by Abraham Kuyper, in Bratt, *Abraham Kuyper: A Centennial Reader*, 279.

26. Den Hartogh, "Varia," 67–68.

27. *De Bazuin*, March 27, 1874. "Kampen. Dinsdag avond l.l. werd het studentencorps met de leeraren der Theol. School en andere uitgenoodigden, waaronder de meeste predikanten en leraren der Hoogere Burgerschool van deze stad, een aangename en nuttige ure bereid. Op uitnoodiging van genoemd corps, was Dr. A. Kuyper in hun midden opgetreden, om zijne lezing te houden over 'Het Calvinisme, oorsprong en waarborg onzer constitutioneele vrijheden.' Met ongewone bedrevenheid wist de Spreker ons in de diepe schatkameren der historie binnen te leiden, om ons dáár den draad van Calvijn te doen zien, langs welken de ware volksvrijheid, van uit Genève over Nederland en Engeland naar Amerika heen, zich had voortbewogen. Boeiend was de wijze van voorstelling, indrukmakend het doen spreken der feiten, wegslepend straks het geven van inzichten en wenken. De Souvereiniteit Gods werd in hare eer krachtig gehandhaafd en in de erkenning dier Souvereiniteit de weg der vrijheid voor kerk en maatschappij aangewezen. Hervorming en Revolutie werden treffend voorgesteld, als takken, somtijds geheel gelijkend op elkaar, maar opgeschoten uit verschillende stam, en daarom in wezen en groeikracht onderscheiden, gelijk ook de vrijheid en de willekeur, de loten, welke uit elk dier takken voortspruiten moeten. Het gehoorde hopen we spoedig te kunnen lezen en weiden er niet over uit. Maar wij zeggen: Onze sympathie voor die beginselen der ware vrijheid! Niet voor reactie, maar voor de rechtontwikkeling dier beginselen! Onze sympathie voor den geachten Spreker, die haar zoo getrouw en waar voorstelde! Onze dank en heilwensch zij hem ook hierbij toegebracht. *Namens het corps*, de Senaat, PH. ESKES, Secr."

28. "Notes, H. Bavinck, 1874." "24 Maart 1874 Dr Kuyper gezien. Hij sprak over het Calvinisme oorsprong en waarborg onzer constitutioneele vrijheden."

29. Valentijn Hepp, *Dr Herman Bavinck* (Amsterdam: Ten Have, 1921), 296.

30. Jotter entitled "Philosophie," HBA, folder 18. This jotter records his likely first exposure to the German theologian Friedrich Schleiermacher, who was presented in the course as a pantheistic philosopher.

31. Dosker to Bavinck, location unknown, spring 1874, in *BHD*. "Heb gij er een van Amelia, stuur dat mij dan eens, opdat ik me in het aanschouwen harer trekken uw geluk moge kunnen voorstellen."

32. "Notulen: 1872 november 7–27 april 1876," Archief van het College van Hoogleraren, Stadsarchief Kampen, item no. 15491.

33. Herman Bavinck, "Autobiographische schets van Dr. H. Bavinck," *De Grondwet*, no. 9, October 6, 1908, 3. "Na het gymnasium te hebben afgeloopen, ging ik een jaar naar de Theol. School te Kampen, waar mijn vader predikant geworden was. Maar het onderwijs aldaar bevredigde mij niet. Zoo ging ik in 1874 naar Leiden, om daar Theologie te studeeren onder de beroemde professoren Scholten en Kuenen."

34. Steketee lost his teaching position at the school in 1882, in close connection to Bavinck's own appointment there. Gleason's account of Bavinck's year in Kampen dwells at length on Steketee's dismissal and claims it was a significant factor in Bavinck's decision to enroll at Leiden: "The dismissal was, in a word, unceremonious. This, too, left a lasting impression on the young Bavinck." Gleason, *Herman Bavinck*, 41. This claim is chronologically puzzling, however, as Steketee was appointed the year before Bavinck enrolled as a student in Kampen and was not dismissed until 1882, by which time Bavinck was already a Christian Reformed minister in Franeker (and stood on the verge of his own appointment at the Theological School).

35. Herman Bavinck, "Inleidend woord van Prof. Dr. H. Bavinck," in *Adriaan Steketee (1846–1913): Beschouwingen van een Christen-denker*, by A. Goslinga (Kampen: Kok, 1914), v. "Het was in de jaren 1873/'74. Ik had den gymnasialen leertijd achter de rug en koesterde eene sterke begeerte, om in Leiden mijne studie voort te zetten en met de moderne theologie van nabij kennis te maken. Maar mijne ouders waren toen pas naar Kampen verhuisd, en drongen er bij mij aan, dat ik althans voor een jaar thuis zou komen en mij als student aan de Theologische School zou laten inschrijven. Ofschool ik daaraan gaarne voldeed, bleef toch het verlangen

mij bij, om eene meer wetenschappelijke opleiding deelachtig te worden, dan de Theol. School toenmaals geven kon; en zoo werd goedgevonden, dat ik in Sept. 1874 naar Leiden zou gaan."

36. F. J. Bulens, "Litt. Examenandi" and "Theol. Examinandi," June 11 and July 12, 1873, Archief van het College van Curatoren, Stadsarchief Kampen, item no. 12821. That Jan Bavinck requested this information is consistent with his own belief that his calling to pastor in Kampen was in service of both the Christian Reformed congregation and the Theological School. See Jan Bavinck, *De zaligheid alleen in den naam van Jezus* (Kampen: J. H. Bos, 1888), 24.

37. Wintle, *Economic and Social History of the Netherlands*, 301.

38. The Athenaeum Illustre would become the University of Amsterdam in 1877. See Gerrit Kalff Jr., *Leven van Dr. G. Kalff (1856–1923)* (Groningen: Wolters, 1924), xiv.

39. Jan Bavinck, "Een korte schets van mijn leven," unpublished, handwritten autobiography, n.d., HBA, folder 445, p. 67. "Onze oudste zoon, die te Zwolle op het gymnasium was, had juist zijn eindexamen gedaan en kwam in Kampen weer bij ons inwonen."

40. Hepp, *Dr. Herman Bavinck*, 83–84; repeated in J. Geelhoed, *Dr. Herman Bavinck* (Goes: Oosterbaan & Le Cointre, 1958), 7.

41. Bremmer, *Herman Bavinck en zijn tijdgenoten*, 18. Gleason translates *De zoete inval* literally as "The Sweet Invasion or Incursion." It is, rather, a Dutch expression with a meaning similar to "Home Sweet Home." See Gleason, *Herman Bavinck*, 38.

42. "Notes, H. Bavinck, 1874." "5 Juni 1874. Besloten, terwijl Ds. Donner, bij gelegenheid van de zendingsvergadering hier was dat ik naar Leiden zou gaan en Ds. D. een huis zou huren."

43. "Notes, H. Bavinck, 1874." "23 Juni. Dinsdag. In een dag naar Leiden heen en terug. De kamer gezien bij Juffrouw Smit Haarlemmerstraat. 't Stond me goed aan. Zoodat ik ze gehuurd heb voor één jaar Ds. Donner ontving mij aller vriendelijk."

44. "Notes, H. Bavinck, 1874." "14–18 July '74 Examen te Kampen. Van de 13 Litteratores 12 doorgekomen (Vonk, Impela) en 1 afgenomen. De 16 Theologen alle er door. Beide examens vielen me zeer mee, ook het theologisch. Toch waren ze niet schitterend. Eskes, Linden evenmin."

45. "Kerknieuws," *De Bazuin*, July 31, 1874. "KAMPEN. Onze geachte Leeraar J. Bavinck, maakte Zondag 26 Juli aan de Gemeente bekend, dat hij eene roeping had ontvangen naar 's Gravenhage. Onze wensch is dat Zew. hier zijn arbeid zal voortzetten, te meer daar hij nauwlijks een jaar onder ons verkeerd heeft. *Namens den Kerkeraad*, C. G. DE MOEN, Scriba."

46. J. van Gelderen and F. Rozemond, *Gegevens betreffende de Theologische Universiteit Kampen, 1854–1994* (Kampen: Kok, 1994), 107.

47. Bremmer, *Herman Bavinck en zijn tijdgenoten*, 20–21.

48. Hepp, *Dr. Herman Bavinck*, 83–84; Geelhoed, *Dr. Herman Bavinck*, 7.

49. Gleason, *Herman Bavinck*, 45.

50. Gleason, *Herman Bavinck*, 46.

51. Henry Elias Dosker, "Herman Bavinck: A Eulogy by Henry Elias Dosker," in *Essays on Religion, Science, and Society*, ed. John Bolt, trans. Harry Boonstra and Gerrit Sheeres (Grand Rapids: Baker Academic, 2008), 15.

52. Bremmer, *Herman Bavinck en zijn tijdgenoten*, 20. "Natuurlijk gaf dit besluit hevige reacties in de Kamper kring."

53. "Binnenland," in *De Standaard*, January 29, 1879, 2.

54. Den Hartogh, "Varia," 69–70. See J. H. Landwehr, *In Memoriam: Prof. Dr. H. Bavinck* (Kampen: Kok, 1921), 9.

55. Alexander de Savornin Lohman, "Donner (Johannes Hendrikus)," in *Nieuw Nederlandsch Biografisch Woordenboek*, ed. P. C. Molhuysen and P. J. Blok (Leiden: A. W. Sijthoff's, 1911), 1:738. The basic pattern of Donner's own life was also one of orthodox Calvinist participation in late modern Dutch culture. He was the pastor of the Christian Reformed Church in Leiden until 1877, when he entered parliament as a member of the Second Chamber.

Chapter 5 Leiden: 1874–80

1. "Ex animo et corpore. H. Bavinck, Theol Stud.," HBA, folder 16.

2. For engagement with this part of Goethe's oeuvre in Bavinck's later writings, see *Philosophy of Revelation: A New Annotated Edition*, ed. Cory Brock and Nathaniel Gray Sutanto (Peabody, MA: Hendrickson, 2018), 10, 28–30, 39, 42–43, 67–68, 88–89, 100–102; "Evolution," in *Essays on Religion, Science, and Society*, ed. John Bolt, trans. Harry Boonstra and Gerrit Sheeres (Grand Rapids: Baker Academic, 2008), 107.

3. "Notes, H. Bavinck, 1874." "24 Sept '74 Met van Deventer, Persille per boot naar Amsterdam, per spoor naar Leiden gegaan."

4. "Ex animo et corpore. H. Bavinck, Theol Stud." "1874. 23 Sept. Met van Deventer, Persille, v.d. Zwaan en Linpers naar Amsterdam en vandaar per spoor naar Leiden gegaan. Genoeglijk maar . . . toch vervelend reisje. Mooi weer, tot we onder een regenbui in L. aankwamen. 't Afscheid van mijn ouders viel me zwaar, vooral hierom, dat ik naar L. ging. Zal 'k staande blijven? God geve het!"

5. Hepp's biography cites a poem published in the 1875 Leiden student society almanac; the poem concludes with the definition of true student life as "vloeken als een echt matroos." Valentijn Hepp, *Dr Herman Bavinck* (Amsterdam: Ten Have, 1921), 33.

6. Jan Jacob de Gelder, *Catalogus van de tentoonstelling ter herdenking van het driehonderdvijftigjarig bestaan der Leidsche universiteit in het museum 'De Lakenhal,' Leiden, Februari 1925* (Leiden: Sijthoff, 1925), 27.

7. "Notes, H. Bavinck, 1874." "24 Sept. In laten schrijven voor de Theologie. Betaald 284 Glds. Begonnen groen te lopen. . . . Besloten geen lid te worden van 't Corps om mijns gewetens wille."

8. "Ex animo et corpore. H. Bavinck, Theol Stud." "Daarna begonnen groen te lopen. . . . Mag ik lid worden als Christen van 't Leidsche Stud.-Corps. 'K twijfelde: Ds. Donner kwam 's avonds te half elf bij me, ried 't me af èn—ik word geen lid, zoo besloot ik. Dikwerf vraag 'k me af, of 't wel alleen en zuiver gewetenshalve was, dat ik geen lid werd."

9. "Notes, H. Bavinck, 1874." "Kosten te Leiden, Collegegeld 270, Lid Corps. 14, Glas bier 5." While this note is undated, the cost of tuition envisaged does not match the actual fee paid in any of his years at Leiden. It is closest to the fee paid in his first year there. See "Kasboek, H. Bavinck," HBA, folder 19. "Uitgaven sedert 23 Sept. 1874 . . . Collegegelden, f. 284."

10. *Almanak van het Leidsche studentencorps voor 1874*, quoted in "Akademie-en Schoolnieuws," *Provinciale Overijsselsche en Zwolsche courant*, December 25, 1873.

11. "Herinneringen aan den Leidsche Dies van 1875," *Het Vaderland: Staat-en letterkundig nieuwsblad*, February 12, 1925. ". . . niet-corpsleden, die biggen werden genoemd."

12. J. M. E. Dercksen, *Gedenkboek der feestvieringen van het driehonderdjarig bestaan der hoogeschool te Leiden* (Leiden: De Breuk & Smits, 1875), 120. Interestingly, the list of signatories prefacing this book (individuals who contributed to the book's preproduction costs) included Bavinck's pastor in Leiden, J. H. Donner (xi).

13. George Harinck and Wim Berkelaar, *Domineesfabriek: Geschiedenis van de Theologische Universiteit Kampen* (Amsterdam: Prometheus, 2018), 68.

14. "Notes, H. Bavinck, 1874." "3 Oct '74 . . . Ik leef veel onder den indruk van de plichten, die ik als Christen hier ter Academie te vervullen heb. God geve mij er kracht toe! Kracht, om niet door woorden slechts maar door daden te toonen, dat ik een volgeling van Jesus ben."

15. "Ex animo et corpore. H. Bavinck, Theol Stud." "3 Oct [1874]. Derde Eeuwfeest van Leidens ontzet; ik was niet feestelik gestemd en had dus niet veel genoegen: zag ik de woelende & kriolende schare, die deze . . . dag slechts dienstbaar achtte voor uitspatting en losbandigheid, dan dacht ik, hoe weinig God toch erkend wordt voor wat Hij ons schenkt. Ik leefde veel onder den indruk der plichten, als Christen hier voor mij te vervullen. God verleene me kracht, kracht om niet door woorden slechts, maar door daden te toonen dat 'k een volgeling van Jezus ben."

16. "Ex animo et corpore. H. Bavinck, Theol Stud." "1 Oct [1874]. Eerste college: bij Bierens de Haan. Goed bevallen maar hij spreekt onduidelijk. 'K kon niet goed begrijpen, dat ik Leidsch student was."

17. For examples of the kind of sermons heard by Bavinck in his Leiden years, see J. H. Donner, *Lichtstralen van den kandelaar des woords* (Leiden: D. Donner, 1883). For a selection of Donner's sermons published posthumously, see H. W. Laman, ed., *Wandelen door geloof: Overdenkingen van de gereformeerde predikanten* (Utrecht: Gereformeerd Traktaatgenootschap "Filippus," 1930). For a sermon delivered by Donner after the death of Godefridus Johannes Lambertus Berends, a Seceder missionary who had converted from Roman Catholicism, see J. H. Donner, *Afgewezen, maar niet teleurgesteld: Toespraak naar 1 Koningen 8:17–19a* (Kampen: G. Ph. Zalsman, 1873). Donner's published sermons are noticeably different from those of Jan Bavinck, which—in their final published form, at least—were more consistently devotional and descriptive, did not make the same use of dialogical rhetoric, and did not aim to deal explicitly with pressing cultural issues.

18. "Ex animo et corpore. H. Bavinck, Theol Stud." "18 Oct [1874]. Zondag . . . O zoo mooi! . . . Jammer dat voordracht, en ook taal en stijl niet harmoniseren met de gedachten, de schoone gedachten, die Ds. Donner heeft."

19. "Ex animo et corpore. H. Bavinck, Theol Stud." "18 Oct [1874]. Zondag . . . Hoe was ik gestemd dezen dag? Een enkel oogenblik voelde ik maar dat zalige van den dienst van Jezus. En 't was mijn wensch om voor Hem te leven maar—die zonde, die zonde. 'K wilde wel voor Jezus leven, doch 't was meer, om mijzelf op den troon te plaatsen, dan oprechte belangstelling in Gods Koninkrijk. 'K weet niet hoe me juist uittedrukken: dat leven voor Jezus moest dan ook 'beloond' worden met eer en roem en aanzien. En dat is toch niet goed! neen."

20. On the history of the Seceders in Leiden, see J. De Lange, *De Afscheiding te Leiden* (Rotterdam: J. H. Donner, 1934).

21. Wilhelmina, Princess of the Netherlands, *Eenzaam maar niet alleen* (Amsterdam: W. ten Have, 1959), 49.

22. J. H. Landwehr, *In Memoriam: Prof. Dr. H. Bavinck* (Kampen: Kok, 1921), 11. "Daar stonden iederen Zondagmorgen de equipages voor de deuren der kerk."

23. Landwehr, *In Memoriam*, 13. "Dat is gebeurd, om u en de uwen niet te compromitteeren."

24. Landwehr, *In Memoriam*, 11.

25. "Ex animo et corpore. H. Bavinck, Theol Stud." "4 Oct [1874] . . . 's avonds Ds. Holster over: Looft God in de gemeente: gij die zijt uit den springaders Israëls. Ps. 68 vers 27. Quid dicam? Na kerktijd bij ds. Holster geweest. Veel volk weinig genoegen. . . . 'K was niet bijzonder opgewekt; ja zelfs bekroop me een weinig spotzucht soms. 'K moet mij daarvoor wachten, want 't is zeer gevaarlijk. De verleiding kleedt zich in allerlei gedaanten. God doe ze mij ontmaskeren en ze schuwen."

26. "Ex animo et corpore. H. Bavinck, Theol Stud." "13 Oct [1874]. Eerste college bij Huygens—tamelijk, id bij Cobet, uitmuntend, id bij Dozij, goed, id bij Land, slecht, id bij de Vries, uitmuntend, id bij Rutgers, tamelijk bevallen."

27. "Ex animo et corpore. H. Bavinck, Theol Stud." "4 Nov [1874] Debating Society. Heemskerk verdedigde stellingen tegen Kuypers: 't Calvinisme, oorsprong, enz. Kuyper was er ook. O, zoo'n genoegen gehad in K's . . ."

28. "Ex animo et corpore. H. Bavinck, Theol Stud." "12 April [1874]. Weer naar Leiden. Tamelijk op mijn gemak. Bede om lust tot studie."

29. "Ex animo et corpore. H. Bavinck, Theol Stud." "20 April Multatuli voor 't eerst gehoord over de verhouding van de in school en huis aangewende pogingen tot volmaking van den mensch, op geestelijk, zedelijk en stoffelijk gebied."

30. Multatuli, *Max Havelaar, of De koffieveilingen der Nederlandsche Handelmaatschappy*, ed. Annemarie Kets-Vree (Assen: Van Gorcum, 1992); ET: *Max Havelaar, or The Coffee Auctions*

of the Dutch Trading Company, trans. Baron Alphonse Nahuÿs (Edinburgh: Edmonson & Douglas, 1868).

31. George Harinck, "The Poetry of Theologian Geerhardus Vos," in *Dutch-American Arts and Letters in Historical Perspective*, ed. Robert P. Swierenga, Jacob E. Nyenhuis, and Nella Kennedy (Holland, MI: Van Raalte Press, 2008), 72.

32. "Kasboek, H. Bavinck," HBA, folder 16. "Uitgaven sedert 12 April 1875 . . . Multatuli (20 April), 1.50."

33. See, for example, Herman Bavinck, *Het Vierde eener Eeuw: Rede bij gelegenheid van het vijf en twintig-jarig bestaan van de "Standaard"* (Kampen: J. H. Bos, 1897), 33, 37; Bavinck, *De Welsprekendheid* (Kampen: Kok, 1901), 9, 15, 23, 30; Bavinck, "Voorrede," in *Het Gebed*, by Frans Kramer (Kampen: Kok, 1905), 1; Bavinck, *Bilderdijk als denker en dichter* (Kampen: Kok, 1906), 143; Bavinck, *Mental, Religious and Social Forces in the Netherlands* (The Hague: P. P. I. E., 1915), 45.

34. *Verslag der Handelingen van de Eerste Kamer*, March 12, 1913, 433. "Ik ben in mijn jeugd getuige geweest, dat het halve jonge Nederland geknield lag aan de voeten van Multatuli en met bewondering tot hem opzag. Ik heb die bewondering in die mate nooit gedeeld, maar één zaak is er geweest, die mij in Multatuli sterk heeft aangetrokken en dat is, dat zijn ziel van verontwaardiging gloeien kon en zulk een verontwaardiging hebben wij menigmaal noodig tegenover toestanden, die in zichzelf onwaardig en onwaarachtig zijn en welke men daarom niet consolideeren, maar zoo spoedig mogelijk in het reine moet brengen." Whether this perspective on Multatuli truly reflects the Leiden-era Bavinck's own thoughts or, rather, the then fifty-nine-year-old parliamentarian's mature perspective on how to handle the works of a noted misotheist in public discourse is impossible to ascertain.

35. James Bratt, *Abraham Kuyper: Modern Calvinist, Christian Democrat* (Grand Rapids: Eerdmans, 2013), 25; Jan de Bruijn, *Abraham Kuyper: A Pictorial Biography* (Grand Rapids: Eerdmans, 2008), 33.

36. De Bruijn, *Abraham Kuyper*, 33.

37. Abraham Kuyper, "The Blurring of the Boundaries," in *Abraham Kuyper: A Centennial Reader*, ed. James Bratt (Grand Rapids: Eerdmans, 1998; first published 1892 by J. A. Wormser [Amsterdam]), 365–66.

38. "Ex animo et corpore. H. Bavinck, Theol Stud." No date. "Kuyper's portret dien dag gekocht."

39. "Kasboek, H. Bavinck." "Uitgaven sedert 12 April 1875 . . . Portret van Kuyper, f. 1."

40. "Ex animo et corpore. H. Bavinck, Theol Stud." "8 Juni [1874] . . . 's avonds met ons vijfen (Wartena, Diena, Snouck, Cramer, en ik) . . . naar Alphen geweest."

41. *De Nederlander, Nieuwe Utrechtsche Courant*, July 7, 1849. "'t Provinciaal Kerkbestuur van Zeeland heeft onlangs, wegens trouwelooze dienstverlating met verzwarende omstandigheden, van zijne bediening als predikant in de Nederlandsche Herv. Kerk, ontzet *J. J. Snouck Hurgronje*, Theol. Doct. en vroeger Pred. te Tholen."

42. Jacob David Mees, *Dagboek: 1872–1874* (Hilversum: Verloren, 1997), 24. Jacob David Mees was a student in Leiden in the 1870s.

43. The dagboek entry on September 24, 1874, lists Baak as one of the students with whom Bavinck had begun to participate in freshers' week. "Ex animo et corpore. H. Bavinck, Theol Stud." "1874, 23 Sept." Baak was the secretary of the 1875 Masquerade Committee. See also "1875," *Het nieuws van den dag: Kleine courant*, May 12, 1874.

44. "Een studentenfeest," *Algemeen Handelsblad*, June 17, 1875.

45. "Ex animo et corpore. H. Bavinck, Theol Stud." "15 Juni [1874]. Maskerade der studenten . . . Mooi om te zien." See also 'Akademienieuws,' *Bataviaasch handelsblad*, April 4, 1874.

46. "Notes, H. Bavinck, 1874." "21 Juni 75 Wouterina gestorven."

47. "Wouterina Arnolda den Dekker 23-07-1851," in *Emmikhoven en Waardhuizen Bevolkingsregister, 1870–1879*, 14:103.

48. Bavinck to Snouck Hurgronje, Kampen, June 28, 1875, in *ELV*.

49. Discussion of their respective progress toward proficiency in Arabic would continue for the next three years, until they both passed exams in Semitic languages, prompting Bavinck to write, "Thankfully, we are [now] free of this burden." Bavinck to Snouck Hurgronje, Kampen, September 24, 1878, in *ELV*. "Gelukkig zijn we van deze zorg bevrijd." In a letter dated August 9, 1876, Bavinck describes Arabic as a subject that "excites [him] very little and that is frightfully dry."

50. "Ex animo et corpore. H. Bavinck, Theol Stud." "13 juli [1875]."

51. "Ex animo et corpore. H. Bavinck, Theol Stud." "27 Sept 1875 Weer naar Leiden na een genoeglijke vakantie. O God: bewaar me in Leiden!"

52. "Notes, H. Bavinck, 1875." "14 Aug Naar huis. Ik was bij W. gelogeerd. Melia niet gesproken."

53. "Ex animo et corpore. H. Bavinck, Theol Stud." "14 Aug [1876] Weer naar huis teruggekeerd. Behalve bij Ds. W. had ik niet veel genoegen op Nieuwendijk."

54. This practice had been common in Leiden from the sixteenth century onward. Pieter Antoon Marie Geurts, *Voorgeschiedenis van het statencollegte te Leiden: 1575–1593* (Leiden: Brill, 1984), 11–12.

55. Bavinck to Snouck Hurgronje, Kampen, September 16, 1875, in *ELV*. "Tegenwoordig drukt me een groote moeilijkheid. Mijne hospita gaat namelijk met november eerstkomende verhuizen. Daar ik van haar de kamer gehuurd hebben en bij haar in kost ben, moet ik ook verhuizen. Nu heeft ze een ander bovenhuis gehuurd in dezelfde straat aan gene zij der Bakkersteeg, met een (volgens getuigenis van ds. Donner, die ze voor mij gezien heeft) mooie voorkamer en slaapkamer daarnaast, en vroeg mij of ik met haar naar de nieuwe woning verhuisde. Hierop had ik niets tegen, dan alleen dat 't nog verder van de Academie en op een min aangenaam gedeelte der Haarlemmerstraat is. Daarom heb ik uitstel gevraagd met mijn besluit, totdat ik in Leiden kom."

56. "Ex animo et corpore. H. Bavinck, Theol Stud." "10 October [1874] Zondag. Ds. Donner sprak over Ps. 34:9. Het was Avondmaal. Voor 't eerst in mijn leven sprak ik aan de tafel des Heeren de openlijke belijdenis uit, dat ik dood ben in zonden en misdaden, maar mijne enige hoop de gerechtigheid van Christus is. O, moge ik mij niet een oordeel gegeten en gedronken hebben! Laat, o God, de wensch om u te dienen, bij mij een waarachtige geweest zijn en dus onberouwelijke."

57. "Ex animo et corpore. H. Bavinck, Theol Stud." "18 Oct. [1875] Verhuisd naar een nieuwe woning, Haarlemmerstraat No. 167A. Beter in vele opzichten."

58. "Ex animo et corpore. H. Bavinck, Theol Stud." "13 Dec. [1875] Was ik jarig en kreeg daarbij van Albert Gunnink een kist (250) sigaren." Bavinck's student receipts book shows that he regularly bought cigars.

59. "Ex animo et corpore. H. Bavinck, Theol Stud." "15 Dec. [1875] Schoolfeest in Kampen, dat met een schoone rede over Plato door Steketee geopend was."

60. "Ex animo et corpore. H. Bavinck, Theol Stud." "16 dec. 1875 A. Steketee, De studie van Plato, met het oog op de theologische vorming. Kampen 1875." This lecture was later published as *De studie van Plato, met het oog op de theologische forming: Rede, uitgesproken, bij het neerleggen van 't rectoraat, den 16en december 1875* (Kampen: G. Ph. Zalsman, 1875).

61. Douglas Hedley, "Theology and the Revolt against the Enlightenment," in *The Cambridge History of Christianity: World Christianities, c. 1815–c. 1914*, ed. Sheridan Gilley and Brian Stanley (Cambridge: Cambridge University Press, 2006), 8:41.

62. "Ex animo et corpore. H. Bavinck, Theol Stud." "1 Maart. [1876] Studenten Stadig en Wessels bij me geweest. Museum v. Oudheden." Cornelis Stadig (1853–1924) had been a student in Kampen since 1871. Cornelis Johannes Wessels (1852–1915) enrolled in Kampen in 1872. See van Gelderen and Rozemond, *Gegevens betreffende de Theologische Universiteit Kampen*, 106–7.

63. "Ex animo et corpore. H. Bavinck, Theol Stud." "<u>1 Mei</u> [1875] Naar Leiden terug. Voortzetting van studie onder aanvallen van twijfel maar ook met gevoel van de innige waarheid, door Christus geopenbaard."

64. Herman Bavinck, *Godsdienst en godgeleerdheid* (Wageningen: Vada, 1902), 13. "Deze ontwikkelingsgang der moderne wetenschap is de oorzaak van het pijnlijk conflict, dat thans allerwege tusschen Christendom en cultuur, tusschen godsdienst en godgeleerdheid, tusschen leven en kennis, tusschen zijn en bewustzijn, tusschen volk en geleerden, tusschen kerk en school wordt aanschouwd. Nergens wordt dit conflict met meer smart doorleefd dan in het hart van den student, die, tehuis in het Christelijk geloof opgevoed, straks op gymnasium en akademie met de moderne wetenschap in aanraking komt. Naarmate dat geloof dieper wortelen heeft geschoten in zijn ontvankelijk gemoed en er levensernst en ideale gezindheid heeft gekweekt, wordt de strijd heviger, waaraan hij straks in en buiten de gehoorzalen der universiteit blootgesteld wordt. Velen zijn in die gevaarlijke crisis bezweken. Zij werden een prooi van den twijfel niet slechts, maar gaven zich ook aan twijfelzucht en vertwijfeling over."

65. "Ex animo et corpore. H. Bavinck, Theol Stud." "<u>27 Mei</u>. [1875] Naar huis gegaan, waar ze zeer blij waren. Voornemen om in Kampen ook examen te doen."

66. Bavinck to Snouck Hurgronje, Kampen, June 6, 1876, in *ELV*. "Te meer nu repetite voor 't examen hier een groot deel van mijn tijd rooft. . . . Met verlangen zie 'k al uit naar 't einde der vacantie, omdat zoo'n geheel nieuw en onbekend terrein zich voor ons opent; zoo vervelend als de colleges op 't laatst me waren, zoo trekken ze me nu aan. Denkelijk zal ik weer wel in Leiden komen."

67. Bavinck to Snouck Hurgronje, Kampen, June 29, 1876, in *ELV*. "Als nieuws kan ik u meedeelen, dat ik me—waarover ge u wel verwonderen zult—in de vorige week heb laten photographeeren. Zoo gij 't goed vindt, zal ik u een volgend maal een portret oversturen, als ik ze dan namelijk heb. Van studie van Hebreeuwsch en Arabisch of theologie komt niet veel. 't Repeteeren van al die dorre vakken—geschiedenis, taalkunde etc—beneemt me haast alleen lust. Na 't examen, dat den elfden juli zal gehouden worden, denk ik een veertien dagen op reis te gaan, om dan de geleden schâ in te halen, en eenigszins me voor te bereiden voor de nieuwe studie, die ons wacht." The photograph in question was sent by Bavinck to Snouck Hurgronje with a letter dated August 9, 1876.

68. This attestation has been preseved in Archief van het College van Curatoren, Stadsarchief Kampen, folder no. 12824.

69. "Ex animo et corpore. H. Bavinck, Theol Stud." "<u>11 en 12 Juli</u>. [1875] Litterarisch Exam te Kampen gedaan: met loffelijk attest erdoor. Soli Deo Gloria—et gratia! Mijn opstel was over: <u>Oorsprong en Waarde der Mythologie</u>, dat me wel beviel en nog tot discussie aanleiding gaf." The original text, "Oorsprong en Waarde der Mythologie," has been preseved in the Archief van het College van Curatoren, Stadsarchief Kampen, folder no. 12824.

70. *Handelingen der drie-en-dertigste vergadering van de kuratoren der Theologische School der Christelijke Gereformeerde Kerk in Nederland* (Amsterdam: P. van der Sluys, 1876), 10. "Na voorafgaand gebed door den president, gaat men op de gewone manier over om over de bekwaamheid der geene, die hun examen hebben afgelegd te oordeelen, met dien uitslag dat, hoewel er een merkbaar verschil van bekwaamheid bij de geëxamineerden is waargenomen, hen allen tot hoogere studiën te bevorderen, met dit onderscheid dat de broeders H. BAVINCK en H. SIJPKENS een diploma zullen verkrijgen met loffelijke vermelding; het overige zevental slechts met gewoon attest."

71. *Handelingen der drie-en-dertigste vergadering*, 8. "H. BAVINCK, over de oorsprong en waarde der Mythologie, J. KOOI, de zes weken voor het examen, J. KOOI, een gesprek tusschen drie litt. studenten, na het hooren eener predikatie, C. STEKETEE, het Germanisme in de Nederlandsche taal, M. SIJPKENS, de Physionomie, H. VAN DER VEEN, niemand heeft mij aan mijn opstel geholpen." These exam scripts have been preserved in Archief van het College van Curatoren, Stadsarchief Kampen, folder no. 12824.

72. "Ex animo et corpore. H. Bavinck, Theol Stud." "<u>28 Juli</u> [1876] . . . met mijn nichtje Dientje naar Vriezenveen (Ds. Verhagen). . . . <u>7 Aug.</u> Met oom Ohman naar Bentheim, Ds. Sundag, de Must, Bad." Although it is possible that Bavinck visited Bentheim in his earlier years, this visit to Sundag is the first known written evidence of Herman Bavinck going there.

73. "Kasboek, H. Bavinck." "7 Aug. Oom Ohman en ik naar Bentheim. 25 Gld gekregen."

74. "Ex animo et corpore. H. Bavinck, Theol Stud." "<u>25 Sept</u> [1876]. Onder veel strijd van buiten weer naar Leiden terug."

75. "Ex animo et corpore. H. Bavinck, Theol Stud." "<u>29 Nov–1 Dec [1876]</u>. Vader hier geweest. 't Stond hem goed aan. Veel genoegen gehad. Hij vertelde mij dat. . . ." The remainder of this entry has been removed from the dagboek.

76. Melis te Velde, *Anthony Brummelkamp: 1811–1888* (Barneveld: Uitgeverij de Vuurbaak, 1988), 414.

77. G. M. den Hartogh, "Varia," in *Sola Gratia: Schets van de geschiedenis en de werkzaamheid van de Theologische Hogeschool der Gereformeerde Kerken in Nederland*, ed. J. D. Boerkoel, Th. Delleman, and G. M. den Hartogh (Kampen: Kok, 1954), 69. "In een volgende vergadering noemde Brummelkamp het 'gedrag' van Ds Bavinck met behelzing tot zijn zoon, lid der gemeente, student der Theol. School, aanstaand predikant, ongepast en onbetamelijk."

78. Den Hartogh, "Varia," 69–70.

79. Harinck, "'The Tares in the Wheat': Henry E. Dosker's Calvinist Historiography of Dutch Anabaptism," in *Religious Minorities and Cultural Diversity in the Dutch Republic*, ed. August den Hollander, Mirjam van Veen, Anna Voolstra, and Alex Noord (Leiden: Brill, 2014), 269.

80. Dosker to Bavinck, Grand Rapids, December 23, 1876, in *BHD*. "Ik dank God, dat ge tot nog toe staande gebleven zijt, te midden van al de aanvallen des ongeloofs rondom u. Wat beweegt toch Herman om *daar* theologie te gaan studeeren, was de vraag, die zich, nolens volens, aan mijn geest voordeed. Leiden, de focus van het modernisme. De namen van Kuenen, Scholten, etc. helaas maar al te zeer bekend. Want kunt ge daar zoeken. . . . Dit eene, mijns inziens, een volledige bekendheid met het plan van aanval, de wapenrusting en sterkte der vijanden. God helpe u, Herman, om standvastig bij uwe keuze te volharden en de heldere geloofswaarheid van ons historisch christendom te kiezen, boven al de flikkerende lichtstralen eener vijandige wetenschap. Toch ge *waagt veel*. Wij zijn beiden vatbaar voor de invloed van schijnbaar logische argumenten. We zijn groeiende, teere planten, die door de storm gebogen worden en gemakkelijk een scheeve richting behouden; gij zult u daar dunkt me te zien moeten terugtrekken binnen de enge muren van eigen opvatting; ge zult te veel verdedigenderwijze moeten te werk gaan, en daardoor wellicht een eenigszins gedrongen opvatting der waarheid *moeten* aannemen, terwijl ge groeien en ontwikkelen kunt, *alleen* door aan te vallen. Zie hier eenige puntjes, die ik gaarne zag opgehelderd in uw volgend schrijven. Wat beweegt u om te Leiden te studeeren? Wat verwacht ge ervan? Wat zegt de algemeene opinie dienaangaande?" Emphasis original.

81. Den Hartogh, "Varia," 70; te Velde, *Anthony Brummelkamp*, 414.

82. Herman Bavinck, "Theology and Religious Studies," in *Essays on Religion, Science, and Society*, ed. John Bolt, trans. Harry Boonstra and Gerrit Sheeres (Grand Rapids: Baker Academic, 2008), 53.

83. "Ex animo et corpore. H. Bavinck, Theol Stud." "<u>26 Sept</u> [1876] worden de theol. colleges geopend, die me bij voortgaande bijwoning in mijn geloof versterken. 'Oprichting van Theologico Sacrum' stellingen van Bruining over de Hervorming. Geopponeerd door Daubarton, mij, Wildeboer en de Hoogh. Voor mijzelven had ik niet veel voldoening wat misschien wel goed was. O God! laat me voor Uw eer strijden!" This note refers to J. Bruining (1853–1943), a fellow theological student at Leiden.

84. "Ex animo et corpore. H. Bavinck, Theol Stud." "<u>3 Maart</u> [1877] Gedineerd bij Prof. de Vries. Heel aardig. <u>18 Maart</u> Zondag—Gesoupeerd bij Prof. Prins. Tamelijk. <u>21 Maart</u> Gesoupeerd bij Prof. de Goeje."

85. "Ex animo et corpore. H. Bavinck, Theol Stud." "16 April [1877] Weer naar Leiden met Nieuwhuis die me meldt dat hij geengageerd is met Juffr. H. Ravenshorst."

86. "Ex animo et corpore. H. Bavinck, Theol Stud." "1 Sept [1877]. Ameliam rogavi."

87. "Ex animo et corpore. H. Bavinck, Theol Stud." "8 Sept [1877] Zaterdag. Met Juffr. Melia gesproken de amore meo es Ameliai et de ira Dionisii. 9 Sept En ecclesia cum Am. iri et mihi numeravit nonnullas difficultates. 10 Sept Feminam ministri v.d. esse debere Christianam mihi dixit. Magnam opem mihi dixit. Tibi Domine gratias ago et precor ut nobis faveas!"

88. "Ex animo et corpore. H. Bavinck, Theol Stud." "30 April [1878]. Een brief ontvangen van Mons. den Boer, die me zijn gesprek meedeelde met A., en hoop gaf dat A. de vraag van 1 Sept. 1877 met ja beantwoorden zal. O God, geef dat dat gebeurt en dat er ook van mijne zijde geen bezwaar kome."

89. "Ex animo et corpore. H. Bavinck, Theol Stud." "3 Mei [1877]. Thiele komt weer terug van Almkerk terug met Kok, die meegeweest was om Dientje de Jong te vragen, maar een weigerend antwoord ontving, (nadat ze eerst het jawoord gegeven had) toen haar moeder er sterk tegen was."

90. Johannes Henricus Scholten, *De leer der hervormde kerk in hare grondbeginselen*, 2 vols. (Leiden: Engels, 1850). For further discussion of Scholten's appropriation of the Reformed tradition, see James Eglinton, *Trinity and Organism: Towards a New Reading of Herman Bavinck's Organic Motif* (London: Bloomsbury T&T Clark, 2012), 13–19.

91. Peter Berend Dirksen and Aad W. van der Kooi, eds., *Abraham Kuenen (1828–1891): His Major Contributions to the Study of the Old Testament* (Leiden: Brill, 1993).

92. "Ex animo et corpore. H. Bavinck, Theol Stud." "6 Juni [1877]. Gedineerd bij Prof. Scholten, aan wiens rechterhand gezeten ik zeer veel genoegen had."

93. "Ex animo et corpore. H. Bavinck, Theol Stud." "21 Juli [1878]. Zondag. 's morgens mijn eerste preek gedaan in Enschede. 't Ging goed. Mijn tekst was 1 Joh 5:4b. Dank zij Uwen naam, o God."

94. Bavinck to Snouck Hurgronje, August 3, 1878, in *ELV*. "Zondag voor acht dagen heb ik te Enschede mijn eerste preek gedaan. Ik voor mij had het liever nog wat uitgesteld, maar mijn ouders hadden het gaarne en een oom en tante van me, die in Enschede wonen, waren er bijzonder op gesteld. Reeds langen tijd geleden had ik het hun beloofd, daar mijn eerste preek te houden en nu de gezondheidstoestand mijner tante wel van dien aard kon zijn dat ze niet lang meer leefde, was dit reden te meer om mijn belofte te volbrengen. Maar daar was natuurlijk veel bezwaar en met 't oog op ons examen groot tijdverlies aan verbonden. Een preek maken was voor mij geen kleinigheid. Toch lukte het eindelijk. Mijn tekst was 1 Johannes 5:4b, dit is de overwinning die de wereld overwint, namelijk ons geloof. En 't uitspreken viel me zeer mee. Ik was zeer kalm en bedaard. Zoodat ik blij ben dat ik het maar gedaan heb, en de grootste zwarigheid ook hierin weer overwonnen is. Toch was ik in zooverre onvoldaan, dat het mij minder inspireerde dan ik gedacht had. Ik sprak niet met dat gevoel voor mijzelf, als ik gehoopt had dat ik doen zou; terwijl de gedachte, altijd zoo ver beneden 't ideaal te blijven staan, me onophoudelijk bijbleef. Maar overigens ging het goed en heb ik tot dankerkentenis overvloedige stof."

95. "Ex animo et corpore. H. Bavinck, Theol Stud." "11 Aug [1878]: Zondag. 's avonds voor 't eerst te Kampen gepreekt . . . 't liep best af. Ook daarvoor U, o God, mijn innige dank."

96. Bavinck to Snouck Hurgronje, Kampen, September 24, 1878, in *ELV*. "Zaterdagavond ben ik in welstand hier aangekomen en zooals te denken was waren mijn ouders zeer verblijd, ook over uw exam, waarmee ze me verzocht hebben uit hun naam geluk te wenschen." The following letter, dated September 29, 1878, also shows that Snouck Hurgronje's parents had sent congratulations to Bavinck.

97. "Ex animo et corpore. H. Bavinck, Theol Stud." "13 Dec [1879] . . . Terwijl ik ook door [Acquoy] tot de beslissing gebracht werd, om een dissertatie te schrijven over de 'Afscheiding.'"

98. Bavinck to Snouck Hurgronje, Kampen, April 8, 1879, in *ELV*. "Scholten . . . vertelde me dat, nota bene, Proost er ook over dacht om een dissertatie te schrijven over de Afscheiding.

Scholten had hem echter gevraagd om dat aan mij over te laten en misschien zou hij dat ook wel doen."

99. Bavinck to Snouck Hurgronje, Kampen, January 6, 1879, in *ELV*. "Met mijn ouders heb ik over mijn reisplan naar een of andere Akademie in Duitschland gesproken. En gelukkig was van hun kant geen bezwaar . . . en zie ik je nog als litteris Semiticus doctor naar Straatsburg gaan." At that time, Strasbourg was a German city.

100. Snouck Hurgronje to Bavinck, Leiden, August 4, 1879, in *ELV*. "Denkt gij nog aan die universiteit een bezoek te gaan brengen? En hoe staat het met uwe Duitsche plannen?"

101. James Strahan, *Andrew Bruce Davidson* (London: Hodder & Stoughton, 1917), 48, 98.

102. Strahan, *Andrew Bruce Davidson*, 261. Strahan notes that Davidson read Dutch "quite well" but was reluctant to speak the language as he found the guttural sounds difficult to pronounce.

103. "Ex animo et corpore. H. Bavinck, Theol Stud." "28 Maart [1879] 1ᵉ deel doctoraal, 's middags 3 uur. 't Ging goed. Als onderwerp voor 2ᵉ deel kreeg ik van Prof Prins: Beknopte aanwijzing van den invloed van Schleiermacher op de uitlegging der H. Schrift. 4 April 2ᵉ deel doctoraat. Om kwart voor vier was alles al afgelopen. . . . Ik kreeg Cum Laude maar had het gevoel dat het minder verdiend was als bij mijn Candidaats. S.D.G." *Nota bene*: S.D.G. is an abbrevation of *Soli Deo gloria* ("to the glory of God alone").

104. I. A. Dorner, *Entwicklungsgeschichte der Lehre von der Person Christi* (Berlin: Schlawitz, 1853); ET: *History of the Development of the Doctrine of the Person of Christ*, trans. D. W. Simon (Edinburgh: T&T Clark, 1861).

105. "Ex animo et corpore. H. Bavinck, Theol Stud." "5 April [1879] . . . paaschmaandag preekte ik in Kampen over Gal. 2:20 waar de kerkeraad mij voor cadeau gaf: Dorner *Geschichte der lehre von der person Christi*, 13 Gld."

106. David Strauss, *Das Leben Jesu, kritisch bearbeitet* (Tübingen: Osiander, 1835).

107. "Ex animo et corpore. H. Bavinck, Theol Stud." "30 Mei [1879]. Vrijdag. 's middags 1 uur naar den Haag gegaan om met Dr. A. Kuyper kennis te maken. Hij was juist uitwandelen, zooals Fabius die bij Kuyper logeerde, ons (Lucasse en ik) vertelde. We besloten in den Haag te blijven, wandelen naar Scheveningen, aten daar en gingen andermaal naar Kuyper die nu thuis was. We bleven bij hem tot half negen spreken met hem over mijn dissertatie (hij ried me klein O. Test. onderwerp aan) over de Vrije Universiteit met haar belijdenis, over de Schriftinspiratie. 't Gaf me weinig licht. Overigens was de ontvangst hartelijk."

108. "Ex animo et corpore. H. Bavinck, Theol Stud." "15 Juni [1879] 's Zondags in Dordt voor de 9ᵈᵉ maal over 1 Joh. 5:4b en 's av. over Gal. 2:20 voor de 11ᵉ maal."

109. "Van 1879 tot 1886," HBA, folder 16.

110. Amelia Jozina den Dekker (1824–96), sister of Arie den Dekker and aunt of Amelia Josina den Dekker.

111. "Van 1879 tot 1886." "5 Oct Mij sterkte en inspireerde de tegenwoordigheid van A."

112. "Van 1879 tot 1886." "8 Oct 's morgens nam ik afscheid bij Juffr. Melia & Mijnh. d. Dekker. 's middags verneem ik dat Mijnh. d. Dekker alleen thuis is met Melia. Ik ga er heen. Juffr. Melia was er maar ging weldra met Melia uit de Kamer. Ik begon met Mijnh. d. Dekker te spreken, vertelde hem heel de geschiedenis, vroeg waarom hij er tegen was, enz. Zijn eenig antwoord was: ik kan geen toestemming geven."

113. Harinck and Berkelaar, *Domineesfabriek*, 87. "Voor dochters van bemiddelde boeren waren theologen, zonder grond of kapitaal, geen goede partij."

114. Smits, *De Afscheiding van 1834*, vol. 8, *Provincie Noord-Brabant* (Dordrecht: J. P. van den Tol, 1988), 141.

115. Smits, *De Afscheiding van 1834*, 8:154.

116. Smits, *De Afscheiding van 1834*, 8:158. The young den Dekker was a vocal and fierce critic of the king's religious beliefs and practices.

117. Bavinck to Snouck Hurgronje, Kampen, November 11, 1879, in *ELV*. "Overigens geen nieuws. Iedere dag is voor mij ongeveer gelijk aan den ander. Maar het huiselijk genot is vroeger

nooit door mij zoo gewaardeerd als thans. 't Zou me niet verwonderen als ik na dit jaar er nog een thuis doorbracht, althans nog niet in de gemeente ging."

118. Bavinck to Snouck Hurgronje, Kampen, November 11, 1879, in *ELV.* "En nu hoop ik dat ge na eenige dagen of weken van ontspanning (die zult ge wel noodig hebben) gelukkiger moogt zijn in het kiezen van een dissertatie-onderwerp dan ik. Lang heb ik er over nagedacht, lang gewikt en gewogen. En na veel weifelen ben ik eindelijk besloten om, zooals ge goed gehoord hebt, Zwingli's ethiek te behandelen. Ik heb dit gekozen, niet zoozeer wijl het me zoo bijzonder aantrok, als wel omdat het me nog het beste leek van alles waarover ik nagedacht had en ik toch ten slotte eens beslissen moest. Gelukkig valt het me onder de bewerking veel mee; het heeft bepaald zijn aantrekkelijke zijde, werpt veel meer vrucht af dan de 'Afscheiding,' en—wat voor mij thans veel zegt—heeft niet die bezwaren, die een ander onderwerp voor mij althans op dit openblik bijna onmogelijk maken. Ik zal dus dit onderwerp wel houden, en ben blij dat ik eindelijk zekerheid heb."

119. Bavinck to Snouck Hurgronje, Kampen, January 6, 1880, in *ELV.* "Had ik een anderen promotor, dan sprak ik zeker nu er al eens met hem over; maar ik denk, prof. Scholten zou me toch niet veel verder brengen. Toen ik eenigen tijd geleden hem schreef dat ik de ethiek van Zwingli behandelen zou indien hij het goedkeurde, antwoordde hij zeer karakterisiek: het is een mooi onderwerp, vooral om aan te wijzen het verband tusschen Zwingli's *verkiezings*leer en zijn moraal. Raadpleeg mijn *Leer der Hervormde Kerk* en nog een paar andere werken, die hij dan noemde. Dit bewijst genoeg dat zoo'n promotor niet veel geeft." Emphasis original.

120. Hepp, *Dr. Herman Bavinck*, 44–46.

121. Scholten to Bavinck, Leiden, November 30, 1879, HBA, folder 2. "Ik heb volmaakt geen bezwaar er tegen dat u de ethiek van Zwingli tot het onderwerp van uwe dissertatie maakt. . . . Zijn moraal staat uit het volstrekte determinisme."

122. Scholten, *De leer der hervormde kerk.*

123. Eduard Zeller, *Das theologische System Zwingli's* (Tübingen: L. Fr. Fues, 1853).

124. Jacob Tichler, *Huldrich Zwingli, de Kerkhervormer* (Utrecht: Kemink en zoon, 1858).

125. Bavinck to Snouck Hurgronje, Kampen, May 12, 1880, in *ELV.* "Voor eenige weken heb ik aan prof. Kuenen mijn manuscript gezonden om het eens in te zien; hij had me dit zelf aangeboden; en na eenige dagen, vier of vijf, kreeg ik het al terug. Met zoo'n spoed had hij dit vervelend werkje verricht. Gelukkig waren er niet heel veel aanmerkingen op, zoodat ik na eenige herziening hier en daar met het laten drukken een aanvang kon maken. Alleen de inleiding stond Kuenen niet erg aan, en mij ook niet; en zelfs na de overwerking is ze alles behalve voor mij zelven bevredigend. Maar zij is nu gedrukt, en gij zult er spoeding zelf over kunnen oordeelen. Aan prof. Scholten, stuur ik op aanraden van Kuenen die er met hem over gesproken heeft, telkens een vel als proef. Hij zendt ze heel gauw terug, zonder eenige andere aanmerking tot dusverre dan taal- en drukfouten, waar hij zorgvuldig op attent maakt."

126. Kuenen to Bavinck, Leiden, October 14, 1879, HBA, folder 2. "De met † geteekende boeken zijn in mijn bezit en tot uw dienst. . . . *T.T.* A. Kuenen." *Nota bene*: the closing "T. T." is an abbreviation for the Latin *totus tuus*, "wholly yours."

127. In that light, I side with Hepp's argument that the Scholten encountered by Kuyper during his studies at Leiden had become a largely spent force by the time Bavinck embarked upon his studies there. Scholten's determinist system still dominated the Leiden school but had lost its sense of novelty by the 1870s. Hepp, *Dr. Herman Bavinck*, 44.

128. For example, Abraham Kuenen, *Critices et hermeneutics librorum n. foederis lineamenta* (Leiden: P. Engels, 1858).

129. Bavinck to Snouck Hurgronje, Kampen, January 6, 1880, in *ELV.* "In vergelijking met voor vijfentwintig jaar is onze school zeer vooruit gegaan. Maar of ze ooit worden zal wat ik soms wensch betwijfel ik. Financieel en zedelijk gesteund door de gemeenten, is ze van haar in elk opzicht afhankelijk en kan ze dunkt mij niet veel meer dan een practische beteekenis krijgen en houden. Zuiver wetenschappelijk kan ze uiteraard nooit worden. Hoezeer me dit soms ook

spijt, ik troost me en kan me ook goed troosten met de gedachte dat ze toch een machtigen invloed kan oefenen op het leven. En dat geeft ten slotte den doorslag."

130. "Van 1879 tot 1886." "21 Mei . . . 's middags kwam er een telegram bij Prof. Scholten voor mij. Dat telegram bevatte dat er in Kampen een telegram van Dr. Kuyper aan mijn adres was gekomen inhoudende, om Zaterdag 22 Mei 's middags 1 uur eene dringende conferentie te komen houden ten huise van Dr. Rutgers." This refers to Frederik Lodewijk Rutgers (1836–1917), whose father, Antonie Rutgers, was one of Bavinck's professors at Leiden. F. L. Rutgers had been appointed professor of church history and ecclesiastical law at the Free University of Amsterdam in 1879.

131. "Van 1878 tot 1886." "21 Mei . . . Ik sprak hierover met Ds. Wielenga, die net in Leiden was, en mij afried een professoraat aan Kuyper's Vrije Universiteit te aanvaarden."

132. Kuyper had been engaged in a long-running public debate on Scripture with Johannes Hermanus Gunning (1829–1905), a leading figure among the nineteenth-century Ethical theologians. See, for example, J. H. Gunning Jr., *De heilige schrift, Gods woord: Antwoord aan Dr. A. Kuyper op zijn "Confidentie"* (Amsterdam: Höveker, 1872); Jasper Vree, "Gunning en Kuyper: Een bewogen vriendschap rond Schrift en kerk in de jaren 1860–1873," in *Noblesse oblige: Achtergrond en actualiteit van de theologie van J. H. Gunning jr.*, ed. Th. Hettema, and L. Mietus (Gorinchem: Ekklesia, 2005), 62–86.

133. "Van 1879 tot 1886." "25 Mei . . . 'Dan neem ik het aan,' zei ik."

134. "Van 1879 tot 1886." "25 Mei . . . Om 8 uur zou ik vertrekken. Maar ik had geen vrede bij 't besluit. Ik kwam er op terug."

135. "Van 1879 tot 1886." "25 Mei . . . Ik kon 't niet aannemen, voelde er hoegenaamd geen roeping toe, en zou, als ik 't aangenomen had, dit alles gedaan hebben om Kuyper's wil en gloriae studio."

136. "Van 1879 tot 1886." "27 Mei . . . 't Was koel afscheid. Ik was verlegen."

137. "Van 1879 tot 1886." "27 Mei . . . Heb ik goed gehandeld? Moest ik 't aangenomen hebben? Geef o God dat der roeping herhaald worde, als ik verkeerd deed, en laat me anders vrede en lust genieten bij 't genomen besluit! Mijn ouders vonden het maar ten deele goed."

138. Dosker to Bavinck, Ebenezer, March 27, 1880, in *BHD*. "Hoe gaat het met uwe Kampen plannen? Wat zijn uwe vooruitzichten daar? Wat zegt gij van voornemens op kerkelijk standpunt?"

139. George Harinck and Wouter Kroese, *"Men wil toch niet gaarne een masker dragen": Brieven van Henry Dosker aan Herman Bavinck, 1873–1921* (Amsterdam: Historisch Documentatiecentrum voor het Nederlands Protestantisme [1800–heden], 2018), 172n23.

140. R. H. Bremmer, *Herman Bavinck als dogmaticus* (Kampen: Kok, 1966), 373.

141. Herman Bavinck, *De ethiek van Ulrich Zwingli* (Kampen: G. Ph. Zalsman, 1880), 1–2.

142. Bavinck, *De ethiek van Ulrich Zwingli*, 107.

143. Bavinck, *De ethiek van Ulrich Zwingli*, 175.

144. Bavinck, *De ethiek van Ulrich Zwingli*, 177.

145. Bavinck, *De ethiek van Ulrich Zwingli*, 179. "Geen der Hervormers is onzen tijd zoo na verwant als Ulrich Zwingli. . . . De eerbiediging van anderer overtuiging."

146. "Van 1879 tot 1886." "10 Juni . . . Naar huis gereden: daar kwam alle theol. professoren bij me, ook Groszen, Acquoy, en Oort. Scholten en Kuen bleven tot over half zes. Lucasse, Snouck, Wildeboer, Cramer en ik dineerden samen in Place Royale. Voor dessert reden we Endegeest nog eens om. Om een uur scheidden wij."

147. *De Heraut*, July 4, 1880.

148. Snouck Hurgronje to Bavinck, Leiden, July 8, 1880, in *ELV*. "Wat heeft *De Heraut* uitvoerig den stand der zaken mêegedeeld wat de benoeming van een professor voor Hebreeuws betreft! Gij vondt zeker die uitvoerigheid minder aangenaam, vooral daar dat alles nu in alle dagbladen de ronde maakt."

149. "Van 1879 tot 1886." "12 Juni . . . En zo gaat alles voorbij en ligt heel de studententijd achter mij. En wat nu? Wat is er voor mij te doen?"

150. David J. Bos, *Servants of the Kingdom: Professionalization among Ministers of the Nineteenth-Century Netherlands Reformed Church* (Leiden: Brill, 2010), 366.

151. Kuyper to Bavinck, Amsterdam, June 18, 1880, HBA, folder 2. "Waarde Doctor, Uw boek ontving ik en het stemde mij tot lof en dank, dat door Gods goedheid zulk een kundig pleitbezorger van de ook mij heilige beginselen was opgestaan. Enger band met u had ik gewenscht, en blijf ik wenschen."

152. *De Bazuin*, June 25, 1880. "In de tweede plaats vermelden wij evenzeer met veel ingenomenheid: DE ETHIEK VAN ÜLRICH ZWINGLI, waarin onze jeugdige vriend Dr. H. Bavinck het bewijs geleverd heeft, dat hij mede zijn stem mag laten hooren onder de mannen der wetenschap. Op dat proefschrift toch verleende hem de Theol. Fakulteit te Leiden haar doctoraat. Dat hij dit doctoraat vroeg van eene inrichting die ja, nog wel met den alouden naam zich tooit van 'Theol. fakulteit,' maar die juist uit de wetenschappen, die zij onderwijst de eigenlijk gezegde theologie d. i. de dogmatiek en de ethiek heeft geschrapt,—wij kunnen niet nalaten te zeggen, dat ons dit ten zeerste smart. Door aan die fakulteit den graad te vragen, stempelen wij zooveel, in ons is de leugen, die daarin schuilt. Eene fakulteit die geene godgeleerdheid onderwijst, maar slechts wetenschappen, die daarmede in betrekking staan, kan naar de aloude beteekenis des woords dien naam niet dragen en dus ook dien graad niet verleenen.—Wij vernemen, dat dezen jeugdigen doctor een professoraat aan de Vrije Gereformeerde Universiteit is aangeboden, maar dat hij er voor heeft bedankt. Intusschen behoort hij mede tot het getal dergenen die zich voor het eindexamen aan de Theol. School te Kampen hebben aangegeven."

153. Jasper Vree, "Van separatie naar integratie: De afgescheidenen en hun kerk in de Nederlandse samenleving (1834–1892)," in *Religies en (on)gelijkheid in een plurale samenleving*, ed. R. Kranenborg and W. Stoker (Leuven: Garant, 1995), 176.

Chapter 6 Franeker: 1881–82

1. "Van 1879 tot 1886," HBA, folder 16. "29 Juli Thiele was sedert eenige dagen ongesteld. Ik bracht hem naar huis. Logeerde op school. Geen nieuws. Bezocht niemand v.d. familie d. D."

2. J. H. Landwehr, *In Memoriam: Prof. Dr. H. Bavinck* (Kampen: Kok, 1921), 20.

3. George Harinck and Wim Berkelaar, *Domineesfabriek: Geschiedenis van de Theologische Universiteit Kampen* (Amsterdam: Prometheus, 2018), 43.

4. Jurjen Nanninga Uiterdijk, *Kampen: Geschiedkundig overzicht en merkwaardigheden* (Kampen: Van Hulst: 1878), 143.

5. "Van 1879 tot 1886." "13 Juli Examen hier in Kampen begonnen. 't Was zeer min. Velen dropen. 16 Juli theol. examen A begon. Eraan deelnamen: ik, Unink, Munnik, Proosdy, v.d. Hoogt enz. 't Ging tamelijk goed. Enkele moeilijkheden over kritiek etc. kwamen er; anders niet. 18 Juli Zondag. Beuker sprak hier 's morgens, Wielenga 's avonds. 19 Juli Examen theol. B. Eerst gepreekt, ik over Mt 15:14ᵃ 't Examen ging goed. Dinsdag 20 Juli middag 5 uur. Balhuizen, Dee, Romein, Steketee gedropen. Ik, Foppens ten Hoor Sr en Jr, Kok, Nijenhuis, Elzenga er door."

6. Valentijn Hepp, *Dr. Herman Bavinck* (Amsterdam: Ten Have, 1921), 83; R. H. Bremmer, *Herman Bavinck en zijn tijdgenoten* (Kampen: Kok, 1966), 35.

7. Hepp, *Dr. Herman Bavinck*, 83. Hepp's citation of Bavinck's "approximate" words: "Waarom men dezen tekst juist *mij* heeft opgegeven, laat zich licht bevroeden. Met opzet heeft men de woorden 'de blinden' weggelaten. Het ontbreekt er nog maar aan, dat men er ook die aan toevoegde. Doch dat dorst men blijkbaar niet aan."

8. Landwehr, *In Memoriam*, 20. "Met de schooner dictie, hem eigen, leverd hij zijn preekvoorstel, dat de bewondering van allen opwekte, misschien ook wel van den ouden Bulens, al kreeg deze ook zijn zin niet."

9. "Nederlandsch Nieuws: bij het cand.-examen van Prof. Bavinck," *Onze Toekomst*, April 19, 1922; "Dr Bavinck kreeg bij examenpreek een bittere pil te slikken," *Friese Koerier*, November 19, 1955.

10. See, for example, "Kerknieuws," *Provinciale en Overijsselsche en Zwolsche courant*, July 22, 1880; "Schoolnieuws," *Het nieuws van de dag*, July 20, 1880.

11. "Kerk- en schoolnieuws," *Leeuwaarder Courant*, July 23, 1880. "De heer Bavinck stelt zich vooreerst niet beroepbaar."

12. "Van 1879 tot 1886." "14 Aug. Naar Zwolle, bij Unink gegeten. Samen 's avonds naar Zwartsluis."

13. "Van 1879 tot 1886." "16 Aug . . . Wij gingen saam naar Zwolle. Ik bleef dien dag bij Unink, ging 's av. naar Kampen."

14. "Van 1879 tot 1886." "18 Sept. 's Morgens naar Franeker, kwam daar aan te half drie, logeerde bij L. Hofstra Jr. Bezichtigde 's middags 't planetarium, stadhuis, portretten etc. 19 Sept. te Franeker gepreekt over Joh 17:19 & Rom 8:28. De kerkeraad sprak er van, om mij te beroepen."

15. On the history of Broek op Langedijk, see Janet Sjaarda Sheeres, *Son of Secession* (Grand Rapids: Eerdmans, 2006), 91–93.

16. For photographs of the city hall and planetarium in Franeker, see A. Loosjes, *Overijssel, Friesland, Groningen en Drente in Beeld* (Amsterdam: Scheltema & Holkema's Boekhandel en Uitgevers Maatschappij, 1927), 73, 114–15, 166.

17. W. B. S. Boeles, *Frieslands hoogeschool en het Rijks Athenaeum te Franeker* (Leeuwarden: H. Kuipers, 1878), 168.

18. The Franeker Athenaeum closed when the number of registered students declined to twenty-five. G. Wumkes, *Stads- en Dorpskroniek van Friesland* (Heerenveen: Nieuwsblad van Friesland, 1917), 9.

19. A. C. J. de Vrankrijker, *Vier eeuwen Nederlandsch studentenleven* (Voorburg: Boot, 1936), 32. "Er was geen academisch ziekenhuis, geen sterretoren, geen behoorlijke verzameling werktuigen voor het practicum natuurkunde (alleen in optische instrumenten was men goed voorzien), er was geen voldoende collectie botanische zeldzaamheden; het theatrum anatomicum op één der bovenlocalen bezat vrijwel niets."

20. "Van 1879 tot 1886." "5 Oct. half vier weer Leiden verlaten. half negen kwam ik in Kampen aan, waar ik vernam, dat er den vorigen dag een beroep voor mij gekomen was van de gemeente Franeker."

21. *De Bazuin*, October 8, 1880. "FRANEKER, den 3 October '80. Heden werd onder de leiding van Ds. K. Kuiper van Ferwerd, door een aan de gemeente Alfabetisch voorgesteld drietal Predikanten, bestaande uit Dr. H. Bavinck, candidaat aan de Theol. School te Kampen, L. van Dellen te Koudum en J. Wessels te Bedum, door de mansleden gekozen Dr. H. Bavinck. Neige de Heere het hart van dien broeder, om met volle vrijmoedigheid de roeping aan te nemen, is de wensch van Kerkeraard en gemeente. Namens den Kerkeraad, J.F. TUINSTRA."

22. "Van 1879 tot 1886." "1 Nov. 's morg. 9 uur naar Leiden, om met D. Donner te spreken over de uitgave der 'Synopsis.' Deze uitgave zal verschijnen onder mijn toezicht; honorarium 150 gld en 20% v. elk exemplaar van 300–500. 's middags weer naar Kampen. 2 Nov. Aangenomen het beroep naar Franeker & bedankt voor dat van Broek op Langendijk." *Nota bene*: although the village's name is now spelled Broek op Langedijk, Bavinck styles it as Broek op Langendijk.

23. Herman Bavinck, ed., *Synopsis purioris theologiae* (Leiden: D. Donner, 1881). This text is available in a bilingual Latin-English edition as *Synopsis purioris theologiae / Synopsis of a Purer Theology: Latin Text and English Translation*, vol. 1, *Disputations 1–23*, ed. and trans. Riemer A. Faber (Leiden: Brill, 2014).

24. Evidence of this effect would appear in print several years later on: see, for example, articles using the *Leiden Synopsis* to contrast Bavinck with Scholten in *De Heraut*, March 23, 1890, and September 28, 1890.

25. H. Beuker, "Bij den overgang 81 tot 82," *De Vrije Kerk* (1882), 3–4.

26. Dosker to Bavinck, Ebenezer [Holland, MI], February 12, 1881, in *BHD*. Emphasis original.

27. Dosker to Bavinck, Ebenezer [Holland, MI], February 12, 1881, in *BHD*.

28. George Harinck, "Inleiding," in *"Men wil toch niet gaarne een masker dragen": Brieven van Henry Dosker aan Herman Bavinck, 1873–1921*, ed. George Harinck and Wouter Kroese (Amsterdam: Historisch Documentatiecentrum voor het Nederlands Protestantisme [1800–heden], 2018), 14.

29. Dosker to Bavinck, Holland, March 23, 1889, in *BHD*. "Ben ik mis, als ik tusschen de regels las, en met u gevoelde en meêdacht."

30. Snouck Hurgronje to Bavinck, Leiden, July 8, 1880, in *ELV*.

31. Snouck Hurgronje to Bavinck, Leiden, September 6, 1880, in *ELV*.

32. Bavinck to Snouck Hurgronje, Kampen, November 13, 1880, in *ELV*. "Zooals ge gelezen hebt heb ik het beroep naar Franeker aangenomen. Het is daar eene tamelijk groote en voor een onervaren kandidaat vrij lastige gemeente. Huiverend, om de practijk in te gaan, had ik gaarne bedankt, maar ik meende me niet langer te mogen terugtrekken en plicht op te offeren aan lust. De intrede is voorloopig bepaald op zondag 6 maart 1881. Ik heb dus nog een poosje tijd, om me op een en ander voor te bereiden. 't Spijt me wel, dat Franeker zoo ver uit de buurt is maar ik hoop toch, als ge van uw buitenlandsch verblijf teruggekeerd zijt, je eens spoedig bij me in de pastorie te zien. Ik reken daar zeer vast op. Zoo heel dikwijls zal 't misschien niet meer gebeuren, dat we elkander ontmoeten; en toch hoop en wensch ik, dat de gelegenheid ervoor zich dikwijls voordoet. Erg blij ben ik, dat ge met uw dissertatie zoover gevorderd zijt. Ik verwacht er spoedig een en ben benieuwd naar den inhoud. Uwe uitnoodiging om de promotie bij te wonen, denk ik niet aan te nemen. Ik heb het, met 't oog op het aanstaand vertrek naar Franeker, erg druk en word zoo langzamerhand in allerlei kerkelijke aangelegenheden betrokken, die in het eerst nogal lastig zijn."

33. Philip Dröge, *Pelgrim: Leven en reizen van Christiaan Snouck Hurgronje* (Utrecht: Spectrum, 2017).

34. See, for example, K. J. Pieters, D. J. van der Werp, and J. R. Kreulen, *Is de Afscheiding in Nederland van het Hervormd Kerkgenootschap, zooals het thans en sedert 1816 bestaat, uit God of uit menschen?* (Franeker: T. Telenga, 1856).

35. Hepp, *Dr. Herman Bavinck*, 91.

36. M. Mooij, *Bond van Vrije Evangelische Gemeenten* (Baarn: Hollandia Drukkerij, 1907), 19.

37. Hepp, *Dr. Herman Bavinck*, 92.

38. Bavinck to Snouck Hurgronje, Kampen, November 24, 1880, in *ELV*. "En zoo hebben wij beiden dan het einde van de academische loopbaan bereikt. 't Kan me alleen maar spijten, dat we zoo ver, zoo ontzachlijk ver in beginsel en in levensbeschouwing uiteengaan. Toch blijft mijne hartelijke vriendschap en warme belangstelling u vergezellen ondanks nog zoo groot verschil van inzicht en overtuiging. Dat dat verschil kleiner zal worden hoop ik, maar zie ik nog niet. Nu ik uit Leiden weg ben, en de moderne theologie en de moderne wereldbeschouwing wat anders in de oogen zie, dan toen ik zoo sterk onder den invloed van Scholten en Kuenen stond, nu lijkt mij veel weer heel anders toe dan waarin het mij toen voorkwam. Ik heb in Leiden veel geleerd, maar ook veel verleerd. Dit laatste kan ten deele schadelijk voor mij gewerkt hebben, maar meer en meer begin ik dat schaedelijke ervan in te zien. Het tijdperk, waarin onze van vroeger meegebrachte overtuigingen in den smeltkroes der kritiek geworpen zijn, is voorbij. 't Komt er nu op aan, de overtuigingen, die wij thans hebben, trouw te zijn en ze te verdedigen met de wapenen die ons ten dienste staan. Maar zoeken wij beiden altijd ernstig en oprecht naar waarheid, dan zullen wij ze vinden ook. Want dit acht ik ontwijfelbaar zeker, zij is er, zij moet er wezen en ontdekt zich aan het oog van wie haar waarlijk zoekt. Vergeef me deze uitweiding. Ze ontvlood me onwillekeurig aan de pen. Het is ook zoo iets ontzachlijk belangrijks, de academische loopbaan achter zich afgesloten te zien. Maar nogmaals, ook namens mijn

vader, met den doctoralen graad geluk gewenscht. Draag hem lang en met altijd toenemende verdienst. t.t. H. Bavinck."

39. Snouck Hurgronje to Bavinck, Strasbourg, December 22, 1880, in *ELV*. "In den tijd van onzen dagelijkschen omgang heb ik nooit den zoo bijzonder sterken invloed van Kuenen en Scholten op u ontdekt, dan in de formeele vragen, d.w.z. ik meende dat uw verblijf in Leiden u steeds ongeschokt gelaten had op dogmatisch gebied, maar u een helderder inzicht dan vroeger had gegeven in de kritische bezwaren tegen de oude Schriftbeschouwing."

40. Bavinck, "Inleidend woord van Prof. Dr. H. Bavinck," in *Adriaan Steketee (1846–1913): Beschouwingen van een Christen-denker*, by A. Goslinga (Kampen: Kok, 1914), v.

41. Bavinck to Snouck Hurgronje, Kampen, January 13, 1881, in *ELV*.

De tijd van het aanvaarden mijner betrekking breekt spoedig aan. Mijne bevestiging en intrede is bepaald op den tweeden zondag in maart. Naarmate het oogenblik nadert, zie ik er te meer tegen op. Er is zoo ontzachlijk veel, dat ik nog wilde onderzoeken en daardoor tot mijn eigendom maken, om er met vertrouwen, met bezieling, met geloof over te kunnen spreken. Maar het is wel waarschijnlijk, dat ik er toch nooit mee zou klaar komen. Misschien geeft mij de omgang met de gemeente, met eenvoudige, vrome menschen, wat de studeerkamer toch niet schenken kan. Neen, het is waar, Kuenen en Scholten hebben op mij (behalve in de Schriftbeschouwing) niet veel invloed gehad, als ge daaronder verstaat het verliezen van geloofswaarheden en het aannemen van andere, van de hunne. Maar zij hebben wel (hoe kon het anders) invloed gehad op de kracht en de wijze, waarmee ik die waarheden omhels. Het naïve van het kinderlijk geloof, van het onbegrensd vertrouwen op de mij ingeprente waarheid, zie, dat ben ik kwijt en dat is veel, heel veel; zoo is die invloed groot en sterk geweest.

En nu weet ik het wel, dat ik dat nooit terugkrijg. Zelfs vind ik het goed en ben ik er waarlijk en oprecht dankbaar voor, dat ik het verloren heb. Er was ook in dat naïve veel, wat onwaar was en gereinigd moest worden. Maar toch, er is in dat naïve (ik weet geen beter woord) iets, dat goed is, dat wel doet; iets dat blijven moet, zal de waarheid ons ooit zoet en dierbaar wezen. En als ik dan soms—heel enkel, want och, waar is het rotsensterke geloof van vroeger tijd nog in onze eeuw?—in de gemeente nog enkele menschen ontmoet, die dat hebben en er zoo wel bij zijn en zoo gelukkig, nu, ik kan het niet helpen, maar dan wenschte ik weer te gelooven als zij, zoo blij en zoo vrolijk; en dan voel ik, als ik dat had, en ik kon dan zoo preeken, bezield, warm, altijd ten volle overtuigd van wat ik zei, ja er één mee, o me dunkt, dan was ik sterk, machtig, dan kon ik nuttig zijn; zelf levend, zou ik leven voor anderen.

On this letter, see George Harinck, "'Something That Must Remain, If the Truth Is to Be Sweet and Precious to Us': The Reformed Spirituality of Herman Bavinck," *Calvin Theological Journal* 38, no. 2 (2003): 248–62.

42. "Van 1879 tot 1886." "18 Dec. Weer naar Kampen terug. Den vorigen dag (Vrijdag) begon de kerstvakantie. Donderdag 16 Dec. hield A Steketee een rede over de bet. der Kunst. 26 Dec. In Kampen 's morg. 2^d kerstdag gepreekt over 1 Tim 1:15 (57). 3 Febr. Donderdag 's av. half acht – tien uur eene lezing gehouden voor de studenten over: het Rijk Gods, het hoogste goed. 6 Maart 's morg. (Zondag) in Kampen gepreekt over Jes. 53:4-6 voor 't laatst voor mijn vertrek naar Franeker (58)."

43. Adriaan Steketee, *De beteekenis der Kunst voor den toekomstigen Evangeliedienaar: Rede, uitgesproken bij het overgeven van het rectoraat den 16en Dec. 1880* (Kampen: Zalsman, 1881). Bavinck's 1881 summary and review of this lecture in *De Vrije Kerk* is important in offering clues as to Steketee's impending (and unexplained) dismissal from the Theological School. In this review, Bavinck noted that some had criticized Steketee for speaking on an "inappropriate" topic (the relationship of the gospel and art) at a public lecture on behalf of the school. Furthermore, he rehearsed Steketee's argument in order to counter the criticism that Steketee had blurred the boundaries of "art" and "gospel" to the point that a minister's ability to carry

out his task would be hindered by ignorance of art. In reply, Bavinck defended Steketee by offering a corrective to his lecture, presenting art as a benefit to ministers, although their work does not depend on it. Bavinck's review closed by inviting Steketee to develop his ideas further in the magazine. Herman Bavinck, "Eene Rectorale Oratie," *De Vrije Kerk* 7 (1881): 120–30.

44. Maarten Noordtzij, *Egyptologie en Assyriologie in betrekking tot de geloofwaardigheid des Ouden Testaments: Rede bij het overdragen van het rectoraat aan de Theologische School te Kampen, den 19den December 1881* (Utrecht: C. van Bentum, 1882). For biographical information on Maarten Noordtzij, see C. Houtman, "Noordtzij, Maarten," in *Biografisch Lexicon voor de Geschiedenis van het Nederlandse Protestantisme* (Kampen: Kok, 1988), 3:284–86; and on his son, see C. Houtman, "Noordtzij, Arie," in *Biografisch Lexicon voor de Geschiedenis*, 3:282–84.

45. "Het rijk Gods, het hoogste goed," *De Vrije Kerk* 7 (April–August 1881): 4:185–92; 5:224–34; 6:271–77; 7:305–14; 8:353–60. For its English translation, see Herman Bavinck, "The Kingdom of God, the Highest Good," trans. Nelson Kloosterman, *Bavinck Review* 2 (2011): 133–70.

46. The lecture itself was only published in singular form posthumously, having been reassembled by his younger brother Coenraad Bernardus (Bernard) in the edited volume *Kennis en leven* (Kampen: Kok, 1922), 28–52.

47. Bavinck, "Kingdom of God, the Highest Good," 134; cf. Steketee, *De studie van Plato, met het oog op de theologische forming: Rede, uitgesproken, bij het neerleggen van 't rectoraat, den 16en december 1875* (Kampen: G. Ph. Zalsman, 1875), 21. Gleason's biography argues that Bavinck only referred to Schleiermacher "because, in a certain sense, speaking in an academic vein is indicative of a young theological student, and Bavinck was no exception," and that Bavinck's thought is otherwise anti-Schleiermacherian (Ron Gleason, *Herman Bavinck: Pastor, Churchman, Statesman, and Theologian* [Phillipsburg, NJ: P&R, 2010], 71). A more nuanced account of Bavinck's theological relationship to Schleiermacher—including critique and appreciation—has been offered in Cory Brock, *Orthodox yet Modern: Herman Bavinck's Use of Friedrich Schleiermacher* (Bellingham, WA: Lexham, 2020).

48. Bavinck, "Kingdom of God, the Highest Good," 153–54.

49. For example, Bavinck, "Kingdom of God, the Highest Good," 159, where the explicit reference to "sphere sovereignty" locates Bavinck in the tradition of Groen van Prinsterer and Abraham Kuyper.

50. *De Bazuin*, February 11, 1881. "Stelle de Heer dezen doctor theologiae verder tot een rijken zegen, zoowel in de beoefening der wetenschap als in de bediening des Woord!"

51. "Van 1879 tot 1886." "11 Maart. Nadat al mijn boeken etc. Dinsdag per spoor naar Franeker waren verzonden, ging ik zelf Vrijdag 's middags; Ik kwam 's avonds half zes in Franeker aan, werd met liefde ontvangen en logeerde bij L. Hofstra Jr. 12 Maart. 's Middags half zes kwamen mijn ouders. Ik was droevig gestemd."

52. "Van 1879 tot 1886." "13 Maart Zondag. 's Morgens werd ik door Vader, naar aanleiding van Jes. 52:7, bevestigd. Roerend plechtig. 's Avonds half zes deed ik intree met 1 Thess. 2:4. Veel, veel volk. (59)."

53. "Van 1879 tot 1886." "Dinsdag 15 Maart . . .'s avonds van dien dag . . . vertrokken mijn ouders weer, die goeden indruk van Franeker meenamen."

54. "Van 1879 tot 1886." "20 Maart. In Franeker gepreekt over Jesaia 53:4–6 en Catech. Vraag 1. (voor 't eerst geheel geimproviseerd, ging goed.) (60 en 61)."

55. The note added by Bavinck to the text of his only published sermon, which indicates that its text was an effort to recall everything he had said in the moment, also signals in this direction. See Herman Bavinck, "The World-Conquering Power of Faith," in *Herman Bavinck on Preaching and Preachers*, ed. and trans. James Eglinton (Peabody, MA: Hendricksen, 2017), 67.

56. "Van 1879 tot 1886." "24 April. 's morgens preekte Unink voor mij over 2 Cor 5:17^a. 't Ging goed. 's middags preekte ik weer over Catech. Vr. 7 en 8. (72 maal). 26 April. Dinsdag. Unink ging 's morgens half negen weer op reis naar Zwolle. Ik ben weer alleen."

57. Henk Nijkeuter, *Geschiedenis van de Drentse literatuur, 1816–1956* (Assen: Van Gorcum, 2003), 42.

58. Bavinck to Snouck Hurgronje, Franeker, June 16, 1881, in *ELV*. "En dat is, dat men altijd 'dominé' is en nooit eens recht vertrouwelijk meer spreken kan."

59. "Van 1879 tot 1886." "26 Mei . . . 300 gld meer als de vorige maal."

60. David Bos, *Servants of the Kingdom: Professionalization among Ministers of the Nineteenth-Century Netherlands Reformed Church* (Leiden: Brill, 2010), 366.

61. "Van 1879 tot 1886." "6 Juni Pinksterenmaandag. 'S morg gepreekt over Efeze 2:19–22. (86) 'S nam. Nanta, vader van vrouw Stekelenburg begraven. 's morg. 10 uur kwam Albert Gunnink bij me, in de kerk, en bleef bij me tot 's avonds 7 uur. 't was erg regenachtig."

62. Bavinck to Snouck Hurgronje, Franeker, June 16, 1881, in *ELV*. "Als ge eens bedenkt, dat ik elken zondag twee keer preeken moet, vier catechisantiën 's weeks heb te houden, verden aan huis- en ziekenbezoek veel tijd moet wijden en dan soms nog een Friesche begrafenis heb te leiden, dan behoeft ge niet meer te vragen, of er voor eigen studie veel tijd en gelegenheid overblijft."

63. Bavinck to Snouck Hurgronje, Franeker, June 16, 1881, in *ELV*. "Wat mij 't moeilijkst in mijn werk valt, is om mij altijd op te heffen tot en te blijven op de ideale hoogte van mijn geloof en belijdenis. O, altijd met het heilige te moeten omgaan, steeds tot gebed of tot dankzegging, tot vermaning of vertroosting geroepen te worden, en dan dikwerf zoo weinig zelf in die telkens wisselende toestanden te kunnen inleven, dat valt hard, kweekt een gevoel van onvoldaanheid en dikwerf van onverschilligheid. Ik begrijp het thans nog beter als vroeger, hoe onder het gewaad van den geestelijke een diep-onheilig, gevoelloos en huichelachtig hart wonen kan. Behalve dit ernstige en drukkende bezwaar van het predikantambt, is er nog een schaduwzijde aan verbonden, die ik ook diep gevoel, en dat is, dat men altijd 'dominé' is en nooit eens recht vertrouwelijk meer spreken kan. Althans zoo gaat het mij. Tot dusver heb ik hier nog niemand gevonden, wien ik dat vertrouwen mag en durf schenken. En dat valt me hard. Thuis ben ik alleen, op mijn kamer, en buiten ben ik altijd de 'dominé.' Zoo ooit, dan heb ik in den laatsten tijd verlangd naar eene vrouw, die mij begrijpen en aan wie ik mij gansch en al toevertrouwen kan."

64. Hepp, *Dr. Herman Bavinck*, 97.

65. Bavinck to Snouck Hurgronje, Franeker, June 16, 1881, in *ELV*. "De gemeente is over het algemeen echter wel goed. Alleen zijn er nog enkele minder aangename nawerkselen van vroeger tijden. Voor eenige jaren stond hier een predikant, die bepaald eene uitzondering maakte in heel onze kerk. Bijzonder scherp van verstand, kon hij 't met onze belijdenis niet vinden, stoorde zich daar ook niet aan en preekte gelijk hij goed vond. Bovendien maakte hij zich schuldig aan zeer groot misbruik van sterken drank—alles te zamen maakte, dat hij eindelijk werd afgezet. Mijn voorganger, Eskes, had met die vrienden van den afgezetten predikant erg te strijden. En nog zijn er, die wel de zonde van dien vroegeren predikant Pieters veroordeelen, maar toch zijne leer nog handhaven. Vandaar is er hier—wat in onze kerk anders nooit voorkomt—nogal verwarring en verschil van meeningen. Vooral de trouwe aanhangers van Pieters zijn wat voornaam, beelden zich heel wat in en meenen knap te wezen. Tot dusverre kunnen ze zich echter in mijne prediking nogal vinden. Vooral zoek ik door gesprekken hen hier en daar, waar ik hun gevoelens afkeur, terecht te brengen. Met geduld en liefde kan er veel gedaan worden."

66. "Van 1879 tot 1886." "17 Juni. 's morg. heb ik in Kampen, waar Curatoren, proff. & studenten allen waren, gepreekt over Joh. 5:17 (97)."

67. "Van 1879 tot 1886." "19 Juli. 's avonds. Preekvoorstellen in de kerk gehouden. Unink deed geen examen, moet nog een jaar wachten."

68. "Van 1879 tot 1886." "8 Aug. 's morg. 10 uur kwam Ds. Wielenga bij mij om . . . met mij te spreken, hoe het met de 'Vrije Kerk' gaan moest. Besloten . . . om van drukker te veranderen, en ander format te nemen. Eindredactie voortaan door mij."

69. "Van 1879 tot 1886." "8 Sept . . . Mooi weer. Veel plezier."

70. "Van 1879 tot 1886." "16 Oct. Munnik bevestigd 's morg. met 1 Cor 3:9 . . . Aangename dag. (124)."

71. Van Proosdy was responsible for the Dutch translation of Ursinus's Latin work on the Heidelberg Catechism. See Zacharias Ursinus, *Verklaring op den Heidelbergschen Catechismus*, trans. C. van Proosdy (Kampen: Zalsman, 1882).

72. "Van 1879 tot 1886." "21 nov. Naar Franeker terug. 's morg. 10 uur kwam onverwacht Proosdij bij mij. Genoeglijke dag."

73. "Van 1879 tot 1886." "13 Dec. Jaardag. Van de gemeente ontving ik vele bewijzen van achting. Van Kamstra, Pars, J. Tamminga, Jule Draaisma, elk 1 kistje sigaren. Van de vrouwen vereenig. een sigarenstel, van eenige jongedochters (Anne Brouwer c.s.) een zijden boeklegger. Van den kerkeraad een stoel. Van de jongedochters (catechisatie woensd. av. 8 uur) een zilveren lepel, vork & servetband. 's avonds kwam de kerkeraad met hun vrouwen bij mij. Aangename dag, stof tot dank aan God bieden te over."

74. Bavinck reviewed the published version of this lecture. See review of *Egyptologie en assyriologie in betrekking tot de geloofwaardigheid des Ouden Testaments: Rede bij het overdragen van het rectoraat*, by Maarten Noordtzij, *De Vrije Kerk* 8, no. 3 (March 1882): 434.

75. "Van 1879 tot 1886." "19 Dec. 's morg. half zeven op spoor naar Zwolle met Unink naar Kampen. Schoolfeest. Degelijke rede van Ds. Noordtzij over de Assyriologie & Egyptologie voor 't O.T. 's avonds gezellige bijeenkomst. Unink ging den volg. dag terug naar Zwolle."

76. "Van 1879 tot 1886." "14 Febr. Kreeg ik brief van Ds. J. W. Felix president Cur. der Vrije Universiteit of ik principieele bezwaar had tegen de aanneming eener eventueele benoeming als Prof. in Hermeneutiek en Exegese van 't N.T. en of ik zoo'n benoeming ernstig zou willen overgeven." Concerning the phrase that I have rendered "*whether I would earnestly consider*," note that in the dagboek entry, Bavinck writes "*ernstig . . . overgeven*" (to surrender . . . earnestly). However, the context, and particularly the answer recorded in the following day's entry (Feb. 16), strongly suggest that he intended to write "*ernstig . . . overwegen*" (to consider . . . earnestly). This hypothesis is all but proved by his use of "ernstige en biddende overweging" (earnest and prayerful consideration) in his letter of reply (preserved in Bremmer, *Herman Bavinck en zijn tijdgenoten*, 39).

77. "Van 1879 tot 1886." "16 febr. Antwoordde ik op de eerste vraag: neen, op de tweede ja; maar dat ik toch zeer waarschl. bedanken zou, om 't belang onzer School, aan wie ik op de a.s. Synode in Aug. gaarne benoemd zou willen worden."

78. Bremmer, *Herman Bavinck en zijn tijdgenoten*, 39–40. "Uwe geërde letteren van den 13den dezer hebben mij niet weinig verrast. Dankbaar ben ik voor de goede gedachten, die U wel omtrent mij koesteren wilt. Op de gestelde vragen geef ik U na ernstig beraad het volgende openhartige antwoord. Principieele bezwaren, die reeds *a priori* het aannemen eener eventueele benoeming mij zouden onmogelijk maken, heb ik niet. De Vrije Universiteit is veeleer door mij in veel opzichten met blijdschap begroet. In haar oprichting eer ik eene daad des geloofs. Eene eventueele benoeming zou dus ook door mij in ernstige en biddende overweging worden genomen. In zekeren zin kon ik hiermee volstaan. Toch zou mijn geweten zich niet gansch vrij gevoelen, indien ik U niet in bijzonder vertrouwen meedeelde, waarom zulk eene benoeming toch vooralsnog hoogst waarschijnlijk door mij zou worden afgewezen. Ik heb mijne Kerk lief. Liefst arbeid ik aan haar opbouw. De bloei harer Theol. School gaat mij na ter harte. Daar is aan die inrichting echter veel, dat dringend verbetering behoeft. De Christ. Gerf. Kerk is daarvan grootendeels overtuigd en zal op de a.s. Synode in Augustus op verbetering bedacht wezen. Eerlijk gesproken, heb ik nu een stil verlangen en hope (het recht tot beide is toch niet enkel aan mijn eerzucht ontleend?) dat die Synode mij eene plaats aanbiede aan hare School. Veel bekorends heeft die plaats zeker niet, maar mij trekt ze aan in het belang der kerk, dien ik dien. Ik weet ook zeer goed, dat die hope, die ik koester, best beschaamd kan en naar sommige gegevens te oordeelen ook beschaamd zal worden. Maar zoolang onze kerk nog niet, door mij op de a.s. Synode niet te benoemen, openlijk verklaard heeft, dat zij van mij aan haar School niet gediend

wil wezen, *zoolang* gevoel ik voor mijzelf geene vrijheid, de krachten die ik hebben mocht, aan haar te onttrekken en aan eene andere inrichting voor Hooger Onderwijs mij te verbinden. Aan haar dus de eerste keuze; daarna ben ik vrij. Hiermede heb ik, naar Uw wensch en den drang van mijn hart, vertrouwelijk en broederlijk mijn antwoord U medegedeeld. Het laatste had ik uit den aard der zaak liefst voor mij zelven gehouden; maar dat kon ik niet, zonder den schijn van oneerlijkheid op mij te laden. Ontvang nogmaals mijn hartelijken dank voor Uwe gunstige gevoelens te mijwaart."

79. "Van 1879 tot 1886." "21 Maart. 's avonds gesproken in de Theol. zaal . . . over karakter, grond, inhoud v. ongeloof."

80. Abraham Kuyper, *Welke zijn de vooruitzichten voor de studenten der Vrije Universiteit?* (Amsterdam: Kruyt, 1882).

81. "Van 1879 tot 1886." "5 Juli . . . Dr. Kuyper te hooren over de vraag: welke zijn de vooruitzichten voor de studenten der Vrije Univ. Schema: Twee opmerkingen vooraf: a) hij sprak geheel voor zichzelf, niet na eenige opdracht v. wie ook. b) de Universiteit is residentie der wetenschap—zorgt niet voor baantjes en postjes der studenten. Drie deelen: 1 Vooruitzichten binnen het kader v. thans: voor artsen, goed; voor philos. litterar. rechtsgel. bijna, tamelijk. voor theologen slecht, van wege de kerk. 2 aan den horizon der verwachtingen—in den staat komt er meer vrijheid; in de kerk echter niet: de Synode moet de vrijheid onderdrukken om te blijven bestaan. 3 naar de profetie des geloofs—kruisdragen, lijden enz. is wat ons, gelovigen, wat den leerar wacht, maar 't loon in de hemelen. Slot was: er waren geen vooruitzichten. Er kwam geen debat van eenige betekenis."

82. Harinck and Berkelaar, *Domineesfabriek*, 89.

83. "Van 1879 tot 1886." "16 Juli . . . Unink Dinsdag, om examen te doen. Hij slaagde."

84. *Verslag van het verhandelde in de Comité-Vergadering der Synode van Zwolle 1882, op Woensdag 23 Aug. in de Voormiddagzitting*, A. Steketee Archive, Historisch Documentatiecentrum voor het Nederlands Protestantisme (1800–heden), folder 17. "In het algemeen ontvingen de Curatoren geen gunstigen indruk."

85. *Verslag van het verhandelde.* "Steketee is niet de man op zijne plaats. Wij zijn met hem teleurgesteld."

86. Harinck and Berkelaar, *Domineesfabriek*, 80–81.

87. Bremmer, *Herman Bavinck en zijn tijdgenoten*, 39–40. "Daar is aan die inrichting echter veel, dat dringend verbetering behoeft. De Christ. Gerf. Kerk is daarvan grootendeels overtuigd en zal op de a.s. Synode in Augustus op verbetering bedacht wezen."

88. "Van 1879 tot 1886." "24 aug. Deze zes moesten zich verwijderen. Bij de stemming hadden <u>Wielinga</u> 39. Beuker 4 <u>Bavinck</u> 39 Hessels 2. <u>Lindeboom</u> 32. Brummelk. 4. Treffend oogenblij voor mij en mijn vader." *Nota bene*: Bavinck misspells D. K. Wielenga's surname at several points in this entry.

89. Jan Bavinck, "Een korte schets van mijn leven," unpublished, handwritten autobiography, n.d., HBA, folder 445, p. 52. "Ik weet nu wel dat in deze bijzonderheid niets buitengewoons is gelegen, en daarom vermeld ik haar ook niet, maar ik voor mij zag den vinger des Heeren er in, en ik dankte Hem er voor, dat mijn zoon, ik zeg niet mij zou opvolgen, maar dat hij de plaats zou innemen, die ik door kleingeloof niet had durven vervullen. Zou ik ook tot mijn bedanken geleid zijn, opdat er gelegenheid voor mijn zoon open zou blijven? Ik weet het niet, maar ik weet wel dat ik sedert dien tijd beter in mijn bedanken heb kunnen berusten."

90. "Van 1879 tot 1886." "26 aug. Weer naar Kampen met Vader. Ik was te vermoeid om naar Franeker te gaan. Ds. Eerdmans ging voor mij en maakte daar mijne benoeming bekend."

91. "Van 1879 tot 1886." "2 Oct . . . In deze week bezocht ik de leden der gemeente in de stad."

92. "Van 1879 tot 1886." "8 Oct. 's Morg. Gepreekt over 2 Tim. 3:14, 15. 's nam. afscheid over Joh. 17:17. Ontzachlijk veel volk. Tuinstra sprak mij toe. Onvergetelijke dag! 232. 233."

Chapter 7   Gathering Materials: 1883–89

1. Herman, "Goed en kwaad gerucht uit Nederland," *Java-Bode*, October 14, 1882. "Daar is in ons land nog zelfstandige studie. Een merkwaardig voorbeeld hiervan leverd de jongste benoeming van drie docenten aan de Theologische School te Kampen, de opleidingsschool—gelijk u bekend is—voor de leeraars der Christelijk Gereformeerde (Afgescheidenen) Kerk. Een der drie was Dr. H. Bavinck, predikant bij de gemeente van genoemd kerkgenootschap te Franeker. Deze jonge man promoveerde eerst vóór een paar jaren met een geleerde Latijnse dissertatie aan de Leidsche universiteit, waar hij ook gestudeerd had. Gedurende zijn ganschen studietijd stond hij als een ultraconfessioneel man bekend, zijn proefschrift getuigde luide van denzelfden geest, en onmiddelijk na het behalen van de doctorale bul onderwierp hij zich aan het proponentsexamen bij de Afgescheidenen. Dat zij den man, die de vuurproef der Leidsche faculteit aldus doorstond, met gejuich binnenhaalden, behoeft nauwelijks gezegd. Laat mij er bijvoegen, dat de Leidsche professoren immer met grooten lof van hem spraken. Maar het verschijnsel is merkwaardig genoeg, kort geleden theologisch student te Leiden, thans docent aan de Theologische school te Kampen." That a traditionally liberal newspaper like the *Java-Bode* was interested in Bavinck's move from Leiden to Kampen via Franeker contradicts Gleason's statement that "the world was not interested in whether Bavinck stayed or left; it was not interested in the history of the CRC in Franeker." Ron Gleason, *Herman Bavinck: Pastor, Churchman, Statesman, and Theologian* (Phillipsburg, NJ: P&R, 2010), 96.

2. Herman Bavinck, *De ethiek van Ulrich Zwingli* (Kampen: G. Ph. Zalsman, 1880).

3. Ulbe Bosma and Remco Raben, *Being "Dutch" in the Indies: A History of Creolisation and Empire, 1500–1920*, trans. Wendie Shaffer (Athens: Ohio University Press, 2008), 293.

4. Bavinck to Snouck Hurgronje, Kampen, November 10, 1882, in *ELV*.

Ik zit thans in Kampen, bij mijne ouders thuis. De couranten hebben u bericht dat de synode onzer kerk, in augustus te Zwolle gehouden, mij met eenparige stemmen benoemd heeft tot leeraar aan hare Theologische School. Half en half had ik dit verwacht; toch vreesde ik voor dien tijd dikwijls, dat het niet gebeuren zou. Dat ik in stilte er naar verlangde, begrijpt ge. Ik zat hoog in het noorden. De gemeente, welke ik diende, beviel mij wel goed; groot was de liefde en achting, die ik in en buiten haar ontving. Er kwam 's zondags veel, zeer veel volk onder mijn gehoor, zoodat de kerk haast te klein werd. En wat het voornaamste van alles is—ik arbeidde er niet zonder vrucht, er werd zegen genoten onder de bediening des Woords. Toch was 't een moeilijke post. 't Was eene groote gemeente. En preeken alleen is niet genoeg; er moest huisbezoek gedaan worden, om treurende te troosten, kranken te bemoedigen, stervenden voor te bereiden, zwakken en neergebogenen op te richten en sterken tot nederigheid te manen. Ik heb het met liefde, met vrucht ook voor eigen hart en leven gedaan, maar niet zonder zelfverloochening en opoffering van wat mij na aan 't hart lag. . . . Ik verlangde dus ondanks al dat goede, waarvoor ik niet genoeg dankbaar kon zijn, naar iets anders, waar ik meende ook meer roeping en lust en geschiktheid voor te bezitten. En dat verlangen is vervuld. Met algemeene stemmen werd ik benoemd. Ik schrift u dit, om u met mij te doen zien het groote vertrouwen, dat ik, eigenlijk tegen alle gedachte en verwachting in, in onze kerk bezit en dat me waarlijk tot diepen ootmoed stemt.

Na de benoeming ben ik nog eenige weken in de gemeente gebleven. Die laatste weken waren in veel opzichten smartelijk. De gemeente was zoo aan mij gehecht. Oud en jong, rijk en arm, in en buiten de gemeente—het speet allen dat ik heenging. 't Greep mij soms aan en deed me vragen of mijn verlangen wel goed en zuiver was geweest. . . . Ik heb in die laatste weken veel geleerd, mijn leven is er door verrijkt geworden. Ik ben blij, dat ik ruim anderhalf jaar in eene gemeente verkeerd heb, en 't volk heb leeren kennen in zijn menigerlei verkeerdheden ja, maar toch ook in zijn diepe godsvrucht en edelen zin voor wat goed is en waar. En nu ben ik al eenige weken in Kampen, bij mijne ouders thuis. 't Kan wonderlijk gaan; toen ik vroeger de ouderlijke woning verliet, dacht ik er nimmer meer dan voor enkele dagen te verkeeren. En nu blijf ik misschien eene geruime poos in huis, want verloofd ben ik nog niet, en het ziet er niet naar uit, dat 't spoedig zal gebeuren. Toch zou ik op een huwelijk niet tegen hebben; 't ligt aan de omstandigheden, niet aan mijn wil of beginsel, dat ik nog vrijgezel ben.

5. In their correspondence in the 1880s, Henry Dosker seems to have misunderstood Bavinck's singleness as having been chosen in principle, leading him to lump Bavinck together with the necessarily celibate Benedictines. See, for example, Dosker to Bavinck, Ebenezer [Holland, MI], March 27, 1880, in *BHD*.

6. Bavinck to Snouck Hurgronje, Kampen, November 10, 1882, in *ELV*. "Ik huiver soms bij de gedachte, wat er op mijn schouders ligt, maar ten andere zijde hoop ik de taak toch te beginnen met lust en moed. Het onderwerp mijner oratie is nog niet geheel zeker. Denkelijk wel: het karakter (wezen) der theologie. . . . Als mijne oratie in 't licht komt (wat nog niet zeker is), zend ik er u een toe; ge kunt dan eens zien, waar ik thans sta. Gelukkig weet ik dat thans *iets* beter dan in Leiden indertijd." Emphasis original.

7. Herman Bavinck, *De wetenschap der H. Godgeleerdheid: Rede ter aanvaarding van het leeraarsambt aan de Theologische School te Kampen* (Kampen: G. Ph. Zalsman, 1883).

8. Bavinck to Snouck Hurgronje, Kampen, January 2, 1883, in *ELV*. "Dat te vernemen scherpt en is van groot belang."

9. Public announcement of the installation was given in *De Bazuin*, December 15, 1882.

10. Jan Bavinck and Willem Hendrik Gispen, *De Christ. Geref. Kerk en de Theologische School: Twee toespraken, gehouden den 9 Jan. 1883 bij de installatie van de drie leeraren aan de Theol. School* (Kampen: G. Ph. Zalsman, 1883), 14–27.

11. H. Mulder, "Lindeboom, Lucas," in *Biografisch lexicon voor de geschiedenis van het Nederlands protestantisme*, ed. D. Nauta, A. de Groot, J. van den Berg, O. J. de Jong, F. R. J. Knetsch, and G. H. M. Posthumus Meyjes (Kampen: Kok, 1988), 3:250–53.

12. R. H. Bremmer, *Herman Bavinck en zijn tijdegenoten* (Kampen: Kok, 1966), 49–53. See, for example, the unflattering remarks on Lindeboom in Abraham Kuyper, (untitled comment), *Heb de waarheid en de vrede lief. Open brief aan Dr. A. Kuyper, hoogleeraar aan de Vrije Universiteit op Gereformeerden Grondslag en redacteur van "De Heraut," alsmede aan de "Heraut"-lezers en alle gereformeerden in den lande, door L. Lindeboom* (Leiden: D. Donner, 1880), 3–6.

13. "Van 1879 tot 1886," HBA, folder 16. "10 Jan. 's middags 12 uur sprak Lindeboom over de Bijbelsche geschiedenis 3 ½ uur. 'S avonds 6 uur Bavinck over de Wetenschap der H. Godgeleerdheid 1 uur."

14. Valentijn Hepp, *Dr. H. Bavinck* (Amsterdam: Ten Have, 1921), 121. "Hij sprak in zulk een snel tempo, dat alles in een goede vijf kwartier was afgeloopen. Als proeve van welspre-kendheid kon deze rede niet gelden."

15. J. H. Landwehr, *In Memoriam: Prof. Dr. H. Bavinck* (Kampen: Kok, 1921), 24, 26. "Wij hadden als studenten groote verwachtingen gekoesterd, maar alles, wat wij hoorden, overtrof die verwachtingen nog. . . . Wij studenten waren vol over die rede."

16. Bremmer, *Herman Bavinck en zijn tijdegenoten*, 46; Gleason, *Herman Bavinck*, 98. Gleason also writes (99) that Bavinck wrote to Snouck Hurgronje "on the same day of his inaugural speech" and "confided some of his concerns about being such a young professor." This does not seem to have been the case. Bavinck's inaugural lecture was held on January 10. The extant letters from Bavinck to Snouck Hurgronje from this period are dated November 10, 1882, January 2, 1883, and February 8, 1883 (see *ELV*). These particular letters contain no reflections on concerns related specifically to Bavinck's youth.

17. Herman Bavinck, "Het rijk Gods, het hoogste goed," *De Vrije Kerk* 7 (April–August 1881): 4:185–92; 5:224–34; 6:271–77; 7:305–14; 8:353–60; ET: "The Kingdom of God, the Highest Good," trans. Nelson Kloosterman, *Bavinck Review* 2 (2011): 133–70.

18. Contrasting the inaugural lecture with the more formulaic earlier publications in *De Vrije Kerk* and his doctoral dissertation, Bremmer views this lecture as the "starting point" in

Bavinck's constructive theological development. In that regard, he neglects "Kingdom of God, the Highest Good" vis-à-vis this particular lecture. R. H. Bremmer, *Bavinck als dogmaticus* (Kampen: Kok, 1966), 373.

19. Bavinck, *De wetenschap der H. Godgeleerdheid*, 5. This claim was made by L. W. E. Rauwenhoff in *Theologische Tijdschrift* (1878), 206; cf. Herman Bavinck, "Theology and Religious Studies in the Nineteenth-Century Netherlands," in *Essays on Religion, Science, and Society*, ed. John Bolt, trans. Harry Boonstra and Gerrit Sheeres (Grand Rapids: Baker Academic, 2008), 283n3.

20. Bavinck, *De wetenschap der H. Godgeleerdheid*, 14, 15, 42.

21. Bavinck, *De wetenschap der H. Godgeleerdheid*, 25. "De Theologie wordt eenvoudig anthropologie; God een ideaal, een beeld, gevormd door den mensch, d. i. een afgod."

22. Bavinck to Snouck Hurgronje, Kampen, January 2, 1883, in *ELV*.

23. Kuenen to Bavinck, Leiden, January 19, 1883, HBA, folder 2. "Am.! Ontvang mijne hartelijken dank voor de toezending van uwe Oratie, die ik met groote belangstelling gelezen heb. Niet met instemming, zooals gij begrijpt. Maar mijne dissensus verhinderde mij niet al lezende op te merken, dat gij uwe opvatting helder, consequent, waardiglijk hebt uiteengezet en verdedigt." *Nota bene:* the Latin *amice* (friend) was a common greeting among the university-educated class of that period.

24. Tiele to Bavinck, Leiden, January 17, 1883, HBA, folder 2. "Al sta ik op een standpunt, hemelsbreed van het uwe verschillende, dit verhindert mij niet u geluk te wenschen met de wijs waarop gij 't uwe hebt verdedigt."

25. Snouck Hurgronje to Bavinck, Leiden, January 24, 1883, in *ELV*.

26. Snouck Hurgronje to Bavinck, Leiden, January 24, 1883, in *ELV*. "Uwe rede nu was gericht tot met u eensdenkenden, bij wie deze met zoo harde woorden genoemde zaken niet bestreden behoeven te worden."

27. Bavinck to Snouck Hurgronje, Kampen, February 8, 1883, in *ELV*. "Maar ook wijl mijn doen een gansch ander was. Dat doel was, om te toonen, wat de theologie naar haar eigen aard is en wezen wil. Theologie is, dunkt mij, kennen van God. Zij geeft het antwoord op de zeer eenvoudige en zeer practische en voor elk mensch, ook den ongeleerdste, belangrijkste vraag: *hoe ken ik God, en hoe krijg ik dus het eeuwige leven?* Zoo opgevat, is er geen ander antwoord mogelijk, dan: alleen uit de Heilige Schrift." Emphasis original.

28. Bavinck to Snouck Hurgronje, Kampen, February 8, 1883, in *ELV*. "Dit is het verschil tusschen u en mij (laat me zoo maar eens persoonlijk spreken): gij wilt door en na onderzoek tot deze stelling komen, ik ga er van uit en ga dan aan 't verder onderzoeken. Ik meen, dat dit laatste moet, zal er ooit van theologie in den eigenlijken zin sprake kunnen zijn."

29. Bavinck to Snouck Hurgronje, Kampen, February 8, 1883, in *ELV*. "Er moet nog iets bij: met mijne Schriftbeschouwing ben ik dus volstrekt nog niet klaar."

30. *De Heraut*, January 24, 1883. "Dat is nu werkelijk gereformeerde wetenschappelijke theologie. Hier is doorgedacht, hier zijn de eerste beginselen weer recht gezet, hier is een weg afgebakend, die tot een uitnemende ontwikkeling leiden kan." For a Seceder reaction to Bavinck's argument, including commentary on Kuyper's critique and praise, see H. Beuker, "Dr Bavincks inaugurele rede," *De Vrije Kerk* 9 (1883): 178–83.

31. Bavinck, *De wetenschap der H. Godgeleerdheid*, 23.

32. Bavinck to Snouck Hurgronje, Kampen, June 26, 1883, in *ELV*; Bavinck to Snouck Hurgronje, Kampen, October 23, 1883, in *ELV*.

33. Bavinck to Snouck Hurgronje, Kampen, June 26, 1883, in *ELV*. "Misschien hebt ge gelezen, dat ik benoemd ben tot lid van de Maatschappij van Nederlandsche Letterkunde. Ik weet niet, aan wien ik die eer te danken heb; ik vermoed, aan prof. Kuenen. Indien dit vermoeden juist was, zou ik hem gaarne daarvoor bedanken. Maar wijl mij er niets van bekend is en heel de benoeming eene pure verrassing is, kan ik dit moeilijk doen. De secretaris dier Maatschappij heet J. J. A. A. Frantzen. Die naam is mij geheel onbekend. Zoudt ge, indien 't niet te veel gevraagd

is, me even *deze week* kunnen inlichten, wie en wat deze secretaris is. Hij schijnt in Leiden te wonen, en gij kent hem zeker wel, althans bij naam. 't Is moeilijk, een brief aan iemand te schrijven, als men niet juist weet, wie die 'iemand' is, vooral met het oog op titulatuur etc. Ge kunt me dus hierin een grooten dienst bewijzen."

34. *Handelingen der algemeene vergadering van de Maatschappij der Nederlandsche Letterkunde te Leiden, gehouden aldaar den 21sten Juni 1883, in het gebouw van de Maatschappij tot Nut van 't Algemeen* (Leiden: Brill, 1883), 91–92.

35. Bavinck's appointment to the society was also a source of pride among the Seceders. See *De Bazuin*, June 29, 1883.

36. Bavinck to Snouck Hurgronje, Kampen, October 23, 1883, in *ELV*.

37. *Handelingen der algemeene vergadering van de Maatschappij der Nederlandsche Letterkunde te Leiden, gehouden aldaar den 19den Juni 1884, in het gebouw van de Maatschappij tot Nut van 't Algemeen* (Leiden: Brill, 1884), 36, 40; Gerrit Kalff, *Het lied in de middeleeuwen* (Leiden: Brill, 1883).

38. "Van 1879 tot 1886." "24 aug. Vrijdag. 's Namiddags. Een brief verzonden aan A. den Dekker, met een ingesloten brief aan A. J."

39. "Van 1879 tot 1886." "'s Middags sprak ik zeer moeilijk voor mij zelf."

40. "Van 1879 tot 1886." "29 aug . . . 's Avonds te 8 uur kwam ik te Kampen. Thuis lag een brief voor mij, niets inhoudend dan mijn ingesloten brief voor A.J., nog ongeopend."

41. Bavinck's sermon was reported on in *De Bazuin*, January 26, 1883.

42. "Van 1879 tot 1886." "11 Aug. 's morgens naar Almelo, Unink was zeer zwak en dien dag weinig opgewekt."

43. "Van 1879 tot 1886." "15 aug . . . op dit uitstapje had ik niet veel genoegen."

44. "Van 1879 tot 1886." "21 Sept. 1883. Jan Hendrik Unink overleden, 25 j. oud. 25 Sept. 1883 begraven Vader heeft de plechtigheid geleid."

45. Herman Bavinck, "Letters to a Dying Student: Bavinck's Letters to Johan van Haselen," trans. James Eglinton, *Bavinck Review* 4 (2013): 97.

46. Bavinck, "Letters to a Dying Student," 100.

47. "Van 1879 tot 1886." "16 Juli . . . Het examen in de dogmatiek was slecht."

48. "Van 1879 tot 1886." "17 juli. Examen en vergadering der Curatoren is afgelopen. 't Onderzoek in de dogmatiek ging vrij goed. De Curatoren waren tevreden."

49. Christiaan Snouck Hurgronje, "Prof. De Louter over 'Godsdienstige wetten, volksinstellingen en gebruiken," *De Indische Gids* 5, no. 2 (1883): 98–108; "Nogmaals 'De Islam en Oost-Indië' naar aanleiding van prof. De Louters brief," *De Indische Gids* 5, no. 2 (1883): 375–80; *De beteekenis van den islam voor zijne belijders in Oost-Indië* (Leiden: Brill, 1883).

50. Bavinck to Snouck Hurgronje, Kampen, October 23, 1883, in *ELV*. "Ik wenschte wel, dat ik ook eens aan 't schrijven kon gaan. Maar het is me nog onmogelijk. Ik moet me eerst in de vakken, die ik heb, goed inwerken. En dat kost tijd en studie. Bovenal is 't me in al die vakken zoo moeilijk, iets te zeggen, wijl niets op zichzelf staat, maar 't eene in onverbrekelijk verband staat met 't ander, en formele kwestiën—waarlijk niet de gemakkelijkste—alles beheerschen. Dikwerf word ik er moedeloos onder. Zoovele vragen van 't hoogste gewicht blijven onopgelost. En de afstand tusschen 't ideaal en mijn krachten is zoo verbazend groot, en schijnt bij voortgezet studie nog grooter te worden. Men zou dan haast besluiten, om maar niets te zeggen en zich op een bescheiden afstand te houden."

51. Eric Bristley, *Guide to the Writings of Herman Bavinck* (Grand Rapids: Reformation Heritage Books, 2008), 44–47.

52. *De Standaard*, December 29, 1883.

53. Bavinck to Snouck Hurgronje, Kampen, February 11, 1884, in *ELV*. "Ik ben zelf maar steeds bezig aan het verzamelen van bouwstof voor eene eigen dogmatiek en ethiek. Dat wil zeggen, dat ik deze thans op de colleges voornamelijk van de historische zijde opvat, en mijzelf en mijne studenten vooral tracht te oriënteeren in het historische gegeven, vooral natuurlijk in

de gereformeerde dogmatiek. Een historische grondslag moet er eerste gelegd zijn, eer aan het optrekken van een eigen gebouw gedacht worden kan."

54. Bavinck to Snouck Hurgronje, Kampen, February 11, 1884, in *ELV*. "'t Komt me ook voor, dat er tegenwoordig op dat terrein ook eenige stilstand is waar te nemen, en dat men noch vooruit kan, wijl de weg almeer wordt afgesloten, noch terug, daar dit nog veel moeilijker valt."

55. Although this letter does not specify what these "terrible occurences" were, he would later make similar and specific observations in vol. 3 of *RD*, when describing the failure of nineteenth-century Ritschlian theology to forge a sustainable path into the twentieth century. "Along with material progress, spiritual poverty increased as well. People again began to see the limitations of culture and, in that connection, the social evils, the defects in education and upbringing, the misery of people's earthly existence." *RD*, 3:555.

56. Bavinck, preface to *Synopsis purioris theologiae*, vi. "Sed tempora mutantur."

57. Christiaan Snouck Hurgronje, *Mekka*, 2 vols. (The Hague: Nijhoff, 1888–89); Snouck Hurgronje, *Mekka in the Latter Part of the 19th Century—Daily Life, Customs and Learning: The Moslims of the East-Indian Archipelago*, ed. and trans. J. H. Monahan (Leiden: Brill, 2006).

58. Bavinck to Snouck Hurgronje, Kampen, June 16, 1884, in *ELV*. "Ik had gehoopt, dat dit binnenkort zou plaats hebben. Zondag 27 juli moet ik namelijk in Delft preeken en ik was voornemens, dan maandag u een bezoek te brengen. Door uwe reis vervalt dit. Ook had ik gedacht, a.s. donderdag de vergadering der Maatschappij van Nederlandsche Letterkunde bij te wonen. Maar ik kan 't zeer moeilijk doen. Ik moet een referaat leveren over de theologie van Chantepie de la Saussaye en ben dus met diens geschriften bezig. Waarschijnlijk dijt dit referaat uit tot een brochure over Saussaye's theologie. . . . Gij zult wel geen tijd hebben, me nog eens voor uw vertrek te schrijven. Ik durf 't ook niet vragen. Maar laat toch 't zij uit Arabië, 't zij na uw terugkeer weer eens iets van u hooren. Van harte wensch ik u eene voor uw studie en leven voorspoedig reis toe. Maar tevens hoop ik dat ge bewaard blijft voor eene waardeering van den islam, als onlangs mr. Van Bemmelen (naar een bericht in 't *Handelsblad*) uitsprak."

59. Pieter van Bemmelen, *L'Egypte et l'Europe, par un ancien juge mixte* (Leiden: Brill, 1884).

60. "Een verdediger van den Islam," *Algemeen Handelsblad*, May 2, 1884. "De heer Van Bemmelen meent dat de Islam in Europa niet goed wordt begrepen, door de schuld zoowel van orthodoxe en moderne protestanten als van ongeloovigen. De Islam is het zuivere monotheisme. . . . De schrijver stelt dus den Islam zeer hoog onder de godsdiensten, vooral als men tot de leer van den Koran terugkeert; hij gelooft in de toekomst van den Islam en spoort de Christenen aan, hem te eerbiedigen, zijn vertrouwen te winnen en tevens de achting van de Muzelmannen."

61. Christiaan Snouck Hurgronje, *Verspreide geschriften* (Leipzig: Schroeder, 1923), 1:284, 2:393; cf. J. Brugman, "Snouck Hurgronje's Study of Islamic Law," in *Leiden Oriental Connections, 1850–1940*, ed. Willem Otterspeer (Leiden: Brill, 1989), 91–92.

62. Allard Pierson, *Dr. A. Pierson aan zijne laatste gemeente* (Arnhem: D. A. Thieme, 1865).

63. Willem Jan de Wit, *On the Way to the Living God* (Amsterdam: VU University Press, 2011), 26; F. H. von Meyenfeldt, "Prof. Dr. Herman Bavinck: 1854–1954, 'Christus en de cultuur,'" *Polemios* 9, no. 21 (October 15, 1954): 109–12; Bremmer, *Herman Bavinck en zijn tijdgenoten*, 142.

64. Pieter Sjoerd van Koningsveld, "Conversion of European Intellectuals to Islam: The Case of Christiaan Snouck Hurgronje alias 'Abd al-Ghaffār,'" in *Muslims in Interwar Europe: A Transcultural Historical Perspective*, ed. Bekim Agai, Umar Ryad, and Mehdi Sajid (Leiden: Brill, 2016), 88–104.

65. Jan Just Witkam, "Christiaan Snouck Hurgronje's description of Mecca," in *Mekka in the Latter Part of the 19th Century—Daily Life, Customs and Learning: The Moslims of the East-Indian Archipelago*, by Christaan Snouck Hurgronje, ed. and trans. J. H. Monahan (Leiden: Brill, 2006), xv.

66. Van Koningsveld, "Conversion of European Intellectuals to Islam: The Case of Christiaan Snouck Hurgronje alias 'Abd al-Ghaffār," 100.

67. Bavinck to Snouck Hurgronje, Kampen, August 3, 1884, in *ELV*. "Bescheidener weg is mij aangewezen, nederiger werkkring toebetrouwd. Misschien dat ik daar niet geheel onnut werkzaam ben. Hooger roeping zou boven mijn krachten gaan; ik ben zelf daar steeds levendig van overtuigd en daarom in mijn kring zeer tevreden."

68. Bavinck to Snouck Hurgronje, Kampen, December 23, 1884, in *ELV*. "Maar daarom kunnen we nog wel van elkander leeren en elkaar nuttig zijn. En juist wijl ik thans altijd onder geestverwanten leef, is mij de controle van tegenstanders die tevens vrienden zijn soms te onmisbaarder."

69. Daniël Chantepie de la Saussaye, *Verzameld werk*, 3 vols. (Zoetermeer: Boekencentrum, 1997–2003).

70. See, for example, Lodewijk Rauwenhoff, quoted in John Halsey Wood, "Church, Sacrament and Civil Society: Abraham Kuyper's Early Baptismal Theology," *Journal of Reformed Theology* 2, no. 3 (2008): 279.

71. Tjerk de Reus, "Op het kompas van De la Saussaye," *Friesch Dagblad*, October 25, 2003.

72. Bavinck to Snouck Hurgronje, Kampen, June 6, 1884, in *ELV*.

73. "Van 1879 tot 1886." "1 juli . . . Ik las referaat voor over Saussaye's Theol. waar geen discussie uit ontstond."

74. Herman Bavinck, *De theologie van prof. dr. Daniël Chantepie de la Saussaye: Bijdrage tot de kennis der ethische theologie* (Leiden: D. Donner, 1884).

75. Bavinck, *De theologie van prof. dr. Daniël Chantepie de la Saussaye*, 95. "Zijne theologie kan de onze niet zijn."

76. Bavinck, *De theologie van prof. dr. Daniël Chantepie de la Saussaye*, 91.

77. For a summary of Bavinck's views on Chantepie de la Saussaye, see Bremmer, *Bavinck als dogmaticus*, 65–72.

78. J. H. Gunning Jr., "Aan Prof. Dr. H. Bavinck," *De Vrije Kerk* 10, no. 5 (1884): 212–20; Herman Bavinck, "Antwoord aan Prof. Dr. J. H. Gunning Jr.," *De Vrije Kerk* 10, no. 5 (1884): 221–27; Gunning, "Aan Prof. Dr. H. Bavinck," *De Vrije Kerk* 10, no. 6 (1884): 277–86; Bavinck, "Antwoord aan Prof. Dr. J. H. Gunning Jr.," *De Vrije Kerk* 10, no. 6 (1884): 287–92; Gunning, "Aan Prof. Dr. H. Bavinck," *De Vrije Kerk* 10, no. 7 (1884): 314–19.

79. Bavinck, "Antwoord aan Prof. Dr. J. H. Gunning Jr.," *De Vrije Kerk* 10, no. 6 (1884): 292. "Want juist omdat het verschil tusschen Ethischen en Gereformeerden loopt over het beginsel der Theologie, over de kenbron en de methode, bestaat er groot gevaar, dat het verschil steeds grooter zal worden, ook in menig punt van de belijdenis, waarin nu nog eenstemmigheid is. De beginselen zijn machtiger dan hunne menschelijke dragers."

80. J. H. Gunning Jr., *Jezus Christus de middelaar Gods en der menschen: Naar aanleiding van dr. H. Bavinck, De theologie enz. door J.H. Gunning jr.* (Amsterdam: Höveker & Zoon, 1884).

81. Bavinck to Snouck Hurgronje, Kampen, December 23, 1884, in *ELV*. "Maar dit wensch ik toe te passen op heel 't menschelijk leven, in al de breedte die het toelaat. En juist dat is het, waarin ik van velen in de Christelijke Gereformeerde Kerk verschil. . . . Ik begin al het nadeelige in te zien van een seminarie en dan nog wel in Kampen. Eene christelijke universiteit zou mijn ideaal zijn; en hoezeer ik in dr. Kuyper veel afkeur, aan zijne grootsche stichting wensch ik zegen en welvaart."

82. Bremmer, *Bavinck als dogmaticus*, 72–114.

83. "Van 1879 tot 1886." "21 Maart. Visite gemaakt bij Prof Gunning."

84. Harinck and Berkelaar, *Domineesfabriek: Geschiedenis van de Theologische Universiteit Kampen* (Amsterdam: Prometheus, 2018), 101. "Mijne heeren, wij hebben het zeldzame voorrecht, prof. Gunning van Amsterdam in ons midden te hebben en ik waag dien hoogvereerden broeder te vragen, of hij mijne plaats wil innemen."

85. "Van 1879 tot 1886." "6 aug. 's Middags Am. alleen ontmoet en gesproken. A.d.D was met Ds. van Goor naar Tilburg."

86. Christiaan Snouck Hurgronje, "Mijne reis naar Arabië," *Nieuwe Rotterdamsche Courant*, November 26 and 27, 1885.

87. Bavinck to Snouck Hurgronje, Kampen, December 9 1885, in *ELV*. "Gelukkig dat in elk geval uw reis niet geheel mislukt is en dat gij zelfs eenigen tijd in Mekka hebt kunnen doorbrengen. Vooral dit heeft mij sterk verbaasd. Toen ik voor uw vertrek bij u was, zeidet ge me, dat Mekka niet mocht betreden worden door ongeloovigen; te nieuwsgieriger ben ik nu om te weten, hoe het u gelukt is de heilige stad binnen te dringen."

88. Bavinck to Snouck Hurgronje, Kampen, January 12, 1886, in *ELV*; Bavinck to Snouck Hurgronje, Kampen, May 7, 1886, in *ELV*; Christiaan Snouck Hurgronje, "Der Mahdi," *Revue Coloniale Internationale* 1 (1886): 25–59; Snouck Hurgronje, "Mohammedaansch recht en rechtwetenschap: Opmerkingen naar aanleiding van twee onlangs verschenen brochures," *De Indische Gids* 8, no. 1 (1886): 90–111; Snouck Hurgronje, "De islam," *De Gids* 50, no. 2 (1886): 239–73.

89. Bavinck to Snouck Hurgronje, Kampen, January 1, 1887, in *ELV*.

90. Bavinck to Snouck Hurgronje, Amsterdam, May 16, 1915, in *ELV*. In more recent scholarship, Joshua Ralston has charted the level of nuanced engagement with Islam in the writings of various Reformed dogmaticians. Of the writers discussed in his work (primarily Turretin, Schleiermacher, and Bavinck), Ralston writes that "Bavinck shows the most interest in Islam and a seeming awareness, however inchoate, of the internal debates and traditions within Islamic thought and practice." Joshua Ralston, "Islam as Christian Trope: The Place and Function of Islam in Reformed Dogmatic Theology," *Muslim World* 107, no. 4 (October 2017): 754–76.

91. Jan Just Witkam, "Copy on Demand: Abū Šubbāk in Mecca, 1303/1886," in *The Trade in Papers Marked with Non-Latin Characters*, ed. Anne Regourd (Leiden: Brill, 2018), 223.

92. Bavinck to Snouck Hurgronje, Kampen, December 9, 1885, in *ELV*. "Wel komt het voor, dat we op elk terrein, ook op wetenschappelijk gebied, leven in een tijd van malaise."

93. Stewart J. Brown, *Thomas Chalmers and the Godly Commonwealth in Scotland* (Oxford: Oxford University Press, 1983).

94. "Van 1879 tot 1886." "14 juli. 't Examen wordt dezen dag bijgewoond door Rev. James Hunter . . . Laurieston Manse, (te) Falkirk (tusschen Glasgow en Edinburgh). Deze gaf mij volgende adressen:

Rev. John Laidlaw DD prof. of Syst. Theol., Free Church College Edinburgh.

Rev. Salmond DD   id.   id.   in Aberdeen.

Rev. Candlich [*sic*] DD   id.   id.   in Glasgow.

Rev. Wm. Binnie DD Prof of Church History, Free Church College, in Aberdeen."

95. Stewart J. Brown, "The Disruption and the Dream: The Making of New College 1843–1861," in *Disruption to Diversity: Edinburgh Divinity 1846–1996*, ed. David F. Wright and Gary D. Badcock (Edinburgh: T&T Clark, 1996), 29.

96. David Wright, introduction to *Disruption to Diversity: Edinburgh Divinity 1846–1996*, ed. David Wright and Gary D. Badcock (Edinburgh: T&T Clark, 1996), x.

97. Alexander Balmain Bruce, "The Rev. Professor Stewart F. Salmond, DD, Free Church College, Aberdeen," *Biblical World* 8, no. 5 (1896): 347–53.

98. "Van 1879 tot 1886." "8 Juli. Plan gevormd naar Berlijn te gaan, waar thans Geerh. Vos is."

99. Harinck has helpfully corrected a claim made in *De Bazuin* in 1829 that Bavinck and Vos were related. This was inaccurate but, according to Harinck, nonetheless "underlines how close they were." George Harinck, "Herman Bavinck and Geerhardus Vos," *Calvin Theological Journal* 45, no. 1 (2010): 20n8.

100. James T. Dennison Jr., introduction to *The Letters of Geerhardus Vos*, ed. James T. Dennison Jr. (Phillipsburg, NJ: P&R, 2005), 14–15.

101. See, for example, Dosker to Bavinck, Amsterdam, August 16, 1888, in *BHD*.

102. For Vos's letters to Kuyper and Rev. J. W. Felix (president of the trustees of the Free University; see chap. 6, under "Opportunities in Amsterdam"), see Dennison, *Letters of Geerhardus Vos*, 116–21.

103. Joris van Eijnatten and Fred van Lieburg, *Nederlandse religiegeschiedenis* (Hilversum: Verloren, 2006), 244.

104. "Van 1879 tot 1886." "Om 9 uur hoorde ik Zeller in Hegels zaal over Logik, dor & droog."

105. "Van 1879 tot 1886." "29 juli . . . en om 12 uur nog van Paulsen, die sprak over Gesch. des geistigen Lebens, Gen 1 v. verwierp, waarschuwde tegen verachting van de leer van 't menschenafstamming van dier, beweerde dat deze theorie veel meer licht wierp in de toekomst, terwijl anders er depravation is."

106. Bavinck interacted with Paulsen at various points in vols. 1–3 of *RD*, with Kaftan, Zeller, and Vos on numerous occasions in vols. 1–4. For an overview, see *RD*, 4:855–56, 870, 890, 894.

107. See, for example, the approving use of Kaftan in *RD*, 1:50–51.

108. "Van 1886–1891," HBA, folder 16.

109. "Van 1886–1891." "14 aug . . . De reis had voor ons beiden nog geen 400 gulden gekost."

110. J. P. N. Land, "Philosophy in the Dutch Universities," *Mind: A Quarterly Review of Psychology and Philosophy* 3 (1878): 87–104.

111. Bavinck to Snouck Hurgronje, Kampen, January 1, 1887, in *ELV*. "Hoe dikwerf verlang ik naar de Leidsche bibliotheek! En hoe gaarne zou ik metterwoon van Kampen naar Leiden of Amsterdam verhuizen. We wonen hier zoo achteraf en worden zoo kleinsteedsch!"

112. Bremmer, *Herman Bavinck en zijn tijdgenoten*, 52.

113. On Kuyper's relationship to Schaepman, see Vincent Bacote, *The Spirit in Public Theology: Appropriating the Legacy of Abraham Kuyper* (Eugene, OR: Wipf & Stock, 2005), 56.

114. George Puchinger and Nico Scheps, *Gesprek over de onbekende Kuyper* (Kampen: Kok, 1971), 25. "Bepalend is *dat* Kuyper, mede door zijn bondgenootschap met zijn roomse tweelingbroeder Schaepman, het regeringskasteel veroverde."

115. "Van 1886–1891." "21 juli. Donderdag. De Curatorenverg. is bijna heel den dag in comité! Men spreekt over de verhouding van Lindeboom tot de andere Docenten. 's Morgens werden Van Velzen en Brummelkamp apart, en daarna Lindeboom afzonderlijk binnengeroepen. 's Middags moesten Cock, Wiel. Noordtzij en ik binnen komen. Ons werd gevraagd over onze verhouding tot Lindeboom enz. Daarna werd L. weer alleen binnengeroepen."

116. Lucas Lindeboom, *Onze roeping tegenover, en onder Rome* (Heusden: A. Gezelle Meerburg, 1890).

117. George Harinck, "Herman Bavinck and the Neo-Calvinist Concept of the French Revolution," in *Neo-Calvinism and the French Revolution*, ed. James Eglinton and George Harinck (London: Bloomsbury T&T Clark, 2014), 21.

118. Willem Geesink, *Calvinisten in Nederland* (Rotterdam: J. H. Dunk, 1887).

119. J. Reitsma, "Passio Dordracena," *Geloof en Vrijheid: Tweemaandeliksch tijdschrift* 21 (September/October 1887): 555–90. Reitsma's pejorative terms were "nieuwerwetsche calvinisten," "herborene calvinisten," "moderne calvinisten," and "neocalvinist."

120. In the 1880s, Kuyper focused on "Reformed" rather than "Calvinist." James Bratt, *Abraham Kuyper: Modern Calvinist, Christian Democrat* (Grand Rapids: Eerdmans, 2013), 172.

121. Harinck has traced the first positive appropriation of this term by a neo-Calvinist to an article by W. H. Gispen in *De Bazuin*, June 26, 1896. See Harinck, "Herman Bavinck and the Neo-Calvinist Concept of the French Revolution," 21n43.

122. Anne Anema, *Calvinisme en rechtswetenschap: Een studie* (Amsterdam: Kirchner, 1897), xvi, 100.

123. Anne Anema, *De grondslagen der sociologie: Een studie* (Amsterdam: Kirchner, 1900), 30.

124. See, for example, F. J. Krop, *Waarom bestrijden wij Rome?* (Leeuwarden: Bouman, 1900), 1; A. J. Hoogenbirk, *Om de kunst* (Nijkerk: Callenbach, 1903), 46; Herman Groenewegen, *De theologie en hare wijsbegeerte* (Amsterdam: Rogge, 1904), 34; Pieter Gerrit Datema, *Zending, een plicht?* (n.p., 1904), 7; M. Beversluis, *De val van Dr. A. Kuyper een zegen voor ons*

land en volk (Oud-Beierland: Hoogwerf, 1905), 10; M. ten Broek, *De geestelijke opwekking in Holland* (Ermelo: Gebr. Mooij, 1905), 9; A. J. Hoogenbirk, *Heeft Calvijn ooit bestaan? Kritisch onderzoek der Calvijn-legende* (Nijkerk: G. F. Callenbach, 1907), 36.

125. In 1887, Geerhardus Vos had left Berlin for Strasbourg in search of a satisfying institutional home, and he corresponded with Bavinck on that matter. Vos to Bavinck, June 16, 1887, in *LGV*.

126. Harinck, "Herman Bavinck and Geerhardus Vos," 23.

127. "Van 1886–1891." "17 juni. Gepreekt in Vlaardingen over Ezech 16:14, Rom 8:14–17 (365. 366). Gelogeerd bij A.W. Schippers."

128. See, for example, *Delftsche Courant*, June 10, 1883.

129. For A. W. Schippers's involvement in the public lower burgher school in Vlaardingen, see, for example, *Het Nieuws van den Dag*, July 9, 1883.

130. "Begravenis A. W. Schippers," *Het Vaderland*, January 24, 1924.

131. "Van 1886–1891." "15 Sept. Naar Schiedam. Gelogeerd bij Mevr. Wedᶜ Vrijland. Mijnheer en Mevr. Schippers van Vlaardigen kwamen 's av. ook. 16 Sept. Gepreekt over Joh. 1:16–18 en Col 3:23 (369. 370). 's avonds waren van Vlaardingen ook gekomen de Juffr. Johanna Schippers, en hare logées Juffrouw Jantine Bos van Wildervank en Juffrouw Geertje Wieringa van Adnard."

132. "Van 1886–1891." "17 Sept . . . Met Mevr. Vrijland gesproken over J."

133. J. C. Schaeffer, *De plaats van Abraham Kuyper in de "Vrije Kerk"* (Amsterdam: Buijten & Schipperhein, 1997).

134. Herman Bavinck, *De katholiciteit van Christendom en kerk* (Kampen: G. Ph. Zalsman, 1888); ET: "The Catholicity of Christianity and the Church," trans. John Bolt, *Calvin Theological Journal* 27 (1992): 220–51.

135. Bavinck, "*The Catholicity of Christianity and the Church*," 224. Compared to Steketee's 1881 lecture on the gospel and art—which was criticized for suggesting that a Christian minister could not carry out his work *without* a knowledge of art—Bavinck's lecture was constructed with far more theological care and may be read as a corrective to it.

136. Abraham Kuyper, *Het Calvinisme en de kunst* (Amsterdam: Wormser, 1888).

137. *De Heraut*, December 30, 1889. "Deze oratie is een meesterstuk."

138. Dosker to Bavinck, March 23, 1889, in *BHD*. "Ik zag den peinzenden Noord, den mobielen Wielenga, den *snuggeren* Lindeboom, den cynischen Cock, den dikken Mulder, den eerwaardigen Van Velzen. Ik zal al de studenten en bestudeerde hunne gelaatstrekken, als gij uw gedachtengang ontwikkelde en uw *ideaal* van het Christendom en zijn missie op aarde ten beste gaaft." Emphasis original.

139. Martien Brinkman, "Bavinck en de katholiciteit van de kerk," in *Ontmoetingen met Bavinck*, ed. George Harinck and Gerrit Neven (Barneveld: Uitgeverij De Vuurbaak, 2006), 307–24.

140. Gunning to Bavinck, quoted in Brinkman, "Bavinck en de katholiciteit van de kerk," 307–8. "Waarom tolereren zij U? . . . Omdat gij een uitstekend geleerde en godvruchtig leeraar zijt, omdat zij u niet missen kunnen . . . wereldlijke utiliteit."

141. Bavinck to Snouck Hurgronje, Kampen, December 22, 1888, in *ELV*. "Mijne oratie hebt ge zeker ontvangen. Bedenk bij de lezing dat ze vooral bestemd is als eenige medicijn voor de separatistische en sectarische neigingen, die soms in onze kerk zich vertoonen. Er is zooveel enghartigheid, zooveel bekrompenheid onder ons, en 't ergste is dat dat nog voor vroomheid geldt. Ik weet wel, het ideaal waar ik naar streef is hier onbereikbaar, maar mensch te zijn in den vollen natuurlijken zin van dat woord en dan als mensch in alles een kind van God—dat lijkt me 't schoonst van alles. Daar streef ik naar."

142. Landwehr, *In Memoriam*, 40. "Nog zie ik Prof. BAVINCK staan in het midden der broederen. Zijn korte zinnen drongen als pijlen in de ziel. Hij geraakte zoo in geestdrift, dat hij

zelfs met den voet op de grond stampte, iets wat hem anders geheel en al vreemd was. Het was een machtig aangrijpend pleidooi om de Synode te bewegen de Concept-acte aan te nemen."

143. Bavinck to Snouck Hurgronje, Kampen, August 7, 1888, in *ELV*. "De theologie over 't algemeen moet op allen die buiten haar staan wel een armzaligen indruk maken. Zeker, omdat de meesten wel zoo ongeveer weten, hoe het *niet* kan en slechts een enkele als dr. Kuyper meent te weten, hoe het wel moet." Interestingly, Bavinck's comments on the state of theology in the Netherlands echo closely Vos's judgment of the same state of affairs in Germany, in a letter written in the previous year: "Most of the students who are now enrolled in the theological faculty certainly would choose other professions if scholarships were as numerous for the more humane professions and an appointment in the future was as certain. It is so bad here that just by looking I can distinguish the theologians from the other students. Personally I would not attach much value therefore to a theological degree earned in Germany." Vos to Bavinck, Strasbourg, June 16, 1887, in *LGV*.

144. *De Bazuin*, March 1, 1889.

145. Bavinck to Snouck Hurgronje, Kampen, February 11, 1889, in *ELV*.

146. D. J. C. van Wyk, "P J Hoedemaker, teoloog en kerkman," *HTS Teologiese Studies* 47, no. 4 (1991): 1069–87.

147. Bremmer, *Herman Bavinck en zijn tijdgenoten*, 62–63.

148. Bavinck to Rutgers, April 5, 1889, quoted in Bremmer, *Herman Bavinck en zijn tijdgenoten*, 63.

149. Idzerd van Dellen, *In God's Crucible: An Autobiography* (Grand Rapids: Baker, 1950), 40.

150. "School en Kerk," *Algemeen Handelsblad*, April 1, 1889.

151. Van der Munnik to Bavinck, Kampen, March 29, 1889, HBA, folder 3.

152. Berends to Bavinck, Amsterdam, April 1, 1889, HBA, folder 3.

153. Bavinck to Hovy, Kampen, April 15, 1889, HBA, folder 3. "Deze afwijzing uwe benoeming doet mij smart, vooral omdat tegenstanders haar allicht ~~zullen~~ toeschrijven aan beweegredenen die de mijnen niet zijn." Strikethrough original.

154. "School en Kerk," *Algemeen Handelsblad*, April 17, 1889.

155. *Kamper Courant*, April 18, 1889.

156. Herman Bavinck, "Dankbetuiging," *De Bazuin*, April 19, 1889. "Misschien verwondert het velen, dat ik de benoeming zoo lang en zoo ernstig in overweging nam. Maar het kwam mij voor, dat ik niet anders mocht doen. Bekend met de omstandigheden waaronder zij plaats had, zag ik haar in een ander licht, dan waarin zij zich aan velen voordeed. Bovendien, de Vrije Universiteit, hoe weinig zij ook nog aan haar naam en doel beantwoorde, is toch vertegenwoordigster en draagster van eene groote gedachte. Zij stelt zich een doel voor oogen, dat elk Gereformeerde heilig moet zijn, de handhaving n.l. van de eere Gods ook op het terrein der wetenschap."

157. Bavinck, "Dankbetuiging." "Eene Universiteit heeft ondanks haar schaduwzijde daarom altijd, naar mij voorkomt, boven eene Theol. School de voorkeur, omdat zij de waarheid Gods, in Christus geopenbaard, tot heerschappij zoekt te brengen op *ieder* terrein van het menschelijk leven."

158. The reasons given by Bavinck in *De Bazuin* were reprinted in *De Heraut*, April 28, 1889.

159. Willem Hovy, "Advertentiën: Vrije Universiteit," *De vriend van oud en jong*, April 28, 1889. "Immers, het universitair karakter der Vrije Universiteit brengt mede, dat haar werkkring zoveel omvangrijker is dan die van een theologische school, hoe verdienstelijk deze ook overigens is."

160. Bavinck to Snouck Hurgronje, Kampen, January 29, 1889, in *ELV*. "Gij schrift nog over eene andere zaak, wier eerste bespreking uwerzijds mij ook vrijmoedigheid geeft, om er mijne meening van te zeggen. Eerlijk beken ik, dat een leerstoel als dien van Rauwenhoff innam, voor mij veel bekoorlijks heeft. Ik ontveins me de bezwaren niet, vooral niet het optreden met *mijne* denkwijze te midden van mannen, die àllen een ander standpunt innemen, en velen ook met

groote wetenschappelijke kracht handhaven en verdedigen. Desniettemin zou zulk eene plaats mij aantrekken door de vrijheid en de rijke gelegenheid, die zij biedt om eigen overtuigingen wetenschappelijk te bevestigen en aan andere mede te deelen. Toch zou ik aan het innemen van zulk een plaats niet hebben gedacht als gij er mijne gedachte niet op *gevestigd* had. Voor het overige geloof ik ook, dat verder nadenken en spreken erover rekenen zou zijn buiten den waard." Emphasis original.

161. Bavinck to Snouck Hurgronje, Kampen, March 15, 1889, in *ELV*. "Maar toch moet mij een woord van dank nog van 't hart voor de aanbeveling van mijn persoon bij het Koninklijk Instituut en voor de Leidsche vacature bij minister Keuchenius."

162. Bratt, *Abraham Kuyper: Modern Calvinist, Christian Democrat*, 218.

163. Bratt, *Abraham Kuyper: Modern Calvinist, Christian Democrat*, 221.

164. Bavinck to Snouck Hurgronje, Kampen, March 15, 1889, in *ELV*. "Ik wilde zelfs de schijn niet geven van mij eenigszins te willen opdringen, en soms had ik berouw over het weinige, dat ik er u over geschreven had. Van de heele zaak hoorde ik verder niets, dan alleen enkele onzekere geruchten over de personen, die door de faculteit waren voorgedragen en waaronder ook ik zou behooren, wat me wel onwaarschijnlijk voorkwam. Eén ding heeft me echter wezenlijk verblijd, dat *gij* mij vervulling dier vacature niet onwaardig keurdet."

165. *Leeuwarder Courant*, March 16, 1889; *Haagsche Courant*, March 18, 1889; *Provinciale Overijsselsche en Zwolsche Courant*, March 18, 1889; *Algemeen Handelsblad*, March 19, 1889. See C. M. van Driel, *Schermen in de schemering: Vijf opstellen over modernisme en orthodoxie* (Hilversum: Verloren, 2007), 22.

166. *De Wakker*, April 27, 1889.

167. "Van 1886–1891." "20 mei. Uit brief van Dinus vernam ik dat Prof. Gunning benoemd is te Leiden. Men zei dat ik met hem op de nominatie stond."

168. George Harinck, "'Eén uur lang is het hier brandend licht en warm geweest': Bavinck en Kampen," in George Harinck and Gerrit Neven, eds., *Ontmoetingen met Bavinck* (Barneveld: De Vuurbaak, 2006), 114.

169. Van Driel, *Schermen in de schemering*, 22.

170. Harinck and Berkelaar, *Domineesfabriek*, 87.

Chapter 8 Writing a Modern Reformation: 1889–1902

1. Wolter Huttinga, "'Marie Antoinette' or Mystical Depth? Herman Bavinck on Theology as Queen of the Sciences," in *Neo-Calvinism and the French Revolution*, ed. James Eglinton and George Harinck (London: Bloomsbury T&T Clark, 2014), 143–54.

2. Herman Bavinck, *De Welsprekendheid* (Kampen: G. Ph. Zalsman, 1889); ET: *Eloquence*, in *Herman Bavinck on Preaching and Preachers*, ed. and trans. James Eglinton (Peabody, MA: Hendrickson, 2017), 21–56.

3. "Van 1886–1891," HBA, folder 16. "23 Oct . . . Johan was niet al te wel."

4. "Van 1886–1891." "25 Oct. Visite gemaakt bij Mevr Vrijland Sr. Johanna Schippers was daar gelogeerd en had ook de lezing bijgewoond. 's Middags na aangenamen morgendrank en diner, om half vijf vertrokken naar Kampen."

5. "Van 1886–1891." "4 febr. 's Morgens naar Amsterdam. Johan was vrij wel, wou niet mee. . . . 20 febr. 's Avonds terug naar huis. Johan was niet wel en ging mee."

6. "Van 1886–1891." "20 febr . . . De studenten verzochten hem niet."

7. *De Bazuin*, April 25, 1890. "Onze geliefde Ouders, JAN BAVINCK EN GEZINA MAGDALENA BAVINCK, hopen den 28sten April a.s. hunne 40-jarige Echtvereeniging te herdenken. *Hunne dankbare zonen*, H. BAVINCK, C. B. BAVINCK, B. J. T. BAVINCK, J. G. BAVINCK, Kampen." *Nota bene*: this note listed Berendinus Johannes Femia's initials incorrectly and also misspells Geziena's name.

8. Pieter Sjoerd van Koningsveld, "Conversion of European Intellectuals to Islam: The Case of Christiaan Snouck Hurgronje alias 'Abd al-Ghaffār," in *Muslims in Interwar Europe: A*

Transcultural Historical Perspective, ed. Bekim Agai, Umar Ryad, and Mehdi Sajid (Leiden: Brill, 2016), 101.

9. Snouck Hurgronje to Bavinck, Weltevreden, July 16, 1890, in *ELV*. *Nota bene*: Weltevreden is now Jakarta.

10. "Van 1886–1891." "1 juni. Gepreekt in Vlaardingen over Joh 8:23, 24 en Joh 9:4, 5 (411 & 412). Ik logeerde bij A.W. Schippers. . . . 's Maandags bleef ik te Vlaardingen tot drie uur. Veel genoten. Johanna. 4 juni 1890. Woensdag. Aan Mijnheer en Mevr. Schippers per brief verlof gevraagd, om aan hun dochter Johanna hart en hand te vragen. 8 juni. Ik ontving verlof, en schreef terstond. 12 Juni. Donderdag avond, ontving ik bericht van Johanna, dat zij mijn aanzoek aannam."

11. "Van 1886–1891." "16 juni. 's Morgens op de trein om 8 uur over Moerdijk naar Rotterdam. Van daar naar Vlaardingen. Ik kwam hier om 2 uur en werd door allen hartelijk ontvangen. Nader kennis gemaakt met Johanna. . . . Met Johanna afspraak gemaakt over wijze v. publiceering onzer verloving."

12. "Schoolnieuws," *De Standaard*, June 16, 1890.

13. See HBA, folder 38. It seems from a letter dated October 21, 1890, that Henry Dosker had received one such engagement card.

14. "Van 1886–1891." "20 juni . . . Daardoor niet ter kerk 's avonds. Met Joh. in 't prieel Gerok gelezen."

15. Karl Gerok, *Palmbladen; Heilige woorden: Ter bevordering van christelijke geloof en christelijke wereldbeschouwing*, trans. C. P. L. Rutgers (Groningen: Zweeden, 1865).

16. Ron Gleason, *Herman Bavinck: Pastor, Churchman, Statesman, Theologian* (Phillipsburg, NJ: P&R, 2010), 139.

17. Cornelia Frida Katz, "Inleiding," *Christendom en Vrouwenbeweging*, introductory issue (1923): 1–7, 20.

18. HBA, folder 40.

19. HBA, folder 11.

20. H. W. van der Vaart Smit to J. A. Bavinck-Schippers, Zuid-Beijerland, October 17, 1927, HBA, folder 11.

21. HBA, folder 11. On the attempts to produce an English-language translation in the 1930s, see John Bolt, "Herman Bavinck Speaks English: A Bibliographic Essay," *Mid-America Journal of Theology* no. 19 (2008): 120–22.

22. "Van 1886–1891." "20 November Bernard en Grietje getrouwd door Vader. Bruiloft niet erg gezellig."

23. Herman Bavinck, "De theologische richtingen in Duitschland" (1884), HBA, folder 41; Bavinck, "Methodologie der theologie" (1883–84), HBA, folder 43; Bavinck, "De leer der verbonden" (1884), HBA, folder 45; Bavinck, "Medulla Theologiae. Dogmaticae. 1884/85," HBA, folder 46.

24. Herman Bavinck, "De Mensch, Gods evenbeeld" (1884), HBA, folder 102; Bavinck, "De kenbaarheid Gods (1888), HBA, folder 106; Bavinck, "De theologie als wetenschap in dezen tijds. Kampen 1889," HBA, folder 107.

25. The unpublished notes on dogmatics are a mixture of dated and undated writings. The volume of dated, unpublished notes on dogmatics increased considerably during the 1890s. See HBA, folders 155–88.

26. For a particularly one-sided picture of this rivalry, see Nicolaas Beets, *Life and Character of J. H. van der Palm*, trans. J. P. Westerveld (New York: Hurd & Houghton, 1895), 16–18.

27. *De Standaard*, July 16, 1890.

28. *Het Nieuws van de Dag*, July 17, 1890.

29. "Samensmelting van doleerenden en afgescheidenen," *Algemeen Handelsblad*, July 12, 1892. "De Theologische School te Kampen zal weldra dr. Bavinck moeten afstaan aan de 'Vrije Universiteit.'"

30. "Van 1886–1891." "16 sept. Docentenvergadering met de Heer Kapteyn. Ik kreeg heel wat minder colleges."

31. Zuidema, "Kapteyn (Johannes)," in *Nieuw Nederlandsch Biografisch Woordenboek*, ed. P. C. Molhuysen and P. J. Blok (Leiden: A. W. Sijthoff's, 1912), 2:647–48.

32. Idzerd van Dellen, *In God's Crucible: An Autobiography* (Grand Rapids: Baker, 1950), 43.

33. George Harinck and Wim Berkelaar, *Domineesfabriek: Geschiedenis van de Theologische Universiteit Kampen* (Amsterdam: Prometheus, 2018), 95.

34. Herman Bavinck, "De Theologie van Albrecht Ritschl," *Theologische Studiën* 6 (1888): 369–403.

35. Herman Bavinck, *Gereformeerde Ethiek*, ed. Dirk van Keulen (Utrecht: Uitgeverij Kok-Boekcentrum, 2019); ET: *Reformed Ethics*, vol. 1, *Created, Fallen, and Converted Humanity*, ed. and trans. John Bolt with Jessica Joustra, Nelson D. Kloosterman, Antoine Theron, and Dirk van Keulen (Grand Rapids: Baker Academic, 2019).

36. Idzerd van Dellen, "In Memoriam: Prof. Dr. H. Bavinck te Kampen," *Onze Toekomst*, August 26, 1921. "Bavinck dicteerde snel. We konden maar korte aanteekeningen maken. . . . Hoe veel gemakkelijker moet het later geweest zijn toen zijn Dogmatiek was gepubliceerd." A clipping of this piece was preserved by Johanna Bavinck after Herman's death. See HBA, folder 40.

37. *De Grondwet*, December 23, 1890. "De NEWS verneemt uit vertrouwbare bron dat Dr. Bavinck, van de Theol. School te Kampen, in den aanstaanden zomer een bezoek aan dit land zal brengen en alsdan vergezeld zal zijn door zijne echtgenoote. Personen, die het weten kunnen, verzekeren ons dat Dr. Bavinck geen echtgenoote heeft."

38. *De Grondwet*, December 30, 1890. "Van de NEWS krijgen wij de verdere inlichting, dat Dr. Bavinck voornemens is om te huwen, voor dat hij in den zomer dit land zal bezoeken."

39. "Van 1886–1891." "15 Sept. 's Morgens had ik met Joh. gesprek over Amerika."

40. Vos to Bavinck, Grand Rapids, June 30, 1891, in *LGV*; see also Harinck, "Inleiding," in *BHD*, 12.

41. Vos to Bavinck, Grand Rapids, June 30, 1891, in *LGV*.

42. Vos to B. B. Warfield, Grand Rapids, June 13, 1890, in *LGV*; Vos to B. B. Warfield, Grand Rapids, July 2, 1890, in *LGV*; Vos to B. B. Warfield, Grand Rapids, August 5, 1890, in *LGV*; Herman Bavinck, "Recent Dogmatic Thought in the Netherlands," *Presbyterian and Reformed Review* 3, no. 10 (April 1892): 209–28.

43. George Harinck, "'Land dat ons verwondert en ons betoovert': Bavinck en Amerika," in *Ontmoetingen met Bavinck*, ed. George Harinck and Gerrit Neven (Barneveld: De Vuurbaak, 2006), 37.

44. "Menu, 17 Juni 1891," in HBA, folder 38. "Menu, 17 Juni 1891. Vermicellisoep. Pasteitjes. Ossenhaas. Snijboontjes. Kalfsfricandeau. Worteltjes. Gebraden kip. Peren. Zalm. Salade. Compôte. Pudding. Taart. Dessert."

45. George Harinck and Marjoleine de Vos, *Wat eten we vanavond? Protestants!* (Amsterdam: Donum Reeks, 2005).

46. The record of their marriage listed in *De Bazuin* mistakenly notes the date as June 2. See *De Bazuin*, July 10, 1891.

47. Valentijn Hepp, *Dr. Herman Bavinck* (Amsterdam: Ten Have, 1921), 209. "2 Juli. Trouwdag. Heerlijk weer. Zonnig en toch Frisch. Mijn ouders, B. en G. (Ds. C.B. Bavinck en zijn vrouw) waren overgekomen. Om 12 uur reed ik van Ds. Sieders naar Mr. Schippers. Om 12¼ uur kwamen de 14 rijtuigen voor. Ruim te één uur op het stadhuis. Getrouwd door Van der Brugge. Daarna om 1¾ uur tot ± 3 uur getrouwd in de kerk door Ds. Sieders, met tekst Ps. 25:6, 7. Daarna naar huis en om 6 uur met rijtuigen naar de "Vriendschap" in Schiedam. Heerlijk diner tot 4 uur 's morgens."

48. Van Dellen, *In God's Crucible*, 40–41.

49. Hepp, *Dr. Herman Bavinck*, 211; R. H. Bremmer, *Herman Bavinck en zijn tijdgenoten* (Kampen: Kok, 1966), 75.

50. 32 De la Sablonièrekade is *rijksmonument* number 23260.

51. Bavinck to Snouck Hurgronje, Kampen, December 23, 1884, in *ELV*.

52. Herman Bavinck, *De katholiciteit van Christendom en kerk* (Kampen: G. Ph. Zalsman, 1888); ET: "The Catholicity of Christianity and the Church," trans. John Bolt, *Calvin Theological Journal* 27 (1992): 224.

53. Herman Bavinck, "Dankbetuiging," *De Bazuin*, April 19, 1889.

54. Abraham Kuyper, "Sphere Sovereignty," in *Abraham Kuyper: A Centennial Reader*, ed. James Bratt (Grand Rapids: Eerdmans, 1998), 488.

55. Jeffrey Stout, "Christianity and the Class Struggle," in *The Kuyper Center Review*, vol. 4, *Calvinism and Democracy*, ed. John Bowlin (Grand Rapids: Eerdmans, 2014), 40.

56. Pope Leo XIII, "Encyclical Letter *Rerum Novarum*," in *The Church Speaks to the Modern World: The Social Teachings of Leo XIII*, ed. Étienne Gilson (Garden City, NY: Image, 1954), 205–44.

57. Abraham Kuyper, "The Social Question and the Christian Religion," in *Makers of Modern Christian Social Thought*, ed. Jordan Ballor (Grand Rapids: Acton Institute, 2016), 45–118.

58. Herman Bavinck, "De Mensch, Gods evenbeeld" (1884), HBA, folder 107.

59. Herman Bavinck, "Welke algemeene beginselen beheerschen, volgens de H. Schrift, de oplossing der sociale quaestie, en welke vingerwijzing voor die oplossing ligt in de concrete toepassing, welke deze beginselen voor Israel in Mozaïsch recht gevonden hebben?," *Proces-verbaal van het Sociaal Congres*, gehouden te Amsterdam den 9–12 November, 1891 (Amsterdam: Höveker & Zoon, 1892), 149–57; ET: "General Biblical Principles and the Relevance of Concrete Mosaic Law for the Social Question Today (1891)," trans. John Bolt, *Journal of Markets & Morality* 13, no. 2 (2010): 411–46.

60. James Bratt, *Abraham Kuyper: Modern Calvinist, Christian Democrat* (Grand Rapids: Eerdmans, 2013), 223.

61. *De Standaard*, December 2, 1891.

62. Tjeerd Hoekstra, "Prof. Dr. H. Bavinck," *Gereformeerd Theologisch Tijdschrift*, July–August 3/4 (1921), 101. "BAVINCK voelde—overeenkomstig zijn aanleg en misschien ook in verband met zijne dogmatische overtuiging meer voor Aristoteles dan voor Plato. Hierin ligt ten deele ook het verschil met Kuyper. In de toekomst zullen deze twee groote geesten herhaaldelijk met elkander vergeleken worden en het nageslacht heeft hier een vruchtbaar veld voor onderzoek. Het komt mij voor, dat een belangrijk punt van onderscheid tusschen deze mannen is, dat BAVINCK een Aristotelische, Kuyper een Platonische geest was. BAVINCK de man van het heldere begrip, Kuyper de man van de fonkelende idee, BAVINCK een bouwer op en uit het historisch gegevene, Kuyper speculeerend met intuitief gegrepen gedachten. BAVINCK in hoofdzaak inductief, Kuyper in hoofdzaak deductief." Hoekstra's article is cited by J. H. Landwehr, *In Memoriam: Prof. Dr. H. Bavinck* (Kampen: Kok, 1921), 58. For repetitions of the "deductive/inductive" descriptions, see R. H. Bremmer, *Bavinck als dogmaticus* (Kampen: Kok, 1966), 13–64; Jan Veenhof, *Revelatie en Inspiratie: De Openbarings- en Schriftbeschouwing van Herman Bavinck in vergelijking met die van de ethische theologie* (Amsterdam: Buijten & Schipperheijn, 1968), 130–33; J. Mark Beach, "Abraham Kuyper, Herman Bavinck, and 'The Conclusions of Utrecht 1905,'" *Mid-America Journal of Theology* 19 (2008): 11.

63. George Harinck and Lodewijk Winkler, "The Nineteenth Century," in *Handbook of Dutch Church History*, ed. Herman Selderhuis (Göttingen: Vandenhoeck & Ruprecht, 2015), 497.

64. Harinck and Winkler, "The Nineteenth Century," 497.

65. See, for example, Lucas Lindeboom, "Het doctoraat in de heilige godgeleerdheid aan de Theologische School der Christ. Geref. Kerk" (n.p., 1887).

66. George Harinck, "Inleiding," in *Mijne reis naar Amerika*, by Herman Bavinck, ed. George Harinck (Barneveld: Uitgeverij De Vuurbaak, 1998), 17.

67. Hepp, *Dr. Herman Bavinck*, 211.

68. *De Bazuin*, December 2, 1892. "Dr. Bavinck, die in zijn stuk, 'een lans gebroken heeft voor het Calvinisme.'"

69. Herman Bavinck, "The Future of Calvinism," *Presbyterian and Reformed Review* 5, no. 17 (1894): 3.

70. *De Bazuin*, June 17, 1892.

71. George D. Mathews, ed., *Alliance of the Reformed Churches Holding to the Presbyterian System: Proceedings of the Fifth General Council Toronto, 1892* (London: Publication Committee of the Presbyterian Church of England, 1892).

72. HBA, folders 66–67.

73. These notes were first transcribed and published in Dutch by George Harinck in 1998. See Herman Bavinck, *Mijne reis naar Amerika*, ed. George Harinck (Barneveld: De Vuurbaak, 1998); see also James Eglinton, "Herman Bavinck's 'My Journey to America,'" *Dutch Crossing* 41, no. 2 (2017): 180–93.

74. Hepp, *Dr. Herman Bavinck*, 213.

75. Hepp, *Dr. Herman Bavinck*, 214.

76. Herman Bavinck, "The Influence of the Protestant Reformation on the Moral and Religious Condition of Communities and Nations," *Mid-America Journal of Theology* 25 (2014): 75–81; first published in Mathews, *Alliance of the Reformed Churches*, 48–55.

77. Thomas Lindsay, "The Protestant Reformation: Its Spiritual Character and Its Fruits in the Individual Life," in Mathews, *Alliance of the Reformed Churches*, 39–45.

78. Bavinck, "Influence of the Protestant Reformation," 79.

79. Bavinck, "Influence of the Protestant Reformation," 81.

80. *De Grondwet*, October 4, 1892. "Dr. Bavinck verontschuldigde zich over zijn gebrekkig Engelsch, zeggende dat het zijne eerste poging was, maar hij had geen verontschuldiging noodig, daar zijne taal zoowel duidelijk en keurig als krachtig was."

81. Hepp, *Dr. Herman Bavinck*, 215.

82. *De Bazuin*, November 25, 1892.

83. Hepp, *Dr. Herman Bavinck*, 220. ". . . naar New-Brunswick . . . College gezien. Dan naar 't Seminarie. . . . Eerst de Library gezien, die zeer goed is. De bibliothekaris was zeer vriendelijk. We zagen vele boeken . . . Chapel gezien. Prof. Lansing bezocht . . . om 1 uur naar den trein. Toen naar Princeton. Naar Prof. B. Warfield. Met hem de gebouwen gezien en een bezoek gebracht bij Patton en McCoch. 't Seminarie heeft 200, 't college 1100 studenten. . . . Bij Warfield gesupperd. Om 7 uur weer op trein naar Philadelphia, waar we 8.13 aankwamen."

84. Louis Albert Banks, ed., *T. De Witt Talmage: His Life and Work* (Philadelphia: John C. Winston Co., 1902).

85. Eglinton, "Herman Bavinck's 'My Journey to America,'" 190.

86. W. Gispen, "Aan een vriend te Jeruzalem," *De Bazuin*, October 28, 1892. "Naar Amerika te gaan is tegenwoordig maar een uitstapje. Doch er kan in een maand of vier heel wat gebeuren."

87. *De Bazuin*, November 25, 1892. "Dr. Bavinck immers heeft in zijn stuk een lans gebroken voor het Calvinisme. . . . Of erkende men slechts de wetenschappelijkheid van Dr. Bavinck's arbeid zonder juist ingenomen te zijn met de positie, die hij verdedigde? Het is mogelijk, dat er sommigen waren, die het Calvinistisch karakter van zijn stuk verdroegen, terwijl zij het als letterkundig voortbrengsel prezen. Maar van allen kan en mag dit volstrekt niet gedacht worden."

88. HBA, folder 67.

89. *Gereformeerd Jongelingsblad*, May 1, 1893; *Amsterdamse Kerkbode*, May 7, 1893.

90. Eglinton, "Herman Bavinck's 'My Journey to America,'" 180.

91. Eglinton, "Herman Bavinck's 'My Journey to America,'" 186.

92. Eglinton, "Herman Bavinck's 'My Journey to America,'" 189.

93. *Jaarboekje van de Jongelingsvereenigingen in Nederland, voor 1894, uitgegeven van wege den Nederlandschen Bond van Jongelingsvereenigingen op Gereformeerden Grondslag* ('s Gravenhage: A. Berends, 1894), 52. "Het kan zijn, dat de beginselen van Scholte en van Raalte

nog doorwerken in Amerika's kerkelijk leven, maar toch zeggen wij ook, dat de grond zoo door Methodistische wateren is overstroomd, dat men maar weinig meer van den grond zien kan en we blijven er bij: 'niet Amerikaansch worden.'"

94. *RD* 1:204. The revision of this line between the first (1895) and second (1906) editions of the *Gereformeerde Dogmatiek* is significant on this point. The first Dutch edition reads, "Het heden schijnt voor den bloei van de Geref. theologie niet gunstig ze tijn" (The present day does not appear to be favorable for the growth of Reformed theology). In the revised, second edition, Bavinck rewrote this line as, "Voor het Calvinisme is er de toekomst niet rooskleurig" (For Calvinism there [i.e., America] the future is not rosy). The phrasing in the first edition gives the impression that Reformed theology's difficulties are general, rather than local. In the revised phrasing, Bavinck preferred "Calvinism" to "Reformed theology" and clarified that the statement applied specifically to America. See *GD*[1], 1:139; *GD*[2], 1:206; *RD*, 1:204.

95. Eglinton, "Herman Bavinck's 'My Journey to America,'" 191–92.

96. Harinck, "Land dat ons verwondert," 39. "Telkens weer zet Bavinck zijn publiek op het verkeerde been, door als binnenstander het buitenperspectief te kiezen. Dat heeft geleid tot irritaties: je weet bij Bavinck nooit precies waar je aan toe bent."

97. Bavinck to Kuyper, Kampen, October 30, 1893, quoted in Bremmer, *Herman Bavinck en zijn tijdgenoten*, 80. "De Oudtestamentische studiën onzerzijds met kracht moeten worden aangevat, en weet ik niemand, die daarvoor thans de aangewezen en tegelijk disponibele persoon zou zijn. Indien er zoo iemand ware, zou ik me terstond terugtrekken."

98. Had this been the case, Bavinck's *Prolegomena* would have been repurposed into a work like Louis Berkhof's *The History of Christian Doctrines* (Edinburgh: Banner of Truth, 1949).

99. Bremmer, *Herman Bavinck en zijn tijdgenoten*, 80–81.

100. Bavinck to Kuyper, January 18, 1894, quoted in Bremmer, *Herman Bavinck en zijn tijdgenoten*, 80–81. "Meer echter dan aan zelfverloochening schort het me aan moed. Ik huiver voor het gewicht der taak die ik op me neem. Alleen de overtuiging, dat dit vak zoo spoedig mogelijk onzerzijds ter hand genomen moet worden, dat er op dit oogenblik geen ander persoon voor disponibel is, en dat misschien door mij op dit gebied nog iets goeds kan gedaan worden, geven me den noodigen moed om voortaan mijne kracht aan deze arbeid te wijden. Natuurlijk zal ik het eerste jaar niet veel meer kunnen doen, dan de studie weer ophalen, die ik sedert mijne komst alhier liggen liet. Ik zal dus zeer bescheiden en klein langs den weg moeten beginnen."

101. Abraham Kuyper, *Encyclopedie der heilige godgeleerdheid*, 3 vols. (Amsterdam: J. A. Wormser, 1894). An English translation, comprising only the introduction to vol. 1 and all of vol. 2, was published four years later: *Encyclopedia of Sacred Theology: Its Principles* [vol. 2], trans. J. Hendrik de Vries (New York: Scribner, 1898).

102. Kuyper to Bavinck, January 24, 1894, quoted in Bremmer, *Herman Bavinck en zijn tijdgenoten*, 79–80.

103. R. H. Bremmer, *Bavinck als dogmaticus* (Kampen: Kok, 1966), 37–45.

104. J. Stellingwerff has claimed that prior to reading Bavinck's *Reformed Dogmatics*, Kuyper had planned to follow the *Encyclopedia* with a work of the same name. However, Stellingwerff provides no sources to prove this claim. J. Stellingwerff, *Kuyper en de VU* (Kampen: Kok, 1987), 176; cf. Dirk van Keulen, "Herman Bavinck's *Reformed Ethics*: Some Remarks about Unpublished Manuscripts in the Libraries of Amsterdam and Kampen," *Bavinck Review* 1 (2010): 43n60.

105. "Krachtsverspilling," *De Heraut*, March 25, 1984. "Te Kampen Dr. Bavinck en te Amsterdam Dr. Kuyper *Dogmatiek* en *Encyclopedie* onderwijzen, en dus beiden hun tijd en kracht hebben te geven aan eenzelfde taak."

106. The only newspaper reference to this approach was made in *De Gereformeerde Kerk*, March 15, 1894. This paper was edited by the former Free University professor P. J. Hoedemaker, who had resigned in 1887. This article was critical of division in the Reformed Churches in the

Netherlands and of Biesterveld's appointment in Kampen, given his lack of scientific education. It made a passing reference to the Free University making another approach to Bavinck.

107. Vos to Bavinck, Princeton, March 28, 1894, in *LGV*.

108. Bratt, *Abraham Kuyper: Modern Calvinist, Christian Democrat*, 235.

109. W. Bakker and H. Mulder, "Petrus Biesterveld," in *Biografisch lexicon voor de geschiedenis van het Nederlands protestantisme*, ed. D. Nauta, A. de Groot, J. van den Berg, O. J. de
Jong, F. R. J. Knetsch, and G. H. M. Posthumus Meyjes (Kampen: Kok, 1988), 3:41–42; Harinck
and Berkelaar, *Domineesfabriek*, 109–10.

110. Harinck and Berkelaar, *Domineesfabriek*, 109.

111. Bavinck to Hovy, May 21, 1895, quoted in Bremmer, *Herman Bavinck en zijn tijdgenoten*, 84. "Midden in dien arbeid af te breken en tot een geheel anderen kring van vakken
over te gaan, eischt eene zelfverloochening waartoe ik niet kan zien, dat ik geroepen ben. . . .
En de leerstoel, dien ik hier bezet, zou naar mijn inzicht lang niet zoo gemakkelijk door een
ander vervuld kunnen worden. . . . Beter ten halve gekeerd dan ten heele gedwaald." Gleason's
biography translates Bavinck's final expression as, "Better half converted than totally lost."
This literal rendering is inaccurate and gives a particularly religious impression to what is an
ordinary Dutch idiom. See Gleason, *Herman Bavinck*, 179.

112. *Nieuwe Vlaardingsche Courant*, November 28, 1894.

113. *De Standaard*, November 27, 1894; *De Standaard*, December 11, 1894; *De Bazuin*,
November 30, 1894; *De Bazuin*, December 11, 1894.

114. Hepp, *Dr. Herman Bavinck*, 209. "'S middags hield ik onze Johanna Geziena ten doop."

115. Bavinck, "The Future of Calvinism."

116. Bavinck, "The Future of Calvinism," 13.

117. Bavinck, "The Future of Calvinism," 20.

118. George Harinck, "The Religious Character of Modernism and the Modern Character
of Religion: A Case Study of Herman Bavinck's Engagement with Modern Culture," *Scottish
Bulletin of Evangelical Theology* 29, no. 1 (2011): 60–77.

119. Harinck, "Religious Character of Modernism," 71.

120. Herman Bavinck, *De algemene genade* (Kampen: G. Ph. Zalsman, 1894), 36. See also
Harinck, "Religious Character of Modernism," 71; James Bratt, "The Context of Herman
Bavinck's Stone Lectures: Culture and Politics in 1908," *The Bavinck Review* 1 (2010): 13–14.

121. Bavinck, "Future of Calvinism," 14.

122. Charles Taylor, *A Secular Age* (Cambridge, MA: Harvard University Press, 2007),
711–27.

123. Augustine, *On Christian Teaching*, trans. R. P. H. Green (Oxford: Oxford University
Press, 1997), 8–10.

124. Bavinck, "Future of Calvinism," 4–5.

125. Bavinck, "Future of Calvinism," 20. Cf. Michael Allen, *Grounded in Heaven: Recentering Christian Hope and Life on God* (Grand Rapids: Eerdmans, 2018), 22–23; Hans Boersma,
Seeing God: The Beatific Vision in Christian Tradition (Grand Rapids: Eerdmans, 2018), 315–53.

126. Bavinck, "Future of Calvinism," 14.

127. Lucas Lindeboom, *Bewaart het pand u toebetrouwd, of de geruststelling in "Opleiding
en theologie" onderzocht en gewogen* (Kampen: Zalsman, 1896).

128. Harinck and Berkelaar have argued that this disagreement contributed to Bavinck's
1894 decision to carry on developing his own dogmatics rather than become an Old Testament
exegete. See *Domineesfabriek*, 113.

129. Maarten Noordtzij, Douwe Klazes Wielenga, Herman Bavinck, and Petrus Biesterveld,
Opleiding en theologie (Kampen: Kok, 1896).

130. Harinck and Berkelaar, *Domineesfabriek*, 111.

131. Abraham Kuyper, *E Voto Dordraceno* (Kampen: Kok, 1894), 2:333. Cf. Gerrit Berkouwer, *Faith and Justification* (Grand Rapids: Eerdmans, 1954), 144.

132. Bavinck, *RD*, 4:216.

133. Herman Bavinck, Abraham Kuyper, and Frederik Rutgers, ed. and trans., *Biblia dat is de gansche Heilige Schrifture bevattende alle de kanonieke boeken des Ouden en des Nieuwen Testaments: Naar de uitgave der Staten-overzetting in 1657 bij de Weduwe Paulus Aertsz van Ravesteyn uitgekomen, in de thans gangbare taal overgebracht door Dr. A. Kuyper onder medewerking van Dr. H. Bavinck en Dr. F. L. Rutgers; Met volledige kantteekeningen, inhoudsopgaven, platen, kaarten, enz.* (Middelharnis: Flakkeesche Boekdrukkerij, 1895).

134. *De Heraut*, September 8, 1895.

135. Tjitze Kuipers, *Abraham Kuyper: An Annotated Bibliography, 1857–2010* (Leiden: Brill, 2011), 253.

136. Kuipers, *Abraham Kuyper: An Annotated Bibliography*, 288.

137. Bavinck, *GD¹*, vol. 1 (Kampen: J. H. Bos, 1895).

138. Herman Bavinck, "Foreword to the First Edition (Volume 1) of the *Gereformeerde Dogmatiek*," trans. John Bolt, *Calvin Theological Journal* 45, no. 1 (2010): 9–10.

139. Bavinck, *GD¹*, 1:iv. "Het oude te loven alleen omdat het oud is, is noch gereformeerd noch christelijk. En dogmatiek beschrift niet wat gegolden heeft, maar wat gelden moet. Zij wortelt in het verleden, maar arbeidt voor de toekomst."

140. G. H. Lamers, *Een woord over dogmatische theologie en dogmatiek* (Amsterdam: W. H. Kirberger, 1876); Lamers, *De leer van het geloofsleven* (Amsterdam: W. H. Kirberger, 1877); Lamers, *De toekomst van de dogmatiek* (Amsterdam: W. H. Kirberger, 1878).

141. J. J. van Oosterzee, *Christelijke dogmatiek: Een handboek voor academisch onderwijs en eigen oefening* (Utrecht: Kemink, 1876).

142. F. E. Daubanton, *Confessie en dogmatiek* (Amsterdam: F. W. Egeling, 1891).

143. P. J. Muller, *Handboek der dogmatiek*, 2nd ed. (Groningen: Wolters, 1908).

144. Quoted in George Harinck, "'Eén uur lang is het hier brandend licht en warm geweest': Bavinck en Kampen," in *Ontmoetingen met Bavinck*, ed. George Harinck and Gerrit Neven (Barneveld: De Vuurbaak, 2006), 115. "Ons bod was feitelijk te hoog; als ik je de condities zeg, zul je verstomd staan over de hooge som. Het werk wordt niet verkocht [aan Bos], maar verhuurd voor het tijdvak van 5 jaar gedurende hetwelk men 800 exemplaren mag verkoopen die door den auteur worden geteekend. Na 5 jaar heeft de Schrijver het recht opnieuwe condities te stellen en opnieuw te verhuren. Voila! Enfin, we hopen ons zonder den grooten professor te redden."

145. "Om reden," *De Bazuin*, October 6, 1895.

146. Bremmer, *Bavinck als dogmaticus*, 37–45.

147. "Bavinck's Dogmatiek," *De Heraut*, June 16, 1895. "Deze twee mannen zijn het eens."

148. "Bavinck's Dogmatiek," *De Heraut*, June 16, 1895. "Evenals de *Encyclopaedie* is ook deze *Dogmatiek* het werk van een feilbaar mensch; menschelijk gebrek er aanklevend. Toch zullen we hier niet op ingaan."

149. For further discussion, particularly concerning Kuyper's private attempts to engage with differences between the *Encyclopedia* and the *Reformed Dogmatics*, see Bremmer, *Bavinck als dogmaticus*, 25.

150. Lucas Lindeboom, *Godgeleerden* (Heusden: A Gezelle Meerburg, 1894), 74. "Hoe is het mogelijk dat mannen als Dr. KUYPER en RUTGERS niet inzien, dat de S.S. Theologia Aldus 'hare eigene woonstede' verlaten heeft? Nog erger is het, dat mannen uit de Afscheiding, uit de Vrije Kerk en School afkomstig, ook al blind schijnen te zijn voor deze zonde en dit gevaar. Is het mede de invloed van de wereldsche, ongoddelijke, gymnasia en universiteiten op de Gemeente en haar zaad? Of is die universiteitsidee op *Geref. wortel* over te planten?"

151. Lucas Lindeboom, "Ingezonden," *De Bazuin*, March 13, 1896.

152. See, for example, Vos to Bavinck, Princeton, December 22, 1895, in *LGV*. Bavinck's criticisms of the second volume of Kuyper's *Encyclopedia* were communicated directly, but privately, by letter. See Bavinck to Kuyper, October 29, 1894, quoted in Bremmer, *Bavinck als dogmaticus*, 24.

153. Arie Theodorus van Deursen, *The Distinctive Character of the Free University in Amsterdam, 1880–2005* (Grand Rapids: Eerdmans, 2008), 51–58.

154. Bratt, *Abraham Kuyper: Modern Calvinist, Christian Democrat*, 233.

155. Bremmer, *Herman Bavinck en zijn tijdgenoten*, 92; Bratt, *Abraham Kuyper: Modern Calvinist, Christian Democrat*, 234; van Deursen, *Distinctive Character of the Free University*, 50.

156. *De Standaard*, June 28, 1895.

157. On the "Seinpost scandal," see Bremmer, *Herman Bavinck en zijn tijdgenoten*, 91–108; van Deursen, *Distinctive Character of the Free University*, 52–53; Gleason, *Herman Bavinck*, 206–24; Hepp, *Dr. Herman Bavinck*, 239.

158. A. F. de Savornin Lohman, *De correspondentie over mijn ontslag als hoogleeraar aan de Vrije Universiteit* (Utrecht: Kemink, 1896).

159. "De Heer Hovy over Mr Lohman's afscheid van de Vrije Universiteit," *De Tijd*, October 22, 1895.

160. Gleason, *Herman Bavinck*, 223.

161. Bratt, *Abraham Kuyper: Modern Calvinist, Christian Democrat*, 233–34.

162. Jan Bavinck, "Een korte schets van mijn leven," unpublished, handwritten autobiography, n.d., HBA, folder 445, p. 71. "Op zekeren avond te huis komende, gaf hij een weinig bloed op, en van dien tijd afaan begon hij te sukkelen en te kwijnen. Wat wij ook deden tot zijn behoud en welke middelen wij ook aanwenden tot zijn herstel, niets mocht baten."

163. Hepp, *Dr. Herman Bavinck*, 238. "26 Dec., 2de Kerstdag, Zaterdag. Onze lieve Johan, die op Zondag 8 Sept. 1895 ten huize van Biesterveld 's avonds een bloedspuwing kreeg, is 's morgens half twee overleden, 24 jaar en 3 maanden oud (25 Sept. '72–26 Dec. '96)."

164. *De Standaard*, December 31, 1896. "Hedenmorgen overleed, na een langdurig en geduldig lijden, in de hope des eeuwigen leven, onze geliefde jongste Zoon en Broeder JOHANNES GERRIT BAVINCK, Docts. in de rechts- en staatswetenschap, in den ouderdom van ruim 24 jaren. J. BAVINCK. G.M. BAVINCK-HOLLAND. H. BAVINCK. J.A. BAVINCK-SCHIPPERS. C.B. BAVINCK. G. BAVINCK-BOUWES. B.J.F BAVINCK. *Kampen*, 26 Dec. 1896."

165. Jan Bavinck, "Een korte schets van mijn leven," 72. "Wij verloren in hem een dierbaren en veelbelovenden zoon en een innig geliefden broeder. Wij waren dan ook allen bitterlijk bedroefd; wij hadden hem zoo gaarne behouden."

166. Bavinck to Kuyper, January 11, 1897, quoted in Bremmer, *Herman Bavinck en zijn tijdgenoten*, 109. "Johan was onze jongste broeder; wij hadden hem allen zoo lief en wij hadden zoo goede verwachting van hem voor kerk en vaderland. Hij had zulk een bescheiden, eenvouding karakter en toch ook zulke kostelijke gaven des verstands en des geestes, dat wij meenden, dat de Heere aan mijne ouders en aan ons in hem een heerlijke gave had geschonken. Maar de Heere heeft gegeven, Hij heeft ook genomen en in beide zij zijn Naam geloofd. . . . Hij was niet ten volle verzekerd voor zichzelf, hij stond aan veel bestrijding bloot, en soms was het donker in zijne ziel. Maar toch ging zijn hart naar den Heere uit, Hij verliet zich op Gods vrije genade; hij wilde van niets weten dan van Jezus Christus en Dien gekruisigd; en zoo is hij heengegaan, ons vooruit, naar een beter vaderland."

167. Berendinus Johannes Femia Bavinck, *De sterfte aan tuberculosis pulmonum in Nederland (1875–1895)* (Kampen: J. H. Bos, 1897). I am indebted to Dirk van Keulen for this observation.

168. Herman Bavinck, *GD*[1], vol. 2 (Kampen: J. H. Bos, 1897); *GD*[1], vol. 3 (Kampen: J. H. Bos, 1898); *GD*[1], vol. 4 (Kampen: J. H. Bos, 1901).

169. *De Heraut*, September 19, 1897. "Wat de gewezen hoogleeraar Muller als Dogmatiek uitgaf, kroop terstond na de verschijning uit schaamte onder den banken weg. Doch hier is nu een *wezenlijke* Dogmatiek, rijp en voldragen, klaar in den vorm, en aan alle bitterheid tegen afwijkende opiniën gespeend." Emphasis original.

170. Bavinck, "Future of Calvinism," 1–24; Bavinck, "Kleine bijdrage tot de geschiedenis der Statenvertaling," *Tijdschrift voor Gereformeerde Theologie* 4, no. 4 (1897): 233–40.

171. Matthew Henry, *Letterlijke en practicale Bijbelverklaring* (Utrecht: Kemink, 1896).

172. Herman Bavinck, *Beginselen der psychologie* (Kampen: J. H. Bos, 1897).

173. Bavinck, *GD*[1], 1:16. "Heel de theologie is door en na Schleiermacher, zoowel onder de modernen als onder de orthodoxen, bewustzijnstheologie." In the second edition, Bavinck revised this statement as, "Since Schleiermacher, the whole of theology has changed, among orthodox as well as modern theologians, into a theology of consciousness." *RD*, 1:78.

174. For an example of Kuyper's engagement with the "theology of consciousness" in 1895, see Abraham Kuyper, "Recensie," *De Heraut*, June 9, 1895.

175. Herman Bavinck, *Philosophy of Revelation: A New Annotated Edition*, ed. Cory Brock and Nathaniel Gray Sutanto (Peabody, MA: Hendrickson, 2018), 168; Bavinck, *Beginselen der psychologie*, 2nd ed. (Kampen: Kok, 1923). For Bavinck's other publications on psychology, see "Ter toelichting en verdediging der Psychologie," *Christelijk Schoolblad* (2 Juni–21 Juli 1899); "Psychologie der religie," in *Verslagen en mededeelingen der Koninklijke akademie van wetenschappen* (Amsterdam: Joh. Müller, 1907), 147–76; repr. in *Verzamelde opstellen op het gebied van godsdienst en wetenschap* (Kampen: Kok, 1921), 55–77; ET: "Psychology of Religion," in *Essays on Religion, Science, and Society*, ed. John Bolt, trans. John Vriend and Gerrit Sheeres (Grand Rapids: Baker Academic, 2008), 61–80; "De psychologie van het kind," *Paedagogisch tijdschrift* 1 (1909): 105–17; "Richtingen in de psychologie," *Paedagogisch tijdschrift* 1 (1909): 4–15; ET: "Trends in Psychology," in *Essays on Religion, Science, and Society*, 165–74; *Bijbelsche en religieuze psychologie* (Kampen: Kok, 1920); ET: *Biblical and Religious Psychology*, trans. H. Hanko (Grand Rapids: Protestant Reformed Theological School, 1974).

176. Bavinck to Snouck Hurgronje, Kampen, December 22, 1888, in *ELV*. "Ik weet wel, het ideaal waar ik naar streef is hier onbereikbaar, maar mensch te zijn in den vollen natuurlijken zin van dat woord en dan als mensch in alles een kind van God—dat lijkt me 't schoonst van alles. Daar streef ik naar."

177. Vos to Kuyper, April 30, 1896, in *LGV*. See also George Harinck, *Varia Americana: In het spoor van Abraham Kuyper door de Verenigde Staten* (Amsterdam: Bert Bakker / Prometheus 2016), 13–15.

178. Abraham Kuyper, *Varia Americana* (Amsterdam: Höveker & Wormser, 1898). For comparison of their observations of America, see James Eglinton, "*Varia Americana* and Race: Kuyper as Antagonist and Protagonist," *Journal of Reformed Theology* 11 (2017): 68.

179. Abraham Kuyper, *Mijn reis was geboden: Abraham Kuypers Amerikaanse tournee*, ed. George Harinck (Hilversum: Verloren, 2009), 60. "Mijn reis was geboden, was noodzakelijk, het hoorde bij mijn leven, het is een deel van mijn taak."

180. Abraham Kuyper, *Het Calvinisme: Zes Stone-lezingen in oct. 1891 te Princeton (N.-J.) gehouden* (Amsterdam: Höveker & Wormser, 1899); ET: *Lectures on Calvinism. Six Lectures Delivered at Princeton University under Auspices of the L. P. Stone Foundation* (Grand Rapids: Eerdmans, 1994).

181. Bavinck to Kuyper, Kampen, April 17, 1899, quoted in Harinck, "Herman Bavinck and the Neo-Calvinist Concept of the French Revolution," 24. "Ik betwijfel wel, of de toehoorders in Princeton, wien deze gedachtenwereld gansch vreemd is, in eens U hebben kunnen voegen in Uwe hooge en breede vlucht. Gij geeft zooveel in een kort bestek, dat alleen wie eenigermate zelf op de hoogte is kan waardeeren wat erin zit."

182. Bavinck, "Future of Calvinism," 23.

183. Bavinck, "Future of Calvinism," 24.

184. Bavinck, "Future of Calvinism," 24.

185. *Provinciale Overijsselsche en Zwolsche Courant*, June 1, 1899. "Het Neo-Calvinisme moet in deze tijd mede gerekend worden . . . De gereformeerde dogmatiek van dr. Bavinck heeft veel invloed bij vele jonge theologen."

186. De Bussy to Bavinck, November 7, 1899. This letter is quoted in Bremmer, *Bavinck als dogmaticus*, 137. Bremmer notes having found it in the *"Bavinck family archive."* However, the letter is not listed in the Bavinck Archive now held in Amsterdam. "Geachte Collega! Ten gevolge van het vertrek van de la Saussaye naar Leiden en verruiling van vakken onder de leden onzer faculteit, zal hier moeten benoemd worden een professor in de dogmengeschiedenis, in de geschiedenis van de leer aangaande God en in de Encyclopaedie. Weinigen zijn er die voor dat professoraat rechtens in aanmerking komen, en als 't er op aankomt ze te noemen dan mag naar mijn meening uw naam niet verzwegen worden. Maar daardoor ontstaat voor mij een groote moeilijkheid. Immers ik heb alle reden om te onderstellen dat U een eventueele benoeming niet zoudt aannemen, en misschien is het u wel niet eens aangenaam genoemd te worden. Zoo kom ik te staan tusschen mijn wetenschappelijk geweten en de eischen der praktijk! De faculteit moet een voordracht opmaken van personen, van wie wij, zonder het hun rechtstreeks te vragen, gissen kunnen dat zij bereid zouden zijn een benoeming aan te nemen. . . . Van de enkelen die ik in de faculteit voorlopig genoemd heb, is u de eenige dien ik om die reden niet durf te noemen, en dien ik dan ook over deze zaak schrijf. Ik wensch aan de faculteit te zeggen, dat ik uw naam op de voordracht niet begeer gesteld te zien *omdat ik mij verzekerd houd dat U daarmee niet gediend zoudt zijn*, en dat u er misschien wel de schouders over zoudt ophalen. Maar dat wil ik u dan toch mededeelen ook. Ik verzoek de inhoud van dit briefje geheim te houden, tot nadat de voordracht van curatoren zal zijn publiek gemaakt, dat waarschijnlijk over 14 dagen zal zijn. De faculteit is nog niet gereed, dus voordat wij aan 't einde van deze weg zijn, hebben wij nog tijd van ademhalen. Geloof mij, met herinnering aan het verzoek dat ik u in Mei deed, en met beleefden groet, uw dw. De Bussy." Emphasis original.

187. Bratt, *Abraham Kuyper: Modern Calvinist, Christian Democrat*, 281.

188. Kuipers, *Abraham Kuyper: An Annotated Bibliography*, 301.

189. *De Standaard*, March 25, 1899; *Rotterdamsch Nieuwsblad*, August 7, 1899.

190. Herman Bavinck, *Theologische School en Vrije Universiteit: Een voorstel tot vereeniging* (Kampen: J. H. Bos, 1899).

191. Herman Bavinck, *Het recht der kerken en de vrijheid der wetenschap* (Kampen: G. Ph. Zalsman, 1899).

192. Herman Bavinck, *Het doctorenambt: Rede bij de overdracht van het rectoraat aan de Theologische School te Kampen op 6 Dec. 1899* (Kampen: G. Ph. Zalsman, 1899).

193. Bavinck to Kuyper, undated, quoted in Bremmer, *Herman Bavinck en zijn tijdgenoten*, 137. Although this letter is undated, its reference to the death of Johanna Kuyper indicates that it was written at some point after August 25, 1899. "Nog altijd wensch ik van ganscher harte, dat het tot vereeniging van beide opleidingsscholen moge komen. Maar mijne hoop op een gunstige uitslag is dit jaar niet versterkt. Misschien is het beste, om voorloping in vriendschappelijke verhouding naast elkander te blijven staan en ieder in eigen kring te arbeiden aan den bloei der kerken en aan de bevordering der theologische wetenschap."

194. Herman Bavinck, "Aan de Lezers van *De Bazuin*," *De Bazuin*, January 5, 1900. "God heeft in de eenheid de verscheidenheid lief."

195. Herman Bavinck, "Moderne kunst," *De Bazuin*, September 21, 1900.

196. Herman Bavinck, "De strijd voor het recht," *De Bazuin*, July 5, 1901.

197. Herman Bavinck, "De oorlog," *De Bazuin*, June 1, 1900.

198. Herman Bavinck, "Calvijn," *De Bazuin*, April 13, 1900.

199. Herman Bavinck, "De eerste doopvraag," *De Bazuin*, May 11, 1900.

200. Herman Bavinck, "Feminisme," *De Bazuin*, March 15, 1901.

201. Herman Bavinck, "Stemrecht der vrouw," *De Bazuin*, March 2, 1900.

202. Herman Bavinck, "De tekst onzer liturgie," *De Bazuin*, January 10, 1902.

203. Herman Bavinck, "Op reis," *De Bazuin*, August 31, 1900.

204. Herman Bavinck, "Dogmatiek," *De Bazuin*, April 26, 1901. "Dan is zij meteen de theologie, die onze tijd behoeft."

205. Herman Bavinck, *De offerande des lofs: Overdenkingen vóór en na de toelating tot het heilige avondmaal* ('s Gravenhage: Fred. H. Verschoor, 1901); ET: *The Sacrifice of Praise*, ed. and trans. Cameron Clausing and Gregory Parker (Peabody, MA: Hendrickson, 2019). This particularly popular work was reissued seventeen times by 1948.

206. Herman Bavinck, *De zekerheid des geloofs* (Kampen: Kok, 1901); ET: *The Certainty of Faith*, trans. Harry Der Nederlanden (St. Catharines, ON: Paideia Press, 1980). See also Henk van den Belt, "Herman Bavinck's Lectures on the Certainty of Faith (1891)," *Bavinck Review* 8 (2017): 35–63.

207. Herman Bavinck, *Ouders of getuigen: toelichting van art. 56 en 57 der Dordsche Kerkorde* (Kampen: G. Ph. Zalsman, 1901). The contents of this book were originally published as articles in *De Bazuin*.

208. Herman Bavinck, *Schepping of ontwikkeling?* (Kampen: Kok, 1901).

209. Herman Bavinck, *De wereldverwinnende kracht des geloofs: Leerrede over 1 Joh. 5:4b, uitgesproken in de Burgwalkerk te Kampen den 30sten Juni 1901* (Kampen: G. Ph. Zalsman, 1901); ET: "The World-Conquering Power of Faith," in *Herman Bavinck on Preaching and Preachers*, ed. and trans. James Eglinton (Peabody, MA: Hendrickson, 2017), 67–84.

210. Gleason, *Herman Bavinck*, 374.

211. Bavinck, "Op reis." "En evenzoo is de tijd van ontspanning, die telkens weer den arbeid des geestes vervangt, een rijke zegen en eene kostelijke gave, die afdaalt van den Vader der lichten. Het hart gaat open en de borst verruimt, het oog verheldert en het voorhoofd ontrimpelt zich, als men voor een tijd den arbeid ter zijde zetten en vrij, naar hartelust genieten mag van de heerlijkheid, welke Gods rijke schepping ons biedt. . . . Reizen blijft een lust en eene rijke genieting."

212. "Van 1886–1891," enclosed fragment. "Zaterdag 18 Aug. Johanna, Hannie, kwamen weer thuis."

213. "Van 1886–1891," enclosed fragment. "16 Nov. Ik moest lezen in Utrecht, maar telegrafeerde het af om de ziekte van Moeder."

214. "Van 1886–1891," enclosed fragment. "26 Nov. Maandag. <u>Moeder</u> 's nam. om 3¾ uur gestorven en Vrijdags 30 Nov. begraven." See also *De Bazuin*, November 30, 1900. Geziena Magdalena Bavinck died on November 26, 1900, at age seventy-three.

215. "Van 1886–1891," enclosed fragment. "8 April. Naar Kampen terug. Intrek in 't nieuwe huis, Vloeddijk."

216. Jan Bavinck, *De Heidelbergsche Catechismus in 60 leerredenen verklaard* (Kampen: Kok, 1903–4).

217. "Recensiën," *De Heraut*, June 7, 1903. "Ds. Bavinck is, trots zijn hoogen leeftijd, naar den geest nog jong en frisch gebleven. Wie de eerste aflevering doorziet, merkt wel, hoe uitnemend goed Ds. Bavinck op de hoogte is met hetgeen in onzen tijd op dogmatisch gebied geschreven is. Voor den dogmatischen fijnproever bieden deze preeken een genot."

218. William Hendriksen, "Translator's Preface," in *The Doctrine of God*, by Herman Bavinck (Edinburgh: Banner of Truth Trust, 1951), 7.

219. Bremmer, *Herman Bavinck en zijn tijdgenoten*, 138.

220. Harinck and Berkelaar, *Domineesfabriek*, 117.

221. Herman Bavinck, "Na de Synode," *De Bazuin*, September 19, 1902.

222. Herman Bavinck, *Blijven of heengaan? Een vraag en een antwoord* (Kampen: G. Ph. Zalsman, 1902).

223. Bavinck, *Blijven of heengaan?*, 6. "En thans staan wij na ongeveer vijftienjarigen arbeid, naar het schijnt, nog even ver als aan het begin. Het is, alsof er in deze zaak een oordeel op onze kerken rust."

224. Lucas Lindeboom and Maarten Noordtzij, "Een woord betreffende de zaak der Opleiding," *De Bazuin*, October 10, 1902.

225. *De Bazuin*, September 5, 1902. "Onder degenen die bij gelegenheid van den verjaardag van H. M. onze geëerbiedigde Koningin opgenomen zijn onder de Ridders in de Orde van den Nederlandschen Leeuw, behoort ook Dr. H. BAVINCK, *Hoogleeraar a. d. Theol. School.*"

226. Bavinck to Kuyper, Kampen, October 8, 1902. "Toch heb ik geen bezwaar, dat Heraut en Bazuin deze week reeds melding doen van de feiten van benoeming en aanneming. Maar mag ik u vriendelijk verzoeken, het, althans ditmaal, bij de vermelding der feiten te laten, en er geen woorden van lof en dank aan te voegen. Hoe meer zakelijk, hoe beter."

227. Herman Bavinck, "Wapenstilstand," *De Bazuin*, October 31, 1902.

228. *Het Nieuws van de Dag*, December 30, 1902.

229. *De Bazuin*, December 12, 1902.

230. Cornelis Veenhof, "Uit het leven van de Theologische Hogeschool 6," *De Reformatie* 30, no. 16 (1955): 123. "Ik had zulk een einde van mijn werken aan de Theol. School me niet kunnen voorstellen. . . . Ik begreep dat ook een Theol. School even wetenschappelijk kan zijn als een Universiteit. . . . Naar de neiging van mijn leven, dan arbeidde ik vroeger en zou ik nog nu veel liever arbeiden aan een Theol. School dan aan eene stichting die den naam van eene Universiteit draagt."

231. Veenhof, "Uit het leven," 123. "Heb ik gezegd en thans herhaal ik het: Ik ben een kind der scheiding en dat hoop ik te blijven. (Daverend applaus)."

232. Veenhof, "Uit het leven," 124. "In der tijd leefde in die kerk de gedachte, we moeten de wereld maar overlaten aan haar eigen lot, en juist omdat ik gekomen ben uit den kring, waaruit ik gekomen ben, gevoelde ik mij genoopt om aan eene Universiteit mijne opleiding te zoeken. Want die kerk liep groot gevaar om terwille der heiligheid des levens de catholiciteit der kerk uit het oog te verliezen. En toen rees de gedachte bij mij, is het mogelijk, die beide te verzoenen?"

233. Veenhof, "Uit het leven," 124. "Maar als men mij vraagt of de V.U. groot zal worden, dan zeg ik, ik weet het niet."

234. Hepp, *Dr. Herman Bavinck*, 283. "Dinsdag 12 uur namen Biesterveld en ik afscheid van de studenten: Rector Noordtzij leidde de samenkomst, Lindeboom zat erbij. Noordtzij sprak tot ons, deelde Seitenhiebe uit over het forceeren na de Synode."

235. Harinck and Berkelaar, *Domineesfabriek*, 117–18.

236. Kuipers, *Abraham Kuyper: An Annotated Bibliography*, 274.

237. Anthonie Honig, *Handboek van de Gereformeerde Dogmatiek* (Kampen: Kok, 1938). Honig dedicated his *Dogmatics* (867 pages) to Charles Hodge, Abraham Kuyper, Herman Bavinck, and Henricus Gravemeijer.

238. Anthonie Honig, "Ter gedachtenis aan Prof. Bavinck," *Gereformeerd Theologisch Tijdschrift* 6 (October 1921): 186. "Bavinck's Dogmatiek zal steeds gerekend worden tot het allerbeste, wat op wetenschappelijk gebied verschenen is."

Chapter 9 Christianity in the Age of Nietzsche: 1902–9

1. Valentijn Hepp, *Dr. Herman Bavinck* (Amsterdam: Ten Have, 1921), 283.

2. Jan Bavinck, "Een korte schets van mijn leven," unpublished, handwritten autobiography, n.d., HBA, folder 445, p. 74.

3. *Amsterdamsche Kerkbode*, February 1, 1902.

4. Herman Bavinck, *Godsdienst en godgeleerdheid* (Wageningen: Vada, 1902).

5. Herman Bavinck, *De wetenschap der H. Godgeleerdheid: Rede ter aanvaarding van het leeraarsambt aan de Theologische School te Kampen* (Kampen: G. Ph. Zalsman, 1883).

6. Bavinck, *Godsdienst en godgeleerdheid*, 56. "Godsdienst en godgeleerdheid staan dus niet tot elkander als moeder en dochter, veel minder nog als dochter en moeder. Veeleer zijn ze twee zusters, die elk in de huishouding van Gods kerk een bijzondere taak en roeping hebben te vervullen. Zij zijn aan Maria en Martha in het huisgezin van Lazarus gelijk."

7. Bavinck, *Godsdienst en godgeleerdheid*, 56. "Maria had het goede deel gekozen, dat van haar niet zou weggenomen worden; en Martha was zeer bezig met veel dienens. Maar ook Martha diende den Heere. En Jezus had ze beide lief."

8. Bavinck, *Godsdienst en godgeleerdheid*, 63. "Mijne Heeren Directeuren. Vanwege de zedelijke gebondenheid, die ik gevoelde aan de Kerk, waarin ik geboren ben, en aan de School, die door haar werd gesticht, ontbrak mij in vroegere jaren de vrijheid, om eene benoeming, een en andermaal door U op mij uitgebracht, op te volgen. Thans echter meen ik te mogen zeggen, dat aan de zedelijke verplichtingen, die te dezer zake op mij rustten, geheel en meer dan genoeg is voldaan. Hoezeer ik er dan ook diep leed over draag, dat ik niet op eene andere wijze en in een anderen weg aan deze Uwe stichting verbonden ben geworden, heb ik Uwe benoeming nochtans met volle vrijmoedigheid aangenomen en betuig ik U openlijk mijn dank, dat Gij deze benoeming op mij, evenals ook op mijn ambtgenoot Biesterveld, hebt willen uitbrengen."

9. Bavinck, *Godsdienst en godgeleerdheid*, 63. "Hier kom ik medewerken aan de verwezen-lijking van een hoog ideaal. Het zal mij tot innige vreugde strekken, als ik naar de mate mijner krachten er eenigszins toe medewerken mag, dat onder Uw beleidvol en energiek bestuur het verband van belijdenis en wetenschap steeds helderder, zoowel theoretisch als practisch, in het licht worde gesteld; dat de verhouding van de Theologische Faculteit tot de Gereformeerde Kerken in deze landen voldoende en afdoende geregeld worde; en dat deze School, door eene spoedige en krachtige uitbreiding van het aantal bezette katheders in de onderscheidene faculteiten, hoe langer hoe meer rechtmatige aanspraak mag doen gelden op den schoonen naam, dien zij bij hare stichting ontving."

10. Bavinck to Snouck Hurgronje, Kampen, January 3, 1903, in *ELV*. "Ik ben geen groot bewonderaar van de Vrije Universiteit en heb voor haar zwakheden en gebreken een open oog; maar hier nam ik, blijvende, den schijn op me van eene overtuiging te zijn [toe]gedaan, die ik niet heb. Hoewel ik er zeer op gesteld ben, dat, bij gemis van eene christelijke overheidsschool, de kerk een sterke zeggenschap hebbe over een theologische faculteit, ik kan het 'beginsel eener eigen inrichting' niet accepteren als een dogma, en vind daarin een onrijpe en wrange vrucht van het separatisme, dat ook in onze Christelijke Gereformeerde Kerk zijn wortelen heeft geslagen. Het heeft mij veel strijd gekost, om te beslissen zooals ik beslist heb. Vele banden hielden me vast. Maar ten slotte kon en mocht ik niet anders. Ik hoop, dat de Vrije Universiteit er eenigszins door in sympathie bij ons volk en daardoor ook in kracht zal toenemen. Een eenigszins volledige universiteit zal ze wel nooit worden. Maar als ze een getal predikanten, litteratoren en juristen mocht afleveren, die op de hoogte van hun tijd staan en tevens mannen van overtuiging en karakter zijn, dan zou ze toch nog in bescheiden mate ten zegen kunnen zijn. En zulke mannen hebben alle partijen, hebben wij vooral noodig."

11. George Harinck, "Abraham Kuyper: De Vrije Universiteit op weg naar de samenleving," in *Verder kijken: Honderdvijfendertig jaar Vrije Universiteit Amsterdam in de samenleving. Zesentwintig portretten*, ed. Ab Flipse (Amsterdam: VU Uitgeverij, 2016), 19–26.

12. Bavinck to Snouck Hurgronje, Kampen, January 3, 1903, in *ELV*. "De droevigste ervaring in het leven is wel de teleurstelling, die men met menschen opdoet."

13. Dirk van Keulen, "Herman Bavinck's *Reformed Ethics*: Some Remarks about Unpub-lished Manuscripts in the Libraries of Amsterdam and Kampen," *Bavinck Review* 1 (2010): 44–45, 51–53. See also Dirk van Keulen, "Ten geleide," in *Gereformeerde ethiek*, by Herman Bavinck, ed. Dirk van Keulen (Utrecht: Uitgeverij KokBoekcentrum, 2019), 9–34.

14. Willem Geesink, *De ethiek in de gereformeerde theologie. Rede bij de overdracht van het rectoraat der Vrije Universiteit te Amsterdam op 20 october 1897* (Amsterdam: Kirchner, 1897), 6. "Deze armoede van onzen tijd aan specifiek Gereformeerde ethische studie."

15. Willem Geesink, *Gereformeerde ethiek*, ed. Valentijn Hepp (Kampen: Kok, 1931).

16. Bavinck to Snouck Hurgronje, Kampen, January 3, 1903, in *ELV*. "Watergraafsmeer . . . bij Amsterdam—in Amsterdam zelf kon ik zoo plotseling geen geschikt huis vinden."

17. Bavinck to Snouck Hurgronje, Amsterdam, November 20, 1903, in *ELV*. "Het bevalt ons hier in Amsterdam zeer goed. Het leven is niet zoo rustig als in Kampen, maar het is rijker aan afwisseling, en de intellectueele kring staat hooger."

18. Joel C. Kuipers, *Language, Identity, and Marginality in Indonesia: The Changing Nature of Ritual Speech on the Island of Sumba* (Cambridge: Cambridge University Press, 1998), 32.

19. Hepp, *Dr. Herman Bavinck*, 290.

20. Hepp, *Dr. Herman Bavinck*, 290.

21. Hepp, *Dr. Herman Bavinck*, 289.

22. Almost all of Bavinck's publications while he was living in Watergraafsmeer were re-editions of earlier works: *De offerande des lofs: Overdenkingen vóór en na de toelating tot het heilige avondmaal*, 3rd ed. ('s Gravenhage: Fred. H. Verschoor, 1903); *De theologie van prof. dr. Daniel Chantepie de la Saussaye: Bijdrage tot de kennis der ethische theologie*, 2nd ed. (Leiden: D. Donner, 1903); *De zekerheid des geloofs*, 2nd ed. (Kampen: Kok, 1903). His book *Roeping en wedergeboorte* (Kampen: G. Ph. Zalsman, 1903) was a compilation of articles that had earlier appeared in *De Bazuin* (ET: *Saved by Grace: The Holy Spirit's Work in Calling and Regeneration*, ed. J. Mark Beach, trans. Nelson Kloosterman [Grand Rapids: Reformation Heritage Books, 2008]). Beyond these, he produced a short article for a Christian periodical ("Wat is wijsbegeerte?" [What is philosophy?], *De School met den Bijbel* 1, no. 38 [1903]: 40, 42, 44–46) and an adaptation of his earlier lectures and booklet on "present-day morality" ("Hedendaagsche moraal," *Tijdschrift voor Gereformeerde Theologie* 10 [1903]: 1–67).

23. Bavinck to Snouck Hurgronje, Amsterdam, June 1, 1905, in *ELV*. "Ik herinner me werkelijk niet, of ik u al eens geschreven heb uit mijne nieuwe woning hier in Amsterdam. Bij ons vertrek uit Kampen waren we tijdelijk, omdat we toen niet ineens een geschikt huis konden vinden, naar Watergraafsmeer gegaan. Maar daar beviel het ons niet best; het was ruim drie kwartier van het gebouw der Vrije Universiteit verwijderd en was bovendien ook een stille, ongezellige buurt. Na veel zoeken vonden en kochten we een perceel in Amsterdam en hebben daar September van 't vorig jaar onzen intrek genomen. Het is een lief klein huis, met een aardig tuintje, dicht bij het Centraal Station en bij het gebouw der Vrije Universiteit, en het bevalt ons tos dusver uitnemend. Maar het is hier een duur wonen; de huizen zijn zeer prijzig en de belastigen zijn hoog. Men moet er heel wat over hebben, om in Amsterdam te wonen. Doch er staat tegenover, dat ik met college geven niet zoo veel tijd verlies en niet zoo afgezonderd en eenzaam leef. Over het algemeen ben ik blij dat ik niet meer in Kampen ben; het was er wel aardig maar ook zeer afgelegen en kleinsteedsch."

24. Herman Bavinck, *Christelijke wetenschap* (Kampen: Kok, 1904). "Thans zijn wij er getuigen van, hoe velen van de uitnemendste natuurvorschers . . . van het atheisme tot het theisme terugkeeren."

25. Herman Bavinck, *Christelijke wereldbeschouwing: Rede bij de overdracht van the rectoraat aan de Vrije Universiteit te Amsterdam op 20 october 1904* (Kampen: J. H. Bos, 1904), 6; ET: *Christian Worldview*, ed. and trans. Nathaniel Gray Sutanto, James Eglinton, and Cory Brock (Wheaton: Crossway, 2019).

26. Frederik van Eeden, *De kleine Johannes*, 3 vols. (Amsterdam: Elsevier, 1979). See also George Harinck, "The Religious Character of Modernism and the Modern Character of Religion: A Case Study of Herman Bavinck's Engagement with Modern Culture," *Scottish Bulletin of Evangelical Theology* 29, no. 1 (2011): 74. On the reception of Nietzsche in the Netherlands, see Jos Gielen, "Nietzsche in Nederland," *De Nieuwe Taalgids* 37 (1943): 19–26; Jaap Kamphuis, *Nietzsche in Nederland* (Ermelo: Woord en Wereld, 1987).

27. Frederik van Eeden, *De nachtbruid: de gedenkschriften van Vico Muralto* (Amsterdam: Versluys, 1909).

28. Herman Bavinck, *Philosophy of Revelation: A New Annotated Edition*, ed. Cory Brock and Nathaniel Gray Sutanto (Peabody, MA: Hendrickson, 2018), 231.

29. Herman Bavinck, *Hedendaagsche moraal* (Kampen: Kok, 1902), 51. "Inderdaad heeft een man als NIETZSCHE in zijne zedelijke wijsbegeerte slechts uiting gegeven aan wat onbewust leefde in veler hart."

30. Harinck, "Religious Character of Modernism," 74.

31. Bavinck, *Christelijke wereldbeschouwing*, 51; cf. ET in Bavinck, *Christian Worldview*, 73.

32. Herman Bavinck, "De hedendaagsche wereldbeschouwing," *De Vrije Kerk* 9, no. 10 (October 1883): 435–61.

33. Herman Bavinck, "Eene belangrijke apologie van de Christelijke Wereldbeschouwing," review of *The Christian View of God and the World, as Centring in the Incarnation*, by J. Orr, *Theologische Studiën* 12 (1894): 142–52.

34. Harinck, "Religious Character of Modernism," 74.

35. Harinck, "Religious Character of Modernism," 74.

36. Marinus de Jong, "The Heart of the Academy: Herman Bavinck in Debate with Modernity on the Academy, Theology, and the Church," in *The Kuyper Center Review*, vol. 5, *Church and Academy*, ed. Gordon Graham (Grand Rapids: Eerdmans, 2015), 64.

37. Herman Bavinck, "Rede over het christelijk onderwijs" (1881), HBA, folder 331.

38. Herman Bavinck, "Middelbaar onderwijs," *De Bazuin*, August 16, 1901.

39. Adriaan Cornelis Rosendaal, *Naar een school voor de gereformeerde gezindte: Het christelijke onderwijsconcept van het Gereformeerd Schoolverband (1868–1971)* (Hilversum: Verloren, 2006), 102.

40. Herman Groenewegen, "Wetenschap of dogmatisme," *Theologisch Tijdschrift* 37 (1903): 385–424.

41. Groenewegen, "Wetenschap of dogmatisme," 413.

42. Bavinck, *Christelijke wetenschap*, 77.

43. Abraham Kuyper, *Principles of Sacred Theology*, trans. J. Hendrik De Vries (Grand Rapids: Eerdmans, 1954), 155–82.

44. Abraham Kuyper, *De gemeene gratie*, 3 vols. (Leiden: D. Donner, 1902–4); ET: *Common Grace: God's Gift for a Fallen World*, 2 vols., ed. Jordan Ballor and Stephen J. Grabill, trans. Nelson Kloosterman and Ed van der Maas (Bellingham, WA: Lexham Press, 2015–17).

45. Bavinck, *Christelijke wetenschap*, 31. "Omgekeerd zijn Christenen nooit zoo enghartig geweest, dat zij al de wetenschappelijke onderzoekingen, door niet-geloovigen ingesteld, als leugenachtig verwierpen . . . want zij gelooven, dat God, dezelfde God, dien zij in Christus als hun Vader belijden, zijne zon laat opgaan over boozen en goeden en regent over rechtvaardigen en onrechtvaardigen."

46. Herman Bavinck, *Paedagogische beginselen* (Kampen: Kok, 1904), 8.

47. Nelle Bakker, *Kind en karakter: Nederlandse pedagogen over opvoeding in het gezin, 1845–1925* (Amsterdam: Het Spinhuis, 1995), 178.

48. Fr. Siegbertus Rombouts, *Prof. dr. H. Bavinck: Gids bij de studie van zijn paedagogische werken* ('s Hertogenbosch: Malmberg, 1922); Bakker, *Kind en karakter: Nederlandse pedagogen over opvoeding in het gezin 1845–1925*, 310n21.

49. Rommert Casimir, "Bavincks paedagogische beginselen," *School en leven* 8 (1906/1907): 38–42, 87–90, 118–23, 177–83, 193–200, 321–27, 465–67; J. H. Gunning Wzn. [Willemszoon], "Prof. dr. H. Bavinck," *Het Kind* 22 (1921): 321–25.

50. Jakob Brederveld, *Hoofdlijnen der paedagogiek van dr. Herman Bavinck* (Amsterdam: De Standaard, 1927); L. van der Zweep, *De paedagogiek van Bavinck, met een inleiding tot zijn werken* (Kampen: Kok, 1935); L. van Klinken, *Bavinck's paedagogische beginselen* (Meppel: Stenvert, 1936).

51. Dr. H. Bavinckschool, Vlaardingen; Protestants-Christelijke Bavinck Basisschool, The Hague; Protestants-Christelijke Basisschool Dr. H. Bavinckschool, Haarlem; Dr. H. Bavinckschool, Dordrecht; Dr. H. Bavinckschool, Hilversum; Bavinckschool, Bunschoten-Spakenburg.

52. Jakob Brederveld, *Christian Education: A Summary and Discussion of Bavinck's Pedagogical Principles* (Grand Rapids: Smitter, 1928); Cornelius Richard Jaarsma, *The Educational Philosophy of Herman Bavinck: A Textbook in Education* (Grand Rapids: Eerdmans, 1935).

53. Guillaume Groen van Prinsterer, *Ongeloof en revolutie: Eene reeks van historische voorlezingen* (Leiden: S. & J. Luchtmans, 1847); Harry Van Dyke, *Groen van Prinsterer's Lectures on Unbelief and Revolution* (Jordan Station, Ontario: Wedge Publishing Foundation, 1989).

54. Herman Bavinck, "Voorrede," in Groen van Prinsterer, *Ongeloof en revolutie*, viii. "Hij geloofde niet alleen in wetten in de natuur, maar zonder fatalisme ook aan wetten in de zedelijke wereld."

55. Bavinck, "Voorrede," in Groen van Prinsterer, *Ongeloof en revolutie*, vii. "Zij ontmoet altijd bezwaren, die, opgerezen uit den aanleg en de behoefte van den mensch, verbonden aan de natuur en aan de ordeningen Gods."

56. Harinck, "Herman Bavinck and the Neo-Calvinist Concept of the French Revolution," in *Neo-Calvinism and the French Revolution*, ed. James Eglinton and George Harinck (London: Bloomsbury T&T Clark, 2014), 27.

57. James Bratt, *Abraham Kuyper: Modern Calvinist, Christian Democrat* (Grand Rapids: Eerdmans, 2013), 302.

58. George Harinck, "'Als een schelm weggejaagd'? De ARP en de verkiezingen van 1905," in *Het kabinet-Kuyper (1901–1905)*, ed. D. Th. Kuiper and G. J. Schutte (Zoetermeer: Meinema, 2001), 270–301.

59. George Harinck, "De Antirevolutionaire Partij, 1905–1918," in *De Antirevolutionaire Partij, 1829–1980*, ed. George Harinck, Roel Kuiper, and Peter Bak (Hilversum: Verloren, 2001), 123.

60. Herman Bavinck, *Christelijke en Neutrale Staatkunde* (Hilversum: Witzel & Klemkerk, 1905), 39. "Want godsdienst en politiek zijn twee en mogen niet worden vermengd. Vermenging van beide is echter iets anders dan handhaving van hun onderling verband; zoozeer vermenging te mijden is, is ook scheiding verwerpelijk."

61. Bavinck, *Christelijke en Neutrale Staatkunde*, 46. "Het ongeloof is van buiten af geïmporteerd en de neutraliteit is een uitheemsch gewas."

62. Bavinck, *Christelijke en Neutrale Staatkunde*, 5. "Toch neemt dit niet weg, dat wij ons van de veranderingen, door zijn aftreden als onze Voorzitter en door zijn optreden als Minister in onze partij aangebracht, klaar bewust moeten zijn. Wij hebben geen belofte, dat na Groen en Kuyper weer een leider van hun talent en energie ons beschoren zal zijn. Met een persoon staat en valt onze partij niet, omdat zij uit beginselen leeft, die den toets der eeuwen hebben doorstaan."

63. Bavinck, *Christelijke en Neutrale Staatkunde*, 5. "Indien het daarentegen verliest, valt het waarschijnlijk voorgoed in verschillende groepen uiteen."

64. Abraham Kuyper, *Nabij God te zijn: Meditatiën* (Amsterdam: J. R. Vrolijk, 1908); ET: *To Be near unto God*, trans. John Hendrik De Vries (Grand Rapids: Eerdmans, 1918).

65. Abraham Kuyper, *Om de oude wereldzee*, 2 vols. (Amsterdam: Van Holkema & Warendorf, 1907); ET: *On Islam*, ed. James Bratt, trans. Jan van Vliet (Bellingham, WA: Lexham Press, 2018).

66. Rumpff to Bavinck, Kampen, May 15, 1905, in HBA, folder 8. "De vaste overtuiging dat een zekere beweging onder de Kamper studenten aan U bekend is en Uwe sympathie heeft, geeft mij moed U te verzoeken ons—een vriend en ondergeteekende—gelegenheid te geven, met U een onderhoud te hebben over bovengenoemde beweging."

67. Harinck, "De Antirevolutionaire Partij, 1905–1918," 130.

68. Bavinck, quoted in Harinck, "De Antirevolutionaire Partij, 1905–1918," 131. "Het huismanskiesrecht een paedagogische waarde heeft gehad; het hield ons volk terug van revolutionaire paden. Doch nu is 't in gerichten zin niet meer toe te passen; dat zou teruggang wezen en tot ontstemming van velen leiden."

69. Quoted in *Nederlands Dagblad*, March 20, 1971. "Kuyper wilde heersen, mijn vader wilde dienen."

70. Bavinck to Snouck Hurgronje, Amsterdam, January 16, 1906, in *ELV*. "Er gaat daarvan dikwerf en op velen een demoraliserende invloed uit. . . . Zoover ik er aan deed, het alleen behartigde uit plichtbesef, niet uit neiging en lust."

71. Bavinck to Snouck Hurgronje, Amsterdam, January 16, 1906, in *ELV*. "De tijd vliegt voorbij en het leven is hier drukker dan in Kampen."

72. For a thorough overview of these debates, see J. Mark Beach, "Abraham Kuyper, Herman Bavinck, and the 'Conclusions of Utrecht 1905,'" *Mid-America Journal of Theology* 19 (2008): 11–68.

73. Bavinck, *Roeping en wedergeboorte*; ET: *Saved by Grace*. See also Aart Goedvree, *Een ondoordringbaar mysterie: Wedergeboorte volgens Herman Bavinck* (Apeldoorn: Labarum Academic, 2018), 120–43.

74. J. L. Schaver, *The Polity of the Churches* (Chicago: Church Polity Press, 1947), 2:34–37.

75. James Hutton Mackay, *Religious Thought in Holland during the Nineteenth Century* (London: Hodder & Stoughton, 1911), xi.

76. Kuyper, *Encyclopedie der heilige godgeleerdheid*, 3 vols. (Amsterdam: J. A. Wormser, 1894); ET: *Encyclopedia of Sacred Theology: Its Principles* [translation of introduction to vol. 1 and of all of vol. 2], trans. J. Hendrik de Vries (New York: Scribner, 1898), 3:389–90.

77. Bavinck to Snouck Hurgronje, Amsterdam, June 1, 1905, in *ELV*. "Alleen hoop ik, dat de achtergebleven Theologische School spoedig naar hier kome en met de Vrije Universiteit vereenigd worde; dan zou aan kleine twisten en verdeeldheden in onze Gereformeerde Kerken een einde komen."

78. Herman Bavinck, *Geleerdheid en wetenschap* (Amsterdam: Höveker & Wormser, 1905), 19. "Als God valt, valt alles, waarheid, wetenschap en kunst, natuur en geschiedenis, staat, maatschappij en huisgezin. Want als er geen God is, is er ook geen idee, geen gedachte meer, waarin de dingen rusten en waardoor ze kenbaar zijn. . . . Alwat uit het verleden ons toekomt, is oud en verouderd, niet alleen de godsdienst en het Christendom, maar ook de moraal en de kunst, heel de wijsheid en beschaving der oudheid. Alles moet nieuw opgetrokken worden, op de basis der moderne cultuur: school en wetenschap, huwelijk en gezin, staat en maatschappij, godsdienst en moraal. Aan hervormers is dan ook geen gebrek."

79. Bavinck, *Geleerdheid en wetenschap*, 28. "Ik zou wenschen dat ze meer en meer een centrum worden mocht van echt wetenschappelijk leven en werken, onderzoeken en nadenken. Ze moet eene vereeniging zijn van mannen, straks ook van vrouwen wellicht, die, door éénen geest bezield, zich kenmerken door vastheid van beginsel, ruimte van blik en geloof in de toekomst."

80. Jan de Bruijn, "'Het krankheidsverschijnsel der zich intellectueel man voelende vrouw': De eerste vrouwelijke studenten aan de Vrije Universiteit," in *Ridders van het Recht: De juridische faculteit van de Vrije Universiteit, 1880–2010*, ed. J. de Bruijn, S. Faber, and A. Soeteman (Amsterdam: Prometheus, 2015), 83–92; H. E. S. Woldring, *Een handvol filosofen: Geschiedenis van de filosofiebeoefening aan de Vrije Universiteit in Amsterdam van 1880 tot 2012* (Hilversum: Verloren, 2013), 55–56.

81. *De Heraut*, July 31, 1898. "Het is daarom mijn hartgrondige wensch, dat de Vrije Universiteit voor het meedoen aan een dergelijke *ontvrouwelijking* der vrouw, ten alle tijde bewaard moge blijven; aan het krankheidsverschijnsel der zich intellectueel man voelende vrouw nimmer schuld moge dragen."

82. *Amsterdamsche Kerkbode*, June 24, 1906.

83. Fenna Tjeerdina Lindeboom, *De ontwikkeling van het strafstelsel in Sovjet-Rusland, 1917–1937* (Rotterdam: Libertas Drukkerijen, 1937).

84. Bavinck to Snouck Hurgronje, Amsterdam, June 1, 1905, in *ELV*. "Mijnerzijds stem ik toe, dat de onderstelling, waarop mijne levensbeschouwing rust, namelijk de waarheid der Heilige Schrift, een moeilijk probleem insluit. Ik kan er eigenlijk dit alleen van zeggen: naarmate ik

langer en dieper leef, bemerk ik, dat ik van het gezag der Schrift niet los kan komen, op dezelfde wijze ongeveer, als ik mij niet aan de autoriteit der denk- en der zedewet ontworstelen kan. Soms heb ik er wel eens de neiging toe, om er mede te breken, maar als ik mij zelf dan goed onderzoek, dan hangt dat saam met het booze in mijne menscheliljke natuur, dan zit er altijd iets in wat niet goed is en voor God niet kan bestaan. En omgekeerd, naarmate ik, laat ik het zoo maar zeggen, vromer gestemd ben en beter oogenblikken doorleef, voel ik mij tot aannemen van en onderwerping aan de Schrift volkomen bereid en geneigd, en heb vrede voor mijn hart. Dat is vrij mystiek, maar alle wereld- en levensbeschouwing worstelt naar mij toeschijnt in zulk eene zielservaring, die aan bewust denken en handelen voorafgaat."

85. Bratt, *Abraham Kuyper: Modern Calvinist, Christian Democrat*, 358.

86. Valentijn Hepp, *Dr. Herman Bavinck* (Amsterdam: Ten Have, 1921), 290.

87. Herman Bavinck, *Bilderdijk als denker en dichter* (Kampen: Kok, 1906).

88. Bavinck, *Bilderdijk als denker en dichter*, 7–8. "Maar bovenal, uit de smarten des levens werd bij beiden het heimwee naar licht en harmonie geboren. Ze zagen opwaarts naar het licht, dat met gouden glans inviel in de sombere diepten van het aardsche bestaan. Ze vingen het in de eerste plaats op uit de openbaring Gods in Zijn Woord; Rembrandt en Bilderdijk waren beiden, elk op zijn wijze, leerlingen des Bijbels en vertolkers van voorstellingen en gedachten der Schrift."

89. In 1905, on the basis of his success as a novelist, the *Algemeen Handelsblad* appointed Israël Querido as a cultural critic with a free rein over his subjects. See Alex Rutten, *De Publieke Man: Dr. P. H. Ritter Jnr. als cultuurbemiddelaar in het interbellum* (Hilversum: Literatoren, 2018), 47.

90. Israël Querido, "Letterkundige kroniek," *Algemeen Handelsblad*, October 3, 1906. "Men ziet uit dergelijke beschouwingen, dat dr. Bavinck meer gaf dan een eenzijdige of dorre biografie van Bilderdijk, den mensch, dichter en denker. Daarom kunnen wij dit werk zeer aanbevelen. Hij stelt ons Bilderdijk nog voor in huisgezin, staat en maatschappij, in zijn geschiedbeschouwing, zijn persoonlijkheid, zijn natuurbeschouwing, zijn denkwijzen over godsdienst, zedelijkheid en recht. En al verschilt men ook nog zoozeer in meeningen, beschouwingen en vooral verklaringen van het geestesleven Bilderdijk's van Bavinck, hij heeft in vele opzichten een belangrijk en goed leesbaar boek over dien reus geschreven."

91. Abraham Kuyper, *Bilderdijk en zijn nationale beteekenis* (Amsterdam: Höveker & Wormser, 1906).

92. "Een vergissing van dr. Kuyper," *Algemeen Handelsblad*, October 10, 1906.

93. Bavinck to Hoekstra, Amsterdam, May 1, 1906, in HBA, folder 8. ". . . en ook op het veld van wetenschap den naam des Heeren groot te maken."

94. H. J. Pos, "Levensbericht Tj. de Boer," *Jaarboek der Koninklijke Nederlandse Akademie van Wetenschappen* (Amsterdam: Koninklijke Nederlandse Akademie van Wetenschappen, 1945–46), 215.

95. See, for example, Tjitze de Boer, "Plato en Aristoteles bij de moslims," *Tweemaandelijksch Tijdschrift* 6 (1900): 306–31; *Geschichte der Philosophie im Islam* (Stuttgart: Fr. Frommanns Verlag, 1901); "De Filosofie van Henri Bergson," *De Beweging* 5 (1909): 225–44.

96. Tjitze de Boer, *Nietzsche en de wetenschap* (Amsterdam: Scheltema & Holkema's Boekhandel, 1906).

97. De Boer, *Nietzsche en de wetenschap*, 47.

98. De Boer, *Nietzsche en de wetenschap*, 50. "Allereerst U, Prof. BAVINCK, toen te Kampen, nu te dezer stede, die filosofischen zin in mij wekte."

99. *GD²*, vol. 1. Under the terms of his contract for the 1895 edition, Bavinck had reserved the right to produce a future revision that could be offered to another publisher. In this case, he moved from Bos to Kok. For an overview of responses to the first edition by Ethical theologians, see R. H. Bremmer, *Herman Bavinck als dogmaticus* (Kampen: Kok, 1966), 100–105.

100. Herman Bavinck, "Het Wezen des Christendoms," *Almanak van het studentencorps der Vrije Universiteit voor het jaar 1906* (Amsterdam: Herdes, 1906), 251–77. This essay was

posthumously republished in Dutch and English: "Het wezen des christendoms," in *Verzamelde opstellen op het gebied van godsdienst en wetenschap*, ed. C. B. Bavinck (Kampen: Kok, 1921), 17–34; ET: "The Essence of Christianity," in *Essays on Religion, Science, and Society*, ed. John Bolt, trans. John Vriend and Gerrit Sheeres (Grand Rapids: Baker Academic, 2008), 33–48.

101. Bavinck, "Essence of Christianity," 48.

102. Bruce Pass, "'The Heart of Dogmatics': The Place and Purpose of Christology in the Theological Method of Herman Bavinck" (PhD diss., University of Edinburgh, 2018), 80; C. S. Lewis, *Mere Christianity* (London: Fontana, 1952).

103. Vos to Bavinck, Princeton, February 21, 1906, in *LGV*.

104. Hepp, *Dr. Herman Bavinck*, 296. "9 April . . . Op dezen dag werd ik in de Kon. Akademie van Wet. tot lid verkozen. Ook werden gekozen Boer, Six en Naber."

105. *Nederlandsch Staatscourant*, December 15, 1906.

106. For a summary of Eerdmans's lecture, see "Vergadering van Moderne Theologen," *Algemeen Handelsblad*, May 3, 1905.

107. *De Heraut*, November 10, 1907. "Prof. Eerdmans weet van de vroegere en de nieuwe Gereformeerde Dogmatiek blikbaar niets af. Hij spreekt hier als een blinde over de kleuren. Kuenen en Scholten zouden zich nooit zoo onvoorzichtig hebben uitgelaten. Maar het geslacht der epigonen heeft van de polemiek blikbaar een andere opvatting. Het is droef, deze decadentie te aanschouwen."

108. Herman Bavinck, *Modernisme en orthodoxie* (Kampen: Kok, 1911); ET: "Herman Bavinck's *Modernisme en Orthodoxie*: A Translation," trans. Bruce Pass, *Bavinck Review* 7 (2016): 63–114.

109. Hepp, *Dr. Herman Bavinck*, 301. "Ik bleef thuis om mijn lezingen voor Amerika te maken."

110. *De Grondwet*, August 11, 1908.

111. "Generale Synode," *De Bazuin*, August 28, 1909. "Werken ook als de Dogmatiek van Dr. Bavinck moeten meer bekend worden."

112. "Generale Synode," *De Bazuin*, August 28, 1909. "Wij voelen ons nog altijd zoo klein; toch zijn wij ook cosmopolitisch van richting *en waardeeren zeer* den band met onze broederen. Er is een neerwaartsche richting in de crisis, die doorgemaakt wordt. De grondslagen der waarheid worden door velen losgelaten. Daarom waakt, staat vast. Bovendien zijn er ook goede redenen ons te verblijden over uwe komst. De overtuiging wordt algemeen, dat 't materialisme heeft teleurgesteld; er is behoefte aan religie. De opwekkingen hebben dus zekere waarde, waarover wij ons met u hebben te verblijden. Dan is er opwaking voor het sociale leven, waaraan wij krachtig moeten mede doen. Eindelijk er is krachtige opleving ter beoefening van de Buitenlandsche Zending. Wij moeten ook langs deze lijn de waarheid des Christendoms meer en meer doen blijken. Hierin kunnen wij meer van u dan gij van ons leeren."

113. *De Heraut*, October 18, 1908. "De reis van Prof. Bavinck naar Amerika op uitnodiging der Princeton universiteit, haalde de banden tusschen Amerika en onze Hogeschool weer nauwer aan en zal voor de doorwerking der Gereformeerde beginselen in het zoo machtige en invloedrijke Amerika zeker goede winste afwerpen."

114. "Vertrek van prof. H. Bavinck," *De Telegraaf*, August 30, 1908. "Ook was ds. J. Bavinck, niettegenstaande zijn hoogen leeftijd (82 jaar), nog bij dit afscheid tegenwoordig."

115. Hepp, *Dr. Herman Bavinck*, 301. "We hebben op deze zeereis van alles bijgewoond, regen, wind, storm, prachtig weer, nevel, wolkensomberheid, onweer, bruinvisschen, noorderlicht."

116. Hepp, *Dr. Herman Bavinck*, 301. "Enorme drukte (hurry) . . . geen rust om tot zichzelf te komen. Voor zieken, gebrekkigen geen plaats. Stad is berekend op sterke zenuwen. Overdreven, schreeuwende reclame. 't Geraas . . . is vermoeiend, zenuwverzwakkend."

117. Hepp, *Dr. Herman Bavinck*, 301. "Dat gaat hier grappig, want van een contract maken is er geen sprake. Herman moet het geheel in vertrouwen overgeven of er iets zal overblijven en daar moeten de vrienden zich nog voor uitsloven om te corrigeren."

118. Vos to Bavinck, Princeton, January 7, 1909, in *LGV*. For commentary on the editorial and translation choices of Vos, Warfield, Steffens, and Dosker, see Cory Brock and Gray Sutanto, "Introduction to the Annotated Edition," in *Philosophy of Revelation: A New Annotated Edition*, by Herman Bavinck, ed. Cory Brock and Gray Sutanto (Peabody, MA: Hendrickson, 2018), xxxi.

119. Hepp, *Dr. Herman Bavinck*, 303. "Mijnheer is een grappige gezellige man, die nooit uitgeput is in geestigheden. Een heel ander type van professor als vader."

120. Theodore Roosevelt, Theodore Roosevelt Papers, series 9: Desk Diaries, 1901–1909, *1907, Jan. 1–1908, Dec. 31; 1909, Jan. 7–Feb. 18*, Library of Congress, Washington, DC. "15.00. Prof & Mrs Bavinck reg. The Netherlands Minister."

121. In 1909, following the end of Roosevelt's presidency, Bavinck compiled a short summary of Roosevelt's time in office. See Herman Bavinck, "Roosevelt's Presidentschap," manuscript, 1909, HBA, folder 67.

122. Bavinck, *Philosophy of Revelation: A New Annotated Edition*, 17.

123. Gordon Graham, "Bavinck, Nietzsche, and Secularization," in *The Kuyper Center Review*, vol. 2, *Revelation and Common Grace*, ed. John Bowlin (Grand Rapids: Eerdmans, 2011), 18.

124. Hepp, *Dr. Herman Bavinck*, 303. ". . . onvermoeid om preeken te horen, doch voor wetenschappelijke lezingen is geen publiek te vinden. Al doet men nog zoo zijn best om eenvoudig en helder te zijn, van geleerdheid of om wat moeite te doen iets in te denken zijn ze bang."

125. Hepp, *Dr. Herman Bavinck*, 306. "De kinderen zijn ruw, ongemanierd, b.v. jonge man wordt niet voorgesteld, loopt zonder groeten de deur uit. Meisje groet niet, lacht ander uit, werpt in gezelschap 't eene been over 't andere, hangt voorover enz., zeer vrij, onafhankelijk, maar ruw onbeschaafd, onverschillig."

126. Herman Bavinck, *Het christelijk huisgezin* (Kampen: Kok, 1908); ET: *The Christian Family*, trans. Nelson Kloosterman (Grand Rapids: Christian's Library Press, 2012).

127. Bavinck to Snouck Hurgronje, Amsterdam, January 3, 1909, in *ELV*. "Zaterdag 12 december bezocht ik hem nog even en sprak enkele woorden met hem, niet denkende dat het zoo spoedig gedaan zou zijn. Maar 's maandags 14 december overleed hij reeds, in den ouderdom van ruim vijfenveertig jaren."

128. Bavinck gave talks on America in Scheveningen (*Haagsche Courant*, May 19, 1909), Appingedam (*Nieuwsblad van het Noorden*, March 4, 1909), and Assen (*Provinciale Drentsche en Asser Courant*, March 23, 1909).

129. Hepp, *Dr. Herman Bavinck*, 309. "Een zuidelijke zei: negers zijn geen mensen. Kanaan ging naar Lod en nam zich daar een vrouw. Die vrouw was een aap."

130. See, for example, George Harinck, "'Wipe Out Lines of Division (Not Distinctions)': Bennie Keet, Neo-Calvinism and the Struggle against Apartheid," *Journal of Reformed Theology* 11, no. 1–2 (2017): 83–85; Jessica Joustra, "An Embodied *Imago Dei*: How Herman Bavinck's Understanding of the Image of God Can Help Inform Conversations on Race," *Journal of Reformed Theology* 11, no. 1–2 (2017): 9–23.

131. Herman Bavinck, "Indrukken van Amerika" (ca. 1909), HBA, folder 66. "Blanken beschuldigen negers van allerlei slechte eigensch. (diefstal v. kippen . . . zinnelijkheid, lynchen; drankzucht, luiheid.) Ik weet niet of blanken met hun prostitutie en alcohol en mammonisme beter zijn."

132. *Rotterdamsch Nieuwsblad*, March 13, 1909. "Ja, in dien toekomst schuilt voor Amerika werkelijk een gevaar—zei spr.—en in de toekomst zal er ongetwijfeld een strijd tusschen zwart en wit gestreden worden, een heete strijd, aangewakkerd door sterke antipathie wederzijds."

133. Bavinck's notes referenced W. E. B. Du Bois's "Die Negerfrage in den Vereinigten Staaten," *Archiv für Sozialwissenschaft und Sozialpolitik* 22 (1906): 31–79. See Herman Bavinck, "Negers" (manuscript, ca. 1909), HBA, folder 67.

134. Hepp, *Dr. Herman Bavinck*, 309. "Beecher Stowe's Negerhut zeer eenzijdig."

135. *Provinciale Drentsche en Asser Courant*, March 23, 1909.

136. *Rotterdamsch Nieuwsblad*, March 13, 1909. "Er schuilt een groot gevaar in de emigratie van heden voor Amerika."

137. Bavinck, "Indrukken van Amerika." "Is Amerika een model land en volk? Wij weten 't niet. Geen enkel toestand is daar settled. Men weet niet, wat ervan worden zal, hoe het zich ontwikkelen zal. Het is alles in the making. Er is the glory of the imperfect, the charm of the impossible."

138. Bavinck, "Indrukken van Amerika." "Evenals de Engelschen voelen zich de Am. een wereldvolk. Save America and you save the world. Door de immigratie zijn de V. St. geworden in geheel eenigen zin the most foreign country and the greatest mission field on the globe. Alle volken hebben hun verwanten in Amerika, en van hen uit gaat de zending voort naar alle deelen der aarde. Evangelisation of the world in this generation, in this century."

139. Brian Stanley, "Africa through European Christian Eyes: The World Missionary Conference, Edinburgh, 1910," in *African Identities and World Christianity in the Twentieth Century*, ed. Klaus Koschorke and Jens Holger Schjørring (Wiesbaden: Harassowitz Verlag, 2005), 165–66.

140. Snouck Hurgronje to Bavinck, Leiden, December 30, 1908, in *ELV*. "Uwe critiek van verschillende stelsels, wereld- en levensbeschouwingen schijnt mij bijzonder scherp en krachtig. . . . Ik ben sceptisch, zonder van scepsis of agnosticisme een systeem te willen maken. Zwak schijnt mij altijd uw standpunt ten aanzien der Schrift, eensdeels omdat daarbij de reusachtige bezwaren, die de meest behoudende en voorzichtige historische critiek oplevert, min of meer genegeerd of weggedoezeld worden; anderdeels omdat het objectief karakter van openbaringen, die door menschenmond gesproken, door menschenhand geschreven, door menscheuitspraak gecanoniseerd, dan toch ten slotte weer subjectief wordt. . . . Neem deze ontboezeming voor hetgeen zij zijn wil: eene openhartige verklaring betreffende een capitaal verschil van iemand, die in waardeering van uw werk voor geen ander onderdoet."

141. Bavinck to Snouck Hurgronje, Amsterdam, January 3, 1909, in *ELV*. "Uwe scepsis begrijp ik. Maar wijl mijne lezingen ook voor anderen dan geestverwanten bestemd zijn, heb ik mij nergens op het gezag der Heilige Schrift als zoodanig beroepen, maar heb ik alleen gezegd: a) zoo en zoo ziet de mensch en de wereld er uit. Zonder eene hoogere en genadige kracht gaat zij te gronde, en b) nu komt daar uit de mond van profeten, Christus en de apostelen, waarvan de kern is: zulk een almachtige en genadige wil *is* er. . . . Dat aan te nemen en als waarheid te erkennen, is zeker eene geloofsdaad, maar waartoe heel de wereld en vooral ons eigen hart ons dringt."

142. Marcus A. Brownson, "The Calvin Celebration in Geneva, and Calvin's City as It Is Today: Personal Impressions," *Journal of the Presbyterian Historical Society (1901–1930)* 5, no. 4 (December 1909): 164–74.

143. Johan de Niet and Herman Paul, "Collective Memories of John Calvin in Dutch Neo-Calvinism," in *Sober, Strict, and Scriptural: Collective Memories of John Calvin, 1800–2000*, ed. Johan de Niet, Herman Paul, and Bart Wallet (Leiden: Brill, 2009), 83.

144. Antonius van der Linde, *Michael Servet: een brandoffer der gereformeerde inquisitie* (Groningen: P. Noordhoff, 1891).

145. Herman Bavinck, "Calvin and Common Grace," in *Calvin and the Reformation. Four Studies*, ed. E. Doumergue, A. Lang, H. Bavinck and B. B. Warfield (New York: Revell, 1909), 99–130; "Calvin and Common Grace," trans. Geerhardus Vos, *Princeton Theological Review* 7 (1909): 437–65.

146. For documentation around his lecture in London, see HBA, folder 8. For accounts of his lectures on Calvin in the Netherlands, see *Nieuwsblad van het Noorden*, April 9, 1909; *Gereformeerd Jongelingsblad*, May 21, 1909.

147. Herman Bavinck, *Johannes Calvijn* (Kampen: Kok, 1909); ET: "John Calvin: A Lecture on the Occasion of his 400th Birthday, July 10, 1509–1909," trans. John Bolt, *Bavinck Review* 1 (2010): 57–85.

148. "Johannes Calvijn," *De Bazuin*, July 16, 1909. "Iets nieuws heeft Dr. Bavinck uiteraard niet gegeven."

149. Snouck Hurgronje to Bavinck, Leiden, July 8, 1909, in *ELV*. "Het is eene huldiging van Calvijns werk, minder geruchtmakend dan de Geneefsche."

150. Hepp, *Dr. Herman Bavinck*, 301.

151. For correspondence from these years, see HBA, folder 10. Archibald Thomas Robertson, *A Short Grammar of the Greek New Testament: For Students Familiar with the Elements of Greek* (New York: Hodder and Stoughton, 1909).

152. Kuyper to Bavinck, Amsterdam, November 9, 1909, HBA, folder 9. "Zeer mijn dank er voor. Het was mij zoo goed, dat gij ook zijn sociale beteekenis voor het volksleven accentueert."

153. *GD²*, vol. 2 (Kampen: Kok, 1908); *GD²*, vol. 3 (Kampen: Kok, 1910); *GD²*, vol. 4 (Kampen: Kok, 1911).

154. Herman Bavinck, *Magnalia Dei* (Kampen: Kok, 1909), 2; ET: *Our Reasonable Faith*, trans. Henry Zylstra (Grand Rapids: Eerdmans, 1956). "Trouwens, die oude werken zijn ook niet meer van onzen tijd. Het verschil van taal en stijl, van gedachtengang en zeggingswijze maakt ze vreemd voor ons. De vraagstukken, die men vroeger als de gewichtigste beschouwde, hebben voor ons geheel of grootendeels hunne beteekenis verloren. Andere belangen, door hen niet genoemd, dringen zich thans op den voorgrond. Wij zijn kinderen van een nieuwen tijd en leven in een andere eeuw. . . . Hoeveel goeds Frankens *Kern*, Marcks *Merg* en Brakels *Redelijke Godsdienst* in vroeger dagen hebben uitegewerkt, ze zijn thans niet meer tot nieuw leven te brengen, spreken het jonger geslacht niet meer toe en wekken onwillekeurig de gedachte, dat het Christendom bij deze eeuw niet meer past. Daarom is er dringend behoefte aan een werk, dat in de plaats van dezen arbeid der vaderen treden kan en de oude waarheid voordraagt in een vorm, die beantwoordt aan de eischen van dezen tijd."

155. Bavinck, *Magnalia Dei*, 3. "En onder hen heb ik weer bij voorkeur gedacht aan al die jonge mannen en vrouwen."

156. Herman Bavinck, "De psychologie van het kind," *Paedagogisch tijdschrift* 1 (1909): 105–17.

157. G. J. van Klinken, "Lucas Lindeboom: Voorman van de christelijke zorg," in *Bevlogen theologen: Geëngageerde predikanten in de negentiende en twintigste eeuw*, ed. Paul E. Werkman and Roelof Enno van der Woude (Hilversum: Verloren, 2012), 123–46.

158. Anthonie Honig, "Algemeene vergadering der Vereeniging tot Christelijke Verzorging van Krankzinnigen in Nederland," *De Bazuin*, October 22, 1907. See also Lucas Lindeboom, *Gereformeerde stichtingen van barmhartigheid in Nederland* (Kampen: Kok, 1927), 12.

159. Bavinck to Lindeboom, Amsterdam, November 28, 1909, HBA, folder 9. "Hooggeachte Voorzitter, zeer vriendelijk zeg ik u dank voor de toezending namens het Bestuur van de gedachtenisrede, door u bij gelegenheid van 't 25 j. bestaan dier V. uitgesproken. Zij geeft een kostelijk overzicht van hare geschiedenis, en kan van vele zegeningen melding maken. Moge ze dienstbaar zijn aan de bevordering van de belangen der Vereeniging, en deze, onder 's Heeren gunst, hoe langer zoo meer tot een zegen worden voor ons volk, gelijk zij het nu reeds 25 jaren in hooge mate was. Hoogachtend Uwdw. H. Bavinck."

160. *Gereformeerd Jongelingsblad*, January 24, 1908. "Bavinck en Lindeboom verschillen. Maar beide arbeiden ze uit eenzelfde geloof en uit dezelfde beginselen." See also *De Heraut*, January 12, 1908; *Amsterdamsche Kerkbode*, January 18, 1908.

161. *De Bazuin*, January 8, 1904. "Daarin wordt het overgaan van Dr. Bavinck van Kampen naar Amsterdam aangemerkt als een rechtmatige staf op de eenzijdigheid en kortzichtigheid van hen, die zich scharen om de minderheid der Arnhemsche Synode. . . . Ten slotte: Dr. W. eindigt met de opmerking, dat Dr. Bavinck heenging om aan de Vrije in een rijk en heerlijk wetenschappelijk centrum te bloeien en voor stampvolle zalen zijn prachtige colleges te geven, terwijl de broeders der minderheid thans een vrij verlaten School hebben. We weten dit, en onze ziel is er over bedroefd. We hadden het zoo gaarne anders gezien."

162. "Een Gedenkdag," *De Bazuin*, January 17, 1908. "En hoe gezegend werkte hij niet door zijne vele geschriften? Onze ruimte laat niet toe ze alle te noemen. Reeds zijne *Geref. Dogmatiek* zegt veel en genoeg. . . . God spare hem nog lang ten rijken zegen voor Kerk en wetenschap!"

163. "Oude Doopsgezinde Geslachten. III. Bavink," *De Zondagsbode*, September 5, 1909.

164. *Algemeen Handelsblad*, November 30, 1909; "Uitvaart van ds. J. Bavinck," *Provinciale Overijsselsche en Zwolsche Courant*, December 2, 1909; Harm Bouwman, "Ds. J. Bavinck," *De Bazuin*, December 3, 1909; *De Grondwet*, December 21, 1909; "Uit Holland," *De Volksvriend*, December 23, 1909.

165. *De Bazuin*, December 10, 1909.

166. Hepp, *Dr. Herman Bavinck*, 311. "'t Was droevige en aangename dag. Belangstelling was treffend."

Chapter 10 Showing His Colors: 1910–20

1. Herman Bavinck, "The Reformed Churches in the Netherlands," *Princeton Theological Review* 8 (1910): 433–60.

2. Bavinck, "Reformed Churches in the Netherlands," 459–60.

3. Anthonie Honig, *De Zending en de scholen* (Zeist: n.p., 1900).

4. *Concept-Zendingsorde voor de Gereformeerde Kerken in Nederland* (n.p., ca. 1902); see also L. Adriaanse, *De nieuwe koers in onze zending, of Toelichting op de zendingsorde* (Amsterdam: Kirchner, 1903).

5. J. P. P. Valeton Jr., *De Nederlandsche zendingsschool* (Utrecht: n.p., 1905), 2, 5. "En wij, wij moeten haar de mannen kunnen aanbieden, die voor die toestanden berekend zijn, Christenen, die den Javaan een Javaan, den Papoea een Papoea, den Alfoer een Alfoer kunnen en willen worden."

6. Bavinck, "Reformed Churches in the Netherlands," 460.

7. Herman Bavinck, "Dr. Bavinck over de zending," *Het Kerkblad der Gereformeerde Kerk in Zuid-Afrika* 12, no. 237 (October 1, 1910): 5–6.

8. For an overview of the history of missionary work in the Reformed Churches in the Netherlands written in this period, see J. H. Landwehr, *Kort overzich van de geschiedenis der Gereformeerde Kerken in Nederland, 1795 tot heden* (Zwolle: Tulp, 1908), 85–93.

9. Quoted in C. Lindeboom, "Speciale opleiding voor de zending?," *De Bazuin*, November 4, 1910. "Speciaal wat de bestudeering van den Islam en van het Heidendom in Indië aangaat. Het Gereformeerde beginsel is hier van zoo groote beteekenis."

10. Lindeboom, "Speciale opleiding voor de zending?" "Nu heeft Prof. Bavinck in zijne rede op den Universiteitsdag van dit jaar bepleit, dat aan de Vrije Universiteit een nieuwe leerstoel zou worden gevestigd, bepaaldelijk met het oog op de Zending en den Evangelisatie-arbeid."

11. Harm Bouwman, "Een leerstoel voor de zending," *De Bazuin*, September 9, 1910. "Prof. Bavinck heeft op den laatst-gehouden Universiteitsdag gepleit voor het instellen van een leerstoel voor de Zending aan de Vrije Universiteit. Terecht heeft hij aangetoond, dat ja de Zendings-geest, de Zendingsliefde en de Zendingsijver ook in onze kringen ontwaakt is, maar dat wij nog maar aan het begin staan van onzen arbeid, dat ons ontbreekt een man, die geheel voor de Zending left, aan haar al zijne krachten wijdt en de aanstaande predikanten voorlicht en met liefde voor de Zending bezielt."

12. H. Dijkstra, *De Macedoniër*, September 1910, quoted in Bouwman, "Een leerstoel voor de zending." "Dat Prof. Bavinck over grooten invloed beschikt lijdt geen twijfel. . . . Twijfel ik niet of wij hebben binnen enkele Jaren eenen leerstoel; misschien wel twee, want de Kerken zullen dan te Kampen wel niet achterblijven."

13. "Schoolnieuws," *Het nieuws van de dag: kleine courant*, November 9, 1910.

14. *Provinciale Drentsche en Asser Courant*, February 24, 1911.

15. Willem Geesink, "In Memoriam: Petrus Abraham Elisa Sillevis Smitt," *Almanak van het Studentencorps a/d Vrije-Universiteit, 1919* (Amsterdam: Herdes, 1919), 68.

16. *Amsterdamsche Kerkbode*, April 30, 1911. "De zendingsdag van de classe Amsterdam zal D.V. gehouden worden op Woensdag 17 Mei e.k. Des namiddags 2 uur zal er in het gebouw van de Maatschappij voor den Werkenden Stand eene bijeenkomst plaats hebben toegangkelijk voor alle belangstellenden, zoowel vrouwen als mannen, waarin Prof. Dr. H. Bavinck zal spreken over de beteekenis der Zending voor onzen tijd."

17. *Amsterdamsche Kerkbode*, May 21, 1911. "Want de Europeesche cultuur kan voor de volken der aarde een zegen zijn, maar zij kan nu ook worden tot een vloek. Als zij, gelijk zij feitelijk doet, den eigen godsdienst der heidenen ondermijnt en hun geen ander en beter geloof in de plaats geeft, verarmt zij hen innerlijk meer dan dat zij hen verrijkt."

18. *Amsterdamsche Kerkbode*, May 21, 1911. "Als deze machtige volken onze beschaving overnemen zonder het Christendom, waarvan zij de vrucht is, ontleenen zij aan onszelven de wapenen, waarmede zij in de toekomst ons bestrijden. En te ernstiger dreigt dit gevaar, wijl Boeddhisme en Mohammedanisme in den jongsten tijd tot een nieuw leven ontwaken en als in het geheim zich toerusten tot een strijd tegen het Christelijke geloof."

19. *Amsterdamsche Kerkbode*, May 21, 1911. "Het schijnt, alsof het eigenlijke Heidendom in de twintigste eeuw allengs geheel verdwijnen zal en dat dan de wereldworsteling zal aanvangen tusschen Boeddha, Mohammed en Christus. Daarom is de zending voor alle Christenen, van wat belijdenis zij ook zijn, in deze eeuw een dure plicht."

20. *De Heraut*, December 17, 1911. "Rekent men toch met het feit, dat dit boek geen stichtelijk boek is, maar een studieboek, dat alleen voor wetenschappelijk gevormden is geschreven; dat de prijs van zulk een werk maakt, dat het zeker niet binnen het bereik van ieders beurs valt."

21. Herman Bavinck, *Handleiding bij het onderwijs in den christelijken godsdienst* (Kampen: Kok, 1913). ". . . allen, die door middel van een niet te uitgebreid en niet te kostbaar leesboek kennis willen maken met den hoofdinhoud van onze Christelijke, Gereformeerde geloofsbelijdenis."

22. Bernardus Eerdmans, *"Orthodox" verweer* (Leiden: S.C. van Doesburgh, 1911).

23. Herman Bavinck, *Modernisme en orthodoxie* (Kampen: Kok, 1911); ET: "Herman Bavinck's *Modernisme en Orthodoxie*: A Translation," trans. Bruce Pass, *Bavinck Review* 7 (2016): 63–114.

24. Bavinck, "Herman Bavinck's *Modernisme en Orthodoxie*," 79.

25. Bavinck, "Herman Bavinck's *Modernisme en Orthodoxie*," 79–80.

26. Bavinck, "Herman Bavinck's *Modernisme en Orthodoxie*," 82.

27. *RD*, 1:116–20. See also Kuyper, *Encyclopedie der heilige godgeleerdheid* (Amsterdam: J. A. Wormser, 1894), 2:276–77.

28. R. H. Bremmer, *Herman Bavinck als dogmaticus* (Kampen: Kok, 1966), 115–47.

29. R. H. Bremmer, *Herman Bavinck en zijn tijdgenoten* (Kampen: Kok, 1966), 248.

30. Bremmer, *Herman Bavinck en zijn tijdgenoten*, 248.

31. Valentijn Hepp, *Dr. Herman Bavinck* (Amsterdam: Ten Have, 1921), 317–18. "Zelfs deed hij eenige jaren vóór zijn dood de belangrijkste dogmatische werken, waaronder vooral oude Gereformeerde theologie, van de hand, 'want,' zei hij mij, 'ik doe daaraan toch niet meer.'" *Nota bene*: the Dutch idiom in question, "van de hand doen," could denote either "to give away" or "to sell."

32. For interaction with this, see John Bolt, "Grand Rapids between Kampen and Amsterdam: Herman Bavinck's Reception and Influence in North America," *Calvin Theological Journal* 38, no. 2 (2003): 266.

33. Hepp, *Dr. Herman Bavinck*, 321–22.

34. Hepp, *Dr. Herman Bavinck*, 319. "Er werd gefluisterd, dat hij het specifiek-Gereformeerd goeddeels zou hebben ingeruild tegen het algemeen christelijke."

35. Herman Bavinck, "Het Wezen des Christendoms," in *Almanak van het studentencorps der Vrije Universiteit voor het jaar 1906* (Amsterdam: Herdes, 1906), 251–77; reprinted in *Verzamelde opstellen op het gebied van godsdienst en wetenschap*, ed. C. B. Bavinck (Kampen: Kok,

1921), 17–34; ET: "The Essence of Christianity," in *Essays on Religion, Science, and Society*, ed. John Bolt, trans. John Vriend and Gerrit Sheeres (Grand Rapids: Baker Academic, 2008), 33–48.

36. George Harinck, "'Eén uur lang is het hier brandend licht en warm geweest': Bavinck en Kampen," in *Ontmoetingen met Bavinck*, ed. George Harinck and Gerrit Neven (Barneveld: De Vuurbaak, 2006), 110.

37. Bavinck, *RD*, 2:501; see also D. A. Young, "The Reception of Geology in the Dutch Reformed Tradition: The Case of Herman Bavinck (1854–1921)," in *Geology and Religion: A History of Harmony and Hostility*, ed. M. Kölbl-Ebert, Geological Society Special Publication no. 310 (London: Geological Society, 2009), 289–300.

38. Bavinck, "Essence of Christianity," 48.

39. Bavinck, *Handleiding bij het onderwijs*, 245–51. Like the four volumes of the *Reformed Dogmatics*, this work is structured around (i) prolegomena (the knowledge of God, general and special revelation), (ii) God and creation (the essence and triunity of God, creation and providence, anthropology), (iii) sin and salvation (sin and death, the covenant of grace, the person and work of Christ), and (iv) the Holy Spirit, the church, and the new creation (pneumatology, effectual calling, the church and means of grace, and the consummation of the world).

40. C. B. Bavinck, "Voorrede bij den tweeden druk," in *Magnalia Dei*, by Herman Bavinck, 2nd ed. (Kampen: Kok, 1931), 1. ". . . die gevonden is in een envelope, met het bijschrift: 'bestemd voor een eventueelen herdruk van Magnalia.'"

41. Herman Bavinck, *Our Reasonable Faith*, trans. Henry Zylstra (Grand Rapids: Eerdmans, 1956).

42. Abraham Kuyper Jr., *Van de Kennisse Gods* (Amsterdam: W. Kirchner, 1907).

43. *De Heraut*, July 7, 1907; *Gereformeerd Jongelingsblad*, August 2, 1907.

44. Willem Jan Aalders, "In Memoriam: Dr. H. Bavinck," *Stemmen des tijds* (1921): 135. ". . . zijn onuitroeibare behoefte aan verzoening, aan harmonie, aan synthese, waarvoor het woord zou kunnen gevormd worden, als het niet reeds bestond: homo sum et nil humanum a me alienum puto."

45. Bavinck to Snouck Hurgronje, Kampen, December 22, 1888, in *ELV*. "Ik weet wel, het ideaal waar ik naar streef is hier onbereikbaar, maar mensch te zijn in den vollen natuurlijken zin van dat woord en dan als mensch in alles een kind van God—dat lijkt me 't schoonst van alles. Daar streef ik naar."

46. Hepp, *Dr. Herman Bavinck*, 321.

47. On this point, Bremmer cites W. J. Aalders's statement, "I doubt strongly whether Dr. Bavinck, in his last years, still accepted everything he had written in the first edition of his dogmatics" (*Herman Bavinck als dogmaticus*, 377), to convey that Aalders suspected that Bavinck eventually distanced himself from his early dogmatic work. Aalders's article, though, recognized that the eventual shape of Bavinck's work in the Amsterdam years reflected the realization of an early commitment to Reformed principles that worked themselves out in the production of dogmatics as well as of Reformed accounts of pedagogy, poetry, psychology, and so on (Aalders, "In Memoriam: Dr. H. Bavinck," 137). The handling of Aalders's writings on Bavinck found in Hepp is more extensive and nuanced than that of Bremmer (Hepp, *Dr. Herman Bavinck*, 324).

48. Hepp, *Dr. Herman Bavinck*, 336.

49. Bavinck to Snouck Hurgronje, Amsterdam, September 1, 1911, in *ELV*. ". . . de benoeming was voor mij een totale verrassing, omdat ik al sedert een paar jaren van politiek terrein me geheel teruggetrokken had."

50. Petrus Kasteel, *Abraham Kuyper* (Kampen: Kok, 1938), 318. "De leeuw was ouder geworden en de welpen kozen eigen wegen."

51. *Kuyper-Gedenkboek 1907* ('s Gravenhage: n.p., 1908).

52. *Kuyper-Gedenkboek 1907*, 25. "Want al gingt Gij naar het tijdperk der Reformatie, het was U toch nooit om repristinatie van het verleden te doen. Gij naamt het verleden wel in U op, maar om het tot een bestanddeel van het heden en van de toekomst te maken."

53. *Kuyper-Gedenkboek 1907*, 22. ". . . want Gij hebt niet alleen persoonlijk voor u zelven eene rijke geschiedenis achter u, maar Gij hebt de geschiedenis van uw leven door uw woord en uw daad ook rijk voor anderen, voor heel ons volk gemaakt."

54. *Kuyper-Gedenkboek 1907*, 98. "Terecht heeft Dr. Bavinck opgemerkt, dat alleen wie *niets* doet, geen fouten maakt."

55. *Kuyper-Gedenkboek 1907*, 25, 39. A report in the *Provinciale Geldersche en Nijmeegsche Court* (October 30, 1907) noted that Bavinck had given a "great speech that honored and thanked the jubilaris [the one whose jubilee is being celebrated]."

56. "Feestrede van Prof. Dr. H. Bavinck," in *Gedenkboek: Opgedragen door het feestcomité aan Prof. Dr. A. Kuyper bij zijn vijf en twintigjarig jubileum als hoofdredacteur van "De Standaard": 1872 1 April 1897* (Amsterdam: G. J. C. Herdes, 1897), 38–52.

57. "Feestrede van Prof. Dr. H. Bavinck," 51. "Zoolang Dr. Kuyper Redacteur van *De Standaard* is—en God geve, het zij lange nog!—zoolang is het principieel belang van de Antirevolutionaire partij in de handen van *De Standaard* veilig."

58. Bavinck to Kuyper, Amsterdam, April 15, 1908, quoted in Bremmer, *Herman Bavinck en zijn tijdgenoten*, 231. "Ik kan niet gelooven, dat Gij die pogingen uitlokt en steunt. . . . Misschien dienen zij voor een tijd de macht der partij; maar aan haar zedelijk gehalte brengen zij eene onberekenbare schade toe."

59. Bavinck to Kuyper, Amsterdam, September 17, 1911, quoted in Bremmer, *Herman Bavinck en zijn tijdgenoten*, 233. "Ik heb ze daarom, in het vertrouwen op den God mijns levens, aangenomen, en bid Hem, dat ik in dat hooge staatscollege nog iets, al is het weinig, tot eer van Zijn naam en tot zegen van ons volk kan doen. Mocht dat niet het geval zijn en de taak te zwaar op mijn schouders wezen, dan hoop ik den moed te ontvangen, om eene plaats te verlaten waar ik niet behoor."

60. James Bratt, *Abraham Kuyper: Modern Calvinist, Christian Democrat* (Grand Rapids: Eerdmans, 2013), 351.

61. *Handelingen van de Eerste Kamer der Staten-Generaal*, December 29, 1911, 127. "Mijnheer de Voorzitter! . . . Onze modern cultuur . . . van het Christendom . . . niet los te maken is."

62. *Handelingen van de Eerste Kamer der Staten-Generaal*, December 29, 1911, 127. "Ik geloof, dat hij in die verwachting zich zal teleurgesteld zien, hoe verder wij de toekomst ingaan."

63. *De Telegraaf*, December 30, 1911. "En, tenslotte, prof. Bavinck verraste ons door een zeer bijzondere gemakkelijkheid van spreken, zoodat hij in dit opzicht heel wat sympathieker is dan z'n ambtgenoot dr. Woltjer, die altijd in een droeven, somberen klaag-toon, en vaak héél onduidelijk, te oreeren staat." This speech was also reported on in *Algemeen Handelsblad*, December 31, 1911.

64. *De Preanger-Bode*, December 31, 1911; *De Sumatra post*, January 2, 1912.

65. Herman Bavinck and Johanna Bavinck-Schippers, addressee unknown, Amsterdam, November 10, 1912, HBA, folder 9.

66. Herman Bavinck, *Het Christendom* (Baarn: Hollandia, 1912); ET: "Christ and Christianity," trans. A. A. Pfanstiehl, *Biblical Review* 1 (1916): 214–36 [this article is not an exact translation]. For the history of the search for the "essence of Christianity," see Hans Wagenhammer, *Das Wesen des Christentums* (Mainz: Matthias Grünewald, 1973).

67. Ernst Troeltsch, *Gesammelte schriften* (Aalen: Scientia Verlag, 1962), 2:391.

68. Bavinck, *Het Christendom*, 11.

69. Bavinck, *Het Christendom*, 5. "Daar bestaan inderdaad talloos vele formuleeringen van het wezen des Christendoms, de Grieksche, de Roomsche, de Luthersche, de Gereformeerde enz., en men kan daaraan nog toevoegen die van Kant en Hegel, van Schleiermacher en Ritschl, van Harnack en Eucken, van Green en Caird en van vele anderen. Doch er bestaat op verschillende punten toch nog eene dankbaar te erkennen overeenstemming."

70. Bavinck, *Het Christendom*, 10–11.

71. Kuyper to Bavinck, Amsterdam, November 12, 1912, HBA, folder 9. "M.i. is het een meesterstuk."

72. *Handelingen van de Eerste Kamer der Staten-Generaal*, April 25, 1912, 495–97.

73. Herman Bavinck, *De taak van het Gereformeerd Schoolverband: Voor onderwijs en opvoeding* (Hilversum: Klemkerk, 1912), 13–14, 20.

74. Herman Bavinck, preface to *Letterlijke en practicale verklaring van het Oude Testament*. vol. 1, *Genesis–Deuteronomium*, by Matthew Henry (Kampen: Kok, 1912), v–xi.

75. Herman Bavinck, "Een brief van zendeling Pieters uit Japan," *De Macedoniër*, September 1912.

76. Herman Bavinck, *Christelijke wereldbeschouwing*, 2nd ed. (Kampen: Kok, 1913).

77. Herman Bavinck, "Christendom en natuurwetenschap," *Stemmen des Tijds* 2 (1913): 343–77; ET: "Christianity and Natural Science," in *Essays on Religion, Science, and Society*, 81–104.

78. Herman Bavinck, "Over de ongelijkheid," *Stemmen des Tijds* 2 (1913): 17–43; ET: "On Inequality," in *Essays on Religion, Science, and Society*, 145–64.

79. Herman Bavinck, "Richtingen in de paedagogiek," *Handelingen van het nationaal christelijk schoolcongres, gehouden op 9, 10, 11 October 1913 te Utrecht* (Kampen: Kok, 1913), 61–69; ET: "Trends in Pedagogy," in *Essays on Religion, Science, and Society*, 205–8.

80. A. Binnerts Sz., *Nieuw-Gereformeerde en Moderne Theologie: Beschouwingen naar aanleiding van de rectorale oratie van Prof. Bavinck, ter moderne theologenvergadering voorgedragen en aangevuld met een Naschrift* (Baarn: Hollandia-Drukkerij, 1912); Herman Bavinck, "Verslag van toespraak gehouden op de vergadering van moderne theologen, op 17 April 1912 te Amsterdam," *Gereformeerd Theologisch Tijdschrift* 13 (1913): 92–93.

81. *Verslag der Handelingen van de Eerste Kamer*, March 12, 1913, 433. "Ik ben in mijn jeugd getuige geweest, dat het halve jonge Nederland geknield lag aan de voeten van Multatuli en met bewondering tot hem opzag."

82. *Congres voor Gereformeerde Evangelisatie op dinsdag 8 en woensdag 9 april 1913 te Amsterdam* (n.p., 1913), 5.

83. Herman Bavinck, "Stellingen: het begrip en de noodzakelijkheid der evangelisatie," *Congres voor Gereformeerde Evangelisatie op dinsdag 8 en woensdag 9 april 1913 te Amsterdam* (n.p., 1913), 8–9.

84. Anthonie Honig, "Evangelisatie," *De Bazuin*, May 16, 1913. "De atheisten van professie, die God den laatsten en grootsten vijand noemen van het menschelijk geslacht." Cf. Bavinck, "The Future of Calvinism," 14.

85. D. E. Boeke, *Gereformeerde Evangelisatie: Indrukken op het Congres voor Gereformeerde Evangelisatie te Amsterdam, 8/9 April 1913* (Amsterdam: Kirberger & Kesper, 1913), 15.

86. Harm Bouwman, "Gedenkdag," *De Bazuin*, January 10, 1913.

87. Boeke, *Gereformeerde Evangelisatie: Indrukken op het Congres*, 20.

88. *Provinciale Overijsselsche en Zwolsche courant*, April 9, 1913. "Evangelisatie is de arbeid van wege de kerk, die zich wendt tot degenen, die vervreemd zijn van het geloof, met de bedoeling hen terug te brengen tot het geloof in Christus. Deze arbeid wordt noodzakelijk geacht."

89. *Handelingen Eerste Kamer der Staten-Generaal*, January 7, 1914, 119–22, 148–51; *Handelingen Eerste Kamer der Staten-Generaal*, March 20, 1914, 484–85; *Handelingen Eerste Kamer der Staten-Generaal*, March 21, 1914, 499.

90. Bavinck, "Inleidend woord van Prof. Dr. H. Bavinck." *Nota bene*: Steketee had died the previous year, on January 18.

91. Herman Bavinck, "Bijbelsche Psychologie," *Orgaan van het Gereformeerd Schoolverband* (4 January 1912–5 March 1914). This article was later republished as the first half of *Bijbelsche en religieuze psychologie* (Kampen: Kok, 1920); ET: *Biblical and Religious Psychology*, trans. H. Hanko (Grand Rapids: Protestant Reformed Theological School, 1974).

92. Herman Bavinck, "De Zending in de Heilige Schrift," in *Triumfen van het Kruis: Schetsen der Christelijke Zending van alle eeuwen en allerlei landen voor ons Hollandsch volk geteekend*, by Henry Beets (Kampen: Kok, 1914), 7–30.

93. Herman Bavinck, "Van schoonheid en schoonheidsleer," in *Almanak van het Studentencorps aan de Vrije Universiteit voor het jaar 1914* (Amsterdam: Herdes, 1914), 121–43; ET: "Of Beauty and Aesthetics," in *Essays on Religion, Science, and Society*, 245–60.

94. *Haagsche Courant*, May 28, 1915.

95. *De Telegraaf*, October 25, 1916; *Algemeen Handelsblad*, January 11, 1917.

96. Anne Anema, Herman Bavinck, Pieter Arie Diepenhorst, Theodorus Heemskerk, and Simon de Vries, *Leider en leiding in de Anti-Revolutionaire Partij* (Amsterdam: Ten Have, 1915).

97. Herman Bavinck, "Death: Theological View," *International Standard Bible Encyclopaedia* (Chicago: Howard-Severance Company, 1915), 2:811–13; Bavinck, "Fall," in *International Standard Bible Encyclopaedia* 2:1092–94.

98. Bavinck to Snouck Hurgronje, Amsterdam, May 16, 1915, in *ELV*. "Godsdienst kan, geloof ik, alleen door godsdienst overwonnen en vervangen worden." This was the phase in Snouck Hurgronje's life in which he publicly stated the rationale behind his "outward Islamic behavior." Snouck Hurgronje viewed religious actions as inherently intransitive: religious behavior need not have a real, direct object—i.e., a deity. Rather, he regarded religious behavior as motivated by self-interest rather than belief. In that light, he viewed his conduct as 'Abd al-Ghaffār as no different from the actions of unbelieving Dutch parents who request baptism for their children in order to procure a higher social status. See Pieter Sjoerd van Koningsveld, "Conversion of European Intellectuals to Islam: The Case of Christiaan Snouck Hurgronje alias 'Abd al-Ghaffār," in *Muslims in Interwar Europe: A Transcultural Historical Perspective*, ed. Bekim Agai, Umar Ryad, and Mehdi Sajid (Leiden: Brill, 2016), 92.

99. Herman Bavinck, "Individualisme en Individualiteit van het kind," *Correspondentieblad van de Vereeniging van Christelijke Onderwijzers en Onderwijzeressen in Nederland en de Overzeesche bezittingen* (1916), 64–72.

100. Herman Bavinck, *De opvoeding der rijpere jeugd* (Kampen: Kok, 1916).

101. Herman Bavinck, *Over het onbewuste: Wetenschappelijke samenkomst op 7 juli 1915* (Amsterdam: Kirchner, 1915); ET: "The Unconscious," in *Essays on Religion, Science, and Society*, 175–98.

102. Herman Bavinck, "De hervorming en ons nationale leven," in *Ter herdenking der hervorming, 1517–1917*, by Herman Bavinck and H. H. Kuyper (Kampen: Kok, 1917), 5–36.

103. Herman Bavinck, *De nieuwe opvoeding* (Kampen: Kok, 1917).

104. Bavinck, *De nieuwe opvoeding*, 29–30, 92.

105. Herman Bavinck, "Het probleem van den oorlog," *Stemmen des tijds* 4 (1914): 1–31; repr. as *Het probleem van den oorlog* (Kampen: Kok, 1914).

106. Bavinck, *Het probleem van den oorlog*, 16. "De Christelijke ethiek laat dus inderdaad geene andere conclusie toe dan deze, dat er goede en rechtvaardige oorlogen *kunnen* zijn." Emphasis original.

107. Bavinck, *Het probleem van den oorlog*, 16. "Zijn recht rust dus niet op het recht van den sterkste, op de deugden van patriotisme, heldenmoed, geduld, standvastigheid, eendracht, offervaardigheid enz., die hij kweeken kan; nog minder op de zegenrijke gevolgen, verruiming van den gezichtskring, verbreiding der cultuur, of zelfs van het Christendom."

108. Bavinck, *Het probleem van den oorlog*, 1. "Wie kan ook aangeven, wat de oorzaak van dezen oorlog is, waarom hij ondernomen werd en waartoe hij dienen moet? Van welke zijde men hem beziet, nergens valt een lichtpunt op te merken, rondom is hij in duisternis gehuld."

109. Bavinck, *Het probleem van den oorlog*, 7–8.

110. George Harinck, "Via veldprediker naar legerpredikant: De protestantse kerken en de wederzijdse doordringing van kerk en leger," in *De kogel door de kerk? Het Nederlandse*

Christendom en de Eerste Wereldoorlog, ed. Enne Koops and Henk van der Linden, eds. (Soesterberg: Aspekt B.V., 2014), 107–31.

111. Maartje M. Abbenhuis, *The Art of Staying Neutral: The Netherlands in the First
World War, 1914–1918* (Amsterdam: Amsterdam University Press, 2006), 196. See also, T. J.
Hagen, "De geestelijke verzorging van onze weermacht," in *Onze Weermacht—van 1914 tot
1918—Extra Nummer van De Amsterdammer Weekblad voor Nederland*, ed. J. A. van Hamel
et al. (Amsterdam: n.p., 1918), 7–10.

112. *Handelingen Eerste Kamer der Staten-Generaal*, June 10, 1915, 312–13; see also *Handelingen Eerste Kamer der Staten-Generaal*, April 25, 1917, 496–98.

113. Herman Bavinck, "De Jongelingenvereeniging in hare beteekenis voor het sociale leven:
Rede gehouden op de 29e bondsdag van de Nederlandschen Bond van Jongelingsvereenigingen
op Geref. Grondslag" (n.p., 1917), 2. "Want de tijden, waarin wij leven, zij ernstig."

114. Bavinck, "De Jongelingenvereeniging," 6. "Alle sociale vraagstukken, hoe ingewikkeld
ze zijn mogen, zijn ten slotte tot deze vier te herleiden."

115. Bavinck, "De Jongelingenvereeniging," 8. "Ik zal mij niet aan profetieën wagen, want
niemand weet, welke toestanden straks na den oorlog intreden. Maar dit durf ik toch wel verzekeren, dat, indien één ding noodig zal zijn, het dit zal wezen, dat er harder dan ooit te voren
gewerkt zal moeten worden, om de geleden schade te herstellen, om weer goed te maken wat
misdreven werd, om er financieel en economisch weer boven op te komen, en om alle krachten
van mannen en vrouwen gereed te maken voor de worsteling, die wij dan niet meer op de slag
velden, maar zonder twijfel op het gebied van economie en politiek zulen hebben te strijden. . . .
Maakt u gereed voor den arbeid, waartoe de toekomst U roepen zal. En verstaat inzonderheid
als gereformeerde mannen de roeping, die in dezen op U rust."

116. J. C. Wirtz Czn., *Bijdrage tot de geschiedenis van de schoolstrijd* (Amsterdam: H. J.
Spruyt's Uitgevers-Maatschappij, 1926), 24, 35, 109.

117. Bavinck, quoted in *Gereformeerd Jongelingsblad*, May 23, 1919. "De Schoolstrijd is
daarom niet uit; maar hij wordt verlegd en moet, terwille van de toekomst van ons volk, verlegd
worden van 't politieke naar . . . 't paedagogisch terrein. Meer dan tot dusver zal het aankomen
op een leven voor en in de school, op rusteloos voortgezette innerlijke reformatie. . . . Als wij deze
roeping niet verstaan en ter harte nemen, dan zou het kunnen gebeuren, dat wij den schoolstrijd
in dit jaar *financieel* hadden *gewonnen*, en *geestelijk* hadden *verloren*." Emphasis original.

118. See, for example, *Friesch Dagblad*, February 6, 1933; *Friesch Dagblad*, December 2, 1937.

119. *Handelingen Eerste Kamer der Staten-Generaal*, May 15, 1917, 618–24.

120. *Handelingen Eerste Kamer der Staten-Generaal*, May 15, 1917, 619. "Het is pure willekeur. . . . Het algemeen kiesrecht is niet algemeen, maar de voorstanders hebben die leuze aan-
vaard, want ze klinkt goed en maakt het aantrekkelijk voor het volk. Het is echter niet algemeen."

121. *Handelingen Eerste Kamer der Staten-Generaal*, May 15, 1917, 621. "De man is nog
altijd een bourgeois, de vrouw nog altijd een proletarier."

122. *Handelingen Eerste Kamer der Staten-Generaal*, May 15, 1917, 621. "Wordt algemeen stemrecht geeischt juist op grond van de *ongelijkheid* en het *verschil* tusschen mannen
en vrouwen."

123. *Handelingen Eerste Kamer der Staten-Generaal*, May 15, 1917, 621. "Wanneer de Zone
Gods een maagd heeft verwaardigd om zijn Moeder te zijn, en wanneer Hij onder het hart van
een vrouw is gedragen en aan de borst van een vrouw is gezoogd, dan is er geen sprake meer
van dat in het Christendom plaats kan zijn voor vrouwenverachting."

124. *Handelingen Eerste Kamer der Staten-Generaal*, May 15, 1917, 622. "Men moet maar
met jonge meisjes van den tegenwoordigen tijd hebben gesproken of haar onder elkaar hebben
hooren spreken, om te weten wat er omgaat in de harten van deze jongedochters. Dat komt
hierop neer: wij hebben eigenlijk niets te doen, en wij verkeeren in de ongelukkige positie, dat
wij moeten zitten wachten op een man die misschien nooit komt, want de huwelijkskansen zijn
verbazend achteruitgegaan. Dat vind ik een verschrikkelijke positie."

125. *Handelingen Eerste Kamer der Staten-Generaal*, May 15, 1917, 622. "Zal in de toekomst de vrouw van het stemrecht zijn uitgesloten enkel en alleen omdat zij *vrouw* is? Dat is de vraag waarvoor wij staan. En daarop durf ik, ook met de Schrift in de hand, niet anders dan een bevestigend antwoord geven: die mogelijkheid is inderdaad voor de vrouw open te stellen."

126. *De Standaard*, June 19, 21, and 23, 1917.

127. Herman Bavinck, *De vrouw in de hedendaagsche maatschappij* (Kampen: Kok, 1918).

128. Kuyper to Bavinck, March 17, 1918, HBA, folder 11.

129. Herman Bavinck, "Politieke rede 1918," 11, quoted in Niels (C. M.) van Driel, "The Status of Women in Contemporary Society: Principles and Practice in Herman Bavinck's Socio-Political Thought," in *Five Studies in the Thought of Herman Bavinck, a Creator of Modern Dutch Theology*, ed. John Bolt (Lewiston, NY: Mellen, 2011), 181.

130. Van Driel, "Status of Women in Contemporary Society," 181.

131. *Nota bene*: the spelling of this surname varies between Ruys and Ruijs across sources.

132. Bremmer, *Herman Bavinck en zijn tijdgenoten*, 264.

133. Herman Bavinck, "Philosophie des geloofs," in *Overdr. uit het Annuarium der Societas Studiosorum Reformatorum, 1918* (Leiden: Donner, 1918), 62–72.

134. Herman Bavinck, *De navolging van Christus en het moderne leven* (Kampen: Kok, 1918).

135. Herman Bavinck, "Klassieke opleiding," *Stemmen des Tijds* 7 (1918): 46–65, 113–47; ET: "Classical Education," in *Essays on Religion, Science, and Society*, 209–44.

136. Herman Bavinck, "Christendom, oorlog, volkenbond," *Stemmen des Tijds* 9 (1919): 1–26, 105–33.

137. Bavinck, "Christendom, oorlog, volkenbond," 13.

138. Bavinck, "Christendom, oorlog, volkenbond," 131–32. "Het Christendom is universeel; het leert, dat heel het menschelijk geslacht van éénen bloede is en dat het Evangelie voor alle volken is bestemd." See also Dirk van Keulen, "Herman Bavinck and the War Question," in *Christian Faith and Violence*, vol. 1, ed. D. van Keulen and M.E. Brinkman (Zoetermeer: Meinema, 2005), 122–40.

Chapter 11 Bavinck's Final Years: 1920–21

1. James Bratt, *Abraham Kuyper: Modern Calvinist, Christian Democrat* (Grand Rapids: Eerdmans, 2013), 373.

2. *Verslag van de Handelingen der Staten-Generaal: Zitting van 21 September 1920–17 September 1921; Verslag van de handelingen van de Eerste Kamer der Staten-Generaal gedurende het zittingjaar 1920–1921* ('s Gravenhage: Algemeene Landsdrukkerij, 1921), 4.

3. *Handelingen Eerste Kamer der Staten-Generaal*, March 13, 1919, 243.

4. Johan S. Wijne, *De "vergissing" van Troelstra* (Hilversum: Verloren, 1999).

5. Herman Bavinck, *Bijbelsche en religieuze psychologie* (Kampen: Kok, 1920), 75. ". . . en met name is toen Friedrich Nietzsche opgetreden, om, met diepe verachting voor de massa, de enkele groote mannen te verheerlijken, die uit de menschheid voortkomen, en voor hen het recht van den sterkste te vindiceeren."

6. Herman Bavinck, Harm Bouwman, and Herman Kuyper, "Rapport voor evangelisatie" (n.p., 1920).

7. Herman Bavinck, "Individueele en Sociale Opvoeding," *Orgaan van het Gereformeerd Schoolverband* (20 May–18 November 1920); Herman Bavinck and H. Tilanus, "Rapport van den Onderwijsraad in zake het ontwerp Lager-Onderwijswet" (n.p., 1920).

8. See, for example, *Middelburgsche courant*, January 28, 1919; *Algemeen Handelsblad*, September 13, 1919; *Het Centrum*, September 27, 1919; *De Telegraaf*, December 12, 1919.

9. Herman Bavinck, "De beroepsarbeid der gehuwde vrouw," in *Tweede christelijk-sociaal congres 10–13 maart 1919 te Amsterdam: Referaten* (Rotterdam: Libertas, 1919), 5–25.

10. J. C. Rullmann, *Onze voortrekkers* (Delft: Naamlooze Vennootschap W. D. Meinema, 1923), 238. "En 's middags—niemand die 't gehoord heeft zal het ooit vergeten!—hoe hartelijk

en eenvoudig, hoe begrijpend en begrijpelijk, heeft hij, de beroemde hoogleraar, toen tot onze meisjes gesproken over de opvoeding der vrouw."

11. Herman Bavinck, "Woord vooraf," in *Calvijn als theoloog en de stand van het calvinisme in onzen tijd*, by B. B. Warfield, trans. C. M. E. Kuyper (Kampen: Kok, 1919), 38. "Zoo staat het Calvinisme voor ons als niets meer of minder dan de hope der wereld."

12. Willem Jan Aalders, "In Memoriam: Dr. H. Bavinck," *Stemmen des tijds* (1921): 140. "Dr Bavinck was een der ouderen en had grooten invloed op den loop der gesprekken en besluiten. Ik zie ons nog den laatsten Zondagavond in de voorkamer bijeen. Er werd vertrouwelijk gesproken over het geloof; hoe veel er toe behoorde; hoe groot de mate van zekerheid moest zijn. Dr Bavinck sprak eerst niet veel. Zijn forsche figuur neigde niet zoo licht tot vertrouwelijkheid. Zij droeg zoo geheel het kenmerk van gecondenseerde kracht en reserve. Maar toen hij eindelijk het woord nam, was dit om te zeggen, dat men zich toch niet moest verbeelden, dat het geloof iets zoo zakelijks en acheveerds was. Althans hij, naar mate hij ouder werd, voelde hoe langer hoe meer, dat er ten slotte maar heel weinig overblijft: een zondig menschenkind, dat zich telkens weer en met dieper behoefte aan Gods genade toevertrouwt. Hij sprak als een groot kind; ontroerd, ontroerend."

13. R. H. Bremmer, *Herman Bavinck en zijn tijdgenoten* (Kampen: Kok, 1966), 265.

14. Arie Theodorus van Deursen, *The Distinctive Character of the Free University in Amsterdam, 1880–2005* (Grand Rapids: Eerdmans, 2008), 30.

15. George Harinck, Cornelis van der Kooi, and Jasper Vree, eds., *"Als Bavinck nu maar eens kleur bekende": Aantekeningen van H. Bavinck over de zaak-Netelenbos, het Schriftgezag en de Situatie van de Gereformeerde Kerken (November 1919)* (Amsterdam: VU Uitgeverij, 1994), 58. "De vorm is totaal menschelijk, van begin tot einde."

16. Harinck, van der Kooi, and Vree, *"Als Bavinck nu maar eens kleur bekende,"* 16. "Ik voor mij vind het beter, om te zeggen, dat de Schrift, het Woord Gods, het *Deus dixit*, de *grond* is van ons geloof, maar het getuigenis des H.G., of misschien nog juister, het door den HG. verlichte oog (hart, oor) is het middel/orgaan, waardoor ik die Schrift als Gods Woord erken en aanneem." For Netelenbos's public response to this particular claim, see *Acta der generale synode van de Gereformeerde Kerken in Nederland, gehouden te Leeuwarden van 24 augustus–9 september 1920* (Kampen: Kok, 1920), 120–21.

17. See also Dirk van Keulen, *Bijbel en dogmatiek: Schriftbeschouwing en schriftgebruik in het dogmatisch werk van A. Kuyper, H. Bavinck en G.C. Berkouwer* (Kampen: Kok, 2003), 175–225, 233–84.

18. Herman Bavinck, "RAPPORT in zake de voorstellen der Particuliere Synodes rakende de Belijdenis," *Acta der generale synode van de Gereformeerde Kerken*, 152–54.

19. Bavinck to Snouck Hurgronje, Kampen, February 8, 1883, in *ELV*. "Er moet nog iets bij: met mijne Schriftbeschouwing ben ik dus volstrekt nog niet klaar."

20. Valentijn Hepp, *Dr. H. Bavinck* (Amsterdam: Ten Have, 1921), 338. "Erg moe."

21. Coenraad Bernardus Bavinck, "Appendix A: Foreword," in *Essays on Religion, Science, and Society*, by Herman Bavinck, ed. John Bolt, trans. Harry Boonstra and Gerrit Sheeres (Grand Rapids: Baker Academic, 2008), 279.

22. Herman Bavinck, *Verzamelde opstellen op het gebied van godsdienst en wetenschap*, ed. C. B. Bavinck (Kampen: Kok, 1921); ET: *Essays on Religion, Science, and Society*.

23. Hepp, *Dr. Herman Bavinck*, 338. "De doctoren schrijven allen, als zij mij in de loop der week bezoeken, rust voor."

24. Henriëtte Kuyper and Johanna Kuyper, *De levensavond van Dr. A. Kuyper* (Kampen: Kok, 1921).

25. Johan Snel, "Kuypers dodenmasker," in *Tussen Kampen en Amsterdam: George Harinck en het Historisch Documentatiecentrum van de Vrije Universiteit 1985–2017*, ed. Wim Berkelaar, Hans Seijlhouwer, and Bart Wallet (Amsterdam: Donum Reeks, 2018), 114–18.

26. R. A. den Ouden and R. C. Verweyck, *Het Kuyperhuis* (Baarn: E. J. Bosch, 1921).

27. Hepp, *Dr. Herman Bavinck*, 338.

28. *Algemeen Handelsblad*, September 3, 1920. "Is prof. dr. H. Bavinck ernstig ongesteld. De toestand is echter niet zorgwekkend."

29. *Algemeen Handelsblad*, September 8, 1920. "Is in de toestand van prof. Bavinck eenige verbetering gekomen; direct gevaar voor 't leven schijnt thans vrijwel geweken."

30. *Provinciale Geldersche en Nijmeegsche courant*, September 13, 1920. "De gezondheidtoestand van prof. dr. H. Bavinck is langzaam vooruitgaande. Er staat hoop op geheel herstel."

31. Quoted in Harinck, "Being Public: On Abraham Kuyper and His Publications," in *Abraham Kuyper: An Annotated Bibliography, 1857–2010*, by Tjitze Kuipers (Leiden: Brill, 2011), ix. See also *Het gereformeerde geheugen: Protestantse herinneringscultuur in Nederland, 1850–2000*, ed. George Harinck, Herman Paul, and Bart Wallet (Amsterdam: Bert Bakker, 2009), 435.

32. *De Telegraaf*, November 29, 1920. "'De Standaard' verneemt, dat de toestand van prof. dr. H. Bavinck de laatste dagen niet merkbaar vooruitgegaan was."

33. *De Tijd*, December 24, 1920. "De toestand van prof. dr. H. Bavinck is zorgelijk."

34. *De Telegraaf*, December 28, 1920. "In de toestand van het Eerste Kamerlid prof. Bavinck in de laatste dagen eenige verbetering ingetreden. De benauwdheden zijn weggebleven. Wel is de patient erg zwak, maar het hart is iets beter."

35. *De Telegraaf*, January 6, 1921. "De toestand van prof. Bavinck blijft zeer zorgelijk; de benauwdheden herhalen zich nu en dan."

36. *Provinciale Overijsselsche en Zwolsche courant*, February 1, 1921. "De toestand van prof. dr. H. Bavinck in de laatste dagen sterk achteruitgaande. Hoop op een herstel wordt niet meer gekoesterd."

37. *De Maasbode*, February 2, 1921. "De patient lijdt vreeselijke pijn." *De Telegraaf*, February 6, 1921.

38. *Nieuwe Apeldoornsche courant*, February 9, 1921.

39. *De Sumatra post*, March 19, 1921.

40. *Haagsche courant*, May 11, 1921.

41. *Rotterdamsch Nieuwsblad*, June 6, 1921.

42. *De Volksvriend*, June 2, 1921.

43. J. H. Landwehr, *In Memoriam: Prof. Dr. H. Bavinck* (Kampen: Kok, 1921), 78.

44. Hepp, *Dr. Herman Bavinck*, 339. "Het . . . leven . . . is . . . vreemd. . . , het . . . sterven . . . nog . . . vreemder."

45. Snouck Hurgronje to Johanna Bavinck-Schippers, Leiden, June 28, 1921, in *ELV*. "Ik ben nog geheel onder den indruk van mijn laatste bezoek: weemoedig, maar stichtelijk tevens. Anders dan vroom heb ik mijn goeden vriend trouwens niet gekend: 1874–1921."

46. Johanna Bavinck-Schippers to Snouck Hurgronje, draft letter, June 28, 1921, in *ELV*, 186n1. "De toestand is precies dezelfde als toen u hem het laatst bezocht. De krachten nemen zeer langzaam af. Nu de toestand eenmaal zoolang op dezelfde hoogte blijft, heb ik hoop dat het einde niet spoedig daar zal zijn."

47. "Mev. Wed. J. A. Bavinck-Schippers," *De Standaard*, June 2, 1942.

48. *De Telegraaf*, July 28, 1921. "Naar wij vernemen, wordt professor Bavinck uiterst zwak. Hoewel zeer geduldig, spreekt hij telkens het verlangen uit, dat de Heere zich spoedig over hem ontferme en hem tot Zich neme."

49. *Algemeen Handelsblad*, July 30, 1921.

50. Tjeerd Hoekstra, "Begravenis Prof. Dr. Bavinck," *De Bazuin*, August 6, 1921. "Hij was een zoon der Scheiding. En een van de wezenskenmerken der Afgescheidenen is geweest, dat ze sterken nadruk gelegd hebben op de vroomheid des wandels, op de heiligheid des levens. Bij enkelen—bij Bavinck niet—kreeg het leven soms een anticultureele tint."

51. They sang from the 1773 "berijmde psalmen." I have quoted the 1650 Scottish Psalter as the closest English equivalent. See *Het boek der Psalmen, nevens de gezangen bij de hervormde kerk van Nederland in gebruik; door last van de hoog mogende heeren Staaten Generaal der Vereeenigde Nederlanden, uit drie berijmingen, in den jaare 1773, gekooren, met de noodige daar in gemaakte veranderingen* (Amsterdam: J. Ratelbrand and J. Brouwer, 1786).

52. Hepp, *Dr. Herman Bavinck*, 341; Bremmer, *Herman Bavinck en zijn tijdgenoten*, 270; Ron Gleason, *Herman Bavinck: Pastor, Churchman, Statesman, and Theologian* (Phillipsburg, NJ: P&R, 2010), 428–29.

53. Abraham Kuyper Jr., "Bavinck-Comité," *De Heraut*, October 2, 1921.

Postscript

1. "Prof Dr H Bavinck" (n.d.), HBA, folder 40. Although this jotter does not identify its author, the handwriting is clearly that of Johanna.

2. Dosker to Johanna Bavinck-Schippers, Holland, MI, August 29, 1921, in *BHD*. "O Johanna, ik had hem zoo innig lief. Wij gingen samen [naar] school, wij vochten samen om dezelfde prijzen in het gymnasium te Zwolle, wij waren samen als jongens verliefd op hetzelfde meisje. . . . Schrijf mij zoo mogelijk eens een regel of wat, hoe, waaraan enz. Herman stierf."

3. *De Bazuin*, October 15, 1921.

4. Dosker to Johanna Bavinck-Schippers, Louisville, March 20, 1923, in *BHD*.

5. A. C. Diepenhorst-De Gaay Fortman, *Wat wil de Nederlandsche Christen-Vrouwenbond?* (Rotterdam: Drukkerij Libertas, 1920), 12.

6. *De Nederlandsche Vrouwenbond tot Verhooging van het Zedelijk Bewustzijn: Ontstaan, Organisatie, en Werkwijze* (n.p., n.d.), 13.

7. *Christelijke Sociaal Congres* (Rotterdam: Drukkerij Libertas, 1919), 4, 8.

8. Cornelia Frida Katz, "Inleiding," *Christendom en Vrouwenbeweging*, introductory issue (1923).

9. See, for example, M. W. Barger, "De vrouw en de studie," *Christendom en Vrouwenbeweging*, series 4, no. 1 (1923); J. R. Slotemaker de Bruïne, "De vrouw en de kerk," *Christendom en Vrouwenbeweging* series 6, no. 1 (1923).

10. *Bouwen en Bewaren*, December 15, 1923.

11. C. B. Bavinck, N. Buffinga, J. Douma, J. H. Sillevis Smitt, and B. Wielenga, *"Ons aller Moeder": Een woord van voorlichting en getuigenis inzake de kwestie-Geelkerken* (Kampen: Kok, 1925).

12. *Algemeen Handelsblad*, April 8, 1926. "Prof. Bavinck nu aarzelde geen oogenblik met te verklaren, dat de synode van Leeuwarden niet naders had kunnen handelen. Hoeveel persoonlijke sympathie hij ook voor ds. Netelenbos had, ds. Netelenbos was niet te handhaven, zeide hij." Herman Kuyper's article was originally printed as "Misleidende leuzen," *De Bazuin*, April 9, 1926.

13. *Algemeen Handelsblad*, January 31, 1928.

14. *De Heraut*, September 30, 1928.

15. Slotemaker de Bruïne, "De vrouw en de kerk."

16. *Rapport inzake het vrouwenkiesrecht aan de generale synode van de Gereformeerde Kerken* (Kampen: Kok, 1927), 8. "De invoering van dit vrouwenstemrecht onder de tegenwoordige tijdsomstandigheden niet zonder gevaar zou wezen met het oog op de onchristelijke emancipatiebeweging, die zich tegen de ordinantie Gods keert."

17. J. Diepersloot and E. L. Smelik, *Een kleine kerk in een groten tijd (De Gereformeerde Kerken in Hersteld Verband)* (n.p., 1937), 44.

18. Herman Bavinck, *Het Christendom* (Baarn: Hollandia, 1912); ET: "Christ and Christianity," trans. A. A. Pfanstiehl, *Biblical Review* 1 (1916): 214–36.

19. John Bolt, "Herman Bavinck Speaks English: A Bibliographic Essay," *Mid-America Journal of Theology* (2008): 121.

20. Herman Bavinck, *The Doctrine of God*, trans. William Hendriksen (Grand Rapids: Eerdmans, 1951).

21. *Tweede Internationaal Congres van Gereformeerden (Calvinisten), Amsterdam 23–26 October 1934, Verslagen* ('s Gravenhage: Martinus Nijhoff, 1935), 187.

22. *De Heraut*, September 8, 1940, quoted in G. van Roon, *Protestants Nederland en Duitsland 1933–41* (Utrecht: Spectrum, 1973), 307.

23. John Bolt, James Bratt, and Paul Visser, eds., *The J. H. Bavinck Reader* (Grand Rapids: Eerdmans, 2013).

24. *De Telegraaf*, June 1, 1942.

25. *Het Volk*, July 3, 1941.

26. James Bratt, *Abraham Kuyper: Modern Calvinist, Christian Democrat* (Grand Rapids: Eerdmans, 2013), 381.

27. Dennis Hevesi, "Johtje Vos, Who Saved Wartime Jews, Dies at 97," *New York Times*, November 4, 2007.

28. *Hier is Londen*, March 26, 1945. Hugo Floris Ruysstraat is named in his honor.

29. For the stories of the Ruys family in World War II, see Historische Kring Bussum, archive no. PRS6015.

30. Peter Heere, Arnold Vernooij, and Jan van den Bos, *De Erebegraafplaats Bloemendaal* (The Hague: SDU Uitgevers, 2005), 319, 821.

31. My translation of the Dutch text on the gravestone.

Appendix 1: "My Journey to America"

1. Bavinck traveled with his Kampen colleague Prof. D. K. Wielenga (1842–1902).

2. The source of this quote is unknown.

3. Isa. 54:10 (my translation of Bavinck's own quotation-from-memory).

4. H. P. Scholte (1805–68), a Secession preacher who led a group of seven hundred immigrants to Iowa, where they founded Pella (1847).

5. S. Bolks (1814–94), a Secession preacher who led a group of immigrants to establish Overisel, Michigan (1848), and who became the preacher in Orange City, Iowa, in 1872.

6. H. Hospers (1820–1901), appointed leader of Orange City in 1871.

7. The Fifth General Council of the Presbyterian Alliance, held in Toronto (September 21–30, 1892).

8. Bavinck placed this sentence within brackets.

9. In the original manuscript, Bavinck left a space for this figure, though he did not fill it in.

10. In the original manuscript, Bavinck left a space for this figure, though he did not fill it in.

11. In the original manuscript, Bavinck left a space for this figure, though he did not fill it in.

12. Bavinck had visited the Rhine Falls, in Schaffhausen, Switzerland, in 1887. Valentijn Hepp, *Dr. Herman Bavinck* (Amsterdam: W. Ten Have, 1921), 136.

13. In 1887 Bavinck traveled along the Rhine. See note 12.

14. Martinus Cohen Stuart, *Zes maanden in Amerika* (Haarlem: Kruseman and Tjeenk Willem, 1875), 1:29–44.

15. William Elliot Griffis, *The Influence of the Netherlands in the Making of the English Commonwealth and the American Republic* (Boston: De Wolfe, Fiske & Co., 1891).

16. Douglas Campbell, *The Puritan in Holland, England and America: An Introduction to American history*, 2 vols. (New York: Harper and Brothers, 1892–93).

17. John Robinson (1585–1625), English theologian and preacher for a group of English Congregationalists in Amsterdam and Leiden. He encouraged the immigration of his congregation to America; the majority of them, the Pilgrim Fathers, immigrated in 1620. Robinson intended to follow them but died in Leiden. In 1891 an American-led initiative saw the erection of a memorial to Robinson in Leiden.

18. Albertus Christiaan van Raalte (1811–76) was a Secessionist preacher and leader of a group of Seceder emigrants who founded a colony in 1847, the center of which was the present-day Holland, Michigan.

19. In the original manuscript, Bavinck left a space for this figure, though he did not fill it in.

20. In the original manuscript, Bavinck left a space for this figure, though he did not fill it in.

21. Bavinck alludes to the beginning of Epistle II of Alexander Pope's 1734 poem *An Essay on Man*: "Know then thyself, presume not God to scan; / The proper study of mankind is Man."

22. Josiah Strong (1847–1926), a Congregationalist preacher and leader among the Social Gospel movement. See Josiah Strong, *Our Country: Its Possible Future and Its Present Crisis* (n.p.: Baker and Taylor for the American Home Missionary Society, 1885). Bavinck cites a later edition of this book (1891).

23. In the original manuscript, Bavinck left a space for this figure, though he did not fill it in.

24. Charles Boissevain, *Van 't Noorden naar 't Zuiden: Schetsen en indrukken van de Vereenigde Staten van Noord-Amerika* (Haarlem: H. D. Tjeenk Willink, 1881), 1:113: "Gisteren had ik na den eten een gesprek met een vader van vele zonen. De jongens gingen op ongedwongene, eenigszins ongegeneerde wijze met hem om. Ze waren niet brutaal, volstrekt niet; maar jongens van 12 tot 14 jaar behandelen hun vader als waren ze academie-vrienden die met hem gestudeerd hadden. De vader was wellicht een weinig beleefder jegens de jongens, dan zij jegens hem, 'doch komt van mijn meerdere beschaving en ervaring,' zeide hij lachend." English: "Yesterday after dinner I had a conversation with a father who had many sons. The lads carried on with him in an easygoing, to a certain extent spontaneous, manner. They were not rude, absolutely not; but boys of twelve to fourteen years old treated their father as though they were friends who had studied with him at the academy. The father was perhaps more polite toward them than they were toward him: 'Never mind my superior refinement and experience,' he said, laughing."

25. Josiah Strong, *Our Country: Its Possible Future and Its Present Crisis*, ed. Jurgen Herbst (Cambridge, MA: Harvard University Press, 1963), 103.

26. Here, Bavinck uses the word *gezellig*, for which no direct English equivalent exists. It denotes a feeling of personal warmth in the company of others.

27. On *gezellig*, see note 26.

28. This word is illegible.

29. Boissevain, *Van 't Noorden naar 't Zuiden*, 1:183. Boissevain devoted a chapter to the press in America and compiled a list of newspapers and magazines available in New York.

30. *Gideon* was a weekly Christian newspaper in print since March 1875, published by J. Wierema te Brielle. It was read in Secessionist circles.

31. Joel Parker (1799–1873) was a Presbyterian pastor and celebrated revivalist preacher in New York.

32. Charles Henry Pankhurst (1842–1933) was a Presbyterian pastor and social reformer. He rose to prominence in New York after preaching against the corruption of the police there in 1892.

33. Thomas De Witt Talmage (1832–1902) was a renowned Presbyterian pastor in New York.

Appendix 2: "An Autobiographical Sketch of Dr. H. Bavinck"

1. The opening two paragraphs were provided by the editor, J. B. Mulder.

Bibliography

The bibliography lists works by Herman Bavinck, in chronological order. The second section includes other primary sources, particularly works by Jan Bavinck and Abraham Kuyper, as well as other correspondence and archival source material; these are also arranged chronologically. The final section lists secondary sources.

Where a Dutch work has also been published in English translation, the information for the translation follows the citation of the original. In following Dutch convention for alphabetization, surnames prefixed with a *tussenvoegsel* (*van*, *van der*, *de*, *te*, *in 't*, etc.) are listed in alphabetical order according to the first letter of the surname, rather than the first letter of the *tussenvoegsel* (e.g., de Jong is listed under *j*, rather than *d*).

On account of the sheer volume of newspaper articles included in the endnotes, which often do not include authors' names, titles, or page numbers (in following the journalistic conventions of their day), only newspaper articles that include the author's name and are introduced by a title are given bibliographic entries. All newspapers cited in the endnotes, however, can be accessed via the online archive of the Koninklijke Bibliotheek: https://www.delpher.nl.

Works by Herman Bavinck

Published Materials

De ethiek van Ulrich Zwingli. Kampen: G. Ph. Zalsman, 1880.

Synopsis purioris theologiae. Leiden: D. Donner, 1881. Partial ET: *Synopsis purioris theologiae / Synopsis of a Purer Theology: Latin Text and English Translation*. Vol. 1, *Disputations 1–23*. Translated by Riemer A. Faber. Leiden: Brill, 2014. Vol. 2, *Disputations 24–42*. Translated by Riemer A. Faber. Leiden: Brill, 2016.

"Eene Rectorale Oratie." *De Vrije Kerk* 7, no. 3 (March 1881): 120–30.

"Het rijk Gods, het hoogste goed." *De Vrije Kerk* 7, no. 3 (April–August 1881): 4:185–92; 5:224– 34; 6:271–77; 7:305–14; 8:353–60. ET: "The Kingdom of God, the Highest Good." Translated by Nelson Kloosterman. *Bavinck Review* 2 (2011): 133–70.

Review of *Egyptologie en assyriologie in betrekking tot de geloofwaardigheid des Ouden Testaments: Rede bij het overdragen van het rectoraat*, by Maarten Noordtzij. *De Vrije Kerk* 8, no. 3 (March 1882): 138–43.

De wetenschap der H. Godgeleerdheid: Rede ter aanvaarding van het leeraarsambt aan de Theologische School te Kampen. Kampen: G. Ph. Zalsman, 1883.

"De hedendaagsche wereldbeschouwing." *De Vrije Kerk* 9, no. 10 (October 1883): 435–61.

De theologie van prof. dr. Daniël Chantepie de la Saussaye: Bijdrage tot de kennis der ethische theologie. Leiden: D. Donner, 1884. 2nd ed., Leiden: D. Donner, 1903.

"Antwoord aan Prof. Dr. J. H. Gunning Jr." *De Vrije Kerk* 10, nos. 5–6 (May–June 1884): 5:221–27; 6:287–92.

De katholiciteit van Christendom en kerk. Kampen: G. Ph. Zalsman, 1888. ET: "*The Catholicity of Christianity and the Church*." Translated by John Bolt. *Calvin Theological Journal* 27, no. 2 (1992): 220–51.

"De Theologie van Albrecht Ritschl." *Theologische Studieën* 6 (1888): 369–403.

"Dankbetuiging." *De Bazuin*, April 19, 1889.

De Welsprekendheid. Kampen: G. Ph. Zalsman, 1889. Reprint, Kampen: Kok, 1901. ET: *Eloquence*. In *Herman Bavinck on Preaching and Preachers*, edited and translated by James Eglinton, 21–56. Peabody, MA: Hendrickson, 2017.

"Recent Dogmatic Thought in the Netherlands." *Presbyterian and Reformed Review* 3, no. 10 (April 1892): 209–28.

"Welke algemeene beginselen beheerschen, volgens de H. Schrift, de oplossing der sociale quaestie, en welke vingerwijzing voor die oplossing ligt in de concrete to-epassing, welke deze beginselen voor Israel in Mozaïsch recht gevonden hebben?" In *Proces-verbaal van het Sociaal Congres, gehouden te Amsterdam den 9–12 November, 1891*, edited by Johan Adam Wormser, 149–57. Amsterdam: Hövker & Zoon, 1892. ET: "General Biblical Principles and the Relevance of Concrete Mosaic Law for the Social Question Today (1891)." Translated by John Bolt. *Journal of Markets & Morality* 13, no. 2 (2010): 411–46.

"The Future of Calvinism." *Presbyterian and Reformed Review* 5, no. 17 (1894): 1–24.

De algemene genade. Kampen: G. Ph. Zalsman, 1894.

"Eene belangrijke apologie van de Christelijke Wereldbeschouwing." Review of *The Christian View of God and the World, as Centring in the Incarnation*, by James Orr. *Theologische Studiën* 12 (1894): 142–52.

Edited and translated with Abraham Kuyper and Frederik Rutgers. *Biblia dat is de gansche Heilige Schrifture bevattende alle de kanonieke boeken des Ouden en des Nieuwen Testaments: Naar de uitgave der Staten-overzetting in 1657 bij de Weduwe Paulus Aertsz van Ravesteyn uitgekomen, in de thans gangbare taal overgebracht door Dr. A. Kuyper onder medewerking van Dr. H. Bavinck en Dr. F. L. Rutgers; Met volledige kantteekeningen, inhoudsopgaven, platen, kaarten, enz.* Middelharnis: Flakkeesche Boekdrukkerij, 1895.

Gereformeerde dogmatiek. 4 vols. Kampen: Bos, 1895–1901. 2nd ed. Kampen: Kok, 1906–11. ET: *Reformed Dogmatics.* 4 vols. Edited by John Bolt. Translated by John Vriend. Grand Rapids: Baker Academic, 2003–8.

With Maarten Noordtzij, Douwe Klazes Wielenga, and Petrus Biesterveld. *Opleiding en theologie.* Kampen: Kok, 1896.

"Kleine bijdrage tot de geschiedenis der Statenvertaling." *Tijdschrift voor Gereformeerde Theologie* 4, no. 4 (1897): 233–40.

Beginselen der psychologie. Kampen: J. H. Bos, 1897. 2nd ed., Kampen: Kok, 1923.

Het Vierde eener Eeuw: Rede bij gelegenheid van het vijf en twintig-jarig bestaan van de "Standaard." Kampen: J. H. Bos, 1897.

"Ter toelichting en verdediging der Psychologie." *Christelijk Schoolblad* (June 2–July 21, 1899).

Theologische School en Vrije Universiteit: Een voorstel tot vereeniging. Kampen: J. H. Bos, 1899.

Het recht der kerken en de vrijheid der wetenschap. Kampen: G. Ph. Zalsman, 1899.

Het doctorenambt: Rede bij de overdracht van het rectoraat aan de Theologische School te Kampen op 6 Dec. 1899. Kampen: G. Ph. Zalsman, 1899.

"Aan de Lezers van *De Bazuin.*" *De Bazuin*, January 5, 1900.

"Stemrecht der vrouw." *De Bazuin*, March 2, 1900.

"Calvijn." *De Bazuin*, April 13, 1900.

"De eerste doopvraag." *De Bazuin*, May 11, 1900.

"De oorlog." *De Bazuin*, June 1, 1900.

"Op reis." *De Bazuin*, August 31, 1900.

"Moderne kunst." *De Bazuin*, September 21, 1900.

Ouders of getuigen: Toelichting van art. 56 en 57 der Dordsche Kerkorde. Kampen: G. Ph. Zalsman, 1901.

Schepping of ontwikkeling? Kampen: Kok, 1901.

De wereldverwinnende kracht des geloofs: Leerrede over 1 John 5:4b, uitgesproken in de Burgwalkerk te Kampen den 30sten Juni 1901. Kampen: G. Ph. Zalsman, 1901. ET: "The World-Conquering Power of Faith." In *Herman Bavinck on Preaching and Preachers*, edited and translated by James Eglinton, 67–84. Peabody, MA: Hendrickson, 2017.

"Feminisme." *De Bazuin*, March 15, 1901.

"Dogmatiek." *De Bazuin*, April 26, 1901.

"De strijd voor het recht." *De Bazuin*, July 5, 1901.

"Middelbaar onderwijs." *De Bazuin*, August 16, 1901.

De offerande des lofs: Overdenkingen vóór en na de toelating tot het heilige avond-maal. 's Gravenhage: Fred. H. Verschoor, 1901. 3rd ed., 1903. ET: *The Sacrifice of Praise*. Edited and translated by Cameron Clausing and Gregory Parker. Peabody, MA: Hendrickson, 2019.

De zekerheid des geloofs. Kampen: Kok, 1901. ET: *The Certainty of Faith*. Translated by Harry Der Nederlanden. St. Catharines, ON: Paideia Press, 1980.

Godsdienst en godgeleerdheid. Wageningen: Vada, 1902.

Hedendaagsche moraal. Kampen: Kok, 1902.

"De tekst onzer liturgie." *De Bazuin*, January 10, 1902.

"Na de Synode." *De Bazuin*, September 19, 1902.

Blijven of heengaan? Een vraag en een antwoord. Kampen: G. Ph. Zalsman, 1902.

"Wapenstilstand." *De Bazuin*, October 31, 1902.

Roeping en wedergeboorte. Kampen: G. Ph. Zalsman, 1903. ET: *Saved by Grace: The Holy Spirit's Work in Calling and Regeneration*. Edited by J. Mark Beach. Translated by Nelson Kloosterman. Grand Rapids: Reformation Heritage Books, 2008.

"Wat is wijsbegeerte?" *De School met den Bijbel* 1, no. 38 (1903): 40, 42, 44–46.

"Hedendaagsche moraal." *Tijdschrift voor Gereformeerde Theologie* 10 (1903): 1–67.

Christelijke wetenschap. Kampen: Kok, 1904.

Christelijke wereldbeschouwing: Rede bij de overdracht van het rectoraat aan de Vrije Universiteit te Amsterdam op 20 october 1904. Kampen: J. H. Bos, 1904. 2nd ed. Kampen: Kok, 1913. ET: *Christian Worldview*. Edited and translated by Nathaniel Gray Sutanto, James Eglinton, and Cory Brock. Wheaton: Crossway, 2019.

Paedagogische beginselen. Kampen: Kok, 1904.

"Voorrede." In *Ongeloof en revolutie: Eene reeks van historische voorlezingen*, by Guillaume Groen van Prinsterer, v–xii. Kampen: J. H. Bos, 1904.

Christelijke en Neutrale Staatkunde. Hilversum: Witzel & Klemkerk, 1905.

Geleerdheid en wetenschap. Amsterdam: Höveker & Wormser, 1905.

"Voorrede." In *Het Gebed*, by Frans Kramer, 1–3. Kampen: Kok, 1905.

Bilderdijk als denker en dichter. Kampen: Kok, 1906.

"Het Wezen des Christendoms." In *Almanak van het studentencorps der Vrije Universiteit voor het jaar 1906*, edited by H. C. Rutgers, 251–77. Amsterdam: Herdes, 1906. Reprinted in *Verzamelde opstellen op het gebied van godsdienst en wetenschap*, ed.

C. B. Bavinck, 17–34. Kampen: Kok, 1921. ET: "The Essence of Christianity." In *Essays on Religion, Science, and Society*, edited by John Bolt, translated by John Vriend and Gerrit Sheeres, 33–48. Grand Rapids: Baker Academic, 2008.

"Psychologie der religie." In *Verslagen en mededeelingen der Koninklijke akademie van wetenschappen*, 147–76. Amsterdam: Joh. Müller, 1907. Reprinted in *Verzamelde opstellen op het gebied van godsdienst en wetenschap*, 55–77. Kampen: Kok, 1921. ET: "Psychology of Religion." In *Essays on Religion, Science, and Society*, edited by John Bolt, translated by John Vriend and Gerrit Sheeres, 61–80. Grand Rapids: Baker Academic, 2008.

"Autobiographische schets van Dr. H. Bavinck." *De Grondwet*, October 6, 1908.

Het christelijk huisgezin. Kampen: Kok, 1908. ET: *The Christian Family*. Translated by Nelson Kloosterman. Grand Rapids: Christian's Library Press, 2012.

Philosophy of Revelation. London: Longmans, Green, 1909. Reprinted as *Philosophy of Revelation: A New Annotated Edition*. Edited by Cory Brock and Nathaniel Gray Sutanto. Peabody, MA: Hendrickson, 2018.

"De psychologie van het kind." *Paedagogisch tijdschrift* 1 (1909): 105–17.

"Calvin and Common Grace." Translated by Geerhardus Vos. In *Calvin and the Reformation: Four Studies*, edited by E. Doumergue, A. Lang, H. Bavinck, and B. B. Warfield, 99–130. New York: Revell, 1909. Also published as "Calvin and Common Grace." Translated by Geerhardus Vos. *Princeton Theological Review* 7 (1909): 437–65.

Johannes Calvijn. Kampen: Kok, 1909. ET: "John Calvin: A Lecture on the Occasion of his 400th Birthday, July 10, 1509–1909." Translated by John Bolt. *Bavinck Review* 1 (2010): 57–85.

Magnalia Dei. Kampen: Kok 1909. ET: *Our Reasonable Faith*. Translated by Henry Zylstra. Grand Rapids: Eerdmans, 1956.

"De psychologie van het kind." *Paedagogisch tijdschrift* 1 (1909): 105–17.

"Richtingen in de psychologie." *Paedagogisch tijdschrift* 1 (1909): 4–15. ET: "Trends in Psychology." In *Essays on Religion, Science, and Society*, edited by John Bolt, translated by John Vriend and Gerrit Sheeres, 165–74. Grand Rapids: Baker Academic, 2008.

"The Reformed Churches in the Netherlands." *Princeton Theological Review* 8 (1910): 433–60.

"Dr. Bavinck over de zending." *Het Kerkblad der Gereformeerde Kerk in Zuid-Afrika* 12, no. 237 (October 1, 1910): 5–6.

Modernisme en orthodoxie. Kampen: Kok, 1911. ET: "Herman Bavinck's *Modernisme en Orthodoxie*: A Translation." Translated by Bruce Pass. *Bavinck Review* 7 (2016): 63–114.

Het Christendom. Baarn: Hollandia, 1912. ET: "Christ and Christianity." Translated by A. A. Pfanstiehl. *Biblical Review* 1 (1916): 214–36. [This article is not an exact (or particularly adept) translation.]

"Bijbelsche Psychologie." *Orgaan van het Gereformeerd Schoolverband* (4 January 1912–5 March 1914).

Foreword to *Letterlijke en practicale verklaring van het Oude Testament*, vol. 1, *Genesis-Deuteronomium*, by Matthew Henry, v–xi. Translated from English. Kampen: Kok, 1912.

"Een brief van zendeling Pieters uit Japan." *De Macedoniër*, September 1912.

De taak van het Gereformeerd Schoolverband: Voor onderwijs en opvoeding. Hilversum: Klemkerk, 1912.

"Verslag van toespraak gehouden op de vergadering van moderne theologen, op 17 April 1912 te Amsterdam." *Gereformeerd Theologisch Tijdschrift* 13 (1913): 92–93.

Handleiding bij het onderwijs in den christelijken godsdienst. Kampen: Kok, 1913.

"Christendom en natuurwetenschap." *Stemmen des Tijds* 2 (1913): 343–77. ET: "Christianity and Natural Science." In *Essays on Religion, Science, and Society*, edited by John Bolt, translated by Harry Boonstra and Gerrit Sheeres, 81–104. Grand Rapids: Baker Academic, 2008.

"Over de ongelijkheid." *Stemmen des Tijds* 2 (1913): 17–43. ET: "On Inequality." In *Essays on Religion, Science, and Society*, edited by John Bolt, translated by Harry Boonstra and Gerrit Sheeres, 145–64. Grand Rapids: Baker Academic, 2008.

"Richtingen in de paedagogiek." In *Handelingen van het nationaal christelijk schoolcongres, gehouden op 9, 10, 11 October 1913 te Utrecht*, 61–69. Kampen: Kok, 1913. ET: "Trends in Pedagogy." In *Essays on Religion, Science, and Society*, edited by John Bolt, translated by Harry Boonstra and Gerrit Sheeres, 205–8. Grand Rapids: Baker Academic, 2008.

"Inleidend woord van Prof. Dr. H. Bavinck." In *Adriaan Steketee (1846–1913): Beschouwingen van een Christen-denker*, by A. Goslinga, v–ix. Kampen: Kok, 1914.

"De Zending in de Heilige Schrift." In *Triumfen van het Kruis: Schetsen der Christelijke Zending van alle eeuwen en allerlei landen voor ons Hollandsch volk geteekend*, by Henry Beets, 7–30. Kampen: Kok, 1914.

"Van schoonheid en schoonheidsleer." In *Almanak van het Studentencorps aan de Vrije Universiteit voor het jaar 1914*, 121–43. Amsterdam: Herdes, 1914. ET: "Of Beauty and Aesthetics." In *Essays on Religion, Science, and Society*, edited by John Bolt, translated by Harry Boonstra and Gerrit Sheeres, 245–60. Grand Rapids: Baker Academic, 2008.

"Het probleem van den oorlog." *Stemmen des tijds* 4 (1914): 1–31. Repr. as *Het probleem van den oorlog*. Kampen: Kok, 1914.

With Anne Anema, Pieter Arie Diepenhorst, Theodorus Heemskerk, and Simon de Vries. *Leider en leiding in de Anti-Revolutionaire Partij*. Amsterdam: Ten Have, 1915.

"Death: Theological View." In *International Standard Bible Encyclopaedia*, edited by James Orr, 2:811–13. Chicago: Howard-Severance Company, 1915.

"Fall." In *International Standard Bible Encyclopaedia*, edited by James Orr, 2:1092–94. Chicago: Howard-Severance Company, 1915.

Over het onbewuste: Wetenschappelijke samenkomst op 7 juli 1915. Amsterdam: Kirchner, 1915. ET: "The Unconscious." In *Essays on Religion, Science, and Society*, edited by John Bolt, translated by Harry Boonstra and Gerrit Sheeres, 175–98. Grand Rapids: Baker Academic, 2008.

Mental, Religious and Social Forces in the Netherlands. The Hague: P. P. I. E., 1915.

"Individualisme en Individualiteit van het kind." *Correspondentieblad van de Vereeniging van Christelijke Onderwijzers en Onderwijzeressen in Nederland en de Overzeesche bezittingen* (1916): 64–72.

De opvoeding der rijpere jeugd. Kampen: Kok, 1916.

"De hervorming en ons nationale leven." In *Ter herdenking der hervorming, 1517–1917*, by Herman Bavinck and H. H. Kuyper, 5–36. Kampen: Kok, 1917.

"De Jongelingenvereeniging in hare beteekenis voor het sociale leven: Rede gehouden op de 29e bondsdag van de Nederlandschen Bond van Jongelingsvereenigingen op Geref. Grondslag." N.p., 1917.

De nieuwe opvoeding. Kampen: Kok, 1917.

De vrouw in de hedendaagsche maatschappij. Kampen: Kok, 1918.

"Philosophie des geloofs." In *Overdr. uit het Annuarium der Societas Studiosorum Reformatorum, 1918*, 62–72. Leiden: Donner, 1918.

De navolging van Christus en het moderne leven. Kampen: Kok, 1918.

"Klassieke opleiding." *Stemmen des Tijds* 7 (1918): 46–65, 113–47. ET: "Classical Education." In *Essays on Religion, Science, and Society*, edited by John Bolt, translated by Harry Boonstra and Gerrit Sheeres, 209–44. Grand Rapids: Baker Academic, 2008.

"Christendom, oorlog, volkenbond." *Stemmen des Tijds* 9 (1919): 1–26, 105–33.

"De beroepsarbeid der gehuwde vrouw." In *Tweede christelijk-sociaal congres 10–13 maart 1919 te Amsterdam: Referaten*, 5–25. Rotterdam: Libertas, 1919.

"Woord vooraf." In *Calvijn als theoloog en de stand van het calvinisme in onzen tijd*, by B. B. Warfield, translated by C. M. E. Kuyper, 5–6. Kampen: Kok, 1919.

Bijbelsche en religieuze psychologie. Kampen: Kok, 1920. ET: *Biblical and Religious Psychology*. Translated by H. Hanko. Grand Rapids: Protestant Reformed Theological School, 1974.

Bijbelsche en religieuze psychologie. Kampen: Kok, 1920.

With Harm Bouwman and Herman Kuyper. "Rapport voor evangelisatie." N.p., 1920.

"Individueele en Sociale Opvoeding." *Orgaan van het Gereformeerd Schoolverband* (20 May–18 November, 1920).

With H. Tilanus. "Rapport van den Onderwijsraad in zake het ontwerp Lager-Onderwijswet." N.p., 1920.

Verzamelde opstellen op het gebied van godsdienst en wetenschap. Edited by C. B. Bavinck. Kampen: Kok, 1921. ET: *Essays on Religion, Science, and Society.* Edited by John Bolt. Translated by Harry Boonstra and Gerrit Sheeres. Grand Rapids: Baker Academic, 2008.

Kennis en leven. Edited by C. B. Bavinck. Kampen: Kok, 1922.

The Doctrine of God. Translated by William Hendriksen. Grand Rapids: Eerdmans, 1951.

Mijne reis naar Amerika. Edited by George Harinck. Barneveld: De Vuurbaak, 1998. ET: "Herman Bavinck's 'My Journey to America.'" Translated by James Eglinton. *Dutch Crossing* 41, no. 2 (2017): 180–93.

"Evolution." In *Essays on Religion, Science, and Society*, edited by John Bolt, translated by Harry Boonstra and Gerrit Sheeres, 105–18. Grand Rapids: Baker Academic, 2008.

"Theology and Religious Studies." In *Essays on Religion, Science, and Society*, edited by John Bolt, translated by Harry Boonstra and Gerrit Sheeres, 49–60. Grand Rapids: Baker Academic, 2008.

"Foreword to the First Edition (Volume 1) of the *Gereformeerde Dogmatiek*." Translated by John Bolt. *Calvin Theological Journal* 45, no. 1 (2010): 9–10.

"The Kingdom of God, the Highest Good." Translated by Nelson Kloosterman. *Bavinck Review* 2 (2011): 133–70.

"Letters to a Dying Student: Bavinck's Letters to Johan van Haselen." Translated and introduced by James Eglinton. *Bavinck Review* 4 (2013): 94–102.

"The Influence of the Protestant Reformation on the Moral and Religious Condition of Communities and Nations." *Mid-America Journal of Theology* 25 (2014): 75–81.

Gereformeerde Ethiek. Edited by Dirk van Keulen. Utrecht: Uitgeverij KokBoekcentrum, 2019. ET: *Reformed Ethics.* Vol. 1, *Created, Fallen, and Converted Humanity.* Edited and translated by John Bolt, with Jessica Joustra, Nelson D. Kloosterman, Antoine Theron, and Dirk van Keulen. Grand Rapids: Baker Academic, 2019. Volumes 2 and 3 are forthcoming.

Unpublished Materials and Manuscripts

Unless indicated otherwise, unpublished materials and manuscripts are held in the Herman Bavinck Archive at the Historisch Documentatiecentrum voor het Nederlands Protestantisme (1800–heden), Vrije Universiteit Amsterdam.

"H. Bavinck, 1872, Zwolle." Folder 16. [Contains entries from 1872 through 1874.]

"Oratio de Historia Atticae Comoediae Antiquae. Elocutus est H. Bavinck Jz. Die III in. Sept. a. MDCCCLXXIII." 1873. Folder 17.

"Philosophie." Folder 18.

"Ex animo et corpore. H. Bavinck, Theol Stud." Folder 16. [Contains entries from 1874 through 1879.]

"Kasboek, H. Bavinck." Folder 19.

"Oorsprong en Waarde der Mythologie." Item no. 12824. Archief van het College van Curatoren, Stadsarchief Kampen.

"Van 1878 tot 1886." Folder 16.

"Rede over het christelijk onderwijs." 1881. Folder 331.

"Methodologie der theologie." 1883–84. Folder 43.

"De theologische richtingen in Duitschland." 1884. Folder 41.

"De leer der verbonden." 1884. Folder 45.

"Medulla Theologiae. Dogmaticae. 1884/85." Folder 46.

"De Mensch, Gods evenbeeld." 1884. Folder 102.

"Van 1886 tot 1891." Folder 16.

"De kenbaarheid Gods." 1888. Folder 106.

"De theologie als wetenschap in dezen tijds. Kampen 1889." Folder 107.

"Menu, 17 Juni 1891." Folder 38.

"Inrichting der gymnasia." 1896. Folder 122.

"Gymnasiaal onderwijs." 1901. Folder 122.

"Bezwaren tegen gymnasiaal onderwijs en hedendaagsche gymnasia." 1903. Folder 122.

"Hoogere burgerscholen." 1904. Folder 122.

"Indrukken van Amerika." Manuscript, ca. 1909. Folder 66.

"Negers." Manuscript, ca. 1909. Folder 67.

"Roosevelt's Presidentschap." 1909. Folder 67.

"Lijst mijner geschriften." N.d. Folder 99.

Parliamentary Speeches

"29 Dec. 1911 n. a. v. de wetsontwerpen tot vaststelling van de begroting van Nederlands-Indie voor het dienstjaar 1912 (4)." *Handelingen van de Eerste Kamer der Staten-Generaal*, 126–28.

"25 April 1912 n. a. v. het wetsontwerp tot regeling van het armbestuur." *Handelingen van de Eerste Kamer der Staten-Generaal*, 495–97.

"12 Maart 1913 n. a. v. het wetsontwerp tot vaststelling van hoofdstuk V (Departement van Binnenlandse Zaken) der staatsbegroting voor het dienstjaar 1913 (2)." *Handelingen van de Eerste Kamer der Staten-Generaal*, 432–34.

"7 Jan. 1914 n. a. v. de wetsontwerpen tot vaststelling der begroting van Nederlands-Indie voor het dienstjaar 1914 (4)." *Handelingen van de Eerste Kamer der Staten-Generaal*, 119–22, 148–51.

"20 Maart 1914 n. a. v. het wetsontwerp tot de definitieve vaststelling van de koloniale huishoudelijke begroting van Suriname voor het dienstjaar 1914 (1)." *Handelingen van de Eerste Kamer der Staten-Generaal*, 484–85.

"21 Maart 1914 n. a. v. het wetsontwerp tot vaststelling van hoofdstuk XI (Departement van Kolonien) der staatsbegroting voor het dienstjaar 1914 (2)." *Handelingen van de Eerste Kamer der Staten-Generaal*, 499.

"29 Dec. 1914 n. a. v. het wetsontwerp tot wettelijke voorziening naar aanleiding van het koninklijk besluit van 2 nov. 1914 (staatsblad no. 514)." *Handelingen van de Eerste Kamer der Staten-Generaal*, 105.

"29 Jan. 1915 n. a. v. het wetsontwerp tot tijdelijke afwijking van de kieswet." *Handelingen van de Eerste Kamer der Staten-Generaal*, 147.

"10 Juni 1915 n. a. v. het wetsontwerp tot aanvulling en verhoging van het VIIIste hoofdstuk der staatsbegroting voor het dienstjaar 1915 (Buitengewoon krediet)." *Handelingen van de Eerste Kamer der Staten-Generaal*, 312–13.

"10 Juni 1915 n. a. v. het wetsontwerp tot vaststelling van nadere strafrechtelijke voorzieningen betreffende veroordelingen, waarbij de straf, tenzij de rechter later anders beveelt, niet wordt ondergaan, de betaling van geldboeten en de voorwaardelijke." *Handelingen van de Eerste Kamer der Staten-Generaal*, 324–28.

"11 Juni 1915 n. a. v. het wetsontwerp tot vaststelling van nadere strafrechtelijke voorzieningen etc." *Handelingen van de Eerste Kamer der Staten-Generaal*, 338–39.

"27 April 1916 n. a. v. het wetsontwerp houdende voorzieningen ten behoeve der statistiek van de in-, uit- en doorvoer." *Handelingen van de Eerste Kamer der Staten-Generaal*, 416.

"26 Mei 1916 n. a. v. verschillende wetsontwerpen ter tegemoetkoming wegens duurte van levensmiddelen." *Handelingen van de Eerste Kamer der Staten-Generaal*, 434.

"15 Mei 1917 n. a. v. het in overweging nemen van veranderingen in het Ilde, IIIde IVde hoofdstuk en in de additionele artikelen der Grondwet, alsmede van art. 192 der Grondwet (Kiesrecht)." *Handelingen van de Eerste Kamer der Staten-Generaal*, 618–24.

"25 April 1917 n. a. v. de wetsontwerpen tot vaststelling van de begroting van het Fonds ter verbetering van de kustverdediging en van de begroting voltooiing vestingstelsel, alsmede van de vaststelling van hoofdstuk VIII (Departement van Oorlog) van de st." *Handelingen van de Eerste Kamer der Staten-Generaal*, 496–98.

"11 April 1918 n. a. v. de wetsontwerpen tot vaststelling van de staatsbegroting voor het dienstjaar 1918." *Handelingen van de Eerste Kamer der Staten-Generaal*, 311–13.

"5 April 1918 n. a. v. het wetsontwerp tot vaststelling van de staatsbegroting voor het dienstjaar 1918, hoofdstuk V (Departement van Binnenlandse Zaken)." *Handelingen van de Eerste Kamer der Staten-Generaal*, 363–64.

"19 Juli 1918 n. a. v. het voorstel van wet Duys c. s. tot verlening van ouderdomsrechten." *Handelingen van de Eerste Kamer der Staten-Generaal*, 755–57, 765–66.

"13 Maart 1919 n. a. v. de wetsontwerpen tot vaststelling van de staatsbegroting voor het dienstjaar 1919." *Handelingen van de Eerste Kamer der Staten-Generaal*, 243–46.

"5 Maart 1920 n. a. v. het wetsontwerp tot voorbehoud der bevoegdheid tot toetreding tot het volkenbondsverdrag." *Handelingen van de Eerste Kamer der Staten-Generaal*, 571–74.

Other Primary Sources

Jan Bavinck

Letters from Jan Bavinck to P. Dijksterhuis, July 18 and 25, August 9 and 22, 1854. Inventory number I–9, 12772. Archief van het College van Curatoren, Stadsarchief Kampen.

Stemmen des heils. Gorinchem: Van Nas, 1863.

De vriendschap der geloovigen met God: Leerrede over Jac. 2:23b. Amsterdam: Van den Bor, 1866.

Het toebrengen van andere schapen tot de kudde van Jezus: Leerrede over Johannes X:16. Amsterdam: Van den Bor, 1867.

Klachte van eene geloovige ziel over de verberging van Gods aanschijn: Leerrede over Psalm 88:15. Kampen: G. Ph. Zalsman, 1868.

Wilt gijlieden ook niet weggaan? Leerrede over Joh. 6:66–69. Amsterdam: Kröber, Heijbrock & Hötte, 1868.

With Helenius de Cock. "Inleiding." *De Getuigenis: Maandschrift in het belang van Waarheid en Godzaligheid*, January 1869, 3–4.

"Houd wat gij hebt": Afscheidswoord aan de Gemeente van Almkerk en Emmikhoven, uitgesproken den 27 Juli 1873. Kampen: G. Ph. Zalsman, 1873.

De bediening des Evangelies een schat, gelegd in aarden vaten: Intreêrede, uitgesproken te Kampen, den 3 Aug. 1873. Kampen: G. Ph. Zalsman, 1873.

With Willem Hendrik Gispen. *De Christ. Geref. Kerk en de Theologische School: Twee toespraken, gehouden den 9 Jan. 1883 bij de installatie van de drie leeraren aan de Theol. School*. Kampen: G. Ph. Zalsman, 1883.

De zaligheid alleen in den naam van Jezus. Kampen: J. H. Bos, 1888.

Davids bede in den ouderdom: Eene overdenking bij gelegenheid van zijne vijftigjarige bediening van het Woord Gods. Kampen: Ph. Zalsman, 1898.

Feeststoffen (voor het Kerstfeest en voor het Oud- en Nieuwjaar). Kampen: Ph. Zalsman, 1900.

Feeststoffen (voor het Paaschfeest). Kampen: Ph. Zalsman, 1901.

De Heidelbergsche Catechismus in 60 leerredenen verklaard. 2 vols. Kampen: Kok, 1903–4.

De algeheele heiliging van de geloovigen, de wensch van de dienaar des Evangelies: Afscheidswoord uitgesproken den 25 Januari 1903. Kampen: Kok, 1903.

Een korte schets van mijn leven. Unpublished, handwritten autobiography, n.d. Folder 445. Bavinck Archive, Historische Documentatiecentrum.

Abraham Kuyper

Het Calvinisme, oorsprong en waarborg onzer constitutioneele vrijheden. Amsterdam: B. van der Land, 1874. ET: "Calvinism: Source and Stronghold of Our Constitutional Liberties." In *Abraham Kuyper: A Centennial Reader*, edited by James Bratt, 279–322. Grand Rapids: Eerdmans, 1998.

Welke zijn de vooruitzichten voor de studenten der Vrije Universiteit? Amsterdam: Kruyt, 1882.

Het Calvinisme en de kunst. Amsterdam: Wormser, 1888.

"The Blurring of the Boundaries." In *Abraham Kuyper: A Centennial Reader*, edited by James Bratt, 363–402. Grand Rapids: Eerdmans, 1998. First published 1892 by J. A. Wormser (Amsterdam).

Encyclopedie der heilige godgeleerdheid. 3 vols. Amsterdam: J. A. Wormser, 1894. ET: *Encyclopedia of Sacred Theology: Its Principles.* Introduction to vol. 1 and all of vol. 2 translated by J. Hendrik de Vries. New York: Scribner, 1898.

E Voto Dordraceno. Vol. 2. Kampen: Kok, 1894.

"Recensie." *De Heraut*, Sunday, June 9, 1895.

Varia Americana. Amsterdam: Höveker & Wormser, 1898.

Het Calvinisme: Zes Stone-lezingen in oct. 1891 te Princeton (N. -J.) gehouden. Amsterdam: Höveker & Wormser, 1899. ET: *Lectures on Calvinism. Six Lectures Delivered at Princeton University under Auspices of the L. P. Stone Foundation.* Grand Rapids: Eerdmans, 1994.

De gemeene gratie. 3 vols. Leiden: D. Donner, 1902–4. ET: *Common Grace: God's Gift for a Fallen World.* 2 vols. Edited by Jordan Ballor and Stephen J. Grabill. Translated by Nelson D. Kloosterman and Ed M. van der Maas. Bellingham, WA: Lexham Press, 2015–17.

Bilderdijk en zijn nationale beteekenis. Amsterdam: Höveker & Wormer, 1906.

Om de oude wereldzee. 2 vols. Amsterdam: Van Holkema & Warendorf, 1907. ET: *On Islam.* Edited by James Bratt. Translated by Jan van Vliet. Bellingham, WA: Lexham Press, 2018.

Nabij God te zijn: Meditatiën. Amsterdam: J. R. Vrolijk, 1908. ET: *To Be near unto God.* Translated by John Hendrik De Vries. Grand Rapids: Eerdmans, 1918.

Principles of Sacred Theology. Translated by J. Hendrik De Vries. Grand Rapids: Eerdmans, 1954.

"Sphere Sovereignty." In *Abraham Kuyper: A Centennial Reader*, edited by James Bratt, 461–90. Grand Rapids: Eerdmans, 1998.

Mijn reis was geboden: Abraham Kuypers Amerikaanse tournee. Edited by George Harinck. Hilversum: Verloren, 2009.

"The Social Question and the Christian Religion." In *Makers of Modern Christian Social Thought*, edited by Jordan Ballor, 45–118. Grand Rapids: Acton Institute, 2016.

Published Correspondence

Dennison, James T., Jr., ed. *The Letters of Geerhardus Vos.* Phillipsburg, NJ: P&R, 2005.

Harinck, George, and Jan de Bruijn, eds. *Een Leidse vriendschap.* Baarn: Ten Have, 1999.

Harinck, George, and Wouter Kroese, eds. *"Men wil toch niet gaarne een masker dragen": Brieven van Henry Dosker aan Herman Bavinck, 1873–1921.* Amsterdam: Historisch Documentatiecentrum voor het Nederlands Protestantisme (1800–heden), 2018.

Miscellaneous Sources

Doop-, trouw-, en begraafboeken (retroacta burgerlijke stand). Inventory no. 308, 44. Stadsarchief Kampen, Kampen.

Hof- und Staats-Handbuch für das Köningreich Hannover auf das Jahr 1844. Hannover: E. Berenberg, n.d.

Vaderlandsche Letteroefeningen, of Tijdschrift van Kunsten en Wetenschappen. Amsterdam: P. Ellerman, 1855.

"Zwolle, Geboorteakte, Aaltje Klinkert, 18-11-1857, Zwolle." Inventory no. 14445, article no. 556. Historisch Centrum Overijssel.

Kuenen, Abraham. *Critices et hermeneutics librorum n. foederis lineamenta.* Leiden: P. Engels, 1858.

Andriessen, P. J. *Een Engelsche jongen op eene Hollandsche school.* Amsterdam: P. N. van Kampen, 1864.

Onze Tolk: Centraalblad voor kunst- en letternieuws 1, no. 8. (January 5, 1870).

Handelingen der Zes-en-twintigste Vergadering van de kuratoren der Theologische School der Christelijke Gereformeerde Kerk in Nederland. Kampen: S. van Velzen Jnr., 1871.

Handelingen van den raad der Gemeente Kampen, 1873. Kampen: K. van Hulst, 1873.

Bulens, F. J. "Litt. Examenandi" and "Theol. Examinandi." June 11 and July 12, 1873. Item no. 12821. Archief van het College van Curatoren, Stadsarchief Kampen.

Mees, Jacob David. *Dagboek: 1872–1874.* Hilversum: Verloren, 1997.

Handelingen der Dertigste Vergadering van de kuratoren der Theologische School der Christelijke Gereformeerde Kerk in Nederland. Kampen: G. Ph. Zalsman, 1874.

Verslag van den toestand der gemeente Kampen over het jaar 1873. Kampen: n.p., 1874.

"Notulen: 1872 november 7–27 april 1876." Archief van het College van Hoogleraren, Stadsarchief Kampen, Item no. 15491.

Handelingen der drie-en-dertigste vergadering van de kuratoren der Theologische School der Christelijke Gerformeerde Kerk in Nederland. Amsterdam: P. van der Sluys, 1876.

Winkler, Johan. "Een en ander over Friesche Eigennamen." *De Vrije Vries* 1, sections 3–4 (1877).

Verslag van het verhandelde in de Comité-Vergadering der Synode van Zwolle 1882, op Woensdag 23 Aug. in de Voormiddagzitting. A. Steketee Archive, Historisch Documentatiecentrum voor het Nederlands Protestantisme (1800–heden), folder 17.

Tiele to Bavinck, Leiden, January 17, 1883. HBA, folder 2.

Kuenen to Bavinck, Leiden, January 19, 1883. HBA, folder 2.

Handelingen der algemeene vergadering van de Maatschappij der Nederlandsche Letterkunde te Leiden, gehouden aldaar den 21sten Juni 1883, in het gebouw van de Maatschappij tot Nut van 't Algemeen. Leiden: Brill, 1883.

Handelingen der algemeene vergadering van de Maatschappij der Nederlandsche Letterkunde te Leiden, gehouden aldaar den 19den Juni 1884, in het gebouw van de Maatschappij tot Nut van 't Algemeen. Leiden: Brill, 1884.

van der Munnik to Bavinck, Kampen, March 29, 1889. HBA, folder 3.

Berends to Bavinck, Amsterdam, April 1, 1889. HBA, folder 3.

Bavinck to Hovy, Kampen, April 15, 1889. HBA, folder 3.

Jaarboekje van de Jongelingsvereenigingen in Nederland, voor 1894, uitgegeven van wege den Nederlandschen Bond van Jongelingsvereenigingen op Gereformeerden Grondslag. 's Gravenhage: A. Berends, 1894.

"Feestrede van Prof. Dr. H. Bavinck." In *Gedenkboek: Opgedragen door het feestcomité aan Prof. Dr. A. Kuyper bij zijn vijf en twintigjarig jubileum als hoofdredacteur van "De Standaard," 1872 1 April 1897,* 38–52. Amsterdam: G. J. C. Herdes, 1897.

Concept-Zendingsorde voor de Gereformeerde Kerken in Nederland. N.p., ca. 1902.

Rumpff to Bavinck, Kampen, May 15, 1905. HBA, folder 8.

Bavinck to Hoekstra, Amsterdam, May 1, 1906. HBA, folder 8.

Kuyper-Gedenkboek 1907. 's Gravenhage: n.p., 1908.

Herman Bavinck and Johanna Bavinck-Schippers to unknown addressee, Amsterdam, November 10, 1912. HBA, folder 9.

Kuyper to Bavinck, Amsterdam, November 12, 1912. HBA, folder 12.

Acta der generale synode van de Gereformeerde Kerken in Nederland, gehouden te Leeuwarden van 24 augustus–9 september 1920. Kampen: Kok, 1920.

"Amelia Josina den Dekker." *Bevolkingsregister, Almkerk, 1910–1920,* 34:96.

"Wouterina Arnolda den Dekker." *Bevolkingsregister, Emmikhoven en Waardhuizen, 1870–1879,* 14:103.

"Zwolle, Registers van overlijden, 1811–1942, Aaltje Klinkert." Inventory no. 15325, article no. 231. Historisch Centrum Overijssel.

Verslag der Handelingen van de Eerste Kamer. March 12, 1913. 's Gravenhage: Algemeene Landsdrukkerij.

Congres voor Gereformeerde Evangelisatie op dinsdag 8 en woensdag 9 april 1913 te Amsterdam. N.p., 1913.

Snouck Hurgronje to Johanna Bavinck-Schippers, Leiden, June 28, 1921. HBA, folder 11.

Dosker to Johanna Bavinck-Schippers, Holland, MI, August 29, 1921. HBA, folder 11.

[Bavinck-Schippers, Johanna]. "Prof Dr H Bavinck." N.d. HBA, folder 40.

Dosker to Johanna Bavinck-Schippers, Louisville, March 20, 1923. HBA, folder 11.

Bolt, John, James Bratt, and Paul Visser, eds. *The J. H. Bavinck Reader.* Grand Rapids: Eerdmans, 2013.

Secondary Sources

Aalders, Willem Jan. "In Memoriam: Dr. H. Bavinck." *Stemmen des tijds* 10 (1921): 129–41.

Abbenhuis, Maartje M. *The Art of Staying Neutral: The Netherlands in the First World War, 1914–1918.* Amsterdam: Amsterdam University Press, 2006.

Adriaanse, L. *De nieuwe koers in onze zending, of toelichting op de zendingsorde.* Amsterdam: Kirchner, 1903.

Allen, Michael. *Grounded in Heaven: Recentering Christian Hope and Life on God.* Grand Rapids: Eerdmans, 2018.

van Alphen, Daniël François. *Reisverhalen en indrukken van een togt via Bentheim (Münster), Hannover, Hamburg, Kiel en Korsör naar Kopenhagen.* 's Gravenhage: J. M. van 't Haaff, 1874.

Anema, Anne. *Calvinisme en rechtswetenschap: Een studie.* Amsterdam: Kirchner, 1897.

———. *De grondslagen der sociologie: Een studie.* Amsterdam: Kirchner, 1900.

Augustine. *On Christian Teaching.* Translated by R. P. H. Green. Oxford: Oxford University Press, 1997.

Bacote, Vincent. *The Spirit in Public Theology: Appropriating the Legacy of Abraham Kuyper.* Eugene, OR: Wipf & Stock, 2005.

Baggerman, Arianne. "Lost Time: Temporal Discipline and Historical Awareness in Nineteenth-Century Dutch Egodocuments." In *Controlling Time and Shaping the Self: Developments in Autobiographical Writing since the Sixteenth Century*, edited by Arianne Baggerman, Rudolf Dekker, and Michael James Mascuch, 455–535. Leiden: Brill, 2011.

Bakker, Nelle. *Kind en karakter: Nederlandse pedagogen over opvoeding in het gezin, 1845–1925.* Amsterdam: Het Spinhuis, 1995.

Bakker, W., and H. Mulder. "Petrus Biesterveld." In *Biografisch lexicon voor de geschiedenis van het Nederlands protestantisme*, edited by D. Nauta, A. de Groot, J. van den Berg, O. J. de Jong, F. R. J. Knetsch, and G. H. M. Posthumus Meyjes, 3:41–42. Kampen: Kok, 1988.

Banks, Louis Albert, ed. *T. De Witt Talmage: His Life and Work.* Philadelphia: John C. Winston, 1902.

Barger, M. W. "De vrouw en de studie." *Christendom en Vrouwenbeweging*, series 4, no. 1 (1923).

Bavinck, Berendinus Johannes Femia. *De sterfte aan tuberculosis pulmonum in Nederland (1875–1895).* Kampen: J. H. Bos, 1897.

Bavinck, C. B., N. Buffinga, J. Douma, J. H. Sillevis Smitt, and B. Wielenga. *"Ons aller Moeder": Een woord van voorlichting en getuigenis inzake de kwestie-Geelkerken.* Kampen: Kok, 1925.

Bavinck, Coenraad Bernardus. "Appendix A: Foreword." In Herman Bavinck, *Essays on Religion, Science, and Society*, edited by John Bolt, translated by Harry Boonstra and Gerrit Sheeres, 279–80. Grand Rapids: Baker Academic, 2008.

———. "Voorrede bij den tweeden druk." In Herman Bavinck, *Magnalia Dei*, 1–4. 2nd ed. Kampen: Kok, 1931.

Beach, J. Mark. "Abraham Kuyper, Herman Bavinck, and the 'Conclusions of Utrecht 1905.'" *Mid-America Journal of Theology* 19 (2008): 11–68.

———. "Introductory Essay." In *Saved by Grace: The Holy Spirit's Work in Calling and Regeneration*, by Herman Bavinck, translated by Nelson D. Kloosterman, ix–xi. Grand Rapids: Reformation Heritage Books, 2008.

Beets, Nicolaas. *Life and Character of J. H. van der Palm.* Translated by J. P. Westerveld. New York: Hurd & Houghton, 1895.

van Bekkum, Koert. "Verlangen naar tastbare genade: Achtergrond, geschiedenis en typologie van spiritualiteit in de Gereformeerde Kerken (vrijgemaakt)." In *Proeven van spiritualiteit: Bijdragen ter gelegenheid van 160 jaar Theologische Universiteit Kampen*, edited by Koert van Bekkum, 131–58. Barneveld: Uitgeverij De Vuurbaak, 2014.

van den Belt, Henk. "Herman Bavinck's Lectures on the Certainty of Faith (1891)." *Bavinck Review* 8 (2017): 35–63.

van Bemmelen, Pieter. *L'Egypte et l'Europe, par un ancien juge mixte*. Leiden: Brill, 1884.

van den Berg, J. "De Spiritualiteit van de Afgescheidenen." In *Gereformeerd Theologisch Tijdschrift* 92 (1992): 172–88.

Berkhof, Louis. *The History of Christian Doctrines*. Grand Rapids: Banner of Truth, 1949.

Berkouwer, Gerrit. *Faith and Justification*. Grand Rapids: Eerdmans, 1954.

Beuker, Gerrit Jan. *Abgeschiedenes Streben nach Einheit: Leben und Wirken Henricus Beukers, 1834–1900*. Bad Bentheim: Hellendoorn KG, 1996.

———. "'The Area beyond Hamse and Hardenberg': Van Raalte and Bentheim." In *The Enduring Legacy of Albertus C. Van Raalte as Leader and Liaison*, edited by Jacob E. Nyenhuis and George Harinck, 23–42. Grand Rapids: Eerdmans, 2014.

———. "German Oldreformed Emigration: Catastrophe or Blessing?" In *Breaches and Bridges: Reformed Subcultures in the Netherlands, Germany, and the United States*, edited by George Harinck and Hans Krabbendam, 101–14. Amsterdam: VU Uitgeverij, 2000.

———. *Umkehr und Erneuerung: Aus der Geschichte der Evangelisch-altreformierten Kirche in Niedersachsen, 1838–1988*. Bad Bentheim: Hellendoorn KG, 1988.

Beuker, H. "Dr Bavincks inaugurele rede." *De Vrije Kerk* 9 (1883): 178–83.

———. *Tubantiana*. Kampen: Kok, 1897.

Beversluis, M. *De val van Dr. A. Kuyper een zegen voor ons land en volk*. Oud-Beierland: Hoogwerf, 1905.

Binnerts Sz., A. *Nieuw-Gereformeerde en Moderne Theologie: Beschouwingen naar aanleiding van de rectorale oratie van Prof. Bavinck, ter moderne theologenvergadering voorgedragen en aangevuld met een Naschrift*. Baarn: Hollandia-Drukkerij, 1912.

Blanning, T. C. W. Introduction to *The Oxford Illustrated History of Modern Europe*, edited by T. C. W. Blanning, 1–10. Oxford: Oxford University Press, 1996.

Bloemendal, Berthold. "Kerkelijke en nationale achtergronden van Duitse studenten in Kampen, 1854–1994." In *Documentatieblad voor de Nederlandse Kerkgeschiedenis na 1800*, no. 85 (December 2016): 62–78.

Boeke, D. E. *Gereformeerde Evangelisatie: Indrukken op het Congres voor Gereformeerde Evangelisatie te Amsterdam, 8/9 April 1913*. Amsterdam: Kirberger & Kesper, 1913.

Boekholt, P. Th. F. M., and Engelina Petronella de Booy. *Geschiedenis van de school in Nederland vanaf de middeleeuwen tot aan de huidige tijd*. Assen: Van Gorcum, 1987.

Boeles, W. B. S. *Frieslands hoogeschool en het Rijks Athenaeum te Franeker*. Leeuwarden: H. Kuipers, 1878.

de Boer, Tjitze. "De Filosofie van Henri Bergson." *De Beweging* 5 (1909): 225–44.

———. *Geschichte der Philosophie im Islam*. Stuttgart: Fr. Frommanns Verlag, 1901.

———. *Nietzsche en de wetenschap*. Amsterdam: Scheltema & Holkema's Boekhandel, 1906.

———. "Plato en Aristoteles bij de moslims." *Tweemaandelijksch Tijdschrift* 6 (1900): 306–31.

Boersma, Hans. *Seeing God: The Beatific Vision in Christian Tradition*. Grand Rapids: Eerdmans, 2018.

Boissevain, Charles. *Van 't Noorden naar 't Zuiden: Schetsen en indrukken van de Verenigde Staten van Noord-Amerika*. Haarlem: H. D. Tjeenk Willink, 1881.

Bolt, John. *Bavinck on the Christian Life: Following Jesus in Faithful Service*. Wheaton: Crossway, 2015.

———. "Editor's Introduction." In *Reformed Dogmatics: Prolegomena*, by Herman Bavinck, edited by John Bolt, 1:11–22. Grand Rapids: Baker Academic, 2003.

———. "Grand Rapids between Kampen and Amsterdam: Herman Bavinck's Reception and Influence in North America." *Calvin Theological Journal* 38, no. 2 (2003): 263–80.

———. "Herman Bavinck Speaks English: A Bibliographic Essay." *Mid-America Journal of Theology* no. 19 (2008): 117–26.

Bos, David. *Servants of the Kingdom: Professionalization among Ministers of the Nineteenth-Century Netherlands Reformed Church*. Leiden: Brill, 2010.

Bos, Emo. *Souvereiniteit en religie: Godsdienstvrijheid onder de eerste Oranjevorsten*. Hilversum: Verloren, 2009.

Bos, F. L. "Velzen, Simon van." In *Biografisch lexicon voor de geschiedenis van het Nederlands protestantisme*, edited by D. Nauta, A. de Groot, J. van den Berg, O. J. de Jong, F. R. J. Knetsch, and G. H. M. Posthumus Meyjes, 2:431–33. Kampen: Kok, 1983.

Bosma, Ulbe, and Remco Raben. *Being "Dutch" in the Indies: A History of Creolisation and Empire, 1500–1920*. Translated by Wendie Shaffer. Athens: Ohio University Press, 2008.

Bouma, H. *Een vergeten hoofdstuk*. Enschede: Boersma, 1959.

Bouwman, Harm. "Ds. J. Bavinck." *De Bazuin*, December 3, 1909.

———. "Een leerstoel voor de zending." *De Bazuin*, September 9, 1910.

———. "Gedenkdag." *De Bazuin*, January 10, 1913.

Bratt, James., ed. *Abraham Kuyper: A Centennial Reader*. Grand Rapids: Eerdmans, 1998.

———. *Abraham Kuyper: Modern Calvinist, Christian Democrat*. Grand Rapids: Eerdmans, 2013.

———. "The Context of Herman Bavinck's Stone Lectures: Culture and Politics in 1908." *Bavinck Review* 1 (2010): 4–24.

Bratt, James. Introduction to "Calvinism: Source and Stronghold of Our Constitutional Liberties," by Abraham Kuyper, in Bratt, *Abraham Kuyper: A Centennial Reader*, 279–80.

Brederveld, J. *Christian Education: A Summary and Discussion of Bavinck's Pedagogical Principles*. Grand Rapids: Smitter, 1928.

———. *Hoofdlijnen der paedagogiek van dr. Herman Bavinck*. Amsterdam: De Standaard, 1927.

Bremmer, R. H. *Herman Bavinck als dogmaticus*. Kampen: Kok, 1966.

———. *Herman Bavinck (1854–1921): Portret van 'n Reformatoriese denker in Nederland*. Potchefstroom: Potchefstroomse Universiteit vir Christelike Hoër Onderwys, 1998.

———. *Herman Bavinck en zijn tijdgenoten*. Kampen: Kok, 1966.

Brinkman, Martien. "Bavinck en de katholiciteit van de kerk." In *Ontmoetingen met Bavinck*, edited by George Harinck and Gerrit Neven, 307–24. Barneveld: Uitgeverij De Vuurbaak, 2006.

Bristley, Eric. *Guide to the Writings of Herman Bavinck*. Grand Rapids: Reformation Heritage Books, 2008.

Brock, Cory. *Orthodox yet Modern: Herman Bavinck's Use of Friedrich Schleiermacher*. Bellingham, WA: Lexham, 2020.

Brock, Cory, and Nathaniel Gray Sutanto. "Introduction to the Annotated Edition." In *Philosophy of Revelation: A New Annotated Edition*, by Herman Bavinck, edited by Cory Brock and Nathaniel Gray Sutanto, xxi–xxxii. Peabody, MA: Hendrickson, 2018.

ten Broek, M. *De geestelijke opwekking in Holland*. Ermelo: Gebr. Mooij, 1905.

Brown, Stewart J. "The Disruption and the Dream: The Making of New College 1843–1861." In *Disruption to Diversity: Edinburgh Divinity 1846–1996*, 29–50. Edinburgh: T&T Clark, 1996.

———. *Thomas Chalmers and the Godly Commonwealth in Scotland*. Oxford: Oxford University Press, 1983.

Brownson, Marcus A. "The Calvin Celebration in Geneva, and Calvin's City as It Is Today: Personal Impressions." *Journal of the Presbyterian Historical Society (1901–1930)* 5, no. 4 (December 1909): 164–74.

Bruce, Alexander Balmain. "The Rev. Professor Stewart F. Salmond, DD, Free Church College, Aberdeen." *Biblical World* 8, no. 5 (1896): 347–53.

Brugman, J. "Snouck Hurgronje's Study of Islamic Law." In *Leiden Oriental Connections, 1850–1940*, edited by Willem Otterspeer, 82–93. Leiden: Brill, 1989.

de Bruijn, Jan. *Abraham Kuyper: A Pictorial Biography*. Grand Rapids: Eerdmans, 2008.

———. "'Het krankheidsverschijnsel der zich intellectueel man voelende vrouw.' De eerste vrouwelijke studenten aan de Vrije Universiteit." In *Ridders van het Recht:*

De juridische faculteit van de Vrije Universiteit, 1880–2010, edited by J. de Bruijn, S. Faber, and A. Soeteman, 83–92. Amsterdam: Prometheus, 2015.

Buys, Marius. *Mr. Jan Rudolf Thorbecke herdacht.* Tiel: D. Mijs, 1872.

Campbell, Douglas. *The Puritan in Holland, England and America: An Introduction to American History.* 2 vols. New York: Harper and Brothers, 1892–93.

Casimir, Rommert. "Bavincks paedagogische beginselen." *School en leven* 8 (1906/1907): 38–42, 87–90, 118–23, 177–83, 193–200, 321–27, 465–67.

Chantepie de la Saussaye, Daniël. *Verzameld werk.* 3 vols. Zoetermeer: Boekencentrum, 1997–2003.

Christelijke Sociaal Congres. Rotterdam: Drukkerij Libertas, 1919.

de Cock, Helenius. *Waarom heb ik mijn kinderen laten vaccineren? Open brief aan de heer D. Wijnbeek.* Kampen: Simon van Velzen Jr., 1871.

Datema, Pieter Gerrit. *Zending, een plicht?* N.p., 1904.

Daubanton, F. E. *Confessie en dogmatiek.* Amsterdam: F.W. Egeling, 1891.

Davies, Guy. Review of *Herman Bavinck: Pastor, Churchman, Statesman, and Theologian,* by Ron Gleason. *European Journal of Theology* 21, no. 2 (October 2012): 176.

Dekker, Rudolf. "Childhood in Dutch Autobiographies, 1600–1850: Changing Memory Strategies." *Paedagogica Historica* 32 (1996): 65–76.

———. Introduction to *Egodocuments and History: Autobiographical Writing in Its Social Context since the Middle Ages*, edited by Rudolf Dekker, 7–20. Hilversum: Verloren, 2002.

van Dellen, Idzerd. *In God's Crucible: An Autobiography.* Grand Rapids: Baker, 1950.

———. "In Memoriam: Prof. Dr. H. Bavinck te Kampen." *Onze Toekomst,* August 26, 1921.

Dennison, James T., Jr. Introduction to *The Letters of Geerhardus Vos*, edited by James T. Dennison Jr., 11–86. Phillipsburg, NJ: P&R, 2005.

Dercksen, J. M. E. *Gedenkboek der feestvieringen van het driehonderdjarig bestaan der hoogeschool te Leiden.* Leiden: De Breuk & Smits, 1875.

van Deursen, Arie Theodorus. *The Distinctive Character of the Free University in Amsterdam, 1880–2005.* Grand Rapids: Eerdmans, 2008.

Diepenhorst-De Gaay Fortman, A. C. *Wat wil de Nederlandsche Christen-Vrouwenbond?* Rotterdam: Drukkerij Libertas, 1920.

Diepersloot, J., and E. L. Smelik. *Een kleine kerk in een groten tijd (De Gereformeerde Kerken in Hersteld Verband).* N.p., 1937.

Dirksen, Peter Berend, and Aad W. van der Kooi, eds. *Abraham Kuenen (1828–1891): His Major Contributions to the Study of the Old Testament.* Leiden: Brill, 1993.

Donner, J. H. *Afgewezen, maar niet teleurgesteld: Toespraak naar 1 Koningen 8:17–19a.* Kampen: G. Ph. Zalsman, 1873.

———. *Lichtstralen van den kandelaar des woords.* Leiden: D. Donner, 1883.

Dorner, I. A. *Entwicklungsgeschichte der Lehre von der Person Christi*. Berlin: Schlawitz, 1853. ET: *History of the Development of the Doctrine of the Person of Christ*. Translated by D. W. Simon. Edinburgh: T&T Clark, 1861.

Dosker, Henry Elias. *The Dutch Anabaptists*. Philadelphia: Judson Press, 1921.

———. "Herman Bavinck." *Princeton Theological Review* 20 (1922): 448–64. Reprinted as "Herman Bavinck: A Eulogy by Henry Elias Dosker," in *Essays on Religion, Science, and Society*, edited by John Bolt, translated by Harry Boonstra and Gerrit Sheeres, 13–24. Grand Rapids: Baker Academic, 2008.

van Driel, C. M. [Niels]. *Schermen in de schemering: Vijf opstellen over modernisme en orthodoxie*. Hilversum: Verloren, 2007.

———. "The Status of Women in Contemporary Society: Principles and Practice in Herman Bavinck's Socio-Political Thought." In *Five Studies in the Thought of Herman Bavinck, a Creator of Modern Dutch Theology*, edited by John Bolt, 153–95. Lewiston, NY: Mellen, 2011.

Dröge, Philip. *Pelgrim: Leven en reizen van Christiaan Snouck Hurgronje*. Utrecht: Spectrum, 2017.

Du Bois, W. E. B. "Die Negerfrage in den Vereinigten Staaten." *Archiv für Sozialwissenschaft und Sozialpolitik* 22 (1906): 31–79.

Van Dyke, Harry. *Groen van Prinsterer's Lectures on Unbelief and Revolution*. Jordan Station, Ontario: Wedge Publishing Foundation, 1989.

———. Review of *Herman Bavinck: Pastor, Churchman, Statesman, and Theologian*, by Ron Gleason. *Calvin Theological Journal* 46, no. 1 (April 2011): 192–97.

Dykstra, Russell. Review of *Herman Bavinck: Pastor, Churchman, Statesman, and Theologian*, by Ron Gleason. *Protestant Reformed Theological Journal* 46, no. 1 (November 2012): 133–37.

van Eeden, Frederik. *De kleine Johannes*. 3 vols. Amsterdam: Elsevier, 1979.

———. *De nachtbruid: De gedenkschriften van Vico Muralto*. Amsterdam: Versluys, 1909.

Eekhoff, W., ed. *Oorkonden der geschiedenis van het Sint Anthonij-Gasthuis te Leeuwarden, uit de 153 en 16e eeuw, Eerste deel, Van 1406–1562*. Leeuwarden: n.p., 1876.

Eerdmans, Bernardus. *"Orthodox" verweer*. Leiden: S. C. van Doesburgh, 1911.

Eglinton, James. "The Christian Family in the Twenty-First Century." In *The Christian Family*, by Herman Bavinck, translated by Nelson D. Kloosterman, ix–x. Grand Rapids: Christian's Library Press, 2012.

———. Review of *Herman Bavinck: Pastor, Churchman, Statesman, and Theologian*, by Ron Gleason. *Scottish Bulletin of Evangelical Theology* 29, no. 1 (Spring 2011): 127.

———. *Trinity and Organism: Towards a New Reading of Herman Bavinck's Organic Motif*. London: Bloomsbury T&T Clark, 2012.

————. "*Varia Americana* and Race: Kuyper as Antagonist and Protagonist." *Journal of Reformed Theology* 11 (2017): 65–80.

van Eijnatten, Joris, and Fred van Lieburg. *Nederlandse religiegeschiedenis.* Hilversum: Verloren, 2006.

Eisenstadt, Shmuel Noah. *Comparative Civilizations and Multiple Modernities.* 2 vols. Leiden: Brill, 2003.

Faber, Riemer, trans. *Synopsis purioris theologiae / Synopsis of a Purer Theology: Latin Text and English Translation.* Vol. 1, *Disputations 1–23.* Leiden: Brill, 2014. Vol. 2, *Disputations 24–42.* Leiden: Brill, 2016.

Fokkema, Douwe, and Frans Grijzenhout. *Dutch Culture in a European Perspective: 1600–2000.* New York: Palgrave Macmillan, 2004.

Fuller, Ross. *The Brotherhood of the Common Life and Its Influence.* New York: State University of New York Press, 1995.

Geelhoed, J. *Dr. Herman Bavinck.* Goes: Oosterbaan & Le Cointre, 1958.

Geesink, Willem. *Calvinisten in Nederland.* Rotterdam: J. H. Dunk, 1887.

————. *De ethiek in de gereformeerde theologie: Rede bij de overdracht van het rectoraat der Vrije Universiteit te Amsterdam op 20 october 1897.* Amsterdam: Kirchner, 1897.

————. *Gereformeerde ethiek.* Edited by Valentijn Hepp. Kampen: Kok, 1931.

————. "In Memoriam: Petrus Abraham Elisa Sillevis Smitt." *Almanak van het Studentencorps a/d Vrije-Universiteit, 1919,* 61–72. Amsterdam: Herdes, 1919.

de Gelder, Jan Jacob. *Catalogus van de tentoonstelling ter herdenking van het driehonderdvijftigjarig bestaan der Leidsche universiteit in het museum "De Lakenhal." Leiden, Februari 1925.* Leiden: Sijthoff, 1925.

van Gelderen, J., and F. Rozemond. *Gegevens betreffende de Theologische Universiteit Kampen, 1854–1994.* Kampen: Kok, 1994.

Gerok, Karl. *Palmbladen; Heilige woorden: Ter bevordering van christelijke geloof en christelijke wereldbeschouwing.* Translated by C. P. L. Rutgers. Groningen: Zweeden, 1865.

Geurts, Pieter Antoon Marie. *Voorgeschiedenis van het statencollegte te Leiden: 1575–1593.* Leiden: Brill, 1984.

Gielen, Jos. "Nietzsche in Nederland." *De Nieuwe Taalgids* 37 (1943): 19–26.

Gispen, W. "Aan een vriend te Jeruzalem." *De Bazuin,* October 28, 1892.

Gleason, Ron. *Herman Bavinck: Pastor, Churchman, Statesman, and Theologian.* Phillipsburg, NJ: P&R, 2010.

Goedvree, Aart. *Een ondoordringbaar mysterie: Wedergeboorte volgens Herman Bavinck.* Apeldoorn: Labarum Academic, 2018.

de Graaf, Gerrit Roelof. "Fides Quaerit Intellectum: 'Het geloof zoekt te verstaan'; Het Kamper studentencorps 'Fides Quaerit Intellectum' in zijn omgang met de 'moderne' cultuur (1863–1902)." *Documentatieblad voor de Nederlandse kerk-geschiedenis na 1800* 28 (2005): 20–35.

de Graaff, W. "Een merkwaardige school in de vorige eeuw." *De Hoeksteen* 11 (1982): 105–12.

Graham, Gordon. "Bavinck, Nietzsche, and Secularization." In *The Kuyper Center Review*, vol. 2, *Revelation and Common Grace*, edited by John Bowlin, 14–26. Grand Rapids: Eerdmans, 2011.

Griffis, William Elliot. *The Influence of the Netherlands in the Making of the English Commonwealth and the American Republic.* Boston: De Wolfe, Fiske & Co., 1891.

Groen van Prinsterer, Guillaume. *Ongeloof en revolutie: Eene reeks van historische voorlezingen.* Leiden: S. & J. Luchtmans, 1847. ET: *Unbelief and Revolution: A Series of Lectures in History.* Edited and translated by Harry van Dyke. Amsterdam: Groen van Prinsterer Fund, 1973–75.

Groenewegen, Herman. *De theologie en hare wijsbegeerte.* Amsterdam: Rogge, 1904.

———. "Wetenschap of dogmatisme." *Theologisch Tijdschrift* 37 (1903): 385–424.

Gunning, J. H., Jr. "Aan Prof. Dr. H. Bavinck." *De Vrije Kerk* 10 (1884): 212–20.

———. "Aan Prof. Dr. H. Bavinck." *De Vrije Kerk* 10 (1884): 277–86.

———. "Aan Prof. Dr. H. Bavinck." *De Vrije Kerk* 10 (1884): 314–19.

———. *De heilige schrift, Gods woord: Antwoord aan Dr. A. Kuyper op zijn "Confidentie."* Amsterdam: Höveker, 1872.

———. *Jezus Christus de middelaar Gods en der menschen: Naar aanleiding van dr. H. Bavinck, De theologie enz. door J. H. Gunning jr.* Amsterdam: Höveker & Zoon, 1884.

Gunning Wzn. [Willemszoon], J. H. "Prof. dr. H. Bavinck." *Het Kind* 22 (1921): 321–25.

Hagen, T. J. "De geestelijke verzorging van onze weermacht." In *Onze Weermacht— van 1914 tot 1918—Extra Nummer van De Amsterdammer Weekblad voor Neder-land*, edited by J. A. van Hamel et al., 7–10. Amsterdam: n.p., 1918.

Harger, Swenna, and Loren Lemmen. *Beloved Family and Friends: Letters between Grafschaft Bentheim, Germany and America.* Holland, MI: Bentheimers International Society, 2007.

———. *The County of Bentheim and Her Emigrants to North America.* Holland, MI: Swenna Harger, 1994.

Harinck, George. "Abraham Kuyper: De Vrije Universiteit op weg naar de samenleving." In *Verder kijken: Honderdvijfendertig jaar Vrije Universiteit Amsterdam in de samenleving; Zesentwintig portretten*, edited by Ab Flipse, 19–26. Amsterdam: VU Uitgeverij, 2016.

———. "'Als een schelm weggejaagd'? De ARP en de verkiezingen van 1905." In *Het kabinet-Kuyper (1901–1905)*, edited by D. Th. Kuiper and G. J. Schutte, 270–301. Zoetermeer: Meinema, 2001.

———. "Being Public: On Abraham Kuyper and His Publications." In *Abraham Kuyper: An Annotated Bibliography, 1857–2010*, by Tjitze Kuipers, vii–xxi. Leiden: Brill, 2011.

———. "De Antirevolutionarie Partij, 1905–1918." In *De Antirevolutionarie Partij, 1829–1980*, edited by George Harinck, Roel Kuiper, and Peter Bak, 123–56. Hilversum: Verloren, 2001.

———. "'Eén uur lang is het hier brandend licht en warm geweest': Bavinck en Kampen." In *Ontmoetingen met Bavinck*, edited by George Harinck and Gerrit Neven, 107–18. Barneveld: De Vuurbaak, 2006.

———. "Groen van Prinsterer en Thomas Chalmers: 'Precious Ties of a Common Faith.'" In *Groen van Prinsterer in Europese Context*, edited by George Harinck and Jan de Bruijn, 43–54. Hilversum: Uitgeverij Verloren, 2004.

———. "Herman Bavinck and Geerhardus Vos." *Calvin Theological Journal* 45, no. 1 (2010): 18–31.

———. "Herman Bavinck and the Neo-Calvinist Concept of the French Revolution." In *Neo-Calvinism and the French Revolution*, edited by James Eglinton and George Harinck, 13–30. London: Bloomsbury T&T Clark, 2014.

———. "Inleiding." In *"Men wil toch niet gaarne een masker dragen": Brieven van Henry Dosker aan Herman Bavinck, 1873–1921*, edited by George Harinck and Wouter Kroese, 11–15. Amsterdam: Historisch Documentatiecentrum voor het Nederlands Protestantisme (1800–heden), 2018.

———. "Inleiding." In *Mijne reis naar Amerika*, by Herman Bavinck, edited by George Harinck, 9–29. Barneveld: Uitgeverij De Vuurbaak, 1998.

———. "'Land da ons verwondert en ons betoovert': Bavinck en Amerika." In *Ontmoetingen met Bavinck*, edited by George Harinck and Gerrit Neven, 35–46. Barneveld: De Vuurbaak, 2006.

———. "The Poetry of Theologian Geerhardus Vos." In *Dutch-American Arts and Letters in Historical Perspective*, edited by Robert P. Swierenga, Jacob E. Nyenhuis, and Nella Kennedy, 69–80. Holland, MI: Van Raalte Press, 2008.

———. "The Religious Character of Modernism and the Modern Character of Religion: A Case Study of Herman Bavinck's Engagement with Modern Culture." *Scottish Bulletin of Evangelical Theology* 29, no. 1 (2011): 60–77.

———. "'Something That Must Remain, If the Truth Is to Be Sweet and Precious to Us': The Reformed Spirituality of Herman Bavinck." *Calvin Theological Journal* 38, no. 2 (2003): 248–62.

———. "'The Tares in the Wheat': Henry E. Dosker's Calvinist Historiography of Dutch Anabaptism." In *Religious Minorities and Cultural Diversity in the Dutch Republic*, edited by August den Hollander, Mirjam van Veen, Anna Voolstra, and Alex Noord, 268–79. Leiden: Brill, 2014.

———. *Varia Americana: In het spoor van Abraham Kuyper door de Verenigde Staten*. Amsterdam: Bert Bakker, 2016.

———. "Via veldprediker naar legerpredikant: De protestantse kerken en de wederzijdse doordringing van kerk en leger." In *De kogel door de kerk? Het Nederlandse Christendom en de Eerste Wereldoorlog*, edited by Enne Koops and Henk van der Linden, 107–31. Soesterberg: Aspekt B.V., 2014.

———. "Wipe Out Lines of Division (Not Distinctions): Bennie Keet, Neo-Calvinism and the Struggle against Apartheid." *Journal of Reformed Theology* 11, no. 1–2 (2017): 83–85.

Harinck, George, and Wim Berkelaar. *Domineesfabriek: Geschiedenis van de Theologische Universiteit Kampen*. Amsterdam: Prometheus, 2018.

Harinck, George, Cornelis van der Kooi, and Jasper Vree, eds. *"Als Bavinck nu maar eens kleur bekende": Aantekeningen van H. Bavinck over de zaak-Netelenbos, het Schriftgezag en de Situatie van de Gereformeerde Kerken (November 1919)*. Amsterdam: VU Uitgeverij, 1994.

Harinck, George, Herman Paul, and Bart Wallet, eds. *Het gereformeerde geheugen: Protestantse herinneringscultuur in Nederland, 1850–2000*. Amsterdam: Bert Bakker, 2009.

Harinck, George, and Marjoleine de Vos. *Wat eten we vanavond? Protestants!* Amsterdam: Donum Reeks, 2005.

Harinck, George, and Lodewijk Winkler. "The Nineteenth Century." In *Handbook of Dutch Church History*, edited by Herman Selderhuis, 445. Göttingen: Vandenhoeck & Ruprecht, 2015.

den Hartogh, G. M. *De Afscheiding en de Theologische School*. Aalten: N. V. de Graafschap, 1934.

———. "De eerste halve eeuw." In *Sola Gratia: Schets van de geschiedenis en de werkzaamheid van de Theologische Hogeschool der Gereformeerde Kerken in Nederland*, edited by J. D. Boerkoel, Th. Delleman, and G. M. den Hartogh, 7–103. Kampen: Kok, 1954.

———. *Onze Theologische School*. Kampen: Kok, 1953.

———. "Varia." In *Sola Gratia: Schets van de geschiedenis en de werkzaamheid van de Theologische Hogeschool der Gereformeerde Kerken in Nederland*, edited by J. D. Boerkoel, Th. Delleman, and G. M. den Hartogh, 60–64. Kampen: Kok, 1954.

Hedley, Douglas. "Theology and the Revolt against the Enlightenment." In *The Cambridge History of Christianity: World Christianities, c. 1815–c. 1914*, edited by Sheridan Gilley and Brian Stanley, 30–52. Cambridge: Cambridge University Press, 2006.

Heere, Peter, Arnold Vernooij, and Jan van den Bos. *De Erebegraafplaats Bloemendaal*. The Hague: SDU Uitgevers, 2005.

Heideman, Eugene. *Hendrik P. Scholte: His Legacy in the Netherlands and in America*. Grand Rapids: Eerdmans, 2015.

———. *The Relation of Revelation and Reason in E. Brunner and H. Bavinck*. Assen: Van Gorcum, 1959.

Hendriksen, William. "Translator's Preface." In *The Doctrine of God*, by Herman Bavinck, 7–9. Edinburgh: Banner of Truth Trust, 1951.

Henry, Matthew. *Letterlijke en practicale Bijbelverklaring*. Utrecht: Kemink, 1896. Translation of *An Exposition of the Old and New Testaments*, first published 1708–10.

Hepp, Valentijn. *Dr. Herman Bavinck*. Amsterdam: Ten Have, 1921.

———. *Levensbericht voor Herman Bavinck*. Leiden: Brill, 1923.

Herman [no first name given]. "Goed en kwaad gerucht uit Nederland." *Java-Bode*, October 14, 1882.

Hevesi, Dennis. "Johtje Vos, Who Saved Wartime Jews, Dies at 97." *New York Times*, November 4, 2007.

Heywood, Colin. "Children's Work in Countryside and City." In *The Routledge History of Childhood in the Western World*, edited by Paula S. Fass, 125–41. London: Routledge, 2013.

Hille, H., and J. P. Neven. "Verheerlijkt en verguisd." *Oude Paden*, March 2001, 42–52.

van Hoeken, C. J. *Antwoord aan den schrijver van: Een woord aan de afgescheidenen uit de hervormden, en aan allen die de waarheid lief hebben*. 's Gravenhage: J. van Golverdinge, 1841.

Hoekstra, Tjeerd. "Begravenis Prof. Dr. Bavinck." *De Bazuin*, August 6, 1921.

———. "Prof. Dr. H. Bavinck." *Gereformeerd Theologisch Tijdschrift* 22, no. 3/4 (July–August 1921): 97–102.

Hofkamp, S. J. *Geschiedenis der Beschaving: Een leesboek voor de hoogste klasse der lagere scholen*. Groningen: M. Smit, 1856.

Honig, Anthonie. "Algemeene vergadering der Vereeniging tot Christelijke Verzorging van Krankzinnigen in Nederland." *De Bazuin*, October 22, 1907.

———. *De Zending en de scholen*. Zeist: n.p., 1900.

———. "Evangelisatie." *De Bazuin*, May 16, 1913.

———. *Handboek van de Gereformeerde Dogmatiek*. Kampen: Kok, 1938.

———. "Ter gedachtenis aan Prof. Bavinck." *Gereformeerd Theologisch Tijdschrift* 6 (October 1921): 186.

Hoogenbirk, A. J. *Heeft Calvijn ooit bestaan? Kritisch onderzoek der Calvijn-legende*. Nijkerk: G. F. Callenbach, 1907.

———. *Om de kunst*. Nijkerk: Callenbach, 1903.

Houtman, C. "Noordtzij, Arie." In *Biografisch Lexicon voor de Geschiedenis van het Nederlandse Protestantisme*, 3:282–84. Kampen: Kok, 1988.

———. "Noordtzij, Maarten." In *Biografisch Lexicon voor de Geschiedenis van het Nederlandse Protestantisme*, 3:284–86. Kampen: Kok, 1988.

Hovy, Willem. "Advertentiën: Vrije Universiteit." *De vriend van oud en jong*, April 28, 1889.

Huttinga, Wolter. "'Marie Antoinette' or Mystical Depth? Herman Bavinck on Theology as Queen of the Sciences." In *Neo-Calvinism and the French Revolution*, edited by James Eglinton and George Harinck, 143–54. London: Bloomsbury T&T Clark, 2014.

Jaarsma, Cornelius Richard. *The Educational Philosophy of Herman Bavinck: A Textbook in Education*. Grand Rapids: Eerdmans, 1935.

de Jong, Marinus. "The Heart of the Academy: Herman Bavinck in Debate with Modernity on the Academy, Theology, and the Church." In *The Kuyper Center Review*, vol. 5, *Church and Academy*, edited by Gordon Graham, 62–75. Grand Rapids: Eerdmans, 2015.

Joustra, Jessica. "An Embodied *Imago Dei*: How Herman Bavinck's Understanding of the Image of God Can Help Inform Conversations on Race." *Journal of Reformed Theology* 11, no. 1–2 (2017): 9–23.

Kalff, Gerrit. *Het lied in de middeleeuwen*. Leiden: Brill, 1883.

Kalff, Gerrit, Jr. *Leven van Dr. G. Kalff (1856–1923)*. Groningen: Wolters, 1924.

Kamphuis, Jaap. *Nietzsche in Nederland*. Ermelo: Woord en Wereld, 1987.

Kasteel, Petrus. *Abraham Kuyper*. Kampen: Kok, 1938.

Katz, Cornelia Frida. "Inleiding." *Christendom en Vrouwenbeweging*, introductory issue (1923).

Kennedy, James, and Jan Zwemer. "Religion in the Modern Netherlands and the Problems of Pluralism." *BMGN—Low Countries Historical Review* 125, nos. 2–3 (2010): 237–68.

van Keulen, Dirk. *Bijbel en dogmatiek: Schriftbeschouwing en schriftgebruik in het dogmatisch werk van A. Kuyper, H. Bavinck en G. C. Berkouwer*. Kampen: Kok, 2003.

―――. "Herman Bavinck and the War Question." In *Christian Faith and Violence*, edited by D. van Keulen and M. E. Brinkman, 1:122–40. Zoetermeer: Meinema, 2005.

―――. "Herman Bavinck's *Reformed Ethics*: Some Remarks about Unpublished Manuscripts in the Libraries of Amsterdam and Kampen." *Bavinck Review* 1 (2010): 25–56.

―――. "Ten geleide." In *Gereformeerde ethiek*, by Herman Bavinck, edited by Dirk van Keulen, 9–34. Utrecht: Uitgeverij KokBoekencentrum, 2019.

van Klinken, G. J. "Lucas Lindeboom: Voorman van de christelijke zorg." In *Bevlogen theologen: Geëngageerde predikanten in de negentiende en twintigste eeuw*, edited by Paul E. Werkman and Roelof Enno van der Woude, 123–46. Hilversum: Verloren, 2012.

van Klinken, L. *Bavinck's paedagogische beginselen*. Meppel: Stenvert, 1936.

Klok, Jacobus, and Hendrik de Cock. *De evangelische gezangen getoetst en gewogen en te ligt gevonden*. Groningen: J. H. Bolt, 1834.

Kok, A. B. W. M. *Dr Herman Bavinck.* Amsterdam: S. J. P. Bakker, 1945.

van Koningsveld, Pieter Sjoerd. "Conversion of European Intellectuals to Islam: The Case of Christiaan Snouck Hurgronje alias 'Abd al-Ghaffār." In *Muslims in Interwar Europe: A Transcultural Historical Perspective*, edited by Bekim Agai, Umar Ryad, and Mehdi Sajid, 88–104. Leiden: Brill, 2016.

Krabbendam, Hans. *Vrijheid in het verschiet: Nederlandse emigratie naar Amerika, 1840–1940.* Hilversum: Uitgeverij Verloren, 2006.

Krop, F. J. *Waarom bestrijden wij Rome?* Leeuwarden: Bouman, 1900.

Kuipers, Joel C. *Language, Identity, and Marginality in Indonesia: The Changing Nature of Ritual Speech on the Island of Sumba.* Cambridge: Cambridge University Press, 1998.

Kuipers, Tjitze. *Abraham Kuyper: An Annotated Bibliography, 1857–2010.* Leiden: Brill, 2011.

Kuyper, Abraham, Jr. "Bavinck-Comité." *De Heraut*, October 2, 1921.

———. *Van de Kennisse Gods.* Amsterdam: W. Kirchner, 1907.

Kuyper, Henriëtte, and Johanna Kuyper. *De levensavond van Dr. A. Kuyper.* Kampen: Kok, 1921.

Laman, H. W., ed. *Wandelen door geloof: Overdenkingen van de gereformeerde predikanten.* Utrecht: Gereformeerd Tractaatgenootschap "Filippus," 1930.

Lamers, G. H. *De leer van het geloofsleven.* Amsterdam: W. H. Kirberger, 1877.

———. *De toekomst van de dogmatiek.* Amsterdam: W. H. Kirberger, 1878.

———. *Een woord over dogmatische theologie en dogmatiek.* Amsterdam: W. H. Kirberger, 1876.

Land, J. P. N. "Philosophy in the Dutch Universities." *Mind: A Quarterly Review of Psychology and Philosophy* 3 (1878): 87–104.

Landwehr, J. H. *In Memoriam: Prof. Dr. H. Bavinck.* Kampen: Kok, 1921.

———. *Kort overzich van de geschiedenis der Gereformeerde Kerken in Nederland, 1795 tot heden.* Zwolle: Tulp, 1908.

De Lange, J. *De Afscheiding te Leiden.* Rotterdam: J. H. Donner, 1934.

Lauzon, Matthew. "Modernity." In *The Oxford Handbook of World History*, edited by Jerry H. Bentley, 73–84. Oxford: Oxford University Press, 2011.

Leo XIII. "Encyclical Letter *Rerum Novarum*." In *The Church Speaks to the Modern World: The Social Teachings of Leo XIII*, edited by Étienne Gilson, 205–44. Garden City, NY: Image, 1954.

Lewis, C. S. *Mere Christianity.* London: Fontana, 1952.

van der Linde, Antonius. *Michael Servet: Een brandoffer der gereformeerde inquisitie.* Groningen: P. Noordhoff, 1891.

Lindeboom, C. "Speciale opleiding voor de zending?" *De Bazuin*, November 4, 1910.

Lindeboom, Fenna Tjeerdina. *De ontwikkeling van het strafstelsel in Sovjet-Rusland, 1917–1937.* Rotterdam: Libertas Drukkerijen, 1937.

Lindeboom, Lucas. *Bewaart het pand u toebetrouwd, of de geruststelling in "Opleiding en theologie" onderzocht en gewogen.* Kampen: Zalsman, 1896.

———. *Gereformeerde stichtingen van barmhartigheid in Nederland.* Kampen: Kok, 1927.

———. *Godgeleerden.* Heusden: A Gezelle Meerburg, 1894.

———. "Het doctoraat in de heilige godgeleerdheid aan de Theologische School der Christ. Geref. Kerk." N.p., 1887.

———. "Ingezonden." *De Bazuin,* March 13, 1896.

———. *Onze roeping tegenover, en onder Rome.* Heusden: A. Gezelle Meerburg, 1890.

Lindeboom, Lucas, and Maarten Noordtzij. "Een woord betreffende de zaak der Opleiding." *De Bazuin,* October 10, 1902.

Lindsay, Thomas. "The Protestant Reformation: Its Spiritual Character and Its Fruits in the Individual Life." In *Alliance of the Reformed Churches Holding to the Presbyterian System: Proceedings of the Fifth General Council Toronto, 1892,* edited by George D. Mathews, 39–45. London: Publication Committee of the Presbyterian Church of England, 1892.

Loosjes, A. *Overijssel, Friesland, Groningen en Drente in Beeld.* Amsterdam: Scheltema & Holkema's Boekhandel en Uitgevers Maatschappij, 1927.

Luther, Martin. *Het regtveerdigend geloof verklaart en bevestigt: In eene verhandeling over Paulus brief aan den Galaten.* Translated by Theodorus van der Groe. Utrecht: A. Visscher, 1870. First published in Latin in 1519.

Mackay, James Hutton. *Religious Thought in Holland during the Nineteenth Century.* London: Hodder & Stoughton, 1911.

Martin, Frederick. *The Statesman's Year-Book: A Statistical, Genealogical, and Historical Account of the States and Sovereigns of the Civilised World for the Year 1886.* London: MacMillan and Co., 1866.

Mathews, George D., ed. *Alliance of the Reformed Churches Holding to the Presbyterian System: Proceedings of the Fifth General Council Toronto, 1892.* London: Publication Committee of the Presbyterian Church of England, 1892.

Mattson, Brian. *Restored to Our Destiny: Eschatology and the Image of God in Herman Bavinck's Reformed Dogmatics.* Leiden: Brill, 2011.

von Meyenfeldt, F. H. "Prof. Dr. Herman Bavinck: 1854–1954, 'Christus en de cultuur.'" *Polemios* 9, no. 21 (October 15, 1954): 109–12.

de Moen, Carol Godefroy. *De Bede van Salomo om wijsheid en wetenschap: Een gepast voorbeeld voor allen, maar inzonderheid voor de dienaren in 's Heeren wijngaard, die met Gods hulp de hun opgelegde taak willen aanvaarden en volbrengen.* Kampen: S. van Velzen Jnr., 1854.

————. "Toelichting." *De Bazuin*, December 22, 1854.

Moltmann, Jürgen. *Man: Christian Anthropology in the Conflicts of the Present*. Translated by John Sturdy. Philadelphia: Fortress, 1974.

Mooij, M. *Bond van Vrije Evangelische Gemeenten*. Baarn: Hollandia Drukkerij, 1907.

Mulder, H. "Lindeboom, Lucas." In *Biografisch lexicon voor de geschiedenis van het Nederlands protestantisme*, edited by D. Nauta, A. de Groot, J. van den Berg, O. J. de Jong, F. R. J. Knetsch, and G. H. M. Posthumus Meyjes, 3:250–53. Kampen: Kok, 1988.

Muller, P. J. *Handboek der dogmatiek*. 2nd ed. Groningen: Wolters, 1908.

Multatuli. *Max Havelaar, of De koffieveilingen der Nederlandsche Handelmaatschappy*. Edited by Annemarie Kets-Vree. Assen: Van Gorcum, 1992.

————. *Max Havelaar, or The Coffee Auctions of the Dutch Trading Company*. Translated by Baron Alphonse Nahuÿs. Edinburgh: Edmonson & Douglas, 1868.

De Nederlandsche Vrouwenbond tot Verhooging van het Zedelijk Bewustzijn: Ontstaan, Organisatie, en Werkwijze. N.p, n.d.

van Nes, A. L. *Woorden van broederlijke onderwijzing en waarschuwing ten opzigte van het gebruik der sterke dranken*. Groningen: J. Oomkens, 1841.

de Niet, Johan, and Herman Paul. "Collective Memories of John Calvin in Dutch Neo-Calvinism." In *Sober, Strict, and Scriptural: Collective Memories of John Calvin, 1800–2000*, edited by Johan de Niet, Herman Paul, and Bart Wallet, 67–95. Leiden: Brill, 2009.

Nijkeuter, Henk. *Geschiedenis van de Drentse literatuur, 1816–1956*. Assen: Van Gorcum, 2003.

Noordtzij, Maarten. *Egyptologie en Assyriologie in betrekking tot de geloofwaardigheid des Ouden Testaments: Rede bij het overdragen van het rectoraat aan de Theologische School te Kampen, den 19den December 1881*. Utrecht: C. van Bentum, 1882.

van Oosterzee, J. J. *Christelijke dogmatiek: Een handbook voor academisch onderwijs en eigen oefening*. Utrecht: Kemink, 1876.

den Ouden, R. A., and R. C. Verweyck. *Het Kuyperhuis*. Baarn: E. J. Bosch, 1921.

Pass, Bruce. "'The Heart of Dogmatics': The Place and Purpose of Christology in the Theological Method of Herman Bavinck." PhD diss., University of Edinburgh, 2018.

Pierson, Allard. *Dr. A. Pierson aan zijne laatste gemeente*. Arnhem: D. A. Thieme, 1865.

Pieters, K. J., D. J. van der Werp, and J. R. Kreulen. *Is de Afscheiding in Nederland van het Hervormd Kerkgenootschap, zooals het thans en sedert 1816 bestaat, uit God of uit menschen?* Franeker: T. Telenga, 1856.

Pos, H. J. "Levensbericht Tj. De Boer." In *Jaarboek der Koninklijke Nederlandse Akademie van Wetenschappen*, 215. Amsterdam: Koninklijke Nederlandse Akademie van Wetenschappen, 1945–46.

Puchinger, George, and Nico Scheps. *Gesprek over de onbekende Kuyper.* Kampen: Kok, 1971.

Querido, Israël. "Letterkundige kroniek." *Algemeen Handelsblad*, October 3, 1906.

Ralston, Joshua. "Islam as a Christian Trope: The Place and Function of Islam in Reformed Dogmatic Theology." *Muslim World* 107, no. 4 (October 2017): 754–76.

Rapport inzake het vrouwenkiesrecht aan de generale synode van de Gereformeerde Kerken. Kampen: Kok, 1927.

Reitsma, J. "Passio Dordracena." *Geloof en Vrijheid: Tweemaandelijksch tijdschrift* 21 (September/October 1887): 555–90.

de Reus, Tjerk. "Op het kompas van De la Saussaye." *Friesch Dagblad*, October 25, 2003.

Rimius, Heinrich. *The History of the Moravians.* London: J. Robinson, 1754.

Robert, Jacques. *The European Territory: From Historical Roots to Global Challenges.* London: Routledge, 2014.

Robertson, Archibald Thomas. *A Short Grammar of the Greek New Testament: For Students Familiar with the Elements of Greek.* New York: Hodder and Stoughton, 1909.

Roegiers, J., and N. C. F. van Sas. "Revolution in the North and South, 1780–1830." In *History of the Low Countries*, edited by J. C. H. Blom and Emiel Lamberts, 275–318. New York: Berghahn Books, 1999.

Rombouts, Fr. Siegbertus. *Prof. dr. H. Bavinck: Gids bij de studie van zijn paedagogische werken.* 's Hertogenbosch: Malmberg, 1922.

van Roon, G. *Protestants Nederland en Duitsland, 1933–41.* Utrecht: Spectrum, 1973.

Roosevelt, Theodore. Theodore Roosevelt Papers. Series 9: Desk Diaries, 1901–1909. *1907, Jan. 1–1908, Dec. 31; 1909, Jan. 7–Feb. 18.* Library of Congress, Washington, DC.

Rosendaal, Adriaan Cornelis. *Naar een school voor de gereformeerde gezindte: Het christelijke onderwijsconcept van het Gereformeerd Schoolverband (1868–1971).* Hilversum: Verloren, 2006.

Rullmann, J. C. *Onze voortrekkers.* Delft: Naamlooze Vennootschap W. D. Meinema, 1923.

Rutten, Alex. *De Publieke Man: Dr. P. H. Ritter Jnr. als cultuurbemiddelaar in het interbellum.* Hilversum: Literatoren, 2018.

de Savornin Lohman, Alexander. *De correspondentie over mijn ontslag als hoogleeraar aan de Vrije Universiteit.* Utrecht: Kemink, 1896.

————. "Donner (Johannes Hendrikus)." In *Nieuw Nederlandsch Biografisch Woordenboek*, edited by P. C. Molhuysen and P. J. Blok, 1:738. Leiden: A. W. Sijthoff, 1911.

Schaeffer, J. C. *De plaats van Abraham Kuyper in de "Vrije Kerk."* Amsterdam: Buijten & Schipperhein, 1997.

Schaver, J. L. *The Polity of the Churches.* 2 vols. Chicago: Church Polity Press, 1947.

Schivelbusch, Wolfgang. *The Railway Journey: The Industrialization of Time and Space in the 19th Century.* Berkeley: University of California Press, 1986.

Schlüter, Dick. "De grensoverschrijdende activiteiten van duivelbanners." In *Nederland en Bentheim: Vijf eeuwen kerk aan de grens / Die Niederlande und Bentheim: Fünf Jahrhunderte Kirche an der Grenze*, edited by P. H. A. M. Abels, G.-J. Beuker, and J. G. J. van Booma, 131–46. Delft: Eburon, 2003.

Schoemaker, J. *Geschiedenis der Oud-Gereformeerde Kerk in het Graafschap Bentheim en het Vorstendom Ostfriesland.* Hardenberg: A. Kropveld, 1900.

Scholte, Hendrik Pieter. "De zesde december." *De Reformatie* 2, no. 1 (1841): 291–97.

————. "Moet in de Nederlandsche Staatsregeling de Bepaling worden Opgenomen, dat de Koning Behooren moet tot de Hervormde Godsdienst?" *De Reformatie* 1, no. 7 (1840): 320–32.

————. "Wet op de Verdraagzaamheid opgesteld door Jefferson." In *De Reformatie* 8, no. 2 (1845): 174–78.

Scholten, Johannes Henricus. *De leer der hervormde kerk in hare grondbeginselen.* 2 vols. Leiden: Engels, 1850.

Schoone-Jongen, Robert. "Dutch and Dutch Americans, to 1870." In *Immigrants in American History: Arrival, Adaptation, and Integration*, edited by Elliott Robert Barkan, 1:59–66. Oxford: ABC-CLIO, 2013.

Sheeres, Janet Sjaarda. *Son of Secession.* Grand Rapids: Eerdmans, 2006.

Slotemaker de Bruïne, J. R. "De vrouw en de kerk." *Christendom en Vrouwenbeweging*, series 6, no. 1, 1923.

Smits, C. *De Afscheiding van 1834.* Vol. 8, *Provincie Noord-Brabant.* Dordrecht: J. P. van den Tol, 1988.

Snel, Johan. "Kuypers dodenmasker." In *Tussen Kampen en Amsterdam: George Harinck en het Historisch Documentatiecentrum van de Vrije Universiteit, 1985–2017*, edited by Wim Berkelaar, Hans Seijlhouwer, and Bart Wallet, 114–18. Amsterdam: Donum Reeks, 2018.

Snouck Hurgronje, Christiaan. *De beteekenis van den islam voor zijne belijders in Oost-Indië.* Leiden: Brill, 1883.

————. "De islam." *De Gids* 50, no. 2 (1886): 239–73.

————. "Der Mahdi." *Revue Coloniale Internationale* 1 (1886): 25–59.

————. *Mekka.* 2 vols. The Hague: Nijhoff, 1888–89.

————. *Mekka in the Latter Part of the 19th Century—Daily Life, Customs and Learning: The Moslims of the East-Indian Archipelago.* Edited and translated by J. H. Monahan. Leiden: Brill, 2006.

————. "Mijne reis naar Arabië." *Nieuwe Rotterdamsche Courant*, November 26 and 27, 1885.

————. "Mohammedaansch recht en rechtwetenschap: Opmerkingen naar aanleiding van twee onlangs verschenen brochures." *De Indische Gids* 8, no. 1 (1886): 90–111.

————. "Nogmaals 'De Islam en Oost-Indië' naar aanleiding van prof. De Louters brief." *De Indische Gids* 5, no. 2 (1883): 75–80.

————. "Prof. De Louter over 'Godsdienstige wetten, volksinstellingen en gebruiken.'" *De Indische Gids* 5, no. 2 (1883): 98–108.

————. *Verspreide geschriften.* 2 vols. Leipzig: Schroeder, 1923.

Spits, F. C. "Problems of Defence in a Non-belligerent Society: Military Service in the Netherlands during the Second Half of the Nineteenth Century." In *Britain and the Netherlands*, vol. 6, *War and Society*, edited by A. C. Duke and C. A. Tamse, 189–202. The Hague: Martinus Nijhoff, 1977.

Spurgeon, Charles Haddon. *Voor iederen morgen: Dagboek voor huisgezin of binnenkamer.* Translated by P. Huët. Amsterdam: W. H. Kirberger, 1870. Translation of *Morning by Morning: Daily Readings for the Family or the Closet*, first published in 1866.

Stanley, Brian. "Africa through European Christian Eyes: The World Missionary Conference, Edinburgh, 1910." In *African Identities and World Christianity in the Twentieth Century*, edited by Klaus Koschorke and Jens Holger Schjørring, 165–80. Wiesbaden: Harassowitz, 2005.

Steketee, Adriaan. *De beteekenis der Kunst voor den toekomstigen Evangeliedienaar: Rede, uitgesproken bij het overgeven van het rectoraat den 16en Dec. 1880.* Kampen: Zalsman, 1881.

————. *De studie van Plato, met het oog op de theologische forming: Rede, uitgesproken, bij het neerleggen van 't rectoraat, den 16en december 1875.* Kampen: G. Ph. Zalsman, 1875.

Stellingwerff, J. *Kuyper en de VU.* Kampen: Kok, 1987.

Stokvis, Pieter R. D. "The Secession of 1834 and Dutch Emigration to the United States: Religious Aspects of Emigration in Comparative Perspective." In *Breaches and Bridges: Reformed Subcultures in the Netherlands, Germany, and the United States*, edited by George Harinck and Hans Krabbendam, 21–32. VU Studies on Protestant History 4. Amsterdam: VU Uitgeverij, 2000.

Stout, Jeffrey. "Christianity and the Class Struggle." In *The Kuyper Center Review*, vol. 4, *Calvinism and Democracy*, edited by John Bowlin, 40–53. Grand Rapids: Eerdmans, 2014.

Strahan, James. *Andrew Bruce Davidson.* London: Hodder & Stoughton, 1917.

Strauss, David. *Das Leben Jesu, kritisch bearbeitet*. Tübingen: Osiander, 1835.

Strong, Josiah. *Our Country: Its Possible Future and Its Present Crisis*. New York: Baker and Taylor for the American Home Missionary Society, 1885.

———. *Our Country: Its Possible Future and Its Present Crisis*. Edited by Jurgen Herbst. Cambridge, MA: Harvard University Press, 1963.

Stuart, Martinus Cohen. *Zes maanden in Amerika*. Haarlem: Kruseman and Tjeenk Willem, 1875.

Sullivan, Elizabeth. "A Brief History of the Collection." In *European Clocks and Watches in the Metropolitan Museum of Art*, edited by Clare Vincent, Jan Hendrik Leopold, and Elizabeth Sullivan, 3–8. New York: Metropolitan Museum of Art, 2015.

Taylor, Charles. *A Secular Age*. Cambridge, MA: Harvard University Press, 2007.

Tichler, Jacob. *Huldrich Zwingli, de Kerkhervormer*. Utrecht: Kemink, 1858.

Troeltsch, Ernst. *Gesammelte schriften*. Vol. 2. Aalen: Scientia Verlag, 1962.

Tweede Internationaal Congres van Gereformeerden (Calvinisten), Amsterdam 23–26 October 1934, Verslagen. 's Gravenhage: Martinus Nijhoff, 1935.

Uitterdijk, Jurjen Nanninga. *Kampen: Geschiedkundig overzicht en merkwaardigheden*. Kampen: Van Hulst, 1878.

University of Amsterdam. *Album academicum van het Athenaeum illustre en van de Universiteit van Amsterdam: Bevattende de namen der curatoren, hoogleeraren en leeraren van 1632 tot 1913, der rectores magnifici en secretarissen van den Senaat der universiteit van 1877 tot 1913, der leden van den Illustrissimus senatus studiosorum Amstelodamensium van 1851 tot 1913, en der studenten van 1799 tot 1913*. Amsterdam: R. W. P. de Vries, 1913.

Ursinus, Zacharias. *Verklaring op den Heidelbergschen Catechismus*. Translated by C. van Proosdy. Kampen: Zalsman, 1882.

Valeton, J. P. P., Jr. *De Nederlandsche zendingsschool*. Utrecht: n.p., 1905.

Vandenbosch, Amry. *Dutch Foreign Policy since 1815: A Study in Small Power Politics*. The Hague: Martinus Nijhoff, 1959.

Vanderlaan, Eldred. *Protestant Modernism in Holland*. Oxford: Oxford University Press, 1924.

van Veen, H. "De Afscheiding en de gezangenstrijd." In *Afscheiding—Wederkeer: Opstellen over de Afscheiding van 1834*, edited by D. Deddens and J. Kamphuis, 117–49. Haarlem: Vijlbrief, 1984.

Veenhof, Cornelis. "Uit het leven van de Theologische Hogeschool 6." *De Reformatie* 30, no. 16 (1955): 123–25.

Veenhof, Jan. *Revelatie en Inspiratie: De Openbarings- en Schriftbeschouwing van Herman Bavinck in vergelijking met die van de ethische theologie*. Amsterdam: Buijten & Schipperheijn, 1968.

te Velde, Melis. *Anthony Brummelkamp: 1811–1888*. Barneveld: Uitgeverij de Vuur-baak, 1988.

———. "Brummelkamp, Anthony." In *Biografisch lexicon voor de geschiedenis van het Nederlands protestantisme*, edited by D. Nauta, A. de Groot, J. van den Berg, O. J. de Jong, F. R. J. Knetsch, and G. H. M. Posthumus Meyjes, 4:74–77. Kampen: Kok, 1998.

Verne, Jules. *De Noordpool-expeditie van kapitein Hatteras*. Leiden: de Breuk & Smits, 1870. First published in French in 1864.

Visser, Eduard. *God, het woord en de tering: Leven en werk van Simon Gorter (1838–1871), met een teksteditie van zijn brieven en een keuze uit zijn proza en preken*. Hilversum: Verloren, 2017.

de Vrankrijker, A. C. J. *Vier eeuwen Nederlandsch studentenleven*. Voorburg: Boot, 1936.

Vree, Jasper. *Enkele aspecten van de Afscheiding in Delfzijl: Gebeurtenissen van toen—een vraag aan ons*. N.p., 1985.

———. "Gunning en Kuyper: Een bewogen vriendschap rond Schrift en kerk in de jaren 1860–1873." In *Noblesse oblige: Achtergrond en actualiteit van de theologie van J. H. Gunning jr.*, edited by Th. Hettema and L. Mietus, 62–86. Gorinchem: Ekklesia, 2005.

———. *Kuyper in de kiem: De precalvinistische periode van Abraham Kuyper, 1848–1874*. Hilversum: Verloren, 2006.

———. "Van separatie naar integratie: De afgescheidenen en hun kerk in de Neder-landse samenleving (1834–1892)." In *Religies en (on)gelijkheid in een plurale samenleving*, edited by R. Kranenborg and W. Stoker, 161–76. Leuven: Garant, 1995.

Wagenhammer, Hans. *Das Wesen des Christentums*. Mainz: Matthias Grünewald, 1973.

Wijne, Johan S. *De "vergissing" van Troelstra*. Hilversum: Verloren, 1999.

Wilhelmina, Princess of the Netherlands. *Eenzaam maar niet alleen*. Amsterdam: W. ten Have, 1959.

Wintle, Michael. *An Economic and Social History of the Netherlands, 1800–1920: Demographic, Economic and Social Transition*. Cambridge: Cambridge University Press, 2000.

Wirtz Czn., J. C. *Bijdrage tot de geschiedenis van de schoolstrijd*. Amsterdam: H. J. Spruyt's Uitgevers-Maatschappij, 1926.

de Wit, Willem Jan. *On the Way to the Living God*. Amsterdam: VU University Press, 2011.

Witkam, Jan Just. "Christiaan Snouck Hurgronje's description of Mecca." In *Mekka in the Latter Part of the 19th Century—Daily Life, Customs and Learning: The Moslims of the East-Indian Archipelago*, by Christaan Snouck Hurgronje, edited and translated by J. H. Monahan, xiii–xxi. Leiden: Brill, 2006.

—————. "Copy on Demand: Abū Šubbāk in Mecca, 1303/1886." In *The Trade in Papers Marked with Non-Latin Characters*, edited by Anne Regourd, 206–26. Leiden: Brill, 2018.

Woldring, H. E. S. *Een handvol filosofen: Geschiedenis van de filosofiebeoefening aan de Vrije Universiteit in Amsterdam van 1880 tot 2012.* Hilversum: Verloren, 2013.

Wood, John Halsey. "Church, Sacrament and Civil Society: Abraham Kuyper's Early Baptismal Theology." *Journal of Reformed Theology* 2, no. 3 (2008): 275–96.

Wright, David. Introduction to *Disruption to Diversity: Edinburgh Divinity, 1846–1996*, edited by David Wright and Gary D. Badcock, vii–xxiv. Edinburgh: T&T Clark, 1996.

Wumkes, G. A. "Bavinck (Jan)." In *Nieuw Nederlandsch Biografisch Woordenboek*, edited by P. C. Molhuysen and P. J. Blok, 10:34–35. Leiden: A. W. Sijthoff's Uitgevers-Maatschappij, 1911.

—————. *Stads- en Dorpskroniek van Friesland.* Heerenveen: Nieuwsblad van Friesland, 1917.

van Wyk, D. J. C. "P J Hoedemaker, teoloog en kerkman." *HTS Teologiese Studies* 47, no. 4 (1991): 1069–87.

Yarnell, Malcolm. *The Formation of Christian Doctrine.* Nashville: B&H, 2007.

Young, D. A. "The Reception of Geology in the Dutch Reformed Tradition: The Case of Herman Bavinck (1854–1921)." In *Geology and Religion: A History of Harmony and Hostility*, edited by M. Kölbl-Ebert, 289–300. Geological Society Special Publication 310. London: Geological Society, 2009.

Zeller, Eduard. *Das theologische System Zwingli's.* Tübingen: L. Fr. Fues, 1853.

Zijdeman, Richard Lindert. *Status Attainment in the Netherlands, 1811–1941: Spatial and Temporal Variation before and during Industrialisation.* Ede: Ponsen & Looijen, 2010.

Zuidema [no first name given]. "KAPTEYN (Johannes)." In *Nieuw Nederlandsch Biografisch Woordenboek*, edited by P. C. Molhuysen and P. J. Blok, 2:647–48. Leiden: A. W. Sijthoff's, 1912.

van Zuthem, Johan. *"Heelen en halven": Orthodox-protestantse voormannen en het "politiek" antipapisme in de periode 1872–1925.* Hilversum: Verloren, 2001.

van der Zweep, L. *De paedagogiek van Bavinck, met een inleiding tot zijn werken.* Kampen: Kok, 1935.

Index